AICPA® PCPS
Private Companies Practice Section

Bull's-Eye!

The Ultimate How-To **MARKETING & SALES** Guide for CPAs

Edited by **Tracy Crevar Warren**

Association for Accounting Marketing

Notice to Readers

Bull's-Eye! The Ultimate How-To Marketing & Sales Guide for CPAs does not represent an official position of the American Institute of Certified Public Accountants, and it is distributed with the understanding that the authors and publisher are not rendering legal, accounting, or other professional services in the publication. If legal advice or other expert assistance is required, the services of a competent professional should be sought.

ISBN: 978-0-87051-871-3

Publisher: Amy Stainken
Managing Editor: Amy Krasnyanskaya
Acquisitions Editor: Erin Howard Valentine
Senior Project Manager: M. Donovan Scott
Cover Design: Nancy Karmadi

BULL'S-EYE

Pronunciation: \'bu̇lz-ˌī *also* 'bəlz-\
Function: *noun*
Date: 1825
a : the center of a target; *also* : something central or crucial **b** : a shot that hits the bull's-eye; *broadly* : something that precisely attains a desired end

Contents

CHAPTER 3
THE INTEGRATION IMPERATIVE: ERASING MARKETING AND BUSINESS DEVELOPMENT SILOS

By Suzanne C. Lowe and Scott Jensen

PART II: GETTING STARTED

CHAPTER 4
THE MARKETING PLAN: AN AUDIT-BASED APPROACH

By August J. Aquila, PhD

CHAPTER 5
DEVELOPING A PERSONAL MARKETING PLAN

By Tracy Crevar Warren

CHAPTER 10

A BUYER'S GUIDE TO HIRING A MARKETING PROFESSIONAL

By Sally Glick

CHAPTER 11

THE FIRM ADMINISTRATOR AS MARKETING DIRECTOR

By Diane Paoletta, CPA

CHAPTER 12

THE CASE FOR UTILIZING A SALES PROFESSIONAL AT YOUR FIRM

By Christopher J. Perrino

CHAPTER 13

THE OUTSIDE CONSULTANT: MORE THAN AN EXPERT

By Cheryl Bascomb

PART IV: MARKETING TECHNIQUES THAT GET YOU NOTICED

CHAPTER 14
WHY SHOULD I CONSIDER ADVERTISING?

By Joe Walsh

CHAPTER 15
SUCCESSFULLY BRANDING YOUR FIRM

By Allan S. Boress, CPA, CVA

CHAPTER 16
GETTING YOUR NAME IN LIGHTS WITH PUBLIC RELATIONS

By Christine Heirlmaier Nelson

CHAPTER 21
NEWSLETTERS THAT GET NOTICED

By Sally Glick

CHAPTER 22
DATABASES THAT FUEL YOUR MARKETING EFFORTS

By Michelle Class

CHAPTER 23
CREATING OPPORTUNITIES THROUGH COMMUNITY ENGAGEMENT

By Karen Love and Raissa Evans   *265*

CHAPTER 24

REFERRAL SOURCE DEVELOPMENT: THE MOST POWERFUL, BUT UNDERUTILIZED BUSINESS DEVELOPMENT TACTIC

By Eileen P. Monesson

CHAPTER 25

UTILIZING SEMINARS TO BUILD YOUR PRACTICE

By Leisa Gill

PART V: THE HANDOFF—CONNECTING THE DOTS BETWEEN MARKETING AND SALES

CHAPTER 27
FROM OPPORTUNITY TO NEW CLIENT

By Gale Crosley, CPA

CHAPTER 28
CREATING PROPOSALS THAT WIN

By Dawn Wagenaar

CHAPTER 29
WIN MORE NEW BUSINESS WITH EFFECTIVE SALES MANAGEMENT

By Rick Solomon, CPA

CHAPTER 30
CROSS-SERVING CLIENTS: INTEGRATING SALES AND SERVICE DELIVERY

By Russ Molinar

CHAPTER 31
SALES TRAINING: THE KEY TO BETTER SERVICE AND BETTER CLIENTS

By Rick Solomon, CPA

PART VI: MEASURING RESULTS, COMMUNICATING, AND REWARDING SUCCESS

CHAPTER 32
IN-HOUSE MARKETING COMMUNICATIONS THAT FOSTER SUCCESS

By Jill R. Lock

CHAPTER 36
DEVELOPING A SERVICE EXCELLENCE PLAN FOR CLIENTS

By Susan Wylie Lanfray

CHAPTER 37
LETTING GO: EVALUATING AND FIRING CLIENTS

By Mark Koziel, CPA

PREFACE
Marketing is Cool Again!

Tracy Crevar Warren
Editor

"Marketing is cool again!" a managing partner of one of the nation's top CPA firms recently quipped. According to the AICPA's 2009 Private Companies Practice Section CPA Firm Top Issues Survey, he is not alone. Marketing is back atop the list of key issues keeping CPAs up at night. Between the rush of work that followed the Sarbanes-Oxley Act of 2002 and the collapse of Arthur Andersen, coupled with the shortage of talent, marketing has not made the survey in several years. Let's face it, many firms haven't had to do much marketing to win new business for some time. Professionals have been focused primarily on getting work out the door, not strengthening their sales and client service skills. For many, marketing competencies have become rusty, even nonexistent, and business development initiatives have been spotty at best.

Although times have changed, practice growth still remains the lifeblood of a CPA firm. Keeping the firm's pipeline full of new business opportunities is essential to success. What has been an easy task for many over the past few years, due to the nature of the environment, is causing concern for professionals and their practices once again.

As we enter a new economy, what made us profitable in the past will not necessarily be what propels us to profitability in the future. To keep up with these changes, our organizations must change. Gaining competitive advantage means new ways of thinking and new ways of doing things. Today's leading firms are looking to embrace new standards for marketing and selling their services. To maximize growth, firms are shifting from the once elusive new business pursuit reserved for the organization's top leaders and rainmakers, to a mission in which everyone plays a part. This requires cultural and operational shifts.

That is why this is the perfect time to publish *Bull's-Eye! The Ultimate How-To Marketing & Sales Guide for CPAs*. Whether your firm is getting back into the full swing of marketing, you are looking for some new ideas to jumpstart your sales efforts, or you are getting serious about business development for the first time, this book is designed for you. Its purpose is to inspire, teach, and provide you with practical insight to help build results-oriented marketing and sales programs in your organization.

Bull's-Eye is a collaboration of 37 of the industry's most successful marketing and sales minds. Collectively these gifted professionals have served as pioneering practitioners inside the profession and as outside advisors and thought leaders for hundreds, even thousands, of CPAs and their firms. They give you an insider's view of what it takes to build business development initiatives that produce results. Through the principles, best practices, and case studies shared in the book, they will help you understand that success doesn't happen by chance, but through careful planning, development, and implementation of well-designed processes, systems, and tools. Be prepared for a journey that explores what is required to make marketing and sales really work in your firm, as you look toward the future. More than a one-time read, *Bull's-Eye* is designed as a comprehensive reference guide to help you and your firm navigate the marketing and business development landscape as you work to build your practice.

Beware! Some of what you are getting ready to read might shock you. Don't worry. It's not as complicated as you might think. Some of its contents are things you already know but need a reminder to dust them off and put them to work again. New concepts and tools are included, too.

In the end, it's all up to you! As you read *Bull's-Eye*, you must decide what you will do with this new-found information. Competitive advantage goes to those who have the courage to put into place what they believe will make a difference.

I encourage you to take purposeful, growth-focused action, get your team involved, and create a prosperous firm that people are proud to call their own.

ACKNOWLEDGMENTS

Bull's-Eye! The Ultimate How-To Marketing & Sales Guide for CPAs is based on the AICPA's *Marketing Advantage* series. Therefore, we wish to recognize and thank the authors of *The Marketing Advantage* (1994) and *The Marketing Advantage II* (1998) for their contributions and original vision, which helped shape this manuscript.

They are as follows:

August J. Aquila, PhD
Barbara A. Bacigalupi
W. Jeffrey Boerger
Clifford M. Brownstein
Melodie Bowsher
Jean Marie Caragher
David W. Cottle
David H. Douglass
Christian P. Fredericksen
Edward J. Gabrielse
Lisa A. Gamze
Warren E. Garling
Carl R. George
Steve Greenberg
Arthur Wm. Hoffman
Herbert M. Kaplan
Tammy A. Linn

Ellen Grayce LoCurto
Patricia M. Luchs
Lynne P Manescalchi
Bruce W. Marcus
Bridget L. Markle
Robert B. Martin, PhD
Francie Murphy
Colette Nassutti
John T. Retterer
Michael A. Schoenecker
Marguerita F. Shea
Frank K. Sonnenberg
James J. Stapleton
Judith R. Trepeck
Kaye Vivian
Troy Waugh
William T. Young

Thanks, of course, to the 37 authors of *Bull's-Eye* for generously sharing their time, insight, and best practices.

In addition, many thanks go to Julie Tucek, president of the Association for Accounting Marketing, and to Granville Loar, former executive director of the Association for Accounting Marketing, for their dedication and assistance in developing the manuscript.

Finally, the support of Mark Koziel and the Private Companies Practice Section was invaluable to ensuring that this book became a reality.

ABOUT THE EDITOR

"I am passionate about helping professionals realize their growth potential. It's ultimately about building a rewarding practice which allows you to do more of the work you love."
—Tracy Crevar Warren

As founder of The Crevar Group, Tracy Crevar Warren advises clients on practice growth, sales, and marketing. A sought-after consultant, facilitator, author, and speaker, her practical, results-oriented approach helps professional services firms win more new business and build more profitable practices. With her proven track record and positive, high-energy style, she inspires and empowers local, regional, national, and international groups to do more of the work they love. Warren is a regular contributing editor for the AICPA's *CPA Insider* and has edited her first book, *Bull's-Eye! The Ultimate How-To Marketing & Sales Guide for CPAs.*

A pioneer in professional services marketing and business development, she has been named as one of *Accounting Today's* Top 100 Most Influential People, and has been inducted into the Association for Accounting Marketing's Hall of Fame. Prior to founding The Crevar Group, she served as the Chief Marketing and Business Development Officer for Dixon Hughes, and helped the firm to grow from less than $10M to one of the nation's largest super-regional firms. Warren can be reached at www.thecrevargroup.com or 336-889-GROW (4769).

ABOUT THE AMERICAN INSTITUTE OF CERTIFIED PUBLIC ACCOUNTANTS

The American Institute of Certified Public Accountants is the national, professional organization for all Certified Public Accountants. Its mission is to provide members with the resources, information, and leadership that enable them to provide valuable services in the highest professional manner to benefit the public as well as employers and clients. For more information please visit www.aicpa.org.

ABOUT THE ASSOCIATION FOR ACCOUNTING MARKETING

The Association for Accounting Marketing (AAM) is the only association in the country formed specifically to act as a catalyst for furthering the marketing and sales efforts of its member firms who seek to expand the business of public accounting. Inherent in this mission is a focus on education, professional skills development and networking to enable its members to increase firm revenues and act as a compass for the rapidly changing competitive environment. The association's 700 members are comprised of marketing and sales professionals, CPAs, consultants, vendors, educators and students that offer products and services to the accounting industry. To learn more about AAM, visit www.accountingmarketing.org.

PART I:
Are You Ready?

CHAPTER 1
Does Your Firm Have the Right Culture for Success?

Tracy Crevar Warren
The Crevar Group LLC

"Change happens when people change. Growth happens when people grow."
—Robert Tomasko

Do you ever wonder why some firms are so successful at marketing and business development, while others struggle?

Is it luck or by design?

If you take a closer look at the successful ones, you will find that marketing and business development does not happen by chance. It is not something their professionals get around to when it's convenient. In fact, it is something they are committed to throughout the year, just like billable time and taking care of their clients. For a growing number of firms, including Ernst & Young, Moss Adams, Lattimore Black Morgan & Cain, Rehmann, Rea & Associates, Barnes Dennig, PKF Texas, and Sobel & Co., to name a few as well as others included in the book, marketing and sales is integrated into who they are and how they do business. It is a part of their culture.

Making a cultural shift requires recalibration, realigning key professionals, and knowledge transfer. That involves sharing a common vision, engagement, infrastructure, accountability, and rewarding success along the way. Because culture shifts do not happen overnight, they also require a tremendous amount of patience and persistence until the new ways of operating become the norm.

In this chapter, we will explore key elements essential to building a marketing and sales culture. We will introduce a model to help you whether you are just getting started, or are looking to take your firm's culture to the next level. This chapter will also set the stage for key concepts, techniques, tools, and insights that will be examined in greater detail throughout the book by some of the industry's most successful practice growth professionals and advisors.

WHAT IS CULTURE, ANYWAY?

Firm culture, simply stated, describes who your firm is, and the way you do what you do in your organization. It can be likened to your firm's DNA. It includes the working environment, how you operate, your organization's personality, how you do business with your clients, how you set your priorities, how you make decisions, what drives your employee's actions, how you deal with problems, and how you embrace change.

When you talk about altering your culture by introducing sales and marketing, it is important to understand that it is not a simple task, which is often the reason why it is faced with resistance. "That's just not how we do things around here." sums it up best. In fact, firms often struggle when they don't take the time to examine how marketing and business development will fit into their own cultures.

> **⚷ Key Concept**
>
> Firm culture, simply stated, describes who your firm is, and the way you do what you do in your organization. It can be likened to your firm's DNA.

3

THREE GS OF PRACTICE GROWTH

To build growth-focused cultures, leading firms are replacing old-school mind-sets and models, which focused solely on driving the bottom-line, with multifaceted approaches. Although a sole focus on bottom-line results may produce results in the short-term, it will not create an environment of acceptance, engagement, and sustainability. The new picture of practice growth is built on an expanded foundation which includes a combination of the three Gs of practice growth. Integrating marketing and business development into your firm's culture is dependent on this well-rounded approach, which includes three key components:

- Growth of the organization
- Growth of its people
- Growth of its clients

Just take a look at how some of the industry's leading firms are embracing growth by examining their missions. Clifton Gunderson's mission is "Growth of our people. Growth of our clients. All else follows." Frazier & Deeter's mission is "To help our clients and people achieve success and realize their potential." Moss Adams' focus is "People. Clients. Safety. Growth. At Moss Adams, we succeed by first helping you succeed."

Not only do these missions guide their firm's growth, but they help define how their marketing and business development initiatives must align with the overall direction of each organization. This clear alignment of marketing and business development initiatives with the firm's overall strategic direction is essential to moving these organizations cohesively toward the achievement of common growth goals. Chapter 3, "The Integration Imperative: Erasing Marketing and Business Development Silos," contains an informative case study on how Moss Adams is changing its culture through the integration of marketing, sales, and client service.

A MODEL FOR CULTURE DEVELOPMENT

Because changing your firm's culture may seem like a daunting task, you might be wondering if there is a road map or a model on which to pattern your firm's culture development as you get started. Good news! We will introduce you to a practical, proven methodology that you can put to use in your firm.

The *Marketing & Sales Culture Development Model* illustrated in Figure 1-1 provides your firm with an easy-to-use framework. It contains seven key components that are essential in culture development and can be tailored to your firm's specific objectives. This tool is designed to help you focus your efforts on building a growth-focused culture while building a rewarding practice for you and your colleagues.

FIGURE 1-1   MARKETING & SALES CULTURE DEVELOPMENT MODEL

1. Vision

One of the most common characteristics of firms with strong marketing and business development cultures is a clear vision of what they want to accomplish. Unlike a culture that focuses on what and where you are now, vision focuses on where you want to go and what you want to become in the future. More than an elusive concept, there is a real understanding of what the team is working toward and what success will look like when it is achieved.

To get started, you must define what you want the firm's marketing and sales culture to look like once it is in place. To develop a clear vision for your firm's marketing and business development culture, it is important to answer the following questions:

- What do you want your firm's marketing and sales environment to look like?
- How will leadership promote and support marketing and sales initiatives?
- Will everyone in the firm be responsible for marketing and/or sales?
- Who will lead your firm's marketing and sales initiatives?
- How will you align your firm's overall goals with your firm's marketing and business development goals to achieve practice growth?
- How will the firm integrate marketing and sales?
- What will marketing and business development success look like?

Once you answer these questions, you can develop a clear vision for the type of marketing and sales culture you are working to build in your firm. It is important to develop a written statement that clearly outlines your vision.

> **⚷ Key Concept**
>
> One of the most common characteristics of firms with strong marketing and business development cultures is a clear vision of what they want to accomplish. Unlike a culture that focuses on what and where you are now, vision focuses on where you want to go and what you want to become in the future.

For example, your firm might outline a vision that looks like the following:

At AB&C CPAs, marketing and sales will become an integral part of our firm's business model and our culture as we work to grow our practice. Success will include the following:

- *Our firm's leadership will actively promote and support the firm's commitment to marketing and sales to grow our practice.*
- *We will strategically align our firm's growth goals with our marketing and sales initiatives and clearly communicate them to the firm.*
- *We will create an environment that encourages active participation from all employees in our marketing and sales initiatives.*
- *We will retain a marketing director to oversee the firm's marketing and business development function and work closely with the firm's managing partner and leadership committee to help everyone take an active role.*
- *We will provide training, coaching and support to our professionals, enabling them to serve as marketing and sales ambassadors for the firm.*
- *We will track our progress against our plans and report on it regularly.*
- *We will celebrate and reward our marketing and business development success regularly.*

As you will notice in the diagram, vision is located at the center of the model. All marketing and business development revolves around this single vision. It is your vision that serves as the beacon to guide all marketing and business development actions and initiatives across the organization.

2. Buy-in, Expectations, & Defined Roles

Successful firms understand that building a growth-focused culture requires more than simply communicating their firm's vision to the team. Even if the managing partner or marketing director has articulated a well-thought out message to the firm's employees, there is no guarantee it will be embraced or acted upon. One of the biggest mistakes that firm leaders often make is thinking that they have gained buy-in because they communicated a brilliant message when, in fact, all that employees heard was, "we are going to build a $25 million practice and business development will be essential to helping us achieve that goal." Although the managing partner understands all that will be involved and all the benefits that can accompany the achievement of this goal, most professionals need more information to embrace it, much less take action.

Buy-In Is Essential

Culture shifts require acceptance and buy-in from individual employees. This buy-in requires trust. Gaining trust takes more than spouting facts and numbers. Although facts can stimulate the brain, you must reach employees' hearts if you are going to be successful in getting them on board. This starts by helping people understand what their organization will look like when the vision becomes a reality, and most importantly, giving them an understanding of what is in it for them.

To gain buy-in, it is important to answer the following questions for your employees:

- Where are we going?
- What will success look like when we get there?
- Why is everyone important to the initiative?
- What is in it for me?
- What will be expected of me?
- What level of support will leadership provide?

Successful leaders have found that answering these questions through powerful narrative and dialogues, such as case studies and stories, help employees understand what this new firm will actually look like and the benefits they can personally expect to receive as a result.

It is important to recognize that employees are disengaged from their organizations now more than ever. A study conducted by the Corporate Leadership Council *Improving Employee Performance in the Economic Downturn – Research Brief - June 2009 revealed the following:*

- Employee Performance Is Declining—The number of employees exhibiting high levels of discretionary effort has decreased by 64 percent since 2005.
- The Disengaged Are Staying—Disengaged employees were 31 percent less likely to quit in 2009 than in 2006.
- High-Potentials Are More Likely to Quit—One out of four employees with high potential plans on quitting in the next 12 months.
- Senior Leaders' Effort Has Dropped—Only 8 percent of senior executives reported high discretionary effort in 2009 compared to 29 percent in the second half of 2006.

Whether they just don't care or they feel their efforts just don't matter, employee disengagement is a real issue in today's workplace. As you look to change your firm's culture, it is important to hone in on this growing trend. The launch of new initiatives can be a turning point for employee re-engagement if you take the proper steps early on to get your team onboard.

Warning! When this essential step of gaining buy-in is overlooked, it is very difficult to achieve wide-spread momentum in marketing and selling over the long-term.

Practice Growth is Everyone's Responsibility

Firms that have built marketing-rich cultures understand that people want to be a part of something bigger than themselves. They realize that professionals yearn to find a place where they not only belong but can make a difference. Yet, they understand that employees outside the executive team often do not feel it is their responsibility to contribute to the firm's growth, nor do they have a clear understanding of how they fit into the mix.

For CPA firms to reach their true potential, it is increasingly important to involve everyone in the growth agenda. That means helping employees to accept that practice growth is everyone's responsibility. A good starting point is to clarify exactly what practice growth means to your firm. Define the broad concept of business development. This definition may be as simple as "everything your firm does to get and keep a client." From there, help employees understand its three key components —marketing, sales, and client service, and what each means to your firm. People have many different understandings of these words, so it's essential to set the record straight by creating a common understanding. How can you expect employees to get involved if they don't really have a clear understanding of what you are talking about?

> **Key Concept**
>
> Firms that have built marketing-rich cultures understand that people want to be a part of something bigger than themselves.

> **Key Concept**
>
> For CPA firms to reach their true potential, it is increasingly important to involve everyone in the growth agenda.

Define Expectations

Professionals often think that just because they are not a great conversationalist, or are not comfortable in front of an audience that they will be lousy at marketing and sales. Convey the message that it takes many different skills to build a successful marketing initiative in your firm. Not everyone has to be great at every aspect, but each person must do their part and leaders need to help them uncover what their part is. It's important to create an environment that enables people to understand the different roles they can play in marketing the firm. Some may be terrific at researching potential prospects, while others might be powerful at developing new leads through speaking and presenting. Some may enjoy the thrill of the new client pursuit, while others might be masterful in developing additional business from current clients as a result of delivering outstanding service.

Although many employees want to get involved in practice growth activities, they simply do not understand how. To jump-start this, define your expectations for them. Build a "business development expectations guide" by level. For example, new staff members are responsible for strengthening relationships with former classmates who have entered the business world as bankers, attorneys, and bonding agents; actively participate in the firm's college recruiting initiatives; and so on. Guidelines should be established for each level of professional within the firm.

Table 1-1 contains some examples of business development expectations that your firm can consider for its professionals by level.

TABLE 1-1   EXAMPLE BUSINESS DEVELOPMENT EXPECTATIONS BY STAFF LEVEL

Associate	Read the firm's Web site and collateral to learn about the firm, the services it provides, and the types of clients it serves
	Attend the firm's new employee orientation
	Learn about the firm's brand and how to bring it to life in your daily routine
	Attend your firm's client service training classes
	Develop a good working relationship with clients

continued

TABLE 1-1   EXAMPLE BUSINESS DEVELOPMENT EXPECTATIONS BY STAFF LEVEL (CONTINUED)

Associate (continued)	Provide good service to clients—be responsive to their needs
	Meet with the firm's marketing director to learn how to get involved in marketing the firm
	Develop new business relationships with former classmates who have entered the business world as bankers and attorneys
Supervisor	Get more involved in the business community by joining a civic group, industry association, or trade group
	Read industry publications to broaden knowledge and skills
	Attend the firm's introduction to marketing training sessions
	Work with the firm's marketing director to develop a personal marketing and business development plan that aligns with your interests
	Seek out a mentor to help strengthen your marketing and business development initiatives and contacts
	Learn how to identify potential cross-selling opportunities for clients—seek opportunities to participate in client calls with partners
	Actively seek the opportunity to participate on sales calls with seasoned rainmakers
	Build relationships with referral sources through more frequent contact
	Write an article for a firm publication or an outside trade publication
Manager	Develop an annual personal marketing and business development plan
	Seek a more active role in civic organizations, industry associations, or trade groups
	Actively work to identify opportunities to provide additional services to clients
	Expand your referral network and strengthen referral relationships through more focused regular activity
	Actively work to retain new clients
	Write regular articles for your firm's newsletter or speak regularly at client seminars and industry sponsored conferences
Partner	Develop an annual personal marketing and business development plan
	Serve in leadership roles for community organizations and industry associations
	Take an active role in uncovering additional needs for clients
	Actively pursue new business development opportunities
	Continue to build your referral network
	Work to mentor younger professionals just getting started in marketing and sales
	Communicate and praise marketing and sales success of others regularly in the firm
Managing Partner	Actively promote the firm's marketing and business development initiatives throughout the firm
	Take a proactive role in developing new business

TABLE 1-1   EXAMPLE BUSINESS DEVELOPMENT EXPECTATIONS BY STAFF LEVEL (*CONTINUED*)

Managing Partner *(continued)*	Work to mentor up-and-coming professionals just getting started in marketing and sales
	Take younger professionals on prospective sales calls and cross-selling meetings with clients
	Find ways to promote the firm to the business community through community and association involvement
	Communicate and celebrate marketing and sales success regularly across the firm

The next step is to work with each individual to outline how they will be involved in marketing the firm. Align individual's interests with specific goals to be achieved. A good way to do this is to help each professional to develop a personal marketing plan. This plan will help individuals focus on those areas in which he or she is comfortable and interested in participating. For example, if a professional is interested in speaking but not yet comfortable with his or her skills, get them involved in Toastmasters. Team them up with other professionals who have made a name for themselves through public speaking and seminars. Once armed with a clear expectation of their roles, professionals are more likely to get started in serving as marketing ambassadors for the firm. For more information, see chapter 5, "Developing a Personal Marketing Plan."

3. Processes & Tools

Although the accounting industry has operated for decades by delivering service offerings based on processes and standards, the same discipline has not always been applied to growing our practices. Can you imagine conducting an audit without a game plan and standards? So, why don't we apply that same logic to our practice growth initiatives? Although standard procedures may not have been necessary to win work in the past, they are increasingly important as competition has strengthened in the hunt for new business. This need is also fueled by the growing number of seasoned rainmakers who will retire over the next decade.

Defined processes and tools help employees feel more comfortable with marketing and sales because they provide a common game plan to follow and skill set to use, just like in an audit or tax engagement. Defined processes and tools also allow employees to maximize opportunities, while minimizing wasted time and frustration. Increased results can be achieved by utilizing best practices and keeping efforts consistent. Clearly defined processes and tools will not only help clarify and manage expectations, but will enable employees to work together toward gaining stronger market share and revenues.

So, what processes and tools should your firm consider? There are many that can be instrumental in building a sound marketing culture within the firm. The trick is to pick a few to start, and add as needed along the way. Consider the following processes and tools for your firm:

- Common definitions of marketing and sales (chapter 2, "Marketing and Sales 101: A Primer for CPAs")
- Marketing, sales, and client service guidelines and expectations by level
- Marketing and sales plans for the following:

    — Firm (chapter 4, "The Marketing Plan: An Audit-Based Approach")
    — Niche (chapter 6, "Marketing an Industry or Service Specialization")
    — Personal (chapter 5)

- Value propositions—messages that define how your company provides value to its clients
- Defined marketing and sales processes (chapter 2)
- Lead generation processes (chapter 27, "From Opportunity to New Client")
- New business pursuit processes (chapter 27)

- Questions on
    - — prospecting (chapter 27)
    - — sales calls (chapter 27)
    - — referral source development (chapter 24, "Referral Source Development: The Most Powerful, but Underutilized Business Development Tactic")
    - — cross-selling (chapter 30, "Cross-Serving Clients: Integrating Sales and Service Delivery")
- Sales pipeline reports (chapter 4)
- Proposal processes and templates (chapter 28, "Creating Proposals That Win")
- Client service standards (chapter 36, "Developing a Service Excellence Plan for Your Clients")
- Cross-selling processes (chapter 30)

More information on these processes and tools is provided throughout the book.

⚷ Key Concept

Defined processes and tools help employees feel more comfortable with marketing and sales because they provide a common game plan to follow and skill set to use, just like in an audit or tax engagement.

---

4. Training & Support

Successful leaders realize that if they expect their employees to serve as marketing ambassadors and contribute to the firm's growth initiatives, it is more important than ever to provide ongoing, practical training and coaching to build the core competencies it is seeking.

Development of regular, ongoing education not only introduces professionals to skills necessary for successful practice growth, but eases fears that may inhibit participation. Here is a list of some of the skills for your professionals to understand, and one day master, as a result of training programs:

- What's involved in an effective sales call and how to conduct one
- How to develop effective referral relationships
- How to effectively communicate the firm's value propositions
- How to bring the firm's brand to life in serving your clients
- How to make more effective presentations
- How to identify additional needs in serving a client and how to help develop those opportunities into new business

An essential part of a firm's training should be to encourage employees to adapt the applications to their own style. This relieves employees of the pressures of having to be just like one of your firm's most seasoned rainmakers and allows them to be more authentic in their approach.

Personal or group coaching sessions with marketing professionals and experienced rainmakers can help employees achieve greater results over time. These sessions can reinforce new skill sets presented in the classroom. In addition, they can help employees adapt concepts and processes to real-life situations, and help make it more comfortable to include marketing and business development into their regular routines. For more information on sales training, see chapter 31, "Sales Training: The Key to Better Service and Better Clients."

⚷ Key Concept

Successful leaders realize that if they expect their employees to serve as marketing ambassadors and contribute to the firm's growth initiatives, it is more important than ever to provide ongoing, practical training and coaching to build the core competencies it is seeking.

Help Professionals Get Involved

It takes more than training to help people get involved in something new, like business development. Just because people go through a training session or two doesn't mean they will just jump right in and get started. Another trait of firms with strong marketing cultures is that they work hard to help their professionals get involved in marketing. This can include making an introduction to a younger colleague of a referral source, or taking them along on a sales call that they might not normally get the opportunity to attend. It might be taking them to visit a Rotary meeting, or helping them navigate their way at an industry function by making an introduction to long-time business acquaintances.

It's important to create an environment that encourages the alignment of experienced rainmakers with those just getting started. Senior rainmakers often take for granted how far they have come in building referral sources and developing new business. It is powerful to help those professionals who are just getting started to understand that it is normal to feel apprehension, and how important concentrated effort and persistence is to emerging a successful rainmaker.

Nothing is more powerful than for the younger folks to hear this straight from those that they look up to, from the firm's successful rainmakers. It's amazing what some good old-fashioned support and a few introductions can do to help build confidence and contacts that can eventually lead to new business for your younger employees. Remember, these young professionals are the future of your firm. It's important to give them every chance to succeed, even if you had to figure out how to do all this "stuff" the hard way.

? Key Concept

It's important to create an environment that encourages the alignment of experienced rainmakers with those just getting started.

5. Communication

Just because your firm has shared your vision, helped others get involved, developed processes and tools, and provided training doesn't mean your job is done. To build marketing and sales into your culture, you must communicate your efforts inside the organization on a regular basis. This communication is often referred to as internal communications or internal marketing. Its purpose is to reinforce this new way of life, help employees understand why their participation is important, and help them learn how they can get more involved. When employees realize that they are an essential part of the firm's success, it helps motivate and encourage them to get involved. It can also introduce or reinforce new concepts that are being offered in training classes, or promote the new classes by highlighting the differences these classes are making in landing new clients.

Internal marketing communication can take many forms, such as face-to-face meetings, internal blogs, podcasts, and e-newsletters, to name a few. Keys to success include focusing on common messages and communicating those messages clearly and regularly. Successful firms have found that by using a variety of communications tools, or channels as they are often referred to in the marketing world, helps get the message out and reinforce it. Employees not only juggle many priorities but also seek and retain information in different ways. So, variety is your friend in successful internal communications. For more information on internal communications, see chapter 32, "In-House Marketing Communications That Foster Success."

? Key Concept

When employees realize that they are an essential part of the firm's success, it helps motivate and encourage them to get involved.

6. Accountability

It's no secret that CPAs and consultants naturally link expectations and plans with results and accountability. As you are working to add marketing and sales to your firm's routine, why should your business development efforts be any different? Take advantage of the accountability factor that already exists and build upon it.

Goals and plans are a waste of time if you do not help people achieve what is outlined in them. Although professionals may balk at you keeping tabs on them at first, they will come to appreciate the care and attention in helping them and the firm to move forward in its growth initiatives.

Review the results that your team's efforts are yielding on a regular basis. Link the goals in the marketing and business development plans with follow up. If someone commits to completing a project by a certain day, follow up with them to ensure they have done it. You might be pleasantly surprised to find that the task has been accomplished and that the professional was overjoyed with their results. On the other hand, you might find that a professional is struggling to get an initiative off the ground and was embarrassed to ask for guidance to help get them started.

There are a number of ways you can build accountability into your regular routine. This can include a recap of activity and comparison against goals at regular niche meetings, management meetings, department meetings, and one-on-one coaching sessions. Tools and processes that you develop such as pipeline reports and marketing plans will provide you with a common measuring stick upon which to report your results.

Remember, there is no one best way to accomplish this. You must find ways that work for you and your firm's leadership team and stick to them until they become a part of your business operations. Successful firms have found that using an integrated approach is often the most effective way to build accountability into the firm's landscape. As marketing and business development become standard fare, your results will start to develop patterns allowing you to have a better understanding of the results you can expect over time.

When you build an environment of accountability into your marketing initiatives, it won't take long for employees to realize that the firm is really committed to it. It will become evident that marketing and sales are here to stay when employees not only witness a new level of activity in the marketing and sales area, but when they see the firm keeping tabs of all the initiatives being put in place. For more information on accountability, see chapter 34, "Marketing and Sales Metrics Matter: Measuring Results, Calculating Return on Investment."

🔑 Key Concept

Goals and plans are a waste of time if you do not help people achieve what is outlined in them. Although professionals may balk at you keeping tabs on them at first, they will come to appreciate the care and attention in helping them and the firm to move forward in its growth initiatives.

---

7. Celebration, Rewards, & Compensation

We have saved the best and perhaps most important point for last. To successfully build a growth-focused organization, leadership must celebrate and reward success. This recognition not only demonstrates management's commitment to the initiative, but it reinforces successful efforts throughout the firm. What is expected and recognized in the organization will become the norm over time. Sadly, we are often so busy that we fail to take time to recognize the very things we work so hard to accomplish. Even sadder, it doesn't take much effort or resources to recognize the success of our people, yet it can carry the most weight in culture shifts.

People love to be recognized in front of their peers for a job well done. In fact, recognition among peers can often surpass monetary rewards. Make this a regular part of your firm's meetings and recognition programs. Have firm leaders recognize the person or persons behind the success and recount how it occurred. It's amazing how this will create a new energy in your firm. Hearing their successes will help inspire and educate others. It is true that success breeds success. Over time, these efforts will become the norm within the organization.

Here are some ideas to consider for recognizing your employees:

- Develop a traveling award such as a "rainmaker trophy" that is given for outstanding marketing and business development achievements. Rotate it from one winner to the next. Employees will not only take pride in receiving this award in front of their peers, but will proudly display it in their office for their peers to see until a new recipient is named.

- Develop an annual awards banquet to recognize outstanding contributions throughout the year. If you already have an awards program but are not recognizing outstanding achievement for marketing and sales, add a new category or two. For example, rainmaker of the year, rookie rainmaker of the year, most referrals received, etc.
- Feature successful rainmakers on your firm's internal marketing blog or intranet. Include video clips of them so others can learn how they achieved the success.

For more ideas, see chapter 33, "Effective Employee Incentive Programs: How to Bring Out the Best in Your Firm."

Compensation for successful marketing and business development is an issue that also must be carefully considered. Some firms elect to provide monetary rewards in the form of compensation or bonuses for sales success, some elect to take away compensation and bonuses for not contributing to the firm's growth, and some consider it to be another part of the job. It is important for your firm to develop clear guidelines for compensating marketing and business development success in a way that fits into your firm's compensation, bonus, and reward structure. Once in place, it is critical to clearly communicate those guidelines to the members of your firm. Adherence to these guidelines is essential to your ongoing success.

? Key Concept

People love to be recognized in front of their peers for a job well done. In fact, recognition among peers can often surpass monetary rewards.

KEYS TO SUCCESS IN CULTURE DEVELOPMENT

Now that we've explored the seven components in building a marketing and sales culture in your firm, let's take a look at some of the keys to success in putting this new model to work.

Leadership Involvement

Tacking marketing and sales onto the firm's list of "to-dos" is one thing, but to truly build it into your firm's culture is entirely different. To be successful at the latter requires the involvement and support of your firm's top leaders. After all, top leaders set the tone for behavior in your firm and are the ones your employees look to for direction and gauging priorities. When employees see the importance that top leaders place on marketing and sales, they will come to understand that it is also a priority for them.

The following are some of the ways in which firm leaders can play an active role in supporting and promoting the firm's marketing and sales initiatives:

- Involvement in initial marketing and sales kickoff meetings
- Regular updates to the firm that highlight marketing and business development success
- Active participation in marketing the firm and bringing in new business
- Coaching up-and-coming rainmakers
- Introducing younger professionals to counterparts of their referral network members
- Taking part in the firm's marketing and sales training programs
- Recognizing and celebrating employees for business development success

More information on leadership involvement can be found in chapter 9, "Your Leadership Makes Business Development Happen."

It Takes Time

Changing your firm's culture does not happen overnight. Just think how long it has taken your organization to become what it is today. Although you may start to see signs of success in a few months, a true shift in the way you do things will take several years to become part of the norm in your firm. This is an area that many firms struggle with in culture development. We live in a society that wants immediate gratification. Unfortunately, changing behaviors doesn't work like that. It is important to not only realize this from the onset, but to set clear expectations with your team.

One of the best places to start is when you are introducing your firm's vision to your employees. Talk about the process and the time and effort that will be involved. Let them know it is something you are committed to for the long-term. Continue to reinforce this message.

> ## ? Key Concept
>
> We live in a society that wants immediate gratification. Unfortunately, changing behaviors doesn't work like that. It is important to not only realize this from the onset, but to set clear expectations with your team.

It's NOT Something You Get Around To

How many times have you heard members of your firm say, "Right after busy season we will get back to building our business"? We've all been guilty of this from time to time. But if you are truly committed to building a marketing and business development culture, you have to eliminate this type of thinking. It is essential to make marketing part of your regular routine. This change in mind set must start at the top. It must be demonstrated and supported. That means you must continue to encourage and reward business development activity even at peak times. You might be surprised at what happens next. It is generally at those peak times when your efforts are rewarded most. Why? Much to our surprise, it is often in those times when we are top-of-mind with people who can hire us to help them.

Break Down Silos

Successful firms are also adopting new business models focused on collaboration across the organization, versus traditional silo-focused modes of operations such as accounting, tax, HR and IT. Department heads are assembling cross-functional leadership teams to help implement the organization's growth goals. This collaboration might include bringing together marketing, sales, IT, and HR professionals to help the firm develop and implement its customer relationship management system. It might involve bringing together heads from all departments to develop client service standards. Or, it might involve aligning niche leaders to kick-off a successful internal marketing campaign. These united efforts help foster greater teamwork and better communication, while eliminating the duplication of efforts produced by old-school silos. For more information, see chapter 3.

For Better or For Worse

Marketing is often one of the first things to go when the economy gets a little rocky. But it's in these turbulent times when we need to be developing new business opportunities the most. Being seen in the marketplace on a regular basis is the key to success. When you fade into the background in tough times, you can be sending the wrong message to the people you want to do business with. Tough times are often when we can help our clients the most.

The best part is that you don't have to spend loads of money to market. It might be as simple as having coffee with a client or referral source to catch up. Maybe it's taking advantage of a social media tool to post an article or invitation to hear you speak at an upcoming event. Get creative. Do what you have to do to stay in front of your audience on a regular basis.

Create a Fun, Infectious Environment

Just because you are in the accounting and consulting business doesn't mean you can't create fun and infectious work environments. What better way to get disengaged employees involved in new marketing initiatives than to make them exciting and yes, fun. People want to get involved in activities they enjoy. Although many professionals may not realize they will enjoy marketing and business development at the on-set, given the right environment even the skeptics can be pleasantly surprised.

Start with the way you introduce your firm's new marketing focus. Do something that will cause your employees to take notice. Maybe it's a dynamic video or a slide show that depicts how far the firm has come, or an "unplugged" aka unscripted session from key members of your firm's leadership team. Consider new ways to bring your traditional training sessions to life. Make celebrations exciting. Why not have some champagne to toast big wins or a cake to celebrate new business in your pipeline meetings?

Your firm's attitudes are reflected in your interactions with clients, prospects, referral sources and recruits. You better believe job satisfaction is related to profitability. Take time to make it fun for your employees. You will be glad you did and they will too!

Create a Movement

Seth Godin's book, *Tribes*, encourages leaders to start efforts or movements that unite people behind a common cause and in turn fuel that effort. People want something to stand for, especially in tough times. Get a few aboard and help the early adopters achieve success. They will tell others. Before you know it, you will have a tribe of professionals on the marketing bandwagon. So go ahead, make marketing and business development a movement in your firm. They will become a part of your firm's culture right in there with billing and client service.

CONCLUSION

Marketing and business development does not happen by chance. It is not something professionals get around to when it's convenient. It is something they must be committed to throughout the year, just like taking care of their clients. Making a cultural shift requires recalibration, realigning key professionals, and knowledge transfer. That involves sharing a common vision, engagement, infrastructure, accountability, and rewarding success along the way. Isn't it time to make marketing a part of the way your firm does business? Starting today, work to build marketing and business development into your culture. You will be rewarded not only with sustainable growth, but a team of professionals who are inspired by the opportunity to make a difference.

ABOUT THE AUTHOR

As founder of The Crevar Group, **Tracy Crevar Warren** advises clients on practice growth, sales, and marketing. A sought-after consultant, facilitator, author and speaker, her practical, results-oriented approach helps professional services firms win more new business and build more profitable practices. With her proven track record and positive, high-energy style, she inspires and empowers local, regional, national, and international groups to do more of the work they love. Warren is a regular contributing editor for the AICPA's *CPA Insider* and has edited her first book, *Bull's-Eye! The Ultimate How-To Marketing & Sales Guide for CPAs*. Warren can be reached at www.thecrevargroup.com or 336-889-GROW (4769).

CHAPTER 2
Marketing and Sales 101: A Primer for CPA Firms

Tracy Crevar Warren
The Crevar Group LLC

Jamie Trayner
LBA Certified Public Accountants, PA

INTRODUCTION

Because marketing and sales skills are not generally a part of most college accounting curricula, many accounting professionals missed out on essential fundamentals needed to successfully compete in today's new economy.

Just imagine you are back in college to audit an important class that wasn't included in your accounting offerings, Marketing and Sales 101: A Primer for CPA Firms.

On day one for example, you might learn that basic marketing and business development theories and principles are generally the same, whether you are promoting a product or a service. There are, however, unique challenges that face professional services firms and therefore, the strategies and tactics utilized in the professional services industry differ from those organizations that market and sell consumer products.

Because you probably don't have time for an entire semester, this chapter is intended to introduce you to some of the essential vocabulary of professional services marketing and sales, discuss some of its unique aspects, and outline key trends for the new economy.

In some cases, the discussion of a particular concept will be quite brief because the topic is addressed in more depth later in the book. In those instances, the goal is to provide you with an introduction and a basic foundation, and then to refer you to the section of the book where the concept is more fully developed.

Finally, while reference will be made to "marketer(s)" and "business developer(s)," it is understood that many smaller firms do not have dedicated marketing and sales professionals on staff. If this is true in your case, these discussion topics will refer directly to your client-serving professionals.

MARKETING AND SALES—IS THERE A DIFFERENCE?

What a perfect topic of discussion for your first day in the classroom. Many people use the terms *marketing* and *sales* interchangeably, not realizing there is a difference between them. But the difference between the two functions is significant. When both functions work in concert, the results can be extraordinary and can significantly impact the growth of the practice. Firms often fall short in having one function without the other, or in having a disconnect between the two.

First things first, let's define the terms so we are all on common ground.

Marketing is defined as follows:

> Marketing is the activity, set of institutions, and processes for creating, communicating, delivering, and exchanging offerings that have value for customers, clients, partners, and society at large.[1]

---

[1] *As defined by the American Marketing Association, 2007.*

Marketing includes the full-range of activities that differentiate your firm in the marketplace, create brand awareness, cultivate a positive image, and elicit the interest of prospects. It encompasses all aspects of strategic planning including research, analysis, and setting business goals for the firm. Marketing also includes the execution of promotional activities (tactics) such as advertising, Web site initiatives, media relations, direct mail, and so on, to meet the goals set forth in the strategic planning. Marketing moves a potential client through the early phases of the buying process from awareness through consideration. Think of marketing as reaching a broad audience of potential buyers.

Selling is defined as follows:

> Selling is what we do when we are in front of a prospective client.[2]

Selling picks up where marketing leaves off. That is, selling encompasses all of the activities required to convert qualified prospects into clients. Here, the effort involved usually centers around a series of face-to-face meetings between one or more members of your firm and a prospective client. Where marketing reaches a broad audience, selling reaches a single audience, the potential buyer.

With so many misconceptions about marketing and sales, it is important to define these terms specifically for your firm and your employees. Help them to understand what each means, and how they relate to the other in growing your practice. A common understanding is the first step in helping your employees get involved.

Key Concept

Many people use the terms *marketing* and *sales* interchangeably, not realizing there is a difference between them. But the difference between the two functions is significant. When both functions work in concert, the results can be extraordinary and can significantly impact the growth of the practice.

Connecting the Dots Between Marketing and Sales

This is a huge concept. Although it may not be on the test, it can surely affect your salary. So pay careful attention.

Successful practice growth requires a coordinated and integrated effort between marketing and selling. While marketing can create new business opportunities for the firm, it is the sales effort that ultimately closes deals and converts opportunities into revenue. If you do not connect the dots between marketing and sales, you have wasted your time and resources on marketing. On the other hand, if you try to sell without the proper marketing, it is a much more difficult task because you have not introduced your firm to your audience.

The handoff between marketing and sales is the place where many firms struggle. For firms to truly maximize their marketing and sales efforts, it is essential to bridge this gap. In chapter 3, "The Integration Imperative: Erasing Marketing and Business Development Silos," we will explore a new model, developed by Suzanne Lowe in her latest book, *The Integration Imperative,* to help firms with this quest. You will also get to examine how one of the nation's top CPA firms Moss Adams is redefining the way it links its marketing and sales functions.

Key Concept

The handoff between marketing and sales is the place where many firms struggle.

A Changing Economy Calls For a More Structured Approach

Because the days of double-digit growth for many firms has faded, most have realized that what made them successful in the past is not what will make them successful in this new economy. As competition for new business is on the rise, leading firms are focusing their attention on a more structured approach to marketing and sales. This

---

[2] *Alan S. Boress,* The "I HATE Selling" Book *(New York: American Management Association, 1995).*

includes well-defined plans; standard systems, processes, and tools; and metrics that tie actions to results. Firms are also working harder to include more people into the practice growth agenda. We will explore these new concepts in much greater detail throughout the book.

The Unique Aspects of Professional Services

Get ready, this is a rather lengthy but important discussion to help position your firm in the marketplace. For starters, what special challenges await an organization that is going to market a service? The easiest way to begin answering this question is to review the distinctive aspects of a service. Let's begin by defining a service.

> A service is any activity or benefit that one party can offer to another that is intangible and does not result in the ownership of anything. Its production may or may not be tied to a physical product.[3]

Furthermore, all services, including professional accounting services, have four distinct yet overlapping characteristics that must be taken into consideration when designing marketing and sales programs. Each poses specific consequences for your firm.

Intangibility

Services are intangible, which makes them extremely difficult to evaluate and compare. Although these services often have tangible results, including for example, an audit report, a buy-sell agreement, a tax return, a business plan, and so on. The initial purchase decision, however, is based solely on something intangible.

This means your clients and prospects can never be completely sure about the quality of your service prior to making a purchase decision. Business owners who rely on their accountants to guide them on issues that affect their profitability and long-term success know there is a great deal at stake when they choose to select a new provider. Therefore, it is imperative that your marketing and sales strategies include doing what is necessary to help prospects have confidence in the service they will receive from your firm so they can know that they are, in fact, making the right choice.

Inseparability

A service is inseparable from its source, namely, the accountant. The intrinsic value of your firm's accounting services simply cannot be separated from the provider of the service. For example, if you have 200 member firm, a client's perception of the firm—positive or negative—will be based solely on the dealings with those he or she has direct contact with on the job. Because building personal, one-on-one relationships is key, marketing the firm as a whole must always be coupled with efforts to communicate the credentials and strengths of the individuals within the firm.

Variability

Although some processes and procedures can be standardized, generally speaking, the quality of a service is highly dependent on the individual who provides it. Most of your clients and prospective clients already recognize and appreciate this fact. (This is the challenge of inseparability.) Clients, once satisfied that they are being well served by a particular member(s) of your firm, will be reluctant to be assigned to another. The opportunities for the marketing effort then need to be focused on educating the prospects on everything about the credentials and reputation of the individuals within your firm, in addition to acknowledging the image and reputation of the firm as a whole.

Perishability

Because services are intangible and are produced and consumed at the same time, they cannot be stored. When service demand is highly seasonal, your organization faces the additional challenge of delivering quality service while coping with the periodic shortages and surpluses in personnel. For this reason, many firms seek to develop service lines that provide off-season work. Certain consulting engagements, for example, can be performed anytime during the year and not only provide a stream of revenue off-season, but they also help ensure that personnel has ample work throughout the entire year.

---

[3] *Philip Kotler.* Marketing Management: Analysis, Planning & Control, 6th ed. *(Englewood Cliffs, NJ: Prentice-Hall, 1988), 477.*

A second challenge with perishability is staying top-of-mind with a client during the off-season, if the only service you provide to some clients is seasonal. If the service only requires that you have contact with the client during the first quarter, you should determine ways to remain in contact throughout the rest of the year. Whether it is through an occasional phone call, lunch meeting, or quarterly newsletter, efforts should be made to solidify your relationship and build loyalty and top-of-mind awareness year-round.

Client-Centered Versus Service-Centered

Now that we've revealed some unique aspects of professional services, it's time to take a look at some different philosophies to providing services. For starters, let's examine the primary differences between the most common two—client-centered and service-centered.

A firm with a client-centered philosophy understands that its skills and services are only meaningful to the extent that they can help the client achieve business and personal goals. By contrast, a firm that is service-centered fails to ask whether or not its services can help the client solve particular problems. These firms focus more on the technical requirements of the service and the process that should be followed instead of the end result the client wants and needs.

When a client-centered firm makes a decision about the services it will offer or the way it will deliver and price those services, it always asks, "how will the proposed change improve our ability to meet our clients' (and prospects') needs, and help fulfill their objectives?" A service-centered firm—one that fails to ask whether or not (and, if so, how) its services can help their clients solve their problems—risks a great deal because it forces clients to draw their own conclusions about whether or not the benefits they seek will ever be received. Because these clients (and prospects) are ill-equipped to judge a firm on technical merit alone, they will be reduced to distinguishing between competing firms on the basis of price alone. So unless you want to win clients by underbidding your competitors, it is best to avoid this situation.

Communicating Value

This subject might be one of the most important lessons in this chapter, so pay close attention. One of the biggest difficulties in providing a service versus a product is the ability to effectively communicate its value to a potential client. Many professionals struggle with how to best accomplish this task. Therefore, it is essential for your firm to work with its employees to help them in the delivery of the message. Your firm must begin by developing clear messages of how it provides value. These messages are commonly known as value propositions. Value propositions should focus on results and outcomes. Once defined, it is essential to teach your employees how to clearly and effectively communicate them to people outside your firm.

> **♀ Key Concept**
>
> One of the biggest difficulties in providing a service versus a product is the ability to effectively communicate its value to a potential client. Many professionals struggle with how to best accomplish this task.

The Marketing Mix

This is one area of marketing that you are likely to be somewhat familiar with, but just in case, let's take another look. Product marketers have long used the "four Ps" (product, price, place, and promotion) to define what they are selling and to craft marketing strategies. Service marketers can and do use the same approach. However, the four Ps are somewhat limited in scope as they relate to the service industry. In the context of services, the marketing mix can be extended to become the "seven Ps."[4] Three additional components of the seven Ps marketing mix model include people, processes, and physical evidence.

---

[4] B. H. Booms and Mary-Joe Bitner, "Marketing Strategies and Organization Structures for Service Firms," Marketing of Services, J. H. Donnelly and W. R. George, Eds. (Chicago: American Marketing Association, 1981).

It is important to note that accounting marketing professionals have varying degrees of involvement in these seven Ps. Take price for example, few marketers are actively involved in this decision, which is generally left to client-serving professionals. Some of the seven Ps have shared involvement between the two groups. It will be interesting to see how this involvement evolves.

Product

Product refers to the services you are selling. A growing number of firms actually sell products, many related to technology. Consider developing a comprehensive list of the products and services your firm offers and then look at your clients' needs. How well do the two fit? The needs of your clients should dictate the depth and scope of your services.

Price

What fee are you asking for your services? More important, what are your clients willing to pay? While competitive pricing is an obvious necessity, especially during tough economic times, the client's appreciation of the value of your services is a key issue. The higher the perceived value in the work you produce, the more a client will be willing to pay for that service. In essence, you can't charge $5,000 for a service that the client feels is worth $2,000. The bottom line is that the more you can do to successfully build a sense of value in the client's mind, the higher your rates can be.

Place

In the product marketing arena, place refers to the wholesale or retail distribution channels where products can be acquired. For an accounting firm, place refers to your office location as well as the quality and character of your facilities. Your office should be readily accessible to clients with convenient parking. Entry ways, hallways, and individual offices should be maintained scrupulously. This does not mean that you have to spend thousands of dollars on extravagant décor, but everything the client sees should be neat, clean, and orderly, and ultimately reflect your firm's brand.

Place can also refer to a virtual office location on the Internet. Many firms now have "client only" sections on their Web sites allowing clients to access documents and in some instances even conduct business transactions in this virtual business environment. In just the same manner that your office is easily accessible to your clients, and is nicely maintained and organized, so should your client only portion of the Web site. This might include an orientation training session to familiarize clients with how the site works and how to successfully navigate this new virtual office.

Promotion

You can offer the finest, high quality service and stellar results for your clients, but it will not benefit you if it is also the best kept secret. A proper mix of promotional tools will enable you to achieve the exposure and subsequent selling opportunities needed to grow your firm. Promotions include an array of activities including advertising, Internet marketing, and public relations, among others.

People

Service businesses revolve around people. You can have the most comprehensive, cutting-edge marketing strategy, but if you do not have the qualified people to implement it, you will not be successful. This includes marketing and sales professionals to develop and carry out the strategy as well as accounting professionals who will provide the client service. The ability to recruit, train and retain the best talent for the marketing, sales, and client service team is critical to your firm's success. Because people are so crucial to your success, you should offer a pleasant working environment and a comprehensive benefits package that helps boost morale, maintains high worker productivity, and reduces attrition.

Process

Process refers to any procedures, mechanisms, and workflow used to assist in delivering services in accounting firms. The process can be considered the whole client experience and can include scheduling staff on engagements, the software programs used to automate procedures, and the delivery of the final product or service.

Physical Evidence

Physical evidence refers to the environment in which the service is delivered. This piece of the marketing mix includes tangible products that help communicate and perform the service and enables clients to make judgments based on tangible goods. This could include how the marketing materials present the firm, the quality and freshness of the Web site, and even how the staff members dress at the office. Physical evidence, among other things, helps create perception—and perception becomes reality in the mind of the client.

The Internet and Social Media Are Changing the Marketing Mix

These are two subjects that you might not have spent much time studying in school but they can have a tremendous impact on the way you grow your practice. Social media and the Web are having a tremendous effect on the traditional components of the marketing mix. Take *place*, for example. Just look what the Internet has done for CPA firms. Not only can clients connect to their firm's Web sites for document sharing and business transactions, but they can attend firm-sponsored Webinars to learn about new subjects to help them run their businesses without leaving their offices. Social networking sites such as LinkedIn, Facebook, and Twitter are providing professionals with new ways to stay connected to their referral sources and other friends of the firm, including alumni. Sites like YouTube are adding a whole new dimension to recruiting with a venue to post videos that can reach potential employees like never before.

Social media and the Internet are changing rapidly and will continue to expand the ways we reach our audiences. The challenge going forward is to find creative ways to put these new technologies to work, enabling your firm to gain competitive advantage in the marketplace. For more information on the Web, see chapter 18, "Guide to an Effective CPA Firm Web Site." For more information on social media, see chapter 17, "Adding Social Media to Your Marketing Mix."

> **⚷ Key Concept**
>
> The challenge going forward is to find creative ways to put new technologies to work, enabling your firm to gain competitive advantage in the marketplace.

Market Segmentation

Until now, the discussion of this chapter has focused on how to organize internally to achieve the best results in client service, marketing, and sales. It's time to now turn our attention outward to the marketplace and examine techniques your firm can use to identify—and then pursue—the most strategic and profitable opportunities for your firm.

The market for accounting and tax services is extensive, far too large and diverse for any one firm to pursue. Therefore, it makes sense to identify the best opportunities for winning new clients prior to launching a marketing campaign. An analytical process known as *segmentation* is an important tool that you can use as you develop a plan.

Segmentation is the process of dividing the marketplace into distinct groups of potential clients. Because your ultimate goal in marketing is to target segments where you can develop superior market position, you can use the segmentation process to help concentrate marketing efforts where the following conditions apply:

- You can readily meet client needs
- An abundance of potential clients exist
- Client fees and profitability are attractive
- Competition is not particularly strong
- You have something to offer that your competitors don't

Before describing segmentation, it is important to define a market segment. In brief, a market segment is any group of businesses or individuals that share a certain set of characteristics, and, therefore, a fairly similar set of service needs. For example, a market segment could be defined as all manufacturing companies in a geographic area, or all private-practice physicians, or even high-net worth individuals with substantial stock portfolios. Possible criteria to define segments include industry, revenue, type of ownership, number of employees, or geographic location. Individuals can be categorized according to age, income, profession, or other socioeconomic factors. The important thing to remember is that, whatever the criteria, each group can be expected to have a fairly uniform set of requirements and expectations when it comes to providing services.

Because the marketplace, when viewed this way, possesses a nearly infinite number of potential market segments, you should start the analysis process by examining your existing client base to determine where your strengths already lie. Exhibit 2-1 lists the questions to assist with this analysis. The advantage of this approach is that you will gain insight into which market segments you can serve profitably, right now. Having clients in a particular segment will make it easier to obtain more clients versus trying to break into an industry in which you are not experienced.

This does not mean that market segments not currently served should be ruled out. In fact, your own knowledge of the local marketplace or your specific interest in a particular area may have already alerted you to some important opportunities represented by rapidly growing—or changing—market segments. Or, you may find that a market segment, while neither growing rapidly nor changing quickly, is not being served adequately by your competitors. In these cases, research that extends beyond the analysis of your own client base may be required. For that matter, you may need to look to outside resources to obtain a clearer picture of some of the segments you already serve. In either case, valuable research data can be obtained through the Internet, business libraries, trade associations, and chambers of commerce. For more on this see chapter 4, "The Marketing Plan: An Audit-Based Approach" and chapter 6, "Marketing an Industry or Service Specialization."

Exhibit 2-1
Marketing Segmentation Analysis of Client Base

As you review your client base, ask yourself the following questions:

1. Which market segments do we serve most often?

2. Which market segments do we enjoy serving?

3. What are the fees for this type of client and how profitable are the engagements?

4. What are the needs of this market segment, and do we consistently meet those needs?

5. How many potential clients within our geographical service area are in this segment?

6. How much experience do we have serving this type of client?

7. How easy will it be to identify and reach potential clients in this segment?

8. How satisfied or dissatisfied are these prospects likely to be with their current accounting firms?

9. What differentiating factor, if any, do we enjoy over the competition in this segment?

10. Is the market already saturated with competitors or is there room for another firm?

FIGURE 2-1* STRATEGIES FOR GROWTH

	Current Products (Services)	New Products (Services)
Current Markets (clients)	1. Client growth strategy	3. Product development strategy
New Markets (non clients)	2. Marketing development strategy	4. Diversification strategy

Figure adapted and reprinted by permission of Harvard Business Review. H. Igor Ansoff, "Strategies for Diversification," Harvard Business Review, September/October 1954. Copyright © 1954 by the President and Fellows of Harvard College, all rights reserved.

FOUR BASIC GROWTH STRATEGIES

Now, it's time to talk strategy. For starters, which growth strategy will your firm employ to most effectively grow your practice? This is not one of those simulation labs that you often experimented with in your college classes. This one is for real. The strategies you will engage in depend, in part, on whether or not you already serve clients in these segments and whether or not you provide all of the services that these segments demand. When it comes to strategic marketing planning, there are four basic growth strategies, each characterized by a unique set of risks and rewards, as illustrated and explained in figure 2-1.

Growth Strategy 1: Client Growth

Sell additional existing services to current clients. This type of client development is also known as *cross-selling* or *cross-serving.* Cross-selling is probably the easiest, fastest, and most cost-effective way to grow your practice, yet it is one of the most overlooked strategies for growth. Some research and advance work is required because you will have to conduct needs analyses to uncover each client's potential demand for services not currently utilized. For more information on this client growth strategy, see chapter 30, "Cross-Serving Clients: Integrating Sales and Service Delivery."

Growth Strategy 2: Market Development

Sell existing services to new clients. This is an obvious and traditional strategy and is usually the main focus of any firm's marketing efforts. Justifiably so, because the primary objective of this strategy is to do for others what you currently do for existing clients.

Because the services you intend to promote are already in place, you will not have to invest the time and financial resources required to bring those capabilities on board. However, you will have to invest dollars in identifying prospects and communicating the features and benefits of your services to those prospects. Unlike growth strategy 1, you will have to absorb the cost of winning new clients. However, the money invested and the time required to see results, will still be less than what is required for growth strategies 3 and 4. For more information on this growth strategy, see chapter 27, "From Opportunity to New Client."

Growth Strategy 3: Product Development

Develop new products (services) and offer them to existing clients. Sometimes your analysis of existing client needs will reveal that you are not providing all of the services they require. In a situation like this, growth strategy 3 becomes a tool not only for generating new revenue, but for preventing client attrition.

In this strategy, you must invest resources in developing (or acquiring) the new skills needed to meet changing client needs. While you do not have the cost of winning new clients, this strategy generally costs more than strategies

1 and 2 because it usually takes longer (and often costs more) to bring new services online than it does to market existing services. This is because, as a rule, new professionals must be recruited and brought on board, facilities must be readied, and equipment must be purchased.

Growth Strategy 4: Diversification

Develop new services and use them to win new clients. As you can imagine, this strategy involves the highest level of risk and may take the longest amount of time to bear fruit. The reasons are obvious—you will be attempting to market services you have not provided in the past and to a market segment you have never served before. The tasks involved are not easy. First, you must successfully identify the target market's service needs. Then, you must bring those service capabilities online. Finally, you must launch a promotional campaign and win new clients.

This strategy only makes sense when you have identified a new market segment with excellent potential and you believe most of the segments you currently serve offer limited opportunity. Finally, you must ensure that the target market is not already well served by one of your key competitors.

Promoting Firm Services

We have covered a lot of territory, but there is a little more ground to cover before you are up to speed. Once you have targeted desirable market segments and determined which growth strategy or strategies to pursue, it is time to develop a promotional plan. The mix of marketing tactics you will use depends in large part on the nature of your objectives. If a primary objective is to retain current clients and sell additional services to current clients, or both, your plan might revolve around getting everyone in the firm to do the following:

- Consistently deliver excellent service
- Maintain regular contact with all key clients
- Find ways to demonstrate a personal interest in each client's affairs
- Take the time needed to understand client's needs, even if all of that time cannot be billed

If, instead your focus is on winning new clients, your plan might include these strategies:

- Increasing awareness of the firm in target markets
- Identifying and cultivating qualified prospects
- Developing a network of referral sources
- Creating opportunities for face-to-face contact
- Developing personal relationships with key prospects
- Delivering proposals and closing

The marketing tactics you employ will be influenced by the kinds of goals and objectives you have established for your firm. Because specific marketing tactics are explored in such detail later in this book, they are not discussed here. Suffice to say that your choices should be governed by an overriding strategy and a set of marketing objectives.

⚷ Key Concept

The mix of marketing tactics you will use depends in large part on the nature of your objectives.

Accountability, Metrics, & Return on Investment

This subject will probably seem the most comfortable of all those we've covered in the chapter up to this point. Contrary to the way CPAs manage their overall practices, over the past decade when it was not uncommon for firms to achieve regular double-digit growth, keeping tabs on their marketing results was just not a top priority for many firms. As a result, many firms have become complacent in measuring lead generation and sales production, not to mention a return on investment (ROI) for marketing activities.

In this new economy, however, internal accountability is more important than ever. Marketing is no exception. If firms want to make marketing and sales a part of their firm's landscape, leaders must measure marketing and sales results in the same manner as they track productivity and billing. Partner groups from firms of all sizes must demand a better accounting of where investments are made and the impacts they have on their organizations' top and bottom lines. While it is difficult to demonstrate an ROI for all marketing activities (for example, advertising), it is important that you find tangible measures to tie overall activities to results. Let's say you report that since the inception of your new integrated marketing campaign, sales calls are up by 10 percent, your opportunities to propose have increased by 15 percent and your overall win rates on new business have increased by 22 percent. For more information on metrics, see chapter 34, "Marketing and Sales Metrics Matter: Measuring Results, Calculating Return on Investment."

INTERNAL MARKETING COMMUNICATIONS

Another marketing fundamental exists that you need to understand in order to achieve positive results. More than executing outside strategies, successful marketing actually begins inside the CPA firm with your employees. If you expect your employees to excel at being marketing ambassadors for your firm, you must show them the way. Internal marketing communications or internal marketing, as it is often referred to in professional services firms, is the sharing of information throughout the organization, enabling your firm to build and support a consistent marketing and sales approach. It includes activities such as teaching your employees what your brand means and how to bring it to life, helping professionals understand how to communicate your firm's value proposition to your clients, and celebrating success when new business is won. A growing body of research amply demonstrates there is a link between internal marketing and profitability.[5] For more information about internal communications, see chapter 32, "In-House Marketing Communications That Foster Success."

FIRM LEADERS MUST SET THE TONE

One last thing before class is adjourned. For all the techniques discussed in this chapter to be successful in growing your practice, this last one is the most important to keep in mind. Marketing and sales are not something that just happen. If you are really going to operate differently, your firm's leaders must set the tone. They must show people the way. They must help people understand how to get involved. They must tell stories of how their firm's employees are achieving success, and give them the praise and recognition for their heroic efforts. When these things all fall into place, your practice will be well on its way to achieving success. For more information, see chapter 9, "Your Leadership Makes Business Development Happen."

CONCLUSION

Now you've been exposed to the fundamentals of sales and marketing. You now know that marketing and selling professional services requires an understanding of a wide array of concepts and mastery of numerous skills. After reading this chapter, hopefully you have a better understanding and foundation, thus preparing you to tackle the work—and reap the rewards—of the process. By understanding your clients, defining your target markets and determining which growth strategy to employ, you have taken the first steps to begin building your firm.

ABOUT THE AUTHORS

See "About the Editor" for more information on **Tracy Crevar Warren**.

Jamie Trayner leads the firm's vision for growth by directing the client service and marketing efforts for all four LBA affiliates: LBA Certified Public Accountants, LBA Healthcare Consulting Services, LBA Retirement Plan Services, and LBA Wealth Management. She works with the firms' leaders to ensure premier, proactive client service and mentors the firms' future leaders as they develop their own client and professional relationships. Jamie is involved with identifying and developing new industry and service niches and for facilitating LBA's involvement and support of local community organizations. She is also responsible for driving the firm's branding and communications efforts and provides marketing consulting services to clients.

---

[5] *Internal Marketing Best Practices Study: The Six Characteristics of Highly Effective Internal Marketing Programs*, FORUM for People Performance Management and Measurement, Evanston, Illinois: Northwestern University, 2006, www.performanceforum.org.

Jamie is the immediate Past President for the Association for Accounting Marketing (AAM) and was named by *Accounting Today* as one of the Top 100 Most Influential People in the accounting industry. She currently serves as Chair of the Marketing Achievement Awards Committee for AAM.

CHAPTER 3:
The Integration Imperative: Erasing Marketing and Business Development Silos

Suzanne C. Lowe
Expertise Marketing LLC

Scott Jensen
Moss Adams LLP

INTRODUCTION[1]

Marketing and business development functions are the most critical engines for the growth of professional service firms. Period. Together these functions propel a firm forward in every way—helping it adapt to the shifting needs of its clients and serving as the springboard for mutually beneficial relationships between experts and clients.

Clients begin forming impressions of the possible effectiveness of their service providers when they first encounter a firm's marketing and business development processes. Clients may ask themselves (sometimes subconsciously), "Has the firm targeted me well? Are its marketing and sales processes well coordinated? How astute is the firm in learning my needs, trying to retain my business, and developing future-oriented solutions that I haven't even considered myself? How well will this firm deliver its services to my company?"

It's clear that firms are expending tremendous effort on a host of initiatives to better themselves in marketing and business development. But collectively, professional service firms are only just beginning to recognize the serious structural and cultural disconnects that hinder their effectiveness in marketing and selling their services. Currently, the majority of professional firms manage their marketing and business development functions from separate functional silos. Most have no overarching structural integration models or cultural integration principles for marketers and business developers to follow, and little or no documented expectations of formal collaborations, shared accountabilities, or documented co-leadership among functions. All too often, in many firms, collaboration between these functions is the result of individual or small team efforts.

This chapter, which is based on excerpts from the book *The Integration Imperative* looks at a fresh approach to erasing structural and cultural silos, an integrated framework, and a case study on Moss Adams that shows how this imperative can and does work.

> ### 🔑 Key Concept
> Professional service firms are only just beginning to recognize the serious structural and cultural disconnects that hinder their effectiveness in marketing and selling their services.

RECONNECTING MARKETING AND BUSINESS DEVELOPMENT WITH THE BUSINESS

"Don't confuse effort with results." It sounds simple enough, right? But for marketing and business development for professional service firms, it has been a challenge to connect the two. In fact, the majority of those firms with marketers and business developers are less than satisfied with the processes they're using to measure their combined efforts. It's still too hard to connect marketing and business development to tangible results.

Even with praiseworthy advances toward more effective evaluation of their go-to market programs, many partner-driven enterprises still find it easy to fall in love with thrilling marketing and business development initiatives that don't connect neatly into the organization's overall strategic goals. Increasingly, executive managers are asking, "Do these activities actually drive revenues? Do they actually sustain the firm in its marketplace? Do they actually help the firm to grow?"

But what about their marketing and business development programs can firm executives and marketers control and improve? Their structural integration, of course.

INTRODUCING THE INTEGRATION IMPERATIVE

When leaders commit to reconfiguring their marketing and business development structures, inevitably, they find that they must first step back and look at every handoff point along the firm's marketing and sales process, at all the capabilities of their staff to perform the tasks required, and at the depth and scope of the administrative infrastructure and cultural norms the firm maintains to support marketing and business development.

Doing so gives leaders an opportunity to reframe marketing and business development *compellingly* and to integrate these functions (and people's individual roles) *effectively*. Figure 3-1 offers just such a view of both elements of the integration imperative concept. It illustrates how an executive manager could lead efforts to embed marketing and business development into every person's function at a professional service firm (PSF).

FIGURE 3-1   THE INTEGRATION IMPERATIVE CHART

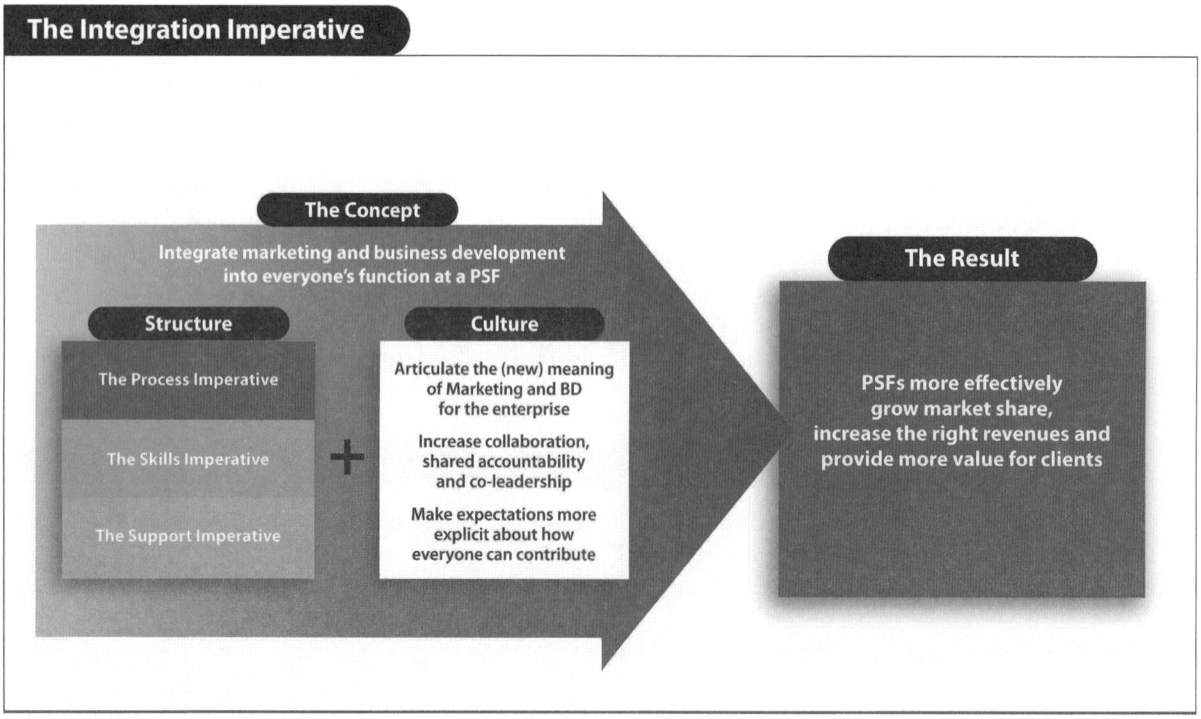

The Integration Imperative

The Concept
Integrate marketing and business development into everyone's function at a PSF

Structure

The Process Imperative

The Skills Imperative

The Support Imperative

+

Culture

Articulate the (new) meaning of Marketing and BD for the enterprise

Increase collaboration, shared accountability and co-leadership

Make expectations more explicit about how everyone can contribute

The Result

PSFs more effectively grow market share, increase the right revenues and provide more value for clients

The *integration imperative* is simple: to achieve marketplace success (beyond mere serendipity, that is), professional service firms must embed marketing and business development into every person's job (although each person will have his or her own role). To overcome the disconnects that exist between marketing and selling processes of today's professional service firms, their executive managers need to devise both structural and cultural solutions.

The bottom line: clients are looking for those firms that develop this kind of integration.

🔑 Key Concept

The integration imperative is simple: to achieve marketplace success, professional service firms must embed marketing and business development into every person's job.

Three Structural Imperatives

The left side of figure 3-1 features three interdependent structural frameworks that, together, would effectively integrate marketing and business development throughout a professional service firm. These are the three structural integration imperatives.

Process Imperative

The first, the *process imperative*, addresses the left-to-right steps in the marketing-to-sales process.

At first glance, it may look somewhat familiar: many firms have created their own versions of this framework. With the process imperative, it's suggested that firms broaden their scope of marketing and business development functions, balance them better strategically, make them more discernible to everyone in the firm, and make them more obviously iterative.

Skills Imperative

The second, the *skills imperative*, is directed at the bottom-to-top pathway of marketing and business development skills growth. Of course many firms have created their own well-recognized career pathways for their practitioners. With the skills imperative, though, it's suggested that firms reframe their advancement pathways—for practitioners and nonrevenue generating staff—to more clearly outline the steps every professional can take toward competency growth in marketing and business development.

Support Imperative

The third, the *support imperative*, frames the lateral working relationships between a professional firm's administrative peers in human resources, information technology, finance, legal, and other operational functions. Many firms already enjoy the results delivered by the friendly, informal working relationships that exist between these support functions and their marketing and business development colleagues. With the support imperative, it is recommended that firms create more formal avenues for function-to-function collaboration, shared accountability, and co-leadership for marketing and business development.

ADOPTING A BROADER FUNCTIONAL PURVIEW FOR MARKETING AND BUSINESS DEVELOPMENT

To build a structure for integrating marketing and business development, executive managers will have to broadly redefine their functions. More specifically, they will have to help those under them adopt new perspectives on what the functions could mean for themselves and their firms.

What does it really mean to "broadly redefine" marketing and business development? Most firms deploy these functions in a much more limited way than they could. For example, in the typical firm the term marketing is used to refer solely to building visibility, promotion, and increasing awareness of and communicating about the firm. In some firms, marketing was—and, for many still is—a back-of-the-house support activity for a firm's sales efforts, with no marketing interface with the firm's clients. In still other firms, marketing actually means selling.

But to be clear, marketing is a one-to-many activity. The optimal scope of marketing in a professional enterprise should be broader, and could even begin to resemble the way in which marketing is deployed in a products company. For example, take the classic four Ps (price, product, position and place) that are taught in many graduate schools.[2] Today, most professional service marketers have no responsibility for at least two of those Ps: price and product. Shouldn't the senior-most marketers have at least advisory responsibilities, if not a lead role in those two areas? What about market and client behavior research? Client satisfaction? Competitive intelligence?

In product or retail companies, these functions are well established. In the professional service arena, they largely have no formal home, much less a home under the marketing umbrella. Because the professional service arena is growing in maturity and competitiveness, and the business focus and experience of senior professional service marketers are deepening, it's time to broaden the term marketing and its purview.

These structural frameworks, when implemented in combination with a deliberate effort to change the culture, form a powerful yet flexible foundation that breaks down a professional service firm's marketing and business development barriers. The result? Professional firms can more effectively grow their market share, increase the "right" revenues, and provide greater value to their clients.

> **Key Concept**
>
> To build a structure for integrating marketing and business development, executive managers will have to broadly redefine their functions and help those under them adopt new perspectives on what the functions could mean for themselves and their firms.

CULTURAL CHANGE MANAGEMENT: THE GLUE FOR NEW STRUCTURAL FRAMEWORKS

However compelling they might look on paper, new structural frameworks, process maps, and skill-level benchmarks won't be enough to erase the marketing and business development silos found in so many professional service firms. They need glue: changes in the organization's culture. Fortunately, cultural change is not viewed with the same trepidation that it might have been even a decade ago.

Cultural change cannot be haphazard or led casually. To influence the change that best serves the firm, leaders will have to embrace principles of change management. The structural framework of integrating marketing and business development will have to be supported mindfully with clearly outlined cultural principles and desired outcomes.

> **Key Concept**
>
> Cultural change cannot be haphazard or led casually.

Three Cultural Integration Imperatives

The middle of figure 3-1 features a set of three interdependent cultural principles that, taken together, will effectively integrate marketing and business development throughout a professional service firm.

The first cultural principle is to articulate the new meaning of marketing and business development for the firm. It addresses a particularly vexing hurdle to integration: definitions of the terms marketing and business development. Adopting an updated lexicon and assimilating it throughout the organization can be a pivotal point for firms striving to integrate marketing and business development. Moreover, a common lexicon is critical to introducing people to a firm's newer and more expansive way of perceiving marketing and business development. It's also vital in reducing the unmatched expectations that are often found among practitioner populations of professional service firms.

---

[2] *Philip Kotler and Gary Armstrong,* Principles of Marketing, *12th ed. (Upper Saddle River, NJ: Pearson Education, 2007).*

The second cultural standard is that of increasing formal avenues of collaboration, shared accountability, and co-leadership on marketing and business development. Structural models are not enough to help professional firms optimally integrate marketing and business development functions. Too often, firms create gorgeous structural frameworks that don't outline formal pathways for collaboration and accountability sharing and co-leadership between practitioners and nonrevenue generating staff. Sure, firms do encourage their people to collaborate or share leadership with their colleagues, but these pathways are often obscure. They aren't expected, just hoped for.

The third cultural paradigm is that executives should make their expectations about how everyone can contribute to marketing and business development more explicit. New lexicons and internal communications techniques are not enough. Leaders must also apply a potent new kind of cultural glue: reviewing and integrating job descriptions, checking and integrating reporting relationships, and reframing performance management guidelines to ensure that people understand how they are expected to work together in new ways toward meeting the organization's revenues, market share, and client added-value goals.

How the Integration Imperative Can Benefit Professional Firms—and Their Clients

Executives continually assess the threats and opportunities that face their firms. Their mandate is to weigh the benefits and risks of investing resources in making changes that might help achieve the organization's goals. At each decision juncture, they consider trade-offs of investing in the improvements they contemplate. If we undertake *this* effort and commit *those* resources, will it make a positive difference in our revenues? Our market share? Our advantage over our competitors? And of course the biggest question, will the effort we are contemplating benefit our clients?

Multiple compelling benefits exist for establishing the structural frameworks and cultural changes in the integration imperative. They can simply be grouped, though, into two areas—internal and external benefits.

Internal Benefits

The first benefit generally addresses the firm's internal advantages, and relates to its own growing revenues, expanding market share, prevailing over rivals, and recruiting and retaining talented people. The internal benefits of integration include the following:

- Integration knocks down the functional silos in marketing, business development, and client service
- Integration is comprehensive
- Integration improves innovation
- Integration is demonstrable
- Integration is flexible
- Integration is measurable
- Integration is customizable
- Integration improves marketing and business development effectiveness

External Benefits

The second area focuses externally on those benefits that clients can directly observe from firms that have embraced the structural and cultural approaches of the integration imperative. These benefits center on the greater probability that clients will enjoy better value propositions and service delivery, and that they will simply find it easier and more enjoyable to do business with firms that have adopted the integration imperative, instead of firms that haven't. These external benefits include the following:

- Integration helps create better client value propositions
- Integration fosters a better understanding of client needs
- Integration promotes better service delivery

The Integration Imperative Can and Does Work— A Case Study

One firm that has made notable progress in better connecting marketing and business development handoffs is west coast-based Moss Adams.

Who's Sailing the Boat? Us or the Economy?

In mid-2006, a group of Moss Adams's office managing partners and industry group leaders gathered in Phoenix, Arizona for the firm's annual leadership meeting. Moss Adams's chairman Rick Anderson said the following:

> We have never proven that we can grow this firm in flat economic cycles. Historically, when the economy expanded, we expanded. When the marketplace hit a downturn, we went flat. I want to change that. We are pretty good at marketing, but we need to get a lot better. We are pretty good at service, too, but we must get better.

Attending the meeting was Scott Jensen, who had just joined Moss Adams as its first ever director of sales. Having previously led regional sales efforts at a much larger accounting firm, Jensen had seen up close what he believed were accounting firms' propensity to expend enormous amounts of marketing resources that ultimately produced minimal or no uptick in awareness in potential buyers, or for that matter, revenues.

Jensen believed Moss Adams's marketing was in many instances disassociated from the firm's overall business processes. Displaying his trademark straight-talk style, Jensen had this to say to his new colleagues:

> Our people, partners, and senior managers too often confuse marketing activity with value. If we put out brochures, if we had ads going out, things would be good. Our people are tempted to have us drum up a lot of marketing initiatives, especially for example, when they see our competitors aggressively launching huge rebranding campaigns. But we have to be very cautious about feeding our egos. For marketing to be really good, it's got to be tied to the business.

> I'd rather have us closer to the dollars. Dollars come from clients. What's the bridge between marketing and service? We've always said our business is a relationship business. Nobody buys Moss Adams because we have the coolest ads. Sure, they might be aware of us because we have a cool ad, or because of our brochures, or because they've attended our events. But few people buy our services because of those things.

Redefining the Way a Professional Service Firm Links Its Marketing and Selling Activities

Jensen did not start out with a focus on structure. Jensen's first order of business was to convince his colleagues that they had to change their behavior. Why change after coming off a record year? Instead of relying on a broad variety of marketing initiatives that they hoped would start the phone ringing with qualified prospective clients, Jensen wanted to see Moss Adams accountants and business consultants demonstrating their personal involvement in initiating and building client relationships.

He decided not to engage Moss Adams professionals in the obvious—a one-time internal training seminar, something the firm had tried in the past. Instead he embarked on a significant internal campaign to introduce them to an entirely new model of growing revenues and expanding market share.

Jensen and the executive team were prepared for a long change management slog. But serendipity stepped in to speed things dramatically. It happened quite by chance during a meeting in the firm's Spokane office. Accompanied by the Moss Adams training leader, Heather Kean, Jensen listened as one of the partners expressed a desire for sales presentation training. Jensen thought this was too limiting, and he marched up to the white board to sketch out his vision of what was more appropriate. What emerged was a rough draft of what became the Moss Adams' Marketing and Business Development Continuum (figure 3-2).

**FIGURE 3-2   MOSS ADAMS MARKETING AND
BUSINESS DEVELOPMENT CONTINUUM**

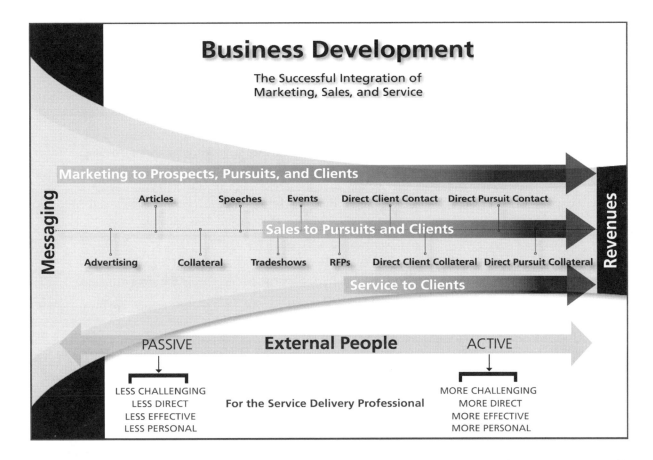

Key Concept

Do not start out with a focus on structure. The first order of business is to convince colleagues that they have to change their behavior.

On the left side, Jensen's rough drawing illustrated the passive tactical vehicles of marketing ("Messaging"), including advertising and articles. Moving to the right of the drawing, Jensen showed at what points different, more active tactics should be used as the personal connection with the prospect becomes closer. The right side of the drawing was labeled "Revenues." He noted that both marketing and business development dealt with messages and while marketing is dominated by statements, business development is dominated by questions.

He was surprised when he heard later about the enormous impact his rough sketch had on his colleagues. Kean explained, "Suddenly people could see the difference between marketing and sales and service, and the interdependence between these functions. Scott presented these ideas with a clarity they hadn't seen before."

The second visual, now called the Moss Adams Marketing and Sales Process, also emerged by chance. In March 2007, Jensen met with the Moss Adams IT group about the firm's efforts to acquire and implement a new client relationship management system. Jensen wanted his new customer relationship management (CRM) system to be built not only around marketing and sales, but also around eventually accommodating how the firm serves its clients. The members of the IT group could not implement a CRM system without understanding Moss Adams' business processes.

Once again, Jensen jumped up to a white board. "I ranted for about 10, maybe 15 minutes. It was boom, boom, boom." "I tried to help them visualize how marketing and sales and service work together, not against each other, and that while we may not have had a documented process, we did have a process." Like before, this now-iconic visual emerged from Jensen's brain about 80 percent complete.

In the final version (see figure 3-3 at the end of the chapter), marketing was placed to the left. It is in charge of initiating and leading broad tactical vehicles to fill the firm's revenue generation pipeline. In the middle is a series of left-to-right stepwise boxes, in a flowchart format, with go/no go decision checkpoints. Along its bottom, the graphic depicts how marketing tactics move qualified leads through the firm's marketing and sales process, and how these tactics help broaden and deepen relationships, from prospect to client to repeat client.

Building New Norms about How to Market and Sell

Despite the enthusiasm and clarity generated from his work, Jensen knew he would not be able to rely on his beautifully formatted process charts or his new internal communications to make his vision come to life. He knew he would have to connect marketing and selling to the ultimate prize: service to clients.

> I knew our people got the message that there is a difference and dependence between marketing and selling. They understood that we cannot effectively sell unless we market, and that we cannot market unless we sell, and finally that without superior service, both are wasted. Marketing is too expensive without selling. Selling is too hard without marketing. But when we market, we send messages to the marketplace. That creates a sense of expectation about Moss Adams.

> So, when we market effectively and sell correctly we establish the basis for serving passionately. Because now our clients know what they believe about us from marketing, and what to expect from selling. From there, it should be easy to fulfill those expectations during the service process.

In order to guide his colleagues' understanding of these complex concepts and their embrace of them, Jensen built a cultural change program around four key elements. These included:

- Training
- Introduction of sales tools or infrastructure
- The pipeline—targets group accountability
- Celebration

Change Requires Commitment

"Culture is a long term proposition and our early results are encouraging," concludes Jensen. "Revenue continues to grow even in this slowing economy. Our pipeline is strong, with more than 2000 identified significant pursuits."

Anderson added, "We sold, albeit a bit poorly, before Scott came. He is the impetus for the improvement, and I could not be happier with the progress we have made. In the end, though, it is not one man, but one firm that makes the difference. We now have the training, the tools, the accountability, and we are seeing the performance."

ABOUT THE AUTHORS

Suzanne Lowe, the founder of Expertise Marketing LLC, is a highly regarded consultant, author, and speaker on professional service marketing strategy. She is the author of *Marketplace Masters: How Professional Service Firms Compete to Win* (Praeger Publishers: 2004), and *The Integration Imperative: Erasing Marketing and Business Development Silos — Once and for All — in Professional Service Firms* (Professional Services Books: 2009). She also publishes a monthly newsletter, The Marketplace Master™ and blog The Expertise Marketplace™. Lowe speaks for leading trade associations and in-house audiences, and writes for premier publications, including the *Harvard Business Review* and *BusinessWeek*. She facilitates Roundtables of Chief Marketing Officers from some of the world's most prestigious professional service firms.

As the Director of Sales for Moss Adams LLP, **Scott Jensen** has passionately constructed a firm-wide integrated business development culture that aligns marketing, sales, and service. His efforts include implementing a sales training and coaching program, building sales tools and infrastructure, establishing the forward-looking accountability inherent in a sales pipeline for all selling professionals, and creating a sense of celebration that promotes the changes and successes.

With a BA from Iowa State University and an MBA from the University of St. Thomas, Scott has more than 12 years experience working in professional services, including Moss Adams, Ernst and Young and Stoel Rives. Prior experience includes almost 20 years as an international arms merchant. He is also a proud father of three adult children (a professor, a naval officer, and an attorney) who still like him and is blissfully married to his high-school sweetheart for almost 32 years.

FIGURE 3-3 MOSS ADAMS MARKETING AND SALES PROCESS

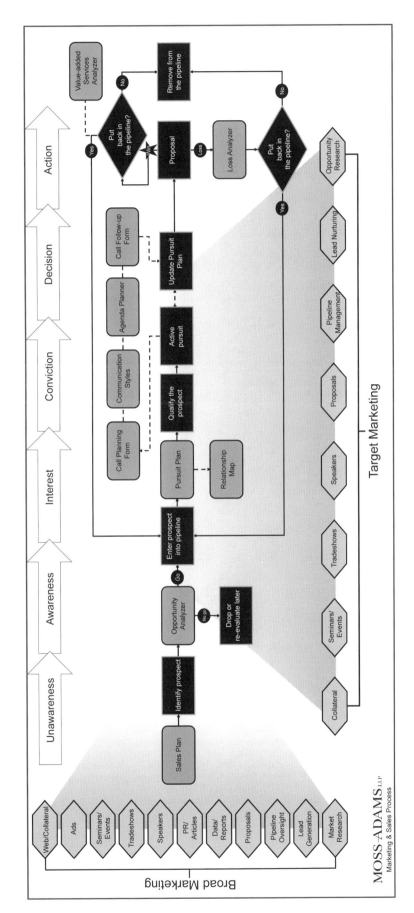

PART II:
Getting Started

CHAPTER 4
The Marketing Plan: An Audit-Based Approach

August J. Aquila, PhD
AQUILA Global Advisors, LLC

INTRODUCTION

Marketing begins with the market. And while that statement may seem simplistic, too many CPA firms spend a great deal of time, money, and effort creating a marketing plan that has little to do with their real market. My 27 years of experience has taught me that CPAs are anxious to jump right into marketing without doing the necessary planning, without really knowing what the marketplace needs or wants, and without having a clear vision for their firm or practice unit.

Successfully investing marketing dollars requires a thorough understanding of your market, the skills of your people, your competitors, and most of all your clients and prospects. This chapter provides both the theoretical and practical knowledge needed to (1) perform a marketing audit, (2) develop a marketing plan, and (3) develop tools to help you implement and manage the plan.

MAKE IT EVERYONE'S PLAN

The major mistake that managing partners and directors of marketing often make is to create a marketing plan without the involvement of everyone who will participate in the firm's business development efforts. Remember that if there is no involvement there is no commitment. While not all of the partners will be wildly enthusiastic about participating in the planning process, embracing a democratic process will help foster an atmosphere of creative thinking and active participation. The more everyone knows about the marketing effort, the faster the firm can embrace a marketing culture and implement the plan.

> **⚷ Key Concept**
>
> Creating a marketing plan without the involvement of everyone who will participate in the firm's business development efforts is a common mistake.

1. Perform a Marketing Audit

Think of the marketing audit as the foundation for a new home. If it is not constructed properly the home will never be stable and the homeowner will always have problems with the house. A well-done marketing plan can infuse your partners with a common sense of purpose and provide the firm with an acceptable rate of return on its invested marketing dollars.

The audit process is designed to examine a number of areas essential to developing your plans. To facilitate the information-gathering process, use survey instruments like those described in appendix 4-1. Areas of focus include the following:

- Organizational, management, and firm issues related to marketing
- Owner and employee perceptions
- Client base and market segmentation

- Trends affecting the key client industries
- Competition
- Client service
- Current marketing activities
- Recruiting and training

With the exception of the first survey, the rest should be completed by those who will have some responsibility for the firm's marketing efforts. Don't forget to gather information from your administrative staff, especially your receptionist.

What is the best way to elicit candid and thoughtful responses from firm members? One approach is to distribute the questionnaires in appendix 4-1 and ask each respondent to fill his or her forms out separately. If you guarantee confidentiality, you might receive more candid, possibly even negative, observations. The important thing is to get at the facts and feelings of your people.

A second approach is to ask an in-house marketing professional or outside consultant to conduct one-on-one interviews. This is usually more effective as a skilled interviewer can rephrase questions and pursue interesting lines of thought. Hence, you will normally get more information from each participant.

A third approach is to bring everyone together in a brainstorming session to discuss the questions on each survey. If you only select this option, make sure you have a skilled facilitator who can keep the discussion focused and ask pertinent open-ended questions. The facilitator needs to draw remarks from everyone in the meeting and prevent any one person from dominating the discussion.

⚡ Key Concept

Think of the marketing audit as the foundation for a new home. If it is not constructed properly the home will never be stable and the homeowner will always have problems with the house.

---

2. Develop a Marketing Plan

Creating the marketing plan includes three key steps. Each will be described in this section. These steps include

- identifying marketing strengths, weaknesses, opportunities, and threats;
- developing marketing objectives and strategies; and
- developing tactical work plans.

Identifying Marketing Strengths, Weaknesses, Opportunities, and Threats

Once the survey instruments have been collected and tabulated, you will be able to identify the firm's internal strengths and weaknesses, as well as external opportunities and threats. This is referred to as a SWOT analysis.

The SWOT analysis should help you identify such items as

- The firm's marketing environment. How prepared are the members of the firm to undertake the marketing initiative?
- The best markets to go after. There are three aspects of a market that must be considered—its needs, its size, and its location.[1]
- The service and product gaps. Can the firm actually provide the services and fulfill the needs of the market it has identified? If there are gaps, they need to be addressed.
- Skills and staffing needs. What additional staff and what new skills will the existing staff need in order to serve the market?
- Pricing and profitability. Each market niche will generate different levels of profitability and pricing levels.
- How much will the market bear and how efficient can you be in getting the product and service to market?

---

[1] *For more information, see* Client at the Core: Marketing and Managing Today's Professional Services Firm, *by August J. Aquila and Bruce W. Marcus (Wiley, 2004).*

Once you have your list of key findings, it's a good idea to present them to all of the key members of the firm for additional comments and feedback. The time you spend in this stage of the process will pay handsome dividends in the future.

Developing Marketing Objectives and Strategies

Objectives

Objectives tell you what you must do to implement your strategies. They must be concrete and realistic. They need to spell out what you want to accomplish. No marketing plan, as Bruce W. Marcus has written, can be developed without a clear view of objectives. Objectives need to be measurable, otherwise how will you know when you have accomplished them.

For instance, you could have marketing objectives in any of the following areas:

- Services—develop a new service niche
- Clients—change the make-up of the existing client base
- Employees—improve employee communication and listening skills
- Internal Processes—improve turn-around time for tax returns
- Financial—grow through acquisitions
- Name Recognition—increase visibility and name awareness
- Financial—obtain a return on investment of 15 percent

Each objective needs to be measurable. Once the general objective is set, then you need to determine how the success of that objective will be measured. The following are some examples of measurable objectives:

- To acquire a two-partner firm with expertise in state and local taxation within the next 18 months
- To increase visibility for our estate planning practice, we will present a series of five seminars to two bank trust departments by the end of 20XX
- To send 50% of our reluctant salespeople through a professional sales training course before the beginning of next year's tax season
- To send Mary Jones, a manager, and Kate Wellington, a new partner, to a leadership training program by December 31, 20XX

Make sure your objectives are relevant and useful by asking the following questions:

- Can we realistically achieve this objective?
- Do any obstacles exist that will prevent us from achieving it?
- Is this objective worth the time and money required to achieve it?
- Can we measure it?
- Can we accomplish it in the time allotted?
- Does it support the firm's mission?

Remember objectives are not cast in stone. While they act as the foundation for designing your marketing program, you should be prepared to change them as conditions and circumstances change.

Finally, to make sure your objectives become everyone's objectives, involve everyone in the goal-setting process. Your people need to know how their daily activities are aligned with the goals of the firm. The more your people participate in the building of objectives, the more they will feel a sense of ownership and they will begin to act as champions of a particular objective.

Selecting Strategies

While objectives tell *what* you plan to do, strategies tell *how* you intend to accomplish the objectives you have set out for yourself. You will find that there are several ways to achieve a goal. For example, you set a goal to increase profitability in the auto dealer niche practice by 10 percent in the next 12 months. Here are some strategies examples to achieve the goal.

Cost reduction. You can further automate the services you are currently providing, thus reducing your cost of service. You could have lower cost personnel do more of the work that previously was done by more senior people. You could also share some of the people in your niche area with other departments in the firm.

Client service. A client service strategy would be not only to strengthen ties with clients but to reduce client turnover. A strategy might be that each owner has to spend five nonbillable hours with clients in order to understand the client's business.

Service delivery enhancement. Perhaps your strategy requires you to improve on the timeliness of delivery. Clients have indicated dissatisfaction with your inability to deliver your services in a timely manner. Reengineering your workflow process or going to a digital environment for working papers may help in this area.

Client profitability. Not all clients are equally profitable. In fact, some may even cost you money to serve them. Knowing which clients add the most to your net income is critical in determining who to serve and how to service them.

Product/service development. Another way to increase the profitability of an area is to offer services that have a higher value to the client. Hence the client will pay more for them. For example, tax planning has a higher value to the client than tax preparation. Strategic planning services or profit improvement is worth more than bookkeeping.

Positioning strategy. In every market there is the most expensive firm and the most inexpensive firm, and everything in between. Where should you position your firm in terms of fees, range of services, reputation, value, aggressiveness, innovativeness, etc.?

Strategy Selection

By comparing the information you now have about your client base and the market, you can determine which market segments to pursue and which to devote little, if any, marketing resources. Figure 4-1 illustrates a standard market segment grid.

FIGURE 4-1 STANDARD MARKET SEGMENT GRID

		Market Attractiveness		
HIGH			1 Highly attractive market Weak Position	2 Highly attractive market Strong Position
LOW			3 Less attractive market Weak Position	4 Less attractive market Strong Position

Firm's Marketing Position

WEAK   **STRONG**

1. *Invest for long-term growth.* When you have identified a highly attractive market segment in which you currently have little or no market share, the best way to respond is to invest for long-term growth. Marketing dollars spent today will not yield short-term results. It will take time for your firm to build up a presence and a reputation in this segment.

continued

FIGURE 4-1 STANDARD MARKET SEGMENT GRID *(CONTINUED)*

2. *Invest to capitalize on existing market dominance.* When a firm dominates a highly attractive market segment, it is in the best of all possible worlds. The firm's main challenge is to win even more market share. It makes excellent sense to invest marketing dollars in this segment (provided that it is still a growing and not stagnant or declining segment) because they should pay back dividends quickly.

3. *Pursue new clients but only the best opportunities.* A firm's response to an undesirable market segment in which it has little presence is to be very selective in its pursuit of new business. Indeed, the firm might only seek out new clients that offer premium profitability or some other compelling reason to do the work.

4. *Manage existing relationships to maintain current market share.* If one of the market segments you presently serve is in decline, your best bet is to service existing clients well, provided they are profitable for the firm, but not to seek out additional opportunities in this segment.

Selecting the right strategy for your firm can be a challenge. There are many ways to achieve your goal and to select the strategies that best suit your needs. Consider these four questions:

- How does the strategy fit the organization?
- Does the firm have sufficient resources to support the strategy?
- Do the economics of the strategy make sense?
- How is the market likely to respond or react to the strategy?

Firms normally pursue more than one market segment at a time. What works for one segment may not work for another. If you pursue more than one market segment, just make sure you have the financial and human resources to execute all of them with excellence.

Developing Tactical Work Plans

Now is the time to develop tactical work plans designed to achieve those objectives. As you enter into this final phase of creating the marketing plan, ask yourself the following questions:

- Do we have all the key people in the firm supporting and committed to the plan?
- Are expectations of what we will accomplish in the first year clearly articulated?
- Have marketing responsibilities been assigned?
- Is part of partner and employee compensation tied to the successful execution of the marketing plan?
- Have we identified marketing and sales training programs for partners and employees?
- Is there a recognition program?

It is essential to develop an integrated and disciplined marketing plan so the various marketing tools work together and support each other. Figure 4-2, the marketing funnel, illustrates the various marketing tools and how they should fit into your plan. The marketing funnel also illustrates how your marketing activities can be orchestrated to draw prospective clients into closer and closer proximity with the firm. And once they become clients, your marketing cannot stop.

Let's review these four categories of marketing activity (broadcast, mid-range, target, and client).

☝ Key Concept

It is essential to develop an integrated and disciplined marketing plan so the various marketing tools work together and support each other.

FIGURE 4-2   THE MARKETING FUNNEL

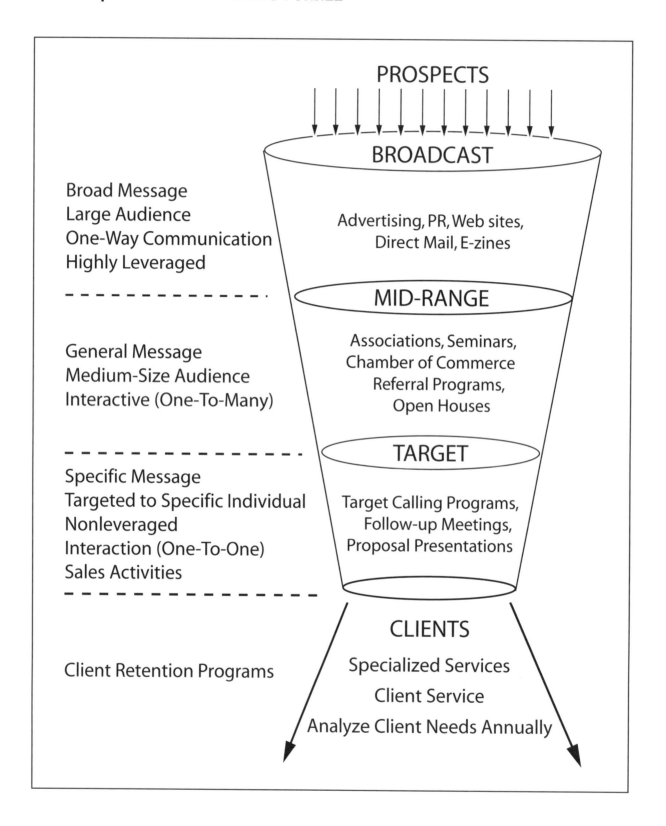

Broadcast-Level Activities

Broadcast marketing, as its name implies, includes those marketing tools that cast out a wide net. They include such marketing activities as advertising, public relations, general direct mail and various types of printed and electronic newsletters, and brochures.

Their main purpose is to create awareness of and interest in the firm and its services. This is a cost-effective way to reach a large audience and is a highly leveraged activity.

Historically, broadcast activities were usually one-way communication—from you to your target audience. However, with the advent of e-mail and electronic newsletters, clients and prospects now have a method of responding immediately. Blogs and Twitter® can fall into broadcast activities or mid-range activities below. For more information on broadcast-level activities, see part IV of the book, *Marketing Techniques That Get You Noticed*.

Mid-Range Activities

Mid-range activities bring prospects that may already be aware of your firm into direct contact with a representative where they can acquire more information that is pertinent to their particular concerns.

Think of seminars, association meetings, chamber of commerce functions, referral source development programs, and open houses as primary examples of the marketing tools that fall into this category. More recently, Webinars have become an attractive and cost-effective marketing tool to reach target markets.

Although these activities reach a smaller audience at any one time, they offer a greater possibility for conveying a more tailored message through a period of questions and answers. And because a firm representative should always be present, the opportunity for two-way communication is enhanced.

Since these activities are not as easily leveraged as those described in the broadcast category, more marketing time is required by firm personnel. In addition, partners and employees will need to develop new and different competencies, such as public speaking skills. For more information on mid-range activities, see part IV of the book, *Marketing Techniques That Get You Noticed*.

Target-Level Activities

Target-level activities are geared toward prospective buyers or prospects, as they are commonly known in business development. Your focus will be on those who are now in the "buying" phase of the cycle. These are prospects that are actively looking for a new accounting and consulting firm but have not yet made their selection.

It is important to note that marketing and sales intersect during this phase. Target-level activities usually involve one-on-one communication and cannot be leveraged. They are extremely important because if you do not perform these activities you will not convert prospects into clients.

The principal activities in this category include follow-up on leads generated by seminars and direct-mail, sales calls, proposal preparation and presentation, and any other face-to-face prospect meeting. For more information on converting prospects into clients and developing winning proposals, see chapters 27, "From Opportunity to New Client," and 28, "Creating Proposals that Win."

Client Marketing Activities

Just because you have been successful in taking suspects, qualifying them as prospects, and finally making them new clients of the firm, you cannot stop marketing to them. Many firms today use what is called a *spotlight* approach in their on-going marketing efforts. This is a disciplined examination of the client's potential unmet needs by the members of the service team. This and other client service activities will help ensure client loyalty and longevity.

By using the marketing funnel concept when you plan your marketing program, you can screen the market selectively for the best possible prospects within your target markets. At the same time, the marketplace is screening you and you need only apply yourself to pursuing those opportunities that offer the highest promise and the greatest return on your investment.

With proper planning, you can eliminate the risk of squandering highly leveraged and costly marketing activities on individuals and companies that may not represent the best opportunity for your firm.

♀ Key Concept

It is not enough to take suspects, qualify them as prospects, and make them new clients of the firm. You must continue marketing to them.

---

3. Develop Tools to Help You Implement and Manage the Plan

Now that the marketing plan is written, the real work begins. A plan is only as good as it is implemented. Implementation is a day-by-day activity. Your implementation strategy needs to focus on who, where, when and how. If the firm's partners are aligned with the marketing plan, it will be easier to get the job done.

Managing the implementation phase of your plan will be a challenge. To be more efficient, consider using the following tools:

Time line for implementation (action plan). This is an overview of the marketing activities you will execute in the next 12 months. Figure 4-3 provides a sample time line (or action plan) for a small tax practice. For each activity in this figure you will want to develop a work plan.

Work plans. Using the time line as a guide, develop a work plan for each marketing activity planned. Figure 4-4 illustrates a sample work plan in support of one activity on the time line—holding an open house. Work plans force you to break each marketing project down into discrete action steps. You also have to assign responsibility for each action item, determine approximately how many hours are required to complete the task, and establish start and end dates. There is also a column for the actual completion date so you can monitor the progress in meeting self-imposed deadlines.

FIGURE 4-3   ACTION PLAN SUMMARY—TAX

ACTION	Jan	Feb	Mar	Apr	May	Jun	Jul	Aug	Sept	Oct	Nov	Dec
Establish Plan Objectives					X							
Identify Target Markets					X	X						
Launch Internal Communications Program											X	
Launch External Awareness (PR) Program											X	
Develop Mid Year Tax Memo				X	X							
Develop Year End Tax Memo/Brochure										X		
Hold Open House											X	
Promote Tax Planning Seminar										X	X	
Develop Financial Services Niche						X						
Obtain Speaking Engagements	X									X	X	X
Develop Key Networking Program							X					
Develop Client Spotlight Program								X				

FIGURE 4-4   WORK PLAN, OPEN HOUSE

Description	Responsible	ESTIMATED HOURS						
		Partners Hrs	Managers Hrs	Staff Hrs	Admin Hrs	Date	Targeted Completion Date	Actual Completion Date
Set Date For Open House	Managing Partner/ Firm Admin	1.0			1.0			
Alert Staff	Firm Admin				0.5			
Circulate Lists Of Attendees	Firm Admin				1.0			
Identify And Hire Beverage And Food Supplier	Firm Admin				3.0			
Prepare Invitations	Firm Admin				5.0			
Mail Invitations	Firm Admin				1.0			
Make Name Tags	Firm Admin				5.0			
Prepare Display Of Materials To Showcase	Managing Partner/ Firm Admin	1.0			1.0			
Circulate Attendee List	Firm Admin				1.0			
Review Parking Facilities	Firm Admin				1.0			
Identify Personnel To Register And Greet Guest	Firm Admin				1.0			
If Low Response, Implement Call Program	Everyone	2.0	2.0	2.0	2.0			
Prepare Opening Remarks	Managing Partner	2.0						
Hold Open House	Everyone	3.0	3.0	3.0	3.0			
Send Out Follow-Up Letter	Firm Admin			2.0	2.0			
Have Debriefing Session	Everyone	2.0	2.0	2.0	2.0			
Total		11.0	7.0	7.0	29.5			

Business development and sales pipeline. Perhaps one of the best tools you can use to help implement the marketing plans and show your partners the results of marketing and business development efforts is to prepare a monthly business development and sales pipeline. This report captures prospects, proposals, and new clients. It can be segmented by partner by type of opportunity. Figure 4-5 provides a basic format that you can easily implement.

Figure 4-5 Business Development and Sales Pipeline

Your Firm Name Here

	Jan-00	Feb-00	Mar-00	Apr-00	May-00	Jun-00	Jul-00	Aug-00	Sep-00	Oct-00	Nov-00	Dec-00	Annual Totals
Prospects													0
Numbers	3	5	2	7									
Dollars	30,000	25,000	17,000	95,000									167,000

	Jan-00	Feb-00	Mar-00	Apr-00	May-00	Jun-00	Jul-00	Aug-00	Sep-00	Oct-00	Nov-00	Dec-00	Annual Totals
Proposals In													0
Numbers	2	2	4	5									
Dollars	18,000	26,000	105,000	35,000									184,000

	Jan-00	Feb-00	Mar-00	Apr-00	May-00	Jun-00	Jul-00	Aug-00	Sep-00	Oct-00	Nov-00	Dec-00	Annual Totals
Proposals Out													0
Numbers	2	2	3	4									
Dollars	18,000	26,000	85,000	45,000									174,000

	Jan-00	Feb-00	Mar-00	Apr-00	May-00	Jun-00	Jul-00	Aug-00	Sep-00	Oct-00	Nov-00	Dec-00	Annual Totals
New Business													0
Numbers	2	1	3	3									
Dollars	26,000	25,000	45,000	30,000									126,000

	Jan-00	Feb-00	Mar-00	Apr-00	May-00	Jun-00	Jul-00	Aug-00	Sep-00	Oct-00	Nov-00	Dec-00	Annual Totals
Totals													0
Numbers	9	10	12	19									
Dollars	92,000	102,000	252,000	205,000	0	0	0	0	0	0	0	0	651,000

RECOGNITION AND REWARD

The selling/business development cycle for professional services can be quite lengthy. To keep momentum going you need to recognize achievements in each of the following five stages, even if the activity does not produce immediate results in the form of new business:

- Generating new leads/prospects
- Setting up follow up meetings
- Meeting with prospects
- Preparing proposals
- Presenting proposals and asking for the work

The type of recognition and reward you offer depends in large part on the culture of your firm. Remember that you get results in the areas that you reward. For more information on incentives, see chapter 33, "Effective Employee Incentive Programs: How to Bring out the Best in Your Firm," and for ways to communicate successful marketing efforts of your employees, see chapter 32, "In-House Marketing Communications That Foster Success."

CONCLUSION

As we have seen, marketing is a process that follows a logical sequence. First, define your market; second, define your firm; third, define the marketing tools you intend to use; and finally, manage those tools. Even with an aggressive and well-executed marketing program, it will still take time to see results.

If you really want to make your marketing program become a reality, follow these basic guidelines:

- Make sure firm leaders have been involved in the process. Remember, no involvement = no commitment.
- Create a culture of accountability.
- Tie marketing results and efforts to compensation.
- Measure and continually monitor the progress of the plan.
- Require monthly marketing activity reports from everyone who has a role in executing the plan.
- Develop internal systems to support the firm's marketing efforts, such as
    — a client and prospect tracking data base
    — tracking systems for new business brought in and referrals received and given
    — revenue growth and new client profitability

Finally, marketing will be successful if you develop a true marketing attitude that places the client at the center of all your activities and systems. With patience, consistency, and commitment the plan can become a reality, and you will reap the benefits of your efforts.

ABOUT THE AUTHOR

August J. Aquila is the CEO of AQUILA Global Advisors, LLC which specializes in succession planning, mergers and acquisitions, compensation plans, and strategic planning for CPA and CA firms. He also heads up Chantrey Capital Advisors, Inc., which assists privately held businesses of between $4 million and $30 million buy or sell their businesses. *Accounting Today* has described August Aquila as "one of the profession's key strategic thinkers." The AICPA has written, "August J. Aquila is one of the country's leading consultants and authorities in the areas of profit improvement, new business development, strategic marketing planning, and management issues for CPA firms." In 2004, 2007, and 2009 he was selected as one of the Top 100 Most Influential People in The Accounting Profession by *Accounting Today*. In 2003 August was inducted into the Accounting Marketing Association Hall of Fame. He won the Lawler Award for the best *Journal of Accountancy* article ("How to Lose Clients without Really Trying") in 1994.

APPENDIX 4-1 MARKETING AUDIT SURVEY INSTRUMENTS

EXHIBIT A4.1
WORKSHEET 1: FIRM PROFILE

This worksheet encourages the firm to answer such questions as "Who are we?" "What is our marketing experience?" and "What is our current makeup and personality?" Questions are also asked about the firm's mission statement, the number of professional staff and their billing rates, how the firm is organized to serve clients, its significant service areas, current marketing activities, fee volume, and governance. The information garnered here is factual in nature, not subjective.

Note: Some CPAs may ask why organization, management, and firm issues are addressed in the course of preparing a marketing plan. If a firm wants its marketing plan to succeed, it must ensure that every aspect of the firm has been structured to facilitate and support it. For example, a CPA firm can unwittingly undermine its own program by maintaining performance standards that only value billable time. This policy, and others like it, can dampen or kill any enthusiasm for the marketing effort.

This worksheet should be completed by the managing owner.

1. Year the firm was founded.
2. Names of founding owners.
3. Number of owners. Staff and corresponding billing rates:

   Owners _____ Billing Rates _____
   Managers _____ Billing Rates _____
   Supervisors _____ Billing Rates _____
   Seniors _____ Billing Rates _____
   Staff_____ Billing Rates _____

4. How is the firm organized to serve clients—by department, industry teams, individual owners?
5. What is the firm's typical client (sales, industry, location, etc.)?
6. Does the firm have a mission statement?
7. Does the firm have a vision?
8. Does the firm have a one-year business plan?
9. What are the firm's current marketing activities?
10. Which of the previously mentioned marketing activities produce the best results?
11. What is the current year's projected fees for the firm?
12. How would the projected fees be broken out by service area (accounting, audit, tax, consulting, financial services) and by client industry?
13. What has been the firm's annual growth over the last five years?
14. What service areas have been growing the fastest?
15. What client industries (niches) have been growing the fastest?
16. What are the firm's specialties?
17. Have there been any mergers/acquisitions in the last five years?
18. How is the firm governed (executive committee, autocratic managing partner, consensus, etc.)?
19. Does owner compensation reward for marketing?
20. How are pricing decisions made (fixed fee, contingency, value, hourly)?

Exhibit A4.2
Worksheet 2: Owner/Staff Profile

This worksheet is designed to unearth the ideas, perceptions, and concerns of the owners and staff. In contrast to Worksheet 1, this worksheet focuses on firm members' perceptions concerning the firm's greatest strengths and weaknesses, as well as its most promising opportunities and significant threats. It also encourages people to express their personal and professional goals.

One of the benefits of this instrument is that it may help you to discover whether or not everybody perceives the firm in the same way and knows the firm's strengths. Often staff members are unaware of all the firm's client services and key selling strengths. If you discover this to be the case in your firm, consider launching an internal communications and training program that disseminates information about the firm's services, mission, objectives, strategies, marketing plan, and core values. For more information about internal communications, see chapter 32.

Plans that succeed are plans that come from your people. The marketing plan cannot just be your plan. It needs to be everyone's plan because people in the firm will only be committed if they feel you have acted on their input.

Each owner and key employee should be interviewed or asked to complete this worksheet.

1. What is your area of expertise?

2. What are the two or three key issues the firm should address in the next 12 months?

3. How should the firm accomplish these issues?

4. What are the major threats facing the firm?

5. What are the major strengths of the firm?

6. What is the firm's mission?

7. What are the firm's core values?

8. Why do clients retain the firm?

9. What are your professional goals?

10. What additional training do you need?

Exhibit A4.3
Worksheet 3: Trends Affecting the Firm

The main objective of this worksheet is to identify significant opportunities and challenges that the firm must confront before launching its marketing program. Firms that are successful in marketing are not afraid to face the brutal reality of their environment.

For example, you might uncover that the firm is losing clients, more clients than it is obtaining. Is this the results of high fees and low value, poor client service, untrained staff, or aggressive pricing by competitors? Problems like this can become serious obstacles to the firm's progress and hamper its marketing efforts, so it is imperative they be identified, discussed, and resolved in the course of the planning process.

1. Rate each of the following from 1 to 10 (1 = no threat, 5 = some threat, and 10 = very strong threat):

    a. Lack of available staff

    b. High staff turnover

    c. Increased sophistication of clients

    d. Fee pressure from clients

continued

EXHIBIT A4.3
WORKSHEET 3: TRENDS AFFECTING THE FIRM *(CONTINUED)*

e. High client turnover
f. Aggressive marketing by competitors
g. Lack of leadership
h. Timeliness of services

2. What opportunities or threats do the situations in item 1 present to the firm?

3. How is the local economy affecting the firm?

4. How are the changing demographics affecting the firm?

EXHIBIT A4.4
WORKSHEET 4: CLIENT BASE/MARKET DEPTH

The purpose of this worksheet is to take a close look at the firm's client base and to determine how it is segmented. One of the key questions this worksheet will help to answer is whether or not there are any market segments in which the firm is already a strong player.

Likewise, it will be possible to determine how much of a presence the firm has in market segments that have been identified as desirable because they are rapidly growing or because they are not well served by any local competitors.

For example, your audit of the firm's client base uncovers the fact that the firm serves a large number of hardwood floor manufacturers. You also discover that some of their needs are operational in nature and the firm has developed a reputation within this industry for solving operational problems quickly and cost effectively. Assuming the industry is growing, these findings should help you draw several conclusions. First, this is a client group you will work to keep satisfied; and second, it is a segment that should be targeted for further development.

The easiest way to start this process is to identify the firm's clients by industry codes. (See the North American Industry Classification System (NAICS) that has replaced the older Standard Industrial Classification System. For more information on databases see chapter 22, "Databases That Fuel Your Marketing Efforts").

The following worksheet can be completed by the firm's chief administrator.

1. Segment and count the client base, using the following criteria:

a. NAICS
b. Annual fee volume
c. Type of service(s) used
d. Segment and count the client base using their annual sales as the criterion:

i. Less than $1 million
ii. $1 million–$4.9 million
iii. $5 million–$9.9 million
iv. $10 million–$19.9 million
v. $20 million–$50 million
vi. More than $50 million

Exhibit A4.4
Worksheet 4: Client Base/Market Depth (continued)

2. List the top industries identified in question 1.

    a. How would you rate the attractiveness of those industries in terms of helping your firm to grow? (Use a scale from 1 to 10, 1 = least attractive, 5 = somewhat attractive, and 10 = most attractive.)

    b. Are they realistic targets for the firm?

    c. Is the target segment large enough?

    d. Does anyone already own the market?

3. For the top industries identified in question 1, how well do you cross-sell services to them?

4. Look at the top 20 percent of your client base (based on fee volume). What services do you currently offer them? What additional services will these clients need?

5. Obtain a NAICS listing of businesses in your geographic market to determine potential new markets to penetrate.

Exhibit A4.5
Worksheet 5: Trends Affecting Key Client Industries

Awareness of the trends affecting key client industries offers two important benefits. First, you will be able to anticipate and plan for emerging service requirements; and second, you will be able to staff accordingly and train your people.

Now that you know which segments predominate in your client base and which ones predominate in your market area, work to identify the challenges and opportunities they face, and the accounting and consulting services each will need as a result. First Research Corporation and IBISWorld are excellent resources for detailed information on industries as well as trade associations.

1. For each of the industries selected determine what changes or trends are occurring that will affect clients and prospects?

2. How will these trends affect the services you currently provide to this segment?

3. How will they affect future services?

4. What opportunities or challenges do these trends create for the firm?

Exhibit A4.6
Worksheet 6: Competition

Knowing who and what your competitors are and do is critical for a successful marketing program. This worksheet enables you to gather vital information about each key competitor. Note that not every nearby CPA firm is a key competitor. And there may be key competitors who are not CPA firms.

For the purpose of this worksheet, focus on those firms you believe are intent on winning clients from the same market segments as you.

1. Who are your key competitors?

continued

Exhibit A4.6
Worksheet 6: Competition (*continued*)

2. For each firm listed in question 1, answer these questions:

    a. Are they larger or smaller than your firm?
    b. How many owners are there?
    c. What are their specialty areas?
    d. What services do they offer that your firm does not?
    e. What are their strengths?
    f. What are their weaknesses?
    g. Who are their biggest and best clients?
    h. How does the firm differ from your firm?
    i. Has this firm taken any important clients from you?

Exhibit A4.7
Worksheet 7: Client Service

Quality client service is in the eyes of the beholder—the client. Only one way exists to determine what kind of job you are doing and that is to ask your clients. With this basic client survey, you will be able to identify what your clients value most about your services. It's also a good idea to have firm members fill out the survey. It can be very enlightening to compare their comments and responses to those of the clients.

    The benefits of having this information go beyond being able to keep clients satisfied and to resolve problems relating to service. Once you know what makes your firm "best," you can communicate this information to prospects.

1. How satisfied are you with the firm's services in each of the following areas (please check one

	Very Dissatisfied	Slightly Dissatisfied	Slightly Satisfied	Satisfied	Very Satisfied
Overall value					
Responsiveness					
Timeliness					
Accessibility					
Understanding your business					
Understanding your goals					
Meeting your needs					

EXHIBIT A4.7
WORKSHEET 7: CLIENT SERVICE (CONTINUED)

2. Would you recommend our firm to others? Yes _____ No _____
3. Have we asked you for referrals? Yes _____ No _____
4. Would you refer us to your trade/professional association? Yes _____ No _____

EXHIBIT A4.8
WORKSHEET 8: PARTNERS' CLIENTS

This worksheet asks the partners to take a quick look at the status of their top five clients. Clients come into the firm in a variety of ways and it can be helpful to learn how the biggest clients were obtained. This worksheet also lets you find out whether the top clients are expected to grow, remain static, or even decline in the years to come.

1. How did you obtain your five biggest clients (in terms of billings)?

    a. Referral from existing client
    b. Inherited client (already a firm client)
    c. Personal marketing effort (explain)
    d. Team marketing effort (explain)
    e. Referral from outside referral source (lawyer, banker, etc.)

2. For each of the clients listed in question 1, do you expect the level of service to

    a. increase,
    b. decrease, or
    c. stay the same.

3. Are these your most profitable clients (cash received less direct cost)?
4. How have your fees for these clients changed over the past three years?

EXHIBIT A4.9
WORKSHEET 9: CURRENT MARKETING ACTIVITIES

The adage that success breeds success is quite true in marketing professional services. It is important to carefully analyze what activities the firm has tried in the past and to know whether or not they are successful. While past performance is no guarantee of future success, you need to find out the comfort level with various marketing tools. For example owners may have a very negative feeling towards sales but think that seminars are a great way for the firm to promote itself.

Ask the owners the following questions:

1. How do you currently pursue new clients?
2. How comfortable would you be in doing other marketing activities such as _____?
3. Who are the best marketers in the firm?
4. Why do you think they are so successful?
5. What would it take for you to become more successful in marketing the firm?
6. How do you keep abreast of what's happening in our marketplace?
7. In which of the following marketing activities are you presently involved?

    a. Advertising
    b. Brochures

continued

EXHIBIT A4.9
WORKSHEET 9: CURRENT MARKETING ACTIVITIES (CONTINUED)

    c. Public relations
    d. Printed newsletters
    e. Electronic newsletters
    f. Web site
    g. Direct mail
    h. Referral source program
    i. Trade shows
    j. Surveys
    k. Speaking engagements
    l. Firm seminars
    m. Webinars

8. Of the activities in question 7, which ones would you personally like to pursue more actively?
9. How should marketing results and efforts be compensated?
10. How can we do a better job at cross-selling our services?
11. How would you rate your selling and closing skills?
12. What marketing and sales training should we provide owners and employees?

EXHIBIT A4.10
WORKSHEET 10: RECRUITING AND TRAINING

The ultimate success of the firm's marketing efforts depends on the efforts and knowledge of the owners and employees. This last worksheet helps you to define the ideal person you want working for the firm and to detail the marketing skills he or she will need to possess in order to be successful in the firm. Use this information to design a professional education program and make it part of the firm's recruiting efforts. It will help all firm members become real marketing stars.

1. What skills and competencies does our ideal recruit possess?
2. Is there someone responsible for the overall training and recruiting program?
3. Have we developed competency tables for each position in the firm?
4. What key marketing and sales skills do we need to develop?

    a. Public speaking
    b. Listening skills
    c. Sales training
    d. Writing skills
    e. Other

Appendix 4-2 Sample Marketing Plan
Marketing Plan For Adams And Monroe

1. Executive Summary

Adams and Monroe entered the 21st century following a decade of impressive growth, in which the firm more than doubled in size. Fees climbed from $3.5 million in 1999 to $8 million in 2009. Fees for 2010 are expected to reach $8.9 million.

We have built our reputation as a firm that is committed to helping our clients succeed. There is no doubt that their success has been the secret of our success. Our client base is primarily limited to just four niches. This way we can truly become experts in the businesses we serve.

We believe that Adams and Monroe is now in an enviable position in the marketplace. We have been able to attract several highly talented professionals from the Big Four firms. Our clients see us as a refreshing alternative to the large firms, who only want to commit their resources to their largest clients.

Smaller firms in the market can still be a competitive threat to us. That is why our marketing efforts need to show potential clients that Adams and Monroe will help them be successful by providing accounting and consulting services that make a difference. It is our challenge as a firm to demonstrate to clients and prospects that we do help them achieve their goals—personal and business.

The critical marketing challenge for the 21st century will be to stand out from the crowd, to be perceived as the firm that provides the greatest value to its clients. One long-time client recently described our advice and guidance as "invaluable to his success." Another wrote, "A&M has become an integral part of our team." If we focus on using our business advisory skills to ensure that our clients perceive and receive great value for the dollars paid, we will be well on the way to attaining the firm's short- and long-term growth goals.

2. Situation Analysis

Over the next year, we will address the need for current market information. Two years have passed since we conducted our last client survey. It has also been two years since our last employee attitude survey was done. We should spend the next year doing research to fine-tune our marketing strategies.

Our recent analysis provides us with the following information on the firm and its markets:

    a. Fourty-five percent of our fees now come from tax compliance and consulting, 25 percent from management consulting, and 30 percent from accounting and auditing services.

    b. The 4 niches we serve continue to grow and our expertise in each becomes stronger each year.

    c. Our clients tell us that we are effective business advisers and we have done a good job of educating them on the range of services we provide.

    d. Clients continue to be price sensitive, but are more than willing to pay for services that help them succeed.

    e. In the list of the top 25 firms in our market we continue to be among the top 10.

    f. Our name recognition has improved over the last 5 years, but there is still room for further improvement in at least 2 of our niche industries.

    g. Privately held businesses continue to expand in our market, offering us many new business opportunities.

    h. Our owners and employees need additional training in selling professional services.

- Strengths
    - One of the largest firms in the market
    - Results oriented
    - Financial resources available for future investment
    - Good name recognition
    - Well known in our niche markets

- Weaknesses
  - Weak image in two niche markets
  - Not developing new services
  - Don't cross-sell effectively
  - Not marketing as aggressively as we should
  - Lack of second generation of industry leaders

- Opportunities
  - Expand range of consulting services
  - Mine existing client base
  - Look for niche merger opportunities

- Threats
  - Resting on our laurels
  - Large regional firms moving into our market
  - Losing key personnel that we want to keep
  - Sarbanes-Oxley regulations apply to non-SEC clients

3. Mission

Simply stated, our mission is to make our clients successful. We provide them with the services or referrals to help them achieve their vision of success.

4. Positioning

Our positioning strategy is critical to the success of our marketing plan because it is important for the market to know who we are and what we do. We want to position the firm as a creative, results-oriented accounting and consulting firm that closely works with clients to help them achieve their goals.

5. Marketing Overview

Marketing is a journey that has no end. The following marketing plan is designed as a road map to help us achieve our marketing objectives and financial goals. It serves as a useful guide to keep us focused. However, some course corrections will realistically need to be made along the way. All of us have an impact on our results and it will take all of us involved to be successful.

6. Marketing Goals and Strategies

a. Develop a firm-wide marketing culture. Our marketing program is designed to help us achieve Adams and Monroe's business development goals. The plan has the most potential for success if we have a high degree of commitment and a positive, aggressive attitude.

   Goal: In the next 6 months partners and managers will develop individual marketing plans. Over the next 18 months we will consider expanding the individual marketing plan approach to all personnel.

   Strategy: Have all partners work with the marketing director and outside consultant to complete individual marketing plans for partners and managers.

b. Position the firm as the go-to firm in the market within our 4 key niches.

   Goal: Generate $500,000 in gross fees from new targeted clients in the next 12 months.

   Strategy: Add industry-specific newsletters for each of the 4 key niches.

   Strategy: Sponsor 2 industry-specific seminars per year for each niche.

   Strategy: Develop a sequel to our name recognition campaign and place it in industry specific publications.

   Strategy: Have bylined articles placed in targeted industry publications—two per industry.

   Strategy: Cultivate industry-specific referral sources.

c. Promote more consulting services to our existing client base. It is far easier to provide additional services to existing clients than to find new clients. By spending more time with clients to identify their unmet needs, we should be able to strengthen our client relationships, help clients be more successful, and improve our bottom line.

> *Goal:* Obtain one additional consulting engagement from 30 existing clients.

> *Strategy:* Spend nonbilled time with clients to identify operational issues we are not currently addressing.

> *Strategy:* Develop case histories of successful consulting engagements.

> *Strategy:* Develop industry-specific client service teams to serve our top clients.

> *Strategy:* Develop sales training at various levels to educate staff about the firm's consulting services.

d. Obtain updated market information to help us fine-tune our marketing program and ensure we are meeting the needs of our clients. The role of marketing research is to provide us with information that helps us define our market, its needs, and new services we need to offer.

> *Goal:* Obtain updated information on clients and prospects in the 4 key niche areas within the next 8 months.

> *Strategy:* Conduct client satisfaction survey in the next 5 months.

> *Strategy:* Use outside market research firm to provide information on our 4 key niches in general and on specific clients as well.

APPENDIX 4-3 MARKETING PLAN TEMPLATE
THE MARKETING PLAN

Economics

- Facts about your industry.
- Total size of your market.
- Growth history.
- Trends in target market—growth trends, client trends, and technology trends affecting your practice.
- Growth potential and merger opportunity for your firm.
- Barriers to entry that keep potential new competitors from your market?

  — High capital costs
  — High production costs
  — High marketing costs
  — Consumer acceptance/brand recognition
  — Training/skills
  — Unique technology/services

- How could the following affect your company?

  — Change in technology
  — Government regulations
  — Changing economy
  — Change in your industry

Services and Products

List all your major products or services.

For each product or service, describe the most important features. That is, what does the product do? What is special about it?

Now, for each product or service, describe its benefits. That is, what does the product do for the customer? Note the differences between features and benefits, and think about them. For example, an estate plan can save taxes; that is one of its features. Its benefits include financial security, peace of mind, and providing for the family.

You build features into your product so you can sell the benefits.

Clients

Identify your clients (business and individual), their characteristics, and their geographic locations; that is, demographics. For business customers, the demographic factors might be

- industry (or portion of an industry)
- location
- size of firm
- quality/technology/price preferences
- other

Competition

What services/products and firms (accounting and consulting) compete with you? List your major competitors, including their names and addresses.

Do they compete with you across the board, just for certain products, certain customers, or in certain locations?

Use Table A to compare your company with your three most important competitors.

In the first column are key competitive factors. Because these vary with each market, you may want to customize the list of factors.

In the "Your Firm" column, state how you think you stack up in clients' minds. Then decide whether you think the factor is a strength or a weakness for you. Now analyze each major competitor. In a few words, state how you think they stack up. In the last column, estimate how important each competitive factor is to the customer. 1 = critical; 5 = not very important.

 After you finish the competitive matrix, write a short paragraph stating your competitive advantages and disadvantages.

Niche

Now that you have systematically analyzed your industry, your services, your clients, and the competition, you should have a clear picture of where your company fits into the marketplace.

In one short paragraph, define your niche, your unique corner of the market.

Marketing Strategy

Now outline a marketing strategy that is consistent with your niche.

Promotion

How do you get the word out to customers?

Advertising

What media do you use, why, and how often? Has your advertising been effective? How can you tell? Do you use other methods, such as trade shows, catalogs, dealer incentives, word of mouth, and network of friends or professionals?

TABLE A   COMPETITIVE ANALYSIS

FACTOR	Your Firm	Strength	Weakness	Competitor A	Competitor B	Competitor C	Importance to Customer
Services							
Fees							
Quality							
Expertise							
Firm Reputation							
Location							
Office Appearance							
Marketing							
Advertising							
Firm Image							

If you have identifiable repeat customers, do you have a systematic contact plan? Why this mix and not some other?

Promotional Budget

How much will you spend on the items listed above?

Should you consider spending less on some promotional activities and more on others?

Pricing

What is your pricing strategy? The lowest price is not a good strategy. Don't compete on fees. Usually you will do better to have average prices and compete on quality and service. Does your pricing strategy fit with what was revealed in your competitive analysis? Compare your prices with those of your competition. Are they higher, lower, the same?

Location

Analyze your location as it affects your clients. If clients come to your firm

- is it convenient? Parking? Interior spaces? Not out of the way?
- is it consistent with your image?
- is it what customers want and expect?

Where is the competition located? Is it better for you to be near them (like car dealers or fast-food restaurants) or distant (like convenience food stores)?

Distribution Channels

How do you sell your products or services?

Has your marketing strategy proven effective?

Do you need to make any changes or additions to current strategies?

Sales Forecast

Now that you have described your services, clients, markets, and marketing plans in detail, it is time to attach some numbers to your plan. Use a forecast spreadsheet to prepare a month-by-month projection. Base the forecast on your historical sales, the marketing strategies that you have just described, your market research, and industry data, if available.

You may want to do two forecasts: (1) a "best guess," which is what you really expect, and (2) a "worst case" low estimate that you are confident you can reach no matter what happens.

Remember to keep notes on your research and your assumptions as you build this sales forecast and all subsequent spreadsheets in the plan. Relate the forecast to your sales history, explaining the major differences between past and projected sales. This is critical if you are going to present it to funding sources.

CHAPTER 5
Developing a Personal Marketing Plan

Tracy Crevar Warren
The Crevar Group LLC

"People with clear, written goals, accomplish far more in a shorter period of time than people without them could ever imagine."
—Brian Tracy

INTRODUCTION

Today's most successful CPAs have realized that one of their most valued privileges is the ability to take control over their careers by filling their days with the type of work they enjoy. This allows these professionals to experience a greater sense of accomplishment, increased levels of job satisfaction, and the ability to make more money. All it takes is a little focus, dedication, and commitment towards common goals. By developing and executing a personal marketing plan, CPAs are able to determine where they want their practices to go and how they will get there.

So why is a personal marketing plan so important? A personal marketing plan is essential to your success for many reasons:

- Enables you to do more of the type of work you enjoy
- Provides you with a focused blueprint to manage the growth of your practice
- Empowers you to be more efficient, maximizing your nonchargeable time
- Enables you to better serve your clients
- Strengthens client, prospect, and referral relationships
- Empowers you to build and strengthen your personal brand
- Enables you to more effectively align with others who have similar goals
- Provides a tool for accountability

This chapter is designed to help demystify the process of developing a personal marketing plan by providing you with an easy-to-use framework. The plan can be tailored to your personal skills, interests, and goals, enabling you to reach your desired outcome. Ultimately, it will help focus your efforts on activities that will empower you to build a rewarding practice.

⚷ Key Concept

Successful CPAs take control over their careers by filling their days with the type of work they enjoy.

FINDING THE TIME

Sure, this all sounds good, but how can you possibly fit another thing into your already hectic schedule? Before you get discouraged, it is important to understand that over 90 percent of what we do is determined by our habits.[1] When our habits and daily routines are not aligned with common goals and objectives, it is easy to get caught up in unnecessary tasks that drain our energy and productivity without realizing it. Putting a personal marketing plan in place will help you re-examine your focus and understand how to replace outdated practices with more efficient ones that enable you to accomplish your desired outcomes.

---

[1] Brian Tracy, *Million Dollar Habits* (Canada: Entrepreneur Media Inc., 2006) 33.

> **⚷ Key Concept**
>
> Putting a personal marketing plan in place will help you re-examine your focus and understand how to replace outdated practices with more efficient ones that enable you to accomplish your desired outcomes.

Conduct Personal Due Diligence

Before putting together a personal marketing plan, it is important to take stock of where you are. If you are like most professionals, you are engaging in a number of successful practice growth initiatives without being aware of it. To determine your best practices, it is imperative to apply those same due diligence principles you use with your clients to your own practice development efforts.

Just as you would do when developing firm marketing plans, start with a SWOT (strengths, weaknesses, opportunities, and threats) analysis. Identify your strengths, weaknesses, opportunities and threats in growing your book of business. The following are significant questions to answer in this due diligence phase:

- Do you have a clear focus for your practice?
- What does success look like?
- What do you want to be known for in the industry?
- What are the most profitable areas of your practice?
- Do you have a well-defined industry or service niche?
- Do you have a well-defined target market?
- How often do you get in front of your clients outside the engagement?
- How do you provide value to your clients?
- What are you doing to position yourself to become "famous" within your target market?
- Do your marketing activities align with the types of clients you are looking to retain?
- Do your clients and referral sources understand your growth goals and how they can help you in expanding your practice?
- What gaps can you fill in the industry?
- How will filling these gaps give you a competitive advantage?
- How will a downturn in the economy affect your practice?
- Are there opportunities to take advantage of this type of market?

It is important to note that conducting this type of strategic assessment or due diligence at various stages of your practice development will enable you to maximize your efforts. It can highlight misdirected initiatives and help redefine priorities, if necessary. Leading professionals continually reassess their actions and are able to rebound from missteps along their journey to achieve profitable, sustainable, and rewarding practice growth.

Build a Solid Foundation and Framework

The personal marketing plan is any easy-to-use vehicle allowing you to add more enjoyment to your professional life by identifying the kind of practice you want to build and the types of clients you want to serve. Effective marketing plans contain seven primary elements including the following:

1. Overall vision of success—supported by clearly defined goals and action plans

2. Clearly-defined target market and competitive advantages

3. Strengthened practice growth core competencies

4. Client management and development

5. Personal brand building

6. Referral relations

7. Clearly-defined sales strategies

We will explore each of these components in greater detail in the following sections.

> **⚷ Key Concept**
>
> Creating a personal marketing plan allows you to identify the kind of practice you want to build and the types of clients you want to serve.

1. Overall Vision of Success—Supported by Clearly Defined Goals and Action Plans

With some strategic assessment work now in place, it is time to turn your attention toward defining where you want to go. Your vision represents what you want to become. It will serve as the foundation for your personal marketing plan. Defining a clear vision is essential to achieving success. Once your vision is clearly in sight, it will be much easier to build a plan and develop strategies that will help you reach your desired destination.

You can now turn your attention toward identifying specific goals that will help you move toward accomplishing your vision. Start by concentrating on a few key goals that you want to accomplish during the year. Three or four goals are ideal. It is often easy to get overzealous when developing a plan, which can result in being overwhelmed and ultimately losing interest.

Goals should be SMART—specific, measurable, achievable, realistic and timely. Consider the following tips as you start setting your goals:

- Define actions necessary to achieve each goal.
- Focus on areas you enjoy and can commit to.
- Determine how much time you have to devote to practice growth and plan accordingly.
- Develop routines.
- Determine a regular time that is best for you to devote to business development (for example, Friday mornings because you are generally in the office—or perhaps you have extra time during the week when driving to and from client meetings).

> **⚷ Key Concept**
>
> Defining a clear vision is essential to building a plan, developing strategies, and achieving success.

2. Clearly Defined Target Market and Competitive Advantages

Another central component of the personal marketing plan is defining your target market. Key elements of this step will become clear as you answer the following questions:

- What does your "ideal" client look like?
- What industry(s) are they in?
- What is your geographic target area?
- How much demand is there for the services that you offer to this market?
- What market share do you currently serve?
- What additional market share are you looking to retain?

With your target market in focus, it is now time to turn your attention toward clarifying the market needs you can fill and the competitive advantages you provide.

- What are the economic indicators that drive this market?
- Is the market likely to change in the near future?
- What common needs can you help your clients resolve?
- What services do they value most?
- Who are your competitors?
- Why do you lose clients to them?
- What advantages do you offer over your competitors?

During this phase, it can be helpful to develop a marketing tool commonly known as a *value proposition* that you can clearly communicate to your clients and prospects. A value proposition is a clear statement of the tangible results a client receives from using your service. It should answer these questions:

- What unique value do you and your product/service provide to clients?
- What problems do you and your product/service solve for your clients?
- What goals do you and your product/service enable your clients to achieve?
- Why do your clients choose to do business with you?

Storytelling is one of the most effective ways to demonstrate your value and competitive advantages. When you bring your value proposition to life by sharing an actual example in the form of a story or narrative, it allows the client or prospect to become a part of the situation and understand the solutions that you can bring to them and their organization.

3. Strengthened Practice Growth Core Competencies

Most CPAs did not plan to spend much time selling when they entered the profession. The rules changed somewhere along the way. Unfortunately, sales and marketing skills have not generally been a part of most accounting curriculums, but this is starting to change. Although some firms are starting to add sales and marketing to their continuing education rosters, it is not the norm.

If you expect success in building the practice of your dreams, there are most likely some skills that need to be learned. These core competencies can include

- lead generation;
- negotiation and closing techniques;
- cross-selling;
- client service;
- networking; and
- presentations skills.

Don't underestimate the importance of developing these essential competencies.

What are you doing to develop and strengthen your skills in these areas? All sound personal marketing plans outline actions necessary to keep existing clients and attract new ones. You will discover that no substitute exists for being able to offer them strategies and solutions that they want and need, as well as being able to communicate them in effective, meaningful ways.

There are a number of options for building these skills should your firm not currently offer them including the following:

- *Reading.* You can get started by simply reading. There are numerous books specifically written for CPAs and consultants who are looking to strengthen their marketing and sales skills.
- *Training sessions.* There are also a number of organizations that provide excellent training programs. Consider bringing some of these professionals into your firm for regular training, or attend one of many sessions that are open to the accounting profession.
- *Podcasts and Webinars.* You will also find that many of these professional trainers and writers offer Webinars and podcasts on their Web sites. These make for excellent listening, either in the office, or while traveling to and from client locations.

With a little training you will find you are more confident in sales situations. Over time, your results should increase significantly.

4. Client Management and Development

Today's business leaders are looking for more from their advisors than ever before in the history of our profession. If you are unable to meet and exceed their changing demands, you run the risk of several scenarios occurring, all resulting in eroding profits. The first of these is losing your current clients to competitors. When this occurs, you not only give up hard-earned profits from existing clients, but you cut off opportunities to reap additional revenues by expanding the scope of the services provided to them based on new needs. Alternatively, you chance falling victim of the commoditization trap, and will have to compete on price.

An essential component of the personal marketing plan outlines strategies for providing outstanding client service. Utilizing it is a spring board from which to develop additional new business for existing clients. There are six dimensions to client management and development, including serving the right clients, strengthening service delivery, building advisory relationships, identifying unmet needs, showing appreciation, and developing a proactive approach to connecting on a regular basis. Deliberate, proactive approaches are the hallmarks of disciplined marketing.

- *Serving the right clients.* One of the most effective ways to eliminate inefficient and unnecessary tasks in your daily routines is to re-examine your client base, making sure you are spending time serving the types of clients that fit your "ideal" client profile. A simple way to determine this is to categorize your clients into A, B, C, and D. Although there are many ways to do this, Bill Reeb outlines an easy-to-use system for this in his book, *Securing the Future—Building a Succession Plan for Your Firm.* (Recently republished as *Securing the Future I: Succession Planning Basics.*) He describes the following client categories:

  — "A" clients are "ideal" clients that comprise approximately 15-20 percent of your revenues. You enjoy working with them on numerous projects and they value your services.
  — "B" clients are those that fit your target profile. You are most likely under-serving them, but they have the potential to generate substantial revenues for you with some effort.
  — "C" clients are good clients. Their work is simple, but they do not generally have additional opportunities for you. Although they pay their fees on time, their revenues are generally small.
  — "D" clients are those that are generally unprofitable, difficult to work with, or require a substantial amount of your time. In other words, these are the ones that you either want to move into A, B or C clients, or you want to get rid of them.[2]

Although it is never easy to sever relationships with long-time clients, it is sometimes necessary to help ensure you are focused on your long-term goals. Your clients will appreciate your honesty if they understand that you are looking out for their overall needs. Should you decide to end your relationships with some of your D clients, consider providing them with names of other professionals who might be a better fit. For more information on this, see chapter 37, "Letting Go: Evaluating and Firing Clients."

⚷ Key Concept

Business leaders are looking for more from their advisors than ever before.

- *Strengthening service delivery.* The level of service you provide to your clients is one of the most valuable things you can offer. In the accounting profession, it is often one of the most visible expressions of how much you value the client. Although many CPAs promise excellent service, they often fall short. Unfortunately, this has been an increasing trend as firms have cut back on staff due to recent economic woes.

  Each client has a different set of expectations for what they consider to be excellent service. The only way to truly provide service that meets or exceeds their expectations is to ask them what they are looking for and tailor an approach around it. This should be done at the beginning of each new client relationship. You should evaluate your delivery at the conclusion of each engagement to help ensure you are doing what you promised and it is in line with their expectations. For more information on this, see chapter 36, "Developing a Service Excellence Plan for Clients."

- *Building advisory relationships.* When you work with clients, you are most likely offering advice or conducting a project that is technical in nature. It is often difficult to develop a relationship with a client that is based solely on its technical aspects. If you can establish an advisory relationship with your client versus one that is solely based on the technical work, you will significantly improve your chances of making the relationship strong and enduring. So how do you move toward this type of relationship? David Maister along with Charles Green and Robert Galford wrote an informative book entitled *The Trusted Advisor* on this very subject. It suggests "none of us begins our career as a trusted advisor, but that is the status to which most of us aspire." The book is based on the premise that the key to a professional's success is not just built on technical mastery, but through the ability to work with clients in ways that earn their trust, gain their confidence,

---

[2] *William L. Reeb,* Securing the Future: Building a Succession Plan for Your Firm *(New York: American Institute of Certified Public Accountants, Inc., 2010).*

and outline the evolution of a client-advisor relationship as follows:

— Subject matter of process expert—may perform with excellence and expertise, but our activities are limited in scope.
— Subject matter expert plus affiliated field—begin to focus on our ability to solve more general problems and not solely on our technical mastery.
— Valuable resource—seen in terms of our ability to put issues in context and to provide perspective.
— Trusted advisor—the highest level. Virtually all issues, personal and professional, are open to discussion and exploration. The trusted advisor is the person the client turns to when an issue first arises, often in times of great urgency (a crisis, a change, a triumph, or a defeat). Issues at this level are no longer seen merely as organizational problems, but also involve a personal dimension.[3]

As you put together your personal marketing plan, it is essential that you address the ways in which you will work with your clients to develop these types of advisory relationships. This begins by demonstrating how much you care about working with them, a concern for their welfare, and a desire to help them to address issues of critical importance. Although these types of relationships will not develop overnight, they have the potential to blossom over time as your practice grows.

• *Identifying unmet needs.* Your best clients can also be some of your best prospective clients. Why? You have already proven yourself to them on previous engagements, and they trust you to help them resolve other issues or needs that they have. Unfortunately, many CPAs lose sight of this important attribute. Instead of looking at client's additional unmet needs as a source of new business, they seek new business from companies they are not currently serving. Developing new clients is far more costly, and it takes more time than nurturing the ones you already have. You can begin to cash in on new revenues by reaching out to your clients following an engagement to discuss hidden opportunities that you uncovered. This is the type of guidance that they are looking for from you, so don't be shy. By identifying these situations and showing your clients how you can resolve them, you will both emerge as winners. For more information on this, see chapter 30, "Cross-Serving Clients: Integrating Sales and Service Delivery."

• *Showing appreciation.* It is easy to get wrapped up in the regular projects you provide for your clients, and fail to take the time to say "thank you" to them. After all, your clients have a choice about whether to work with you. Showing an appreciation for their work helps reinforce their decision to continue the relationship with you. Although a simple "thank you" may be enough, consider options such as the following:

— Honor special events with cards or gifts

o Birthdays
o Anniversaries
o Company milestones
o Honors and achievements

— Attend client-hosted events
— Send breakfast, lunch, or fresh-baked cookies when they are facing deadlines

• *Developing a proactive approach to connecting on a regular basis.* Like the unmet promises of excellent client service, many CPAs promise to take a proactive approach in working with their clients. They vow to be available not only during the engagement, but to reach out to them throughout the year. Also like the outstanding client service promise, many CPAs have good intensions, but often fall short of this goal. In fact, this is one of the biggest complaints that clients make about CPAs today. Failure to take a proactive role with your clients can open the door for your competitors who have been trying to get in. When you develop good habits of being in front of your clients, it creates many opportunities for you to provide additional services.

If your work with certain clients is sporadic, it is important to reach out to them on a regular basis. Your frequency of contact should depend on the type of client that it is, and the potential it holds. You may decide to reach out to your A clients once a month, your B clients every two months, and your C clients quarterly. You can supplement telephone calls and in-person meetings with e-mails, newsletters, invitations

---

[3] Maister, David H., Green, Charles H., and Galford, Robert M. The Trusted Advisor *(New York: Free Press, 2001).*

and articles that might be of interest. As you reach out to your clients, you will not only demonstrate how much you care about them, but you will strengthen your relationships with them. It will also help you to generate new opportunities for work along the way.

> **Key Concept**
>
> Failure to take a proactive role with your clients can open the door for your competitors who have been trying to get in.

5. Personal Brand Building

A number of years ago, Bob Bunting, the former managing partner of Seattle-based Moss Adams coined the phrase "famous person." The term refers to a CPA or professional striving to build a name for themselves inside a specific area in which they are focusing. For example, this could take place in an industry such as construction or in a service such as business valuation and litigation support. Emerging as a "famous person" is accomplished by utilizing various marketing techniques such as public speaking on specific issues, writing articles on these same matters and being involved in various groups and trade associations that face these issues. Over time, the professional will become famous, almost like a celebrity among the targeted group. They will become known for their industry knowledge or subject matter expertise, and as a result become a sought after advisor for the sector.

This strategy is still referred to today in the accounting profession. It is also known as personal brand-building. It employs many of the same techniques that organizations use to build their brands. Successful brand-building techniques include an integrated combination of activities such as writing articles, speaking, positioning one's self as a resource for the media, and serving in leadership roles on boards and committees. As you are developing your personal brand, it is important to focus your attention on areas in which you are interested, avoiding those in which you are not comfortable or don't wish to pursue. To develop a brand that is known for what you have outlined in your personal marketing plan, it is essential to develop clear, consistent messages that you communicate to your audience. For more information on branding see chapter 15, "Successfully Branding Your Firm."

- *Write or speak.* Seek opportunities to write or speak about the issues or problems that the specific sector is facing, and offer techniques to help overcome them. Look for opportunities within your firm to write articles for your organization's newsletter or to speak at upcoming seminars. Reach out to professional and trade associations to be considered to write for their publications and to teach at their educational programs. They are always looking for new contributors.
- *A resource for the press.* Many CPAs avoid the press because they are not familiar with how the press operates. Developing a relationship with members of the media is much like developing a relationship with referral sources. Reach out to them and get to know them over breakfast or lunch. Volunteer to serve as a resource when they are writing stories about your area of expertise. Offer story ideas as new developments occur. Keep focused on the value that your insight can provide to their readers. Avoid being self-serving at all costs. If you pursue this technique, be aware that the press operates on short deadlines, requiring you to quickly respond to their requests. For more information, see chapter 16, "Getting Your Name in Lights With Public Relations."
- *Association involvement and leadership.* Another widely-used branding strategy is to become famous in a particular circle by assuming a leadership role in a professional or trade association. Your active participation on a board or committee allows you to work closely with other industry leaders on common projects. Your involvement will make a strong statement to those around you. For more information on this, see chapter 23, "Creating Opportunities Through Community Engagement."

6. Referral Relationships

Referrals continue to be the number one way that CPAs develop new leads. These referrals come from a variety of sources, with clients often atop the list. Other providers of referrals include attorneys, bankers, brokers, bonding and surety agents, IT professionals, trade association executives, and other professionals within your own firm. Successful marketing plans can help you prioritize and manage your relationships with these referral sources over time.

Clients can be the best source of new business leads because they understand the value that their CPA brings. In fact, there is perhaps no greater proof of a client's satisfaction with your work than their willingness to assume the risk that accompanies making a referral. It is important to realize that your clients are often eager to help you as a way to say "thank you" for what you have done for them, but they may need a little prompting to do so. It is up to you to decide whether to ask directly for referrals from your clients. If you choose to move forward with this strategy, the most difficult part is getting the courage to ask for the referral. Why? For most it is the fear of rejection, or appearing too pushy. Don't feel alone though, many CPAs face this same angst.

To be successful at developing client referrals requires a change in mindset. The next time a client praises you for a job well done, don't just stop at "thank you." Be purposeful in your interest to build your client base. For example, you might respond to well-deserved praise with "Thank you, John. Your kind words mean a great deal to me. I am grateful to have you as a client and enjoy working with you. In fact, I would like to have a few more clients just like you. If you have others in mind that might benefit from working with me, I would welcome the opportunity to meet them." This might also be an appropriate time to share some elements of your personal marketing plan with them. Ask for their advice. Take advantage of the opportunity to let clients know that you are always looking for a few new clients just like them. You might be surprised at their response. "I didn't realize you were looking for new business." If you don't take the initiative, you may never reap the rewards.

As you look for referrals beyond your client base, reach out to other professionals that serve similar types of clients. You might start by getting to know the advisors of your top clients, if you don't already know them. They will most likely be open to a meeting with you because you share common clients. They will recognize your ability to introduce them to similar types of decision makers at other companies in which they are pursuing. During your meetings with these professionals, learn all that you can about their practices. Understand who their "ideal" clients are, and what those clients value from a relationship with them. Share the focus of your personal marketing plans with them so they have a clear understanding of the type of practice that you are working to develop. This will help them to provide meaningful referrals. Your ability to reciprocate is equally important as you look to develop long-term relationships with these professionals. Learn where their focus is, and how you can best help them to accomplish their growth goals. Don't overlook other professionals in your firm that have the potential to become good referral sources for new work. Treat them with the same attention that you would an outside professional.

Here are some tips to consider when you receive a lead from a referral:

- Take the time to say "thank you."
- Keep your client or referral source informed about how things are progressing with the potential new client.
- When you retain the client, express your appreciation with a thank you letter or a gift, as appropriate. It is important to personalize the acknowledgement for the recipient. If you are uncertain about their special interests, call their assistant and let them know what you are planning to do.

  — Give a gift certificate for their favorite restaurant.
  — Send a gift basket with some of their favorite food items.
  — Offer tickets to a theater production.
  — Give tickets to a sports event.
  — Give a round of golf.
  — Provide a day at the spa.
  — Reciprocate with a referral—it is often the best way to express gratitude.

For more information about developing referral relationships, see chapter 24, "Referral Source Development: The Most Powerful, but Underutilized Business Development Tactic."

⚷ Key Concept

Referrals continue to be the number one way that CPAs develop new leads.

7. Clearly Defined Sales Strategies

As your personal marketing plan begins to produce results, you will find yourself with a number of new business opportunities or "leads" as they are called in the sales arena. To make the most of your hard work, it is important that you develop an organized approach to turning these leads into new clients. If not, you run the risk of losing out on potential new revenues. As you work to strengthen your sales skills through additional training, you will most likely discover some proven techniques to help you become more successful.

Since the prospect has never retained your services, all they have to base their decision to hire you on is what they have read or heard about you. It might be the helpful information you shared with them in a recent seminar, or in an article. It may be praise from another client, or glowing comments from a referral source. Therefore, it is important for you to use every opportunity with prospects to your advantage. Here are some helpful hints to get you started.

- Do your homework—learn all you can before making the visit.
- Show your leadership abilities, and be respectful of their time.
- Ask purposeful questions to understand their needs and demonstrate your knowledge.
- Be able to communicate your competitive advantages.
- Use stories to help your prospects understand your capabilities.
- Use passion as a competitive advantage—demonstrate your interest in them and their business.
- Determine if they have the potential to become an "ideal" client.
- Use your meetings, phone calls, correspondence, and proposals to demonstrate the type of advisor you would be, if selected.

For more information on this subject, see chapter 27, "From Opportunity to New Client."

Many CPAs fail to appreciate the amount of time and frequency of contacts required to "close" a sale in today's competitive environment. In fact, many CPAs feel rejected if they leave the first or second meeting without a signed engagement letter from the prospect. As you adopt a more formal approach to marketing and business development, it is essential to develop a realistic understanding of how long the sales process can take. Sales cycles can vary widely from a few weeks to more than a decade. It takes an average of five sales calls to close a $35,000 piece of business.[4]

Live Your Plan

As we have discovered, a personal marketing plan is the blueprint that outlines where you want to take your practice and how you want to go about getting there. When you are ready to start developing your plan, you will find a personal marketing plan template at the end of this chapter in exhibit 5-1. Beware, your plan is simply words on paper if you do not believe in it and live it each day. Take a lesson from the industry's most successful professionals and have the courage to turn your dreams into reality. The rewards will be great if you have the discipline to stay on course. As Walt Disney said, "The way to get started is to stop talking and start doing."

Track Your Results

It is critical to be able to see the results that your efforts are yielding, once your personal marketing plan has been deployed. By tracking key practice growth indicators, you will be able to measure your return on your investment (ROI). Indicators that you may want to track include the following:

- How many appointments do you go on per month?
- How many leads do your client seminars produce?
- How many calls result in the opportunity to propose?
- What are the win rates for your proposals?

After your plan is in place for a while, these results will start to develop a pattern allowing you to have a better understanding of the results you can expect over time. For more information on this, see chapter 34, "Marketing and Sales Metrics Matter: Measuring Results, Calculating Return on Investment."

---

[4] *Cahners Research,* Evaluating the Cost of Sales Calls in Business to Business Markets (2001) 7-8. *Information pulled from 23,341 businesses surveyed.*

More rainmakers are utilizing the tracking tools of a customer relationship management system or contact management software these days. There are many products on the market with features to make ongoing follow up with your prospects easy, and simplify the tracking process. For example, these systems will help you to keep track of your contacts in a much more organized way. This will become increasingly important to you as your list of prospects grows and it is more difficult to remember what was said in a meeting, or what you promised you would do for the contact during the meeting. It will also make your next contact with the prospect more meaningful when you can easily look back, for example, on what was discussed at the lunch you had with Mary last month.

HOLD YOURSELF ACCOUNTABLE

You work hard to help your clients be accountable to you. It is important to put this principle in place for yourself. Many of today's most successful practitioners allow themselves to be accountable in certain areas to someone else. Whether it is to another partner, a marketing director, or an outside coach, increasing numbers of successful CPAs are reaching out to others to help keep them on track in achieving their goals. They understand that the secret to their success lies in their ability to stay focused throughout the year, not just when it is convenient.

So how does this accountability relationship work? Once you have established your growth goals, reach out to someone that you feel comfortable in giving permission to check in with you regularly. This can be accomplished over the phone, during a breakfast meeting, or over lunch. The key to this relationship is to find whatever works best for you. You will be amazed at how something so simple can help boost your ability to stay focused over the long haul.

Key Concept

Many practitioners allow themselves to be accountable in certain areas to someone else, such as another partner, a marketing director, or an outside coach.

CELEBRATE SUCCESS

One of the most overlooked areas in marketing professional services is taking time out to celebrate hard-earned accomplishments. We get a new client, and without even taking time to celebrate our hard work, we move right into the next big project. Perhaps it is the nature of our business, or the way things have always been done. But if you are going to reap the true rewards of your plan, it is important to take time out, if only briefly, to reflect on how the accomplishment was achieved. Thank others who had a hand in your win. Enjoy your victory, and know that there is more to come.

By developing a clear focus and good habits, you now hold the key to your success.

REFERENCE

Collette P. Nassutti, *Marketing Advantage: How to Get and Keep the Clients You Want* (New York: American Institute of Certified Public Accountants, Inc., 1994) chapter 1.

ABOUT THE AUTHOR

See "About the Editor" for more information on **Tracy Crevar Warren**.

Exhibit 5-1
Personal Marketing Plan

Name_____ Effective Date_____

Vision/Purpose/Goals

What does successful practice growth look like to you?

What are your overall marketing goals?

What marketing goals would you like to accomplish this year?

1._____

2._____

3._____

How much would you like to grow your business by the end of: Year 1   Year 2

New Clients $_____ $_____

Additional Services to Current Clients $_____ $_____

Total New Business $_____ $_____

Brand/Value Proposition

What unique value do you and your product/service provide to clients?

What problems do you and your product/service solve for your clients?

Why do your clients choose to do business with you?

Target Market

Describe the profile of your "ideal" client.

Where are your "ideal" clients located?

What are the biggest issues facing your "ideal" clients?

Who are the thought leaders/centers of influence in your target market?

Who are your competitors? Why do you lose business to them?

Marketing Strategies

What marketing strategies do you use to build your business? Which are most effective and why?

Are your marketing strategies putting you in front of your "ideal" targets on a regular basis?

Are there strategies you need to change or eliminate in order to effectively grow your practice?

What is the single biggest opportunity you have to grow your business this year?

What is the biggest obstacle you have to overcome to achieve your growth goals? How will you do this?

continued

EXHIBIT 5-1
PERSONAL MARKETING PLAN (*CONTINUED*)

Action Plans

List your specific marketing and sales goals for this year and the actions needed to accomplish each below:

Goal:_____

Actions To Achieve Goal	Start Date	Frequency	Completion Date

Goal:_____

Actions To Achieve Goal	Start Date	Frequency	Completion Date

Goal:_____

Actions To Achieve Goal	Start Date	Frequency	Completion Date

EXHIBIT 5-1
PERSONAL MARKETING PLAN (*CONTINUED*)

Professional & Civic Involvement

List any organizations with which you are currently involved. Indicate how you and the firm benefit from your involvement, and how you can enhance your image within the organization(s).

Rank	Organization	Leadership Positions	Benefits/Future Plans
1			
2			
3			

Indicate any organization(s) you wish to join or become involved in over the next year and what you hope to gain from your involvement.

Rank	Organization	Reason for Involvement	Action Plan
1			
2			
3			

Core Competency Development

This is an opportunity for you to identify and develop the skills that will help you better serve your existing clients and gain new business.

Core Competency Area	Your Action Plan	Target Date(s)

continued

EXHIBIT 5-1
PERSONAL MARKETING PLAN (*CONTINUED*)

Your Personal Network

Top 10 Clients

Name/ Organization	Relationship	Frequency of contact	What else can you do for them?	What can they do for you?

Top 5 Referral Sources

Name/ Organization	Relationship	Frequency of contact	What can you do for them?	What can they do for you?

EXHIBIT 5-1
PERSONAL MARKETING PLAN *(CONTINUED)*

Top 5 Prospects				
Name/ Organization	Relationship	Frequency of contact	What can you do for them?	What can they do for you?

By signing your name below, you are making a commitment to your Personal Marketing Plan, which will guide your professional growth and development.

Signature_____Date _____

Chapter 6
Marketing an Industry or Service Specialization

Jean Marie Caragher
Capstone Marketing

Introduction

In order to compete in the accounting profession in the new century, firms must focus their energies on building industry and service specializations, or niches. The evidence is clear. Two-thirds of *Accounting Today's* 2009 Top 100 Firms cited industry specializations as an area in which their firms are increasing business. Client survey results tell us that industry knowledge is one of the main reasons why prospects select a CPA firm. Industry specialization has been cited as a factor of local firms' ability to survive and prosper.

The many benefits of niche marketing include high profitability, services that are of high value to clients, more easily identified prospects, and work that is not seasonal. Finally, niche services lend prestige to your practice. Niche marketing can also provide personal and professional challenges and rewards. In fact, industry consultant David Maister asserts that you can only become successful if you care about what you are doing.

There are benefits and risks associated with niche marketing. Therefore, do your homework before you decide to utilize a niche marketing strategy for your firm. Review this chapter carefully before deciding whether your firm is ready to market an industry specialization.

> **⚷ Key Concept**
>
> Client results tell us industry knowledge is one of the main reasons why prospects select a CPA firm.

Benefits of Niche Marketing

The following list includes short descriptive summaries of the benefits of niche marketing.

- *High profitability.* Niche marketing offers higher profitability for two reasons. First, clients are willing to pay a higher fee for industry expertise. Second, there is less danger of losing clients if your firm is the industry specialist.
- *Economical.* Marketing dollars are being spent on specific niches rather than random efforts.
- *High-value services to clients.* Firms specializing in an industry niche have the ability to offer services far beyond an audit and tax return. There are often opportunities for consulting engagements that benefit the client's bottom line.
- *Easily identified prospects.* By utilizing basic market research techniques, firms can identify prospects by geographic area, sales, number of employees, Standard Industry Classification (SIC) code or North American Industry Classification System (NAICS) code, and CPA firm. This information can then be used to define your market.
- *Fewer geographical barriers.* Being known as an industry specialist opens the door to clients outside your local marketplace. The skills and services offered by your firm can be leveraged to build your client base in other geographic markets.

- *Personal and professional challenges and rewards.* Being known as an industry specialist provides opportunities and exposure for your partners and professional staff. Also, building a book of business is an effective career path to become a partner.
- *Easily identified competition, and strengths and weaknesses.* While researching your prospects, determine the CPA firms that currently serve these companies. Then, research the CPA firms to find their industry specialists, marketing products, and industry involvement.
- *Prestige.* A reputation as a specialist in a specific industry makes your firm more valuable to your clients and leads to additional marketing opportunities, for example, published articles, speeches, and leadership positions in trade associations.
- *Year-round work.* By expanding the range of services offered to clients, it is more likely that you will provide services on a year-round basis, unlike traditional, seasonal accounting work.
- *Increased knowledge of your clients.* By focusing on a specific niche you are also able to focus on continuing professional education (CPE), trade association memberships, and outside reading on topics of need and concern to your clients. This in turn makes you better able to serve your clients' needs and more valuable to them because you have an enhanced knowledge of their industry.

Dangers of Niche Marketing

The following list includes short descriptions of the dangers of niche marketing.

- *Misidentifying the niche.* Research is very important when identifying your niche. Be sure there is truly an opportunity by defining the niche by industry or industry segment (for example, electrical contractors) in a particular metropolitan area, sales range, and number of employees.
- *Misdirecting the message to the niche.* Define the message you will send to your clients and prospects. For example, it would not make sense to be known as a high-cost provider in a not-for-profit niche.
- *Relying too heavily on one niche.* The danger here is a downturn in a particular market (for example, real estate) that could adversely affect the future of your firm if that market represents the majority of your client base.
- *Services may not recur each year.* Consulting services may be one-time projects that would need to be replaced by new consulting services to continue growth.
- *Increased travel is necessary to reach prospective clients in narrower markets.* Your geographic market may expand as opportunities for new business increase. This may result in increased revenue for your firm but may also result in increased staff turnover.

This chapter will cover how to develop and implement a strategic marketing plan for each niche, and how to avoid the common obstacles of niche development. First, let's briefly cover how to select an industry niche.

> **Key Concept**
>
> Niche marketing is the decision to use a mix of marketing tools to address a specific target: a niche in the market.

How to Select an Industry or Service Niche

Niche marketing is the decision to use a mix of marketing tools to address a specific target: a niche in the market. The place to start in selecting a niche is to conduct a marketing audit of your firm. For a detailed discussion of this topic, see chapter 4, "The Marketing Plan: An Audit-Based Approach."

The key areas on which to focus are the following:

1. *An analysis of your firm's client base.* Segment your clients by SIC or NAICS codes. Then, for each industry, calculate the gross fees, net fees, realization, average fees billed, average hours billed, average billing rate, and number of clients. Also, analyze your client base by sales volume, geographic location, and services provided. Graph this information to give an accurate picture of your client base. This will show you in which industries you are spending the most time, earning high fees, experiencing high collection rates, offering a variety of services—all opportunities for niche market development. It will also show unprofitable industries, those you should avoid.

2. *An analysis of your firm's current services and skills.* In addition to traditional accounting, auditing, and tax services, what services is your firm competent in providing? What services does your firm provide that your competitors do not provide? Do your partners and professional staff have the skills to build a niche or should you consider hiring an industry specialist?

3. *The trends affecting your clients.* Talk with experts and clients in the industry to understand its service needs and hot buttons. Trends that influence an industry niche can create opportunities for additional firm services, expand the scope of services to existing clients, and provide services to new clients experiencing the same trends.

Using the information gathered in your marketing audit, answer the following questions prior to pursuing a particular industry or service specialization:

1. Is pursuing this niche consistent with your firm's mission?
2. Is there a market? Is the market size sufficient to generate revenue goals? Is there a market demand? Will clients and prospects be willing to buy these services?
3. What are the current growth rate trends for this industry?
4. Is there a champion within your firm to lead the effort for each niche?
5. Can your firm deliver? Can your firm meet the market's perceived needs? Are additional resources needed to deliver? Are they accessible? A dissatisfied client can undo the benefit to your firm of having sold its services to that client.
6. Do you have enough knowledge about this industry? If not, what more do you need? Where can you get it?
7. What kinds of clients do you like to spend time with?
8. What fees can you expect?
9. Can you anticipate premium pricing or value billing?
10. Can your firm reach the target market?
11. Do the individuals in your firm have a network of referral sources to obtain work in a specific niche?
12. What level of manpower and resources will your firm need to enter this niche and service prospects?
13. What firms in your marketplace are currently providing services to this industry? What are your competitors' strengths and weaknesses?
14. What marketing effort will your firm have to make to enter this niche and serve prospects?
15. Will your firm's size affect its ability to succeed in a particular niche? Keep in mind that certain industries are predisposed to Big Four firms.
16. Are there other obstacles?

According to *Accounting Today* research, the trend in providing niche services is as shown in table 6-1.

TABLE 6-1   NICHE SERVICE TRENDS

	2002	2003	2004	2005	2006	2007	2008	2009
Attest services	—	—	55%	67%	76%	86%	87%	80%
Business valuations	78%	77%	72%	89%	72%	82%	82%	74%
Litigation support	73%	71%	73%	69%	76%	78%	75%	73%
Forensics/fraud	55%	60%	60%	56%	76%	77%	75%	72%

continued

TABLE 6-1   NICHE SERVICE TRENDS *(CONTINUED)*

	2002	2003	2004	2005	2006	2007	2008	2009
Estate/trust/gift tax planning	77%	71%	65%	66%	72%	74%	82%	68%
International	40%	39%	51%	44%	76%	68%	72%	68%
SALT	—	—	—	—	—	54%	63%	65%
NFP	51%	52%	60%	60%	68%	55%	63%	58%
Business management for wealthy individuals	56%	57%	55%	63%	51%	62%	71%	56%
M&A	61%	52%	53%	63%	65%	68%	55%	52%
Technology consulting	53%	48%	44%	40%	50%	46%	53%	47%
Sarbanes-Oxley compliance	—	—	63%	77%	76%	67%	53%	46%
Employee benefits	55%	47%	48%	41%	51%	49%	53%	42%
Business recovery/ recession advice	—	—	—	—	—	—	—	41%
PFP	53%	59%	52%	47%	47%	46%	57%	39%
Cost segregation	—	—	—	—	50%	54%	51%	38%
Investment advice/ services	53%	48%	48%	39%	43%	45%	37%	35%
IFRS consulting	—	—	—	—	—	—	—	34%

More than half of *Accounting Today's* 2009 Top 100 firms identified the following industries as areas in which they increased their business:

- Manufacturing, 76 percent
- Nonprofit organizations, 68 percent
- Real estate, 66 percent

- Construction, 62 percent
- Professional services, 62 percent
- Pension plans, 61 percent
- Technology, 59 percent
- Healthcare facilities, 58 percent
- Wholesale/distributors, 54 percent

DEVELOP A STRATEGIC MARKETING PLAN

One of the key factors of a successful marketing program is a written plan. The plan should start with your firm's mission, vision, and core values. The mission statement is your firm's basic purpose, what it is trying to accomplish. The vision for your firm is where you see your firm in the future, including net revenue, number of employees and offices, and new products and services. Core values are the essential and enduring beliefs of your firm.

The situation analysis describes the current status of your firm, the niche market you wish to pursue, and your competition. This information was gathered during your firm's marketing audit.

Objectives need to be developed. As mentioned in previous chapters, objectives should be SMART—specific, measurable, attainable, realistic, and timely. The strategic marketing plan should include three-year objectives for the firm, revised annually. Each niche area should have one-year objectives, reviewed quarterly. Specific strategies are then identified to obtain your objectives. Make sure that your objectives and strategies state the specific tasks, deadlines, and those responsible for making it happen.

> **Key Concept**
>
> A written plan is critical to the success of a marketing program.

Kinds of Opportunities

The following are the four types of opportunities your firm can pursue, each with its own level of risk.

1. *Market penetration.* Better known as cross-selling, market penetration is providing existing services to existing clients. This is the least risky opportunity since you are already familiar with the service and the clients. For example, you may be developing a niche in the construction industry. Currently, succession planning is a firm specialty. This is a service needed by and could be offered to your builder and contractor clients.

2. *Market development.* Provide existing services to new clients. This is a bit more risky since you need to learn about a new market segment. For example, you may currently offer retirement planning services to your current clients. This is a service needed by and could be offered to new business prospects.

3. *Product development.* Provide new services to existing clients. This is also a bit risky since you need to learn a new service area.

4. *Diversification.* Provide new services to new clients. This opportunity is the most risky since you are moving into a new line of business. Sarbanes-Oxley compliance work has provided many regional and local firms with opportunities to expand their bottom lines.

More detailed information on these types of opportunities is provided in chapter 2, "Marketing and Sales 101: A Primer for CPA Firms."

Implement the Strategic Market Plan

There are many success factors critical to the effective implementation of your strategic market plan. The more of these factors that exist within your firm, the more likely the plan will succeed. These factors include the following:

1. *Active support from the managing partner or director.* The managing partner or director must support the strategic market plan with time, dollars, and personal commitment.

2. *Commitment to and ownership of the plan by the entire group that will be responsible for its implementation.* Without total commitment, it is easy for your strategic market plan to fall off course and things to return to "business as usual." Hold monthly meetings to review the progress of each niche group. This will help keep your efforts on track.

3. *One person who will be the "driver" of the plan.* This is the person who makes sure the plan stays on schedule. Your firm's marketing director is an excellent candidate to fill this role.

4. *The group who will be the visionary force behind the plan.* This is the group that provides the overall view and much of the input in developing the objectives and strategies. It should consist of one or two technical partners who are knowledgeable in the industry, assigned staff members, and a marketing-oriented partner or marketing professional.

5. *An internal marketing awareness and mind-set within the firm.* It is important for everyone in your firm to understand the purpose of your strategic market plan and to be knowledgeable about the services offered by your firm and the promotional materials available to market these services. Share your goals in firm meetings and internal publications. Explain the why and how of your goals and what they mean to each individual in the firm. Everyone in your firm is a potential salesperson; everyone needs to know what they are selling. For more information on internal communications, see chapter 32, "In-House Marketing Communications That Foster Success."

6. *Integrated marketing tools.* Analyze how the various marketing tools will work together. The goal is to maximize all the marketing opportunities by selecting the best marketing mix. Marketing tools include but are not limited to brochures, Web sites, proposals, newsletters, seminars, Webinars, speeches, direct mail, e-mail, blogs, telemarketing, news releases, articles with by-lines, media interviews, advertising, sponsorships, organization memberships, surveys, and mixers with clients, prospects, and referral sources. When developing a niche, it is important to gain name recognition. Brochures, Web sites, newsletters, organization memberships, advertising, sponsorships, and news releases can help you do that. Seminars, Webinars, speeches, and mixers can help you generate leads, if you are better known in the marketplace. For more information about integrated marketing tools, see part IV of the book, *Marketing Techniques That Get You Noticed.*

7. *Project management tools.* This is a system to track the status of your plan's implementation and budget. This system can be a simple as a spreadsheet outlining the specific activities and deadlines of your plan, and the date on which each activity was accomplished. You'll also want to track the expenses incurred including promotional materials, CPE, entertainment, seminars, and advertising to ensure that you stay within budget. Be sure to communicate this within your firm on a regular basis.

8. *A recognition and reward program.* These will differ from firm to firm. Determine what kind of program will work best with your people and culture. An Atlanta-based CPA firm initiated a recognition and reward program. A marketing activities list was developed and points assigned for each activity. Each level of personnel, from administrative staff to shareholders, was assigned quarterly and annual point goals. Monthly, quarterly, and annual prizes were awarded. Plus, at year end, those who had achieved their minimum annual point goals were eligible to earn redemption credits, which could be used to claim additional prizes.

   Not only did the firm achieve nearly 15 percent growth, the recognition and reward program encouraged an increase in marketing activity.

   Recognition and reward programs can be as simple or elaborate as the firm sees fit. In addition to offering monetary bonuses for new clients, firms may offer other prizes like dinners or tickets to a concert or show. Recognition can be given in the firm's internal newsletter and on signs and plaques hung in the office. In his book, *1001 Ways to Reward Employees,* Bob Nelson offers many other suggestions including parking spaces, movie passes, and electronic equipment in addition to offering guidance on developing recognition and reward programs.[1] For more information on employee recognition programs, see chapter 33, "Effective Employee Incentive Programs: How to Bring Out the Best in Your Firm."

---

[1] Bob Nelson, 1001 Ways to Reward Employees *(New York: Workman Publishing Co., Inc. Revised 2005).*

COMMON OBSTACLES IN NICHE DEVELOPMENT

The common obstacles in niche development include not knowing where to start, lack of partner commitment, lack of a champion, perceived lost opportunities, and lack of communication. A discussion of each obstacle follows.

Not Knowing Where to Start

The place to start is to make a commitment to a niche marketing strategy. Then, follow the steps in this chapter to determine the niche(s) to pursue, identify the champion, and write a strategic marketing plan for the niche. Learn from CPA firms outside your geographic market. Membership in the Association for Accounting Marketing entitles you to an online directory of firms willing to share niche marketing information.

Many accounting firm associations have developed niche marketing programs for their member firms. Members meet and share ideas and skills. Promotional materials such as brochures and newsletters are produced. Also, they utilize industry specialists from other member firms to assist in both current client and new business opportunities.

Firms can join a *power network*, a network developed to market a specific industry. The Alliance of Professional Associations (APA) is a national association management company for CPA Associations whose members serve clients in niche-specific markets. APA currently manages six CPA associations including CPA Auto Dealer Consultants Association, Community Banking Advisory Network, National CPA Health Care Advisors Association, CPA Manufacturing Services Association, Not for Profit Services Association, and the Real Estate and Construction Advisors Association. APA helps firms enhance and expand their practices through education, networking, and marketing and is currently working with over 300 CPA firms in their niche-specific associations.

Since 1980, PDI Global, Inc. has been a leader in providing niche marketing newsletter programs, financial planning guides, marketing collateral, and practice development consulting services for accounting and consulting firms. From client surveys and its work with more than 2,500 firms throughout North America, PDI Global has identified the factors that determine the success of a niche practice.

"There is a direct correlation between an individual's willingness to bet his or her success on the success of the niche, and the niche's actual success," says Allan D. Koltin, CPA, PDI President and CEO. "Also, marketing skills are more important than technical skills in building a profitable niche practice. Simply put, partners who equip themselves with good tools and proactively go after new business get it."

Interestingly, neither firm size nor the number of its clients are important factors in successfully starting a niche practice. Having a base of clients in a particular industry is helpful, but marketing is by far the most critical ingredient in developing a niche.

Firms have also joined forces with other firms specializing in an industry to form a power network, most notably Auto Team America (ATA). Organized in 1991, ATA currently has 11 members that serve over 2,000 auto dealerships nationwide.

Firms can also form an alliance with a consulting organization that provides services to a specific industry. This enables a firm to offer services to clients and prospects that it would be unable to provide.

> **Key Concept**
>
> The common obstacles in niche development include not knowing where to start, lack of partner commitment, lack of a champion, perceived lost opportunities, and lack of communication.

Lack of Partner Group Commitment

Rarely will you receive 100 percent commitment from all partners for any initiative your firm would like to undertake. It is important, therefore, that the firm's managing partner and those partners who are interested move forward with a niche marketing effort despite resistance. The reward for these efforts will be reaped in new business. Partners who are not interested in marketing an industry specialization must specialize in a technical area (for example, international tax) to maintain a role in their firms.

Lack of a Champion

An important point for you to keep in mind is that *without a champion you do not have a niche.* The champion must be a person with influence, but does not have to be a partner. One possibility is a manager who is interested in building his future in the industry and becoming a partner in the firm. The champion is not necessarily the driver of the strategic market plan. The driver is a role that can be effectively played by the firm's marketing director.

If the champion does not exist in your firm, consider hiring the champion from another firm or industry.

> **♀ Key Concept**
>
> Without a champion you do not have a niche.

Perceived Lost Opportunities

Research conducted by McKinsey & Company on market dominance states that ranking in the top 3 in any market is critical to achieving marketing efficiency. The top 3 firms in each market will get the opportunity to sell 70 percent of the time. The opportunity to sell for the firm in fourth place drops to 40 percent. Niche marketing will allow your firm to break up the market and be in the top 3 firms for selected niches. By utilizing a focused niche marketing approach, your firm will increase its number of opportunities for new business while also improving its closing success.

Lack of Communication

The champion and visionaries of your strategic marketing plan are key to its implementation. It is important to communicate your progress throughout the entire firm and to celebrate the successes. This will help build a sense of enthusiasm within your firm and enhance the commitment to a niche marketing strategy.

CONCLUSION

In an age where accounting and auditing fees are shrinking and consulting fees are rising, it is apparent that CPA firms must change their way of thinking or perish. A niche marketing strategy will allow you to offer your clients value-added services at premium fees. It will challenge your partners and staff. It will focus your energies on the greatest opportunities for growth for your firm.

Your challenge is to conduct a marketing audit of your firm, determine the niche areas with the greatest opportunities, select your champion, write your strategic marketing plan, implement, and follow through. You may find that marketing an industry specialization is an effective method of growth for your firm.

ABOUT THE AUTHOR

Jean Marie Caragher is president of Capstone Marketing, focused on providing marketing consulting services to CPA firms since 1998. Services include Brand Surgery^SM, marketing plan development and implementation, retreat facilitation, and training. Reach her at 757.673.6826 or jcaragher@capstonemarketing.com.

Exhibit 6-1
Sample Strategic Marketing Plan

Situation Analysis

Current Status of the Firm

Smith & Jones is a local, independent CPA firm with one office in the state of North Carolina. Formed in 1987, the firm has grown to annual net revenue of $6 million, 8 partners, and 50 professional staff. This growth has enabled the firm to retain many talented partners and professional staff who are excited about continuing the success of the firm.

The firm has recently made a commitment to developing a niche marketing strategy and conducted a marketing audit to determine which niches to pursue. The manufacturing industry was identified as an opportunity due to the volume of manufacturing in the state as well as the firm's solid client base. Also, John Doe, partner, has made the commitment to lead the manufacturing industry services group.

Smith & Jones currently serves 25 manufacturing industry clients, representing $500,000 in fees, and 8.3 percent of firm revenues. This client base can be segmented as follows:

NAIC Code Classification	Number of Clients	Net Fees	Average Fee	Average Hourly Rate	Realization
Furniture	10	$200,000	$20,000	$110	86%
Machinery	5	$150,000	$30,000	$122	88%
Transportation Equipment	10	$150,000	$15,000	$135	92%

Services provided to manufacturing industry clients currently include assurance, tax, business valuation, operational reviews, production and inventory control, manufacturing shop floor flows and controls, and research and development tax credits.

Prospective Clients

Prospective clients include privately-held manufacturing companies in the state of North Carolina (excluding chemicals and tobacco products) with sales between $2 and $50 million.

[This section should include the specific number of companies by type of manufacturing and sales range. Sources include www.hoovers.com, www.zapdata.com.]

Growth Goals (in thousands)

Due to current economic conditions, Smith & Jones estimates 5 percent growth per year.

Figure 6-1

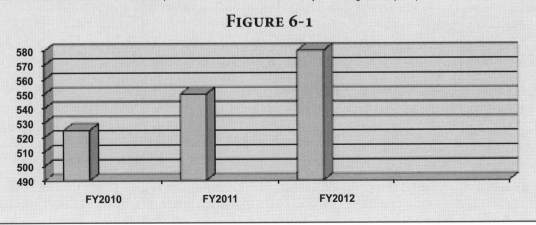

continued

Exhibit 6-1
Sample Strategic Marketing Plan (continued)

Competition

Although several other CPA firms offer services to manufacturing clients in North Carolina, a market leader does not exist. The firm's main competitors are North and South, LLC, Williams, Lane & Company, P.C., and the local office of a Big Four firm. The strengths and weaknesses of these competitors are shown in the following table.

Firm	Strengths	Weaknesses
North and South, LLC	Strong marketing Aggressive	Quality of service
Williams, Lane & Company, P.C.	Good reputation in manufacturing More established niche	Limited range of services
Big Four	Promotes multiple office locations Breadth and depth of services	Pricing

Industry Outlook

The North Carolina manufacturing industry includes more than 10,000 companies with combined annual revenue of $157 billion. Manufacturing employs about 623,300 with an annual payroll of $21 billion. Major manufacturing subsectors include chemicals ($27 billion); beverage and tobacco products ($21 billion); food products ($13 billion); and transportation equipment ($12 billion). Manufacturing contributes $78 billion to the gross state product, representing 20 percent of North Carolina's total gross state product. Issues impacting manufacturers include raw material, labor, and energy costs; foreign competition; labor, pollution, and foreign trade regulations; supplier and customer consolidation; capital equipment and facility expenses; quality control; and labor relations. North Carolina manufacturing industry annual exports total about $23.4 billion.

[This section should also include industry information for your particular geographic area. This can be obtained through trade associations, industry and business publications, and services like www.firstresearch.com.]

Objectives and Strategies

1.   Build a prospect database by January 31, 2010.

Task	Responsible Person(s)	Deadline
Download list from source.		
Research additional contacts for each company, e.g., CFO, controller.		

Exhibit 6-1
Sample Strategic Marketing Plan (continued)

Task	Responsible Person(s)	Deadline
Add e-mail addresses for all contacts.		
Update list.		

2. Develop a networking plan for referral sources by February 28, 2010.

Task	Responsible Person(s)	Deadline
Identify top tier bankers and economic development directors.		
Send introductory letter.		
Follow up by telephone to arrange meeting.		
Debrief results of meetings.		

3. Distribute a quarterly newsletter to manufacturing industry clients, prospects and referral sources starting March 2010.

Task	Responsible Person(s)	Deadline
Research newsletter vendors and writers; make selection.		
Create/update database for newsletter mailing.		
Distribute newsletter.		
Add PDF file to Website.		

continued

EXHIBIT 6-1
SAMPLE STRATEGIC MARKETING PLAN (CONTINUED)

Implementation/Timetable

[Name of niche champion] is responsible for the implementation of the marketing plan. The status of the plan's implementation will be monitored at regular marketing meetings.

[List specific marketing activities in this chart.]

January 2010	February 2010	March 2010

April 2010	May 2010	June 2010

July 2010	August 2010	September 2010

October 2010	November 2010	December 2010

Evaluation

The manufacturing niche group champion and the firm's managing partner will review the Strategic Marketing Plan on a quarterly basis.

Budget

Marketing budget line items may include the following: advertising, consultants, direct mail, membership dues; postage; promotional items; proposals; research; salaries; seminars; sponsorships; subscriptions; technology; training; Web site, Webinars, and miscellaneous.

[An actual plan must include a detailed budget that will allow for the effective implementation of the Strategic Marketing Plan. For more information, see chapter 8, "Budgeting Techniques for Today's CPA Firms."]

CHAPTER 7
Marketing for the Multi-Office Firm

Katie Tolin
Rea & Associates, Inc.

INTRODUCTION

Marketing the multi-office firm creates unique challenges that are not experienced in the single office setting. Things that are easy in a single office, like scheduling a meeting, become complicated projects to organize when multiple offices are involved. More complex issues, like market strategy and developing a solid brand, are true challenges since conditions vary greatly by market. In order to successfully market a multi-office firm, it is important to understand the fundamental differences that exist between it and a single office firm. The marketing of a multi-office firm is complicated by the following:

1. *Different markets.* Each office competes in a different market. As a result, marketing analysis and strategy for each office will vary.

2. *Varying expertise.* The service capabilities, including specialties and niches, will vary by office as will the marketing tactics implemented. There are obstacles to overcome when offering and delivering services in a market when the firm specialist is located hundreds of miles away.

3. *Accountability challenges.* Reporting relationships between team members are complex, which makes it harder to keep track of what people are doing to hold them accountable.

4. *Communication difficulties.* With multiple locations, it's imperative to ensure consistency and uniform messaging, but it's challenging to find the right time, location, and channels to do so.

This chapter will further explore these challenges and provide some guidance for those responsible for marketing a multi-office firm.

CREATE A FIRM MARKETING PLAN

Whether your firm is a single location or one with multiple offices, the most effective way to market your firm starts with the development of an overall game plan, a marketing plan. This plan outlines objectives, strategies, and actions necessary to achieve them. It moves from big picture to specifics.

A single-location firm often establishes its marketing strategy with relative ease compared to the multi-office firm. Actually, the multi-office firm's situation runs counter to each of the single-office advantages. The following are some of the complications a multi-office firm faces when developing a marketing plan:

- It does not have all of its resources in one geographical location
- The marketplaces in which the firm competes are spread out and firm presence is not within a single geographical market
- Decision makers are not under one roof making it harder to develop strategies
- Any analysis performed is complicated because it may not be able to be completed on or in a single location
- Communication and decision making can be logistically complicated and expensive

Considering those challenges, developing a marketing plan for the multi-office firm is extremely important, and it needs to tie directly to the firm's overall strategic plan. The success of the entire firm stems from what the individual offices accomplish; however, each individual location needs to understand what the firm as a whole is trying to achieve so it can identify and define the specific role it will need to play to help the firm as a whole reach its goals.

In addition, any niches and specialties the firm develops may be able to be marketed successfully in a number of the multi-office firm's markets. These specialties often become a true firm effort as many resources are shared amongst offices to form the niche team and deliver the specialty services. To illustrate the importance of these niches and the role they play in the firm's success, they too must be included in a firm marketing plan, even if they have marketing plans themselves, so an individual office can determine what role it will play in both selling and completing any of the specialty work.

To shape the firm's performance goals and measures, the core business strategies and critical success factors for the firm must be identified along with the critical behaviors that partners and professionals must demonstrate in order to achieve these success factors. By identifying a small number of important, shared and high-impact strategies and success factors, and the corresponding human behaviors, skills, and knowledge that will be necessary to achieve the strategies, the firm can consolidate resources and increase effectiveness. Performance measures can then be assigned to activities and outcomes can be measured.

> **Key Concept**
>
> Core business strategies, critical success factors, and critical behaviors must be identified in order to shape the firm's performance goals and measures.

TAKE MARKETING LOCAL

After developing goals and strategies for the firm, identify the specific tactics each individual office will implement to help the firm achieve its overall goals and the budget that will be needed to do so. The office plans should include specific actions and a timeline for completion. It is also imperative that responsibility be assigned to specific team members and a system for accountability implemented.

To establish a local marketing strategy, the firm needs to analyze the following in each of its markets:

- Core competencies—its people's talents and deliverables
- Marketplace—who and where the buyers are
- Market demand—the services most needed in that marketplace and how those services are packaged to best relate to buyers in that area

The core competencies may vary by location even though technology available today has made it easier for offices within a firm to share team members and complete work for clients on the other side of the globe. These variances may come from the breadth of competencies, the array of service capabilities that an office team has to offer, or from the level of expertise in the service line.

The individual marketplace in which each firm office competes will differ depending on geography and competition. It is important that a firm understand these differences so they can be taken into consideration when developing marketing strategies. For example, an office may decide not to push its auto dealer expertise in a market where there is a lot of competition. Rather, the office could build its expertise in banking, where there is less competition, to gain more market share and revenue.

Market demand for the services offered will also vary depending on the office's location and skills in packaging and promoting the services to the market, as well as buyer awareness and office expertise. Pay attention to what the marketplace is saying so each office of a multi-office firm can determine those areas where they can have the biggest impact.

The challenge is that not all locations need to have the same nature and degree of activity and influence. The size, market sophistication, and experience levels of professionals in one office may starkly contrast with those of another. The marketing strategies for each location may vary, and each office may have a diverse set of products and services that are performed, location by location.

Before developing a local marketing plan, perform a SWOT (strengths, weaknesses, opportunities, and threats) analysis, a market analysis, and a services portfolio analysis to better understand each individual office and the needs of the market. Here's what a firm can gain by completing these analyses:

- *SWOT analysis.* Identify strengths, weaknesses, opportunities, and threats for each office and for the firm as a whole. This will help each office see not only how it is positioned but also how it is positioned relative to the firm.
- *Market research.* Because each office operates in a unique market, it's important to understand the characteristics of that marketplace. Things like household income, dollars spent on accounting services, and other economic trends will impact strategy. By calculating current market share and completing a competitive analysis, it can be determined how much that office can realistically grow.
- *Industry analysis.* This analysis looks at the individual office's capabilities to serve a given industry compared to the size and breadth of the industry and how the office packages the services it offers the industry. The idea is to qualify the market characteristics and office competencies to meet what the market is demanding. From this the firm can determine what is most critical from a market demand and service delivery standpoint and make investment decisions accordingly.
- *Services portfolio analysis.* This analysis poses challenges for the multi-office firm because the competencies that buyers in a given industry are seeking may not reside in the office location nearest the buyers. Or perhaps none of the offices have developed industry specific expertise, and the competencies for the entire firm are unfocused. The firm's challenge is to determine the most promising intersections of markets and service capabilities and decide how to invest resources to market them. Start by looking at current revenue for each office. Determine how much revenue is generated from each service line and industry. This will illustrate what expertise currently exists within an office so the firm can identify what will be necessary to develop and extend the market-service mix.

Even though it is imperative that a firm market itself as a whole, it is extremely important to look at each office separately. By understanding the local marketplace, knowing who the firm's competition is and how it differs, and comprehending a firm's core competencies, both the individual office and the firm's management will know how each particular location can best help the firm meet its goals.

> **♀ Key Concept**
>
> Market your firm as a whole, but examine each office separately. Understanding the local marketplace, the firm's competition, and the firm's core competencies ensures that each location knows how to best help the firm meet its goals.

PROMOTE INDIVIDUAL MARKETING

Personal marketing plans in a multi-office firm are extremely important to help team members realize their role in the firm's marketing and growth process. All the firm's partners should have an individual marketing plan and a firm may want to consider extending the requirement to all professional staff. These plans add accountability to actions, especially if they are tied to compensation. In a multi-office firm this helps ensure that all professionals, even though they work in different locations, are evaluated on their unique contributions to the firm.

An individual marketing plan allows team members to identify specific actions they want to accomplish in a set period of time. Designed correctly, it will uncover what a practitioner is good at and motivated to do, while contributing value to the office. Community involvement, speaking opportunities, article development, building client relationships, and referral source contacts are common areas included in these plans. However, they should go into as much detail as possible and include specific revenue goals and a prospect list with an action plan.

An individual marketing plan is best accompanied with personal coaching, a role often assumed by a member of firm management or the marketing director. The involvement of firm management in this process is imperative if these actions are directly tied to compensation, as they should be. A professional services coach is quite similar to a sports team coach; they both encourage their team members to work toward achieving a goal and provide the moral support and guidance needed to do so. Plus, if an individual is off track, the coach can direct them back to where they need to be in order for the individual to best contribute to the firm's success. While coaching sessions are easier face-to-face, the multi-office firm can still take advantage of this important marketing element with telephone conferences. For more information on personal marketing plans, see chapter 5, "Developing a Personal Marketing Plan."

Establish Marketing Systems and Processes

Marketing systems are programs that are used to gather and process information and make the data available to others to help in prospecting, marketing, and lead generation. Establishing marketing systems to compile and track marketing information and progress is very beneficial in a multi-office firm; however, the processes around the systems will determine overall success. For example, developing a firm pipeline to track current opportunities may make perfect sense. However, if adding new leads and updating the information contained in it are not part of standard operating procedures, the pipeline won't work as desired and may not be worth the effort put into establishing it.

There are four primary groups of marketing administration systems. The character and complexity of the components will vary by purpose and system sophistication, even though the underlying functional purpose remains the same. These groups with their chief components are as follows:

1. Market intelligence

    a. Market research
    b. Buyer behavior information
    c. Prospect lists
    d. Competitor information
    e. Marketing plan, budget, and timelines

2. Result tracking

    a. Firm, office, niche, and personal marketing plans
    b. Close ratios (wins vs. losses)
    c. Budgets and forecasts
    d. Financial results by market segment, service, and location
    e. Marketing audit
    f. Analyses: marketing expenses-to-revenues and leads-to-proposals-to-wins

3. Client information

    a. Client database
    b. Referrals in and out
    c. Client satisfaction surveys
    d. Revenue analysis (services purchased and related dollars)

4. Marketing tools and tactics

    a. Pipelines
    b. Schedules
    c. Document files (letters, proposals, etc.)
    d. Pricing for services and supplies

Before implementing any marketing system, be sure to examine the following:

- *Purpose.* Does the information collected align with firm strategies? Will it be used in decision making?
- *Set up.* What is practical in terms of time and expense?
- *Maintenance.* Who will gather and input information? What is the source of technical help? Who will update and "clean up" data and the coordinating linkages both locally and centrally?
- *Expansion.* How will firm needs change? What impact will technology make on the system now and in the future?

- *Analysis/Interpretation.* How will the data be used? Who will do the analysis? In what way will data be shared with firm management and other team members?

> ### 🔑 Key Concept
>
> Marketing systems are programs that are used to gather and process information and make the data available to others to help in prospecting, marketing, and lead generation.

It's important to first make sure there is a compelling purpose behind setting up and maintaining the system. If the information gathered for these systems will be used in decision-making, consider developing them. If the information won't change decisions made in the individual offices or the firm, there is no rationale for installation. Equally important is to make sure there is a resource at each location committed to performing routine maintenance. With technology today, it's easy to maintain systems from a central location, but someone will be needed in individual offices to help with updates and routine maintenance. This is where the importance of specific processes around how the system will be updated, maintained, and utilized becomes imperative. Unless someone assumes ownership for the system at the office level and everyone knows specifically how to update and use it, success will be limited. Finally, consider how closely the decision making aligns with the firm's top strategies and critical success factors. To the degree that the information affects the firm's critical behaviors, the system rationale becomes stronger. Of course, this is true for any system introduction, but in the case of a system that resides in or is used by multiple offices, the investment and complexity of operation grows considerably.

Many well-designed systems fail because people do not learn how to use and maintain them. While the marketing staff is typically responsible for setting up and maintaining marketing administration systems, in the multi-office firm these systems may be carried out in each individual office by a staff accountant, administrative assistant, or marketing coordinator. In any of these situations, the person responsible for this function must be trained for the role they have, whether that be in performing administrative support duties or interpretation and analysis of data.

COMMUNICATE REGULARLY

In a multi-office firm, it is critical to continually communicate the marketing goals for the firm and offices, and the current status in attaining them. The following methods can be used for doing this:

- *Internal newsletter.* The firm should have a periodic marketing bulletin that describes the initiatives undertaken across the offices. This may be a separate newsletter dedicated solely to marketing or a portion of another newsletter that may include general firm information. Be sure to mention new marketing tools and highlight how an individual can roll them out. Team members participating in initiatives should be acknowledged and progress and outcomes shared with all. It must be produced consistently with the objective to keep people upbeat, informed and mindful of marketing's role in their daily lives. These newsletters are often sent electronically, but they could be distributed in paper format during meetings or directly to individuals' mail boxes, posted on bulletin boards, or set out in lunch rooms and other internal gathering places.
- *Intranets.* While they look very similar to Web sites, intranets are restricted to internal use. They are typically placed on internal servers or are password protected so they can only be accessed by firm members. This tool is a resource for firms. Not only can it share pressing news that people need to know at a moment's notice, but it becomes a library of sorts, hosting documents that team members need—including marketing documents. An intranet can house many of the firm's marketing tools from proposals to articles to sales collateral along with instructions for use.
- *Audio/Video conferencing.* Getting people to travel to meetings is a painstaking experience in a multi-office firm. Many of the meetings that were once done face-to-face can now be done on the phone and by computer. Technology exists for people to call in from multiple locations, on-demand, for an audio meeting very cost effectively. They can also view material needed for a meeting right on their computers, which is a good way to ensure that everyone on the call can see exactly what is being discussed. Video conferencing allows multiple locations to meet via live audio and video. It serves as a conference and not simply a video phone

call. While this was once extremely expensive and is still a significant investment, saved travel costs and reduced time requirements have made this a viable option for the multi-office firm. It's a great tool to expand communications from a simple office level to a firm-wide one where the managing partner can communicate to everyone at one time while also providing a way for offices to work together on marketing initiatives.

- *Internal blogs.* Externally, blogs allow firm professionals to show their expertise to readers. Internally, they are used by firm management to communicate firm-wide. The managing partner, or any other designee, can provide updates on current marketing efforts, financial performance, and strategic efforts. By reading the comments posted by readers, firm management can keep its fingers on the pulse of what's happening within the organization.
- *Podcasts.* These audio or video digital files are used as a marketing tactic by many firms, but they are also a great tool for internal communications. Messages from firm leadership can be recorded and employees can download them at a time that's convenient to them. They are also great training tools to share processes with current employees and basic company information to new employees.
- *Office marketing meetings.* On an office level, meetings should be held to discuss new work obtained, upcoming events, marketing successes, and tools for professional development. These meeting are also a great avenue to share firm-wide information at a local level. It's important for team members to learn from each other by discussing specific marketing goals and strategies and to witness firsthand what to do and what not to do in specific instances. If a regular meeting cannot be held, find other ways to communicate marketing news within an office.
- *Partner meetings.* Local, regional, and firm-wide partner meetings should carry news about what's working in individual offices so that locations can serve as resources for one another. Demonstrating the results that are being achieved in the firm heightens the partners' receptivity to marketing in their own location.
- *Pipeline meetings.* Those responsible for business development within a firm, including all partners, need to meet regularly to discuss current opportunities. These can be done face-to-face within an office and via phone or video conference regionally or firm-wide. Communication ensures there is no duplication of efforts and allows for people to identify ways they can help others in the firm with opportunity pursuit. It adds accountability to the business development process, too.
- *Strategic committees.* Niche or specialty industry groups and other specific committees within a firm that generate and implement marketing and client service ideas can be a powerful communication source. Since these committees have specific marketing goals, they must communicate with each other regularly to discuss progress and revamp strategies when needed. They must then share their efforts firm-wide so individual offices know what resources are available to them.
- *Marketer's report.* The marketing department is not exempt from communicating what it has accomplished. A summary of priorities achieved, projects, budget results and overall performance with marketing, strategic and business goals may help some partners understand how the firm's marketing efforts have impacted firm accomplishments. This communication also reinforces strategic priorities and shows how they translate into marketing activity and ultimately business results.

🔑 Key Concept

In a multi-office firm, it is critical to continually communicate the marketing goals for the firm and offices, and the current status in attaining them.

The bigger the firm, the more important a role communications play. Team members want to be informed of what is going on in the firm and where the firm is going in the future. After all, professional services professionals are intelligent, inquisitive, and focused individuals by nature, and their careers are at stake. By communicating firm, region, and office goals, all team members are able to buy into the marketing process and feel confident that they are part of a goal-attaining organization. This will help the firm develop younger team members into stronger professionals and firm supporters in the years to come. For more information, see chapter 32, "In-House Marketing Communications that Foster Success."

FOCUS ON ACCOUNTABILITY

Success starts with goal-setting, and a multi-office firm is no exception. However, equally important to goal setting is defining performance measurements that allow everyone to know that the goal has been reached, and defining a system to hold individuals accountable for reaching established goals. Although goal setting is the universal starting point for all public accounting firms, the need for clear goals, performance expectations, and accountability is heightened in the multi-office firm. Not only are the functions of the marketing department widely interpreted by the personnel in the different offices, but there may be confusion as to the role each individual, office, or department may play in the action process. Further, it is essential that measurable outcomes are prioritized and tracked to reinforce the priorities of the firm, region, or economic unit.

Developing a system to keep track of what individuals accomplish is the heart of accountability. The system should take care to not just reward numbers, but rather the efforts and actions taken by individual team members. Communications is the key to a well developed accountability plan. Team members need to answer to someone, usually a member of firm management, to demonstrate that they are working toward established goals. Accountability triggers results. For more information about tracking marketing initiatives, see chapter 34, "Marketing and Sales Metrics Matter: Measuring Results, Calculating Return on Investment."

Key Concept

Developing a system to keep track of what individuals accomplish is the heart of accountability.

CREATE A BRAND

One of the best marketing strategies any accounting firm can implement is to create a consistent brand. A brand helps define the organization and communicates a single firm message to both internal and external publics. However, in a multi-office firm, a brand takes on an even more important role. With offices spread out across the state, nation, or world, it is easy for the individual offices to operate as independent practices under a single firm name rather than as a single entity.

To ensure that all offices in a multi-office firm have the same identity, create one. This is more than a logo and a tag line, too. It's a firm's story and how that story plays out in the interactions people have with its employees. A solid brand always starts with a solid story to which people can relate, and a firm may want to get feedback from existing clients, prospective clients, and employees as part of the brand development process. A wide range of opinions will give the firm true insight into current brand strengths and provide guidance as to what identified areas are integral to the brand.

Start by developing a story for the firm. Determine what is unique about its employees in terms of character, its overall identity and the values it exhibits. Know specifically how the firm solves business problems and what exactly firm professionals can educate others on. Understand the firm's vision, especially why it is in existence beyond making money, and why the firm is the best one to help the right organizations. From this, write a story for the firm and be prepared to tell others not only what the firm is, but why it is.

The story must then be relayed to employees. Think of employees as walking, talking billboards and use them to create a consistent brand. Providing brand training is an important step since these employees are the ones who bring the brand to life during encounters they have with clients and others in the marketplace. It's important for all firm personnel to see exactly where they fit into the firm's story so it can be passionately shared with others. In professional services firms, the talents, skills, and personalities of the people delivering the services are what people buy. Tax returns and financial statements are a few of the end products delivered to clients, and that's an important part of the process. However, the hard truth is opinions are formed about a firm through direct interactions people have with its employees, and those thoughts are then confirmed by a quality work product. People deliver a brand to other people.

Differentiation is a key element in a firm's brand. The story told and the image that story creates must not look like another. Today, a fair price, quality work and solid service delivery are standard operating procedures—

people expect these from all firms automatically. It's the inspiration one gets from the story and how people emotionally connect with it that will separate one firm from another. The firm's value proposition, or what it can deliver to customers, will differentiate the firm from the competition if the same messages are used consistently.

In a multi-office firm, the brand should primarily come to life through the people. It is further illustrated in marketing collateral that contains common messages and themes that tell the firm's story. The different variations of the marketing material developed for the firm should have the same "look" and "feel," and it should be used consistently by each office. The primary marketing collateral that can be developed to define a brand and illustrate the firm's story include the following:

- *Logo and tagline.* One of the primary elements of creating a brand is logo and tagline development and use. To help strengthen a brand in all offices and within the markets in which they compete, use a logo and tagline consistently on all marketing collateral the firm produces. The same is true for use of corporate colors. National retailers always use the same colors on everything, from the sign on the front of the store to the shopping bag they send their buyers away with. This is a calculated decision because of the impact it has on brand. A brand style guide is a great way to create that consistency as it spells out in specific detail how and when to use the logo and what formats are acceptable. All successful brands utilize and enforce brand guidelines.
- *Stationery.* The same letterhead, envelopes, business cards and other stationery pieces should be used by each office with as few changes as possible. The most obvious changes would be to the individual office's contact information.
- *Brochure.* There is much debate as to whether or not a firm brochure has outlived its life cycle, as there are many pros and cons to consider in today's electronic era. Any firm that decides to use a brochure will see this marketing piece as a key element in brand development. The uniqueness of the piece, the design elements, and the tone of the text will help a firm set itself apart from other firms. The same holds true with brochures and sell sheets targeted to specific services and industries. They help create a firm's brand while also showing expertise in a specific area, and are needed even if firms opt against a general firm brochure. For more information on brochures, see chapter 20, "Guidelines for Effective Brochures."
- *Web site.* A firm's Web site is one of its most important marketing pieces and has moved from a luxury to a basic marketing tool that firms are expected to have. With the increased number of Web users, the use of search engines is on the rise as Internet users attempt to find the exact information they are looking for. This change in behavior means that a Web site is often a prospect's first encounter with the firm and from which initial opinions are made. This makes it important for a firm to optimize its site for search engines. Whether a firm simply uses a Web site as an electronic brochure or if they have built it into a revenue generating tool, the site has to be able to be found by the end user via a search engine. Plus, a Web site is an important element in defining a brand and often serves a primary way to communicate with existing and prospective clients. For more information on Web sites, see chapter 18, "Guide to an Effective CPA Firm Web Site."
- *E-mail templates.* The number of e-mails employees send and receive in a given day is staggering. A firm should take advantage of this situation and use e-mail messages as another way to build a brand. This can be done simply by establishing a signature line format everyone in the firm must follow. There is also technology in existence that helps firms establish more graphically appealing electronic letterhead templates. Attaching marketing messaging, like seminar announcements and recognition received, to outgoing e-mails provides another channel that can be used to create awareness.
- *Blogs.* Many firms are illustrating their brands further by developing a blog that allows professionals within the firm to post commentary on specific issues. These commentaries are typically posted in reverse chronologic order and can be searched by topic, author, or date, and readers can add their own comments to the postings. Blogs create a dialogue with clients, prospective clients, and the media while allowing the firm to illustrate thought leadership in the areas they wish to show expertise. Real Simple Syndication, or RSS, feeds are common on blogs and they allow new content to automatically be delivered to people who want to get it in the format they choose. In an environment where marketing pieces get lost in the sea of messages out there, this technological capability helps firms get information directly to people who truly want to receive it.
- *Social media.* To build upon the concept of creating dialogue, social media (that is, Facebook, LinkedIn, and Twitter) allows firms to let their brands play out in social communities. Communications are disseminated through social interactions on the Web or through Web-based technologies. The way these communications take place, along with how firms respond to the communication of others, allow the brand to play out in real

time. As with a blog, in the social media realm, firms have the luxury of interacting with people who opt to receive the firm's messages. For more information on social media, see chapter 17, "Adding Social Media to Your Marketing Mix."

> **⚷ Key Concept**
>
> A brand helps define the organization and communicates a single firm message to both internal and external publics. In a multi-office firm, a brand takes on an even more important role.

GENERATE FIRM-WIDE MARKETING MATERIAL FOR LOCAL USE

When marketing multiple offices, the firm strives to achieve a balance between meeting the unique needs of each individual office and its market and attaining economies of scale inherent in developing marketing approaches for the overall firm. Marketing should focus on a strategy that benefits more than one location. Take care to create marketing pieces that can be used by all offices, even if it means eliminating addresses and phone numbers. Often firms rely solely on a Web site address since it typically doesn't vary by location.

While using specific data that may date the piece was once avoided like the plague, on-demand printing has made that issue null and void. Printing only small batches of marketing material means modifications can be made when offices are added or information changes. It also allows for specific information to change on a set number or pieces while the firm can still obtain volume pricing. For example, a firm can split a 5,000 piece print run among 5 offices with each office's specific contact information included only on the pieces it will use.

In addition, partner and staff time spent doing marketing tasks can be minimized by providing ready-to-use marketing materials and program kits to each office. All marketing pieces do not need to look exactly alike, but should rather have similar elements that convey and uphold the firm's brand. Here are some examples of firm generated marketing materials that can be used on the local level:

- *Newsletters.* Printed newsletters are a great way to reach a large audience at a reasonable cost. They are used to reinforce the firm image and educate clients, referral sources, and team members about timely issues as well as services and capabilities. While some firms elect to produce these newsletters completely in-house, others purchase them from outside sources that can customize them with the firm's logo and possibly some content generated by the firm. Despite the method a firm elects to use, the key to effectively using a newsletter is to have an up-to-date mailing list. If sending out a large quantity of newsletters, be sure to contact the local U.S. post office for rules regarding bulk mail. The post office requires that a mailing list be checked by a licensed vendor for accuracy before it is used and then periodically after that. Also, when developing mailing lists, make sure that certain groups of people can be identified to receive information that is relevant to them. For example, individuals in the construction industry should be able to receive a newsletter with content that applies specifically to them, while manufactures on the mailing list don't receive the construction related content. For more information on newsletters, see chapter 21, "Newsletters That Get Noticed."
- *E-newsletters.* Since sending material electronically is extremely cost-effective, electronic newsletters continue to grow in popularity. They allow firms to send content to a large audience without the added printing costs of a traditional newsletter or the turnaround time needed for the printing and mailing process. There are numerous platforms that can be purchased that help with the layout, which should be branded to the firm, and the mailing of the newsletter. Other vendors sell article content as part of their platform to help firms that struggle with writing it themselves. Mailing list development, and the ability to sort this data by buyer group, is just as important as with print newsletters. However, e-communications present unique challenges. First and foremost, e-communications must comply with laws that guide electronic communication, the most prevalent being the CAN-SPAM Act of 2003. The key to compliance is making sure the people who receive the newsletter have asked to get it. Contact the Federal Trade Commission for guidance. In addition, there can be complications to sending e-newsletters from the same domain name (that is, @yourfirm.com) used for other firm e-mail messages. There are many best practices for e-communications that should be researched before sending newsletters electronically.

- *Presentation material.* Folders or other methods used to present marketing pieces to prospects and tax returns, financial statements, and other work product to clients should also convey the firm's brand. Same with presentation slide templates used in face-to-face presentations and Webinars.
- *Advertising slicks.* A portfolio of ad slicks can be developed by the firm and modified for local office use. These ads can vary from those specifically designed for general branding of the firm to those selling specific niches or specialty services. While most publications prefer electronic copies, ad slicks can also be developed on paper if that's what is required in a specific situation.
- *Professional biography template.* In a professional services setting, bios are used to communicate professional, educational, civic, and personal information about team members to the public. While some firms continue to use a very traditional format for these bios, many firms are beginning to add creative flair to the information to help support the firm's brand and give insight into the unique personality of each professional. Develop a template so everyone's bio looks the same regardless of location.
- *Speaker sheets.* CPAs often look for opportunities to speak to their clients and prospects. This sheet provides background and contact information for the speaker as well as a list of recent presentations made and those that can be made. By distributing these sheets to seminar and event planners, professionals are asking to be considered as a speaker, and a speaker sheet will increase odds for success.
- *Testimonials.* Testimonials have become important marketing pieces that highlight a firm's success with a specific client. The look and uses vary from a single quote used in an advertising campaign to a full case study that is given to prospects. These testimonials can be used locally to promote successes and to assist in communicating both capabilities and possible results.
- *Media relations kit.* This kit should include a series of sample press releases for common occurrences like promotions and passing of the CPA exam. In addition, it will highlight the individual media outlets (that is, local newspapers, business and industry journals and radio and television stations) that the firm targets for communication. Individual offices should also be given guidance on how and when they are able to communicate with the media. This includes designating one person, perhaps a marketer or senior partner, as the spokesperson for the office because speaking in one voice is critical. As part of an overall media relations program, specific goals can also be set as to what type of coverage the firm would like to receive in which outlets and on what topics; however, some of these tasks will probably be handled by marketing staff in coordination with individuals in the local offices.
- *Article database.* The articles developed for newsletters as well as those published in business and industry journals can be repurposed for use on the firm's Web site, in other newsletters, for other publications, and for meetings with prospects. By developing a database of all content written, firms can keep track of where articles appeared and how they have been used. This ensures the greatest return for the investment of time that went into article preparation.
- *Letter file.* A file of sample letters used in various practice development efforts, such as follow-ups to seminars, luncheons, or the first meeting with a prospect, should be compiled in a format that can be shared with all offices and updated as new letters are developed.
- *Proposal bank.* Guidelines on both the form and content for proposal preparation should be included in a proposal bank. These guidelines should incorporate layout format, including margins, headings, table of contents, and use of tabs and covers. Most importantly, the bank should file proposals and include useful sort options (that is, by industry, services proposed, location) while also noting whether the proposal resulted in a "win" or a "loss" for the firm. It's also important to establish guidelines as to what proposals can be prepared at the local level and which are to be developed by a firm's marketing staff. Those proposals that have larger than average revenue or may be strategically important to the firm may require the added expertise of a marketing professional. For more information about proposals, see chapter 28, "Creating Proposals That Win."
- *Seminar planner.* This guide on how to plan, implement, and follow-up after seminars should include samples from previous seminars to aid the planning process. In addition, the planner should include worksheets for the seminar's theme, objectives, and budget along with a planning time frame. Include a checklist that lists all the issues that need to be addressed to ensure that no detail is overlooked and provide guidance on how to calculate a return on investment for post event analysis. For more information on seminars, see chapter 25, "Using Seminars to Build Your Practice."

- *Tradeshow planner.* Instructions should be given on how to determine whether an office should participate in a given tradeshow, and if so, what the pre-show, during show and after show tactics should be considered. Guidelines may also cover how to design an exhibit or how to use exhibit displays owned by the firm. Give the personnel in attendance tips on how to conduct themselves during the show, and spell out how information gathered at the show should be used post event, like adding names to mailing lists and tracking leads. Be sure to include information on how a return on investment should be determined. For more information on tradeshows, see chapter 26, "Building Opportunity Through Tradeshows."

These are just some of the possible ready-to-use marketing material options. Other tools that lend themselves to this format include surveys, bulletins, "how-to" booklets and training sessions. These materials cannot simply be distributed to the local offices, but must be accompanied with instructions, including in what circumstances assistance from the marketing department must be obtained. The key point with firm generated marketing material is to develop packaged solutions that answer broad-based needs and are easy to implement at the local level.

DEVELOP A MARKETING AND BUSINESS DEVELOPMENT STAFF

In a multi-office firm, there is usually one individual who assumes the role of overseeing the firm's marketing strategy as a whole. For some firms it is a partner and for others it is a marketing director. The marketing director's primary function is to be a roving educator and interpreter, the glue that binds the area offices and niches together in their efforts to grow.

Depending on the firm's size, there may be a marketing manager for a region or marketing coordinators in individual offices, or both. Or a firm may build an internal marketing team by expertise where different people have different skills—writing, public relations, marketing research, graphic design, etc.—that are pulled upon to help the firm meet its marketing goals. The larger the firm, the more likely its department will be built by skill set in each region. Despite how a department is structured, these marketing professionals help administer the marketing programs and work with and support the marketing director. It is important to note that all the members of a marketing department, and most notably the marketing director, are important members of a firm's entire team and the marketing director should play an important role in the strategic and growth plans for the firm.

As an alternative or addition to an in-house marketing department, some firms may consider outsourcing various marketing functions, like newsletter development, advertisement development and placement, and media relations to an advertising or public relations agency. These outside consultants also provide consulting services if firms need additional resources. While this is a great way to get specialized assistance with marketing efforts, a firm must closely evaluate the costs and value associated with outsourcing. Depending on firm size and layout, it could be feasible to add personnel to the marketing department to handle these functions at a lower cost. However, there are some benefits to working with an outside firm that must also be considered.

> **⚷ Key Concept**
>
> The marketing director's primary function is to be a roving educator and interpreter, the glue that binds the area offices and niches together in their efforts to grow.

Using an outside agency provides accessibility to a much larger team with a wide range of creative ideas. In addition, an outside agency adds a layer of accountability since consultants push professionals to meet deadlines. Since the firm's practitioners comprehend the need for efficiency when paying for services, they are usually more receptive to providing timely assistance when needed. Finally, outsourcing provides objectivity and honest feedback, which may be helpful in specific situations. When a firm considers outsourcing marketing functions, the pros and cons must be carefully considered to help ensure the decision benefits the firm as a whole and the individual offices. For more information on retaining outside consultants, see chapter 13, "The Outside Consultant: More than an Expert."

While some partners expect the members of the marketing department to relieve some of their burden and actually "do" sales and marketing for them, that should not be the case. Although marketers can help partners with their marketing by helping them understand a prospect's needs, supplying them with tools and coaching to enable them to achieve results, partners should still be doing the significant marketing and sales activities themselves.

However, firms that employ business developers use these professional sales people to enhance their sales efforts. Business developers are typically not accountants, and they have training and experience in selling. They have the skill set to generate leads themselves, help develop existing opportunities the firm may have, and coach others within the firm on how to best close a sale. Because of their unique skill set, business developers can help partners develop specific strategies for each opportunity and help them re-strategize, as needed, throughout the sales process. The nature of selling a professional service puts CPAs in a stronger position to close opportunities, but the hand-off between the sales person and the partner is a tricky process. If it is not done right, the chance for loss is heightened. Partners must approach the lead with the same formality and dedication that the business developer did in order to keep the process moving forward and not undo all the business developer's hard work. For more information about business developers, see chapter 12, "The Case for Utilizing a Sales Professional at Your Firm."

Marketers and business developers must work together closely for optimal success. While marketers generate leads, the business developers will be eager to follow-up on them. Together, the two professionals, with very different skill sets, know where the opportunities lie within a given market. Marketers can gain insight from what the sales staff is learning in the marketplace that will help with segmenting, targeting and positioning the firm best for potential buyers. When the firm gets the opportunity to submit the proposal, sales will feed information to marketing for the proposal. This synergy should result in more wins, and revenue, for the firm.

The success of the marketing and business development departments depends primarily on the relationship between the professionals and the managing partner or to whomever they report. A strong relationship with management is vital because the managing partner

- sets the vision for what marketing and business development is suppose to achieve.
- controls the purse strings and other resources.
- can lend credibility to efforts by linking them to other meaningful practice goals and initiatives.

The managing partner and the marketer and business developer as a team come across as very powerful. The sense of team reinforces a commitment to marketing and sales efforts by indirectly saying, "This is important, as important as any other thing the firm is currently working on." When people observe that the marketer and business developer are spokespeople, and in some regards deputies, for the managing partner, they begin to see the inherent connection between the firm's marketing and sales activity and its business goals. For more information about integrating marketing and sales, see chapter 3, "The Integration Imperative: Erasing Marketing and Business Development Silos."

> **Key Concept**
>
> The managing partner, marketer, and business developer make a powerful team, one that reinforces the firm's commitment to marketing and sales efforts.

Conclusion

Marketing in the multi-office firm takes on a whole new set of challenges that single locations do not have to face. More coordination between the firm's central leadership and local leaders is needed. The use of well-defined plans, systems, and tools enable the multi-office firm to carry out its marketing initiatives in a much more efficient and cohesive manner. Keys to success include the development of an overall strategic plan and the establishment of well-defined systems and processes. Regular communications and a focus on accountability help the firm to realize its goals. The development of an overall brand helps the firm develop clear marketing messages inside the firm and out, and aids in the development of effective marketing communications. Additional marketing professionals are also crucial to effectively managing the process. Yes, many of the areas that multi-office firms need to pay attention to are best practices for firms of all sizes, but it is even more important for the multi-office firm to do them well to ensure success. It definitely requires additional work, but in the end, multi-office firms that recognize their uniqueness and strive to operate and present themselves as one firm, will achieve even greater marketing results.

ABOUT THE AUTHOR

Katie Tolin is the marketing director for Rea & Associates, Inc., an Ohio-based firm, where she oversees marketing, public relations, business development, and product management for the firm and its 11 offices. Active in the profession, she serves on the board of directors for the Association for Accounting Marketing and writes and speaks on topics related to practice growth. Prior to joining Rea in 2003, she spent 5 years in legal marketing. She holds a BSBA from Ohio Northern University, graduating with distinction, and a MA from Emerson College in Boston. Katie can be reached at katie.tolin@reacpa.com.

CHAPTER 8
Budgeting Techniques for Today's CPA Firm

Art Kuesel
PDI Global, Inc.

INTRODUCTION

In this chapter, we'll explore the budgeting process for marketing expenditures. We'll cover items like why you should budget and how much, as well as some more advanced topics such as where to spend and how to track and measure return on investment on your marketing expenditures. Whether you're a partner in a growing CPA firm with new marketing responsibilities, or a marketing professional with a few years under your belt, this chapter will help you improve your overall marketing budgeting and tracking processes.

WHY BUDGET FOR MARKETING EXPENDITURES AT ALL?

Just like tax planning and forecasting is done to assist clients in planning, budgeting, and managing their taxes, marketing budgeting helps CPAs plan, budget, and better manage their marketing expenditures. It's not that you don't know that budgeting is the right thing to do, but maybe you just need a little help getting started in this quasi-foreign territory. If you're just beginning to explore the concept of marketing budgeting, here are just a few reasons that may convince you it's the right thing to do.

- *Marketing is a component of a profitable CPA firm.* To effectively plan for profitability in your practice, you need to have a solid plan for revenues and expenditures. If you aren't truly planning for your marketing expenses, you will probably approach them with a minimalist attitude. You may attempt to minimize the surprise marketing expenditures, potentially to an ineffective level (in this case doing "something" is not always better than doing "nothing"). This may result in wasted money and agonizing decisions that plague your otherwise successful practice.
- *Budgeting for marketing in advance reduces disagreements later.* If you and your partners get together at the beginning of your fiscal year and agree on a marketing budget that makes sense for your firm, there will be fewer arguments down the road, when the expenditures make their way to the general ledger. You will still have to meet on a regular basis to discuss these expenditures, but knowing what you have to spend within an approximate time frame will help you and your fellow partners come to agreements faster and more efficiently regarding these expenditures.
- *Marketing is a strategic activity.* Marketing is a strategic function of your business and should be planned for appropriately. Because properly applied marketing dollars generate revenue and increase awareness of your practice, it is only natural that they should be given the same importance as any other area of your business.

> **♥ Key Concept**
>
> Marketing budgeting helps CPAs plan, budget, and better manage their marketing expenditures. Properly applied marketing dollars generate revenue and increase awareness of your practice, therefore they should be given the same importance as any other area of your business.

HOW MUCH SHOULD I BUDGET?

This question can only be answered with another—what are your objectives? Defense toward client attrition, client maintenance and ongoing education, and practice growth are three separate and distinct objectives that require different and unique marketing strategies and tactics, which affect the level of budgeting necessary. Knowing what you want to accomplish from your marketing budget is key to establishing your budget. Before you're ready to establish your budget, let's review some of the most common budget mistakes as well as the only truly effective method of determining your marketing budget.

- *Mistake #1: Budgeting based on what others are doing.* If you're like many CPAs, you are likely interested in "what others are doing." While this can serve as a guide, it should certainly not serve as the rule. There are several reasons why this is a bad model to follow, which include the following:
  — Your competition has different goals and objectives
  — You may be interested in different types of marketing activities (more expensive or less expensive) than your competitors
  — Your focus should be leading in marketing, not following
- *Mistake #2: Budgeting based on what you can afford.* This method will create inconsistencies that go against the principles of marketing effectiveness. It further encourages you to spend (perhaps foolishly) when times are good, and cut back when times are rough. This model of budgeting will result in poor outcomes and disappointment in your marketing expenditures.
- *Mistake #3: Budgeting based on past sales.* This is a poor method of budgeting because you're essentially looking in the wrong direction. Marketing is a forward thinking, strategic planning discipline that makes you look at what you want your practice to become, not what it has been in the past.
- *The ONLY correct way: Budgeting based on projected revenues.* Projected or targeted revenues are the only true method of accurately planning and budgeting for the future. This is because you must determine where you want to be, and then craft your marketing plan and budget to accomplish that objective. For example, if you want to generate $100,000 in cross-selling opportunities this year, you then must facilitate and plan for the type and number of activities that drive toward your goal.

The amount of your marketing budget needs to be established after you determine what your projected revenues will be. Then, you can effectively build your objectives and marketing activities that build toward that revenue goal. Even if you only want to "maintain" your practice, you must still invest in marketing "maintenance" activities that will help ensure that you keep your clients in the years to come.

⚷ Key Concept

Marketing is a forward thinking, strategic planning discipline that makes you look at what you want your practice to become, not what it has been in the past.

BUDGET CATEGORIES AND ALLOCATION METHODOLOGY

Now that you've been convinced that a marketing budget is the right thing to do, and you've determined your revenue goals and objectives for the coming year, you're ready to begin allocating your budget. A marketing budget is easier to establish if you break it into major and minor categories. Following in table 8-1 is a marketing budget sample, which details the most common major and minor categories for a CPA firm marketing budget.

TABLE 8-1 MARKETING BUDGET SAMPLE

Marketing Budget Category	Sub-Category
Advertising	Design/Concept/Development
	Print Placements
	Radio Placements
	White/Yellow Pages
	Online Placements
	Industry/Trade Directories
	Obligatory/Misc
Community/Association Involvement	Chamber Memberships
	Industry/Trade Group Memberships
	Key Sponsorships
	Participation/Attendance Fees
Philanthropy	Key Sponsorships
	Corporate Donations
Marketing Communications	Firm Brochure
	Niche/Practice/Industry Pieces
	Logo/Tagline Development
	CV/Profiles

continued

TABLE 8-1   MARKETING BUDGET SAMPLE (*CONTINUED*)

Marketing Budget Category	Sub-Category
Web site	Design/Concept/Development
	Updates
	Search Engine Optimization Program
Client/Prospect/Referral Communication	Client Newsletter (General)
	Niche Newsletter
	E-Newsletters
	Printing/Postage/Fulfillment
	Direct Mail
Events	Key Sponsorships
	Seminars
	Trade Shows
	Trade Show Booth
Other Internal or Client/Prospect/Referral Communication	Year End Tax Guide
	Tax and Regulatory Updates
	Direct Mail
	On-Hold Client Messaging
	Annual Report
	Intranet/Internal Newsletter

TABLE 8-1   MARKETING BUDGET SAMPLE (*CONTINUED*)

Marketing Budget Category	Sub-Category
Business Development	Marketing/Sales Training
	Partner Coaching
	Proposal Templates
	Referral Events
Marketing Research	Market Perceptions Study
	Database Subscriptions
Public Relations/Media Relations	PR Firm Assistance
	Press Photos
	PR Recovery Plan
	Reporter/Editor Entertainment
Client Appreciation	Holiday gifts
	Sports/Entertainment Events
	Golf Outing
	Open Houses
Client Satisfaction Initiatives	Client Survey
	Client Interviews
	Post-Engagement Surveys
Branding	Trademark/Legal Expenses

continued

TABLE 8-1   MARKETING BUDGET SAMPLE (*CONTINUED*)

Marketing Budget Category	Sub-Category
Promotional Items	Pens/Padfolios/Etc
	Logo Apparel
	Trade Show Giveaways
Recruiting	Recruiting Brochure
	Recruiting Microsite
	Trade Show Booth
	Recruiting Giveaways
Miscellaneous	Partner Discretionary Funds
	Freelancers
	Consultants
	Speakers/Trainers

Budget Allocation

Now that you know the common categories that comprise a marketing budget, you need to know how to allocate it. It is nearly impossible to propose a "common" allocation because each situation is entirely different based upon the different objectives and goals of each practice. Further, trying to determine a common allocation for marketing expenditures would be basing marketing budgeting on what others are doing. The best way to show you how to build your actual marketing budget is to go through a hypothetical example. Please review exhibit 8-1, "Marketing Budget Case Study," at the end of the chapter.

Tracking Techniques

There are a few ways to track your marketing investment, to make sure it is generating the results you budgeted and planned for. While not every marketing activity is measurable, many are, and ways exist to capture your results in a summary document that can substantiate your annual marketing budget. Consider a *New Client Origination Inquiry*. Every time you get a new client, you can ask the relationship executive how the firm earned the client. Allow for several levels of influence. Your results may look like this:

New Client A:	Primary Influence—Hot topic seminars 2 and 3 Secondary—Advertisements in newsletter
New Client B:	Primary Influence—Referral from lawyer Secondary—Sales skills of Audit Manager Secondary—Direct mail pieces

For more information about tracking and measuring results, see chapter 34, "Marketing and Sales Metrics Matter: Measuring Results, Calculating Return on Investment."

Time Budgeting

Another issue to contend with is time. If your firm doesn't have a marketing coordinator or director, the marketing activities must be carried out by administrative personnel, staff, seniors, managers, directors, and partners. The best way to manage the time allotment for marketing is to establish a goal number of hours for each level of personnel and measure and monitor that goal monthly. Divide your major marketing initiatives up among a group of "champions," who are ultimately responsible for their implementation. Have the champions build their implementation teams from the pool of firm employees or practice employees available. Then, employees carry out their marketing tasks along with their billable responsibilities—as long as they are meeting both hour goals (marketing and billable), things should run smoothly. Finally, as a reference point, the level and volume of activity proposed in the case study earlier in the chapter would probably need to have a dedicated marketing coordinator or marketing director to implement and monitor.

CONCLUSION

Marketing budgeting can be as precise and strategic as the preparation of a tax return. In fact, for marketing to be effective, it truly has to be. If you can avoid the caveats to marketing budgeting, you should be successful in building your first marketing budget. Remember to start with the big picture and determine what your revenue goals and objectives will be. Then, work up to those goals by building marketing activities that will achieve the desired result. Know the pool of marketing activities that you can choose from and assign budgets and expectations for each one. With solid strategy, good planning, and periodic review you will see results from your marketing budget.

ABOUT THE AUTHOR

Art Kuesel, Director of Consulting Services for PDI Global, Inc., specializes in helping CPA, law, and financial services firms meet their marketing, business development, and growth goals. He especially enjoys developing marketing programs that produce significant, measurable, and revenue-enhancing results. With more than 10 years of experience working for CPA firms in a marketing and business development function, he brings an inside perspective as well as industry best practices to each firm he works with. Contact Art at 312.245.1745 or akuesel@pdiglobal.com.

EXHIBIT 8-1
MARKETING BUDGET CASE STUDY

Today you are a $4,000,000 firm, composed of three practice areas, four partners, and a revenue breakdown of the following:

Tax and Accounting Services	$ 2,500,000
Technology Help-Desk Services	$ 500,000
Audit/Assurance Services	$ 1,000,000
Total	$ 4,000,000

Last year you spent $100,000 on marketing, but your firm only grew in revenue by 1 percent, or about $40,000. As the marketing partner, you are taking some heat about the lackluster results from your fellow partners. However, you convince them that this year things will be different because you've recently read a book chapter about how to develop an effective marketing budget. After much convincing, they reluctantly allow you to propose a plan to spend marketing dollars this year.

Because you and your partners are interested in growth for the firm, you start at the top and decide that 10 percent top line growth will be your goal for the year. Looking at the practice areas you have, and trends in the industry and marketplace, you target $100,000 growth for Technology Help-Desk Services and $300,000 growth for the Audit/Assurance practice.

Technology Help-Desk Services

Because this practice area consists of 100 percent reoccurring revenue, your goal will be easier to achieve than if it consisted of some nonreoccurring revenue. You want to make sure your existing clients are satisfied, so you would like to implement the following maintenance activities to keep your clients happy and hold on to your $500,000 of reoccurring revenue:

1. Publish a "tips for using the help-desk" bulletin/e-bulletin 12x per year	$ 4,800
2. Host a client roundtable 4x year to discuss hot topics	$ 1,600
3. Take your five best clients to one baseball game each over the summer	$ 1,750
4. Send a client survey to every Technology Help-Desk client	$ 1,500
5. Send holiday gifts to each one of your Technology Help-Desk clients	$ 3,000
	Total: $12,650

And, to grow your Technology Help-Desk practice by $100,000 to $600,000, you would like to implement the following New Business Generation activities:

1. Host an informative seminar on IT trends 3x per year	$ 9,000
2. Publish a Help-Desk Newsletter/e-Newsletter (4x) for your	
3. prospects/referral sources	$10,000
4. Produce a repetitive direct mail campaign (8x) to a targeted group	
5. of prospects	$ 2,000
6. Join a technology association and work toward a leadership position	$ 1,000
	Total: $ 22,000

Audit/Assurance Services

Because this practice area consists of 90 percent reoccurring revenue your goal will be a bit harder to achieve than with Technology Help-Desk Services. You essentially start the year with only $900,000. To achieve your top line 10 percent growth goal of $1,300,000, you will actually need to bring in new revenue of $400,000. Again, you want to make sure your existing clients are satisfied, so you would like to implement the following maintenance activities to hold on to your $900,000 of reoccurring revenue:

EXHIBIT 8-1
MARKETING BUDGET CASE STUDY (CONTINUED)

1. Publish an Audit/Assurance client newsletter/e-newsletter 4x year $ 7,500
2. Invite 24 Audit/Assurance clients to your firms' golf outing $ 4,800
3. Take your 10 best clients to one hockey game each in the fall $ 5,200
4. Do a client interview with the top 30 Audit/Assurance Services clients $ 1,500
5. Host Executive Briefings (12x) designed to educate clients on trends $ 3,600
6. Publish a manual that assists clients in getting ready for an audit $ 2,500

Total: $ 25,100

And, to grow your Audit/Assurance practice by $400,000 to $1,300,000, you would like to implement the following New Business Generation activities:

1. Produce a repetitive Internal Audit direct mail/e-mail campaign (8x) $ 4,000
2. Host receptions with your referral sources (6x) $ 3,600
3. Send your top Audit Manager to an outside sales course $ 3,500
4. Sponsor the Independent Auditor's Association Annual Dinner $ 5,000
5. Host seminars (4x) for prospects/referrals on hot topics in the industry $ 12,000
6. Run advertisements in an association magazine/newsletter (8x) $ 4,000
7. Engage a PR firm to assist you in getting published/quoted in publications $ 12,000

Total: $ 44,100

Marketing Budget Summary	Amount	Goal
Technology Help-Desk Services Maintenance	$ 12,650	100% Retention
Technology Help-Desk Services Growth	$ 22,000	$100,000 in new revenue
Audit/Assurance Services Maintenance	$ 25,100	100% retention
Audit/Assurance Services Growth	$ 44,100	$400,000 in new revenue
Total	$103,850	

Case Study Summary

Once you've completed the previously mentioned planning steps for your practices and the activities that will accomplish your goals, your partners will have a hard time arguing with the validity of your strategically allocated marketing budget of $103,850. Because successful marketing is built on repetitive activities, you will not see equal results in all months during execution of your marketing activities. Don't get nervous if you don't see results in the first six months of your marketing efforts, The power of marketing typically comes after multiple positive experiences have been achieved with your target audience. Finally, if you haven't achieved the results you are looking for after a certain time period, changes can be made to your approach. It can often take 6-9 months of activities, as outlined in the case study, to generate measurable results.

PART III:
Building the Team

CHAPTER 9
Your Leadership Makes Business Development Happen

Melinda Guillemette
Melinda Motivates

INTRODUCTION

Psssst.

Hey, you. Yeah, you. The managing partner.

Seen your marketing plan lately? Know who's supposed to be doing what? Any idea whether they're doing it?

Ah, well. You've been busy. Hours to bill. Jobs to manage. A firm to run.

Here you are, the managing partner of your firm. You have a very skilled team of technicians and support professionals, and you might have a capable, energetic marketing director. Maybe you've spent more money than you'd like to count sending yourself and your partners to business development training. All of you want to make more money, get new clients, get more engagements from current clients, and do interesting work. But it isn't happening.

If this scenario strikes a familiar chord, it's probably because your marketing leadership has taken a back seat to all the other day-to-day demands of managing a practice. Is this completely understandable? Absolutely. Is it wise in the long term? Certainly not.

Without your marketing leadership, the best laid plans, the most finely crafted strategies, the most honorable intentions are meaningless. Without marketing *leadership*, there is no marketing *following*. The result is that only the most senior partners are bringing in business. As those senior partners retire, your firm's longevity and stability can come into question.

Many tools exist to develop business in a CPA firm. You can write and execute marketing plans, create communications and advertising strategies, and redesign Web sites, to name a few. However, real marketing success boils down to individual behaviors and tendencies, not just firm policies. If professionals are inclined toward giving great client service, they will do so with or without written guidelines. If they are inclined toward bringing in new clients, they very likely will do that with or without a cookie-cutter plan.

The most effective marketing leadership strategy is to find out what each individual does well and feels comfortable doing, figure out how to apply that to the firm's goals, then support individuals with the right tools and appropriate training. This is harder than it sounds, particularly when trying to determine how different skills should be compensated. A few guiding principles might help.

> **⚷ Key Concept**
>
> The most effective marketing leadership strategy is to find out what each individual does well and feels comfortable doing, figure out how to apply that to the firm's goals, then support individuals with the right tools and appropriate training.

PRINCIPLE 1: MONEY TALKS

Let's face it. Everything that happens in a CPA firm is driven by compensation. If professionals aren't compensated for doing something, they are unlikely to do it. So the first thing to do is to build marketing efforts and results into your firm's compensation plan.

If you want to create a true business development culture, you have to demonstrate that bringing in clients will make individual firm members more money. You have to show that *not* bringing them in will limit personal income.

Set out clear career paths for team members. Then let them know that the firm's top-paid professionals are those who bring in the business. Those who learn how to do that will have the opportunity to become partners more quickly than those who don't. You must appeal to individual self interest when exercising effective marketing leadership.

PRINCIPLE 2: MONEY TALKS, BUT IT ISN'T EVERYTHING

Keep in mind that successful business development cultures consistently recognize and reward not only the results, but also the efforts to bring in clients. The best marketing leaders know that most human beings respond more strongly to public praise than they do to a few dollars. The praise you give them is what they will remember long after they have spent the bonus money for hitting certain business development targets.

In most firms, people are usually rewarded for actually getting clients in the door, but they are not rewarded or recognized for what it takes to get clients there—relationship-building, networking, community service, teaching, speaking, writing, or referral source development. All these activities require time and effort, and they happen in addition to, not instead of, billable work.

To pique professionals' interest in business development, some firms are instituting incentive programs, where individuals or teams can earn points for activities like those mentioned previously. Such programs are still relatively new, so we can't predict their long-term effectiveness. In the short term, they raise the level of marketing awareness and often increase enthusiasm for the process. Sometimes, they even result in new clients. For more information on incentives, see chapter 33, "Effective Employee Incentive Programs: How to Bring Out the Best in Your Firm."

While additional work is the most obvious result of an incentive program, the more subtle result should be to recognize and reward the efforts of those who make an attempt at business development. These tangible rewards can be relatively inexpensive. The real reward—and it costs nothing—is public recognition and affirmation. It is wondrous what a simple "good job" will do to motivate people.

🔑 Key Concept

Your staff will respond to public praise more strongly than to a few extra dollars.

PRINCIPLE 3: TRUSTING EACH OTHER IS GOOD BUSINESS

You and your team need to critically review efforts and results. To do this effectively, a high level of trust must exist among leadership, partners and up-and-comers. Trust is built by sharing time and experiences and by creating an environment that supports brainstorming and risk-taking. All of this fosters clarity of thought, communication, and action.

Meet regularly with your partners and senior team (both formally and informally) and get to know them. It's amazing what you can learn in a relatively short time if you are paying attention. Share your perspectives and experience; tell them your professional story (and, if you want to, your personal story). Encourage their questions and answer them in a way that makes people feel richer for asking. Their trust in you will grow, and their willingness to learn from you will increase.

After you have established trust, talk clearly with individuals about business development. Discuss and negotiate (don't dictate) what they can do to increase the firm's top line and what you will do to support their effort. Get their agreement and their commitment. Reward their success, and recognize their efforts publicly and privately. When their efforts flag or fail, it is important to give them the time and support they need to get back on track.

PRINCIPLE 4: YOUR BEHAVIOR SPEAKS LOUDER THAN YOUR WORDS

This rule applies to all areas of a firm's practice, but particularly to business development. Younger partners and employees will model behavior on what they perceive has made the firm's leaders successful. If your firm's leaders are sitting at their desks all day every day, crunching numbers and avoiding calls from clients, your followers will imitate that behavior. By the same token, if the firm leadership is regularly visiting clients, participating in community activities, and developing a strong referral network, your employees will begin to do the same.

Not only must you as a leader develop business; you must create the firm's marketing programs (with the marketing director if you have one) and ensure they are carried out. And then you must recognize and reward all those who participate, including those who demonstrate marketing efforts and those who actually bring in business.

Day-to-day, your responsibility as the marketing leader is to:

- be the same person every day. Leaders don't have the luxury of moodiness.
- be consistently optimistic while acknowledging the truth of any situation.
- criticize privately and praise publicly.
- say "thank you" to someone who has exerted marketing effort.
- ensure that your firm celebrates its marketing successes throughout the firm.

PRINCIPLE 5: KNOW WHEN AND HOW TO COMMUNICATE

If you want to increase your firm's marketing productivity, it is important to be a skillful communicator. Remember that when it comes to business development activities, it is not possible to over-communicate internally, assuming you are doing so truthfully, concisely, and compellingly. Everyone in your firm should know what's going on and why. Everyone should hear about business development successes. Use e-mail, telephone, internal newsletters, and intranets to spread the word. For more information on internal communications, see chapter 32, "In-House Marketing Communications That Foster Success."

Most people have an easier time spreading the good news than addressing the bad news. The tendency is to treat both situations the same way. It is more useful, however, to remember, as stated earlier, to praise publicly and criticize privately. When an individual is not meeting his or her commitments to business development (or any other commitment, for that matter), you as the marketing leader have the responsibility to address the specific issues with that individual. It is normal to want to gloss over specificity and avoid discomfort by making general statements in senior level meetings (for example, "We all need to get on the ball and start meeting our commitments to this effort"). This approach is unproductive. In using it, you manage to ignore those who are not doing what they said they would do and to offend and discourage those who are. It is far more useful to deal with the discomfort of one-on-one conversations than to issue general appeals for improvement.

⚷ Key Concept

Being a skilled communicator is key to increasing your firm's marketing productivity.

PRINCIPLE 6: MONITOR YOUR FIRM'S MARKETING

We've all heard it a thousand times: "Accountability is essential to success." Absolutely true.

It is also true when it comes to business development. Individuals must be accountable for their own marketing success. But what does "accountable" really mean in this context?

Of course, being accountable means the individual takes personal responsibility for implementing his or her individual marketing plan. But the other part of the equation must be that the firm is living up to its end of the bargain by supporting and monitoring the individual's effort.

This is where marketing activities can run into roadblocks. It is human nature to create a marketing plan and immediately forget about it. It's as though the mere creation of the plan, the writing of the words, will make business development happen. Knowing this very human response, it is essential that you and other marketing leaders in your firm play the role of monitor, mentor, and conscience.

You or a delegated marketing leader should scan individual action plans at least every month to be sure deadlines are being met. It is important that you contact individuals ahead of deadline to remind them of tasks they committed to and to see what progress they have made. This way, you can encourage and offer help, rather than scold them for a missed deadline. Nearly everyone responds more productively to praise than criticism, particularly when they have ventured into a new area such as business development.

> **? Key Concept**
>
> Individuals must be accountable for their own marketing success.

PRINCIPLE 7: HIRING THE RIGHT MARKETING HELP MAKES A BIG DIFFERENCE

Too often, firms hire a marketing director or marketing coordinator without giving it enough thought. Before you begin your search, decide what the position itself should involve, then what skills are appropriate and how much you are willing and able to pay. Only then should you begin your search for an individual who fits your specific requirements.

The bulk of marketers for accounting firms are creative, energetic, able people who implement strategies created by someone else—either the partners or high-level senior marketing staff. There is a smaller percentage of marketing practitioners who are higher level operators—those who either create the strategies for their firms, or who collaborate in their creation with firm partners. These individuals work at the executive level, and they are paid accordingly.

A very small percentage of marketers are a combination of the two. These are often people who have worked their way up through the professional services marketing ranks by learning the tasks, earning the trust of partners, and then teaching these tasks to others as they progress along their career paths. A handful of them have become partners in their firms.

The trick is to know what kind of marketer you need before you hire. If you are looking for a do-er and hire someone who is mostly a thinker, you will be disappointed. You can expect the same result if you want an executive and hire a neophyte.

Just like CPAs, all marketers are not alike. You wouldn't be likely to hire an accountant without thinking through the firm's needs and an individual's ability to fill those needs. Employ the same level of thought and due diligence when hiring your marketing professional. For more information on hiring a marketing professional, see chapter 10, "A Buyer's Guide to Hiring a Marketing Professional."

PRINCIPLE 8: LEADERS MAKE LEADING LOOK EASY

If you want to instill confidence in the firm's marketing leadership, it is important to make those around you comfortable and secure. No matter how busy you are, make time and find the energy for employees to discuss marketing ideas with you. Keep your door open (literally and figuratively) as much as you can. When you are asked, "Do you have a minute?" Answer "yes" whenever possible. If the answer has to be "no," follow the negative with "why not drop back by around 2:00?" or something similar. You are no less busy than anyone else; in fact, you almost certainly have more to do. But somehow you must make time to fit it all in, and you must do so without obvious effort.

If you want people to perceive you as a leader, you must exude self-discipline. Be graceful and gracious under pressure. Be absolutely engaged in the moment, regardless of other demands. And enjoy a good laugh now and then, especially if it is at your own expense.

Finally, become your firm's business development champion, both in your own activities and in motivating others. Plan your firm's marketing activities, communicate the firm's goals to *everyone* in the firm, and make sure marketing tactics are executed. Stay focused and optimistic. Recognize and reward everyone involved in the process. Celebrate the firm's achievements and progress.

If you apply these eight simple principles to your firm's marketing efforts, you will almost certainly reap the tangible benefits of business development: more clients, more interesting work, and more money. Some might say the intangible benefits that ensue—stronger, more trusting relationships among partners, more effective communications firm-wide, and a generally more optimistic culture—are the real icing on the cake.

ABOUT THE AUTHOR

As the owner of Melinda Motivates, **Melinda Guillemette** helps professionals find, create, and sustain relationships by communicating more effectively. Through speaking and consulting engagements, business people learn to communicate intentionally, authentically, and clearly. Speaking, facilitation, and training are her passions. She has addressed scores of professional associations, law firms, and accounting firms. In 2004, Melinda was inducted into the Association of Accounting Marketing Hall of Fame. She lives happily with her husband and dog in beautiful Corrales, New Mexico. You can reach her at mguillemette@comcast.net.

CHAPTER 10
A Buyer's Guide to Hiring a Marketing Professional

Sally Glick
Sobel & Co., LLC

INTRODUCTION

For many accounting firms, marketing has become a basic component of doing business profitably. Most accountants—even those who manage the firm's business affairs—have no formal training and little experience in the field. They have logically concluded that hiring a professional is the best way to ensure the firm's long-term success in marketing.

But what kind of marketing professional is right for your firm? Should it be a senior management-level marketing director with 10 or more years of relevant experience? Or a highly skilled marketing coordinator who isn't required to do planning, but can efficiently carry out marketing programs devised by senior partners? Or maybe you need something in between? Once you have determined what kind of professional you need, how do you find him or her? What about salary and compensation, expectations, evaluations, and creating a career track?

The goal of this chapter is to help you determine what kind of marketing professional you need, and then conduct a search and qualification procedure that ensures your final candidate will fit into your firm. It may seem like a lot of work, but consider this: a skilled and motivated marketing professional who genuinely cares about your firm can have a tremendous impact on the bottom line. He or she can help ensure that the firm's marketing initiatives are strategic, targeted, and consistent. Their very presence can introduce new energy and new ideas that can revolutionize the firm's approach to marketing, new business development, and client service.

Even when you plan to hire only a junior-level marketing professional, you should approach the process with as much thoroughness as you would when looking for a new partner. Why? Because the stakes are high. The right candidate will make you feel like you have entered into a partnership made in heaven; the wrong candidate will make you want to give up marketing altogether.

> ### ⚷ Key Concept
>
> A skilled and motivated marketing professional can have a tremendous impact on your firm's bottom line.

ARE YOU READY TO HIRE A MARKETING PROFESSIONAL?

Contrary to what some might believe, it is a mistake to assume that the size of a firm will determine a firm's readiness for hiring—and making good use of—a marketing professional. Instead, key variables include management's preparedness to confront the tough issues that a marketing planning process will inevitably bring to the fore, the firm's culture and commitment—including availability of time and a financial investment, as well as a clear sense of what it wants to achieve in the way of marketing and business development.

To be sure your firm is ready, ask yourself the following questions:

1. Do our partners believe marketing is a necessary business function, requiring the same level of attention and resources as client service, billings, and employee recruitment? If marketing is viewed as a necessary evil—

little more than an administrative function—then that is all it will ever be. Marketing must be viewed as a logical extension of the firm's mission and goals, a tool for helping the firm to achieve long-term growth and improve profitability.

2. Do we recognize that a skillful marketing professional will try to touch every aspect of the firm, seeking changes that will make it more client- and service-centered? A good marketing professional will analyze every aspect of your firm, looking for ways to improve client satisfaction. Your marketing professional may recommend change in areas as diverse as client billing, hallway lighting, and signage. You need to be ready to listen—and when appropriate—to institute change.

3. Do we understand the difference between sales and marketing and as such do we have realistic expectations for the results our marketer will deliver regarding new business generation?

4. Is our managing partner (or partner in charge of marketing) prepared to guide the marketing professional's efforts? In most accounting firms, the managing partner is already overburdened with work. To be successful, a marketing professional will require the insights, leadership, and support that only the managing partner can provide as well as the credibility across the firm that comes when the marketing professional has the managing partner's support.

5. Do we have a clear sense of what we want to accomplish? In other words, have we completed a written marketing plan? If you have not put a plan together, you can work with your new marketing professional to do so; however, before hiring anyone you should have some idea of what you want to accomplish in terms of growth. The partners and other decision makers at the firm can openly and honestly discuss what they expect of a marketing professional, even if it is just a list of bullet points. An example is as follows.

   We want

   a. a written marketing plan to act as a blueprint to guide us.
   b. a review of our existing logo, materials, and Web site to ensure consistency and a true reflection of our firm's culture.
   c. individual partner and niche specific plans and action steps.
   d. marketing and networking training for our next generation of leaders.
   e. assistance in improving our proposal process and the proposal template.
   f. implementation of a customer relationship management (CRM) system.

   Any of these tasks are reasonable to expect from the marketing professional you hire, but the more sophisticated your expectations are, the more likely it is that you will require a director level professional rather than a coordinator or manager. Going through this procedure helps you realize what kind of marketer fits your firm's needs.

6. Are we prepared to invest the time, money, and firm resources necessary not only to hire a marketing professional, but to fund his or her programs? Once you hire a marketing professional, your marketing expenditures will extend beyond his or her salary and compensation. The programs dictated by your marketing plan will require capital outlays. And the professional will require some kind of administrative support—usually a full-time secretary—along with office space and computer resources.

7. Do we all recognize that the outcomes of the marketing and branding activities will have firm wide and community wide impact, not necessarily measured only in new business? Effective marketing builds client retention as well as developing new business. Effective marketing also builds a strong name for your firm with referral sources. In some cases, all the efforts that are made to brand the firm and create a reputation in the community as a leading firm will not contribute to bottom-line profits. Branding is not selling, but it will ultimately create a powerful message that will translate into new business. With that in mind, it is more realistic to view most marketing expenditures as long-term investments in the future of the firm. It is important that everyone in the firm, especially the partners, appreciate and accept this fact. This does not mean you shouldn't scrutinize marketing outlays, or ask for a statement about the potential return on investment. Marketing efforts today may create opportunities that do not materialize for months, or even years, and in some cases you may not even realize that new business opportunities are resulting from current marketing activities because a direct correlation doesn't exist.

To sum it up, a marketing professional is not a miracle maker, and cannot accomplish significant results without the support and active participation of the firm's partners and senior staff. Making marketing work takes time, money, and sweat equity—everybody's sweat.

> **⚲ Key Concept**
>
> Marketing must be treated as an extension of the firm's mission and goals, a tool for helping the firm to achieve long-term growth and improve profitability.

> **⚲ Key Concept**
>
> A marketing professional cannot accomplish significant results without the support and active participation of the firm's partners and senior staff.

DEVELOPING A JOB DESCRIPTION

Nothing is ever as simple as it seems. This is certainly an appropriate comment to make about developing a marketing professional's job description, because much depends on what you want to accomplish in the area of marketing and what kind of role you expect the marketing professional to play. This is when the importance of having a marketing plan already in place comes into play.

Does the firm want to generate more face-to-face selling opportunities, or concentrate on launching new services? And do you want a marketing professional who can go out and generate new business leads, or simply edit proposals and keep track of partner activity? Should the person play the role of visionary, administrator, coach, or able assistant? These questions aren't easy to answer, but they will help you find the ideal candidate whose greatest strengths are in the areas that matter most to your firm.

The following "Job Description and Skills Level Checklist" covers the marketing skills you might look for in a marketing professional. Use it as a basis for designing your own job description and establishing skill requirements. As you review the checklist, ask yourself these questions:

1. Given our firm's marketing objectives, do we require a professional who possesses skills in this category?
2. If the answer is yes, what level of skill is needed?
3. How will we ascertain that a candidate possesses the required skill and to a sufficient degree?

See appendix 10-1 for several sample job descriptions.

Job Description and Skill Levels Checklist

General Description

Begin by developing a one- or two-sentence position charter for this role. Here are some examples:

> Senior level: Works directly with the firm's management group to help ensure the firm's continued growth and prosperity by designing and implementing appropriate marketing strategies.

> Junior level: Supports senior marketing staff and the firm's management group in carrying out selected marketing strategies.

Specific Responsibilities

Research and planning. What role is the marketing professional expected to play in the firm's marketing planning process? Assuming the firm has recently completed a general marketing plan, the professional could assist in developing industry-specific or service-specific strategies. Because market research is a vital component of good planning decisions, this skill should be required. Consider the following requirements:

> Senior level: Excellent grasp of marketing theory for professional services firms. Experienced in guiding similar organizations through the marketing planning process. Includes conducting relevant internal and external research, collating research findings, report preparation, and facilitating planning meetings. Knowledge of and experience with research techniques.

> Junior level: Good grasp of marketing theory for professional services firm. Able to assist with internal and external research, collating findings, and report preparation.

Public relations. Do you plan to retain an outside public relations (PR) firm? If this outside agency will be charged with planning and carrying out most of the firm's PR programs, then the in-house professional's experience in this area need not be as extensive. However, if yours is a large multi-office firm, a marketing professional with extensive PR experience can help you make the most of the agency you have retained.

If your marketing professional is going to handle PR on their own, try to determine what the scope of the PR program will be before hiring. A firm with plans for holding press conferences, releasing specialized economic reports, and hosting events will require someone with considerably more expertise than a firm looking for a few byline articles on tax subjects, along with arranging speaking engagements for senior partners.

> Senior level: Excellent grasp of PR, its tools and constraints. Extensive experience (preferably with a PR firm) in planning, launching, and evaluating PR campaigns for professional services or related businesses (financial institutions, real estate, services). Strong ties to the local media.

> Junior level: A good grasp of PR and its tools. Experienced in preparing and issuing press releases, maintaining media lists, placing byline articles, and arranging speaking engagements.

Advertising. As was the case with PR, your first questions should be, "Do we plan to do any advertising?" and "Will we be using an outside agency?" CPA firm advertising is as diverse as any other aspect of marketing, and can range from placing straightforward announcements regarding new partners and services, to more sophisticated campaigns designed to target specific industries and stimulate their interest in the firm and its services.

As was the case with PR, the skills required to act as liaison with an ad agency are far less than those required to plan, test, and launch year-round campaigns. So think carefully about these two questions before establishing your requirements.

> Senior level: Strong grasp of advertising fundamentals. Experience with advertising concept development, copyrighting, design fundamentals, and media planning. Also knowledgeable about prelaunch testing and post-campaign evaluation methods.

> Junior level: Understands the role advertising can play in promoting professional services. Has experience writing and placing simple announcement-type ads.

Client service and client satisfaction. Does your plan call for measuring client satisfaction and working actively to improve service? Do you feel managers and senior staff need help assessing their clients' service needs? What about all of the firm's "client contact points": its system for handling incoming calls, client communication tools (such as newsletters, tax alerts, guides, and other timely, relevant information), client billings, the condition of your offices? Consider these requirements:

> Senior level: Experience in designing survey instruments and administering client satisfaction surveys, preferably for service—or better yet, professional service—businesses. Proven ability to translate findings into workable action items that can be executed by the service provider. Thorough understanding of service excellence theory in the professional services arena.

> Junior level: Able to assist with administering client satisfaction surveys and tabulating results. Good grasp of service excellence theory.

Training. Since marketing and business development are not strong core competencies for CPAs, your firm might want to offer this type of training to your professionals. A firm with goals of achieving client service excellence may well require client service training for its partners and staff. What roles will the marketing professional play?

Only a senior-level professional should be expected to develop and implement a comprehensive program.

Senior level: Proven experience with assessing skills, designing training programs, leading seminars, and evaluating results.

Junior level: Able to assist firm management in conducting a search and evaluation of trainers and training programs.

Business development, including proposals. Business development is a broad category that includes background work, such as targeting industry associations and professional groups that might yield new clients, and frontline activities, like generating new leads for partners and managers to pursue, and then producing proposals and making presentations. These activities should take place whether or not you have a marketing professional on board. But when you do, how will they be expected to contribute?

Senior level: Excellent grasp of the professional services selling cycle, including proposal development. Personal experience with selling. Able to guide strategic planning on key proposals, help assemble proposal team, assist with sales training, and assist with determining prospect's needs. Knowledge of local marketplace sufficient to identify key organizations that should be pursued by the firm.

Junior level: Able to assist with proposal writing and development, tracking, and postmortem evaluations.

Internal and external communications. Internal communications can refer to something as uncomplicated as writing an internal marketing newsletter or an internal marketing blog to developing a complex system of policies to disseminate marketing information, encouragement, and incentives throughout the firm. External communications refers to preparing firm brochures, along with newsletters, special tax letters, announcements, seminar invitations, and so on.

If you are just beginning to tackle these areas of marketing, a senior-level marketing professional experienced with concept development, planning and budgeting, writing, artistic direction, and production supervision would be invaluable.

Senior level: Outstanding written and oral communication skills. Good understanding of human resources and incentive plan design. Extensive background in preparing brochures, newsletters, Web sites, bulletins, and other collateral. Experienced with concept development, planning and budgeting, writing, artistic direction, and production supervision.

Junior level: Excellent writing and editorial skills. Journalism background and knowledge of desktop publishing software a plus.

Budgeting and administration. This category includes budget development and administration, as well as supervision of marketing support staff, working with graphic artists, printers, PR and advertising agencies, and consultants, and utilizing computer data services.

Senior level: Strong grasp of budgeting and basic accounting principles. Able to develop a budget, monitor expenditures, foresee problems, and make appropriate adjustments. Able to supervise marketing support staff, and experienced in managing outside vendors, including artists, printers, agencies, and mailing houses.

Junior level: Able to assist in monitoring specific line items for cost containment. Able to identify potential problems for partner resolution.

When you have reviewed all the descriptions above you can consider which of these fits your needs, and based on the content, what specific skills will be necessary to accomplish the tasks.

SALARY AND COMPENSATION

Now that you have formulated a job description, the next step is to establish a salary range and to determine what other forms of compensation and benefits the marketing professional will receive. Much will depend on circumstances that are unique to your firm. Consider the following issues as you determine compensation:[1]

---

[1] Accounting Marketing/Sales Responsibility and Compensation Survey—2006 *(Kansas City, Missouri: Association for Accounting Marketing [AAM] 2006). An updated survey will be conducted in 2010.*

- Salary is directly related to the type of accounting firm and the role within the firm. It is also based on geography. Northeast firms and midwest firms tend to pay more than in the south and west.
- Prior to assuming their current position, respondents had work experience in the following areas: professional service marketing (32 percent); finance/insurance/real estate (22 percent); PR and communications (22 percent); business services (23 percent).
- 93 percent marketing professionals hold 4-year degrees; 27 percent hold a graduate degree (Masters or PhD).

RECRUITING: WHERE TO LOOK

Now that you have a job description and a compensation package, you are ready to begin looking for a candidate. In the following paragraphs are some options to consider.

Both the Association for Accounting Marketing (AAM) and the Legal Marketing Association (LMA) maintain national job referral services.[2] For a modest fee, these associations will advertise your job listing in publications sent to all current members via Web postings and e-blasts. They may also be able to refer you to reliable headhunters or some other assistance.

Local PR and marketing organizations are another good resource, and include the Public Relations Society of America (PRSA), Women in Communications, Inc. (WICI), and the American Marketing Association (AMA). You can also try the LMA because the law firm marketers could easily transition to accounting firms. Local career action centers also post job notices, and may help you to screen resumes they have on file.

Reach out to your online networks on LinkedIn, Facebook and Twitter. These social media sources are proving to be a valuable source for potential candidates.

Advertising, though frequently overlooked, can be productive. Large metropolitan dailies with large readerships should help you locate most of the candidates within local reach.

Finally, don't overlook your colleagues and referral sources. Put the word out that you are looking for an experienced marketing professional. They may be able to put you in touch with qualified candidates they were not able to hire.

HOW TO QUALIFY YOUR CANDIDATES

With luck, you will enter into this phase of your search with reams of resumes. A preliminary review should help you sort out a group of viable candidates. The next step is to compare each candidate's skills and experience with the firm's job description. This should allow you to cut the list down to about five to seven candidates who may be called in for interviews.

During the interview, ask to see the candidate's portfolio. A portfolio is evidence of the candidate's prior work experience and skills. It may include sample press releases, along with clippings of the stories the releases generated. Expect to see brochures, newsletters, seminar announcements, Web sites, and so on. Feel free to ask questions about the items that interest you. How were they used, and what did the candidate's client/employer think about the results the product generated? Obviously, a candidate for a junior-level position will have considerably less to show you than a senior candidate. Nevertheless, it is important to find out what the candidate has done. Ask them how they would work with your firm to enhance the culture, build the brand, and create a marketing driven philosophy. See what kind of energy, passion, and tangible ideas they have to offer.

Personal chemistry is another critical component, one that is not easily quantified, but might come out in an interview. The candidate's leadership, sound judgment, and decision-making abilities may also reveal themselves in face-to-face meetings. A great marketing professional has to be creative, offer viable options, and aggressively pursue opportunities that are consistent with firm goals. The marketing professional must be a can-do person, confident, open-minded, and positive, and able to affect compromise.[3]

---

[2] *For more information about AAM and its services, write to AAM headquarters, 15000 Commerce Pkwy, Suite C, Mount Laurel, NJ 08054, 856.380.6850, www.accountingmarketing.org.*

For more information about the Legal Marketing Association (LMA), write to LMA headquarters, 401 N. Michigan Avenue, Suite 2200, Chicago, IL, 60611, 312.321.6898, www.legalmarketing.org

[3] *Adapted from the* National Association of Law Firm Administrators White Paper, Series Two, *published October 1990.*

TEN QUESTIONS TO ASK DURING THE INTERVIEW[4]

1. Describe your most significant marketing accomplishment (at your most recent place of employment).
2. On a scale of 1–10, rate your mastery of these marketing areas: market research, planning, PR, advertising, client service, business development, communications, budgeting, and administration. Which of these activities do you enjoy the most?
3. What has to happen for marketing to work in a professional services environment?
4. What is your style of day-to-day operations?
5. What kind(s) of material and personnel support do you require?
6. Were you responsible for profit and loss in your previous position? If the answer is yes, describe.
7. How will you persuade partners and senior staff, who are not 100 percent sold on marketing, that they should participate?
8. Describe your experience working with consultants and other outside agencies—public relations, graphic artists and printers, and others.
9. What kind of authority and review structure do you think you should work under?
10. What are your greatest strengths? Weaknesses?

HOW TO KEEP YOUR MARKETING PROFESSIONAL

The harsh reality of professional services marketing is that many marketing directors and coordinators leave their place of employment after a brief tenure. A recent survey of professionals suggested that the following were the main reasons marketing professionals left their firm:

- Partners were not perceived as being in full support of the marketing effort.
- While given the responsibility for marketing, the marketing professional was not accorded a commensurate level of authority.
- Marketing professionals were excluded from partner meetings.

In addition, marketers who do not report to the managing partner or a high level senior partner with real authority in the firm have a higher tendency toward failure. Those without a plan or a budget also have a harder time "selling" and "defending" their ideas internally.

Basically, the obstacles that force turnover are the lack of support, credibility, and respect. While the average turnover rate is high, there are some things you can do to beat the odds.

1. Ensure that the marketing professional is granted a level of authority commensurate with his or her responsibility.
2. Be realistic about how much a single person can accomplish. See to it that the professional has appropriate professional support in the form of a highly skilled administrative or marketing assistant. (Most productive marketing professionals will require a full-time secretary, at the least.)
3. Grant the marketing professional the rights and privileges of his or her rank. If you hire a $100,000 per year marketing director, his or her office should be comparable to that of a middle-level partner. Even if you hire a junior-level marketing coordinator, avoid actions that will cause firm members to perceive him or her as a secretary.
4. If the marketing professional has never worked for an accounting firm, develop an orientation program designed to bring him or her up to speed on such matters as the profession's ethics with respect to confidentiality and objectivity, firm structure and administrative matters such as time and billing, the difference between local accounting societies and the AICPA, the role of various rule-making bodies and codes such as FASB, SEC, and GAAP/GAAS, and trends in the profession such as the impact of critical legislation like the Sarbanes-Oxley Act.

---

[4] *The author gratefully acknowledges the contribution of William B. Henegan, President of MarketLead, a marketing consulting firm based in Washington, D.C.*

5. Allocate funds for continuing professional education comparable to those granted to a CPA. Various universities and professional associations offer specialized courses that will help the professional stay abreast of the latest developments and techniques in the field. The professional should also be encouraged to participate in relevant professional associations and take full advantage of accounting marketing educational programs delivered by AAM, the annual conference, and the quarterly AAM High! teleconference series.

6. Most importantly, find a way to create a career path within your firm. This is perhaps the most difficult challenge of all. Where does a senior-level marketing professional go? It is now possible to consider offering an equity position in the firm. And what about junior-level staff? If they are intelligent and persevering, they may be able to move from a junior- to a senior-level position. Of course, it will also be important to know what your firm needs and to find out what the professional wants.

EVALUATING THE MARKETING PROFESSIONAL'S PERFORMANCE

Evaluation is the process of determining the value or degree of success in achieving a predetermined objective. Firm management and the marketing professional should work together to set measurable objectives for all aspects of the marketing program. With clearly defined benchmarks in place, the marketing professional will be in a position to respond meaningfully to two key questions: "How much did it cost?" and "What did we get for our money?"

Some standards for evaluating marketing efforts include the following:

- Budget accountability
- Achievement of specific goals
- Results as measured in terms of dollars gained, profit realized, impact made, responses or viable leads generated
- Deadlines reached

The person to whom the marketing professional reports—presumably the managing partner—should conduct the review. Other partners and key personnel can be asked to contribute. Performance reviews should be held every 6–12 months, or whatever is in keeping with how the firm's other professionals are evaluated. In the initial year or so, the firm's expectations should be tied to what was realistically within the professional's control. For instance, a first-year review might focus on the quality of programs developed, as well as the strategic use of time, while subsequent reviews might emphasize specific outcomes obtained, such as increases in revenues or profits, increases in proposal opportunities, and so on.

> ### ⚲ Key Concept
>
> Firm management and the marketing professional should work together to set measurable objectives for all aspects of the marketing program your vision.

CONCLUSION

It is critical that you begin your search only after deciding what the firm wants to accomplish in the area of marketing and how your prospective marketing professional should be able to help you.

Remember, however, that the marketing professional can never be expected—nor should they be asked—to assume the partners' share of the responsibility for marketing. Instead, the marketing professional and the partners must work together as a team to strengthen both the firm's marketing and selling capabilities and to improve the bottom line.

ABOUT THE AUTHOR

Sally Glick is a Principal of the Firm and the Chief Growth Strategist at Sobel & Co., LLC. In that role she has responsibility for the firm's branding and marketing communications as well as connecting the dots between marketing initiatives and the firm's growth strategy. Glick was named Accounting Marketer of the Year for 2003 and served as the President of the Board of Directors of the Association for Accounting Marketing (AAM) in 2004. She has also been listed on *Accounting Today's* list of Top 100 Most Influential People in Accounting for 2004, 2005 and 2006. She also hosts a blog on Accountingweb.com focusing on marketing advice for CPA firms. She had the honor of being the first non-CPA woman to appear on the cover of *Practical Accountant,* a publication for the accounting profession, in August 2002. In 2007 she was inducted into the Association for Accounting Marketing's Hall of Fame.

Closer to home, she was selected as one of the NJBIZ 25 Women of Influence for 2005 in New Jersey and was selected as one of the Top 50 Women in Business in New Jersey in 2008. Glick currently serves on the boards of the Commerce and Industry Association, the Executive Women of New Jersey and Temple Beth Am. She is also on the advisory board for ADP's CPA Services Group in New Jersey.

Sally received her undergraduate degree from Northwestern University in Evanston, Illinois and was selected their alumni merit winner of the year in 2008 for the School of Continuing Studies. She earned her MBA at Lake Forest Graduate School of Business Management in Lake Forest, Illinois.

APPENDIX 10-1: SAMPLE JOB DESCRIPTIONS

JOB DESCRIPTION 1: SENIOR-LEVEL POSITION

Title: Director of Marketing and Practice Development

Position Charter:

Works directly with the firm's management group to help ensure the firm's continued growth and prosperity by designing and implementing appropriate marketing strategies. Reports to managing partner or partner in charge of marketing.

Responsibilities:

1. *Research and planning.* Plans and oversees execution of all marketing research needed to make strategic marketing decisions at the firm, office, and service level. Evaluates results of research studies, and recommends appropriate action to the firm's management group.

2. *Public relations.* Plans and oversees the firm's PR programs, including media relations activities, firm-sponsored seminars, and public speaking engagements for partners and staff. Evaluates results and recommends future action. Prepares contingency or crisis plan for dealing with the press in the face of negative publicity.

3. *Advertising.* Manages the firm's advertising activities, and supervises any outside advertising agencies retained by the firm. Responsible for assessing the firm's ongoing need for advertising and developing each campaign's key objectives and messages. Directs all creative work and plans media buys. Monitors results of advertising campaign and prepares internal status reports for firm management.

4. *Communications.* Assesses the firm's need for communications programs, such as Web sites, client newsletters, direct mail, and distribution of firm brochures. Also responsible for any in-house communications relating to marketing. Acts as project manager and senior editor on all projects, and directs the efforts of both in-house staff and outside contractors, including writers, graphic artists, printers, and mailing houses. Responsible for estimating and controlling costs.

5. *Client satisfaction.* Plays an active role in ensuring that the firm's standards of service excellence are clearly defined—and met. Participates in the design of training programs, standards, and incentives. Also plans and executes client satisfaction surveys and is responsible for survey instrument design and survey execution. When results are tabulated, prepares a report, including recommendations.

6. *Business development.* Supports partners and managers in all phases of the business development cycle, from targeting pertinent business organizations to generating leads and issuing proposals. Acts as coach and adviser to staff below the level of partner and works as adviser to partners.

7. *Budgeting and administration.* Develops and then oversees the firm's marketing budget. Responsible for preparing—or soliciting—estimates of all projects before they are approved, and for cost containment and quality control through the program's life. Supervises the firm's other marketing personnel.

8. *Other.* Serves as a member of the firm's management team, and participates in decisions affecting the firm's growth, direction, finances, and personnel. Serves on local and national boards and committees of relevant accounting and marketing associations. Attends partner meetings, especially when marketing is an agenda item.

Qualifications:

1. Holds a bachelor's degree in a relevant field. An MBA is preferred.
2. Has five or more years experience working as an in-house marketing professional for other accounting firm(s).
3. Other work experience includes PR, advertising, communications, or sales management.
4. Possesses an excellent grasp of marketing theory as it relates to the professional services environment.
5. Management-level experience in the fields of sales, finance, operations, and human resources preferred.
6. Extensive experience with research, planning, and execution of specific marketing programs, controlling costs, and evaluating outcomes.
7. Possesses outstanding leadership and oral and written communication skills.

JOB DESCRIPTION 2: JUNIOR-LEVEL POSITION

Title: Marketing Coordinator/Marketing Manager

Position Charter:

Supports the firm's management group in carrying out selected marketing strategies. Reports to the managing partner or the partner in charge of marketing.

Responsibilities:

1. *Public relations*

    a. Assists in carrying out specific PR programs, as directed by the firm's senior marketing professional or the managing partner. If a PR agency is retained, acts as liaison with the agency. Prepares press releases and maintains an up-to-date media mailing list.

    b. Responsible for logistics relating to the firm's special events, including seminars, open houses, and off-site activities.

2. *Communications*

    a. Acts as assistant editor for all firm-generated communications, including Web sites, client newsletter mailings, and in-house briefs. Supervises production, acts as liaison with graphic artists, writers, and printers, and directs mailing.

    b. Maintains inventory of the firm's promotional literature. Is responsible for notifying management or the senior marketing professional if reprints are needed. Makes materials available for seminars, public speaking opportunities, and other needs.

    c. Coordinates all mailings and e-mailings to clients, including overseeing production, printing, and distribution. Researches bulk mail and business reply options at the request of management. Responsible for the quality and accuracy of the firm's marketing-related mailing lists.

3. *Special events.* Responsible for logistics relating to the firm's special events, including seminars, open houses, and off-site activities.

4. *Business development.* Maintains the firm's business development database or customer relationship management (CRM) system and prepares management reports concerning the status of the firm's proposals, leads, and new clients.

5. *Administrative.* Provides support to the firm's marketing partner on an as-needed basis, including handling phone calls and correspondence, editing and writing marketing materials, maintaining marketing files, databases and CRM systems, and generating reports for management.

Qualifications:

1. Holds a bachelor's degree in relevant field.
2. Has three or more years experience in marketing, communications, PR, advertising, or journalism.
3. Possesses outstanding oral and written communication skills.
4. Is able to organize and carry out a wide variety of tasks in a timely fashion, and knows when to consult with management about setting priorities.
5. Is comfortable taking direction from several supervisors and negotiating their requirements.
6. Demonstrates sound judgment, is detail oriented, and understands the CPA's code of ethics with respect to handling sensitive or confidential information.
7. Demonstrates ability to work with little direct supervision.
8. Is proficient with business office equipment, including personal computers and word processing software.

For more sample job descriptions, contact the Association for Accounting Marketing at www.accountingmarketing.org.

CHAPTER 11
The Firm Administrator as Marketing Director

Diane Paoletta, CPA
Friedman LLP

INTRODUCTION

More and more accounting firms are hiring full-time marketing professionals to plan and implement marketing programs. At the same time, many smaller firms—driven by economic constraints—are examining other options. One alternative used by a number of firms is to ask the firm administrator to assume the lead role in planning, executing, and overseeing the firm's marketing efforts. In a recent survey of members conducted by the Association for Accounting Administration (AAA) 38 percent of those members surveyed reported having significant marketing responsibility in their firm.[1]

Is this a viable option for your firm? Would you be better served by hiring a part-time dedicated marketing professional, or retaining the services of an outside consulting firm? Only you can make the final decision, so proceed with caution. Before you do, you should be able to answer the following questions:

- Does your firm administrator have an interest in leading your firm's marketing functions?
- Does your firm administrator posses the skills to direct your marketing functions?
- Will your firm administrator be able to effectively balance this new responsibility without compromising current duties?
- Will partners and other professionals allow the firm administrator to effectively make the transition to this new responsibility?
- What support will the firm administrator need from other employees to effectively execute this new role?
- What additional costs will be involved?

Each of these questions and issues are examined on the following pages. Taken together, the information and advice contained in this chapter is designed to help you determine whether asking the firm administrator to serve as marketing director is the right choice for your firm.

QUALIFYING THE FIRM ADMINISTRATOR

One of the biggest qualifiers for firms looking to add marketing to their administrator's agenda is his or her interest in taking on the responsibilities. Does your firm administrator have an interest in leading your firm's marketing initiatives? A genuine interest in marketing is the first consideration. Many firms have found that marketing is indeed an interest to their administrators.

Other natural qualifiers for administrators as marketers include being able to hit the ground running because he or she most likely has a good grasp of the firm's capabilities, its people, and its policies. In addition, the administrator generally has the insider's advantage of having already earned the respect and trust of the partner group and may be able to shorten the sometimes lengthy accreditation process that a newly-hired marketing professional almost always undergoes.

Unfortunately, the characteristics that make someone an excellent administrator do not necessarily make them a successful marketing professional. For example, the administrator may lack the clout and leadership skills needed

---

[1] *The AAA Resource Center (Dayton, Ohio: Association for Accounting Administration, 2008).*

to guide the partners and professionals in marketing the firm, and will therefore still need to prove him/herself in this new role. This is an essential consideration in making such a move in your firm, because it can have a significant impact on effectiveness of your marketing program and ultimately your results.

As far as the requisite skills are concerned, most firm administrators already possess skills and experience in the areas of program design and administration, budgeting, and human resources. However, these same administrators may lack fundamental marketing skills and know-how. While it is true that weaknesses in marketing skills could be dealt with through continuing professional education, it can take years for the firm administrator to gain the skills needed to lead your firm's marketing.

While training can help qualify the administrator for the role of marketing director, it is not an absolute substitute for an experienced marketing professional. Many of the successes that marketers experience come from a combination of skills and experience. Training may help administrators accomplish some marketing tasks; however, it may not be enough to accomplish all types of marketing activities, such as developing comprehensive marketing programs. Marketing programs aimed at accomplishing larger firm goals, such as developing a new practice area, include a mix of various marketing tactics designed to work together in this effort. The firm will need an experienced marketer's judgment to effectively develop these types of programs. When deciding on whether to use an administrator or hire a marketing professional to do your marketing, keep in mind that the marketing activities that can be accomplished may be limited by that choice.

Finally, while your firm administrator is acquiring the requisite marketing skills needed, you may have to utilize outside consultants to complete special projects and provide guidance in the interim. If this happens fairly often, you may end up spending more money, at least in the short term, than if you had hired an experienced marketing professional in the first place.

> **♀ Key Concept**
>
> A firm administrator must have a genuine interest in marketing in order to be considered for the role of firm marketer.

> **♀ Key Concept**
>
> The characteristics that make someone an excellent administrator do not necessarily make them a successful marketing professional.

DEVELOP A LIST OF RESPONSIBILITIES

To determine which option will be the best and most cost effective for your firm, begin by developing a list of the marketing activities the administrator will be asked to handle. Next, determine the skills and abilities that are required to carry them out. Finally, assess the administrator to determine how well-equipped he or she is to do the job.

As you develop an activities and skills list, your best resource will be the firm's marketing plan. The marketing plan is used to support the firm's overall business goals, such as the firm's growth. This document is usually the first step when initiating any marketing activities and will help you determine what the administrator will be expected to do. The number of activities that can be executed under the marketing plan may be limited by the time allocated to the marketing role and experience of the administrator. This limitation could have an impact on how much of the firm's overall business goals can be realistically attained. Therefore, when identifying the marketing activities that an administrator can perform based on skills, abilities, and time constraints, be sure to properly align these activities with the firm's goals to help ensure that expected results are obtained, and to clearly communicate these goals to the administrator.

If a marketing plan is not currently in place at your firm, you may want to retain the services of a marketing consultant who has the savvy to strategically align the firm's goals with a tactical marketing plan.

When complete, the activities and skills list can be used to develop a job description. For more information about the tasks routinely assigned to the individual in charge of marketing, refer to chapter 10, "A Buyer's Guide to Hiring a Marketing Professional."

EXAMINING CRITICAL ISSUES

After you have developed a job description and assessed the firm administrator's potential, it's important to address the following issues and decide how you will handle them.

Reassignment of Tasks and Workload

Most firm administrators are hired because a firm's partners have realized that firm management is not being given the attention it deserves. The administrator is often asked to assume responsibility for accounting and finance for the firm, personnel (including administering payroll, benefits, hiring and firing), the information technology department, supplies, equipment and maintenance, continuing education, library management, and so on. It is safe to say that firm administrators almost always have more work than they can handle. Therefore, without clear and realistic guidelines of the administrator's duties and responsibilities for handling marketing in addition to the administration function, the administrator's workload may become too heavy for one person to handle, resulting in a decline in the administrator's overall performance. Some questions to consider when setting up these guidelines include the following: Which of these tasks will the administrator be allowed to delegate? Who will take over those projects the administrator cannot handle?

The administrator should be solicited for input when determining how much additional work can be handled and when setting priorities to determine workload capacities. This will not only help ensure more efficient results but also generate positive morale given that the administrator's workload will increase.

> **⚷ Key Concept**
>
> The administrator's overall performance may decline if clear and realistic guidelines for duties and responsibilities are not set. Handling marketing in addition to administrative duties could result in a workload that is too heavy for one person.

How Will the Administrator Choose Between Firm Management and Marketing Priorities?

Whenever the administrator is in charge of the firm's marketing efforts, there is always the chance that marketing will take a backseat to administrative duties. This is especially true if the firm has instructed the administrator to allocate only a portion of his or her time to the marketing effort. It is a good idea to establish general guidelines concerning the relative importance of various marketing and administrative tasks. At the same time, the firm administrator should also be able to meet regularly with the firm's managing partner or executive committee so priorities can be reviewed regularly and special situations can be dealt with in a timely manner. The administrator, along with the managing partner or executive committee, should review the firm's goals in light of any changes to the marketing activities to determine if they are being compromised in some way.

While this discussion pinpoints one of the shortcomings of asking the firm administrator to direct the firm's marketing efforts, consider the alternative, which is having the partners struggle ahead—each partner attempting to execute one component of an overall marketing strategy. By redirecting the firm's marketing activities to the administrator, a firm can at least reap the benefits of centralizing its efforts.

Reporting Relationships

Most firm administrators report to the managing partner, or, in smaller firms, to the partners as a group. In the case of a multi-office firm, administrators frequently report to the partner in charge of the office.

When the firm administrator assumes responsibility for marketing, he or she should continue to report to one individual, preferably the same person who directs firm management efforts. This should be the case even when the firm also has a marketing committee.

The administrator's title may also need to change. Since the administrator is handling both the administration and marketing, the title "Firm Administrator" may not accurately reflect the responsibilities that the administrator is assuming and his/her hierarchical level within the firm. Alternative titles might include "Director of Firm Administration and Marketing" or "Firm Administrative and Marketing Director." The title can also be an important aspect of the administrator's ability to carry out certain marketing efforts. For example, it can be a significant communications point when dealing with outside parties, such as the media when implementing a PR campaign. The title can also help better position the administrator within the firm when working with partners in this new role, especially when persuading them to do their marketing activities.

Authority

The administrator must be granted enough authority to carry out his or her work without being hamstrung by a system of approval that requires review of every action and decision. If the firm's management is explicit in stating its requirements (usually through the overall marketing plan) and has outlined budgeting parameters, the administrator should be able to execute specific projects without a great deal of supervision. As mentioned previously, a change in the administrator's title with more cache would also serve as support for the administrator's authority.

Performance Reviews

Many firms tie their administrator's performance to his or her ability to achieve specific predetermined goals. Before employing the same approach in evaluating marketing performance, it is important to note that many of the outcomes of marketing are, in fact, intangible or—at best—difficult to quantify especially, in the short-term. For example, the firm might launch a PR program in the hopes of improving public awareness of its services. Yet, it is difficult to measure the results of such a campaign. Therefore, an analysis of the administrator's performance should be based largely on how successfully the PR campaign was *implemented*.

Compensation

Often, administrators who take over marketing do not receive an automatic increase in salary. Some administrators will shoulder the added responsibility without complaint. But is it fair to ask them to? Firms should consider offering a salary increase to the administrator. Would you ask a tax professional to take on substantial additional responsibilities without proper compensation? To expect the administrator to increase his/her workload by performing another significant discipline and not receive additional compensation may subsequently lower the administrator's morale and result in lower work performance. A compensation adjustment is especially needed if the firm administrator is not able to delegate some of his or her current workload to another employee. In deciding on the amount of compensation adjustment, firms should view the marketing activities as valuable to the firm in that they are ultimately instrumental in helping the firm bring in new business and grow.

Continuing Education

Most firm administrators will have had little, if any, formal training in marketing. To help them get started, consider arranging for them to attend marketing seminars and courses. The AICPA and state societies both offer programs on marketing, as does the Association for Accounting Marketing, and most community colleges offer courses on a variety of subjects from market research to communications. Some organizations also host Webinars, sponsor libraries, and sell video and audio tapes, which administrators can view at their convenience. The firm may want to consider retaining the services of an outside consultant to provide ongoing marketing coaching for a limited period, possibly the first six months to a year, as the firm administrator makes the transition. As mentioned earlier the consultant would also be instrumental in the early stages of marketing plan development and implementation.

Career Path

Where does the firm administrator go from here? The administrator's career path has historically been one of uncertainty. There is usually only one administrator in a firm, with limit to his or her scope of responsibility and compensation. Some administrators have increased their value to the firm by providing billable services to clients, and as time goes by it is possible that more and more administrators will be asked to become shareholders or principals.

But the administrator who also assumes responsibility for marketing may not have any time to bill work to clients. Certainly, over time the administrator's efforts will yield tangible results in the form of new clients, new work, and—presumably—a higher rate of profitability. These kinds of results would probably not go unrewarded.

Taking on the marketing role, along with the administrative role, could open up new opportunities for the administrator. Overtime as the administrator becomes more experienced in marketing, while continuing to assume the administrative responsibilities, he/she can possibly advance to more of an executive role, such as chief operating officer. This management level is usually given a wider scope of authority and has seasoned staff reporting into it, such as a marketing director and administrative manager. Another opportunity for the administrator is to pursue a full-time career in marketing, transitioning all of his or her time to the marketing effort. Marketing directors have had similar executive level opportunities, such as becoming chief marketing officer, or can move into a more focused marketing role that has a broader, more firm-wide, scope, such as director of firm strategy or director of practice growth. In addition, marketers have moved up to the role of principal or shareholder, expanding their responsibilities and authority. Administrators have the ability to enjoy that type of career advancement with the addition of the marketing role.

In some cases, where the administrator is seeking advancement and the firm is not ready to offer a higher-level position, the administrator may need to move to another accounting firm that is larger and more diversified to achieve increased responsibility and opportunity. Although this is not always the case, larger firms typically will provide the administrators with a wider range of activity, a larger marketing budget, and a greater degree of autonomy.

⚷ Key Concept

Taking on the marketing role, along with the administrative role, could open up new opportunities for the administrator.

Costs

The most obvious benefit of asking the firm administrator to serve as the marketing director is that you can avoid the cost of adding another full-time position to the firm's payroll. On the other hand, a firm administrator who is already fully employed cannot be expected to shoulder new responsibilities without being assigned some additional support staff. So, while you may have saved yourself the cost of a full-time marketing coordinator or director, it may be necessary to hire an office manager, bookkeeper, or administrative assistant to help the firm administrator.

To be sure you have considered this decision from all angles, ask yourself the following questions:

1. What would it cost us to hire a full-time marketing professional? How does this cost compare with the cost of hiring (or assigning) new support staff for the firm administrator?
2. Will the firm administrator receive an increase in salary or other compensation as a result of assuming responsibility for marketing?
3. If we ask the administrator to handle marketing, what special training will he or she require? What is the cost of that training?
4. What marketing tasks will the administrator be unable to execute? If we have to use outside contractors, what can we expect our cost to be?

In weighing the costs, firms need to account for any expected increase in revenue that could result from the administrator's marketing tasks. Firms also need to take a realistic view when structuring the organization in this manner and ask themselves if the firm administrator can successfully carry out the dual role or if the existing role will be compromised in an effort to keep costs at a minimum.

KEY TO SUCCESS

Firms considering using their administrator to take on this dual role should address the following points when making their decision:

- *Identify firm goals.* Goals should be realistic and should be communicated to the administrator, executive committee and partner group.
- *Develop a marketing plan that supports the firm's goals.* The plan should include the needed resources (staff and budget) to carry out the marketing plan. Assess whether goals need to be revised at this point and recommunicated.
- *Solicit ideas from the administrator on how to make the transition work.* The administrator is most familiar with the administrative tasks and can help the firm estimate the amount of work that can realistically be performed by one person or whether additional resources are needed. Also, consider hiring a consultant to help with the transition by taking on the marketing role temporarily and providing guidance to help the administrator adjust to the new dual-role.
- *The firm should periodically reassess expectations in terms of workload and accomplishments from both the administrative and marketing functions.* The firm should communicate changes in priorities to the administrator since the tendency will be to work on the administrative tasks and push back the marketing activities when the workload becomes too heavy. This will undermine the original intent of carrying out the needs of both functions with one individual.
- *Communication is critical at every level.* The managing partner, executive committee, partner group, and firm administrator all need to be on the same page in terms of projects and expectations. Two-way communication between the administrator and firm's partners is one of the most important elements to a successful outcome.

CONCLUSION

Marketing is a slow, methodical process that requires a considerable amount of persistence and patience before delivering tangible results. It is also a critical function to the firm's growth, one that requires dedicated support and resources.

When an accounting firm hires a marketing professional, or asks its administrator to assume responsibility for directing its marketing efforts, a tendency exists to look for results in the very short-term. However, the reality is that one can expect to wait from six months to a year before marketing begins to impact the firm's bottom line. When your marketing director is also the firm's administrator, it is doubly important to maintain perspective and to be patient. Because the administrator will not be devoting 100 percent of his or her energies to the marketing effort, it may even be longer before the firm sees some positive results. Therefore, aligning the firm's objectives with the marketing activities will help to set realistic expectations of the firm's marketing efforts and help ensure desired results are obtained.

There is no question that a firm's marketing program can move more quickly if a full-time marketing professional is hired. However, many smaller firms cannot afford to exercise this option. For these firms, asking the administrator to direct their marketing efforts will at least help the marketing effort to move forward. Overtime, this organizational structure should be reevaluated to determine if it is still the appropriate way of operating. Combining the administrative and marketing tasks under one person may become inappropriate as the firm grows or as needs change. At that time, hiring a dedicated marketing director may be worth considering.

ABOUT THE AUTHOR

Diane Paoletta, CPA, MBA, is the Director of Marketing at Friedman LLP. Over the course of a 20-year career, Diane has helped firms in a variety of industries, including professional service firms, financial services, and telecommunications, both public (Fortune 500) and private firms, identify and pursue marketing opportunities, enhance revenue and profitability, and achieve business goals. Diane also coaches partners and management on business development skills through her self-developed networking class series. She holds a Bachelor of Science from State University of New York in Albany and an MBA from University of Massachusetts.

CHAPTER 12
The Case for Utilizing a Sales Professional at Your Firm

Christopher J. Perrino

Barnes Dennig

INTRODUCTION

What role can the sales professional play in helping an accounting firm develop new business? Many CPAs have struggled with this question, wondering how they would reconcile their need to improve the firm's ability to gain new clients with their appreciation for the fact that, in the professional services arena, the service and the service provider cannot be separated.

The answer is simple. While a sales professional has much to offer, he or she must play a supporting role in the business development process. Accountants will always have direct contact with prospects because they are, in a sense, "the product." The effective sales professional acts as a powerful ally, helping you to achieve the best possible results at each step in the sales process, from initial contact and pre-qualification to fully understanding the prospect's needs and securing the prospect's commitment to engage your firm.

How would a sales professional work in your firm? There are literally dozens of variables to consider. This chapter reviews some of the most important factors, posing a series of questions that a firm's management group should consider before committing itself. Topics include assessing the firm's ability to make good use of a sales professional, developing a job description, recruiting, managing and motivating the sales professional, and compensation. A simple cost-benefit analysis of hiring a professional sales professional may be an effective tool to prove the value of the sales professional. It is, however, important to look at the total, life-time value of recurring business from a new client (that is, the projected annual fees multiplied by the average tenure that your firm retains clients—the industry average is purported to be just seven years; however, many firms experience twice this figure). Then, the sales professional's compensation might be more fairly compared to the product of this equation.

ARE YOU READY FOR A SALES PROFESSIONAL?

Would your firm make good use of sales professional? To find out, ask yourself the following questions:

- Do you feel you are not getting enough opportunities to meet with high-quality prospects right now?
- Have firm revenues reached a plateau, with the exception of inflation rate adjustments?
- Have you seen an actual decline in the amount of new work you can cross-sell to existing clients?
- Are you losing market-share (are competitors growing faster than your firm)?
- Is the local market mature, with only negligible new company formation and inflow?
- Are your competitors relatively aggressive in pursuing new business, and are they initiating contact with your clients?

- Do your partners and staff need to invest more time and effort in practice development but can't seem to get out of the office?
- Is your firm's culture progressive? Does the firm encourage new ideas and employ a strategic, investment-oriented approach to practice management?
- Are new services or niches being launched at your firm?
- Is the managing partner able to manage the expectations of the other partners well enough to allow the sales professional 18 to 24 months to prove his or her true value?

An accounting firm that answers most of these questions in the affirmative is very likely to benefit from hiring a qualified sales professional. Equipped with the right skills and resources, a sales professional can help you achieve the growth that is vital to retaining clients and staff while positioning the firm for the future. The sales professional accomplishes this outcome in a number of ways—as described later in this chapter—but most importantly, by identifying and pursuing qualified prospects and helping partners and staff to deploy the most effective business development tactics and close on more new work. In addition, many firms find that the sales professional's ability to bring a fresh set of eyes (and ears) to prospect meetings is invaluable to fully understanding the prospect's needs.

Box 12-1	The following experience of a mid-size firm is a good example of the different perspectives and actions a business developer brings to the table.

The business developer was coaching a partner through a new opportunity but discovered, over a period of weeks, that the prospect hadn't called, as the banker had promised. The partner called the banker once or twice to ask for permission to call the prospect directly, but was a bit uncomfortable calling the banker again. The business developer asked to take over using the partner's upcoming vacation as a chance to intervene while allowing the partner to save face. After numerous calls to the banker over several weeks, the banker quickly said we were welcome to call the prospect all along and he asked, "is that the only reason you called me?" Clearly the banker had the heart of a business developer. The prospect became one of the partner's larger clients and the partner dubbed the business developer a "pit bull" for merely following his training and being politely persistent.

Firms contemplating hiring a sales professional sometimes wonder if it is a professional thing to do. Would clients, contacts, and business colleagues accept such a move, or would they disapprove? These may still be valid concerns.

[Many readers will no doubt have questions about the laws and ethical regulations governing the use of sales professionals. In general, compensating employees for their efforts on a performance basis, whether chargeable time or new business, is accepted, while the payment of commissions or finder's fees to independent third parties is strictly prohibited. Because each state tends to interpret the laws governing this issue in its own way, readers are advised to check with their state society or state board to learn what is permissible and what is not.]

First, let's look at the notion of professionalism. Being a professional calls for adherence to a set of commonly accepted work methods and standards of integrity. If you hire an individual whose character and sense of professional behavior is in alignment with the standards set for the firm as a whole, then he or she will generally be accepted by clients, prospects, and firm members quite quickly. This can be easily ascertained by calling previous clients of the candidates for the professional sales position to ask about why they liked doing business with this person.

There is also the question of whether or not a business developer can actually succeed at selling accounting firm services. After all, how can nonaccountants understand the nuances of a CPA firm's services well enough to do a good job of selling them? The answer is simple, but not so obvious. They don't have to! They do, however, have to be an expert on why and how people "buy" accounting services.

A good sales professional should have an excellent grasp of the essentials of your services—what they are, how they are delivered, and, in general, how much they cost. The sales professional must also be capable of identifying a prospect's needs and explaining why the firm is the right choice to meet those needs. However, because the sales professional is generally teamed with a practitioner when meeting with prospects, a complete mastery of the technical intricacies of accounting is not required. In fact, too much technical detail too early in the sales process can actually short-circuit the sales process by focusing on Financial Accounting Standards Board, Statements on Auditing Standards, generally accepted accounting principles, and generally accepted auditing standards rather the prospect's strategies, goals, worries, and profits.

In some instances, the business developer's referral source relationships may be stronger than those of the firm's partners. One such tale involves a business developer receiving an e-mail from a banker who refers the firm to one of the area's largest architects. The banker asks the business developer to choose the partner with the best skills and personality for the job. The business developer is given detailed background information to help choose the partner with the right fit. Additional instructions are given for setting up the initial meetings with the CEO of the prospect company. To optimize partner group harmony, the business developer involved the managing partner in the decision process related to choosing which relationship partner would be involved in the new business pursuit. As a result, the matchup was successful and the firm won the new business thanks to a coordinated effort between the business developer, the referral source, and the firm's managing partner.

In essence, the sales professional initiates the action and then works in a complementary fashion with the accountant to convert the prospect into a client. A team approach to professional selling really works because it doesn't require all accountants to be Dale Carnegie or Zig Ziegler—they can focus on problem solving—not what step comes next in the sales process.

Some CPAs fall in the trap of wanting their proposal to "sell" the client on the firm's capabilities. One business developer in Chicago knows this is a trap that leads to commoditization and decisions based on price alone. Face-to-face meetings and relationship development are key to winning new business—not fancy and lengthy prose in a proposal. She coaches the partners around this simple truth by reciting her mantra, "meet more, write less."

While sales professionals can play a key role in helping accounting firms achieve their business development objectives, they cannot do it alone. It's very important for all firm professionals, especially partners, to understand that their responsibility for cross-serving clients as well as referral source and prospect development will in no way be reduced when the firm hires a sales professional. Rather, the efforts of all will be optimized.

Keep in mind that hiring a sales professional may not cure a sales drought any more than buying a new golf club will cure a slice. Just as a quality firm's reputation will give the sales professional something of great value to bring to the market, the opposite is also true.

♟ Key Concept

A sales professional can help you achieve the growth that is vital to retaining clients and staff while positioning the firm for the future.

DEVELOPING A JOB DESCRIPTION

When you decide to hire a sales professional, you must define your expectations and his or her role. While each firm's requirements will vary, depending on what they are trying to accomplish, the sales professional's duties may include some or all of the following:

- *Research.* Identifying and targeting prospects using specific qualifying criteria (the firm's ideal prospect profile) established by the firm's management, in concert with the business developer.
- *Lead generation.* Generating qualified leads through direct mail, community involvement, telephone work, referral source development, and other networking, and marketing tactics. (Careful consideration needs to be employed here to delineate how the sales professional's role in lead generation differs from the role of the marketing department.)
- *Pre-screening.* Qualifying prospective clients prior to getting accountants involved in the selling process in order to maximize the accountant's personal time spent in selling. Keen business sense and research abilities are needed for this function.
- *Tele-prospecting.* Writing professional, thought-provoking letters of introduction regarding the firm and its services; developing phone scripts; contacting and engaging prospective clients in a preliminary fact-finding session; appointment scheduling; creating and maintaining prospect dialogue records in the firm's customer relationship management system.
- *Sales process development.* Documenting and formalizing the firm's process for pursuing leads and converting them into clients.

- *Sales process optimization.* Adding sales acumen to each face-to-face selling scenario. This is accomplished by assisting the accountant in asking questions designed to fully develop the prospect's needs and buying motivations, differentiating the firm from its competitors, understanding and anticipating sales obstacles, and guiding the process to a logical conclusion in a persistent but professional way.
- *Sales management.* Tracking new business opportunities, conferring with partners on the best next step in the process, keeping accountants and the prospect on track, and being the subject matter expert on how to win new clients are some of the aspects of this role.
- *Strategy development.* Determining the overall approach to be utilized for each specific opportunity and assuring execution of the strategy.
- *Coaching.* Offering on-going advice to accountants on how to better apply their unique talents to all aspects of the sales process. Tips and pointers can be offered based on the first-hand observation of the accountants in real-world sales situations.
- *Proposal analysis.* Assisting with the creation of persuasive documents with significant eye appeal that differentiate the firm, show the depth of the firm's ability to solve problems, and are customized to document the specific solutions that the firm will provide to address the needs and challenges of each prospect.
- *Follow-up.* Maintaining regular contact with prospects, in the form of letters; articles of interest; telephone conversations; invitations to firm, sporting, chamber of commerce, social and cultural events; lunches; and so on. This role can be of great value and is a clear way the sales professional can demonstrate return on investment (ROI).
- *Measuring results.* Producing periodic management reports that detail efforts as well as wins and losses.
- *Formal sales training.* Depending on the sales professional's background and aptitude, he or she might be able to present formal sales training sessions or facilitate roundtable discussions at the firm to catalyze knowledge transfer from the sales professional to partners and from partners to less experienced staff.

Box 12-2	Let's look at a case study that illustrates how the sales professional would carry out some of these duties, working in tandem with one or more of your firm's accountants.

The newly hired sales professional begins identifying prospects that fit the firm's ideal profile. Thereafter, contact with prospects is initiated through networking with bankers or attorneys to seek a referral, organizational involvement, or various marketing programs, which can generally be lumped under the heading of "cold calling." When a lead is generated, the sales professional works to set-up an initial meeting. The sales professional and the accountant go out together and make the initial sales call. During the meeting, the sales professional ensures that all of the questions necessary to fully discern the prospect's needs and concerns are asked. The sales professional may also field any of the prospect's nontechnical questions and help the accountant handle challenging questions (sometimes called objections). In general, his or her goal is to work in close partnership with the accountant, clarifying and emphasizing important points as needed, all the while positioning the accountant, and the firm, to have a unique and desirable approach to the prospect's challenges.

Back at the office, the sales professional leads debriefing meetings and strategy sessions to determine how best to meet the prospect's needs. Plans are developed for interim meetings with the prospect's decision makers to build the relationship, develop the needs, and understand how to navigate the prospect's decision process successfully. Then, the sales professional may help write and assemble a proposal. If a tangible opportunity is not uncovered at the first meeting, the sales professional finds creative ways to nurture the relationship over the long term to position the firm as a resource to the prospect in the future. Overall, the sales professional assists in qualifying prospects, getting the accountant in the door for a meeting with the prospect, facilitating the face-to-face nuances of the sales presentation, and ensuring proper follow-up.

The sample job description, exhibit 12-1, may be helpful as you work to prepare your own.

EXHIBIT 12-1
SAMPLE JOB DESCRIPTION

Title: Business Development Director

Position description: Creates new business opportunities for the firm by identifying and initiating contact with prospect companies and potential referral sources; provides sales support to partners and managers on new client solicitations; reports to managing (marketing) partner. Develop/improve the firm's sales opportunity development process and assure execution of it.

Duties and responsibilities: Target, research, and establish/maintain contact with prospects that fit the firm's ideal profile. Determine and implement appropriate prospect development strategies, such as approach letters, and initiate appointments via phone calls, e-mails, etc. Develop networking relationships with bankers, attorneys, consultants, and others who regularly interface with targeted prospects. Attend and participate in various business and community organizations, as well as relevant trade industry functions, in order to generate leads for the firm. Create or oversee the creation of proposals. Coach firm personnel to increase their knowledge and understanding of the sales process.

Professional and personal qualifications: Basic understanding of business, accounting, and marketing. Strong communication skills; professional image and demeanor; proven success in selling professional or technical services; professionally persistent, goal oriented, and ethical; long-term client/customer relationship-building experience required.

RECRUITING

Because it may not be easy to locate a sales professional who already has experience in selling for other accounting firms, you may have to look to other, related industries for candidates. Former banking and commercial finance company business development officers, commercial insurance brokers/agents, and institutional stockbrokers may have the ability and contacts to make them strong candidates who will produce ROI quickly. Computer and software salespeople may also prove to be good candidates—especially those who sell enterprise resource planning (ERP) and accounting packages. Payroll service sales reps may also have some appropriate qualifications. In fact, any sales professional with extensive experience calling on CFOs, and other C-Suite executives may be a good candidate. These professionals are usually highly trained in consultative selling, and are typically quite good at developing qualified leads, through various avenues. Also, since they may have had experience in selling services or products that are financial/accounting related, they could already possess a basic understanding of your business. For these sales professionals, the biggest hurdle may be in adjusting to the management environment of a partner-owned business. He or she may also need to adjust to being alone on a "sales island" relative to the rest of the firm's daily activities.

⚑ Key Concept

It may not be easy to locate a sales professional who already has experience in selling for accounting firms. You may have to look to other, related industries for candidates.

How to Find the "Right" Person

Volumes have been written about how to conduct an employee search, so we do not attempt to reproduce that knowledge here. However, a few tips may be beneficial:

- If you have a human resources director in-house, he or she should be able to help you identify the best ways to cast the net. His or her experience with recruiting in the local marketplace should prove quite useful.
- Running an advertisement in local business periodicals or the daily paper or local/national job posting Web sites may be fruitful. But plan this campaign carefully, in order to control costs.

- Get the word out to as many of your clients, referral sources, and friends as possible. Also, ask your vendors' reps if they know of people who are qualified for the position.
- Consider posting the position with the Association for Accounting Marketing's Job Bank—an e-mail bulletin that goes to hundreds of accounting marketers and sales professionals. It can be found at www.accounting-marketing.org/jobs.asp.
- Consider hiring the sales professional away from your competition.
- Another option is to retain a headhunter or a consultant who can help you in clarifying your requirements and in conducting the search and qualification process. While this is probably the best option available to you (and the most costly), be sure this individual has worked with professional service firms in the past.
- Use social media to get the word out on your search. This is proving to be an effective resource to find qualified talent.

A note of caution—if you're considering "promoting" your marketing director to this position, or worse yet, asking your marketing director to "do this too," think again. Although this tactic can be successful, it can also set-up your marketer for failure if he or she doesn't have the experience or aptitude for the job. To illustrate this point, would you suddenly ask your top tax expert to add auditing to his or her workload or switch specialties?

> **🔑 Key Concept**
>
> Take caution when considering offering the sales position to your marketing director. It can set-up him or her up for failure if he or she doesn't have the experience or aptitude for the job.

Interviewing and Qualifying Candidates

Here are a few suggestions on getting to know the top candidates before making a final decision. See exhibit 12-2 at the end of this section for a sample list of interview questions.

- Learn about the candidate as a person: What are his or her personal traits and motivations? Will the candidate mesh with the personalities and culture of your firm?
- Learn all you can about the candidate's approach to selling and what makes him or her a great sales professional. Explore the candidate's sales training background. Is he or she an advocate of the Sandler sales system, Miller Heiman, Huthwaite, solution selling, or one of the other better-known sales training programs?
- Ask questions about the candidate's experience. For example, what kinds of people and organizations did he or she sell to in the past? How much does the candidate know about the businesses you have targeted? What was the average amount of time required to move from identifying a prospect to completing the sale? Whenever possible, ask the candidate to quantify his or her answers and tell stories about actual experiences and situations that illustrate the answers to your questions.
- Get a feeling for how well the candidate understands the unique characteristics of professional services and how those attributes influence the selling process.
- Consider the candidate's experience with selling services vs. products. Also, does the candidate have experience selling a product or service that resulted in a long-term relationship vs. a one-time transaction? Experience with services that result in an on-going relationship is a significant plus.
- Identify the candidate's level of knowledge about the accounting industry in general, and about your firm and its services in particular. This will show how quickly the candidate could be expected to get up to speed. It also demonstrates the candidate's degree of preparation for the interview. This is key since prospect meeting preparation, researching and qualifying are big parts of the job.
- Make sure you inform the candidate about the dynamics of working for a partnership instead of in a corporate structure. Does the candidate understand that he or she may be sales managing and coaching the "boss?"

Who should be involved in interviewing candidates and making the final selection? Because this is such an important matter, you should employ the same protocols used whenever the firm is making any key decision. For example, if the firm's partnership is willing to accept the managing partner's decision, then only his or her input is needed. If, on the other hand, important decisions are usually made by the partnership group as a whole, then it might be best for all of the partners to meet with the top candidates and vote on the final selection. Additionally, the firm's marketing professional should be involved in the selection process and provide insight on the candidate's abilities, experience, and fit with the rest of the firm's practice growth team.

Since the candidate is selling the ultimate product—himself or herself—these other considerations may be helpful to keep in mind:

- Was the candidate able to establish rapport with the interviewers quickly and professionally?
- Was the candidate concerned about his or her fit with the firm?
- Was the candidate appropriately interested in the salary and benefits of the position (but not pre-occupied with money or uncomfortable discussing the subject)?
- Did he or she answer your questions concisely, on-point, and thoughtfully?
- Did the candidate ask good, relevant questions that kept the meeting moving forward?
- Did the candidate listen intently to the answers to his or her questions?
- Did the candidate exhibit "closing" behaviors near the end of the interview such as restating his or her fit with the firm's needs, suggesting logical next steps, etc.?
- Most importantly, would you feel comfortable buying professional services from the candidate?

The more of the questions above that were answered with a "yes," the better the candidate may be for the position.

EXHIBIT 12-2
SAMPLE INTERVIEW QUESTIONS

- What aspect of sales do you like most?
- It is rare to get an immediate "yes" from prospects. What do you do in these situations?
- Tell me about your training.
- What have you done to become a better sales professional?
- What are some of the things in sales that you find difficult to do?
- What do you know about our firm and its services?
- Do you ever take work home?
- What special characteristics should I consider about you as a person?
- What special skills and techniques are required to be successful setting appointments on the phone?
- What do you consider your greatest strength?
- How much time do you spend on the telephone or in front of prospects in your current job?
- What types of personalities do you sell to and work with in your current job?
- Are there any business or social situations that make you feel awkward?
- Describe your personality.
- How do you gain an understanding of a client's needs?
- How do you organize your day-to-day activities?
- What kind of rewards are most satisfying to you?
- In your current job, how long does it typically take from initial contact to close the sale?
- Describe a typical day.
- Have you ever developed a new territory for an employer?
- How many prospects do you like to handle at one time?
- What do you feel are the personal characteristics of successful salespeople?
- Do you set goals that are easy or difficult to reach?
- What do you dislike most about sales?
- If a partner came to you with a complaint about the way you were doing things, how would you react?
- What would you do if you could not resolve the matter?
- How would you describe an optimal work atmosphere?
- If you could make one constructive suggestion to your current management, what would it be?
- How do you deal with disagreements with others?
- Describe the best manager you ever had.

continued

Exhibit 12-2
Sample Interview Questions *(continued)*

- How do you deal with it when you lose in a sales situation?
- Describe the most innovative win you ever participated in during your sales career.
- Describe the longest sales pursuit you were ever involved in. What did you do to keep the process moving?
- Why are you the ideal candidate for this position?
- Describe in detail each step in the sales process, as you see it.
- Describe persistence. Do you have those qualities?

Helping the Sales Professional to Be Successful

Once you've hired a sales professional, the real work begins. While it may be tempting to let a seasoned sales professional operate independently, this is not advisable. The old sales poem for the sales professional's first day, "Here's your desk, there's your phone. Good luck kid, you're on your own," does not pass for best practices these days. Keep in mind that hiring a sales professional is an investment in the future of the firm. As such, it is extremely important that you work closely, and patiently, with the sales professional, to ensure he or she understands the firm's values, culture, goals, target markets, resources, and expectations. You must work together to develop the best possible strategy to utilize the sales professional's strengths relative to the strengths of the firm. With this in mind and depending on the service mix of your firm, hiring a sales professional who will report for duty between January 1 and April 15 may be unwise.

What kinds of goals are realistic? Again, because so many variables exist that are unique to your firm, it is difficult to offer precise guidelines. Much will depend on the skills and experience of the sales professional you have hired. Also, the marketplace, and the types of prospects you will be targeting, will play a key role. For instance, will the sales professional be asked to help the firm build up a new practice area, or simply expand a service that is already in place? Will he or she be expected to sell transaction-oriented consulting engagements, which may require a shorter gestation period, or mostly audit work, which is more relationship oriented, and may take longer to win? Bear in mind that greater patience with the sales professional's performance must be exercised if he or she is selling relationship business as opposed to transaction business. As such, goals must be adjusted accordingly.

As stated earlier, the sales professional is not a savior or turn-around specialist. The sales professional's goals can be much more aggressive if the firm's existing marketing tactics result in significant leads or if he or she will inherit a substantial pipeline of qualified leads or if he or she already has extensive bank or attorney relationships. If none of these conditions exist when the sales professional is hired, then sales goals will need to be created to reflect the person's learning curve or the timeline of the firm's marketing plan implementation.

⚲ Key Concept

While it may be tempting to let a seasoned sales professional operate independently, this is not advisable.

To develop realistic goals, and then to quantify them, you must begin by ascribing some value to all the activities the sales professional will be asked to do. This extends to the quality of efforts, not just the quantity of sales. It also includes what the sales professional helps others in the firm to achieve. For example, if you have decided the sales professional is responsible for guiding junior firm members and helping them develop business development skills, then this too must be considered when the sales professional's performance is being evaluated. So, in the early months or years of the sales professional's tenure with the firm, it may make sense to grade his or her performance on the quality and quantity of activities, as outlined in the business development plan, as well as tangible results.

Also, don't confuse sales with marketing, as noted earlier. Too often the sales professional is asked to be involved in planning the firm's seminars, newsletters, brochures, advertisements, and so on. The net result is that the sales professional is asked to be a hybrid—part sales professional, part marketing director—who may not be especially effective in either capacity due to time constraints.

This is not to say that the sales professional and marketing department should not work together. In fact, the sales professional will have an improved chance for success if a marketing professional and a marketing plan are already in place, as both can provide him or her with important strategies and direction in prospecting for new clients. Furthermore, each can support the other's efforts in certain areas. For example, the marketing professional can support the sales professional's efforts by providing background information on specific prospects culled from commercial databases. The sales professional can, in turn, relay any intelligence gathered on the street concerning market demand for a new service, competitor strategies, or the growth potential of a new or emerging market segment. For more information on integrating sales and marketing, see chapter 3, "The Integration Imperative: Erasing Marketing and Business Development Silos."

The marketing and sales professionals should meet frequently to fine-tune the firms' overall practice growth strategy. Each brings a different but equally valuable perspective to the table that, if fully integrated into the firm's overall strategy, will help the firm's messages resonate with the market. In addition, consideration should be given to holding regular meetings together with the managing partner so these insights can be honed and implemented firm-wide.

Generally and depending upon the levels of experience of the sales professional and marketing director, it's better to have the sales professional report to the managing partner or marketing partner—not to the marketing director. These roles should be at equal levels since their day-to-day duties vary so much.

Whatever standards you choose to employ, remember to give the new sales professional a fair chance. It will take a while for him or her to achieve any significant results, so the first year may not look that great on paper. However, the increased prospecting activity and contacts will pay back in future years. In fact, it's not unusual for some prospects to engage the firm after four, five, or six years of professionally persistent follow-up by the sales professional.

The idea that employing a sales professional is an investment in the firm's future cannot be overstated. To carry this concept further, consider that most investors lose money in the stock market at some point. The wise investor with patience and utilizing a long-term strategy may sell a particular stock in favor of another but doesn't get completely out of the market at the first down-turn. So it is that the wise managing partner may find that a particular sales professional is not performing and must be replaced. However, one should be cautious not to abandon the concept of employing a sales professional based on a bad hire. This is sometimes referred to as "throwing the baby out with the bath water." The sales professional concept has worked for a great number of other firms and, with the right approach and some patience, it can work for you too.

> **Key Concept**
>
> Employing a sales professional is an investment in the firm's future.

MANAGING AND MOTIVATING THE SALES PROFESSIONAL

While in many instances the sales professional acts as a leader and a standard-bearer, he or she must also have someone in the firm to turn to for advice, mentoring, and leadership. That person should be the firm's managing partner.

If the firm has multiple offices, it may be preferable for the sales professional to report to someone located in the same office, such as the partner-in-charge. This person—the managing partner or the partner-in-charge of the office—should also be responsible for evaluating the sales professional's performance and for helping him or her to overcome any obstacles that come up in the course of the work. Examples of such an obstacle might revolve around the failure of firm accountants to

- be willing to work with the sales professional on new business opportunities,
- follow-up on leads,
- provide feedback on technical aspects of proposals or approach letters, or
- develop and maintain referral source relationships.

There may also be situations where conflicts can arise between the sales professional and the marketing director, requiring the counsel or intervention of the managing partner or partner-in-charge.

In addition, the managing partner should work hard to keep the sales professional "in the loop." The sales professional can feel isolated and even unappreciated if he or she is taken for granted or inadvertently excluded from informal lunch groups, etc. It's important for there to be firm-wide recognition that the sales professional has as much experience in his or her profession as a senior manager or partner has in accounting or tax. The sales professional needs respect and interaction—lest he or she feel like a "hired gun."

Compensation

Now, on to the interesting part. What is the optimal mix of salary, bonus, and commission that will keep your sales professional motivated? Most firms should expect to pay a top candidate an amount equivalent to what they pay their managers, senior managers, or, in some cases, partners.

While some firms have utilized a commission-only compensation plan, many accomplished sales professionals may not be willing to take the position when they bear all the financial risk. In fairness, it would be difficult for them to do so, as they could not reasonably be expected to earn significant commissions within the first 12 to 24 months of service. Since the goal is for the sales professional to focus on high-quality, profitable prospects, the compensation program must reflect this. An all commission plan would motivate the sales professional to bring in any work he or she could scrounge up, without regard to quality, in order to keep from starving! In fact, many firms have utilized one kind of compensation program for the first 12 to 18 months of the sales professional's tenure, and then introduced a more results-oriented system at the end of that period.

Commission and bonus systems vary widely but generally include the following:

- 5 to 20 percent of the first year's fees collected, depending on the amount of the base salary.
- Some percentage of the expected amount of fees for the first year (depending, in part, on the size of the fee and whether or not the work is recurring). As a rule, 100 percent of the commission is paid out in the year the revenues are generated, although some firms pay the commission out over a two- to three-year period.
- Other plans pay a tiered commission schedule such as 15 percent of first year fees generated by a new client, 10 percent of second year fees and 5 percent of third year fees. This is in recognition of the fact that most clients are retained over a long period of time, yet the sales professional may only be rewarded in year one.
- Other plans utilize a significant salary and a structured bonus plan. The bonus is usually a percentage of the salary and is tied to tangible and pre-established measures such as total dollar amount of new work won, total number of new prospect relationships established, etc.
- An override bonus can be established and tied to overall firm profitability.
- One school of thought says that the salary should be two-thirds of the total compensation with the bonus potential being about one-third. This structure is good for encouraging long-term relationship building on the part of the sales professional.
- Firms wanting to encourage the start-up efforts of a new sales professional may opt for paying commissions on the value of the proposal opportunities the sales professional is able to generate for the firm. In this case, there is frequently a ceiling on the amount that can be paid, such as 5 percent of the proposal amount, up to $2,000 per proposal. The firm retains quality control because the sales professional only receives a commission on the proposal opportunities the firm chooses to pursue.
- Bonuses in addition to commissions are generally only paid out when the sales professional has reached or exceeded targeted production quotas, or other performance measures, for the year. Or, alternatively, the bonus may be tied to the firm's profitability, as mentioned previously.

Two areas of caution:

- Take care not to create a system that puts the sales professional in direct competition with the partners and accountants for commission and bonus dollars. This is likely to doom the sales professional to failure and taint any future efforts to utilize a sales professional with the partner group.

- Resist the urge to make the compensation plan overly complex. The easier it is for the sales professional to understand how commissions and bonuses are earned, the more motivating the plan will be.

Whatever approach you use, be sure to compensate fairly based on tangible activity that is within the control of the sales professional (for example, leads versus wins in the first year or so and allowances made for "strategic" use of time). Keep in mind that the old adage, "You get what you pay for" is good advice when determining compensation for a sales professional. It's a challenge to budget for what could be a six-figure position. But, it's important to look at the impact on firm revenue over a 5 or 10 year period when determining the true value of the sales professional's contributions.

> ⚑ **Key Concept**
>
> Do not to create a compensation system that puts the sales professional in direct competition with the partners and accountants for commission and bonus dollars.

TENURE AND CAREER TRACK

Will your sales professional contribute enough to become a long-term asset of the firm, and therefore merit consideration as a principal? If the answer is "yes," and if the sales professional is interested in this type of advancement, you will have to create some kind of career path. Ultimately, this opportunity to advance may be a key ingredient in retaining a quality sales professional for the long term. Many firms have admitted sales professionals as well as marketing professionals to the ownership ranks and many more have considered it. As such, it is not an unprecedented move and, therefore, worthy of serious consideration.

CONCLUSION

Accounting firms of every size are employing salespeople with greater and greater frequency, and with good reason. Hiring a sales professional can be the most powerful strategy a CPA firm can use to acquire new clients and to catalyze its business development efforts. It is also an excellent way to facilitate the introduction of new products or services targeted to a specific market segment or niche. As specialty and boutique firms proliferate, "traditional" firms are under pressure to keep pace.

Growth may be harder to come by over the next few years, as in the recent past. Utilization of a sales professional may be the right move now to help assure that your firm moves ahead and stays ahead in the years to come. Because a sales professional's efforts can be clearly quantified and the results more precisely measured, the utilization of a professional sales approach will continue to grow among accounting firms of all sizes.

While it's true that the initial years after deciding to hire a sales professional will have their share of challenges, managing partners must summon the courage to unabashedly defend their decision as in the best, long-term interests of the firm. If recent trends continue, the question of why a firm should hire a sales professional will likely change to *why not*.

ABOUT THE AUTHOR

Chris Perrino serves as Principal, Business Development at Barnes Dennig in Cincinnati, Ohio. He works directly with the firm's owners on opportunity management and sales coaching while assuring implementation of business development strategies. He has presented on business development topics at the Association for Accounting Marketing conference, the AICPA Leadership Forum, the Association of Accounting Administrators conference and the Ohio Society of CPAs conference. He has over 20 years of business development experience and is a graduate of Thomas More College.

Chapter 13
The Outside Consultant: More Than an Expert

Cheryl Bascomb
Berry, Dunn, McNeil & Parker

Why Do It?

There are a variety of reasons to expand your firm's marketing and sales efforts: increased visibility in your market, new market entry, strategic use of new media, or increased market share through a focused sales effort. Unfortunately, your firm's marketing resources may be fully tapped with existing projects and responsibilities, your team may not possess the skill set for supporting the expanded marketing efforts, or you simply may not have marketing or sales professionals on board. Whatever the reason, hiring a consultant can be an enormously successful strategy to solve your marketing and business development issues.

This chapter will take you through the process necessary to increase your success in choosing and working with an outside marketing or sales consultant. We'll cover the steps to take before you begin your search for a consultant, how to qualify and select a consultant, the types of engagement arrangements to consider, and some keys to success in working with the consultant.

What Services Can You Outsource?

While every firm's situation is unique, some areas lend themselves to working with an outside consultant more readily than others. Consider bringing in outside resources into the process early on if

- you are introducing a new and substantially different product or service from what you currently offer.
- you are changing your approach to business development/sales or have increased your growth goals substantially in a short period of time.
- you have a short term, resource-intensive project, like a client appreciation or anniversary event that will take focused resources with specific expertise.
- you want to "test the waters" for a new area before incurring the structural expense of a new department or new employee.
- you are ready to hire a new marketing or sales professional.

Table 13-1 contains a list of services that are commonly provided by outside consultants. As you will notice, the chart is broken down into three primary categories—marketing, sales, and client service—to help you better pinpoint your needs.

TABLE 13-1   SERVICES COMMONLY PROVIDED BY OUTSIDE CONSULTANTS

Marketing	Sales/Business Development	Client Service

• Marketing audits/plans
• Marketing professional recruiting/outsourcing
• Marketing research
• Integrated marketing campaigns
• Marketing/communication development
  —Advertising/branding
  —Collateral
  —Direct mail/newsletters
  —Web sites/blogs
• Copy/ghost writing
• PR/media placement
• New product/service roll-out
• Post-merger marketing
• Niche marketing campaigns
• Internal marketing campaigns
• Infrastructure development
• Culture development
	• New client pursuit strategies
	• Lead development
	• Cold calling
	• Proposal tools/development
	• Sales processes
	• Sales tools
	• Staffing/hiring sales professionals
	• Outsourced services
	• Sales training/coaching programs
	• Cross-selling coaching
	• Large opportunity strategy
	• Customer relationship management systems
	• Sales incentive programs
	• Compensation structure
		• Mystery shopper
		• 360° Evaluations
		• Client satisfaction survey instruments
		• Client satisfaction surveys and analysis
		• Client service standards and program development
		• Client service training and coaching
		• Focus group facilitation

Step 1—Before You Reach Out, Set Goals, Set Expectations

Unless you have more business than you can handle and are meeting all your growth goals, generally an opportunity exists for taking on additional marketing and sales efforts. Determining whether those resources come from inside the firm or outside in the form of consultants (or some combination of the two) depends on your objectives and your constraints. For a successful engagement you need to be clear about both.

Be sure everyone (or everyone who has a major stake in the outcome) has the same understanding of why the firm is hiring an outside consultant and what they expect to see as a result of the engagement. Some of the things to consider include the following:

1. *Create Your Goals.* Can you articulate the goals in terms of measurable, definable outcomes and is everyone in agreement? Is there a time-frame to achieve the goals? If you haven't agreed on the answers, taking the time to come to agreement on this before you start interviewing consultants is critical to the success of your efforts. If you don't have the benefit of a group to help you, write down what you think the goals should be; share them with your colleagues or the person most accountable for marketing and sales in your firm. Get the buy-in of your firm's leadership. Understand your budget and the expected time frame (that is, constraints). Make sure that everyone is clear about why you want to hire a consultant and what you expect them to achieve.

2. *Are Your Expectations Realistic?* Are the measures something the consultant can affect directly or only indirectly? For example, if the goal is increased numbers of large case sales, does the consultant have the

ability to deliver that or do others have a critical role in that effort as well? Should the goal be increased opportunities for large case sales or increased qualified leads for large case sales rather than purely increased large-case sales?

3. *What are your constraints?* Most of us have more time to apply to any given work than we do money or people, but all are likely to be constraining factors. If any are limited (and most likely all of them will be), make sure to discuss the specific limits with the group so that you can be clear about them with the consultant as you develop a budget and time frame. Although there would seem to be a law of nature that money and time are inversely proportional in any given project, it's worth coming to agreement on your specific constraints nevertheless.

Whatever your goals and constraints, you must be specific. The more tangible you make these expectations the less likely there will be disappointment or hard feelings at the end of the process. For example, a goal of having a marketing plan of action to provide services to the construction industry in your geographic region and a list of key prospects at the end of 6 weeks is much clearer than saying you want help focusing on marketing your firm to the construction industry.

Step 2—Finding the Right Fit

More than anything else, you want someone who brings the right skills to help you grow your business, whether it's through the development of a strategic marketing plan, a strong ad campaign or the retention of a new business development professional.

A good professional services consultant who is skilled in marketing plan development, for example can provide what your organization needs to turn your agreed-upon marketing goals into tangible results. They not only know marketing and sales theory and practice, but understand the elements critical to success when implementing a business development program for a professional services firm. If your firm is smaller and doesn't have a dedicated marketing person on staff, you might want to use a consultant for general marketing support and advice. If you have a dedicated marketing and sales employee or group, you can use a consultant to address certain types of marketing and sales endeavors that your firm's marketing professional(s) cannot do on his or her own without additional resources or skills. For example, many accounting firms hire outside resources to provide advertising creative, handle large-scale media buys, re-design the Web site, or provide sales training.

The type of consultant you hire very much depends on what kind of results you are looking for. You want to make sure the consultant's skills and experience match those required to do the job. Developing an effective Web site requires very different skills from creating a strategic marketing plan or executing a lead-generation campaign.

Know Your Firm's Culture

Understand and be able to describe the nature and characteristics of your firm, including the firm's personality (difficult as that may be to articulate). This will allow you to define for others the kinds of activities that your firm will tolerate well and those that they would find difficult to manage. For example, is your firm very conservative and traditional in taste or manner of expression? An advertisement or prospecting letter that works for a conservative firm is likely to be a poor choice for a firm that has a higher tolerance for risk or wants to stand out from the crowd.

Set Your Parameters

These are the rules of engagement and the limits within which you and the consultant must work. Be prepared to lay them out clearly in the beginning to make sure the expectations for fees, scope, and other things are in alignment. Parameters include your budget for the project, the scope of the project, and who will be the primary point of contact in the firm for the consultant. Make sure you and the consultant know how decisions will be made (Will they be made by the primary contact? By a committee? By the Managing Partner?) and how this can affect the timing or progress of the project. For example, if your decision committee meets only once a week or once a month, that is important to know in creating a timeline for deliverables. Nothing can sour a consulting relationship faster than unclear or unrealistic expectations.

> **♀ Key Concept**
>
> The type of consultant you hire depends on the kind of results you are looking for. Make sure the consultant's skills and experience match those required to do the job. Expertise and focus can vary depending on the skills and interests of the individual consultant and the consulting firm.

Step 3—How to Locate Prospective Consultants

The best recommendations come from people who are in a situation similar to yours. Start with colleagues in other (but preferably noncompeting) firms. If your colleagues share a similar philosophy of doing business, chances are the consultants they recommend will be compatible with your firm. If you don't know who to call directly, check out local, state, and national accounting organizations you belong to (for example, Association for Accounting Marketing, AICPA, CPA networks, state societies) or chapters of associations for the kind of service you are looking for (for example, The Ad Club, Maine Public Relations Council). Members of these associations are happy to help and are likely to know the reputations and be aware of the track records of the consultants you are considering.

If geographic issues are a problem, the timing is not right, or the fit is not a good one, the consultant him or herself will often recommend others who can do the work that is right for you, and do it more readily or closer to your location.

Step 4—Qualifying a Consultant or Consulting Firm

Once you have clearly established your goals, expectations, and parameters for the project, you are ready to find and evaluate candidates. Your needs and the scope or specialty requirements of your project will dictate whether you should be supported by a number of professionals who can bring to bear the resources of an entire organization or whether you need a single consultant, who, if needed, can pull together the right group of people with the right skills to meet your needs.

Just like a CPA firm, you will find that expertise and focus can vary depending on the skills and interests of the individual consultant and the consulting firm. Some consultants and consulting firms provide a wide array of services, while others are more boutique specialty shops with very narrow areas of expertise. Some consultants serve as general contractors, pulling from a hand-picked team of subcontractors to deliver just the right service to meet the client's needs. And others have a full staff on board. One thing is consistent, most all of them have Web sites that outline their qualifications. A growing number have blogs too. So take a look online, it's a great place to start your qualification process.

Step 5—Selection Criteria for Your Marketing Effort

1. *The right skills.* You want to be sure, above all else, that the consultant you hire is capable of delivering the results you expect in the way that you expect them. Identifying what skills to look for is worth taking a little extra time on the front end to make sure your consultant has the right expertise to deliver the program. Consider both the amount of experience with the task or area of your project, and the softer skills needed to deliver it well. The softer skills include things like writing and persuasive verbal skills, credibility with your partners, consensus-building skills, and interpersonal interaction skills. You don't want to lose the message because the messenger was the wrong choice.

   Jot down and prioritize the skills you think are necessary for the work and then ask the consultants you speak with to do the same. Do your lists match? Are there different or missing criteria? Discussing why the consultant identified the skills he or she did can be very enlightening. Sometimes there are valid reasons to include or look for a skill that you didn't have on your list. Consider it carefully and be open to new information, but be aware when arguments for particular skills are self-serving for the consultant. As the expression goes, if you have a hammer, everything is a nail.

2. *Ability and willingness to teach you.* Unless it's a very specialized area of skill (such as creative development) or you are completely outsourcing the project, you should expect to learn a great deal from your outside consultant during the course of the project. Look for the consultant who, from the start, talks about how marketing and sales expertise will be shared with you and your firm members and openly shares their ideas and opinions.

3. *Innovative and creative.* Because much of good marketing flows from the ability to look at the familiar and see something new, your consultant must be creative and willing to suggest alternate courses of action that go well beyond the familiar.

4. *Professional service or accounting marketing experience.* Marketing and selling accounting services is very different from marketing and selling consumer products or lower-price point service items. While marketing principles apply to services and products alike, it is important for a consultant to have experience with the sales cycle associated with professional services and the relationship development component of marketing. They should also understand the key factors that engender client loyalty in professional service buyers so that the prospects and results of the work are aligned with the kind of long-term client relationships that apply to your firm.

5. *Knowledge of your market.* This may be more of a requirement when your marketing effort is focused on penetrating a new niche or creating a market for highly targeted services. A consultant's appreciation for vertical niche marketing is a pivotal issue for efforts that focus on a niche, new or existing. If the consultant addresses the proposed work too broadly or doesn't tailor the message to the defined geographic area, industry group, or consumer segment, then it is unlikely that you'll achieve the results you are looking for.

There are other areas that may be important to you and will vary by the type of work you require from a consultant and your firm's personality, your previously identified constraints and goals, and the project's parameters. These include

- pricing and fees for the value provide.
- understanding the general economics and ownership structure of accounting firms.
- familiarity with your technology or with new technology appropriate to the marketing project selected. For example, do they do all their creative work in a software program that doesn't translate well to your working environment?
- personality fit and an ability to feel at ease with the consultant and that you can trust them with proprietary information about your firm.

Step 6—Check References, Review Work Samples

Once you've narrowed down your choices to a select few, or even just one, it's important to get the perspective from their other past or current clients about the quality of their work, working style, delivered results, and skills. Don't hesitate to ask for references and contact information or, in the case of graphic or Web site work, a portfolio or writing samples as well. Ask the consultant or consulting firm for references who have hired them for engagements similar to what you plan to do so that your comparisons are more realistic.

Be thorough in your reference checking. You are getting references from the prospective consultant, so these all should be very good. However, every engagement has room for improvement and probing for those areas may give you a good sense of the strengths and weaknesses of the consultant.

Here are some sample questions to ask references:

- Why did you choose to hire this consultant?
- Did he/she/they deliver the results you expected? Why or why not?
- Did the consultant work well with the other people in your firm?
- Was he/she/they easy to reach and responsive when you had questions or changes?
- Did the engagement provide the value you expected? Were the fees what you'd expected or did they change during the course of the project? (*Note*: this does happen, often for good reason)

- What recommendations or strategies did the consultant suggest that you or your firm decided not to follow?
- What were the best and worst aspects of working with this consultant?

If you will be doing any graphic work, make sure you review samples of past projects or material in addition to talking to references. When you review the portfolio, consider the following:

- If you see only full-color glossy publications, then be concerned that the consultant only works with high-budget projects. If that's appropriate for your firm, then fine. Otherwise, ask to see other material.
- Look for variety in the portfolio. This is a good indication that the consultant delivers marketing solutions tailored to the needs of the client. Publications should be geared towards the audience that you want to address in terms of graphics and writing style.
- Check for how well the identity or brand of an organization is visually maintained through a family of publications, advertisements, or electronic communications. Analyze how the organization's logo and typography have been applied.

Personally interview each finalist (or representative from the larger firms) to ensure that you are comfortable with how he or she engages you, how well the candidate thinks on his or her feet, and how he or she presents him- or herself to you and others. Will he or she be credible to the decision maker's in your firm?

Hiring the Consultant: What Type of Payment or Fee Arrangements Make Sense?

Most consultants will meet with you to develop a clear sense of the work, scope the project, understand your outcomes, and give you a more-or-less fixed fee for the work. Some will provide only an hourly rate for specific services (for example, copyrighting or PR work), but most will provide you with some combination of the two. It is common for consultants to ask for retainer fees up front, especially if they have not worked with you in the past. These fees can range from a nominal amount up to half of the estimated fees for the proposed project. This retainer fee demonstrates to the consultant a commitment on your firm's part for the work to be done.

Our strong advice is to negotiate, negotiate, negotiate—not necessarily to get the lowest price, but to make sure you're receiving the best value. The more specific your goals, the more often you are able to tie them directly to the payment. For example, if you are hiring a public relations firm to increase the turnout and success of your manufacturing accounting seminar, you might work with the firm for a low base fee and have bonus payments tied to specific attendance milestones, the media sponsorships, or whatever your goals point to in terms of defining success for the work. If on the other hand, your objective for the project is to develop a marketing plan and provide coaching to your partners and managers in helping them work toward the specified goals, you might settle on a flat fee up front and an incremental fee linked to how well your firm's professionals achieve their defined goals. This might also include assessments to your firm for failing to work toward specific goals outlined.

> **⚲ Key Concept**
>
> The more specific your goals, the more often you are able to tie them directly to the payment.

Keys to Success

1. *Agree to the deliverables and the timeline.* Having your goals and your budget in place before your consultant is on-board makes this effort immeasurably easier.

2. *Give the consultant access to the experts as much as possible.* If you are working on a campaign for your business valuation group, bring the marketing consultant in to hear directly from the group what their needs are and how they see their group, their market, etc.

3. *Communicate often.* Status updates to your managing partner or the group responsible for the marketing work is important. If things look likely to be delayed or things might go over budget, let them know and help them understand why that is happening. Effective and regular communication with the outside consultant is critical to the success of the project, keep them focused in the right direction, answer questions, etc.

4. *Make decisions as efficiently as possible.* Things are going to come up, planned or unplanned, that need a decision in fairly short order to keep things on track. Group decisions are difficult. Talk to the person or group in charge of the initiative and work out a good process for what kinds of decisions need to be made by certain individuals and what need to be made by the whole group or key leaders.

CONCLUSION

Hiring the right marketing or business development consultant can be the start of a fruitful and positive relationship for you and your firm. Take the time to make sure that the fit is right, that the skills are there and you and your firm are in agreement about what will be delivered for the price.

Good marketing and business development can result in many indirect, positive benefits beyond the expected results, including improved morale, easier recruiting and improved retention, and increased business opportunities from existing clients. Realizing those extra benefits is well worth the investment in time and money that a qualified professional consultant requires.

ABOUT THE AUTHOR

Cheryl Bascomb is the Marketing Director for Berry, Dunn, McNeil & Parker, the leading certified public accounting and management consulting firm headquartered in northern New England with offices in Portland and Bangor, Maine and Manchester, New Hampshire.

PART IV:

Marketing Techniques that Get You Noticed

CHAPTER 14
Why Should I Consider Advertising?

Joe Walsh
Greenfield/Belser

INTRODUCTION

From the Mcgraw-Hill Web site, one can download the company's famous "The Man in the Chair" ad. (You can view it at http://www.mcgraw-hill.com/aboutus/advertising.shtml.) On the site you learn that "the ad, designed in 1958, stands as one of the most effective and influential works in the genre. The ad, recognized as the #1 B-to-B ad of all time by *Business Marketing* in September 1999, continues to make the compelling case for the value of B-to-B advertising in the sales cycle." Why? Because it has a message that is simple and compelling. And a bottom line lesson that accounting and other professional service firms can apply today.

In the ad, the curmudgeon of an executive looks directly at the reader and states:

"I don't know who you are.
I don't know your company.
I don't know your company's product
I don't know what your company stands for.
I don't know your company's customers.
I don't know your company's reputation.
Now—what was it you wanted to sell me?"

As it matures, the accounting industry continues to experience significant consolidation. But it's still a highly fragmented sector with plenty of competition for the same work. The fact is, many prospective clients are not aware of your firm, much less familiar with why you are a smart choice for them. Even some of the better-known local and regional firms are recalled, unaided, by less than 20 percent of buyers. Compare that to the Big Four—a brand unto itself—who go to market with awareness levels in the 85 percent range.

Why should you care about your firm's awareness levels? Simple. If you're not called to the table, you can't sell your services. Done the right way, advertising helps you penetrate the word-of-mouth network that dominates accounting firm selection. Smart advertising can increase name recognition and recall, putting you in a circle of consideration for new work, even from existing clients. Bottom line: awareness leads to preference and preference leads to choice.

> **Key Concept**
>
> Many prospective clients are not aware of your firm, much less familiar with why you are a smart choice for them.

MORE REASONS WHY GREAT FIRMS ADVERTISE

For many of us who have a certain affection for the profession, advertising may seem unprofessional, even unseemly. Moreover, we may suspect that advertising is unnecessary given that a professional service is a relationship business like no other. We may also believe that advertising is ineffective. Finally, we have little confidence that we can measure the return on our investment. All good reasons to debate the tactic. So what drives successful firms to advertise?

1. The competition and the fact that they are good, too.

   If you believe that you are alone in offering terrific expertise and great service, then there is no reason in the world to advertise. But you're not. There are many top-shelf professionals out there doing fine work. Furthermore, the population of professional service providers is growing and the competition is keen—one good reason why great firms advertise.

2. Misperceptions and the fact that perceptions often lag behind reality.

   Clients and prospects don't stay up at night studying your service list on your Web site or carefully parsing the differences between yours and other great firms. Unless you take control of market perception, market perception controls you. Put another way: define yourself or someone else will. Perceptions of who you are and who you serve today typically trail reality by a few years. The primary goal in advertising is to bring the market up-to-date with the value you bring and the capabilities you have right now.

3. The desire to affect the emotions of choice.

   Buyers pay $50,000+ for a Lexus when a Scion will get you there just as quickly, but the $35,000 difference is paid for prestige. Legal buyers will pay the law firm Skadden Arps two to three times the cost to do the deal that another law firm may be able to do just as well, but the difference is paid for certainty. The same thinking can be applied when a CFO chooses the Big Four, for example. The lesson? Purchasing decisions are predominantly emotional decisions, not rational ones. Far and away, the most difficult advertising (and broader branding) challenge you face is to identify—and focus on—the emotional need you fill. Even advertising won't affect perceptions unless you explain the benefit of working with you versus another service provider. Advertising is a great medium for making an emotional connection and differentiating your firm.

4. They need to get their own people aligned and on board.

   An overlooked and critical audience (in more ways than one) for advertising is your own people. An advertisement is the distillation of a market position, so the exercise alone is worth the effort, if for no other reason than to get accounting, tax, and consulting professionals in one or in far-flung offices on the same page. Add the critical employees that support their efforts and it becomes clear that in no small measure our "Ads Are Us." If everyone in the firm is pulling in the same direction, you are certain to get there faster than your competitors.

5. They recognize their clients want to hear from them, too.

   Existing clients frequently report they are glad to see their firm's ads in industry publications where they are focused. Why? Because they are proud to be associated with industry leaders. In addition, research persistently shows that clients (and prospects!) wear their industry hat first when they approach; they are wondering, "What do you know about my industry and its trends, opportunities and troubles?" Industry knowledge trumps practice area expertise (all things being equal) every time. So a key goal is to affirm to existing clients that they have made the right choice; in other words, advertising is in part post-purchase confirmation.

6. Because they're people who need people (sorry, Barbara).

   Great firms advertise because the future of their firm is the talent that chooses them. Attracting experienced hires and merger candidates is critical to most strategic growth plans. Attracting the best and brightest accounting students is also very important. Advertising can ease the effort to bring talent in the door. In fact, we've heard again and again that firms feel the most obvious benefit they perceive as coming directly from advertising is support of recruiting marketing efforts.

> **⚲ Key Concept**
>
> The primary goal in advertising is to bring the market up-to-date with the value you bring and the capabilities you have right now.

> **⚲ Key Concept**
>
> An overlooked and critical audience for advertising is your own people.

REALITY CHECK: WHAT ADVERTISING DOES NOT DO

Advertising is not designed to make the phone ring. Advertising, like all marketing, is designed to "precondition the sale"; it provides air cover for the ground troops. Advertising does not sell, but does create the platform for a relationship. Advertising does not close the deal, but does define the reasons why one should consider your firm over another. Advertising does not grasp your prospect's hand in a friendly grip but does create a personality for the firm, an image that you can live up to… or disappoint. Advertising can work hard on your behalf if you let it.

> **⚲ Key Concept**
>
> Advertising does not sell, but does create the platform for a relationship.

THE STICKY QUESTION OF RETURN ON INVESTMENT

Return on investment (ROI) is the logical question every businessperson should ask. And the logical answer is unsatisfying, but here it is: no matter what someone promises you about measuring return on investment, don't believe it. You can't. There are simply too many variables to create an effective equation. For example, create an integrated marketing campaign that includes advertising and you may discover your sales soar. But this may also be because your service hit the market in stride or that the economy went on a tear or that one new hire opened hitherto closed markets. Even the most devoted accountant cannot confidently ascribe this result to that tactic.

The one exception to this rule is in online media, which we'll discuss in the following paragraphs. A more linear relationship exists between Google ad words and real leads, for example. But again, that medium is an exception, which helps to explain Google's success and market cap.

MOVING FROM WHY TO HOW

As you reflect on why advertising makes sense and debate its value in your firm, remember that business-to-business (B-2-B) advertising, especially professional services advertising, is profoundly different from, and profoundly the same as, consumer product advertising. In taste tests prior to release, Coca-Cola found New Coke preferred by 83.3 percent of its testing populations. A sure winner? Actually, New Coke is considered one of the immense marketing blunders of the past half-century. How could such a smart giant misstep?

The answer is Coca-Cola forgot what it was selling. It doesn't sell thirst-quenching. It sells a relationship. Anyone can sell sugar, water, and food coloring. Even though testers liked New Coke, consumers felt betrayed. The product with which they had a long relationship disappeared. No business-to-consumer (B-2-C) marketers really sell soap, sneakers, or tires. Nor do accountants sell tax returns or lawyers briefs. You sell the promise that you'll identify a client or prospective client's problem and solve it. That is, the best B-2-B or B-2-C ads are about the market, not about us.

HOW DO WE DO ADVERTISING RIGHT?

Great advertising, like anything great, requires courage. Unfortunately, the courage needed to stand out from the crowd is in perennial short supply within the world of professional services—which speaks more to the nature of accountants, lawyers, and consultants than to your marketing acumen. Accountants, for instance, are trained to help spot and manage risk (among other things), while marketers tend to break new ground. Fortunately, the courage needed to do something distinct and bold can come from understanding how advertising works to reinforce or change the image of your firm. It all begins with a concept called *positioning*. And while it's easy to explain, it's very hard to practice.

What Is Positioning?

Positioning is as fundamental to marketing theory as the theory of gravity is to physics. The theory informs how a firm should run its business as well as how a firm should market its accounting, tax, and advisory services.

Al Ries and Jack Trout introduced the theory of positioning in a series of articles in *Advertising Age* in 1972, which they later collected into the marketing classic, *Positioning: The Battle for the Mind*. Ries and Trout observed the behavior of buyers to learn (a) how they learn, (b) how they store information in memory, and (c) how they retrieve stored information from memory.

Positioning is, in fact, a theory of human memory applied to consumer behavior. Advertisers study their own positioning and the positions of the competition to learn how to influence the consumer, not merely to recall their product or service, but to remember it in a positive light.

Winning the Battle for the Mind

Ries and Trout start with a fact we all know and experience: We live in an "overcommunicated" society. We receive over 3,000 messages a day—from the radio or television when we wake up to the morning newspaper at breakfast to the signs we see on the way to work to the things we read on and offline to the mail spilling out of our in-box.

To protect ourselves from this rush of stimuli we react the only way we can—we tune out. We select only a small portion in each category of product or service, organizing those few (usually only three or four) names in precise order in our minds, like rungs on a ladder. Typically, those three or four names we remember are the market leaders. They have won the battle for the mind.

Prove it? Back to the soft drink world. The market leaders are Coke, Pepsi, and Cadbury/Schweppes (Canada Dry Ginger Ale, Seven Up, Dr. Pepper, etc.). Those three companies have something like 45/30/15 percent market shares respectively—a not unusual mix for market leaders in any field.

Name a beer. The market leaders are Budweiser, Miller, and Coors. Name a long distance service. The market leaders are AT&T, Verizon, and Sprint. All the other brands in both those fields are competing for the rest of the pie—which could still be worth a good living but, nevertheless, is not at the level of the market leaders.

Positioning involves much more than we have room for here—the mechanics of memory, the analysis of current market position, the positions available for your firm and how to develop a positioning strategy. But it's an important art and science. Perhaps the best way to begin to understand positioning is to analyze one accounting firm's brand and advertising campaign and how it was developed.

CASE STUDY: DIXON HUGHES

The Situation

A clear market void, smart management, focused expansion and opportunistic mergers have solidified Dixon Hughes' place as the dominant Southeast regional CPA firm (top 20 nationally) and leader in select industries from coast-to-coast.

Their campaign development begins with the following key fact about the market:

In a push to focus on larger clients, the Big Four left smaller middle market public and private companies under-served, despite their need for world-class audit, tax and consulting services. Dixon Hughes (and other fine firms) have helped fill the void, offering the resources of the largest firms plus the relationships and attention clients crave.

In undertaking a complete rebranding program and building a new ad campaign, Dixon Hughes sought to take this message to market in a unique and compelling fashion. They also sought to increase awareness of the firm in its home and newer markets, position the firm as a safe (and wise) choice, and differentiate itself—all in a way that earned the attention of busy executives, recruits, and the firm's own people.

The Dixon Hughes Creative Solution

In its ad campaign and all other marketing touch points (Web site, brochures, direct mail, newsletters, announce-ments), word pairings make Dixon Hughes' proposition clear. The straight-up, left side words highlight cre-dentials. The handwritten right side handles the personal service style. Reason meets emotion. The pairings are reinforced with custom-built images tied to the firm's new "positively unique" tagline. And all of the elements come together in a lighthearted competitive joust with the Big Four. The ads run in the Southeast edition of *The Wall Street Journal* and several city business journals across the region. A flight of direct-mail pieces—the print ads reconfigured—add frequency and reach to the print insertions. They are staged to hit executive desktops in advance of the firm's telemarketing outreach efforts.

Practice brochures extend the brand and invite the scanning reader (the only kind we have in business to busi-ness marketing). Industry-centric images and word pairings cover four-panel brochures, such as the ones created for Dixon's national dealer services group. Charts, graphs, and tables deliver substantive information visually. The copy is all about clients and their issues instead of a recitation of service offerings. Nice!

When sales calls are landed, Dixon Hughes' professionals arrive with impressive pitch materials, created on-demand, to share the firm's stories in formal presentations and one-to-one conversations.

Samples of the campaign and other marketing touch points can be viewed at http://greenfieldbelser.com/cas-estudies/396/dixon-hughes.

INTERESTED IN BUILDING YOUR OWN UNIQUE ADVERTISING OR BRAND CAMPAIGN? HERE'S HOW

The process requires many stages—all enlivened by the passion of your people to help you enunciate and market your organization's unique strengths and identity. Here are the major steps followed by Dixon Hughes and other professional service leaders.

- *Form a committee.* Yes, you read that right, form a committee. Building consensus is an essential—and often overlooked—part of the process. And it is especially important when your product is your people. A com-mittee helps vet strategy and creative options and pave the way for a successful launch internally. The goal is to develop and educate apostles for the campaign.
- *Dig deep.* You and/or your agency partner need to audit (collect, catalogue, and critically review) all of your existing materials and those of your competitors. Look for any tangible and intangible evidence to evaluate current marketing communications efforts. Among them are (1) key messages—how your organization and your competitors have chosen to "sell" yourselves to date; (2) overall quality of the marketing materials—strength (or weakness) of the creative approach, quality of copywriting and imaging, richness of production values, etc.; (3) obvious inconsistencies in the presentation of service and product offerings and the market-ing message; and (4) completeness of substantive information (Is the message convincing?).
- *Interview your own people.* The next step is, in many ways, the springboard for all else to come. You need to unearth and articulate your organization's spirit—the individuals, history and soul that drive your work and culture. This is done with interviews. Think of a representative sample that includes your ruling body, rainmakers, culture bearers, and rising leaders who will move you into the future. You want to know how they do things, not just what they do. Remember, the goal of advertising or broader branding is to discover, articulate and present your organization's personality—its resources, expertise, modus operandi, style, and aspirations.

- *Trust but verfiy—tap or field market reseach.* Hopefully, your people will tell good stories and share a clear understanding of their markets and marketing challenges. But don't stop there. If you have access, you should draw on proprietary or syndicated research in the markets where you have offices or interests. Dixon Hughes chose to commission original awareness and favorability research to put hard numbers to hunches about marketing problems and opportunities. They also interviewed existing clients as a reality check on the organization's self-perceptions (Note: the interviews yielded many of the testimonials used in the ad campaign and other brand work).
- *Create a clear, concise and compelling communications brief.* This is without question the most important document in the process. It is the distillation of all that you have heard and learned about the organization. You should insist that this information be reduced to one page, vetted by your committee, and agreed to before any concept or creative work begins. After all, how can one explain a firm like yours on an airport billboard if you can't explain it and its core proposition on a single page? Your brief will guide work throughout the creative process and be used again and again as a touchstone for the evolving creative.
- *Redesign and realign.* With a clear, approved brief in hand, it's now time to reach into the creative tool kit to solve marketing problems or align your organization's messaging with opportunities in the marketplace. Whether it's a new identity system, Web site, ads, sales material, or a recruitment campaign, the idea is to find a creative way to bring your firm's story to life and connect it with the goals of your clients, prospects, and people. As you review creative, ask yourself three things: (1) Is it true to the communications brief? (2) Is the takeaway clear and compelling? (3) Is the approach interesting enough to breakthrough an abundance of clutter?
- *Prelaunch the campaign internally.* Once the brand is prepared to launch, it's important, if not imperative, to roll it out internally with fanfare and explanation. Many tactics to do this exist that may include internal presentations at retreats; full internal campaigns, where you deck the halls with your creative, construction of intranet sites; distribution of chotchkes; creation of brand books and standards guides; and completion of conversational branding workshops. But the key lies in getting your people familiar and comfortable with the messages you are taking to market—all in a way, of course, that makes your firm unique.

Where Do We Run Our Ads?

You've decided on advertising, developed ads that can't be ignored, and have a position or promise of value different from others. Where do you run these ads? This is a vital question. Here are steps to developing a hot media plan.

1. Put as much energy and thought into your media plan as you do into your message.

    Your media planning demands as much creativity as your ads. Ads can accomplish many things, but no single publication can achieve all those things at once or equally well. Choices must be made. That's why it's called a media plan.

2. Clearly define and prioritize your goals.

    Is your top goal

    a. increasing your firm's name awareness among services buyers of all types?
    b. selling a specific service in one geographical region or industry?
    c. attracting accounting students to on-campus interviews?
    d. building attendance for a seminar?

    A clear understanding of your goals should guide the development of the creative work, of course. But your goals should also guide your selection of media. Smart advertisers begin the creative process with the potential media in mind. For example, a small budget and highly targeted media led one professional services firm to create a card to be inserted in the publication rather than simply print on the regular pages of the publication. It stood out like a sore thumb, earning lots of attention. Bingo.

3. Define your buyers.

    If your goal is to increase name awareness, for example, you'll want to reach a variety of buyers and influencers. They could be

    a. C-Suite executives at large companies—CEOs and CFOs who confirm or ultimately control the hiring of outside firms.
    b. entrepreneurs and small business or middle market business owners.
    c. government officials, who could be clients or frequent referral sources.
    d. other professionals—even competitors.
    e. recruits and laterals.
    f. your own people.

    The more closely you define your targets, the more effective you'll be in managing your media dollars. Note, it's important to stratify your targets into primary, secondary, and tertiary levels. This will help you make budgeting decisions.

4. Follow your buyers throughout their day.

    You know who they are. But where do they go for their news about the industry or services like yours? Why not ask them? Ask which media they read and where they spend time on the Web. Be prepared for some surprises. New media sources appear every year. Clients will often be reading the hot new industry newsletters, magazines, or blogs before you've even heard of them. What you learn by talking with a few clients won't be statistically valid, but it will be useful when analyzing publication pitches, agency recommendations, and your own hunches.

5. Start with your competition. ("You're kidding right?")

    You may not realize how much your competition can help you. For example, in a beauty contest, if buyers have never heard of you, smart competitors will tell them, "Never heard of 'em!" shaking the buyer's confidence in their short list. So advertise in your own trade press. If you do a good job in differentiating your firm, you'll find that same "competition" to be a source of referrals. Be known as an industry leader inside the industry. The added advantage of accounting industry trades is that they reach experienced hires and possible merger partners, who are often as interested in the measure of your marketing commitment as they are in your firm's other strengths.

6. Reach for the sky.

    National business media (both on- and offline) build brand awareness and name recognition over a wide spectrum of readers—from Fortune 500 executives to Wall Street leaders to venture capitalists. Their wide distribution, though less-highly targeted than industry pubs, delivers greater prestige. Reach is an important aspect of your media plan. The goal is to maximize reach and repetition, but even the most lavish media plan must make choices between the two. Therein lies the art of the media planner.

7. Look under your feet.

    Local publications are the ticket if you define targets geographically. If your town is fortunate enough to have a business journal (eponymously, the Business Journals or Crain's), you'll find their cost lower than the general news source and usually a better value to boot. City magazines are expensive but the perfect choice for some services, particularly when they employ sales-boosting editorial gimmicks like "The Top Professionals Under 40." Don't disdain religious, arts, and civic organization publications if they fit into your plan. In fact, consider everything. Media planning usually suffers from too little creativity, not too much.

8. Put your ear to the ground.

    That's not a stampede you're hearing but commuters on their way in and out of town. Womble Carlyle, a leading law firm that's emerged from the Southeast, has turned its iconic bulldog Winston into a spokesdog on commercial radio, to the delight of drive-time listeners in several major markets. Winston also appears in elevators in downtown office buildings, on display ads in business-focused news Web sites, on busy airport billboards and in print publications. Womble is a case in point example of following your audience through their day.

9. Fly through the air.

    Broadcast can be your strongest tool in building an image or changing the image of your firm—think Archer Daniels on PBS. But broadcast is not for everyone. Don't limit your thinking to PBS. Head for the narrowly-focused cable channels and the powerhouse CNN. If CNN is targeting your market for ad sales, you'll find them a willing partner in working with you to develop creative packages that include more than just broadcast, including participation in important seminars.

10. Go online (but not all-in online).

    Five years ago, you would have read discouraging advice about online advertising on these pages. No longer. As the audience has grown and become more reliant on the Web for news and information, advertisers are flocking to the Web—often at the expense of their investment in broadcast and print. This entire chapter could be devoted to the promise of search engine optimization (your organic results on search engines), search engine marketing (pay per click ad words that appear at the top and in the margins of organic search results), and Web display ads. But three points are imperative: (1) Online is an area you need to have in your media plan, (2) Buying on line is an evolving science, and (3) You need to find the right balance between on- and offline media.

11. Put your heads together.

    We believe that conferences should be part of your media plan. If you're going to spend the time and money to show up, make a showing as well. Because many firms put these dollars in a separate budget, they seldom show up as part of a comprehensive media plan, but they should.

12. Take flight.

    Ads don't move along in lockstep like soldiers. Smart plans move more like infantry—run across the field for three weeks, then dig in for a month, run, dig in. In advertising, this kind of schedule is called "flighting." Create a splash, for example, around the kickoff of the school year, go steady through November, then go dark in December with a big push at the beginning of the new year. In other words, the monotone march of advertising placements is neither useful nor natural.

13. Advance patiently, then hit the long bomb and spike the ball.

    Even the NFL complains that sports metaphors are tired and overused. Whatever. We're trying to drive the message home. A spike is a period of time where your ads are big and seen by your tightly focused target everywhere. A spike could be scheduled around four major seminars, for instance. IBM uses this steady-as-she-goes approach with its weeklong schedule on CNN and other news shows, followed by a blockbuster buy on Sunday football broadcasts. That's a spike!

14. Hit 'em where they ain't.

    If types of media or specific outlets are chock full of competitors (like your local businesss journal), try a different medium, especially a novel one. First movers typically gain press attention from thinking differently than the pack. Said again, think as creatively about the media as you do about the message.

15. Brace yourself.

As you narrow your options, you'll be listening to pitches, scrutinizing costs, and weighing the claims of media possibilities. The proposals all sound good. Every publication can cook up glowing demographics and amazingly low cost-per-impression numbers. But ask the following questions:

    a. How many copies of each issue do they actually print?
    b. How are they distributed?
    c. Are they actually read?
    d. What's the evidence that they are passed along?

By the way, have you wondered why magazines have mostly disappeared from the shuttle flights? It's because publications were using this distribution channel to inflate their circulation numbers (and thus their advertising rates) until some smart lawyer brought the hammer down.

Circulation reports in the media kit are just a starting point. You'll need independent information to evaluate a medium. If you have time to do some analysis, here are tools that can help:

    a. BPA Worldwide audits the circulation of business-to-business publications, as well as general-interest business periodicals. BPA also provides trend reports and analysis.
    b. Audit Bureau of Circulations supplies audits of print (newspapers and consumer magazines) circulation and readership, and Web site activity. ABC maintains a database of circulation and readership information.
    c. SRDS offers a database of media rates and contact data on more than 100,000 U.S. and international media properties.
    d. Market research companies provide advertising, circulation and editorial studies to advertising agencies, corporations and consultants. Erdos & Morgan, for example, performs custom studies such as brand equity research and subscriber surveys.

♀ Key Concept

Put as much energy and thought into your media plan as you do into your message.

CONCLUSION

Most professional services firms concern themselves with substance and scorn preoccupation with branding form in their advertising and other communications. But, if only substance was important, magazines would publish typewritten articles, and the C-suite would choose the unappealing and unlikable advisor as easily as the appealing and likable CPA. Buyers—even those who buy complex, relationship-based business services—are not immune to the form. Good design and high creativity delivers logic and emotion. And, whether we like it or not, people make buying decisions in part based on form or comfort. Form does not rule over substance; neither does substance rule over form. Use them both, just like Dixon Hughes.

ABOUT THE AUTHOR

Joe Walsh is a life-long professional services marketer who got his start in the field in 1987. He offers clients a wealth of brand positioning, market research, creative development and media planning skills. Based in Portland, Maine, he is a principal and creative director with Greenfield/Belser, the nation's leading brand strategy and design firm focused on accounting, consulting, and legal service providers. He works with marketing-challenged clients of all shapes and sizes across the U.S. and around the world. Before joining Greenfield/Belser in 2002, he was an Andersen partner with responsibilities ranging from global brand management to local office marketing.

CHAPTER 15
Successfully Branding Your Firm

Allan S. Boress, CPA, CVA

Allan S. Boress & Associates

INTRODUCTION AND PURPOSE

The purpose of this chapter is to

- describe exactly what branding can—and cannot do for you,
- show you the traps of branding,
- help you decide exactly what should be branded in your firm, and
- provide some keys to success as you get started.

WHERE DID "BRANDING" COME FROM?

It is generally accepted that the American economy entered a completely new phase of development and progress after World War II called *consumerism*. If you study modern American history, you will find that the primary reason the Allies won the war (headed up by the U.S.) was we had the ability, capacity, creativity, resources, and drive to *make more stuff than the other guys*.

President Roosevelt tapped Henry Kaiser, the famous industrialist, to head up the massive transition from a peacetime economy to war effort practically overnight. The auto industry, airline industry, household appliance industry—just about every form of consumer or business production—was transferred and transformed to making munitions, planes, jeeps, bullets, and bombs. Everything we take for granted was rationed or unavailable; gas, food, tires, nylon stockings, new cars. Imagine… Kaiser transformed the economy from peacetime to wartime in a few months. His famous quote was "Problems are only opportunities in work clothes."

My dad told about the Battle of the Bulge. He said that if you looked up you couldn't see the sun or clouds as the entire sky was filled with our airplanes bombing Germany. That's lots of "stuff"!

Why is this important? It's just a little background to our subject. You see, American manufacturers were stuck with all sorts of leftover manufacturing capacity after WWII that they had to utilize or lose to waste.

What was their answer? Create a tremendous, unprecedented demand for consumer goods. Consumerism was born: the drive to create the intense desire to buy everything possible to satisfy one's sense of self.

How? Through advertising, marketing, any kind of promotion you can think of (think "Happy Meals") and BRANDING. The culture of selling products to the American public dramatically shifted to a much more aggressive, create-a-demand-where-one-didn't-exist-before mode, than ever before ("You have bad breath…," "Aren't you glad you use Dial Soap? Don't you wish everyone did?"). You may find it hard to believe, but people in the U.S. didn't always bathe everyday with deodorant soap and use mouthwash until Madison Avenue created the demand.

The last decade saw people driving leased cars they couldn't afford, living in homes that could easily house another family or two, watching a "home theatre" (often paid via a second mortgage), and eating out on a mere weeknight for $80. These excesses were in no small part due to 60 years of increased sophistication of consumerism.

A BIT ABOUT BRANDING

I was raised in the 1950s. My mom was way ahead of the curve. We had the first TV set of anyone in the family or neighborhood. She knew that if she stuck me in front of the Admiral,[1] she would have a built-in babysitter.

Being an only child, I watched one heck of a lot of TV. I remember watching commercials as much as anything from the time I was two and three years old.

One commercial, which played over and over, year after year, was by an association called "The Brand Name Council." I can still see the lady on the screen, with the 1950s permed hair and modest dress: "Do you buy brand names when you go to the store? Make sure to buy ONLY brand names to insure quality for your family!"

And so it went. Brainwashing the American people to buy only well-known, well-advertised items. And it worked.

How many times have you overpaid for Raisin Bran to leave the generic version on the shelf for much less?

Do you realize that there are large, sophisticated companies who specialize in "private branding" and most often offer the same high quality you expect from Kellogg's? Many of these companies sell the exact same product that is then "branded" and simultaneously this same product appears on the shelves under a generic or store name. I used to buy gas back in Chicago from an outfit called "Gas City." They were about five cents less a gallon. Who did they get their gas from? Amoco!

What are you paying the extra 50 percent to 100 percent at the supermarket for? Branding! Actually, you're paying for the advertising, promotion, sales force, and administrative overhead that come with creating and selling a branded product.

And, most importantly, *you're paying to overcome your fear of buying something you haven't heard of.*

That's the power of branding.

WHAT IS BRANDING?

A *brand* is *a* readily recognizable name, image or product. *Branding* is linking the firm name with a concept or area of practice with a goal to "own the market" for that niche, product or service.

An obvious example is the name "Lexus" linked with the product "automobile" and the concept "highest quality."

The idea is that when the name of the product, service, or firm is mentioned, seen, or heard, a POSITIVE idea and feeling pops into one's head automatically. Lexus wanted to, and does to a great extent, own the position of being the foremost luxury car sold in the U.S.

Here's another example, as it relates to a service provided: "Ritz Carlton." What went off in your mind? Ritz Carlton does, in fact, own the position of premiere luxury hotel.

A brand is a promise of what you can expect from a company's product or service. For example, you know what you will get when you purchase Heinz ketchup, but what about the bargain brand? Will it have that same thick, rich taste and texture you expect from Heinz? How will a Big Four audit vary from a regional or local firm's audit?

A great example of branding in the professions is a New York firm based on Long Island. In New York if you mention, Grassi & Company, people will think and say "construction expertise." The feeling you will get is "they know what they are doing in our business." Arthur Andersen, once considered the premier firm in the world, had the strongest branding of all the big firms. When they created Andersen Consulting (merely naming the consulting branch of the already existing firm and creating a separate marketing strategy for it versus the accounting/tax side), the other firms laughed and Andersen partners got rich.

It is possible, of course, that some of your associates or partners might not want to create this kind of brand name recognition for a particular niche. They would rather be known for nothing, than well-known for something so they don't miss any business that might accidentally wander through the door.

Always remember, in order to retain your sanity, that professionals are not primarily "business people," although they all think they are. They are primarily "technicians," great at doing their job, not necessarily running a business, managing and motivating people, marketing, and selling—you get the idea.

So how do you accomplish branding your firm, branding a niche, and making sure you don't lose every possible client who might come in contact with you?

Quite simply, just brand the firm name and the niche at the same time. For instance, if Lou Grassi's firm

---

[1] *Admiral Appliances was one of the early manufacturers of televisions.*

decided to go into the investment banking business, they could create a new brand, "Grassi Capital." Or if they wanted to pursue financial services, then "Grassi Financial."

The smart idea is that if the branding your firm does actually helps get a client in the door, then one has the opportunity to cross-sell other services to the client (just like they do at the Big Four and other large consulting firms).

> **Key Concept**
>
> A brand is a promise of what you can expect from a company's product or service.

WHAT BRANDING IS NOT

Successfully branding your firm, or niche, does not replace humanity. Branding doesn't make the sale for you. It is definitely NOT the final determining factor in hiring a firm.

People buy people; they don't buy a "brand" because you are selling an intangible service, not soup. This is why the Big Four firms lose business to firms you never heard of (and neither did they). The ultimate decision to do business when buying a service is based upon interaction between human beings. Personal chemistry is 50 percent to 80 percent or more of making the sale.

WHY CPA FIRMS ARE PLACING SUCH IMPORTANCE ON BRANDING

Many positive attributes exist from a well-branded product or service.

1. It provides more sales opportunities.

    The hope is that a firm that can successfully brand itself will find that it is on the short list of companies or organizations who need their assistance.

    This can happen because it's a lot easier to access information about a product or service when you remember the name of the people who do it! If the audit committee of the bank decides it wants a Big Four name on its audit, four firms should immediately come to mind. Here in the Orlando area, if a local governmental body or health care facility wants a new accounting firm, Moore Stephens Lovelace will come up first. This is because of years of positive branding investment.

    It's widely accepted that when opportunities occur in certain service areas, certain firms are always going to the party because they are well known, or branded for that niche.

2. Opens the door wider.

    Branding makes you and the firm more memorable because they have heard of you and therefore the name of the firm (or product) is embedded in their mind.

    If one works for a branded or well-known firm, and introduces him or herself, there is a certain amount of recognition and credibility associated with that person.

3. Branding allows firms to own their position now before someone else takes it.

    If you are first ones in, or the ones with the most positive recognition, you will preclude a certain amount of your competitors from sucking up market share because of your brand. That's why at the turn of the millennium all those dot-coms spent fortunes promoting themselves—so they could own their position in their market. Best success examples of owning positions: Amazon and eBay.

Of course, the company that still owns the fast-food market is McDonalds. They were one of the very first ones in and hit the market hard with a specific concept and targeted a marketplace to brand into.

Nobody owns the discount brokerage business like Charles Schwab. Of course, his competitors laughed at him when he opened his doors 30 years ago. Look how long and hard ScottTrade and TD Ameritrade have been trying to steal their market share.

Please understand that just because you own a position doesn't mean you will hold it (think Cadillac). Caddies used to be the ultimate car anyone in America wanted to buy, now it may or may not make someone's top five. Notice how Cadillac and Lincoln have had to reinvent themselves (rebrand themselves) to compete and stay viable with their new looks, rock song jingles, and emphasis on a younger buyer.

Unless you continue to market and promote the brand heavily, continually look to improve the product, and keep your best people, someone else who sees an opportunity that isn't being capitalized on properly, or the management has gotten spoiled, lazy, cheap, and reactive will jump on the situation and steal your place of prominence.

The best example of this is one we are living now. American carmakers once owned 90 percent plus of the domestic market. Cars went relatively unchanged, except for cosmetics, in the 1950's, 60's and early 70's. Then along came Volkswagen, followed by the Japanese giants. They saw an entire industry that was a fat, sitting duck. Thirty-five years after people started switching in droves to foreign carmakers because of better quality and features, Detroit is still trying to catch up and would have gone under, save a generous government.

Another great case in point is Apple. Fabulously profitable in the late eighties, but after being forced out of his own company, Steve Jobs took time off and Gilbert F. Amelio, formerly of National Semiconductor Corporation, took over. Coming from an old, established company, Amelio didn't have the driving entrepreneurial spirit of Jobs, and the company concentrated more on profits than innovation. The net result was that Apple was in decline until the Board brought back Jobs and his visions to reinvent Apple as a leader of cutting edge technology far beyond laptops and Macs.

⚷ Key Concept

Just because you own a position, doesn't mean you will hold it.

---

4. Branding removes some of the fear of doing business with you.

    When you have a well-known name, it is human nature to feel less fear about doing business than if nobody has heard of you.

    For a lot of years, the auto repair business was identified with hucksters. Then the smart people at Midas and AAMCO came along and branded mufflers and transmissions and wound up owning their position. Now people take their cars to them before someone else to this very day.

    "Oh yeah – I've heard of you," is a VERY powerful statement when it comes to removing someone's fear of doing business with you.

5. It automatically implies a certain level of quality.

    Going back more than 50 years of consumer brainwashing, humans are presold on something well-known and assume a certain level of quality psychologically because they are familiar with the name.

    The effort and cost behind branding reinforces to the buyer that the expertise (or quality) exists to merit the brand.

And higher perceived quality is more likely to result in willingness to pay HIGHER PRICES!

6. It's easier to bring out new products or services.

Would it be easier for Honda to bring out a new car model or Rover?

7. A great tag line can be used forever.

If you come up with a great tag line, one that is associated with what you do and who you are, you can use it forever and people will automatically think of you when they hear it or see it.

"Good to the last drop."

That particular tag line was a comment by President Teddy Roosevelt after drinking a cup of Maxwell House coffee over 100 years ago. And they still smartly use it.

Another great example is what the DeBeer family monopoly did to greatly increase the demand of diamonds. Diamonds are NOT the most precious stone. However, you wouldn't know that if you looked at the tag line created years ago which still holds power: Diamonds are forever. And a good tag line is forever, too.

In the mom and pop income tax business, H&R Block still dominates. Their "We Got People" campaign is brilliant in its simplicity and attraction to one's emotions because everyone wants someone with insider knowledge to help them in difficult situations.

8. Easier to attract quality recruits.

Many people like to work for well-known firms so they can brag to their buddies and families who they work for. It's discouraging and demeaning to proudly tell your Uncle Lou that you just got your job at the XYZ firm and he says "Who?"

9. Easier to spread word-of-mouth advertising.

Word-of-mouth advertising has always been the most powerful form of marketing. Movies rely on it. Even a film that gets bad reviews in the media can score at the box office if the target market tells their friends.

Other businesses rely on it too.

Of course, word-of-mouth advertising is easier if people can remember the name of your firm! And that is accomplished by branding a simple, easy to remember name over a long period of time. Also, when the good word is passed along, if the person receiving the recommendation has heard of the firm or the product that has been branded, they can more easily assimilate the information and are more likely to take action.

10. Can parlay the brand into other products or services with presold perceived quality.

My first foray into real-world sales came immediately after college when I went to work for Alberto Culver in Chicago. Our hottest product at that time was something called "Alberto Balsam" shampoo. Stores couldn't keep it on the shelves. What made balsam so important as a shampoo additive? Who knows? Who knows what balsam really is? The fact was they had a neat ad campaign with a good looking and amiable hairdresser. They dumped huge sums of money into this brand promotion. The balsam thing was a new idea that people hadn't heard of yet.

After about a year of getting rich off of the shampoo, they figured people just might buy Alberto Balsam HAIRSPRAY. Well, of course they would and did. Next came the Alberto Balsam deodorant. That was a stretch. What people were willing to put on their heads, they weren't going to spray under their arms. A short time after this, the Balsam franchise expired and Alberto Culver came up with another device to sell stuff.

What's the point? Once you build perceived quality and name recognition into one brand, you can transfer that perceived value into another—*as long as the consumer or client sees a viable relationship.* There is no way Alberto Culver would have sold that much shampoo if the balsam name weren't on it. Similarly, Lexus could bring out a motorcycle and do well with it, but not necessarily ice cream.

The television series *Law and Order* and *CSI* are other marvelous examples of superior branding because their spin-off shows are also hits.

This concept worked like a charm the second time as the former Andersen Consulting rebranded itself as Accenture before the Andersen/Enron catastrophe and has continued to invest in its brand to dominate its market.

> **Key Concept**
>
> It's widely accepted that when opportunities occur in certain service areas, certain firms are always going to the party because they are well known, or branded for that niche.

THE DOWNSIDE OF BRANDING

Partners in accounting and other professional service firms tend to love the concept of branding. Often that's because they see it as some kind of miracle drug for marketing, which in their minds, if done correctly, would further remove them personally from the marketing process. This way they could sit at their desks and never feel at all guilty about it because their firm, service, or niche was now "branded."

When branding alone doesn't bring gobs of new business through the door (because of a lack of active and appropriate participation in the process), they then blame the marketing people—they knew it wouldn't work!

Let's take a look at the traps of attempting to brand your firm or niche.

- *Your branding needs to be consistent with the message you are trying to convey, your services, physical plant, and people.*

Here's one way for people to notice you; promote a certain service and level of quality in your marketing and advertising, and then have the actual delivery of the product be something else.

Buyers can't be fooled for long. As a CPA firm, whatever you choose to brand, the impressiveness of the brand will not exceed the actual quality of service or product over time. In other words, the existence of a good brand won't last if you don't deliver accordingly.

Good brands can be spun around to bite you when the brand becomes associated with poor quality or bad situations. Fixing it is usually impossible.

Will Citigroup ever recover from the banking meltdown? How hard will it be for AIG to recapture its once prominent position in the insurance industry?

We have seen firms invest fortunes in branding, pursuing a higher-class clientele, a better paying customer. Unfortunately, nobody ever told their people how to dress or groom and many times their offices look much less than impressive. That'll get you noticed.

- *Branding takes time and investment.*

Professional people in general (technicians) often don't understand that marketing, branding, getting a message across, breaking through the muddle, TAKES TIMES AND REPEAT EXPOSURE.

Some firms in the accounting/consulting profession are renaming themselves to represent a more holistic approach to taking care of their clients' financial situation. Smith, Jones, and Xavier, CPAs, now call themselves "SJX Financial."

If changing their name and the way the phone is answered is all they do (not changing the way they do business or deal with clients), there will be no effect regarding branding financial services, only confusion in the marketplace and trashing a recognized name.

Marketing is an INVESTMENT, not a cost.

Professionals must be patient with the process, and realize it's going to take three to five years to create an effective brand with the appropriate monetary investments and impressions in the marketplace. Smart firms do not retreat from the branding and marketing wars, they surge ahead to capture more market share as their competitors count their pennies. Look at how Verizon and News Corp have bumped up their advertising and promotion in the recession that began in late 2007.

- *Once branded, it is hard to reinvent the brand image.*

If you do decide to brand your firm, the image you create and embed in the minds of your clients, referral sources, and others will be tough to change.

A great case in point was the attempt to reposition CBS several years ago. In 1996, CBS decided it didn't like its traditional demographics of viewers mostly over 35, or even older, and wanted to morph itself into a clone of Fox, who had a very strong presence in the 19-35 age bracket.

So, CBS started bringing out Fox-clone shows that season. Immediate result? Its traditional audience felt abandoned and ratings plummeted.

⚷ Key Concept

It can to take three to five years to create an effective brand with the appropriate monetary investments and impressions in the marketplace.

HOW TO DO IT SUCCESSFULLY

In 25 years of consulting to this profession, I have discovered certain key success factors in creating a powerful brand. They are as follows:

1. Exactly what is it that you want to brand? Is it your firm, a product, a niche?

    The more specific it is about what it is you want to brand, the easier it is. You need to determine exactly the characteristics of what it is you are trying to brand.

2. What message do you want to convey?

    Exactly what message do you want to put across when people come in contact with your brand?

    Some idea should pop into the client's mind when they come in contact with your brand.

    Is it

    a. quality?
    b. efficiency?
    c. speed (think Nike's "Swoosh")?
    d. caring?
    e. integrity?
    f. a specific expertise?

A successful brand CANNOT be all of those things, just like Outback Steakhouse doesn't mean anything beyond good ribs, chicken, and steak. If YOU can't define it, don't expect others to understand it or define it for you.

3. What FEELING do you want to impart?

    What FEELING do you want people to get when they see it, hear it, and come in contact with it?

    Do you notice that the feeling you get from the brand "Mercedes" is different than the feeling you get from the brand "BMW"? Both of those brands describe well-made, German cars that are expensive. But the FEELING you get is different. Mercedes looks to create a feeling of efficiency, sturdiness, and precision. Where BMW wants you to feel sporty, fun, exciting.

    People buy for emotional reasons; this aspect of branding cannot be underestimated. Emotional comfort and satisfaction must be considered.

4. Get lots of input.

    It is best to get lots of input during the branding process from those you are trying to influence: clients, referral sources, and recruits. This is because you are hopefully going to create something PERMANENT.

    Unfortunately, most firms spend most of their efforts eliciting responses from the partners, who often know much less about such subjects than do the people you are trying to influence.

    Conversely, young people on staff *can* be excellent sources for ideas as they are not yet skeptical and overly stodgy in their ideas and habits.

    The more input you get, the more buy-in you will have once the brand is brought out.

5. Your brand must be CONSISTENT.

    Based on what it is you want, your brand and accompanying message and feelings must be constant with those target clients and existing clients you want to influence.

    The way the office looks, the way your people look and act, the quality of work, product, and reputation for service are all going to have to be in harmony with what you are trying to convey.

    Don't fool yourself into thinking that the brand will overcome inadequacies in these areas.

6. Invest lots of money.

    Successful branding doesn't come cheap. If you work for people who are overly thrifty, chances are your branding efforts will fail because they the necessary monetary investment in the branding process will not be made. Since the vast majority of CPA firms don't have branding specialists on board (the marketing director may not have the necessary expertise), consider retaining the services of a firm that specializes in brand development.

    Chances are you are going to need a new logo, one that is memorable, simple, and conveys the message you want. Get the best graphic designer you can afford.

    New brands require new stationary, new brochures, new newsletter design, and new business cards. Branding is not, however, a one-time cost.

    However, building a new brand, or reinvigorating an existing one, is much more than a good logo and advertising. It invokes everything your firm stands for.

    One Big Four firm redesigned their age-old logo and spent $30 million on the re-branding process. Another firm in the same profession is spent $90 million to further impress their target market with their brand. Other firms in smaller markets have branded for considerably less. A minimum cost for a mid-sized firm might be $150–$250 thousand initially with further expenditures in subsequent years. The most expensive component of branding is advertising.

7. You will need a GREAT LOGO.

A logo ties your name and service together in a visual. It has to exemplify what you are trying to convey. Take a look at what Dixon Hughes has done (www.dixon-hughes.com). Their tagline, "positively unique" ties nicely into their careers page that emphasizes "real work and real fun."

The best logo I ever saw was for the First National Bank of Chicago, later First Chicago Corp. Just by seeing this elegant, unforgettable emblem, you knew immediately who and what it represented. Of course, it has since been trashed through the multiple mergers and buyouts that industry has gone through.

8. KISS: Keep It Simple Stupid.

Smart firms shorten their name to make it memorable. It is Impossible for one to brand a long, tedious, multiple name firm.

Usually, every partner wants his or her name on the door and many times when a new member is admitted to the partnership, they change the name of the firm! This won't work! Keep it simple!

9. The branded name must remain the same.

The name has to stay the same forever!

Every time you change a name you are taking a huge risk and have to undergo the branding process all over again. It took KPMG at least 10 years—and tens of millions of dollars—to overcome the 75 years of branding of the name Peat Marwick.

Take, for example, what happened to what was once the largest selling import car company in the United States. Datsun sold more imported cars in 1983 than anyone else. Then they changed their name to Nissan, and fell to third place where they still reside.

10. Get it out there every place you can.

Once you have established the visual aspect of your brand, your logo, get it everywhere on everything all of the time.

Splatter it all over your Web site, e-mails, blogs, tweets, LinkedIn postings, stationary, office, ads, special shirts the people wear, stuff you give away over and over again.

The brand is now the focal point of everything you do. Nothing should conflict with the brand image you are trying to create. The more the marketplace sees it and comes in contact with those people who represent it, the sooner it will be accepted and turned into a powerful marketing and client retention force.

ⓘ Key Concept

People buy for emotional reasons; this aspect of branding cannot be underestimated.

A Case Study of Presidential Proportions: Obama Diet Soda

Andrew Breitbart is a *Washington Times* columnist and author of *Hollywood, Interrupted: Insanity Chic in Babylon.* He has his own popular news portal, Breitbart.com. Breitbart described President Obama's election by saying "we just bought a new soft drink, and we haven't tasted it yet."

Pretty radical, but some might say right on the money. Unlike any other political candidate in history, President Obama was marketed as a consumer product, a brand.

Can this apply to CPA marketing? Let's take a look at some of the obvious tactics:

- *Sell into the pain.* People vote their pocketbooks—period. The McCain campaign could never communicate how lower taxes help the economy and raising them hurts everyone. Any econ grad knows this. Years and years of history prove it. Instead, McCain's campaign talked about Obama's association with certain people. Who cares when I can't pay my bills?

- *The look of the package.* I have maintained for years that dress, grooming, car, office, and quality of marketing materials must all be coordinated for the target niche one wants. The Obama campaign certainly had this licked—smooth, cool, and confident. People buy things they want to be associated with. The Obama campaign was going for a young voter that had never participated much in politics. Therefore, they marketed Obama like a fancy automobile, one the buyer would want for themselves. McCain, on the other hand, is an old man and looks it. Who wants to be associated with that?

  Consider the visual effects of the "package." If the office, the people, what they drive, and how they look are not in congruence with the desired message and what you want for clients, you lose. Even Obama's logo was cool. Do you recruit? Use their consumer product ideas for that. Also, emulate the Obama campaign for reaching targeted audiences under 30 or people in leading edge industries.

- *The message.* Keep it simple and repeat it over and over. McCain never could communicate a consistent message. Obama's was change, hope, and peace. What's yours? What consistent message is your firm sending to its targeted clientele? One of the worst things a firm, or business, can do is change its message. Once you do, all of the goodwill and awareness created by the previous campaign goes away. Think "baseball, apple pie, and Chevrolet." What's happened to their sales since they dropped that? It made it patriotic to buy their car.

- *Avoidance of technical competence as a sales point.* I've known for years, as supported by all of our surveys since the mid 1980's, that technical competence—and fees—usually rank at or near the bottom for most decisions to hire CPAs, far below the human, personality, and relationship side. Obviously, the Obama campaign knew this as well. How else can you explain the election of someone to the most important post in the world with no executive experience?

- *Perfectly targeted niches.* The Obama campaign knew exactly who they were going after, and hit them hard the way they wanted to be marketed to. How does your targeted market want to be marketed to? Have you asked?

- *What's your Obama channel?* Did you know Obama's campaign had its own television channel on Direct TV? (Maybe you weren't the target market.) How ingenious is that? What are you doing that is out-of-the-box?

  We once had a client years ago, a sharp marketer with a degree in psychology, who developed a CD of songs specifically targeted to college grads (they did campus recruiting). How cool is that? Unfortunately, her bottom-line oriented partners insisted she spend next to nothing on the production, forcing her to use songs like "Nine-to-Five" from 20 years ago, instead of the more expensive stuff college grads were listening to. How dumb is that? Amazingly, it still was effective as it separated them from other CPA firms. How much better would it have been if the partners got their heads out of their wallets for a change and instead popped for the music the kids would play repeatedly in their frat house, in their car, and for their friends?

Lesson for CPAs? What can you do that is extraordinary to draw attention to yourself and your firm? Do you have a radio show? A published book? A video of your people being interviewed and telling how great it is to work at the firm and all the positive things they do for clients?

The Obama campaign has proven once and for all that marketing and branding works, if it is extremely well thought out and executed for a specific targeted audience. Is yours?

CONCLUSION

Branding is a powerful tool that will help you, your firm, and your services stand out from the competition. It can help create a preconceived notion of value.

Branding, even when effective, does not replace humanity. Just because one represents a powerfully branded product, doesn't mean they can remove themselves from the personal marketing process. People still buy people, not brands.

ABOUT THE AUTHOR

Allan Boress, CPA, CVA is author of 12 published books on marketing and selling professional services. He has consulted internationally to over 500 CPA firms. Visit www.ihateselling.com

Chapter 16
Getting Your Name in Lights With Public Relations

Christine Heirlmaier Nelson
Ingenuity Marketing Group, LLC

Introduction[1]

A few years ago, a major accounting client of ours retained us to build a public relations (PR) campaign. Those in client circles knew them for their certain niche, but the accounting client actually had three or four other industry niches. As they warmed up to the idea of promoting certain experts in their firm to the media, we started positioning their experts, brainstorming topics in each niche, and targeting local media.

A PR prospect summed up the result by enviously commenting to us, "We want to be like ABC CPAs. They're everywhere."

How does a firm move from relative obscurity to high visibility in the marketplace?

PR, of course.

Just as we no longer define marketing by advertising, PR has gone beyond news releases and sponsorships. The average daily newspaper doesn't have the news hole or staff to write "about" your firm. The average business magazine or blog is looking for fresh, relevant content; a new twist on traditional ideas; or a timely piece of advice.

In the cyber age of media, your firm has more opportunities to become a respected resource for hot topics in your industry—a thought leader with a story to tell. The trick is knowing how to design a compelling idea that speaks to your customer and intrigues the media messengers. Once you understand the game, the return on investment (ROI) is light years beyond any form of advertising.

This chapter is designed to help the busy CPA gain insight on today's best PR strategies. We've combined some of our best practices (without giving away all our trade secrets) to help you ramp up your story and brand.

After reading this chapter, you may experience a powerful shift in your perceptions about self-promotion and business development. Just take a deep breath and think about the story your ideal clients need to hear.

Be the Expert

Many of our clients initially object to calling themselves experts. Most people think they have to know EVERYTHING to be an expert. And those who think they know everything say that "expert" is an improper description in the public accounting industry.

What if being an expert was simply a state of mind? Try it on like a ridiculously expensive suit. You might like it. Positioning yourself as an expert through PR doesn't require you to change your brochures or promise a certain outcome. You do need to believe that you are highly trained in a particular area of public accounting and have knowledge that is of vital importance to your clients, industry, or society. More people could benefit from what you know. PR allows you to share that knowledge with many more people than you can reach in prospect meetings or seminars.

The first step in your PR strategy is to decide what you know. Accountants often tell us, "Tax. We do tax." That's a start, but it's not a very compelling story.

---

[1] *This chapter was originally published by the AICPA as* Get Your Name in Lights: Practical PR for the Busy CPA *(AICPA 2009). It is reproduced here with permission.*

Let's dig deeper. One of the accounting firms we've worked with has a unique niche in forensic accounting. NOW we're getting somewhere. We've worked with clients who know a ton about not-for-profit issues. Other firms may investigate fraud or provide business valuations or advise on high net worth estates. Digging further, we begin to see unique knowledge on which to build a PR strategy.

A competitive figure skating accountant? Hey, I want to know more!

> **Key Concept**
>
> A sales pitch will turn off a reporter faster than an accounting newsletter titled, *Audit This.*

The best experts see themselves as resources to their clients as well as the media. This point comes as a great relief to introverted CPAs who turn pale at the idea of self-promotion or sales. In reality, reporters and editors dismiss comments like, "You should write about us!" Oh yeah? Why?

Media in all its forms today thrives on the next good story. A good story has three punches:

- Character
- Tension
- Resolution

We're oversimplifying it, but it may help you to think of your story character as your ideal client. The tension comes from the challenge or need they are experiencing. The resolution comes from the knowledge you deliver through this character.

For example, a client is concerned about how he is going to retire when no one in the family is interested in taking over the company. At risk is a family tradition of 35 years, loyal clients, and a valuable service. An accountant well versed in succession planning could offer advice on improving operations to increase the perceived value of the company, developing leadership within, seeking outside leaders, or strategizing on a future merger or sale. The how-to of this dilemma is a story you've probably seen frequently in business journals. The people quoted in those journals are gaining credibility, increasing brand recognition for their firm's knowledge in this area, and getting leads on business owners with a similar problem. It's a hot topic. Any client issue coming across your desk more than once could be a PR hot topic.

If you think of your firm as a story, you also could create a compelling angle by discussing a problem your firm experienced, the tension it created, and how you solved it or moved past it. This honest storytelling can be a great help to other business owners and have a positive PR effect. Prospects are looking for the real deal. They want to know if they can trust you, work with you, and like you. When you are in the people business, showing some vulnerability and humanity is an attractive selling point.

KNOW YOUR AUDIENCE

In the old days, an ad in the local newspaper or a shingle on Main Street was all you needed to attract buyers. Now the buyers are checking you out long before you are aware of them. They may or may not contact you, depending on how you rate against hundreds of other choices or against two other references from their attorney. A multi-pronged approach to PR, known as strategic saturation, is highly recommended.

Knowing your audience is key in PR. You need to know whom you want to serve and find out where they get their information. It's better if you have more than one target audience or niche in order to expand PR and business opportunities. If your firm is targeting empty nesters for estate planning, you also might have a niche in risk management or personal financial planning. The empty nesters might get some of their information right now from the Internet, but they also get it from friends and family, consumer magazines, and their attorney. They're listening to the money show on public radio during their commute. They also may have joined an online discussion group to ask questions about insurance and investments.

Do some research. Ask current clients where they get their information. Ask them who they talk to, what they read, how they learn about new services, how they choose advisors or vendors, what's in their bathroom magazine rack, what they listen to on the radio, if they are Internet surfers or real surfers. Know their hobbies and interests to get an idea of where they spend their time and how to reach them; lifestyle and sports media might be as important in your plan as a business publication.

> **⚷ Key Concept**
>
> If your clients are those representing businesses, find out what magazines are in their lobby, what associations they belong to, where the decision makers golf or dine out, how they research vendors, what keeps them awake at night, and who they trust for good advice.

By asking a few questions, you will begin to see whom you need to talk to and where you need to share your knowledge to get in front of your target audience. Get into the habit of asking every client and referral source about their research habits, goals, pet peeves, and challenges. For example, "What are some of your challenges regarding professional development of young professionals?" Think about how your knowledge could support them and bring resolution.

MEET THE MEDIA

Lots of misconceptions exist about the infamous and faceless entity known as THE MEDIA. To clear the misconceptions, let us introduce you.

"Hi, I'm a journalist. I've been trained to be objective and gather expert opinion and statistics from all sides that relate to the story angle I'm building. I don't often interject my own opinion into a piece. I don't take gifts or a free lunch even though my pocketbook is tight. And I don't have a lot of time."

"Hi, I'm a radio talk show host. I need to fill airtime with witty conversation and experts who know their stuff and can explain it quickly while being charismatic and interesting. A clear resonating voice helps, too. I can interview you from your home or you can come into the studio. I like gifts that I can try out and talk about on the air. I also like it if you have a book or product to promote or give away that we can link to on our Web site to drive listeners there."

"Hi, I'm a television morning show host. I have maybe 30 seconds to interview you, so you need to be on your toes, camera polished, and here by 4:00 a.m. with a good sense of humor and something interesting to say. We'll link your book or Web site to our news site, and please don't wear plaid!"

"Hi, I'm a blogger. Send me something cool to write about and I'll tell thousands (or millions) of people about it. I need tons of fresh content to drive traffic. I'll *trackback* to your Web site or blog and add your blog to my *blogroll*."

Whoa. Where did that last one come from? Yes, blogs are now part of the media machine, along with magazines and electronic newsletters. They are quoted in the news, entered as evidence in court cases, talked about, linked to, and definitely relevant to your PR plan. Social media is growing exponentially, including social networking on Facebook, LinkedIn, and MySpace. These sites are becoming the new virtual Rolodex. More on that later.

For now, let's talk about each of the traditional media first and how to leverage them.

Print Media

A midsized accounting firm is expanding its services to support environmentally conscious businesses and wants to get attention from the local daily newspaper and business publications. The firm's marketing director could send a press release announcing the new practice, but a savvy director also would send along several story ideas such as "Five ways to save on taxes by going green" or an article about how accounting firms can leverage the green revolution.

Highlighting your knowledge of hot topics or anticipating a hot topic is more powerful than a grand opening announcement.

In addition to daily and weekly newspapers, print media includes general interest, lifestyle, business, and niche publications. By understanding your market for prospects and referral sources, you will know which publications will get you in front of the right audiences.

Those in print media are looking for informative articles that help their readers live or work better. They don't want a sales pitch about your company or products unless it's something revolutionary or designed to save the planet from aliens. So you need to create a pitch that is relevant to the audience and informative. Most articles also allow a short bio or photo of the author, or both, to accompany the article.

Some people feel comfortable contacting the appropriate editor by phone; others prefer e-mail. Either one is acceptable, but most editors and reporters prefer an e-mail pitch. Just explain the idea and why it would be relevant to the publication's audience or why it relates to trends and current events. You really don't need to send a formal press release for story ideas; this typically requires an attachment that your reader may not open. If you insist on sending attachments, make them PDFs or Word documents.

Our preference is to send a short e-mail pitch introducing our firm and the idea. In about a week or two, we follow up with the editor by e-mail or phone if we haven't heard anything. We don't nag or plead if we don't get a response. It's the nature of the PR game to win some and lose some. Plus, reporters and editors are very busy like you. The important thing is to maintain rapport with your contacts.

In addition, more publications are accepting submissions by professionals on relevant topics. Get to know the publication you are targeting and look for these access points: case studies, book reviews, commentary, question and answer, and columns. Talk to the managing editor or business editor about whether they accept submissions and for what areas of the publication. Request writer's guidelines so that you submit the piece to the appropriate contact and follow the font, length, bio, and photo requirements. Information about submissions and writer's guidelines also may be on the publication's Web site.

> ## ⚲ Key Concept
>
> If you can write, you have a huge advantage for getting into print. If you can't, hire a writer. Businesses and politicians do it all the time and no one seems to mind (or notice). Some media take issue with ghostwriting, so make sure hiring one doesn't go against policy. If hiring a ghostwriter is prohibited, find a good editor.

The single categorical **don't** when pitching print media is pitching the same story to competing publications in the same market. They'll get wind of it eventually, and they'll question your integrity. Every reporter wants to be first and exclusive on a good story. Show them that you value their job beyond a huge media splash. If you build the relationship well through unique ideas that fit their publication and deliver quality information on time, these same busy reporters and editors will start calling **you**.

Radio

I was doing an interview with my hometown radio station a few years back when the radio host asked me if I'd ever tried to ripen bananas in a paper bag. My children's book used ripening bananas as a way to teach young children about patience. I admit I'd never heard of such a practice, but learned quickly that this irrelevant question can be a goldmine for promotion or make me look like an idiot.

Radio hosts often will throw guests an unrelated question for entertainment effect, so be prepared to bring them back to topic with phrases such as, "Well, I'm here to talk about X," or "Did you mean to ask me about X?" Jokes and humor are encouraged to engage the audience. I countered by laughing, "Well no, but that would defeat the lesson of patience in the green bananas, don't you think?" This light retort brought the host and audience back to my expertise and key message.

The great thing about radio is that you can do an interview with anyone while in your pajamas. A lot of interviewers conduct interviews by phone. Just make sure to turn off your radio before a live interview so you don't get feedback. The show assistant will remind you about it 10 times if you forget.

Find out the name of the program director or main contact for the radio show you are pitching. A media kit or news release is preferable in this case to showcase your experience or background. In the media kit, include a bio of each advisor or spokesperson you are promoting, a list of topics they can speak about, a firm profile or summary, and contact information. You also may include copies of past media coverage. Even though it's radio, e-mail the host professional photos because it somehow helps in their decision process, and they can post your photo on their Web site. If you have a face for radio, as Garrison Keillor would say, don't worry. It's your topic that really sells the pitch.

Include a list of various topics you can speak about related to seasons, current events, and hot topics of the moment. For example, during tax season a radio show might want last-minute tax tips to pass on to listeners. If you have a background in housing trends or mortgage valuations, you might pitch an interview on figuring out what your home is really worth and if homeowners should be concerned. Keep in mind that radio shows are typically speaking to the consumer. *Your ideas must appeal to a broad audience.*

Radio shows like quick tips, so tip lists on different topics are a good way to get their attention. If you have authored a book related to your experience, include that information and your firm Web site in your news release or media kit. You also should mention this information a couple times during the interview.

> **Key Concept**
>
> It's okay to repeat things on radio. Have at least three key points prepared and fit them in wherever appropriate.

Radio shows also like to highlight local events, fundraisers, contests, and promotions. It adds value, timeliness, and relevance to the interview. Make sure to mention any related events and promotions.

Canvas your market for various talk radio opportunities, from local news stations to public radio. Send out your media kits and plan to follow up with new ideas each season.

Television

So you want to be on CNN? We tell clients the same thing about this desire that we tell them about hitting the front page of the *Wall Street Journal*: "Think globally but publicize locally." Put your greatest PR efforts into a form of media that is accessible and visible to prospects. Don't chase *Time*. Even if you got print, it may result in little more than bragging rights.

Like print reporters, television journalists are looking for unique stories that affect the general public. In addition to breaking news, they will have how-to segments on money, education, politics, health and medicine, relationships, home and garden, lifestyles, human-interest profiles, and community events.

Pitch the reporters or anchors of the show directly. E-mail works best. Introduce yourself and provide a list of 5 to 10 headlines or topics that you can speak about with authority. Like radio people, television people like quick tips, a new twist on an old idea, ways to make life easier, as well as commentary and analysis on current events that affect their market.

When big news happens, think about how your knowledge and experience could help reporters frame the issues and provide advice. Send them an e-mail that explains three to five key points you could make to help people understand the issues surrounding the news. If you work with manufacturers, what could you contribute to the dialog about jobs, quality, and trade deficits? If you serve the not-for-profit sector, what could you advise people to think about financially when giving to or joining an organization?

Once you get the interview, your interviewer may ask you to arrive at some crazy hour like 4:30 a.m. If you're lucky, you'll get about one minute of airtime, but it will probably be less. If you have long hair, make sure to pull it back so your face is visible from any camera angle; you won't know when they are switching camera views. Wear glasses that are antireflective and wear neutral solid colors so your clothing doesn't detract from your face. Speak clearly and slowly. Keep your answers short. Like you would for a radio interview, prepare two or three key points to emphasize during the television interview.

> **Key Concept**
>
> Mention your book, event, or firm Web site for more information. Give those details to the anchor ahead of time to repeat and post on the station's Web site.

Now that you understand the realities of meeting and becoming friends with the media, leverage the resulting exposure into additional PR opportunities. Find out how in the next section.

WRITE OR SPEAK—OR BOTH!

Write or Hire Right

Top ways to leverage articles are as follows:

- Get published in print and electronic media
- Link to articles from your Web site or request PDFs of the article to post on your site
- Get reprints of articles and send them to clients and prospects
- Blog about articles on your blog or other blogs, and link to the articles
- Include articles in your media kit and business and speaking proposals

Good PR is consistent, relevant, and credible. Consistency comes from regular media and public engagement. You must have information that is relevant to your audience. You build credibility by getting published, writing, or speaking about your knowledge.

If the idea of writing fills you with dread, consider dictating your thoughts to a ghostwriter. PR agencies have a team of experienced writers who can quote you an estimate for writing articles, blog entries, and columns for a variety of uses. They should be able to write it in a format that fits the style of media: journalistic, footnoted, or conversational. For longer projects, such as a book or e-book, you should hire a writer with that kind of experience. Ask about hiring by the hour versus hiring on retainer to gauge the ROI of a longer engagement. We recommend PR retainers of at least six months to generate effective results because you should plan written and electronic publications between one month and one year in advance.

Speaking for Fun and Profit

Top ways to leverage speaking are as follows:

- Include speaking experience in proposals to get more speaking opportunities
- Offer live or taped teleseminars and Webinars through various services
- Turn taped speeches into MP3 files and podcasts for prospects and clients to download
- Have yourself videotaped and create video files for your Web site on different topics

Believe it or not, you **can** be a public speaker. Of course, some people enjoy the idea of speaking more than others do. We're just going to throw it out there because many experts build huge credibility by getting in front of their target audiences and talking about what they know with enthusiasm.

♀ Key Concept

Enthusiastic mastery of your topic is half the battle to successful public speaking. The other half is overcoming your fear of uncontrollable shaking, sweating, forgetting what you were going to say, rejection, and thrown fruit.

Even the most introverted expert can learn to speak publicly through a combination of training and practice. Speaking opportunities vary from professional meetings and events to civic organizations, training, and seminars sponsored by your firm. If you want to take baby steps, look for opportunities to be part of a professional panel. Usually in a question and answer format with a facilitator, this form of speaking is less intimidating than taking the stage solo. Plus, you usually get to sit behind a table, which protects you from the thrown fruit.

Although videotaping sounds like adding insult to injury for the reluctant speaker, it is another way to expand PR options. As you may have noticed, it's becoming an online world. People are getting their information in a variety of formats to use when it's convenient for them. The more convenient you make it for people to learn about you, the more success you'll generate. It's also easier for them to decide to hire you when they can see you in action. It provides the human engagement that a wicked smart article can't.

Blogs, Social Networking, and Electronic Media

Yes, some see the Internet as a vast and impersonal entity that increases our isolation from others and leads to an apocalyptic cybernetic uprising. Some see it as a new pathway of human connection.

Every day, people are reconnecting online with high school classmates, former colleagues, and old neighbors. Parents are finding support and ideas from other like-minded parents to work with their children's illnesses and behavior. Companies are sharing their goals and getting feedback from a vast sample of customers.

Your future clients might live in Hoboken, NJ, or Haiti. As an expert author, you can speak to them directly online. Is that scary or exciting? Welcome to Web 2.0 and virtual PR.

We hate to lump electronic media into one category, but it's changing so fast that it's difficult to provide evergreen tips. Let's throw caution to the wind and dive in anyway.

The big buzz in PR is social media. From YouTube to Facebook, LinkedIn, and Second Life, people are building their online presence beyond the firm Web site. Social networking sites are like a living Rolodex; the more connections you make with others, the more your influence and business development potential can grow. Obviously, the younger people in your firm are more native to this form of communication because they've been posting information, music, and photos for years now. But old dogs like me (35 to 70-something) have joined in too.

Although we've heard about some firms that discourage staff from posting to social networking sites or blogs due to brand erosion or fear of what young people might post on their profiles, it's a phenomenon that's difficult to prevent. Plus, it can be beneficial when you manage it well.

You can link profiles on these sites to your Web site to boost search engine rankings. Create consistently branded firm and job descriptions so that anyone posting a profile can easily cut and paste them.

Here are a few other ways to get those external links:

- Write a blog or create a microsite and link it to your site.
- Comment on relevant industry blogs, and include your URL to draw readers to other information on your Web site.
- Publish articles and podcasts with online media that link to your site.
- Include your URL in online association membership lists.
- Ask clients to link to your site's Tools or Resources pages.
- Ask colleges and universities to include a link to your Careers page as part of college fair publicity.

The amount of electronic media opportunities available just in your industry is staggering. Bloggers and electronic publishers are starving for fresh and relevant content. You have a wonderful opportunity to feed them your knowledge, increase your credibility, and build your brand.

⚑ Key Concept

If you're not ready for a firm blog or you sense that it won't have good ROI right now, ask other industry bloggers to write about your firm. Getting mentioned in other blogs is a good way to direct eyeballs to your site. Offer to be a guest blogger just like you would contribute an article to a magazine.

To find the right blogs and online media, begin a general search of topics that relate to your firm's knowledge base such as "CPA publications online." Like any PR campaign, simply define your target audience, determine the purpose of each online tool, begin interacting with the people behind the tool, and determine the best connections.

Rule Cyberspace

What's the benefit of integrating online PR with traditional PR? For one thing, it's promoting your firm 24 hours a day, 7 days a week. For another, it's immediate and viral. An article posted on one blog can travel to millions of people in seconds. Finally, it can be highly targeted and niche specific. You can speak directly to prospects who are interested in audits of chinchilla farms, if you do audits of chinchilla farms.

The hub of online marketing and publicity is your Web site. How you identify each page of your site is important. How many arrows you have pointing to your site is important. Rather than using your company name as the title at the top of each page, provide a reason that users might go there. "Find a manufacturing consultant" immediately tells search engines and users the relevance of that page. You can even include a subheading such as "Business Valuation, Succession Planning, Cost Controls" to further identify your services.

These days, search engines are much smarter. They give less or no attention to meta tags or site keywords (computer-speak coding that search engines read to find out about your site) and are instead crawling through the content of the pages for common, relevant phrases. Consistent descriptions of firm strengths and services on each page of your Web site are now critical.

People will search for a phrase like "distressed real estate valuation Minneapolis" if they understand that service and need it in Minneapolis. If you provide this niche service in a certain city, it should appear in your Web site content, preferably more than a few times. Include your contact information on every page. Forget popular and flashy. Be relevant.

Keep your content fresh. The world of new content options is vast, including blogs, e-books, articles, videos, and audio clips. Your top priorities when creating new content should be freshness, relevance, convenience, professionalism, and branding. You may know your field and offer a great culture, but if you don't show that through your Web site, visitors will get easily distracted or disappointed. This holds true for high bandwidth Web site "widgets" that don't add value—like animated graphics or pretty introduction pages. They are slow to load and delay viewers from what they really want. Like a bad sales pitch, Web site widgets will distract readers, and you'll lose them before you get to the good part.

> ### Key Concept
>
> Remember, one or two paragraphs of simple content speaking directly to your audience will beat the bells, whistles, and fancy widgets of Web site design every time. But attractive design with branded colors and easy navigation communicates professionalism and convenience.

Luckily, you don't need to be a techno nerd to take advantage of online publicity. Many services will send mass e-mails with your press releases to targeted media and bloggers, track your favorite blogs, syndicate your Web site content for interested readers, and create downloadable audio and video clips. If homeschooling moms from Topeka, KS, can do it, so can you. (See the Resources Guide at the end of the chapter for a list of tools to help you get started.)

For example, to keep track of the blogs you like, use real simple syndication (RSS) to subscribe to them. Then sign up through a blog reader like Google Reader so that you receive a copy of each new post either at the blog reader's home page or by e-mail.

If you want your firm to look accessible and tech savvy, use audio and video clips as PR tools. Podcasts, for example, are short audio programs that people can download to their MP3 players and listen to while traveling or mowing the lawn. Suddenly, your knowledge is portable and convenient. They hear your voice and get to know you better.

Digitally record key parts of your speeches and presentations and post them on your Web site, YouTube, or Vimeo. Video clips are like a warm handshake before people ever call or meet you. Just make sure that the sound and video are high quality. Also, host your videos on your site, not on a video Web site. We found an accounting firm Web site that had posted a video of the managing partner, and when his video ended, another video popped up called, "Dancing Naked With Disco Lights." Don't allow the video site to make your site look cheap and showy.

The potential for placing positive PR in front of the right people online is unprecedented. Neither a gatekeeper editor nor publisher can stand in your way. You can speak directly to your audience in a variety of ways whenever you wish. Anyone in your firm can be an author or an expert source. Going viral by spreading your knowledge quickly, conveniently, and cost effectively is a good thing for your firm.

For more information on blogs, social networking, and the Internet, see chapter 17, "Adding Social Media to Your Marketing Mix," and chapter 18, "Guide to an Effective CPA Firm Web Site."

BUILD YOUR RAH-RAH FACTOR

Think about the image of a rock star. This is someone who commands attention without saying a word. This person has built up a following of raving fans who follow their every move. When the rock star walks into a room, heads turn and they are instantly recognized.

It might seem like a stretch to apply this vision to an accounting firm, but it is possible with the right PR strategy. If you can take a risk (I know, a scary word) and incorporate some fun, humor, or play into your communications with clients and prospects, they will remember you. Help them enjoy the experience of your firm and people.

The rah-rah factor is about engaging your clients and prospects in your business in a fun or creative way.

One strategy that many print publications use is to host various business awards. These awards are similar to awards given by associations and civic organizations. Some of the benefits to the publication include attracting more business readership and selling advertising in the award special sections. Just as importantly, it increases reader engagement and goodwill.

Winning one of these awards can provide a great deal of publicity for your business through award winner announcements, a list of past award winners, a plaque or trophy for your office lobby, and publicity of the actual award event. Plus, you gain bragging rights for press releases and your Web site.

Many of the nomination forms or applications don't take long to fill out. If the award requires a nomination, request this from one of your most loyal clients who can share a success story related to the award. If an application is required, you can find much of the requested information internally. The form usually notes which information the media will keep confidential. If that's not clear, ask.

Awards and contests aren't just for the media. Your company can create its own award or contest to highlight a pet cause, service strength, or company transition. Ask clients to name your next great product and how they might use it. Have them share a humorous story related to the holiday season. It doesn't have to relate to your business; it just needs to be fun and engaging.

Another way to engage clients is to request reviews and testimonials. Ask them why they think you're great or why they continue to hire you. Get approval to use those statements in various marketing materials and on your Web site. It's best if the clients agree to use their real names and companies, but firms with confidentiality issues could use a generic description to describe the client. You could simply say, "Client since 1983" to focus on the client's longevity. Just avoid labeling it "anonymous" because it looks like you made up the testimonials. By the way, don't make them up.

> ### Key Concept
>
> If anyone in your company has published a book that is available for purchase through an online bookseller, ask readers to write reviews and rank the book. It boosts the book's standing and exposure online and is another way to build your rah-rah factor with clients.

Finally, throw a party. Well, more specifically host an event that celebrates a milestone in your company, showcases the knowledge of your firm, or honors clients. This can include anything from a niche services seminar to an anniversary or moving party to a book signing. It creates goodwill and gives clients a chance to get to know you and your company on a more informal level. Don't expect the media to show up at your event, but if they do, it's a bonus! Hand them some punch and give them a tour.

CONCLUSION

Well, now that you know everything we know about publicity (except a few of our super secret, no-fail PR tricks) you can get out there and be the firm that everyone complains is "everywhere." When the competition is talking about you with envy, you have arrived at PR nirvana.

Namaste. (No, that doesn't mean "No comment." Look it up on Wikipedia.com. While you're at it, create your own Wikipedia page.) It's time for sassy self-promotion, people!

RESOURCES

Online Media

- **Technorati.** Collection of the latest posts of your favorite blogs in one central location by category. www.technorati.com

- **Alltop.** Collection of top news stories from thousands of credible Web sites organized by subject. www.alltop.com

- **LinkedIn.** Social networking site just for professionals. Post a profile, answer expert questions, join a virtual group, and connect with new business leads. www.linkedin.com

- **Facebook.** Social networking site with a younger and less professional feel than LinkedIn but still used to research contacts and companies. www.facebook.com

- **YouTube.** Short video clips of daily life and opportunities to promote your business. www.youtube.com

- **Del.icio.us.** Online bookmark manager that lets you bookmark sites and content that you love and recommend it to others. This is an opportunity to get your site linked and recommended. www.delicious.com

- **Typepad.** Subscription-based site that gives you an easy way to create a blog for your firm. www.typepad.com Google also has a free one called Blogger. www.blogger.com

Media Research

- **Mondo Times.** Database that allows you to search for relevant media in a particular market to build a PR plan. www.mondotimes.com

- **PRNewsWire.** Comprehensive database of media where you can send targeted press releases and build your own preferred media lists. www.prnewswire.com

- **ProfNet.** Query system to receive topical requests from the media and send your own to experts. www.profnet.com

- **Help a Reporter Out (HARO).** Free reporter query service that allows you to keep up with what reporters want by sending you two or three HARO e-mails a day. www.helpareporter.com

- **Businesswire.** One of the largest press release distribution services. www.businesswire.com

- **Medialink.** Web 2.0 meets PR strategy: Distribute your news release, video, and audio to the media. www.medialink.com

- **Google.** Tools to enhance your Web site, earn revenue, and keep track of your favorite blogs. Check out its offerings under the "More" tab where you'll find GoogleReader to scan blogs quickly, Google Alerts to track publicity for your firm, and Google Sites for group Web site development. www.google.com

- **K.D. Paine's PR Measurement Blog.** One of the most comprehensive blogs in the world about all kinds of PR available and how to measure the ROI of each. http://kdpaine.blogs.com/kdpaines_pr_m/

- **Xinu.** Database of Web statistics, including your Web site's search engine ranking. www.xinureturns.com

Books

- *The New Rules of Marketing & PR: How to Use News Releases, Blogs, Podcasting, Viral Marketing & Online Media to Reach Buyers Directly,* by David Meerman Scott

- *Get Slightly Famous: Become a Celebrity in Your Field and Attract More Business with Less Effort,* by Steven Van Yoder

- *Primal Branding: Create Zealots for Your Brand, Your Company, and Your Future,* by Patrick Hanlon

ABOUT THE AUTHOR

Christine Hierlmaier Nelson is a communications consultant and former journalist who leads the public relations team at Ingenuity Marketing Group, the quintessential marketing strategy, public relations, and training firm for the people of professional services. She is also the author of a children's book, a blogger, speaker, and shameless self-promoter who has landed the pages of *Redbook*, *Parents*, *First for Women*, *Woman's World*, and several online parenting and lifestyle sites. A bit of a rebel, she ran her own freelance writing company for small businesses for nine years. She is now happily writing and strategizing for professionals around the country. Contact Ingenuity at at 651-690-3358 or visit wwww.ingenuitymarketing.com.

CHAPTER 17
Adding Social Media to Your Marketing Mix

Joe Rotella
Delphia Consulting, LLC

INTRODUCTION

The Web is continually affecting marketing strategies and tactics. Traditional marketing channels, by their very nature, are highly controlled, one-way messages—created by marketing departments and directed at the consumer. The "original Web," or Web 1.0 as it is known, made it easier than ever for prospects to learn about products, services, or providers. Back then, most of the information available was published by the provider so the message and brand was highly controlled.

Today's Web, Web 2.0, reflects a paradigm shift in the way the internet is being used, from *presenting* information to sharing to collaborating and building a community of interest *around* information. Forester describes Web 2.0 as a set of technologies and applications that enable the efficient *interaction* between people, content, and data. The interaction is what makes these technologies different. The interaction is usually referred to as social media—conversations facilitated by technology.

This chapter is designed to help you understand how social media is changing the marketing landscape, introduce you to the five most common social media channels used for business and provide you a three-step strategy to add social media to your marketing mix.

MARKETING IS CHANGING

With the onset of social media, CPA firms and their marketing departments no longer control the message. Power is shifting to the client, the consumer. Individuals can influence the perception of a brand and buying decisions of their online friends through such online media as LinkedIn, Facebook, Twitter, and blogs.

Social media is profoundly different from standard marketing channels such as print, radio, and TV. Web 2.0 channels might be better seen as marketing "engines" rather than "channels." These engines can energize and add power to marketing messages, helping those messages to spread from one person to another (that is, viral marketing). "Word-of-mouse" marketing is amplified online where it's easy to pass on a message to hundreds of contacts and friends around the world in a fraction of a second.

Many employers view social media channels such as LinkedIn, Facebook, Twitter, and blogging as ways for the younger generation to have fun and stay connected with friends and colleagues. As a result, they often view social media as a distraction for their employees while at work. They believe it leads to lost productivity and profits. But what many employers have yet to understand is that there's also an opportunity here to use these technologies to positively affect, and even grow, their business. Just consider these statistics to understand how the business landscape is shifting, and the role that social media is playing in these shifts:

- In various surveys, more than 80 percent of business-to-business (B-2-B) buyers say they like to find their vendors online.
- Over 93 percent of Americans online expect companies to have a social media presence and 91 percent say consumer content is the number one aid to making buying decisions.[1]

---

[1] *JC Williams Group*

- 87 percent trust a friend's recommendation over a review by a critic.[2]
- Social network users are three times more likely to trust peer opinions over advertising in purchase decisions.[3]
- IT buyers trust social media more than any other source.[4]

These statistics show that the marketing landscape has changed. "The traditional marketing model is being challenged, and (Chief Marketing Officers) can foresee a day when it will no longer work."[5] Now is the time for you to consider using Web 2.0 technologies, like social media, to enrich your online B-2-B experience.

Key Concept

With the onset of social media, CPA firms and their marketing departments no longer control the message. Power is shifting to the client, the consumer.

Key Concept

Don't use social media because it's popular. Use it because it can boost your marketing reach.

FIVE SOCIAL MEDIA CHANNELS WELL SUITED FOR CPA FIRMS

There are 100's of social media Web sites or services on the Web today, and many on the horizon. Given limited resources, it's important to carefully decide what channels are appropriate for your practice and are likely to produce the highest return on investment. Channels come and go as the underlying technology evolves and people's preferences change, so it's important to invest your resources strategically. The following five channels are most commonly used for business:

1. *YouTube.* A free video sharing Web site founded in 2005 that has become one of the most popular sites in the world. Registered users can upload and share an unlimited number of videos, each up to approximately five minutes in length. Accounts of registered users are called "channels" and can be branded to incorporate the user's logo and colors. Videos can be played on the YouTube Web site or embedded directly into another Web site, such as an organization's primary marketing site. So YouTube can be considered a free video hosting and streaming service. CPA firms are using video to present recruiting information; facility tours; client testimonials; and software demonstrations, tips, and tricks.

2. *LinkedIn.* Founded in 2002, LinkedIn is a business-oriented social networking site mainly used for professional networking. Registered users build their network of contacts, people they know and value in business, by sending out or accepting "connection" requests. Introductions to new contacts can be made through your connections. This "gated-access approach" is intended to build trust.

   a. Registered users can present information about their current status, current position, past positions, and education in their profile.
   b. Your connections can post a recommendation to your profile, telling others about their experience working with you.
   c. People use LinkedIn to find jobs, people, and business opportunities recommended by those in their network.
   d. Employers can list jobs and search for candidates. Job seekers can review the profile of hiring managers and potential employers.

---

[2] *MarketingSherpa.*

[3] *Jupiter Research.*

[4] PJA IT Social Media Index.

[5] McKinsey Quarterly, *2005, Number 2.*

    e. Professionals use Linkedin to stay in touch with referral sources such as bankers, attorneys, and brokers.

    f. Firms are using Linkedin to stay in touch with their alumni by creating alumni groups.

3. *Facebook.* A free social networking Web site with over 300 million registered users worldwide as of September 2009.[6] Registered users can invite other users to be their "friend." Once a friend request is accepted, they become part of the user's network. Friends can send each other private messages or write on each other's *wall*—a message area owned by a user that can be viewed by all their friends. Additionally, users can join networks organized by city, workplace, school, and region. Personal pages can also include applications ranging from games to suggested reading lists. Business can also have a presence on Facebook by creating a business page or group.

    a. Registered users can become a "fan" of a business or organization. By doing so, they will receive notices when the business posts new information.

    b. The visual design of Facebook pages is limited to the Facebook brand; white pages with blue boxes. However, a company page can include its company logo as an identifying mark.

    c. Business pages have significantly limited use of applications. Most business pages are used to present company information, news, events, photos, and videos.

    d. A proprietary development language called "facebook markup language (FMBL)" can be used to provide additional components, such as a list of resource Web site links, on a business page.

4. *Twitter.* A free micro-blogging service created in 2006 that enables registered users to send and read messages known as *tweets*. Tweets are text-based posts of up to 140 characters displayed on the sender's profile page and delivered to the sender's subscribers who are known as *followers*. Registered users can send and receive tweets via the Twitter Web site, Short Message Service, or external applications (for example, TweetDeck or Twhirl). A February 2009 Compete.com blog entry ranked Twitter as the third most used social network.

    a. The visual design of a registered user's page on Twitter can be customized to match their brand.

    b. Twitter users may create a 48x48 pixel image or "avatar" that is displayed on their page and, in most applications, alongside the messages they send.

    c. Businesses use Twitter to send messages about their latest news, upcoming events, articles, deadlines, and tips or techniques.

    d. It is possible to embed recent tweets directly on a Web site, making it possible to provide the timely content associated with Twitter on what may typically be a less dynamic site.

5. *Blogs.* Typically thought of as an online diary, a blog (short for *web log*) is usually maintained by an individual with regular entries or posts. Posts are commonly displayed in reverse-chronological order. A key component of a blog is the ability for readers to comment on and subscribe to content. As of June 2008, blog search engine Technorati was tracking more than 112.8 million blogs. Businesses can use a blog posts to share commentary, descriptions of events, news or announcements, or links to other Web site content.

SOCIAL MEDIA ADOPTION STRATEGY

An understanding of the most common social media channels is not enough to integrate social media in to your marketing plan. It's important you understand how social media differs from traditional media. In many ways, you approach social media marketing as you would approach social engagements in real life.

    Social media communities often remind me of a neighborhood hangout where people routinely gather, know one another, and have built relationships slowly over time. The hangout or community has a culture. If you want to become part of the community you first understand the culture, then start contributing to the community and

---

[6] *www.facebook.com*

then gradually you can expect to benefit from being a part of the community. Following this pattern, approach social media marketing in these three steps:

1. *Listen.* Listen to the community to learn about the culture. In time, you'll begin to understand what's talked about and what isn't, how "chatty" the community is, what behaviors are well received and what ones are not, and what information most interests community members.

2. *Serve.* Once you get a feeling for the culture of an online community you can start to contribute. Contributing means more than blatantly promoting your products and services. It involves sharing information that nurtures community members. If the information you share has value to the community, they will get to know you, like you, and trust you—key emotions that play a significant role in purchasing decisions.

3. *Engage.* Actively participating in multi-way conversations with community members; discussing, learning, questioning, challenging, listening, growing, and benefiting from being part of a virtual community.

? Key Concept

It's important to understand how social media differs from traditional media. In many ways, you approach social media marketing as you would approach social engagements in real life.

---

1. Listen

You've probably heard the statistic many times. The most significant reason clients leave one provider for another, coming in at a whopping 68 percent, is "perceived indifference." Simply put, clients don't feel like their service provider cares about them.

Clients want to be heard and want to know you understand their needs and wants. If you've worked to position yourself as their "trusted advisor" they may even expect you to know their needs and wants better than they do. Showing that you really understand your clients and their industries can help you deliver exceptional service— the kind of service that separates you from your competitors and creates intensely loyal clients.

The incredible surge of social media means more and more people, including your clients, are sharing their thoughts and feelings on the Web. And, it continues to gain momentum. While individual Web sites or tools come and go, the overall trend is toward faster and faster adoption of social media. According to a 2009 survey of 2,253 adults by Pew Internet & American Life Project, one third (35 percent) of American adult Internet users have created a profile on an online social network. This is 4 times as many as 3 years ago.

Tune your listening skills to focus on information you can use. Listening to everything all your clients say on the Web would be nice, but unrealistic. Focus on your most profitable clients and on things you can use to make a difference in your service delivery. Don't forget prospects and referral sources too.

? Key Concept

Clients want to be heard and want to know you understand their needs and wants. Showing that you really understand your clients and their industries can help you deliver exceptional service—the kind of service that separates you from your competitors and creates intensely loyal clients.

Five Things to Listen for on Social Media

1. *Complaints*

   Some clients have trouble being candid with their service provider, no matter how many times we ask if they are OK. Unfortunately, some of those clients have no trouble posting their frustration on the Web. When you hear a complaint, do something about it. Bring a solution to the table and show your problem solving skills. In many cases, the most loyal clients are ones that have had a bad experience that was promptly resolved.

2. *Needs*

   If you're listening carefully, you could catch wind of a need. Someone sharing a "pain" or "gain" is an opportunity for you to rise to the occasion and help. Even if you don't directly offer a solution, you might be able to refer them to a partner in your firm, or even another provider. A true trusted advisor sometimes offers advice that doesn't put a penny in their pocket.

3. *Successes*

   Everyone loves to be recognized when they've achieved a goal. A word of "Congrats!" to a client that has won an award, closed a big deal, or made a difference in the community shows you are listening and take pride seeing your clients succeed.

4. *Praise*

   If you hear a client say something nice about you, thank them! A hand-written thank you note for a glowing comment is going to make them feel appreciated. It might also give you the opportunity to ask for a testimonial for your Web site or a recommendation on LinkedIn.

5. *Tips and Trends*

   A key component of social media is sharing—finding useful information and passing it along. As you listen you will come across information that might interest your clients. For example, if you listen to *#nonprofits* on Twitter you will frequently see posts with links to articles showing how nonprofits are using technology to fulfill their missions. You could pass those same links along to your nonprofit clients through social media, e-mail, or a newsletter.

How do you listen to all the chatter on the Web and find what's important to your clients and in the industries you serve?

Four Free Tools to Help You Listen to the Conversation

1. *Google Alerts*

   Set up alerts to monitor your top tier clients as well as your organization's name and the names of your client-facing staff. You can also monitor trends in a particular industry that you serve, and keep up with what your competitors are doing. Google does the work of *crawling* or continuously examining the Web to find mentions and sends that information to your e-mail inbox.

2. *LinkedIn Network Updates*

   As you build your LinkedIn network, include your clients, prospects, referral sources, association leaders, and even the media. As a member of Linkedin you will receive updates about the members of your online network. These updates will begin to provide you with insights in to their world. Profile updates could indicate a single promotion or reveal a broader reorganization. Status updates often include glimpses in to current projects. Events could show you where your clients are going to get their information.

3. *Monitter*

   It seems like more and more professionals are sending a 140-character "tweet" on Twitter about everything from what they did that morning to an interesting article they read. Keeping track of it can be overwhelming. Beyond the integrated search of Twitter apps like Twhirl and TweetDeck, Monitter (www.bbmonitter. com) provides real-time monitoring of the Twittersphere. Tweets can give you insights into competitor offerings by letting you listen to what they are talking about. By monitoring Twitter for keywords related to your services or industry niches, you might hear someone talk about a pain their experiencing or a need they have and uncover a prospect.

4. *Technorati*

   Billed as the "leading blog search engine," Technorati helps you find postings that can provide insights to challenges your clients are facing or what industry trends are heading their way. Blogs play an important role in building positive or negative word-of-mouth when it comes to purchasers making decisions about products and services by helping to shape readers' perceptions and behaviors. Blogs focused on the accounting profession, such as *CPATrendlines* (Rick Telberg, Editor), can help you stay current. Industry blogs can help you spot tips and trends that could influence the services you offer or promote.

Listening is the first step toward integrating social media in to your marketing plan. Listening is a form of business intelligence. It lets you spot trends, learn about prospects and clients, and hear what people really think. Effective listening can help you understand the industries you work with, what your clients are doing, what challenges they face, and where they are succeeding. This is valuable information for both pre-sales and account management.

Key Concept

Listening is the first step toward integrating social media in to your marketing plan.

---

2. Serve

Once you're comfortable listing to the community, you can begin to serve its members. Serving an online community nurtures relationships with the community members. It's a long term view that demonstrates you care about the people that are part of the community. You give more than you take and you help others succeed.

CPAs and marketing professionals sometimes struggle with "giving." Many have repeatedly heard "you can't give it away for free." They perceive information as proprietary assets and work to collect more than they share. If someone wants to learn from them, they must trade something of equal or greater value; a name to add to a mailing list, an address to send a white paper, an so on.

Many CPAs and marketers have also learned to work to find openings in a conversation that enable them to promote their organization's products and services. No matter where the conversation flows, they find an opportunity to bring it back to what they have to promote. Bette Midler's character in *Beaches*, CC Bloom, portrays this well when she says, "But enough about me, let's talk about you... what do YOU think of me?"

Pushed to the extreme, these behaviors are rude and annoying in real world conversations. They are also rude and annoying in social media. If you are on the receiving end of this type of dialog in the real world you're likely to work to find some way of excusing yourself from the conversation. In social media, it's easy to walk away. "Unfriending" someone on Facebook or "unfollowing" someone on Twitter only takes a few simple mouse clicks. And given the acceleration of social media messaging, it's very easy for one person to quickly tell others what a bad experience they had.

The "Rule of Thirds" for Social Media Content

To avoid becoming an "ear-sore" on social media, follow the advice of Dale Carnegie who once said "It's much easier to become interested in others than it is to convince them to be interested in you." The "rule of thirds" for social media content can help you heed his advice.

- *Self promote*—One third of your content can promote your products and services. Share what's going on at your firm, news, events, accolades, successes, and public relations messages.
- *Share*—Pass along information *your community* will find valuable, as another third of your content. Think about what books or articles would be helpful to others. Share information about industry related events or deadlines. Pass along "news you can use" that was passed to you. A key component of social media is sharing and the benefits are clear; people like people who share. You'll also establish yourself as someone "in the know" who helps others succeed.
- *Chat*—Social media is about conversation and there is a place for chit-chat, even when you're using social media for business. So, a third of your content should help facilitate conversations. Create a dialog by engaging in the conversation. Share your own thoughts and ask others what they think. Respond to questions. Ask others how they are doing, just as you would in a real world conversation. This builds online social capital and the more of that you have, the better off you'll be in the long haul.

3. Engage

Fundamentally, Web 2.0 and social media are about conversations made efficient by technology. And, once again, the virtual world has similarities to the real world. The art of conversation takes knowledge, practice, and patience.

As you move along the social media marketing adoption curve from listening through serving you'll naturally have the opportunity to engage with community members in meaningful conversations. If you've listened carefully and done your homework, you know what people are interested in. You've chatted enough so people know and like you. You've provided enough nurturing content so people have begun to trust you. Now you can participate and even start more meaningful conversations with community members.

- Help *further topical discussions* by asking clarifying questions or providing your thoughts on what others have asked.
- If you disagree with something being discussed, consider whether your response will help continue the conversation or be perceived as argumentative. While it's critically important to be authentic in social media, it's also challenging to convey when you aren't face-to-face with someone or talking over the telephone. If you're confident your views will contribute to healthy discussion, share them.
- Be careful when playing "devil's advocate." It requires great care to use this technique as a way to *keep the conversation moving*. If used too frequently, you could be perceived as disagreeable or even hostile.
- Know when the conversation is over. Even the best conversations run out of content or interest. When you sense that is happening, it might be best to let it happen.
- Consider using lulls in the conversation as a way to *start a new dialog*. Ask a question or start a dialog that helps further your business goals.

> **⚑ Key Concept**
>
> As you move along the social media marketing adoption curve from listening through serving you'll naturally have the opportunity to engage with community members in meaningful conversations. If you've listened carefully and done your homework, you know what people are interested in.

MEASURING RESULTS

Unlike traditional marketing, which is about velocity, *social media is about acceleration*. Traditional marketing metrics center around how many people received your message at any given point of time, just like you measure velocity at an instance in time. We measured "impressions" and were often able to do so with relative ease. We could count how many brochures were distributed or estimate the readership of a given publication.

In contrast, *social media metrics consider the influence of a given network* and how the message distribution grows over time. For example, a "tweet" that goes out to 400 followers might be retweeted several times, eventually reaching tens of thousands of people. A key consideration in social media marketing is how the message spreads over time, just like acceleration measures speed over time.

> **⚑ Key Concept**
>
> Unlike traditional marketing, which is about velocity, social media is about acceleration.

CLEAN HOUSE FIRST

Remember, once you're an active part of the Web community, it's likely visits to your organization's Web site will start to increase. A major goal of social media marketing is to drive traffic to your Web site. No one is going to buy your products or services from something they read on Facebook or a 140 character message they saw on Twitter. Social media channels help support your marketing funnel. Social media marketing isn't intended to replace all your other marketing channels. In online marketing, the *real due diligence happens on your Web site* and in person-to-person interactions.

Listening on social media can help you understand what your target audience expects and you can use that information to continuously improve your marketing messaging, including your Web site.

As you nurture the online community by providing valuable information, you have opportunities to drive traffic to your Web site to read articles, whitepapers, or case studies. As that starts to happen, it becomes even more critical that your Web site meets your organization's business goals while providing users with an exceptional user experience.

Before you start driving traffic to your Web site with social media marketing, take some time to audit your Web site. Ask yourself questions like the following:

- Are you confident your current Web site provides visitors with exactly what they need and expect?
- Is the information useful to your target audience?
- Does it differentiate your organization from other organizations?
- Does it present your organization's personality or brand well?
- Is it designed to acquire new clients? Retain current clients? Recruit talent?
- Can visitors conduct business with us 24×7×365 over the Web (that is, downloading a white paper, joining an e-mail list, or registering for a Webinar/seminar any day at any time)?

Remember, online communities are like your neighborhood hangout, and your Web site is like your home. As in the real world, take care to make sure your home is ready for company before inviting people over for a visit. You can only make a first impression once. For more information about Web sites, see chapter 18, "Guide to an Effective CPA Web site."

Join the Conversation!

It's likely that social media marketing will require a significant shift in your organization's culture as stakeholders learn the power of social media, come to grips with a loss of message control, and understand the commitment required to remain part of this new community. You'll also need to think carefully about how you measure the return on investment of digital media marketing tools so you can continually revise your plans to maximize your efforts.

To some, Web 2.0 technologies, including social media, can feel like the "bright shiny thing" that pulls them in with childlike enthusiasm. Others perceive social media as a waste of time and completely inappropriate for business use. We saw similar reactions in the early stages of e-mail's adoption. Now we can't imagine a business that doesn't embrace the use of e-mail. And just like e-mail, social media channels can be used effectively or frivolously. How well your organization uses social media marketing for business is up to you.

Key Concept

It's likely that social media marketing will require a significant shift in your organization's culture as stakeholders learn the power of social media, come to grips with a loss of message control, and understand the commitment required to remain part of this new community.

Conclusion

To successfully add social media to your firms marketing mix, you must start with a clear understanding of your marketing goals, resources, and constraints. Then build and adopt a social media marketing strategy based on that understanding. Select channels that help you reach your target audience and then *listen, serve,* and *engage.* Measure your results and adjust your strategy based on your findings to maximize your return on investment. Done well, you'll reap the benefits of accelerated messaging and deeper relationships with prospects, clients, and referral sources.

ABOUT THE AUTHOR

Joe Rotella is chief technical officer at Delphia Consulting where his team helps clients define, design, and build an exceptional Web presence, from their Web site to social media marketing strategies and tactics. According to Bob Scott, he's "something of a one-man think tank, has been doing more innovative things with the Internet than anyone I've met yet." When he's not working, geocaching, speaking, or riding his Vespa scooter, he's busy tweeting or posting to his blog, www.JoeRotellaSays.com.

CHAPTER 18
Guide to an Effective CPA Firm Web Site

D. Michelle Golden
Golden Practices Inc

INTRODUCTION

The Web has evolved greatly in the 10–15 years that professional firms have invested in their online presences, yet few firms do more than scratch the surface of the Web's potential for their business development. Web sites no longer echo firm brochures—they are a tool through which to powerfully build your firm's reputation.

Your firm's Web site creates the first impression many potential clients or prospective employees have of your firm. The same is true for journalists, trade association representatives, and others seeking experts to quote, speak, or direct business to. If visitors don't like what they see, valuable opportunities may pass you by.

Can you answer all these questions with a definitive "yes"?

- Is your firm's Web site generating the results it could be?
- Are you reaching the right audiences and delivering the right messages?
- Does your site align with your firm's business development goals?

If not, this chapter will help you to

- know your audience(s),
- clarify the purpose of your site, and
- effectively approach development.

⚷ Key Concept

Your firm's Web site creates the first impression many potential clients or prospective employees have of your firm.

KNOW YOUR AUDIENCE(S)

Great marketing begins with this imperative first step: identify all your unique target audience groups. You'll then develop a "persona" profile for each group. Your eventual Web site effectiveness hinges on addressing each unique persona in appropriate, relevant ways through content.

Establishing purpose-oriented goals and priorities for your Web site is easier when you think in terms of goals by persona. Create a small committee to identify personas and their unique needs through the exercise to follow. First, identify all desired site visitors and, later, you may decide some aren't important enough to distinctly address with your site.

Before zeroing in on your audiences and personas, examine this excellent example of a university's personas shared by author David Meerman Scott.[1] For universities, prospective students are the core audience, second are their parents. More groups are current students, alumni, current faculty, prospective faculty, and high-school counselors who are influential in student placement.

---

[1] *D.M. Scott,* The New Rules of Marketing and PR. *(Hoboken, New Jersey: John Wiley & Sons, Inc., 2007).*

Each audience has its own set of reasons—drivers—for visiting the site. Sometimes, the messages sought by the different audiences might seem to be at odds. A university wants to attract students with promises of exciting lifestyle, while simultaneously reassuring parents they are making a wise investment by sending their kid to that school. It wants to inspire people to attend and support athletic and art programs, move alumni to contribute, and provide support for current students in registration, on-line education, access to faculty, and interaction with each other. These are some goals by persona.

For CPA firms, prospective clients are a core audience, as are potential employees. Additional groups are current clients, referral sources, alumni, trade association leaders, and the media. Your firm certainly has more. Each persona has unique informational needs and different reasons to contact you. Even within a single organization, your sales messaging ought to be targeted to the stakeholder persona you are addressing. In a nonprofit organization, the CFO, executive director, and audit committee member will have very different motivations for ultimately hiring your firm.

Breaking each audience down to individual people and roles is how you create your personas. Get as micro as you can, recognizing that within a particular audience, there can also be subsets. For example, a university wants to position itself somewhat differently to recruit high-school seniors versus grad students. This is not unlike a CPA firms' need to simultaneously appeal to both college grads and experienced, lateral hires. While a college senior might respond with hope to your promises of fabulous work-life balance, a lateral may be skeptical knowing based on past experience. To be most effective, your Web site would offer separate hubs for these two groups. Always be honest and authentic in both because one persona may, at any time, read the others' intended content.

How easy is it for different types of visitors to quickly determine where they should go on your firm's site? In our university example, we note this key fact: when representatives of their defined audience groups visit the Web site, they can quickly identify where they should go. University sites almost unfailingly have menu items for "alumni," "parents," "students," "faculty," and one for "athletics." From each of those pages, the intended audience can find a full spectrum of pages that will be most relevant to *them*. This is called a "hub" approach and prevents visitors having to comb through information that doesn't pertain to them.

> **♦ Key Concept**
>
> Each audience has its own set of reasons—drivers—for visiting your site.

Is Your Site Audience-Centric?

Until recently, CPA firms haven't been particularly audience-centric, which sends a strong message to the site visitors that these firms are more concerned with themselves. Your firm's sitemap should not be a mere reflection of the firm's organizational chart: audit, tax, consulting, business valuation, technology—the departments or service lines of the firm. This is an unhelpful firm-centric approach because readers are left to fend for themselves, clicking from service to service, unsure of whether a service is appropriate for them. This would be the equivalent of a university having main level tabs listing "humanities" "arts" and "engineering" (their products) rather than staging them through hubs for their personas. When information is delivered in an audience-centric manner, you reinforce the concept that the reader comes first.

A firm's presentation reflects its culture and values. When information is delivered in an audience-centric manner, you reinforce the concept that the reader comes first. There is a bold contradiction when a firm says customers come first, but its presentation is firm-centric. What you do in your approach will override whatever you claim as a philosophy.

A positive evolution, more firms now feature pages for the industries they serve. The next step is to apply the "hub" approach, described previously, by creating spokes linking industry pages to other relevant areas of the site such as the industry's service team; industry-specific articles, tools, and resources; events geared for that sector; and credentials pertinent to those readers.

Bottom line: don't look to other accounting firms for Web site best practices. At present, there are few good role models, so it is the blind leading the blind to some degree. As General George S. Patton said, "If everyone is thinking alike, then somebody isn't thinking."

> **Key Concept**
>
> When information is delivered in an audience-centric manner, you reinforce the concept that the reader comes first.

Content Strategies

Content is defined as all the text—the words and phrases—found anywhere on a Web site. Ultimately, your firm's Web goals surrounding prospects, current clients, referral sources, and prospective employees should center largely on *meaningful* differentiation through the content. Claims of being different, specialized, trustworthy, and timely are not adequate; firms need to *show* they possess these traits.

Positioning your firm as hire- and referral-worthy is achieved best through substantiating your claims of expertise—demonstrating knowledge, capabilities, and thought-leadership with evidence. Ways to do this are to (1) share articles or whitepapers, (2) create a blog with strong content, (3) illustrate results through case studies and testimonials, and (4) list organizations or publications to which the firm has contributed to the advancement of ideas and practices or shown other significant commitment.

Before you begin to develop the rest of your content, three great favors you can do for your firm's next Web site (as well as brochures and proposals) are the following:

1. Eliminate one-size-fits-all content—information diluted to the degree that it is applicable to all, and not specific to any.

2. Omit content that is pie-in-the-sky or wishful thinking—nonbelievable content calls your otherwise accurate content into question.

3. Rid yourself of any text, especially statements or claims, also found on other CPA firm Web sites. Instead of differentiating your firm, the repetition reinforces your sameness.

How to Create Meaningful Content

Firms' service and industry pages generally feature text about the firm's services, types of organizations it serves in that area, and a bulleted list of "solutions" the firm delivers. Sometimes, on industry pages, firms describe a few key challenges faced by those within the sector.

While it's good to contain key words and phrases related to the services you deliver and solutions you apply, your content can go one better. The purpose of *meaningful* content is to satisfy, reassure, and resonate with the reader through its quality and depth, hopefully to trigger an action. Having the right information on the page accomplishes two tasks well: (1) it satisfies people you direct to your site *and* (2) draws unknown people to your site through search engines. Consider the following analogy:

> Walking through your living-room barefoot, late at night, your foot painfully greets a heavy object—uttering a few choice words, you stagger to bed. When you awaken, your big toe is swollen and badly bruised. You think it might be broken and aren't sure if you need medical care. You turn to the internet.
>
> It's important to remember that humans don't all use search engines the same way. Some would search "swollen bruised toe." Others might search "is my toe broken?" and still others may search "symptoms and treatment of a broken toe." The point is that few search "splint" or "ibuprofen" (solutions) to find the information they need. Nor would people be likely to search "kicked the coffee table in the dark" (root cause) or "turn on a light" (prevention).

FIGURE 18-1 SEARCH LOGIC

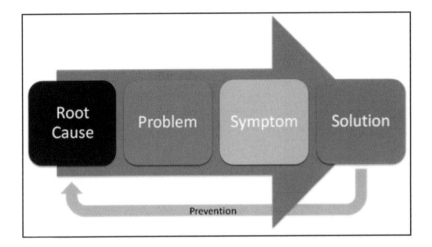

Today, as illustrated in figure 18-1, firms list solutions and sometimes discuss the root cause, but they seldom venture down the path of those middle areas—symptoms and problems—despite the fact that these are the areas with which their audiences could most identify. Though people like to self-diagnose, we don't always know what we need even as we're staring at that shelf of solutions (prescriptions). When problems are big, we rely on experts to diagnose the problem, identify the root cause, and prescribe treatment. Your content most helps readers, and simultaneously draws the most organic search traffic, when you discuss their symptoms and problems that call for the solutions you provide.

Because content is what attracts readers through search results, companies whose sites don't contain phrases to draw enough search results sometimes pay to increase their search rankings. Ironically, when visitors delivered through paid search land on sites lacking compelling content in the first place, they won't find much to compel them to buy or act. Good, strong content is the best solution.

> **Key Concept**
>
> The purpose of meaningful content is to satisfy, reassure, and resonate with the reader through its quality and depth, hopefully to trigger an action.

Identifying Your Readers' Needs and Situational Triggers

Once each persona is identified, it's time to think about their concerns, needs, symptoms, and problems (collectively called "situational triggers") that would drive them to your site. Listing these triggers is the first step in future content development. During this process, it is helpful to humanize your personas, and even to name them. For example, "nonprofit executive director, like 'Donna'" or "sixth-year prospective hire, 'like Tim.'" As you more personally visualize the person you've named, you can more fully consider his or her needs and perspective. Don't hesitate to ask your real-life Donna or Tim if your perceptions of their positions and needs are accurate.

This trigger identification process, illustrated in figure 18-2, establishes the core messaging applicable in all your marketing-related endeavors.

FIGURE 18-2 TRIGGER IDENTIFICATION PROCESS

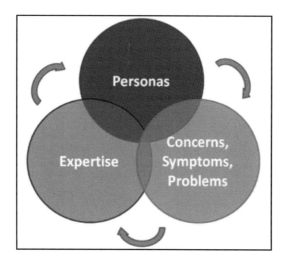

Box 18-1	Exercise A—Personas and Needs

Step 1 – List all desired target visitors.

Step 2 – Within each type, study to determine if there are subtypes. The results comprise your "personas." This is the time to personalize or name them.

Step 3 – Brainstorm to list needs, concerns, problems, or symptoms for each persona. Think through specific situational triggers that might inspire them to visit your site.

Once your firm knows its potential audiences, prioritize them for clarity when it comes to making strategic choices about which specific personas to address in your site and to what degree. You may not be able to accommodate all identified personas—this will depend on your resources and goals, which we'll discuss in the following section.

CLARIFY THE PURPOSE OF YOUR SITE

With your audiences clearly in focus, it's time to turn your attention toward your site's purpose. For each of your personas, define your goals. What do you want to accomplish related to their site viewing and actions? How will you know if your objective is met? At what point will it be appropriate to measure or judge? Within your content and visuals, how can you address each persona's triggers that you defined previously? And then how can you inspire them to take actions that will move the interaction from digital to personal.

Second to the content aspect of your goals is Web site design and features. Design and features should support the delivery and clarity of the message and make interaction easy. Do not allow these secondary considerations to distract from or dilute the content. Fancy features and superficial beauty cannot compensate for substance of message. When you have the right combination of content, design, and features, your purpose is fulfilled.

When it comes to choosing the design elements and features of your next Web site, options are limited only by imagination. Because differentiation is important, study other Web sites cautiously. Look far beyond what other professional firms do. Glean ideas from product-based sites, service-related sites, news sites, entertainment sites, and luxury lifestyle sites. Open your mind to depart from all preconceived notions of what a CPA firm site "should be."

You may already have some ideas in mind for site features and styles. Before you find yourself married to them, consider how CPA firm Web sites are currently used.

How People Use CPA Web Sites Today

If you think your Web site exists primarily for clients, think again. A lot of firms talk about investing in pricey features for a client-only portion of the Web site. Only about 1 percent of clients return to a firm's site after hiring them. When they do, it's usually to find an address or phone number.

Firms think about adding a payment feature or a document storage tool so clients can get their electronic documents without bothering the firm to send copies. These ideas are quite firm-centric.

Firms also envision putting valuable content and tools behind this client-only wall. This is exactly opposite of what your content strategy should be. Put your content and tools out front where people can see how brilliant and generous you are. Recognize that other audiences use your site a lot more than clients ever will. Clients expect you to personally impart any and all important information to them. Everyone else wants to be able to find it without, or before, having to interact with you.

Most CPA firm Web site visitors are job seekers. Second are prospective clients or referral sources—particularly looking at biographies. Least visited are firms' services pages. It's entirely probable that clients seldom visit because of a lack of updated content. If you want more traffic from current clients, first decide why (define your goal), then in accordance with your goal, create appropriate content to attract them back to your site regularly.

Usability and Navigation

Usability means the site works well for most without overly frustrating people. Don't sacrifice usability for design; usability must always trump "sizzle."

Entire books are written on this topic. Navigation should be intuitive, fast, and nearly invisible. *Don't Make Me Think! A Common Sense Approach to Web Usability*[2] is a fitting resource for partners and marketers embarking on a Web site redesign. It even includes a section called, "Help! My boss wants me to ___," wherein Krug addresses several of the types of disputes that arise between the partners, marketers, and developers. The book remains highly relevant despite being a few years old.

Flash

Until a few years ago, Flash intros were popular with site owners, but not so much for users. "Skip intro" buttons are the second most clicked on the Web (the "back" button takes first place). There's no better way to alienate visitors than by making them pause to gain access to your site. Flash animation is also a barrier-to-entry for search engines as they try to index your site's content. They cannot "see" or follow links on content that is embedded in Flash or other graphics, so deeper pages of your site cannot be indexed. This is the unfortunate state of sites where design choices rendered the site less effective at achieving the firm's marketing objectives. Flash is still a useful and interesting tool to use within a page, but don't embed content or any navigational elements within it.

Accessibility

To avail your Web site to sight-impaired visitors and other persons with special needs, build your site to meet the requirements of Section 508 of the Rehabilitation Act. According to the 2000 Census data shared by the U.S. Census Bureau, 57 percent of the 30.6 million people between the ages of 21 and 64 who are disabled are employed. While "508 compliance" is only mandatory for federal agencies, the efforts are greatly appreciated by those for whom access to much of the Internet is limited. Your programmers should know how to do this. Good usability practices not only make the experience better for site visitors, they also garner better search engine results.

Budgetary Considerations

It is wise to have a rough project budget in mind for your Web site, early-on. The main pricing elements will be: content; design; development or programming; and photography, video, or other graphical production. Project management, if your agency offers it, is usually bundled into design or development. To aid in planning, some rough market prices (as of 2010) are included.

---

[2] S. Krug, Don't Make Me Think! A Common Sense Approach to Web Usability, Second Edition. *(Berkeley, CA: New Riders Publishing, 2006).*

Content, if outsourced, can be the most expensive component of your site. Good writing is hard to find. In reading this chapter, you'll see how incredibly important it is to get it right. If writing in-house, be sure to fully appreciate the value of the hard work your team is sure to do. If outsourcing, expect to pay somewhere between $500 and $1500 per page of content. Less is more with Web site writing, so a longer page is not necessarily a better page and the shorter page content may cost you more. Brevity in messaging is an art. Consider the importance of clear, concise messaging in a 15-second advertising spot. Recall the (translated) quote by Blaise Pascal in *Lettres provincials, letter 16*, 1657: "I would have written a shorter letter, but I did not have the time."

Design is not expensive in the scheme of things. Design includes creating graphics, usually in Adobe® Photoshop®, to be used with consistency throughout the site. The firm should expect to own the rights to these files and should obtain a copy of the originals. Designers will explore ideas with the firm prior to creating compositions. A few initial concepts are created and one or two are refined before the firm makes its final decision. Design is complete at this point unless specialized graphics are required within the site. The design phase can be as quick as one to two weeks or can stretch out much longer, depending on the firm's review and approval process. Design costs tend to be directly related to the number of unique page layout "templates" needed and number or complexity of special graphics. Expect to spend $2,000 to $5,000 in design fees for an average CPA firm site.

Development typically costs more than design. Costs vary depending on whether the firm will use an off-the-shelf Web editing software or a more robust content management system (CMS). A CMS is an administrative back-end to your site which provides the nontechnical user an easy interface for making future updates. Development can start at a couple thousand dollars for a site without a CMS or can exceed $50,000 if a custom CMS is built from scratch. Some developers can tailor existing CMS programs for less, but expect to pay at least $20,000 to $30,000 if a CMS is desired. A CMS may be a worthwhile investment if your Web site will feature more than 25 professionals or if you plan to add content regularly and updates are performed by someone without adequate programming knowledge. Look for CMS pricing to come down in future years, especially as open-source options change the competitive landscape. Weigh the pros and cons of portable versus proprietary when you consider the platform your site is built upon. Expect to pay extra for programming if you want to capture any visitor data, or need features such as event registration. A number of excellent plug-ins (prebuilt tools) are available to developers that eliminate the need to reinvent the wheel, so discuss with your vendor the possibility of leveraging these wherever feasible, potentially saving the firm tens of thousands of dollars.

Imagery should include good photography. It's a sound investment when your products are your people because strong impressions are critical. If your photos are more than 3 years old, or someone would fail to recognize you in person after viewing it, invest in a retake. Budget about $100 per person, though package deals might be available. Nonexclusive stock art ranges from $10 to over $300 each, and purchasing exclusive rights to art is much more expensive. To include video on your site, prices vary from nearly free to quite high for production and editing. For a professionally produced video, estimate about $10,000 for a 3–5 minute piece. If budget is an issue, consider more casual YouTube-type videos, which even major corporations find acceptable (though don't set videos to auto-play).

Key Concept

It is wise to have a rough project budget in mind for your Web site, early-on.

Box 18-2	Exercise B—Site Brief

Before issuing a development request for proposal (RFP), convene your Web oversight committee to create a site brief. Internally, this document serves at least three purposes:

1. Internal consensus on total approach before your marketing department, designer, and developer get started

2. Iron out the approval process (tip: don't run everything through the full partner group)

3. Define all critical needs before asking anyone to price your project (otherwise proposed pricing is sure to change)

continued

| Box 18-2 | Exercise B—Site Brief *(continued)* |

Your Site Brief

Project Background & Goals

Define the Web site's objectives, success metrics, schedule requirements, internal resources, constraints, corporate identity assets, and so forth.

- Who are the decision makers and what is the approval process?
- Who, exactly, is responsible for what?
- What specific outcomes will make this project successful?
- What specific challenges do we anticipate? (For best results, include in your planning committee any partners likely to pick apart the project later)
- Will the Web site reinforce an existing branding or marketing strategy? How exactly?

Target Audience, Content, & Functionality

Define the intended target audience, products and services offered, content sources, intended update schedules/frequency, and functional requirements.

- What types of personas do you want to attract? What are their demographics, user tendencies/sophistication, and compelling content needs?
- What are your specific action goals for each persona?
- Where will content come from? Will it be new, repurposed, or both? Prepared/collected by whom?
- What types of legacy systems/databases are in place? What new ones are needed?

Development Parameters

Define all technical parameters, timing, and testing/installation responsibilities.

- Identify any graphical elements desired.
- Is there a need to collect data? Which data and how do you plan to use it? (Affects the level of sophistication needed in collecting it.)
- Will a CMS be desired for easier site management?
- Will anyone need training in order to update the site?
- Does the firm want to incorporate any social media technologies such as blogs and Twitter feeds?
- Will custom photos and graphics be a predominant design element?

Maintenance Plan

Once live, it's important to keep your site fresh. A maintenance plan is essential. Consider these items on the front end, and finalize assignments as your sitemap phase (discussion to follow) concludes and you know exactly what pages will be where.

- Who will initiate changes for each section?
- What processes are currently in place to capture needed changes?
- What processes should be developed to capture new content opportunities?
- Will changes be made "as needed" or on a schedule (for example, once per month)?
- Who will collect and submit changes to the Webmaster?
- Who will update which content? (Assign by page and include frequency.)
- Who will proof changes after they are made and final-approve?
- How frequently will the site be thoroughly reviewed for stale content and necessary updates? (Quarterly is recommended.) And who is responsible for the review?

Effectively Approach Development

Once your parameters are defined, you're ready to move toward the development phase of your Web site. To make the process smooth and efficient, you should designate a project manager whose role is to provide clear task definitions and oversee all aspects of completion.

Large design or development firms provide project managers to work with your firm's key point of contact. But CPA firms tend to be a bit fee-sensitive, so they usually select smaller design firms that are less likely to have professional project managers on staff. Smaller Web agencies are just as eager to please and can be every bit as savvy in design and programming, but they do tend to be a little less organized in the process.

If the firm is willing to pick up the project management role, great savings can be had. A cost to the firm exists in doing this—one that doesn't show on the income statement. Proceeding without a dedicated project manager almost guarantees time and cost overruns. Should you take on this role, using the processes and checklists in this chapter can spare you from some pitfalls, and keep you on track.

> ### ♟ Key Concept
>
> To make the process smooth and efficient, you should designate a project manager whose role is to provide clear task definitions and oversee all aspects of completion.

Realistic Timelines

A high risk-factor for Web site project success is adhering to the planned timeline. The project timeline outlines realistic content, design, and launch timing. Your project duration depends on the scope, but most sites can be developed in 60 to 120 days.

It's no small task keeping busy CPAs accountable for timely reviews and approvals. A good, solid project plan lets everyone know all the pieces and when they are expected. Seeing the entire plan, particularly dependent tasks, educates about impact of delays on project completion. Provide ample time padding around typical CPA deadlines.

Declining morale is another troublesome aspect of project delay. When there are significant delays, the firm and outside vendors may become disenchanted and suffer project burn-out. As enthusiasm wanes, launching with genuine excitement is more difficult. Staying on time is best for everyone.

Sitemap Diagrams

The preproduction sitemap is the complete outline of your Web site. It's where you merge your ideas and expectations with your budget. The sitemap is a very important scope-defining tool, so this is not the place to shortcut, figuring you can tweak it later. Carefully depict every page and subpage so you and the developers know exactly what is included. This attention to detail also helps everyone see which pages require content, the type of content needed, and other functionality necessary, page by page.

A good sitemap documents all navigation choices and accounts for the results when following each path. Always build your sitemap around the user experience.

Page name choices affect navigation, usability, and search engine rankings. Avoid lengthy page names, which are difficult for readers to grasp quickly. Long names also pose design challenges that may limit your firm's page layout options. In naming pages, buttons, and links, don't be vague, use jargon, or deviate from well-recognized standards like "home" and "contact." Being decisive about word usage in the sitemap phase saves money as renaming after design starts can increase project costs.

The sitemap is the site's strategic overview, driven by your goals. It, in turn, drives final project pricing. Companies that quote a development price without a final sitemap are essentially guessing and scope change is probable. If you complete your sitemap before you issue a RFP, your quotes will be much more accurate.

> **🔑 Key Concept**
>
> The preproduction sitemap is the complete outline of your Web site. It's where you merge your ideas and expectations with your budget.

Writing for the Web

Depth, originality, and usefulness of your content determine the degree to which your site attracts new business. Focus on the persona-based content strategies discussed earlier.

To create customer-centric content, take care not to begin sentences with, or overly use, "we" and "our." Repetition of the firm's name should be avoided, too. Mentioning your firm name or using the word "we" from time to time is okay, but try to mention others first, thus indicating they are your priority, not your firm. For example, say "Your needs come first" instead of "We put your needs first." A tool exists to help evaluate a site's self-centeredness. The "We We Calculator" is found at http://www.futurenowinc.com/wewe.htm.

Online writing is much different than writing for print. People simply don't read vast amounts of on-screen text. People scan Web text instead of reading it word-for-word. This is why, though the Web offers limitless "space" for content, brevity is critical. Use of visual aids like headings, subheadings, bold, bullets, and links are very effective for getting people to the meat of your message. Speaking of meat, there is no place for fluff on the Web. Fluff is jargon, buzzwords, and gobbledygook—worse than no information at all, so strike every sentence and word that isn't essential to making a strong point or how humans talk. Personality and authenticity—even in corporate writing—is the appropriate style for the Web.

Rules to live by when writing Web (and e-mail) content:

- Less is more. Be concise.
- Keep sentence structure simple and sentences short.
- Use an active voice in the present tense versus passive and past-tense (for example, "He works with Fortune 100…" instead of "He has worked with…")
- Never "borrow" words from other sites.
- Paragraphs should be between 1-3 sentences, at a maximum, for easier skimming.
- Don't let worries of vertical scrolling discourage you from breaking up text (it is no longer a *faux pas* to require some scrolling on a Web page).
- Use links to highlight and to take the user to further information.
- Link text should be more than just "click here." Anchor text (the clickable text in the link) should be descriptive.
- Use headings, subheadings, and white space—it looks better and is more user-friendly because it is easier to skim.
- Don't use all capitals in body text—it is the equivalent of a shout.
- For ease of reading, avoid italics, using them for emphasis or foreign words only.
- Left justify text. Don't center it or use full justification.
- Don't underline text unless the text is actually a link; it causes confusion.

> **🔑 Key Concept**
>
> Depth, originality, and usefulness of your content determine the degree to which your site attracts new business.

Keywords

Keywords are the terms or phrases that people enter into search engines to find information they seek. In performing exercise A, you will identify many pertinent keywords to weave into your content in order to attract the targeted personas to your site. Most search engines place heavy emphasis on the actual text of a Web page. Where possible, use these keywords in links, titles, and subtitles—the same strategies that help readability also positively affect search engine rankings.

Well-crafted and frequently updated content is the real key to building and sustaining traffic to your Web site. The search engines are designed to detect quality content, if you make sure to have that, you have optimized your Web site for search.

A professional Web copywriter will test terms for you and verify that certain word choices are better than others. You can do this, too. If you're not sure what words are key for your various personas, some experimentation is useful. These tools can help:

- Wordtracker Keyword Tool: http://freekeywords.wordtracker.com
- Google Tools: http://www.google.com/trends
- https://adwords.google.com/select/KeywordToolExternal

Search Engines

User studies show that most people don't look past the first page of returned search results, and rarely go deeper than the third page. With 10 results per page, there is a lot of competition for the first 10 spots, and a bit less for the next 20.

Search engine optimization (SEO) is a marketing strategy used to improve the position of a site when searches for certain words are performed to increase the volume and quality of Web site traffic. SEO efforts generally involve a site's coding, presentation, and structure, as well as fixing problems such as those mentioned in the content strategies section, which prevent search engines from fully indexing the site.

Webmasters aspire to understand major search-engines' ranking methodologies, but search engine developers don't release the details of their algorithms because they don't want programmers to be able to game the system. They only share loose guidelines as to what will increase or decrease rankings and they change back-end details often. One thing that remains consistent is that search engines seek to ensure users find the Web sites with the most useful content, so the typical model for algorithms gives heavy preference to sites that appear to contain a great deal of content about the searched topic.

Since the perfect SEO recipe is kept secret, Webmasters often experiment with small changes to determine what Web site elements most impact rankings. Once a particular step is confirmed to make a difference, it can be described as "white-hat" or "black-hat" SEO. White-hat strategies play by the rules of the engine algorithm and they keep the user experience as the first priority. Black-hat strategies break the rules and don't help the user.

Search engines continue to hunt for sites that employ new deceptive techniques and may decrease such sites' rankings or even remove their listings completely. Be wary if you decide to hire an outside company to perform search engine ranking improvement services. If your vendor employs unseemly tactics to increase the site rankings, your site could suffer seriously. In every case, the best SEO strategy is rich, focused, authentic content.

> **⚿ Key Concept**
>
> Search engine optimization (SEO) is a marketing strategy used to improve the position of a site when searches for certain words are performed to increase the volume and quality of Web site traffic.

Analytics and Tracking

Once your site is built, you will want some idea of how it is being used and which elements are most effective. Robust tracking software is available for purchase and most Web hosts offer pared down tracking for free. The best free tool is Google Analytics. Analytics enables you to sort and view traffic data by a number of different variables such as date range, referring Web site, entry page (a special campaign you run might bring visitors to a special page so you can track response rates). You can set up customized, automated reporting for easier monitoring of Web stats.

When you assess visits, note that hits are not sufficient as a goal for your site. You are looking for conversions or actions in the direction of conversion (for example, outreach, downloads, subscription to content, or event registration). Also monitor patterns of navigation within your site. If some pages have better action rates than others, study what's different between the pages. Just looking at hits doesn't tell you enough about what you are doing poorly or well. Developers refer to hits as "How Idiots Track Success." That's not nice, but it illustrates the relative unimportance of hits.

Launch

The launch of your Web site is exciting. The end is near! As your launch gets closer, prepare yourself to experience feelings of despair that the project will never end. This is normal. A Web site project is a sizable undertaking.

After all your hard work, reports of small bugs or typos can detract disproportionately from positive feedback. Once the technical quality is verified through testing, the site is ready for internal review including final proof-reading and acquainting team members with your new electronic presence. A fun way to accomplish these tasks quickly is to run a firm-wide contest over three or four days. Here's how:

1. Invite everyone to read the site and report any typos/issues.

2. The person who turns in the greatest number of valid corrections wins a $50 gift certificate (consider runner up prizes, too).

3. In the event several turn in the same "error," credit goes to the first person reporting it.

Postlaunch Maintenance Plan

Web sites aren't meant to remain static. To attract readers and maintain high search-engine rankings, your site needs to continually offer new content. You don't need to change or rewrite every page, or renovate pages that are working well, but the firm should select at least a few pages to revise frequently (not counting your employee listing). Some suggestions include the following:

- Incorporate blogs or blog-type content in industry, tools, and press-room sections.
- Revisit your "case studies" and "day in the life" and "events" sections at least quarterly.
- Update bios to add new experience and qualifications, memberships, and activities, at least annually.
- Ensure your Maintenance Plan (created in exercise B) is up to date and diligently followed.

Key Concept

Web sites aren't meant to remain static. To attract readers and maintain high search-engine rankings, your site needs to continually offer new content.

Get Started!

In the age of social media and digital marketing, your Web site can be the cornerstone of your effective electronic presence. It's exciting to watch your firm grow through online marketing as the business world adopts new processes to investigate and procure professional services.

When you apply these concepts, your new successful Web site will be the result of investing great-thinking in the strategy phase of your site and addressing your own personas in appropriate, relevant ways through your content. Enjoy the process and have fun—let your passion for your practice and those you serve shine through—your Web site will be exceptional as a result!

ABOUT THE AUTHOR

President of Golden Practices Inc, **Michelle Golden**, CPF, is an educator, certified professional facilitator, strategic advisor and author. Recognized as the accounting profession's thought leader in Internet and social media marketing, she teaches professionals how to have an extremely effective electronic presence, and is commissioned by the AICPA to write the social media toolkit for their PCPS members. Michelle won AAM's 2007 Marketing Achievement Award for results generated via the first multi-author CPA firm blog. Having built or directly influenced more than 1/3 of existing CPA blogs, she continues to be the catalyst behind blogging in the accounting profession. Michelle can be reached at michelle@goldenpractices.com.

CHAPTER 19
Effectively Using Direct Mail

Marsha Leest
CCH, a Wolters Kluwer business

INTRODUCTION

When the concept of accounting firm marketing first became accepted, some firms shunned the idea of direct mail marketing while others viewed it as a panacea. Large mailings of 2,000, 5,000 or even 10,000 pieces were not unusual, and a measurable response rate convinced other firms that direct mail was a good way to increase their client base. Generally, these mailings were simple business solicitations. These mass mailings faded away as the accounting industry began to rely on sophisticated marketing professionals who recognized the inherent value in targeting specific prospective clients. At the same time, the Internet's role in marketing became more prevalent as digital direct mail gained overwhelming popularity across all industries. Now, the definition of "direct mail" is much broader, and includes both traditional mail and digital direct mail delivered to desktops as well as a variety of mobile devices.

The "call me today" letters that defined early direct mail marketing efforts changed as the marketing of professional services matured and evolved. Today, direct mail has found its place as part of an overall integrated marketing approach, used to increase name recognition (also called "branding," see chapter 15, "Successfully Branding Your Firm"), improve the firm's image, and raise awareness of specific services. No longer just letters, comprehensive direct mail campaigns include newsletters, postcards, industry-related client alerts and articles, tax updates, invitations to seminars and other firm events delivered through several different methods.

Even firms that do not recognize it as such are most likely using direct mail. For example, a solo practitioner who sends out tax organizers each year, whether by snail mail or e-mail, is utilizing direct mail to reach his or her clients.

Used wisely, direct mail can help your firm accomplish a number of other things, including the following:

- Increase name recognition among potential clients and potential referral sources
- Maintain and enhance client contact in support of client retention efforts
- Support ongoing niches

Still, it is important to remember that clients need to have a serious reason—fee dispute, service issue, or personality conflict—before they will change accountants. Like most other marketing strategies employed by CPA firms, a direct mail campaign can open the door to qualified prospects, paving the way for an individual CPA, or a team of CPAs, to capture the prospect's interest and win an engagement.

WHY DIRECT MAIL SHOULD BE PART OF YOUR OVERALL MARKETING STRATEGY

Direct mail can be a very efficient method of reaching a target, especially when it is part of an integrated marketing campaign that utilizes various marketing and communication channels. You may be as brief or as expansive as you wish, and you can zero in on almost any target audience. Unlike some other marketing programs, direct mail puts you on equal footing with competitors of all sizes; each one of you has only a few seconds to convince the reader to keep reading.

One of the most important upsides to direct mail is that its shelf life is infinite. Strike a nerve in your reader and they are likely to keep the information until they need it.

As an added benefit, if you use first class postage, you will get return mail. This will allow you to update your database. The same is true with e-mail tracking tools that allow you to see which e-mails "bounced" or did not reach the intended recipient. You can follow up to see if they have a new e-mail address or have a SPAM blocker that is preventing your e-mails from getting through to them.

> **⚑ Key Concept**
>
> Direct mail can be a very efficient method of reaching a target, especially when it is part of an integrated marketing campaign that utilizes various marketing and communication channels.

THE METHOD

There are a number of direct mail vehicles to consider for your marketing mix:

- *Snail mail.* The traditional, tried and true regular mail method still is used.
- *Overnight mail.* Providers such as the U.S. Post Office, Federal Express, and United Parcel Service (UPS) promise overnight mail delivery.
- *E-mail.* When e-mail first came on the scene, it was regarded as the best direct mail delivery method ever created. There was so much e-mail marketing that software developers produced filters to weed out anything that could be viewed as spam (also called junk mail). It became such a big problem that the government got involved and enacted the CAN-SPAM Act, which sets the rules for commercial e-mail, establishes requirements for commercial messages, gives recipients the right to have you stop e-mailing them (that is, allows them to easily opt out of receiving e-mail from your firm), and spells out tough penalties for violations. Other laws may also apply, so be sure to check with legal counsel before initiation of an e-mail marketing campaign.
- *Social media channels.* Twitter, Facebook, LinkedIn, and the like have changed the way people communicate. Some may contend that contact via social media is not truly direct mail, but no one can dispute the fact that receiving a written message announcing an upcoming seminar, for instance, is a direct communication. Social media can be considered yet another tool in the direct mail arsenal.

According to the Print Council and DM-News/Piney Bowes 2008 Direct Mail Survey of more than 1,000 US consumers, age 18 and up, from 10 major metropolitan areas found that more than 8 out of 10 survey respondents (85 percent) say they review their USPS mail daily.

- Half of all respondents report greater enjoyment reviewing the mail received in their home mailbox versus e-mail. This includes consumers age 18 to 39, with 52 percent reporting greater satisfaction in reviewing mail received through the USPS compared to e-mail.
- Two-thirds of the consumers surveyed said they are examining their mail more closely for coupons and offers than they did a year ago.
- Half of all respondents say they have requested promotional materials from companies over the past six months. Direct mail is the preferred way to receive offers.

Medium	Preferred Method for Receiving Promotional Materials
Direct mail	78%
E-mail	63%
Newspaper inserts	52%
Web sites	34%

Keep in mind that there was a period where faxes were an important part of direct mail campaigns. They are rarely, if ever, used today. Things change. To get the best results from your firm's direct mail program, be sure to monitor trends and new developments and adapt your direct mail campaign accordingly so it can be as effective as possible.

> **♀ Key Concept**
>
> According to the Print Council and DM-News/Piney Bowes 2008 Direct Mail Survey of more than 1,000 US consumers, age 18 and up, from 10 major metropolitan areas found that more than 8 out of 10 survey respondents (85 percent) say they review their USPS mail daily.

DETERMINING THE GOAL OF YOUR DIRECT MAIL CAMPAIGN

Several conventional marketing caveats exists that are as applicable to a direct mail campaign as to all other aspects of your firm's marketing program:

1. Eighty percent of your business comes from 20 percent of your clients.

2. It is more cost effective to focus your efforts on selling new services to your existing clients.

3. The more personalized the mail piece the better received it is.

4. It generally takes 5 "touches" to convert a prospect into a client.

These principles should be a major consideration when taking the first and most important step in a mail campaign: determining your goal. For instance, a direct mail campaign can be used to

- enhance name recognition,
- increase visibility in the marketplace,
- touch clients and potential clients a certain number of times in a set time period using nurture or drip marketing,
- educate clients/potential clients,
- cross-sell services,
- sell specific services,
- reach potential referral sources,
- promote events,
- increase contacts and referral sources, and
- create opportunity for leads and new business

DEVELOPING THE CAMPAIGN

Once the campaign's goal is established, it is time to plan how to roll out the campaign. That means the following:

- Determining the scope of the campaign. Things to consider include
  - the source of the list/target audience;
  - the number of touches the campaign will involve; and
  - the nature of the mail pieces. For example, if it is a mailing to prospective clients in a particular niche, the campaign might include a newsletter or tax alert to acquaint the target audience with your name, a letter, and a postcard. If the campaign's goal is cross-selling services to existing clients, one letter or questionnaire may be all that is needed. These messages may be delivered using either traditional snail mail or e-mail.

- Establishing a budget. Things to consider include the following:
  - Design, writing, printing and mailing may be outsourced or done in house. Depending on whether experienced marketing staff is available, it may be more efficient to outsource all or part of the project.
  - You may mail to an existing client list or purchase or license a list. Part of the budget will need to go for cleaning/scrubbing the list. Be aware that this part of the process can be quite time-consuming.

— Snail mail or e-mail is another consideration. An ongoing debate exists over which is more effective, but there is no contest about the cost differences. E-mail is very inexpensive, but postage is a big cost, since, as a rule, first class postage should be used. Hand applied stamps are a nice touch, too. Indicia can be used for newsletters and the like. Many firms use a combination of these two delivery methods, basing their choice on what is being mailed.

Given the high cost of overnight and first-class mail, most direct mail advertisers opt for bulk rates. If you are interested in this option, contact your local post office and ask for information about the various bulk mail options available.

In most cases, using bulk postage means you need to purchase an annual bulk permit from the post office or use the permit of a local printer or mail house. Also, some presorting and classification is required. Variables include the first 3 digits of the zip codes, 9 digit zips, carrier route selections, or weight. Although you can save up to 10 cents per mailed piece, remember to factor in the labor cost associated with presorting. If you are working with a mail house, you can ask them to prepare a cost comparison for you.

First-class postage takes 1-3 days for delivery. Local third-class (bulk rate) takes 2 to 12 days, with third-class in other areas taking 5 to 30 days (12 to 20 day average). If you choose the latter option, figure the lag time into your initial production timetable, as well as into the offering itself. If you have a return envelope in the mailing, use business reply or first-class postage on the envelope.

— Promotional items/giveaways.
— Staff time for follow-ups and telemarketing costs need to be allotted.

- Determining the approval process. This may depend on the firm's culture. If all partners need to approve the mail piece, you may need to have an opt out contingency tied to a certain date. Otherwise, the entire process may be held up by a partner who does not respond by a certain date. Alternatively, responsibility for each mailing may be limited to one or two partners.

- Roll-out and follow-up. Generally, mailings to prospective clients should be rolled out in stages of no more than 100 mailers at a time. This allows personal follow up by the partner, sales professional, or a telemarketer. If telemarketers are used, they need to be coached about (1) the goal of the campaign, (2) the nature of the mailing, (3) the history of the firm, (4) brief bios of the partner(s) who sign the mail piece and (5) any freebies or giveaways being offered. Properly coordinating this type of campaign can result in a higher return rate.

Whatever the vehicle(s), keep in mind that the design of each piece should be consistent with your firm's brand.

- Deciding on the timing of the mailing. Things to consider include the following:
    — Are there any time sensitive issues that need to be considered (for example, tax filing dates)?
    — Any calendar sensitive issues (for example, holidays)?
    — Generally, mailings should be timed so the mailing does not arrive on a Monday or the day after a holiday.

- Scheduling the mailing. Things to consider include the following:
    — Start preparations at least six weeks before the mail date to allow time for writing, design, printing, and approvals.
    — Keep in mind that mailhouses and other vendors may be allotting a specific time to complete your project. If you are late, you may have to wait until a new time slot opens up.
    — Be sure to allow enough time if promotional items need to be ordered.

- Define the list. Regardless of the method used, your focus in list development should always be the quality, not the quantity of the names on that list. Keep in mind that it can be quite difficult to gather e-mail addresses. It is a good practice to include a request for an e-mail address on your firm's client intake form. (For additional information on list development, see chapter 22, "Databases That Fuel Your Marketing Efforts")
    — *In-house lists.* Clients, potential clients, referral sources, event attendees. Be sure all lists are updated and life changing events (marriages, births, deaths, etc.) are reflected.

— *Purchased lists*. Lists may be purchased or licensed from many sources, including established list brokers (for example, Dun & Bradstreet, Hoover's, magazines in specific niche areas, and membership associations. Often, purchased lists may be downloaded directly from the list broker's Web site. Lists also may be purchased or licensed on CD. *Marketplace* is an example of such a list. Whether you use an in-house list or a commercial list, there are a wide variety of selection criteria to choose from, and the process of developing these criteria can be quite involved. You may therefore wish to rely on the services of a marketing consultant or a mailing list broker to ensure your list really does contain the names of your most likely prospects. Here are two brief examples that may help you understand the importance of defining list selection criteria:

If you are planning to promote personal financial planning services, you might select a mailing list based on the following criteria:

> All heads of household…ages 45–65…with annual incomes in excess of $100,000…
> residing in zip code areas 55331, 56342, 56332.

If you plan to target large employers, you might try the following criteria:

> All corporations…with 25 or more employees….in zip code areas 55393, 55321, 55800.

— *Cleaning/scrubbing*. This can be a time consuming process, depending on the quality of the list. It is important to review the data for the following items:

  - o Client names
  - o Duplicate names
  - o Duplicate titles
  - o Similar names (that is, possible misspelled names)

— *Maintaining*. List maintenance is an ongoing process that requires cooperation from everyone who deals with clients. For e-mail messages, it is important to delete names that bounced back.
— *Aging*. Lists get old. They need to be updated regularly to reflect life changes—changes in addresses, jobs, job titles, marital status, and so on.

WHAT KIND OF RESPONSE DO YOU WISH TO ELICIT?

Before drafting the content of the direct mail piece, you need to determine what kind of response you want the mailer to elicit, such as

- do you want interested prospects to request a more detailed brochure?
- do you want them to call in and schedule a meeting?
- do you want to leave the offer open-ended and say that you will contact them?
- do you want them to click through to read more about a topic in a digital mailing such as a newsletter?
- do you want them to click through to learn about a partner who is considered an industry expert in a particular niche area?

No matter what your goal is for the mailing or the method of delivery, be prepared to handle the response. Have receptionists and secretaries standing by to take the calls, and make sure they are briefed ahead of time. If you offered to send more information, make sure the material is ready to go before the campaign is initiated. Many firms fail to give this part of the campaign adequate attention, and there is nothing more disastrous than the inability to respond quickly and professionally when you have stimulated interest in your product or service.

Now it is time to turn toward drafting the letter.

🔑 Key Concept

No matter what your goal is for the mailing or the method of delivery, be prepared to handle the response.

Guidelines for Drafting the Message

The Letter

As stated earlier, anything mailed to a client, referral source or prospect, whether using snail mail or digital delivery, may be classified as direct mail and a direct mail letter is perhaps the most difficult to craft. The most important thing to remember when writing the letter is that it should focus on the recipient's needs rather than the firm's qualities. This means the letter should touch the receiver's "hot buttons," use language that will appeal to them, and be laid out in a way that will catch their interest.

In effect, the document should be viewed as a written version of a sales presentation. As such, it must fulfill the following requirements:

- Attract the reader's (prospect's) attention. It is a good idea to use the firm's stationery. Other options include specially printed stationery for client alerts or tax alerts. Your printer can help you choose paper with the appropriate weight and texture. The important thing is raising brand awareness by carrying the firm's look across all mail pieces. If your budget allows and it suits the goal of the mailer, you may choose to use more than one color ink.
- Begin the copy with a headline. This opening sentence is extremely important. It is here that you either win or lose the reader's attention. A strong headline can increase the response rate (or the open rate for an e-mail communication). Another device that helps to increase readership is positioning a summary of the offer immediately above the salutation.

  What goes into a headline? A statement of your offer, a request that the reader respond, a statement of what the reader will receive when he or she responds, and a brief summary of the one or two key benefits provided by the product or service being offered. The headline should be able to say all this in about 20 to 30 words. Use grabber words like *How, How to, Learn, Find out, Discover, Solve* or *Solution.* Here's an example:

  > "Send for our free financial planning kit that shows how you can reduce your taxes $3,000 this year by starting your own Keogh retirement plan."

  When using a digital delivery system, the subject line acts as the headline. If the reader isn't captivated by it, there is a good chance he or she won't read the rest of the message. This highlights a major difference between print and digital copy: with print copy, the reader had the opportunity to scan the entire document; using digital copy, the reader usually sees only the subject line and a sentence or two.

  If your prospects keep reading after the headline/subject line, they are probably interested in what you have to offer. Now your challenge is to get them to act.

- Make it as personalized as possible. Address the letter to a specific individual; write the copy so that the name or the name of the recipient's company appears in the body of the text. (But be careful. If someone named Robert never goes by "Bob," be sure your communication doesn't begin with "Dear Bob.") Close with a personal signature. Remember, this letter is intended to be personal. Someone with a high rank in your firm, like the managing partner, or better yet the partner in charge of the client, should sign the letter.

  — Although the letter functions as a type of sales presentation, it should possess most of the attributes of a well-written piece of personal correspondence. The reader must feel at all times that he or she is being addressed as an individual, by an individual. For example, use "I want to tell you about our new service…" instead of "We are pleased to announce…." As you review the benefits of your offer, make sure each is backed up with substantial proof.

    Because most people will not read through the body copy from start to finish, the letter should be designed to make it easy to find the information being sought. Use short paragraphs whenever you can, and indent them for easy readability. Margins and spacing should be similar to those used in a business letter. You can use emphasis devices, such as italics or boldface, as long as you don't overdo it. Bulleted and numbered lists are other good devices for drawing attention to the important points you are making.

    What kind of response do you want to elicit? Do you want interested prospects to request a more detailed brochure, or do you want them to call in and schedule a meeting? Think carefully about the kind of action you want people to take. Emphasize the importance of responding to the offer within a given time frame. Rephrase your request that the prospect respond, usually at the end of the text, and then again in the postscript.

— Be as brief as possible and still get your message across:

o First paragraph—always a current issue of concern

o Middle paragraph—how your credentials can help

o Final paragraph—Call us or we'll call you

- Arouse interest in your offer, perhaps by including a deadline for response or a link to a form to be filled in.
- Persuade the reader that the offer is valid by reviewing features, benefits, and proof of your claims (for more information on features and benefits, see chapter 28, "Creating Proposals That Win").
- Use a postscript. This is another method of gaining the reader's attention in a print piece. It is intended as a tease to get them to keep reading. Generally, a postscript offers just enough information to make the reader to go back to the beginning of the letter and read the headline offer. Here's an example:

"We are the only firm to complete 10 such transactions in 12 months."

or

"Don't forget the special bonus you'll receive if you respond by June 8."

Keep in mind that writing for hard copy is significantly different than writing for e-mail. With hard copy, everything you want to say needs to be in front of the reader. With e-mail, the writing needs to be more headline driven, inviting readers to click through to read more about any given topic.

The Envelope

While it is a good idea to focus most of your energies on the text of the mail piece, it is also important to remember that the envelope, as well as any mailed response card, will influence the prospect's response. They are all components of the selling process:

The envelope offers a first impression of your company while the letter represents the sales presentation, that is, the message you wish to convey.

The Reply Card/Click Through Form

A reply card can be compared to a salesperson's request for an order. In an e-mail, the reader needs to click through to get to the form to be filled out. In both, be sure the form is written so that you can gather the information that is most important to you, such as an e-mail address or the reader's title.

⚷ Key Concept

Keep in mind that writing for hard copy is significantly different than writing for e-mail. With hard copy, everything you want to say needs to be in front of the reader. With e-mail, the writing needs to be more headline driven, inviting readers to click through to read more about any given topic.

⚷ Key Concept

Key elements of successful campaigns include firm buy-in, scrupulous planning, specific target audience, careful execution, consistent follow-up, and management of expectations.

Use the Clear Only If Known Principle

How do you know when your copy is ready? First, review it using the clear only if known (COIK) principle. It is imperative that the copy be intelligible to a layperson who knows nothing about the subject you are discussing.

In other words, do not overestimate the knowledge of your audience, but do not underestimate their intelligence either. As a general rule of thumb, your copy should be directed to the reading ability of an 18-year-old, and approximately 75 percent of the words should contain five letters or less. Second, hand the letter over to several other people in your firm for a thorough critique. Ask people who are not already familiar with the service you are writing about.

Social Media Copy

Writing for social media distribution is quite different than writing for hard copy or e-mail. Social media uses abbreviations that are particular to digital communications. For instance, "U r" rather than "you are." This is impacting how English is written in a number of venues, but it is not considered proper for business communications. That said, social media channels such as Twitter limit the number of characters in a correspondence (140 in the case of Twitter), and that makes using such abbreviations very tempting.

The Importance of Proofreading

Sending out a document that contains errors is the easiest way to turn potential clients away. Once we are intimately involved in the project, our brains are programmed to read what we think we see and it is very easy to miss an extra word, a wrong word, etc.

Consequently, it is important to have someone who was not involved in the writing process review the copy. Other successful proofreading methods include reading aloud, preferably to someone who is following a written copy of the document, or reading the document backwards.

Tracking Results

Since there is no expiration on the shelf life of a direct mail piece, tracking responses is an ongoing process. New clients, prospects, and those who call or e-mail with inquiries may be responding to a hard copy or digital mailer they received. One of the best ways to track this is simply to ask how the person got the name of your firm. Anyone who might answer the call, from the receptionist to a partner, should be trained to ask this question of all first time callers.

Tracking the accuracy of the mailing list is simple since first class mail sent to an incorrect address generally is returned within three weeks after it is mailed. Tracking e-mails is fairly easy as well. E-mail distribution systems such as iContact, Constant Contact, and Ennect allow users to track results on an ongoing basis. You can find out which links were clicked on most often, how many people opened the e-mail, whether the e-mail was forwarded and who opted out of receiving further communication. Your marketing director can use this information to adjust the mailings to the interests of the audience, making it as targeted as possible.

> **⚷ Key Concept**
>
> Since there is no expiration on the shelf life of a direct mail piece, tracking responses is an ongoing process.

Calculating Return on Investment

Calculating your return on investment (ROI) can be tricky because, as stated earlier, direct mail doesn't expire. If someone is interested in what you have to say, they can keep the communication forever. Nevertheless, there is a real dollar cost associated with any direct mail campaign, and it is important to know how successful your investment is. The formula presented in exhibit 19-1 provides a general measure of ROI.

It is impossible to count the number of recipients of hard mail who actually read it versus the number who simply throw it in the trash. That isn't necessarily true for e-mail. With e-mail you can track the number of recipients who open any e-mail sent in HTML format. This can be a little tricky, since it sometimes is difficult to differentiate between readers who actually opened the message and those who previewed it.

There are other things you can measure with e-mail as well. For instance, it is easy to track the number of recipients who click on a link in the e-mail and how many times the e-mail is opened or forwarded to someone

EXHIBIT 19-1
CALCULATING ROI

Input

1. Number of pieces being mailed

2. Total cost of program

   a. Stationery and printing

   b. Mailhouse/postage

   c. Cost of creating the mail piece (for example, time cost of inhouse writer, cost of outside writer, subscription to e-newsletter content)

   d. Telemarketing

3. Expected response rate (%)

4. Expected engagements

5. Average fee for each expected engagement

Results

6. Number of responders ÷ Cost of program = Cost per response

7. Number of engagements ÷ Cost of program = Cost per new client

8. Revenue from new engagements ÷ Cost of program = Cost per piece

else. Measuring the number of readers who click through to read more about a specific topic is very helpful in deciding what topics to cover in future mailings.

For more information on calculating ROI, see chapter 34, "Marketing and Sales Metrics Matter: Measuring Results, Calculating Return on Investment."

CONCLUSION

Direct mail campaigns are a relatively inexpensive way to reach a large but carefully selected audience. Best practices are to research who you are mailing to, so that your mail piece is heavily targeted to a specific audience. Examples of such audiences include companies in a certain geographic area who meet the financial criteria of your firm's ideal client, or everyone on your client list who might benefit from a new service you are offering. Once you have identified who truly is a good prospect for your firm, you can then follow up with more personal and more costly marketing tactics, including a face-to-face sales presentation.

Even if you are not selling something, consider using some of the techniques discussed in this chapter. These are great ways to strengthen the impact of all of your communications, regardless of whether you are issuing newsletters, seminar invitations, or customized year-end tax planning letters.

Planned communications and follow up are the keys to success. One excellent mailer doesn't make a good campaign. Generally, an integrated marketing campaign best practice follows a four to six week timeline between mailings. Remember, shelf life is infinite, so results can trickle in over time.

ABOUT THE AUTHOR

Marsha Leest is the editor of CCH's *CPA Practice Management Forum* and a co-author of *How to Manage Your Accounting Practice: Taking Your Firm From Chaos to Concensus* (6th edition, CCH 2009). A nationally recognized expert in the field of accounting firm marketing, she has an extensive background in accounting and law firm marketing as well as in professional publishing. Her experience as an in-house marketing director for a top 25 accounting and business consulting firm coupled with the knowledge she gained as a consultant gives her a unique perspective of the industry.

CHAPTER 20
Guidelines for Effective Brochures

Amy M. Clutter
Heard, McElroy & Vestal, LLP

INTRODUCTION

A nationwide survey of accounting marketing directors, conducted by the Association for Accounting Marketing revealed that 95 percent of them are strategically involved in the development of their firm's brochure, while 60 percent outsource this function.[1]

This suggests that brochures are a standard component of the CPA firm's marketing communications arsenal.

It's easy to understand why. Brochures can help to increase a firm's visibility and improve the public's understanding of its strengths and services. Used in conjunction with a well-thought-out marketing and business development plan, they can also help to open doors and create new selling opportunities.

In this chapter, we review how to plan, design, and produce brochures that function effectively in a variety of marketing and selling situations.

⚷ Key Concept

Brochures can help to increase a firm's visibility and improve the public's understanding of its strengths and services.

SELECTING THE TYPE OF BROCHURE

When it comes to deciding what kind of brochure you need, much depends on how you intend to use it and on whom you expect to give it to. Accounting firms tend to rely on one or more of the following types of brochure, so we discuss each of them in turn and how they can be used.

Firm Brochure

Also referred to as a *firm overview* or *capabilities statement*, a firm brochure details the firm's history, background, and credentials; reviews its services; and describes the types of clients served. Together with a customized cover letter, a firm brochure can be mailed or e-mailed to prospects that have requested information about the firm. It can be attached to a proposal document or used as a handout at seminars and trade shows. You can use a firm brochure as a background piece in a public relations program or give it to new firm members as part of their orientation package.

Service Brochure

Service brochures usually describe just one of the firm's practice areas, and in much greater detail than in the firm brochure. It is not necessary to produce service brochures for each of your firm's practice areas. Instead, consider

---

[1] Accounting Marketing/Sales Responsibility and Compensation Survey—2006 *(Kansas City, Missouri: Association for Accounting Marketing, Inc., 2006).*

developing them only for the practice areas that require an added level of marketing support or areas that you are primarily focusing on growing.

Suppose your firm has recently developed an IT consulting practice. Because it is a relatively new service, prospective—and even existing—clients may not know that much about your firm's capabilities. You may not be able to accommodate their need for information within the scope of a general firm brochure. This is an excellent situation in which to consider developing a service brochure. By producing a piece devoted exclusively to one practice area, you would be able to describe each of its service components in detail and incorporate case studies and client testimonials as needed.

Industry-Specific Brochure

Whereas service brochures profile one of the firm's practice areas, industry-specific brochures describe all, or nearly all, of the firm's services, just like the general firm brochure. However, they are geared to the interests of a particular industry, profession, or interest group.

Suppose your firm has developed a niche in serving the accounting needs of physicians and dentists. You could develop a brochure that highlights the interests and concerns of the professionals in the market segment and reviews each of the firm's services that might be of value to them.

Monograph

Monographs usually address a specific technical topic. Think of a monograph as an in-depth, feature-length article that has a long shelf life (six months to one year, minimum). Pocket tax guides, retention schedules, planning checklists are good examples that fall into this category.

How would you use monographs? Suppose you have a prospect that is especially interested in your firm's tax services. You could e-mail or mail him or her, a pocket tax guide along with a firm brochure. You can also use them to convince existing clients to try additional services. For example, if a client requests information about applicable business deductions in the current year, you could combine a telephone call or letter with sending him or her a copy of your monograph on the subject. That way, the client receives a timely and personalized response, along with a lasting reminder of your responsiveness and expertise.

Whether your firm chooses to develop one, two, or all of these types of brochures, make sure all firm literature, including brochures, flyers, monographs, and newsletters have the same look and feel. Your brochure materials do not have to be identical, but they ought to carry forward the same basic color and design schemes, so they can be recognized, at a glance, as coming from your firm. By embracing this philosophy, you begin to achieve an identity for your firm, also known as a brand, and it becomes possible to use a variety of pieces together and have them still be visually appealing.

E-brochure

The electronic brochure (e-brochure) is now a popular approach to marketing a product or service. The benefits of an e-brochure can be appealing to many, especially when cost is a factor. Benefits include the following:

- Saves time and money. Saves on production, printing, and distribution costs associated with traditional print documents; changes can be made without major print rerun costs
- Easy distribution. Can be distributed via CDs, DVDs, or downloaded from Web sites; can be linked to Web site pages, e-mail addresses, and all contact details can be listed; Recipients can pass it on easily to friends of the firm and associates
- More dynamic than print. Can integrate animated and Flash graphics to make more interesting pages.

MANAGING THE PLANNING PROCESS

In an ideal world, you could help ensure everyone's satisfaction with the final product by soliciting his or her input and suggestions throughout the brochure development process. While it is an excellent idea to keep all partners well informed on the project's objectives, costs, and progress, you would have very slow going if every partner's approval was required at each turning point of the project.

Instead, consider establishing a representative brochure committee and making it responsible for the product from start to finish. The committee's members should be chosen by the partner group, and then entrusted with making the majority of the planning decisions involved. A committee leader should be designated to guide the group's efforts, and act as liaison with the managing partner or the partner in charge of marketing. The most likely candidate for this role is the marketing director or coordinator. This person should be responsible for moving the planning and development process forward as quickly as possible and should report only significant planning decisions to the partner group. The committee head should also be in charge of developing the project budget and managing costs.

DEVELOPING GOALS AND OBJECTIVES

When you develop a brochure, it is not enough to know what you want to say. You must also think about what your *target audience* wants to hear. Getting a brochure to the right people is one thing. Getting those people to open the brochure, read it, and act on it is quite another.

Begin the planning process by answering the following questions:

- How will this brochure be used? Will it be sent to prospects, employed in direct mail campaigns, used in proposals? Will it be something you leave behind after meeting with a prospect? Will an electronic copy be posted on the firm's Web site? Will it be e-mailed to potential clients or referral sources?

  Tip. Develop a complete list of the ways you want to use this brochure and then prioritize it. It may not be possible to shape the brochure for all desired purposes, so at least make sure it can be employed in the ways that are most important to your firm.

- What kinds of people will be reading this brochure? What are they like? What are their tastes and preferences?

  Tip. Even if the piece you are developing is a general firm brochure, you should be able to identify some common characteristics in your client base. You may need to do some research, but given the amount of money you will invest in the brochure, it is well worth the effort. Bring clients or prospects together into focus groups (these are discussed in detail in chapter 35, "Gaining Client Feedback to Strengthen Your Practice,") or hold one-on-one interviews. Learn about their needs and concerns, what they value most in your firm, and try to discover their aesthetic preferences. For instance, if your target market is made up mostly of individuals who are baby-boomers, and are concerned about retirement issues, the brochure's imagery should reflect that fact.

- What does your target audience need to know about the firm?

  Tip. Again, through focus groups and interviews, you should be able to identify one of several specific benefits that your target market is looking for in an accounting firm. When you begin work on the brochure, you should then find ways to demonstrate how and why they will receive those benefits as a result of choosing your firm. What differentiates you from your competitor(s)? Use your brochure to set yourself apart.

- What do you want readers to think, and do, after they have read the brochure? For instance, do you want them to call in for an appointment, or request more information on specific service areas?

  Tip. While getting a prospect to come in for a face-to-face meeting tends to be the highest priority, there may be instances where you would want to email or send an initial low-cost brochure designed to weed out unlikely prospects, followed by a lengthy and more expensive brochure that really explains your service or product. In this case, you should be planning both the introductory and follow-up brochures concurrently. If, instead, you do want to solicit a request for an appointment, make sure your firm is equipped to handle the response promptly and efficiently.

♦ Key Concept

When you develop a brochure, it is not enough to know what you want to say. You must also think about what your target audience wants to hear.

WORKING WITH OUTSIDE WRITERS AND ARTISTS

Searching For and Qualifying Specialists

When it comes to writing copy for the brochure, some CPAs may be tempted to go it alone, believing they know their company and services best. While it is true that no one understands accounting services better than technical familiarity. It requires the ability to translate and then communicate key concepts and benefits in ways that are interesting to nonaccountants and those unfamiliar with your firm.

A good brochure also contains strong graphic elements associated with your firm's brand—a judicious and carefully planned use of color, photos, illustrations, and layout—that convey a message in their own right. The text and design have to work with respect to utilizing your firm. It takes a natural creativity and years of experience working with words and images to accomplish these kinds of outcomes, so it is usually best to go with the pros.

How do you find the best writer and graphic artist for your project? It may take a little time, but the results will be worth the effort. Good freelance writers and graphic artists are out there, if you know where to look. Start by asking clients for references, or talking with attorneys or bankers whose brochures and marketing communications programs you admire. If there is an advertising organization or marketing group in your area, they may be able to refer you to members who specialize in marketing collateral for professional service firms.

Once you have located some interesting candidates, schedule face-to-face interviews. Ask to see samples of their work and find out how the idea for each piece originated. Most artists and writers have a certain style that carries into everything they do. Ask yourself if the style meshes with the image you want to convey. Also, find out if they have any experience working with accounting firms or other professional services. This can be an advantage, as they will already know a little about what you will be trying to get across to readers. Finally, consider how well you get along with the candidate. You have to work together quite closely, so it is imperative you can communicate clearly and comfortably.

Useful Tips for Working with Freelance Professionals

Graphic Artist

Let your graphic artist know up front what kinds of images and ideas you want to put across. For instance, do you want the brochure to convey the image of a young and rapidly growing organization, or one that has been around for 50 years and is serious and reliable? If you are having trouble telling the graphic artist how you want the brochure to look, show him or her some samples of brochures—preferably from other professional service firms—that have impressed you in the past. Always ask for at least two, preferably three, proposed designs. If you aren't impressed with any of them, say so. It's too expensive to change your mind later on. Remember that your firm is unique, so your brochure doesn't need to—indeed, shouldn't—conform to some standard for the accounting industry. Dare to be different.

Professional Writer

When using a professional writer, there is an almost irresistible urge to micromanage their work and edit every line of prose. Obviously, it is your brochure, and your name is going on the cover. But try to avoid unnecessary editing, that is, making changes only for the sake of change and not because the change will actually improve the copy's quality.

Marketing Consulting Firm

If you would rather not search for artists and writers, another approach is to retain a marketing consulting firm. One advantage of working with such an organization is that you can get all of the outside services you need from one provider. Most of these consulting firms can handle copywriting, brochure design, and printing. While this approach represents one-stop shopping for all the specialists you need, you should, nevertheless, carry out some form of appraisal of the style and skills of the writers and artists who will be assigned to your account.

Once you have hired an outside writer and graphic artist (or have retained a consulting firm), take the time to convey the firm's general marketing and communications objectives, along with your goals for the brochure project. All outside specialists should be supplied with detailed information about the firm, along with copies of current brochures, newsletters, and, if possible, sample proposals and engagement letters.

The Cost of Hiring Specialists

If you do use outside specialists, what will it cost? Nearly all writers, graphic artists, and consulting firms bill for time and expense—just like accountants. Most will be happy to prepare a detailed project estimate. In general, the more precise you can be about your requirements, the easier it will be for them to give you an accurate quote.

A writer's estimate will probably include references to time spent in planning meetings with your firm, research and interviews, copywriting, editing, and final revisions. The estimate should also include billing terms and a general timetable for completing the project.

A graphic artist's estimate is likely to be much more detailed, as more types of expenses must be included in the proposal. The estimate might include references to time spent in design and production, as well as out-of-pocket expenses, including typesetting charges, stock photo charges, and use of subcontractors for illustrations or custom photos, and mechanicals.

Hourly billing rates vary. A writer or graphic artist who is just starting out may bill anywhere from $40 to $60 per hour or more, while a professional with very strong credentials and an impressive portfolio might bill at between $80 and $100 or more per hour, depending on the kind of work being performed and the geographic location. While it is generally true that you get what you pay for, don't assume an extremely high billing rate assures the right brochure for your firm. As suggested earlier, it is far more important that you like what that specialist does for you and the two of you can work together well.

DESIGN CONSIDERATIONS

While it is recommended that brochure design be entrusted to a professional graphic artist, it is still important that you understand what the design should ultimately accomplish. First and foremost, you want to get prospects interested in your business. This process of engagement has to begin when someone first glances at your brochure. The brochure's cover, even the way your firm name is displayed, should be attractive and intriguing enough to compel the viewer to turn the page and begin reading.

Think of the brochure as an invitation, not a catalog of firm services, a user's manual, or a handbook. While it's tempting to provide prospects with a lot of information about your firm, if you tell them too much, they will have no incentive to meet with one of your professionals. Going back to the invitation analogy, your goal is to convey just enough information about the firm that the prospect is impressed with the firm's capabilities, but must also know more before he or she can make a purchasing decision.

In essence, your goal should be to elicit a dialogue, rather than to answer every unspoken question a prospect might have about the firm. With words and images, you want to say enough, but just enough, to interest the reader in making some kind of contact with your firm. Finally, you want readers to feel good enough, and well informed enough, about the firm to call for an appointment, but not so well informed that they only need to ask you, "How much?"

> ⚷ **Key Concept**
>
> The process of engagement begins when someone first glances at your brochure.

WRITING THE TEXT

As was the case with brochure design, it pays to be an informed consumer. The list in exhibit 20-1 should help ensure that your brochure contains good copy.

EXHIBIT 20-1
THE HALLMARKS OF GREAT BROCHURE COPY

1. *Use complete sentences.* Don't fall into the advertising lingo trap of using phrases and sentence fragments instead of complete, coherent sentences.

2. *Less is more.* Be brief and to the point. Simple and straightforward.

3. *Beware of technical jargon.* There is an overwhelming urge to show off technical ability by using technical language. Avoid this trap by keeping the reader in mind at all times.

4. *Write the way you talk.* Pretend you are writing a speech that you will use before a live audience. Writing for the ear is an old radio secret that makes for great copy.

5. *Vary sentence length.* Your opening lines should be short. Make the next sentence a little longer, but don't forget to vary the length of the next sentence after that.

6. *Use callouts.* Callouts are highlighted quotes from your main text. They are great to look at and help to catch the reader's attention.

7. *You can quote them on that.* Potential clients enjoy reading what current clients have to say about your firm.

8. *Break it up.* Paragraphs of text can be boring. Use quotes, lists, bullets, and callouts to make your prose easier to read and understand.

9. *Be fresh.* Even when you're writing about something you love—like the firm—writing can become a chore. Tackle the job when you're fresh and full of ideas, usually first thing in the morning.

10. *Don't be afraid to ask for help.* If you are unsure about the quality and clarity of some prose, ask others to review it. Your peers can review the text for accuracy and completeness, and a few carefully chosen clientscan help you clarify features and benefits.

WORKING WITH PRINTERS

To find a qualified printer, follow the same guidelines outlined for locating writers and graphic artists. Ask people you know and trust if they can refer a company they have used before. Examine the brochures of local law firms, banks, insurance companies, and even other CPA firms. If you find something you like, try to learn more about the printer who did the work. Always ask these printers for references, and then call and ask about the printer's service and timeliness, and whether or not the project came in within budget.

Your writer or graphic artist may also be able to refer printers to you.

It may be tempting to rely on a client who is in the printing business, but you should only do this if your client is truly the best qualified to do the job, and you can maintain an arms-length relationship with him or her throughout the lifetime of the brochure project.

Once you have narrowed the field of printers down to three or four, ask them to submit cost estimates. Don't just look at the bottom line: One printer's final fee may include far more features and service components than another's. Take the time, and ask the questions, that will enable you to judge the quality and scope of the printers' service. Learn about the printers' scheduling practices, and ask for deadlines for delivering specific segments of the project, such as layouts, proofs, and the final product. Find out whether or not there will be an extra charge for delivery. Finally make sure the printer has arranged for you to deal with one key representative through the production process.

Putting a Project Out to Bid

Before you can put a project out to bid, you must develop a detailed description of how you want the brochure to look when it is printed. This description is usually ref rred to in the industry as a specifications sheet (or request for quotation [RFQ]). Many printers have their own version of this form, and the one shown in exhibit 20-2 is merely an example.

To fill out an RFQ, you should familiarize yourself with some printing industry jargon. We have provided definitions of the terms employed in the sample RFQ, and you can always ask your printer or graphic artist for help in understanding and in filling it out. Sometimes a tour of a printer's shop, which includes a discussion of the work that would be performed on your behalf, can help you get a feeling for why certain processes cost what they do.

While preparing an RFQ may take some time, there are several important benefits to be derived. First, a comprehensive RFQ is also a detailed project description. Getting it all down on one or two pieces of paper may help you evaluate the quality of the decisions you are making. Second, an accurate RFQ will improve your chances for receiving accurate printers' estimates. You will also be able to make detailed comparisons of competing printers' bids. A detailed RFQ also enables the printer to do a better job of identifying costs and spotting issues that might lead to cost overruns later on. Finally, a well-prepared RFQ assures the printer you are an informed consumer and recognize and expect quality in the work he or she provides.

EXHIBIT 20-2
REQUEST FOR QUOTATION[2]

Item: _____   Date: _____

Contact: _____   Date quote needed: _____

Business name: _____   Date job to printer: _____

Address: _____   Date job needed: _____

Phone: _____   E-Mail: _____

Please give: _____ firm quote _____ rough estimate

_____ verbally _____ in writing

Quantity: 1) _____ 2) _____ 3) _____

Size: flat trim size _____X_____ folded/bound size _____X_____

Pages: # of pages _____ _____ self-cover _____ plus cover

Design features: bleeds _____ screen tints: # _____ reverses: # _____ edges: # _____

_____ comp enclosed

continued

[2] *Eric Kenley, Mark Beach,* Getting it Printed: How to Work With Printers and Graphic Arts Services to Assure Quality, Stay on Schedule, and Control Costs, *(Cincinatti, OH: North Light Books, 2004).*

Exhibit 20-2
Request for Quotation (*continued*)

Art:

_____ printer to typeset (manuscript and rough layout attached)

_____ complete electronic art provided _____ program & version

Mechanicals—color breaks: _____shown

Halftones: _____ halftones #: _____/_____ duotones #: _____

Proofs:_____ page_____

composite color_____

_____ b&w _____ color laser _____matchprint_____

_____ Press Proof Requested

Paper:	Weight	Name	Color	Finish	Grade
Inside:	_____	_____	_____	_____	_____
Cover:	_____	_____	_____	_____	_____

Ink:
Inside: _____Cover: _____

Binding: _____

Packing/Shipping: _____

Filling Out a RFQ: Glossary of Terms and Advice on Making Selections

Item. Here you should indicate your firm's description of the project, such as general brochure, computer consulting brochure, or retirement planning monograph.

Contact. This is the name of the person at your firm who has primary responsibility for working with the printer.

Business name/address/phone/e-mail. This is more information about your firm. The telephone number should be that of the contact person.

Dates. "Date" refers to the date you are submitting the RFQ. "Date quote needed" refers to the date the printer must submit a final quote. "Date job to printer" refers to the day you will be able to deliver all artwork and instructions to the printer. "Date job needed" refers to the date the finished product must be delivered to your office. "Date job needed" can also be referred to as "turn time."

Unless you are working under a "drop dead" deadline, it's best to negotiate the last two dates with the printer. Otherwise, you run the risk that the printer will either charge you more for a rush order or will work quickly to meet the deadline and cut corners—perhaps sacrificing quality—in order to accommodate your deadline.

"Please Give." A "firm quote" is the printer's commitment to a price on the project as it is described in this RFQ. However, it is not unusual for the job's specifications to change once or twice over the life of the project, so be sure to find out how those changes will affect the bottom line.

A "rough estimate" is just like it sounds. If you are contemplating a project and are still at the stage where you are comparing several alternative approaches, this type of RFQ is much more fair to your printer, because he or she will not have to spend as much time coming up with an accurate estimate.

Always ask for the estimate, especially a "firm quote" estimate, in writing.

Quantity. Quantity refers to the number of brochures you want printed. The first quantity number you give should represent your ideal quantity, with second and third volumes requested in order to determine whether or not there is a price break worth taking. In fairness to the printer, the print quantities you put down should represent numbers you are seriously contemplating.

Ordering the right number can be a challenge. The last thing you want to do is run out of an important marketing brochure just when you need it most. On the other hand, you don't want to find out it is outdated while you still have 5,000 copies sitting in a storeroom. As you consider how many copies to order, try to envision how, and through what channels, the brochure will be distributed. For instance, you should include any upcoming direct mail campaigns, seminars, conferences, and trade shows in which the brochure would be used. Also think about whether the brochure will be used in proposals and prospect meetings. Print enough copies to last two years.

Size. Size refers to the dimensions of the brochure, such as 8 ½ x 11 inches, when it is folded and finished. A project consisting of a single flat sheet should be described by its trim size, such as 8 ½ x 11inch flier. Items such as brochures should be described by the dimensions of their pages after being bound and trimmed.

When it comes to choosing the size of a brochure, make sure it is one that will be easy to handle, display, and fit into envelopes you already have in stock or can order for a reasonable amount of money. Always find out what the postage will be before committing yourself.

Pages. This refers to the number of pages in the finished brochure. It almost always includes the cover. "Self-cover" means that the cover consists of the same paper as the inside pages. If the cover paper is different from paper inside, the product is said to be "plus cover."

As a rule, brochures should not exceed eight pages, including the cover. You should be able to tell your story within this limitation. If you have more to say, you may want to consider breaking the information down into separate components, and developing two or more brochures.

Design Features. This is your opportunity to indicate whether there will be bleeds, screen tints, and reverses, as well as how many. It is a good idea to enclose a sketch whenever any of these features are included in the brochure.

"Bleeds" refer to areas in the brochure where printing extends to the edge of the page after it has been trimmed.

A "screen" is an area where the ink is applied at less than 100 percent density. Screens are often placed behind or underneath text in order to highlight it, or make it stand apart from other text printed on the same page. They can also be used to make the brochure look like more colors were used, because a 60 percent screen of a given color can look quite different from 100 percent screen or a 12 percent screen.

A "reverse" is an area in the brochure where the type is white (that is, no ink is applied), and the area immediately surrounding it appears in black or some other color. In other words, ink is applied around the text.

Art. Here is your chance to tell the printer about the condition of the materials you will provide. Options include the following:

- "Printer to typeset": You are instructing the printer to arrange for the copy to be typeset, and to finalize all art features
- "Complete electronic art provided": Artwork can be sent in electronic format such as TIFF, JPEG, or PDF. The printer will need to know what program and version were used to create the piece.

Most jobs are delivered as prepared for the printer to typeset.

Mechanicals—color breaks. This feature applies only to multicolor printing. Your graphic artist should be handling this detail.

Halftones. When prepared for printing in a brochure, photographs can be reproduced as halftones. Halftones are used in black and white photos and the printer usually charges by the number needed, regardless of size. Therefore, it is only necessary to indicate the number of black and white photos that will appear in the brochure.

If you decide to use photos in the brochure, choose action shots that illustrate an active firm, on the move and growing. Avoid head and shoulder shots; they're boring. Don't be afraid to take photos out of your office. Consider shooting some of them in clients' offices. Avoid using photos that are already a year or two old, as they may become obsolete quickly.

Proofs. It is recommended that you request any kind of proof appropriate to the job. Again, consult with your graphic artist about what your particular project requires.

Press Proof Requested. When primarily checking color, you can request to see a proof straight off the press. There is usually an additional charge for this.

Paper. To specify a paper, it is usually a good idea to indicate its weight, name, color, finish, and grade, as in "80# supercoat white gloss cover." The feel of a brochure is as important as its overall appearance and content, so it pays to be tactile in your approach to selecting paper stock for the text and cover. Choose a paper that reflects the image you want to project. For instance, while glossy color brochures speak of a firm's success, rich linen stocks exude traditional values and qualities. Both messages are positive, so just be sure you know what message you are sending.

Cover stock should be substantial enough to convey a feeling of quality. The weight, feel, and texture of the paper are as important as its color.

When it is time to make a selection, ask for a full page of the stock—enough to get a feeling for it. Don't try to make a judgment based on a clipped corner of a sample booklet page.

A good printer will help you to shop around for a well-priced paper. He or she should also tell you how much waste to expect because papers run in different sizes, and the way the brochure is printed can influence how much paper is cut and thrown away.

Try to select a paper stock that is fairly widely used, so you can be assured it will still be around in a year or two, when you order reprints. Ask the printer to order extra stock, in case there are any problems during the printing run.

Ink. When you identify the colors you want used, you should always indicate a name and number from a color matching system, such as Pantone Matching System (PMS), a check standard trademark for color reproduction and color reproduction materials owned by Pantone, Inc. By utilizing a color-coding system, you can ensure that your printer will deliver a finished product using precisely the colors you had intended.

When you specify the ink color, you will also need to indicate whether or not there will be any varnish, whether it should be gloss or dull, and whether it will be flood or spot coverage. You must also give the printer a rough idea of ink and varnish coverage expected on the press sheet. Moderate coverage would be inking on 25 percent to 65 percent of the sheet.

Remember that the colors can appear to change when applied to different kinds of paper. In some instances, the ink will be absorbed into the paper; in other cases, it will rest on top, forming a smooth and complete coat. Consult with your printer or graphic artist on whether the paper and inks you have chosen may interact in ways you are not expecting. You can also ask for a drawdown, which means you want to see the ink applied to the actual paper that has been specified for your project.

A brochure that only uses two colors (in addition to black) can look like it has more if you employ a technique called highlighting that is achieved by printing text in black, with bullets and chapter heads in one of the other colors used. Screened intensities can also make the brochure appear to have more colors than the two or three you are actually using.

Avoid high contrast between the color of the ink and the color of the paper, especially when it is light copy on a dark background. Black ink on glossy white paper might be attention getting, but is hard on the eyes. Also, choose ink colors that won't go out of date in six months. Traditional grays, blues, and dark greens will outlast the mauves, roses, and teals. Finally, check that the colors chosen for this brochure will coordinate with any other firm materials already in place.

Binding. Bindery refers to how the brochure is going to be folded and then stitched or stapled, usually at the spine of the piece (like a book).

Packing/Shipping. This refers to how you want the brochure shipped, how many brochures per carton, and so on. Since having the boxes of brochures shrink-wrapped can help protect the brochures while they are in transit, you may want to ask for this option.

One last note: before authorizing the print job itself, find out who will be liable if the final product is unsatisfactory. If the graphic artist has been responsible for selecting the printer and developing the specifications, he or she may be accountable if something goes wrong. However, this is not always the case. Whether you have chosen to work directly with the printer, or through a graphic artist, it is a good idea to get things in writing before the project goes to press.

DEVELOPING A BUDGET

It is difficult to offer clear guidelines on how much a specific brochure should cost, since there are so many variables to consider. Adding photos, or increasing the brochure's length, page size, or printing volume will cause prices to increase. So do your homework.

It's not uncommon for the larger national and international accounting firms to spend over $100,000 on a complete collateral package, including brochure, one-page biographies of key partners, service and industry brochures, and a pocket folder to hold them all. On the other hand, a tri-fold flyer detailing the firm's services can be designed and printed for as little as $200—depending on paper stock and quantity.

TIMETABLE

Rome wasn't built in a day, and your brochure won't be produced in a week. Expect an eight-page brochure to take four to six weeks and a simple flyer or services brochure to take about 8-10 working days. With new digital printing capabilities, it is possible to get materials printed in a shorter amount of time. It is important to note that digital printing may not produce the same quality as traditional printing methods. Your graphic advisors will be able to discuss available options to help you make the best decision. It is important to consult with your graphic artist, writer, and printer at each phase of the project to ensure the piece is moving along as scheduled.

CONCLUSION

By defining your marketing and communications objectives at the outset and by being a savvy consumer, you can assure your firm will get its money's worth from a brochure. But always remember to be realistic about how the brochure will contribute to the firm's marketing efforts. A brochure can be a valuable tool to reinforce a firm's image, to introduce a firm service, or to simply serve as an awareness piece. It is up to you, however, to close the sale.

RECOMMENDED READING

Beckwith, Harry. *The Invisible Touch: The Four Keys to Modern Marketing. (New York, NY: Business Plus, 2009).* Finke, Gail. Creative Edge: Brochures. (Cincinnati, OH: North Light Books, 2000).

Kenley, Eric, Mark Beach. *Getting it Printed: How to Work With Printers and Graphic Arts Services to Assure Quality, Stay on Schedule, and Control Costs. (Cincinatti, OH: North Light Books, 2004).*

Sullivan, Jenny. Brochures: Making A Strong Impression: 85 Strategies For Message-driven Design. (Rockport Publishers, 2007).

The Accounting Firm Brochure: A Primer. (Albany, NY: NEWKIRK Products, Inc., 1989).

The Best of Brochure Design 8. (Rockport Publishers, 2006).

ABOUT THE AUTHOR

A member of Heard, McElroy & Vestal, LLP's marketing department, **Amy Clutter** is hands on in all areas, including business development, public relations, and the overall marketing piece. She thoroughly loves the diversity of her role, and loves watching her peers get excited about what marketing can do and be for the firm as a whole.

Chapter 21
Newsletters That Get Noticed

Sally Glick
Sobel & Co., LLC

Introduction

If you're like most people, you receive one or two newsletters in some format every day—from civic organizations, trade and professional associations, your employer, and every type of business including banks, brokerage houses, and the boutique down the street.

Many of these publications get dumped in the wastebasket unread or are quickly deleted from your inbox. Why? Because people simply lack the time to read everything that crosses their desks or appears in the morning e-mail, even if it provides important information.

Yet newsletters can be one of the most useful marketing tools a CPA can employ. They provide a means to establish an accountant's credentials or reinforce his or her credibility as an authority with specialized knowledge. Newsletters are also an economical and effective method of strengthening the CPA-client relationship, eliciting extra business from existing clients, and introducing the firm to prospective ones.

But all of these benefits occur only *if a* publication is well written, well read, and distributed to the appropriate audience. Whether printed on paper or sent via e-mail, each publication only gets a few seconds to prove its worth to the reader before he or she decides to read it or discard it. The sooner valuable information is introduced, the more likely it is that the reader will spend the time to read further.

The ideal newsletter features a crisp style, simple format, and accurate "insider" content. Instead of repeating generic information that is easily accessible elsewhere, its articles explore information from a unique perspective, offer judicious advice, and reference key resources for business owners and their advisors. Most importantly, they convey relevant and timely information firms believe to be critical to their readers' personal and financial well-being.

E-mail and print newsletters can play an active role in your business development strategies. In this chapter, we will discuss how you can create a powerful newsletter, or just improve on an existing one. All of the following steps are appropriate for both printed and electronic newsletters.

> ### ♀ Key Concept
>
> The ideal newsletter features a crisp style, simple format, and accurate "insider" content.

Step 1: Define Your Goals and Objectives

To begin the goal-setting process, ask yourself what results you expect to get from the publication. Write a short description or mission statement for the newsletter, and then follow through with a list of objectives. Some examples follow below.

Most CPA newsletters are geared toward the interest of the firm's corporate clients, their senior managers and advisors. They usually contain articles covering tax and accounting issues and general business information as well as details on specific industry trends and challenges, as we will discuss below. Important clients are often profiled and firm developments featured, such as a new partner or service. These general newsletters are an excellent way to cross-sell services.

When sending any newsletter today, however, it is important to be sensitive to the IRS ruling 7216 which prohibits the sending of any marketing materials, including newsletters, to a firm's tax-only clients. If you are performing other services, you can mail or e-mail newsletters as you always have, but if you only perform tax related services, the information you send must be restricted to tax items only. For anything else, you must obtain the written permission of your tax client. This is a confusing area and much has been written on it already. Additional information is available through the Association for Accounting Marketing and the AICPA.

A significant number of CPA firms also publish newsletters targeted to clients and prospects in a particular industry such as health care, nonprofits, manufacturing, real estate, or hospitality. The more targeted the newsletter's information, the more likely it is to be valuable—and thus more likely to be read. Less frequently, a publication may be directed toward a particular service niche like mergers and acquisitions, valuations, estate planning, fraud and forensics, or bankruptcy.

While considering goals and objectives for your newsletter, remember to consult the managing partner or local office partner-in-charge throughout the planning process. The support of the firm's management is vital to a new newsletter project's success.

Sample mission statements are as follows:

> The XYZ newsletter will communicate financial and business information to clients, prospects, and other business leaders or influencers, designed to stimulate interest in our firm and its services.
>
> or
>
> The XYZ newsletter will communicate relevant accounting, business, and legal information to clients and prospects of the firm's litigation practice designed to stimulate awareness of, and interest in, our firm's capabilities in this area.

Sample objectives include the following:

- Keep the firm's name before clients
- Draw readers to the firm's Web site and blogs
- Acquaint readers with the company's services and facilitate cross-selling
- Motivate readers to hire the firm
- Present the firm's employees in a positive light
- Publicize important due dates
- Keep readers informed of recent developments affecting them
- Address specific problems of reader concern

Do not overload the newsletter with too many objectives—three to five is sufficient. And be realistic about marketing outcomes; rare indeed is the newsletter that can bring in new clients all by itself. Instead, your newsletters are one component of an integrated mix of tactics, all designed to build your brand and make a connection for your firm in the marketplace it serves. At best, you will stimulate interest in the ideas you are presenting and motivate readers to call your firm for more information. It will be up to your firm's receptionist and professional staff respectively to direct that call and convert it into a business opportunity for the firm.

Key Concept

It is important to be sensitive to the IRS ruling 7216 which prohibits the sending of any marketing materials, including newsletters, to a firm's tax-only clients. If you are performing other services, you can mail or e-mail newsletters as you always have, but if you only perform tax related services, the information you send must be restricted to tax items only.

⚷ Key Concept

Your newsletters are one component of an integrated mix of tactics, all designed to build your brand and make a connection for your firm in the marketplace it serves.

STEP 2: IDENTIFY YOUR AUDIENCE

Although this step may seem obvious or simple, identifying your newsletter's audience is a very important step. Clients, prospects, members of the local or trade media and centers of influence, of course, are the intended readers. But only by taking a closer look at those clients can you know what topics interest them.

Is the newsletter to be sent to lawyers or cement manufacturers, entrepreneurs or CFOs, small business owners or CEOs? Create a brief profile of your typical client or prospect and describe his or her interests and problems. If client records are computerized, you can classify targeted readers by the size of their business and by SIC code. Perhaps you will find that the bulk of your client base is made up of manufacturers, retailers, construction contractors, and auto dealerships. In that case, an article about IRS audits of not-for-profit organizations may not be of much use, while a story about independent contractors could be very timely.

With specialty publications, it is doubly important to understand who your readers are and what they want to know. Nothing is worse than discussing a topic that was hot six months ago, or one that has little relevance to the individuals targeted by the newsletter. A group of industry advisers (clients, naturally) can act as an informal editorial board for you to help you identify current topics and emerging trends in their field. Consider the following tips as you define the audience of your niche newsletter:

- Keep content very targeted to the needs of industry
- Send to other influencers in the industry
- Use membership lists from industry trade associations
- Send to trade association executives

STEP 3: DECIDE WHETHER TO PRODUCE OR PURCHASE

While the majority of this chapter addresses how to produce your own newsletter, buying a commercial newsletter that is researched, written, and published by outside vendors is a very popular alternative approach, especially for a CPA firm with limited personnel resources. These publications are usually custom imprinted with your firm's logo or artwork so they appear to be produced in-house.

You can typically buy the exclusive rights to the newsletter for a particular geographic territory for a set number of issues. This is an important consideration, as you would not want your clients to receive the identical publication from a rival firm!

There are a number of sources for purchasing newsletters, including the AICPA, PDI Global, and BizActions, but there are many more wonderful sources for you to explore if this alternative is best for your firm.

To ensure that the newsletter reflects your firm's personality, you may want to consider making further modifications. For example, you could enclose a laser-printed supplement, customize one article in each issue, or purchase the right to reprint the articles in your firm's existing newsletter format.

Clearly, the advantage of utilizing a newsletter service is that the time required to plan, write, and produce the firm's newsletter can be kept to a minimum. On the other hand, your firm will have probably little or no control over the editorial content of the publication, and you may find the newsletter does not adequately address the unique needs and interests of your target audience. Therefore, the decision to utilize a newsletter service should be accompanied by careful research to determine how the publication's editorial content is planned, researched, and written. In this way, you will be able to determine which service provides articles that will be of greatest interest to your firm's clients.

While each newsletter service is unique, the following observations apply to most, if not all, of them:

- Most services provide a newsletter that is geared to the personal and business interests of a firm's tax, accounting, and audit clients. Many also offer a wide array of industry—and service—specific publications.
- The basic tax/business newsletter is usually four to six pages long, printed in two or four colors, is issued on a quarterly or bi-monthly basis, and allows for the CPA firm's name, logo, address, and phone number on the front page. Several services allow for additional customization, including choice of colors and the insertion of news articles and photos.
- Almost all services offer regional exclusivity for the duration of the subscription period. If you live in a large metropolitan area, find out if any CPA firms have a territory adjacent to yours.
- The fee usually includes a one time set-up or licensing fee, a per-copy charge based on the number of newsletters ordered, and a nominal shipping fee. Additional customization may entail extra charges.
- The costs quoted to you do not include labeling, postage, and handling, so be sure to calculate those charges on your own.
- Many services offer the option of selling you their articles on disk, ready to dump into your own in-house newsletter format.
- You should be able to e-mail a PDF version to readers who prefer an electronic version.
- You should be able to have the PDF available on your Web site with each new issue.

You should also consider electronic newsletters that are interactive. Once a reader clicks on to a story, perhaps reading more about "Compensating Nonworking Family Members" for example, you can capture the e-mail address as well as the length of time spent on the article. This data can help you understand your audience and provide improved content based on the interest level you are tracking. This newsletter can also have hyper links that take the reader from the newsletter back to your Web site, to register for an event they just read about in the newsletter, or learn more about your firm.

If you want to compare the costs of an in-house newsletter with that of a newsletter service, exhibit 21-1 contains some important considerations. Note, however, that only you can assess the relative quality and usefulness of the articles written and the quality of production methods and materials used. To consider the cost of e-mail versus paper mail, factor in the charge by the provider less the costs of printing and postage that you would typically incur.

 Key Concept

> The advantage of utilizing a newsletter service is that the time required to plan, write, and produce the firm's newsletter can be kept to a minimum.

Step 4: Develop a Plan and a Budget

Each planning decision you make influences the final cost of the newsletter and is extremely easy to underestimate. When you sit down to develop a plan and associated cost estimates, consider the following factors and issues.

Quality and Image

What kind of image do you want to project and what level of quality do you want to achieve? A newsletter can be classic and conservative, friendly and down to earth, or sophisticated and high tech.

Choices concerning image and quality influence every other decision made about the newsletter, from choosing a name and picking a paper stock to setting the tone of the articles. And, of course, the more sophisticated and high quality the image, the higher the costs.

When you reach this planning crossroads, revisit the newsletter's marketing goals and target audience. Remember your readers' tastes and preferences, and think about what you want them to do, or think, as a result of reading your newsletter. This will help you make the right choices. If you aren't certain about the kind of image you want to convey, look at other newsletters and think about the images they project.

Exhibit 21-1
Cost Comparison Worksheet—
In House Newsletter Vs. Newsletter Service

	In House	Service
Editorial:		
Planning		
Research and interviews		
Writing and Editing (use tillable rate for those involved)		
Production:		
Layout		
Typesetting		
Proofreading		
Revisions		
Photos and illustrations		
Printing:		
Volume color charges		
Special handling		
Postage and Handling:		
Mailing list management		
Printing the list		
Labels		
Labor to apply labels and postage		
Cost of postage		
Totals:		

Length and Frequency

A newsletter is, by definition, brief. Most are four to six pages long, but can range comfortably from two to eight pages. As a rule, the fewer the pages, the more often you can publish. For instance, a two-page newsletter may go out monthly, while an eight-pager might be mailed as little as twice a year. Many accounting firms publish quarterly.

Even publishing four times a year requires a lot of effort. Before committing to a more frequent schedule, make sure you can handle the work load and the pressure that accompanies quick turnaround. Be careful about mailing too often. A weekly mailing might put your firm's newsletter into the pest or junk mail category, especially if it is designed to promote services.

Page Size

The standard page size for printed newsletters is 8 × 11 inches. This is a convenient size because it fits into standard business envelopes, files, and folders. Legal, tabloid, and smaller sizes can be used, but you should have good reasons for exercising one of these options, as they may entail higher production and mailing costs.

Scheduling

Building a workable schedule and adhering to that schedule is crucial if you want to get your newsletter out on time. To build a timetable, begin by deciding when you want clients to receive each issue. Now work backward, allocating time to the mailing process, production, finalizing rough drafts, and making initial assignments. Solicit input from everyone who will play a role in producing it, from writers, printers, and designers to your in-house committee of reviewers. Of course, delays are the norm, but your readers will come to expect the newsletter at a certain time, so make sure everyone who produces the newsletter understands how important it is to adhere to the timetable.

Quantity

If you need 3,000 newsletters for your mailing list, consider ordering an additional 200 to stock the reception area and to have available as handouts for seminars, to include with proposals, and for distribution at tradeshows or at partners' speeches. If a client was featured in an issue, order extra copies for the client.

Distribution

Who will you send these newsletters to, and how will they get there? Clients, centers of influence, and key prospects are an obvious choice. But don't forget referral sources, past and present, along with firm alumni, selected journalists, lost prospects, program attendees (nonclients) and executive directors of key business groups. To keep them informed, every member of your staff should also receive a copy.

If you have enough clerical staff and can build the longer delivery time (two to three weeks) into your schedule, why not take advantage of the savings by mailing bulk? Since some direct mail experts feel that bulk mail is often discarded unopened, you may also consider first class pre-sorted by ZIP code. This is cost effective and does not have the stigma of bulk mail.

Current Mailing Lists

Keeping any mailing list current with postal addresses and e-mail addresses is not an easy task. Mailing houses update their lists six or more times a year because people move and change jobs so often. Your list will be outdated in no time unless you have "Address Correction Requested" printed on the envelope or under the mailing label so the U.S. Postal Service will return those that were undeliverable.

Here are some suggestions for keeping current:

- Send postcards to your mailing list for updating contact information semi-annually
- Include a request for new contact information with your annual tax organizer mailing
- Lists can be purchased from industry publications and trade associations
- Zapdata and other business list brokers sell names and contact information
- infoUSA has lists of high net worth individuals

To keep e-mail lists current, you can use tracking features to help you keep tabs on your respondents. Most new distribution tools contain a feature entitled "bounces." These are the e-mails that do not reach your intended recipients. This is generally due to several things. First, spam blockers have intercepted it. This means you will have to contact them about adjusting their e-mail settings so they can receive your newsletters. Don't worry, it's an easy fix. Second, their e-mail address has been changed or omitted. That likely means they have a new e-mail address or they have left the company. A phone call can help you find out the information you are seeking on these bounced recipients so you can keep your lists up-to-date.

Project Management

Even though many people in your firm may contribute to the newsletter's success, it is important to assign one person the responsibility of producing the newsletter. Ideally, choose your marketing director or one of his or her staff. You may also want to consider forming a newsletter advisory committee. This group can be helpful in suggesting topics and sources as well as providing the essential review of all articles for technical accuracy. Limit the number of committee members to three to five people, or you may find the review and approval process too cumbersome.

Key Concept

It is important to assign one person the responsibility of producing the newsletter.

Writing and Editing

Some editors believe it's best to do as much as possible within the firm, asking partners and other CPAs to write byline articles, having the clerical staff handle distribution, and even producing the newsletter through desktop publishing software packages. If you can persuade the firm's professionals to write newsletter articles, you have created a way for clients to become better acquainted with those individuals and their special expertise. But many partners and managers are just too busy. And it may not be cost effective to ask a high-priced professional to sacrifice billable time in order to prepare an article.

The most obvious alternative is to hire a professional writer to plan and produce the articles for each issue. Other options include subscribing to a newsletter service and utilizing only selected articles, hiring a professional writer to interview the designated firm expert on a subject and ghostwrite an article, and establishing a feature exchange with other similar accounting firms outside your region. If you purchase a newsletter, you need to distribute it internally so that the partners and staff are familiar with the information being presented to your readers.

Tips for the Editor

- Read, proof, then reread and reproof your drafts for errors.
- Always have someone new proofread the final version.
- Verify numbers, dates, names, titles, prices, totals, and addresses.
- Double-check captions, alignments, page numbers, headlines, and subheads.
- Use a table of contents if the newsletter has more than four pages.
- Establish regular columns or sections.
- Be crisp and to the point.
- Avoid a jumbled, crowded look.
- Strive to write a lead that grabs the reader.
- Cut out clichés or try to twist them in some original way to give them new meaning or sparkle.
- Avoid racial and sexual bias in writing. Use *business executive* or *owner* instead of *businessman, staffed* instead of *manned,* and never be coy as in "the attractive Ms. Wilson."
- Instead of label headlines, try to use a verb that comments on the story or teases the reader. Think of the headline as a sentence without a period.
- When in doubt, keep it simple.

- Always use some type of grid system to lay out the newsletter.
- Design each page to follow the path of the eye on a page.
- Underlining words or phrases acts as a brake to the eye. Use boldface instead.
- Use captions under photos, and if appropriate, under illustrations.
- Don't use all caps in headlines.
- Don't be rigid. There's an exception to every rule.

Design and Production

When it comes to design and production work, there is the question of whether or not an in-house team can produce the desired level of quality. And at first glance, purchasing a desktop publishing system may seem like a money-saving proposition. But producing elegant, technically correct, and visually appealing print ready pages takes more than knowing how to operate a software package. Are you prepared to invest in hiring a staff member who has the appropriate graphic arts skills? And what will this individual do when he or she is not working on the newsletter? Using outside professionals may actually save money in the long run, and will almost always ensure a higher level of accuracy and quality in the finished product.

How do you find and qualify writers and graphic artists? Ask for references from your peers, associates, and the local chamber of commerce. Interview the top candidates and review their portfolios. Explain your requirements and try to get a feel for their working style. Some designers are extremely gifted but may not serve you in the way you like. It is worth doing the extra work to make sure the designer you hire will be a team player who will become an integral part of your team.

Color and Images

Colored inks can help make your newsletter more visually appealing, but they can also make it more costly. Using one color in addition to the standard black ink for text can greatly enhance the newsletter's appearance, without too much added cost. A second color (after black and one color) may increase your total cost up to approximately 15 percent. This is an area where print versus electronic creates a cost savings; there is obviously no additional charge for color when producing an electronic version.

Printing Method

As suggested earlier, a high-quality publication depends on commercial offset printing because it delivers sharp clear text, along with vivid color and crisp photographs. Quick printers and photocopiers save time and money, but won't deliver the same quality. While digital printing is vastly improved, you need to consider a number of factors. Can an outside digital printer provide the quality you are seeking at a reasonable price? If printing is done in-house you must factor in the cost of time, paper, and wear and tear on your equipment. On the surface this may appear to be a cost savings but ultimately it may not reduce your expenses significantly, especially if you have a large mailing list.

To find a printer, ask for recommendations. Graphic designers are an excellent resource because they can recommend printers they have employed in the past. Specify every printing job in writing and accompany specifications with a dummy or sample. To be sure you are getting a fair quote, get bids from at least three printers. To estimate costs, the printer needs to have a great deal of information; the more precise you can be in describing the project, the easier it will be for the printer to provide you with an accurate cost estimate. For more detailed information on preparing a request for quotation and the terms frequently employed by printers and graphic artists, refer to chapter 20, "Guidelines for Effective Brochures."

Once the newsletter is in production, always ask to see a blue line (press proof) before your newsletter goes to press, especially if you are implementing complex graphic techniques. (Try to minimize the need for any corrections at this stage; it's expensive.) Ask for the cost per issue and per year and about payment terms. Your graphic artist can also get this information for you. Just remember, if the graphic artist manages the printing process for you, and handles the press check, you can expect an agency markup on the printing charge (the markup is usually 15 percent). The advantages of this approach are that the designer is experienced in supervising the printing process and will be responsible for the press check. You can even negotiate for the designer to assume responsibility for any problems that arise—just make sure you make this agreement in writing first.

Keep in mind that there are different concerns to focus on when planning an electronic newsletter. These newsletters can come in template format or can be customized. In selecting to send your newsletter by e-mail you will not have to focus on printing and mailing costs but you will have to consider distribution channels and the use of a provider who can e-mail hundreds, or even thousands, of newsletters on your behalf. Many companies provide sites to build and distribute e-newsletters including iContact and Constant Contact. BizActions and PDI Global provide e-newsletters for the accounting industry. They have a good understanding of the rules, the process, and the practical approach to this vehicle.

The topics mentioned previously affect the cost of producing your newsletter. The following planning issues, although of equal importance, are treated separately because they have little—or no—impact on the cost.

Step 5: Select the Name

You are going to live with the name of your newsletter for a long, long time, so try not to rush the decision-making process. Hold some brainstorming sessions with your in-house committee, look at the names other accounting firms are using, pick adjectives that describe your company, and thumb through a thesaurus. You can also ask other people in the firm for ideas; try holding a "Name the Newsletter" contest.

Your newsletter's name should be creative but not too cute. It also must be distinctive and easy to pronounce and reflect your firm's personality. In addition, it should be consistent with the look of your other materials, including print brochures as well as the design of your Web site. Everything should be consistent as you build a powerful brand. Choose a name that helps to position the newsletter. Here are some examples:

- *Tax Outlook*
- *Management Focus*
- *The Resource*
- *Tax Roundup*
- *Footnotes*
- *Perspective*
- *Alert*
- *Tax and Financial Ledger*
- *Scoreboard*
- *Accounting Alert*
- *Newsline*
- *Matters of Fact*
- *Monitor*

Once you have chosen a name, work on a descriptive phrase that helps identify the newsletter's purpose. For example, a newsletter entitled *Litigation Update* could be followed by the phrase *Forensic Accounting Newsletter*. If you are developing a family of newsletters, the mast head or titles can be coordinated so that they show continuity and emphasize the firm-wide brand.

Step 6: Determine the Design and Editorial Content

Planning the newsletter's design, masthead, and editorial content is an exciting process because every element of the final product says something about the personality of your firm and what it stands for and enhances your branding campaign by creating a consistent image.

Nameplate

The nameplate is the most visible and permanent design element of the newsletter. The designer needs to know whether you want color before producing preliminary sketches. Choose the three you like the most and ask the designer to produce final designs. The managing partner and in-house review committee should be asked for input, and it may be worthwhile to solicit opinions from future readers too.

Page Layout and Style Guide

The next step is page layout. Create a format that can be used in issue after issue, with minor modifications allowed for different story lengths and photos and illustrations. You may want to establish sections or regular columns and set benchmarks for how long each type of article should be. Other layout features include standing heads, a table of contents, and the firm's logo, which should be displayed prominently on the first page. Also, each issue should include a masthead, which is the box that delineates the firm's name, address, fax and phone numbers, plus the name of the editor and others responsible for writing and producing the newsletter. If you utilize an electronic format, the reader will see up to four or five synopses of articles and can then click to select those that are most interesting and relevant to read in full. This presents different challenges than for a print newsletter.

Establish policies for how industry jargon is to be handled, and set rules concerning spelling, punctuation, using numbers, and grammar. Always use the correct form for titles, departments, other companies, and products. Be consistent.

Content

When it comes to article topics, add value by presenting real information that readers' need to operate their organizations and reach educated decisions. You do not need to blatantly promote the firm if you are using articles that share pertinent information, the firm will sell itself. Your clients want to be associated with a top-notch firm, which becomes obvious in the high level of expertise that is embedded in your articles. The following are some ideas on what to publish:

- Choose articles and stories that serve your readers. Inform them of new trends and pending legislation and suggest appropriate planning strategies. This is an excellent medium for showcasing a particular partner's technical expertise, so try to have him or her write the article.
- Remind clients of imminent deadlines. For instance, if your newsletter is published quarterly, include a tax calendar covering the following four-month period.
- While some firms like to feature clients, others are very concerned about insulting clients not covered, or the potential for adverse publicity later regarding the highlighted client.
- Eliminate articles that "sell" the firm. Your best sales tool is an informational article that demonstrates your value and expertise.
- Consider polling your readers for article ideas they would like to see in future issues.
- Include a disclaimer that says the information presented is for information purposes only, and clients should consult a professional before taking action.

Finally, be cautious about presenting a point of view. Newspapers want to stir up controversy. You are trying to inform readers and acquire new clients, not alienate them. If you are worried about having enough story ideas, set up a file and monitor the media year round. National and international stories can be localized. A firm member's speech or article for an outside publication can be reprinted (always make the appropriate attribution).

> **¶ Key Concept**
>
> When it comes to article topics, add value by presenting real information that readers' need to operate their organizations and reach educated decisions.

Subject Lines

Once good copy is in place, you must attract the attention of your readers. Good subject lines are the key to success. In a recent issue of *BizMarketing*, BizActions outlined some solutions to get your e-newsletters noticed and opened.

The goal of the subject line is to get your reader's attention in a professional manner. E-mail newsletter creation can be as enjoyable as it is rewarding. Get more readers to open your e-newsletter with a good subject line.

Consider these ideas[1]:

- Avoid a poorly constructed subject line. Your filter is probably full of e-mails with subject lines with ALL CAPITAL LETTERS. Or that scream for attention with an exclamation mark! Or two!! You can use a general or default subject, but instead consider using the lead article as your subject line. If you use an out-sourced newsletter, the publisher may provide you with one or more of the article titles in advance.
- One method of creating a good subject line is to frame your article with a question. For example, if your lead article is on the safety of assets being held in financial institutions, the subject line could be "How Safe Is Your Money?" or "Is Your Money Safe?" Your readers will mentally answer the question. And their answer may lead to them opening so they can read more.
- An alternative can be to make a benefit statement out of your lead article's subject. Using the same example as mentioned previously, the subject line could simply be "Keeping Your Money Safe." If they think they have a problem, and you can help them solve it, they'll want to read more.
- Combining topics of several articles can also be effective. Just keep each description short, as in three to four words. An example: "New Tax Law, IRA Beneficiaries, Cash Is King."
- You can also choose a default subject line for your e-newsletter. When doing so, try to include fields that will personalize and change each issue, such as the reader's first name and the date your newsletter is distributed. For example, "Hello David. Here is our current newsletter for September 9, 2009."

STEP 7: GET READER FEEDBACK

Once you get the newsletter under way, you will probably want to know whether or not anyone is reading it. If they are, what do they think? And is the newsletter actually achieving the objectives you set out for it?

A readership survey is one way of getting feedback and making sure the newsletter is meeting its goals. Here are several approaches you might want to consider:

- Send an electronic survey to all newsletter recipients. Keep your questions to a minimum; 5–10 is ideal.
- Send out a questionnaire (no more than one page) and enclose a prepaid business reply envelope or an electronic survey link.
- Enclose a simple self-mailer, postcard size, in the next issue of the newsletter. See exhibit 21-2 for a sample.
- Use both multiple-choice and open-ended questions and leave room for comments and suggestions for future issues.

EXHIBIT 21-2
SAMPLE QUESTIONNAIRE

[Your CPA Firm Name]

In order to create a better newsletter, we kindly ask you to take a moment to answer a few questions regarding the [Firm/Newsletter name]. Your feedback is important to us, and we thank you for your assistance.

Do you find the [newsletter] interesting to read? Yes ___ No ___

Do you find the [newsletter] informative or useful? Yes ___ No ___

Do you find the topics relevant to you? Yes ___ No ___

What additional topics would you like to see addressed in upcoming issues?

Do you find the [newsletter] design easy to read? Yes ___ No ___

Which aspects of the [newsletter] do you like the most? _____

Which aspects of the [newsletter] do you like the least? _____

How often would you like to receive the [newsletter]?

    Quarterly _____ Bimonthly _____ Take me off the list _____

Additional comments: _____

---

[1] "What Makes a Good Subject Line," BizActions (Potomac, Maryland: BizMarketing e-newsletter, October 28, 2009) www.bizactions.com.

Another technique is to bring together a focus panel made up of current and intended readers, and ask them what they think of the newsletter. Focus group research is a tried and true marketing research technique and can be valuable; however, it is expensive and best conducted by experts.

CONCLUSION

Newsletters should never be static. A good editor is always tinkering, changing, and improving the publication to keep it fresh and in touch with its readers. Remember to validate your innovations by testing them through reader feedback.

A final word of caution: don't let the firm management team view the newsletter as the whole marketing effort. Even a well-written and award-winning newsletter is but one element in a coordinated marketing effort. No one reads a newsletter and shouts, "Eureka! Let's hire that firm!" At the very best, a newsletter can inspire a reader to obtain more information by contacting your firm.

ABOUT THE AUTHOR

Sally Glick is a Principal of the Firm and the Chief Growth Strategist at Sobel & Co., LLC. In that role she has responsibility for the firm's branding and marketing communications as well as connecting the dots between marketing initiatives and the firm's growth strategy. Glick was named Accounting Marketer of the Year for 2003 and served as the President of the Board of Directors of the Association for Accounting Marketing in 2004. She has also been listed on *Accounting Today's* list of Top 100 Most Influential People in Accounting for 2004, 2005, and 2006. She also hosts a blog on Accountingweb.com focusing on marketing advice for CPA firms. She had the honor of being the first non-CPA woman to appear on the cover of *Practical Accountant,* a publication for the accounting profession, in August 2002. In 2007 she was inducted into the Association for Accounting Marketing's Hall of Fame.

Sally Glick earned her undergraduate degree from Northwestern University in Evanston, Illinois and her MBA from The Lake Forest Graduate School of Business Management in Lake Forest, Illinois.

CHAPTER 22
Databases That Fuel Your Marketing Efforts

Michelle Class

Barnes Dennig

INTRODUCTION

Databases of years ago were nowhere near as sophisticated as the databases of today. In accounting firms across the world, major investments are being made to update time and billing systems and marketing databases. In some circumstances, the time and billing systems contain a marketing module that helps enhance new business within the firm. However, having a time and billing system incorporated with all the necessary (and evolving) marketing capabilities is difficult to find.

The long-term viability of accounting firms will increasingly depend on the willingness of CPAs to invest in databases that can provide powerful marketing intelligence, whether it is one system or multiple. Customer relationship management (CRM) software packages are proving more beneficial for the business-to-business (B-2-B) community. In its infancy, CRM systems were nothing more than stand-alone data collection systems. However, today, they are much, much more than that. Many CRM systems have the capabilities to integrate with an accounting firm's time and billing software, which saves on collecting and maintaining redundant data. Additionally, CRM packages are now able to speak to other programs, such as an e-mail system. Reminders or follow-up messages can be set up in a CRM system and received in a user's e-mail inbox. This functionality was not available in the past.

Consider a sole practitioner with 10 small business clients. As a change in business tax deductions is signed into law, the practitioner instantly makes a series of assessments:

- Which of the 10 clients will be affected by the new law?
- Which of the client companies affected will undertake a planning project designed to mitigate, or take advantage of, the new provisions?

The practitioner then calls each client selected and guides them through this process to discuss the new law, suggests a planning meeting, and finally, schedules the work. With only 10 clients, there is limited need for a CRM system or marketing database. The CPA can store all of the necessary information in an excel spreadsheet and can easily assess each company's situation.

But what happens when the number of clients increases to 20, 200, or 2,000? Or what about multiple variables, such as realization rates and staff utilization? What happens when a firm must make critical decisions about developing new industry or service niches, and determining how much to invest in making them successful? With a well-crafted marketing database or CRM system, you can anticipate client and prospect needs, as well as referral source needs, and so maximize client service, sales efficiency, and ultimately, firm profits.

Here are some examples of how accounting firms use their marketing databases to improve the bottom line:

1. One firm tracks the birthdates and income levels of all tax clients. When they reach the ages of 50, 55, 59+, 62, 65, and 70+ they are approached with planning suggestions related to retirement and estate planning.
2. Another firm tracks the gross sales of its business clients and compares those figures to the industry's regional and national averages. Clients who are falling at or below the average are offered additional consulting services to boost profits.
3. A third firm measures its own employees' performance by evaluating the amount of nontraditional services they have been successful in selling to clients.

4. Yet another measures its market share by comparing the number of clients it has in a given industry to a commercial database of all comparable businesses within target geographic and volume parameters.

5. Many firms also use databases of clients, prospects, referral sources, personal contacts, and local businesses for mailing of targeted marketing materials.

The marketing applications described in the previous list usually rely on a single table of information that can be sorted by the desired characteristics. Within the past five years, the sophistication of databases has become extraordinary. Not only can information be pulled from a single source of information, but now by building relationships with a primary key or field, such as ID number, databases can be "relational" and pull sources of information from many different tables.

For example, suppose you want to identify the 50 most promising manufacturing prospects from a large list of businesses in a specific geographic area. Since your best bet is to do more of what you already do well, you would begin by looking at your personal records to identify the companies you already serve most efficiently and profitably, then find companies who fit your ideal client profile. Without a database management system, you would have to review your time and billing system, realization reports, and staff utilization data manually to arrive at an answer. Then, you'd have to perform market research to locate the companies who would be prospective clients. Imagine how much easier it would be to structure a query that would automatically link, then search each of these files electronically, then deliver a list of those clients who met all of the criteria you had established. From that information, you would know which types of clients you serve most profitably, and would be able to use this information to decide which prospects to target first.

So far, we have reviewed a number of ways to use a marketing database or CRM system, some simple, others more complex. The rest of this chapter shows how to build a marketing database using client information that is already available to you in your electronic files or time and billing software. Then, we'll discuss new features that can broaden the power and usefulness of your existing marketing database(s). Finally, we'll discuss relational databases (or CRM databases) and the power and flexibility they offer in designing marketing databases.

A word of advice—since the idea of databases has spread like wildfire amongst accounting firms, there may be a rush to develop programs uniquely suited to everyone's needs. Before this happens, make sure your firm develops and follows a uniform database philosophy, so that data can be shared with little inconvenience. For example, you may want to specify who has rights to create tables, queries, forms, or reports in the database, then identify and educate those individuals on the importance of consistently entering key variables, such as client number and client name. A database is only as good as the information obtained, therefore, ensure consistent data entry and identify a champion of the database (this will help ensure that all reports will be flawless and without error).

Key Concept

With a well-crafted marketing database or CRM system, you can anticipate client, prospect, and referral source needs, thus maximizing client service, sales efficiency, and firm profits.

Key Concept

A database is only as good as the information obtained, therefore, ensure consistent data entry and identify a champion of the database.

Client Databases

For most firms, the first and most important client database is the system used to manage time and billings. While many are not designed to support marketing (and those that can are still evolving and working out the kinks), it almost always contains the basic client information needed to begin a marketing database, as shown in exhibit 22-1.

EXHIBIT 22-1
BASIC CLIENT INFORMATION

Client number
Client name (aka, company name)
Primary contact
Address
Primary phone
Primary fax
Primary e-mail
Web site
Engagement partner
Engagement manager
Fiscal year end month
Entity type (S corp, C corp, individual, and so on)
NAICS code (aka, SIC code)
Billings (year, month, and so on)
Status of client (active, inactive, on hold, and so on)

Once this information is exported into a separate document, it can be developed as the beginning of your marketing and business development database. Please note: many firms elect to maintain a separate database for marketing purposes or at least a separate one for prospective client information. While a second database means that some basic information will be redundant, marketing databases can quickly expand and require significant amounts of management and processing time. This work is usually best handled by someone who is directly involved in the marketing or business development process.

It never fails that newly exported information will require some scrubbing and cleansing. To facilitate the cleaning process, each record must be in a consistent format. For example, the primary contact field may have been entered in many different ways. You might find "Joan Jenkins" in one record, then "Smith, Howard" in the next. Or "Sanders, Ms. Elisabeth," followed by "Dr. and Mrs. James Johnson." To solve this dilemma, break the primary contact field down into separate fields, as shown in exhibit 22-2. The time required to reformat the information in your new database may range from a few hours to many days, but it will be time well spent.

With the fields shown in exhibit 22-2, a number of useful reports can be generated. For example, e-mail addresses can be generated for e-newsletter distributions. Labels and custom-addressed letters and envelopes can be prepared for mailings. A report can be printed that lists all clients billed a minimum (or maximum) amount by a partner. A report showing cash flow contribution by partner—by month, quarter, year—can be created. But, don't stop now! By adding three new fields (NAICS codes, fiscal year-end, and total revenue of a client) you'll be on your way toward building a more powerful marketing and business development database.

EXHIBIT 22-2
SUGGESTED DATABASE FIELDS

Client number
Salutation (Dr., Mr., Mrs., Ms.)
First name
Middle initial
Last name
Client name (aka, company name)
Address
City
State
Zip
Phone number
Fax number
Email
Billings (year, month, and so on)
Engagement partner

Exhibit 22-2
Suggested Database Fields *(continued)*

Additional fields:
NAICS codes
Fiscal year-end month
Total revenue of client

NAICS Codes

NAICS (North American Industrial Classification System) replaced the U.S. Standard Industrial Classification (SIC) system. According to the U.S. Census Bureau, the NAICS reshapes the way we view our changing economy. The designations, developed jointly by the U.S., Canada, and Mexico, to provide new comparability in statistics about business activity across North America, help to differentiate between types of businesses.

The codes are made up of two- to six-digit numbers, each representing a higher level of differentiation within a certain area of industry. The first digit is the most general discriminator and the sixth digit, the most specific. As a rule, classifications at the second, third, and fourth digit levels are the most useful. Here is an example:

31	Manufacturing
311	Food Manufacturing
3111	Animal Food Manufacturing
31111	Animal Food Manufacturing
311111	Dog and Cat Food Manufacturing
311119	Other Animal Food Manufacturing

When assigning a code in a database, be sure to use one that describes the primary business of the client (for example, a manufacturing client at your firm could easily be tagged in the general category of 31, Manufacturing; however, if your geographic area has an abundance of manufacturers in the food arena, then the 311, Food Manufacturing, category may be more applicable to you). Another consideration is if a client has a significant secondary business activity (say, 10–25 percent of gross revenues) come from 3111111, Dog and Cat Food Manufacturing, then a new field should be added to the database, Secondary NAICS code.

While an engagement partner should be consulted on assigning an NAICS primary or secondary code, a single person should be responsible for ensuring that the codes are assigned consistently. This will help to identify the companies who may be affected by legislative laws that may be pertinent to the functionality of their business.

Fiscal Year-End

While this information is usually well known by the engagement team and is part of the tax return and financial statements, it should nevertheless be entered into the database. An important item to note: information that stays inside the engagement partner/manager's head is not easily accessible; get it into the database for all to utilize.

Revenue and Size of Client

The revenue of a client, as indicated by gross or net annual sales and the number of employees, should also be added to the database. In evaluating these two factors, annual sales and number of employees, both are useful to determine your ideal client profile and to evaluate how your clients are doing. The rule of thumb is that each employee equals about $100,000 in sales. This can be calculated by the following formula:

$$\frac{Gross\ margin\ (or\ gross\ profit)}{Total\ \#\ of\ employees}$$

With this calculation, conclusions can be made regarding your ideal client (and average client size) and the prospective clients that you may be targeting.

Now that you have added this new information into the marketing/business development database, what can it tell you? With the NAICS code, revenue/size of client, and fiscal year-end month in place, the billing potential of a particular prospect can be estimated by reviewing average billings made to clients with similar characteristics. Or, turn the process around. Look at your most profitable clients and ask if they have any features in common, such as size, industry category, or service utilization. Once the answer is known, development (or in some cases confirmation) of the ideal future client profile can be completed. We cover this application in greater detail later on in this chapter.

Mailings/E-mail Campaigns

As noted earlier, the most common use of a marketing or business development database is to support e-mail campaigns or postal mailings to clients, prospective clients, referral sources, and others. Again, with the NAICS code, fiscal year-end month, and revenue/size of companies in your database, e-mails/mailings can pinpoint those individuals with the greatest need for the information. For example, an announcement of a new tax ruling that affects manufacturing companies with sales in excess of $5 million. A list (query) can be prepared for distribution almost instantaneously. And you will be assured that all of the clients who fit into this category have been notified. You can also utilize this type of information as a prospecting tool—companies love free information and if a personal relationship has been established (and your firm is #2 in their eyes), why not extend the information to them on your firm letterhead or firm template (if electronic)?

Your database also allows you to personalize e-mails and mailings. Cover letters can be addressed to the CFO, and the name of the client's engagement partner can be printed below the signature line. To ensure that the mailing is followed by a telephone call, you can provide each partner with a list of the clients (or prospective clients) he or she needs to call. Creating a report that includes the name of the person receiving the letter, along with a phone number, can be easily generated too. The most difficult part of this process is ensuring the follow-up calls are made in a timely fashion.

> **? Key Concept**
>
> The most common use of a marketing or business development database is to support e-mail campaigns or postal mailings to clients, prospective clients, referral sources, and others.

ENHANCING DATABASES/CRM SYSTEMS

Once the marketing/business development database is created, most firms will want to continually incorporate information about prospective clients and friends of the firm. Typically, the friends include attorneys, bankers, insurance professionals, firm alumni, and other potential referral sources.

This is an excellent idea, but to help ensure these aren't included as prospective clients, be sure to customize a field that will allow you to divide the list by clients, prospective clients, referral sources, and others, as needed. The benefit of creating a field for these categories is that when something of interest to attorneys comes up, you can develop a special mailing or e-mail distribution just for that group of contacts quickly and easily.

You can also add the names of companies or individuals who have no direct connection with the firm, yet. Remember, these may be your business associates and a valuable asset to the firm in the future. In order to avoid unnecessary clutter, someone in the firm (perhaps a marketing professional or administrative professional) should confirm all additions represent real potential clients for the firm. Establish criteria and stick to it—putting clutter into your database will only make reporting on results more difficult.

Who should be asked to find the companies or individuals who fit your inclusion criteria? If your firm is broken into niche industries or services, it's important that this function become part of your monthly or quarterly meetings. This will also help ensure that the "top prospects" are being contacted and educated about your firm on a constant basis. An example of this process would be

1. establishing criteria for identifying potential clients.
2. having the marketing person research the company to ensure it meets all criteria.
3. discussing the company during your monthly/quarterly meetings to see if anyone has a connection to the company (this could also be an e-mail to the entire firm).
4. identifying the person(s) who will be responsible for keeping proactive communication with the company.
5. reporting on or updating status on each company during the monthly/quarterly meetings (or via some electronic process). Many firms utilize CRM systems that allow the user to enter notes about the account. If used exclusively, these systems can be very beneficial to the growth of a firm. If used sparingly, these systems are a waste of money and in many cases valuable time.

Another way to expand your database is to consider adding data available from commercial listings (such as a Dun & Bradstreet list or various industry specific database sources). These listings are available for nearly all metropolitan areas for a minimal cost. Most offer a number of selection criteria, including the following:

- Geographic location, by zip code
- Type of business, by primary and secondary NAICS code
- Size of business, by number of employees, or by revenue
- A contact at the company, with title or function
- Phone numbers and/or addresses of each contact

You can expect to pay about $3.00 per record to capture the number of employees, sales estimate, and key personnel. If that's not in your budget, sign up for a free membership at www.referenceusa.com to find "some" data (not as thorough as D&B, but less expensive). In general, the more information you want to gather about each company, and the more accurate you want it to be, the more you will pay.

The least expensive lists are those compiled from your area's chamber of commerce or the telephone company's white or yellow pages. These directories may not be verified annually (if at all) and have a comparatively high error rate. They also have the fewest selection criteria, so you may not get what you need. The more expensive lists usually have a guaranteed accuracy rate and offer many selection criteria. As a rule, their information is gathered and periodically verified through phone calls to company executives.

Lists can be purchased for a one-time-only use, or leased, generally for a one-year period with quarterly updates. In either case, vendors work to enforce their contracts by "seeding" fictitious names in the list, so they can monitor how often their customers use them. Be sure you understand the terms of your contract when you acquire one of these lists.

There are many lists, and many list vendors. Some specialize in households; others focus on business listings. While some vendors will sell directly to end users, your best bet is to work with a broker or an information retrieval specialist. Both of these intermediaries can help you identify and clarify your requirements prior to making a purchase.

Importing, merging, and purging the new records into your marketing database will be fairly straightforward. However, as the number of records in your database increases, so does the clean-up work that goes with it. At some point, consider utilizing a mail house, or service bureau to create a cost effective and desirable solution to your mailing needs. Don't hesitate to call these places and ask to speak to someone—even if it's a small job. They'll gladly discuss with you your options and in the process, you'll become educated on what must be done to become more efficient and effective with your mail campaigns.

DATA INTEGRITY

Remember the adage that a chain is only as strong as its weakest link. You must take steps to ensure that data entry into the marketing/business development database is highly accurate. Here are some suggestions for how you can accomplish this:

1. Employ skilled data-entry personnel. Don't let this get passed off to temporary help—it'll only cause more work, if it's done incorrectly.
2. Have a consistent person (or process) for entering data and have others check the database periodically for updates.
3. Ensure the entire firm is aware of the importance of correct information. Without it, our clients, prospective clients, referral sources, and others may endure a negative perception of your firm. An example of how incorrect data can hurt is the client who passed away last year who is still on the mailing list. This quickly turns into a personal issue for the beneficiary. By keeping a clear process, this will not be a recurring event.

As additional listings are merged into the database, it becomes increasingly necessary to test for duplicate names. For example, when you solicit names from partners for the friends of the firm list, they will probably give you the name of every person in their handheld device (or rolodex, for those who still use them).

Remember, the merge/purge process is an absolute necessity each time there are additions to the database. Consider scheduling such a procedure every three months to ensure correctness.

Annually, sort and print the database by engagement partner (or team, whichever works at your firm), and ask everyone to carefully check for updates. Finally, remember that if mailings go out first class, the postal service will help to verify the accuracy of the addresses. (With first class, undeliverable mail is returned to the sender.)

Developing an Ideal Client Profile

Profiling helps you determine whether there are any common characteristics—objective or subjective—among your most valuable clients. It is important to know what these characteristics are because they serve as a type of filter as you search for the most desirable prospects. Here are some examples of the criteria you might employ:

1. The client is healthy and growing, and has stable or expanding marketshare.
2. The client's demand for services is well balanced: It contains a mixture of repeat and transaction-based work; the work is performed throughout the year; most of the work can be leveraged to staff. Also, consider realization rates in order to determine the value of the client.
3. The client's management team is stable and competent, gets along well with your partners and managers, and the work is challenging and interesting to your most valued staff members.
4. Most of the work performed for the client is immune to competitive pricing.
5. The industry the client is in is healthy and growing.

How do you collect the information needed to answer these questions? Some of it is readily available in the time and billing software or the client file. You can obtain undocumented information by preparing questionnaires for your partners to fill out. Once again, remember to extract the information from your partner's and manager's heads. Finally, industry trend information can be obtained through census data, industry projections, regulatory agencies, and business information databases.

When you are finished, look at those clients who have met all, or most, of the criteria established. What do they have in common? Do they come from separate, but somehow related, industries? Are they all professional service companies, such as physicians, dentists, attorneys, or real estate brokers? Are their primary customers similar? What about the characteristics of the ownership group—public or privately held or perhaps all family-run businesses? Whatever the common characteristics, they form an important component of your selection criteria in targeting prospects to pursue.

⚷ Key Concept

Profiling helps you determine whether there are any common characteristics—objective or subjective—among your most valuable clients.

The Model for an Ideal Client

While profiling involves looking inward at your existing client base, modeling involves looking for businesses that possess all, or nearly all, of the characteristics of an ideal client. At its core is the assumption that both parties, the CPA firm as well as the client, should be discriminating in their search. A poor fit can only result in client dissatisfaction and reduced profits for the firm.

In attempting to profile groups of prospects, you have to look to various sources for the information you need. Begin by reviewing data available in directory listings, industry research, as well as begin participating in industry associations, if applicable. Additionally, once you have collected research on the company, call and schedule a meeting to learn more about their company. Not only will you have your foot in the door, you'll have a much better idea if they are a fit for your firm.

Conclusion

Accounting firms committed to long-term viability continually invest large amounts to improving their time and billing systems, as well as their marketing and business development databases or CRM systems. They have already come to understand that the purpose of database marketing is to predict client and prospect behavior in order to maximize sales efficiency, client service, and to increase firm profits. The development and maintenance of this information is costly and time consuming. But those who undertake the effort understand that the investment will make the difference between success and mere survival.

ABOUT THE AUTHOR

Michelle Class has over 11 years of strategic marketing experience, working as the Marketing Director for Barnes Dennig (15 partners, 105 staff; Cincinnati, Ohio). She leads the marketing initiatives and strategies the firm develops to market their full menu of services to existing and new clients. Additionally, she is responsible for planning and managing the 20+ seminars annually designed to educate attendees on the happenings in their industry, and overseeing and improving the four industry-specific compensation and benefit benchmarking studies.

CHAPTER 23

Creating Opportunities Through Community Engagement

Karen Love
Pannell Kerr Forster of Texas, P.C.

Raissa Evans
Pannell Kerr Forster of Texas, P.C.

"We cannot live only for ourselves. A thousand fibers connect us with our fellow men; and among those fibers, as sympathetic threads, our actions run as causes, and they come back to us as effects."
    —Herman Melville

"Our commitment to the community, not the transaction, is our recipe for success. When we lose sight of this, we lose our bearing."
    —Pannell Kerr Forster of Texas, P.C.

INTRODUCTION

Making a commitment to participate in your community is one of the most effective ways to grow a CPA practice. Far more than traditional networking, community engagement and big-picture corporate social responsibility (CSR) can open doors to opportunities that set your practice apart. Any practice, regardless of size, can establish some level of community outreach.

CSR is important for several reasons. First, there's the altruistic view expressed by Melville in the opening quote to this chapter. Connecting with the community will come back to you in many ways.

Second, CSR can help your practice establish its unique brand. Participation in community outreach helps people see your company in a positive light. It can also open up opportunities to talk about what your company does, and what it cares about.

Third, there is the effect of CSR activities on everyone who works for your company—especially your new recruits. When they have a choice, younger workers will opt to work for a company that allows them to participate in meaningful (and yes, fun) community philanthropy projects.

Yet every CSR program needs a solid business purpose and strategy first. "This is not the time to carry on marginal activities or to waste resources on initiatives that do not contribute to your future," warns Art Bowman, editor of *The Bowman Accounting Report*,[1] "It is the time to put your faith in those activities that will build your future."

This chapter offers a framework for building a CSR strategy from the inside out, in a very deliberate way. You'll find tactics you can apply to your practice right away. You will see examples of innovative community involvement and how these initiatives can help a CPA practice establish its unique brand. You will learn how community

---

[1] *Bowman's Accounting Report*, August 2008.

engagement can contribute to practice growth and how to measure its return on investment (ROI). You'll also find ideas for outreach opportunities to consider as you start or expand your CSR efforts.

Benefits of engagement for your practice include the following:

- Any size company can benefit
- Nimbleness and alignment trump time and money invested
- Every team member becomes ambassador for the firm
- Appeals to altruism
- Supports employee retention
- Fits into life-work balance prized by employees and prospective employees
- Enhances practice brand and establishes niche
- Contributes to practice growth

Key Concept

Making a commitment to participate in your community is one of the most effective ways to grow a CPA practice. Community engagement and big-picture corporate social responsibility (CSR) can open doors to opportunities that set your practice apart.

1. CSR Is a Strategy

CSR starts inside your organization, and becomes a natural outgrowth of the values your practice holds. The key to making these activities successful is to define an overall strategy and follow it just like you would a business plan.

Give your CSR strategy the same thoughtful consideration you would give any new business strategy. It needs to be backed by research and planning, implemented, and then evaluated. It should also have a place in your budget, however small. (It typically comes out of the marketing budget, which represents 3–5 percent of net revenue, but varies widely.[2]) While one department may be responsible for developing the CSR programs, everyone in the practice should play a role.

CSR initiatives should match the strengths of your practice. At PKF Texas, for example, one of our specialties is serving technology companies. So part of the strategy developed by our Practice Growth (business development) group was to sponsor a "Fast Tech 50" award program. We enlist members of the firm at all levels to assist with parts of the program. That gives us visibility among technology firms and a reason to communicate with decision makers at every technology company in the area. Our support of this competition fits our focus, and it sets us apart in the marketplace.

"Strategic positioning means performing different activities from rivals or performing similar activities in different ways," states Michael E. Porter in an article on business strategy in *Harvard Business Review*. "Otherwise, a strategy is nothing more than a marketing slogan that will not withstand competition." [3]

So how can you use what you already have *inside* your practice to become more fully engaged *outside* your practice? And how do you make sure your company does it differently, and better, than your competitors? You'll find steps to developing a successful CSR strategy in the sections that follow.

Key Concept

Community outreach and CSR initiatives can include sponsoring an event, raising funds for charitable causes, doing pro bono work, or serving on the boards of community organizations. While those are among the opportunities you should consider, some of the most valuable CSR opportunities take a little more work to discover—or create from scratch.

---

[2] *Association for Accounting Marketing (AAM)*

[3] *Michael E. Porter, "What Is Strategy?" Harvard Business Review (November–December 1996).*

2. PLAN AND PREPARE

Like any business strategy, community engagement strategy should have the elements of research, planning, implementation, and measurement.

First, Look Within

Poll your employees to learn who in your organization has personal connections to community organizations, school volunteer groups, professional associations and special causes. Having a personal connection is an authentic way to launch a CSR effort. If employees have a say in which organizations to support, they will be more willing to participate in volunteer projects.

In our practice, for example, a number of employees have a personal interest in supporting heart disease education, prevention, and cures. So we enlist a multigenerational company team to participate in a fundraising walk for the local chapter of the American Heart Association. We build excitement for the program with competitions and prizes, and that excitement spills over into our interactions with clients and the community.

Identify Gaps in the Community

Discovering needs in your community is an important part of your background research. Talk to the leaders of organizations in your community to learn what gaps exist.

Questions to guide your research include the following:

- Are volunteers scarce?
- Are leadership positions going unfilled?
- Do they seek major donors for a capital campaign?
- Do they need knowledgeable speakers, trainers or accounting advice?
- Are there opportunities to judge award programs or serve on advisory committees?
- Do they need a place to hold board meetings or programs?
- Might they benefit from an introduction to one of your clients?
- And—this is very important—What are your competitors already doing?

Look within your practice to connect the dots, keeping in mind that the best strategy will serve those needs in a way that is different than what anyone else is doing.

Box 23-1   **How We Found the Gap and Filled It**

One of the organizations we participate in is the Greater Houston Partnership (GHP), a large chamber of commerce organization. Several of our young professionals (YPs) joined the business development committee of the GHP and reported back that there was a lack of YP representation within the partnership. Our team members were by far the youngest members of their committee. They identified this underrepresentation as a gap and we began working on a strategy to fill it.

Our firm's approach to marketing can be likened to a spider web, with different initiatives interconnecting to form a whole. This gives us the ability to use one program continuously without having to "spin a new web." By tweaking or adding another piece to the web, it grows organically. Our approach to using our YPs is no different; it is another part of our perpetual outreach into the marketplace.

To solve the GHP's lack of YP participation, we presented a business plan for the creation of a YP group to the GHP leadership. We felt we were in a good position to lead this effort, building upon the success we had already had bringing next-generation workers together within the company. While the creation of the group took some time, it finally gelled when we enlisted YPs to help with the GHP's World Trade Soiree. The young professionals brought a wealth of new ideas to promote the event. They planned the first-ever After Party following the soiree, and used social media, including a YouTube video, to generate "buzz." The Soiree had record attendance, and the YPs gained a foothold in the GHP organization by showing what they were capable of doing.

Make It an Organized Effort

Who should "do" CSR? Everyone in your company should have an opportunity to participate in some way. When you sign up to help with a community fundraising campaign of any kind, create an employee task force to handle communication and logistics for the effort. Set a high, but reachable fundraising goal. Then provide incentives for employees who reach their personal fundraising goals. For example, create some excitement by letting employees donate $10 for the privilege of wearing jeans and sneakers to work; or award an extra day of vacation to the firm's top fundraiser.

Your company benefits by bonding together to support a great cause, and the community benefits from your willingness to support a charitable organization.

Matches and Mismatches

Outreach efforts can fail when there is a mismatch between your company and the program, when expectations are not clearly defined, when employees get too busy to do nonbillable work, or when follow-through on either side isn't done. Commitments on both sides should be in writing.

Leadership support of a company's CSR efforts is essential. Some companies include community involvement or participation in professional associations as part of their employees' career goals.

CSR efforts should not be done in a "Lone Ranger" style. If your company's name is associated with an effort, or an employee is participating on your company's behalf, accountability is essential. (This applies even to partners of the firm. CSR should be a collaborative effort within the company, not a haphazard, spur-of-the-moment episode.) A one-person activity may sometimes be appropriate, but if no one inside the company is aware of it, that activity will be an ineffective use of the company name or resources.

At PKF Texas, we hold a "B4UGo" (Before You Go) meeting. It's a brief orientation about what we expect our team members to accomplish at a particular meeting or event. They're expected to report back to the director of practice growth, and to follow through on commitments and contacts they make. We also equip them with materials to leave behind, if appropriate, or plan other ways to add value to their participation.

How to Add Value to Your CSR Activities

Are the community groups you support doing something extraordinary? Help them brag about it. Use the communications vehicles you have available to you: a print newsletter, e-mail, news releases, or social media.

Here's an example of a blog posting by one of our directors, who is actively engaged with Rice University and the Rice Business Plan competition.

Rice University Graduate Entrepreneurship Program Ranked No. 5 in the US

> *Great news! Rice University has been named the number five for Graduate Entrepreneurship Programs by the* Princeton Review *and* Entrepreneur Magazine. *This year they jumped from 16 to five. That's 11 spots! I've posted their press release below. Congratulations![4]*

Another way to add value is to offer printed resources—not promotional materials—to the groups you interact with. These can have your branding on them, but they should be useful, educational and informative. Examples are article reprints about tax law changes for charities, white papers, newsletters with business tips, or a compilation of materials gleaned from your executives' speeches or presentations.

One of our most successful "leave-behind" items is "The Entrepreneur's Playbook." It's a small glossy-covered booklet containing excerpts from a weekly business advice radio show we host. Topics include cash management, recruiting, budgeting, fraud prevention and engaging next-generation workers. We also make an audio version of the shows available via our Web site.

---

[4] *www.FromGregsHead.com*

3. WEARING YOUR AMBASSADOR HAT

It's not enough to have employees or partners attend a fundraiser, pass out a few business cards, and dash back to work. Everyone should be tuned in to the CSR strategy and goals of your firm, and be on the lookout for new opportunities that fit.

When wearing the ambassador hat for the firm, each person is responsible for representing the firm in a positive light, and for finding new opportunities to *serve,* not *sell.* Yes, those cards should be exchanged whenever appropriate. The exchange should be accompanied with phrases like "I'll follow up with that resource for you," or, "I think you and Tracy should connect, I'll pass this along to her today." The ideal ambassador—the one who is welcomed at any event—serves as a connector of people and resources.

4. TRACKING YOUR RESULTS

CSR results can and should be measured. Decide up-front what is within your ability to track, and make sure your employee volunteers are aware of what is being tracked when they return and report their community activities. Examples of things that can be tracked are overall attendance at events, number of companies represented, funds raised, and the dollar value of employee volunteer hours invested.

Tracking ROI for community engagement activities can be done using a spreadsheet to capture results of each team member. More complex customer relationship management systems may also be used if available. The type of system used isn't nearly as important as making it easy for team members to report their activity. The key is to track results consistently over time, so that ROI trends emerge from the data. Share the results at regular meetings so team members can see their progress. For more information about results tracking, see chapter 34, "Marketing and Sales Metrics Matter: Measure Results, Calculate Return on Investment."

Emphasize employee accountability and responsibility for following up on leads that their service may generate. Some companies tie in the accomplishment of CSR goals to an employee's pay-for-performance plans. This can be a very effective way of encouraging results-oriented activities.

Another way to track and prove results is to enter a successful CSR effort into a local, regional, national, or international awards competition. Putting together awards entries can take some time, but the payoff can be enormous. An award serves as independent public recognition of your programs. It reinforces and differentiates your brand. It showcases your firm's talent, and can help you attract new clients and employees.

Winning an award for a community engagement effort is not only great for team morale, it reinforces the value of CSR investments all the way to the top of the firm. Landing an award—or a whole shelf full of them—is a sure way to gain some extra visibility for your firm. Use traditional and social media to toot your horn about every award and its significance. Then keep those plaques and trophies polished and on display throughout your offices.

5. INCORPORATING OUTREACH STRATEGIES INTO YOUR CORPORATE CULTURE

Ideally, your company's CSR initiatives enlist the willing support of everyone in your company. It won't always be possible to get everyone on board. Yet when community engagement is a part of your firm's written mission, individual employee goals, and corporate brand, it will be easier to attract employees and partners who value CSR.

Who's Your Champion?

Find or groom a "champion" within your company who will model and support effective community engagement. You may know someone who already demonstrates leadership in this area, or you may need to help someone discover their "inner volunteer" by encouraging them to take a leadership role in a small outreach project. Reward their efforts and accomplishments with recognition company-wide, along with new opportunities to lead.

Engaging the top-level executives in your firm may be a challenge, yet their participation is essential. Look for opportunities that are clearly aligned with your CSR strategies, and set up win-win scenarios that can be leveraged to create visibility for the executive and the company. (Sorting cans at the food bank is probably not where you want to put your CEO, but addressing the board of directors of the food bank on tax matters might be perfect.)

Among the other opportunities you might seek for your partners are as guest bloggers, experts on business-related TV and radio programs, judges for student business competitions, advisory board members for nonprofit groups or educational institutions, or keynote speakers for special events.

> **⚲ Key Concept**
>
> Team members should be encouraged to begin building their centers of influence early in their careers.

Preach What You Practice

Extend the value of your community engagement efforts by telling employees, customers, prospects and the business community how you are serving and why. Include these messages in all of your company communications vehicles, from a sign in your lobby to photos on your Web site.

To make sure your employees are engaged from the very beginning, incorporate messages about your company's culture of community participation in the information you give prospective hires and newly-hired employees. It should be a part of employee orientation and reinforced on an ongoing basis.

At PKF Texas, our culture perpetuates the professional *and* personal development of our entire team, including our young professionals (YP). YPs are the future of our firm. The advantage of focusing on the development of our people, and not tolerating "empty suits" is an engaged, motivated workforce.

Celebrate Successes

Celebrate the successes of your employees and teams by recognizing them at gatherings, in your newsletter, in company news releases, and with special awards or privileges. For instance, in your newsletter, you might have a spotlight section to highlight the personal involvements of one employee each issue. Or, externally, consider nominating your internal talent for community or business recognition awards relevant to your industry or specialty. Even an end-of-busy season party or team lunch can acknowledge hard work and a job well done. These accolades serve as retention vehicles. They contribute to the intangible climate of the workplace.

6. Finding New Opportunities

Be flexible and nimble as you scan the business horizon for new opportunities for community engagement and partnering. Constant change means you'll need to re-adjust your CSR strategies regularly.

Consider allocating a percentage of your budget for unexpected opportunities. These may come in the form of new programs you decide to create, or for responding to sudden community needs. This "Opportunity Fund" should be defined in your budget, allowing you to respond quickly when funds are needed.

When you create an outstanding community outreach program, your competitors are going to catch on. If they decide to copy your program or move in on your CSR "territory," you'll know it's time to establish something new.

We have changed tactics and expanded our CSR programs numerous times. When we won a "best places to work" three years in a row, we decided to become a sponsor of the program instead of a participant. Then, when the program became saturated with our competitors, we shifted our sponsorship and founded a "40 Under 40" program with a local business magazine to recognize up-and-coming business leaders. This allowed us exclusive access to the award winners and gave us opportunities to begin building relationships with them.

We have also sought and found an excellent business alignment when we partnered with a university entrepreneurship business plan competition. This puts us in an excellent position to scout new talent or prospective future clients from dozens of prominent universities. It also associates our firm name with entrepreneurship.

7. Expanding Your Horizons: Perpetual Outreach

Planned and perpetual outreach initiatives, rather than occasional one-shot efforts, will help you achieve your CSR goals.

Look for opportunities within your firm and throughout your community. Consider these types of groups as avenues for expressing your firm's commitment to the community. Scan your business community's events calendars and you'll find plenty more, such as

- Chambers of commerce
- Economic development groups
- Tourism bureaus (destination marketing organizations)
- Professional associations
- University foundations
- Research foundations
- Alumni associations
- Minority business associations
- United Way organizations
- Health-related nonprofit groups
- Environmental and green causes
- Small business development groups
- Speakers' bureaus

Conclusion

With clear goals that express your firm's values, attention to community needs, participation of all team members, tracking of results, and readiness for new opportunities, your firm can establish its unique brand, maintain competitive advantage, achieve long term practice growth and make lasting improvements in your community. Let the outreach begin.

ABOUT THE AUTHORS

Karen Love found the accounting marketing world in the mid 1990's, when business development was a word rarely heard in our industry. Operating in the 4th largest city in the United States with an environment of entrepreneurship and international flavor, Karen's innovative practice growth strategies and inside-out approach to practicing what she preaches has enabled the professionals at PKF Texas to infiltrate virtually every organization in Houston and internationally. Karen has mentored and blazed the trail for other accounting marketing professionals in her more than 15 years in the industry, and has been recognized as one of *Accounting Today's* 100 Most Influential People, a Marketer of the Year by the Association for Accounting Marketing (AAM), and was inducted into the AAM Hall of Fame in 2009. Her passion for corporate social responsibility began with her work on the Texas State Board of the American Heart Association, and continues to be an essential element of her leadership at PKF Texas. Her greatest joy is leading the PKF Texas Practice Growth team. Karen can be reached at klove@pkftexas.com.

Raissa Evans is the Senior Manager in the Practice Growth department at PKF Texas, where she has worked alongside Karen Love since 2003. With a background in technology, she brings nontraditional business acumen to the team. Active in the community, she is a member of a number of organizations, including the American Marketing Association, the Houston Interactive Marketing Association, and with Karen, co-founded the AAM Houston Chapter. She currently sits on the national Board of Directors for AAM. A member of the firm's Pipeline team, the *Leading Edge Magazine* and PKF University taskforces, Raissa is a key contributor to PKF Texas' internal culture through her project management skills and resourcefulness. Working closely with the Human Capital and Technology departments she provides input into shaping programs that will benefit the firm's internal and external clients. Raissa can be reached at revans@pkftexas.com.

CHAPTER 24

Referral Source Development: The Most Powerful, but Underutilized Business Development Tactic

Eileen P. Monesson
Cowan, Gunteski & Co., P.A.

INTRODUCTION

In today's competitive environment, developing new business opportunities can be a challenge for CPA firms. Even though most firms use traditional marketing approaches, such as printed collateral (for example, brochures, direct mail, flyers, newsletters), and promotion (for example, advertising, seminars, telemarketing, media), the development of a strong referral network is still the best way to engage new business.

According to a market research study of 231 buyers of professional services conducted by RainToday.com entitled *How Clients Buy: 2009 Benchmark Report on Professional Services Marketing and Selling from a Buyers Perspective,*[1] nearly 80 percent of business owners are very or somewhat likely to identify and learn more about professional service providers from a colleague's referral. Bill Cates, the author of *Get More Referrals Now!* states in his book, "The way of the world is meeting people through other people, and the referral is the warm way to get into people's lives. When you need to find a painter do you go to the phone book first? No, you ask friends and neighbors for recommendations. Your best clients want to meet you through an introduction from someone they already trust. That is why the referral process should be your primary method for attracting new clients."[2]

In the business development process, it is important for CPAs to demonstrate the value that you can bring to the relationship. Since prospective clients tend to view audit and tax services as a commodity—something that they must do to meet lender and IRS requirements, it is essential that you "provide evidence that you will deliver on your promises. This is where the referral comes in. When a prospecting client meets you through a referral, the evidence is already high. It's as if the referral source has testified on your behalf. This is why meeting you through a colleague or friend is their preferred method. Your buyers would rather meet you through a referral. The endorsement and testimony of others makes them feel much more comfortable opening their door to you and giving you their business."[3]

Successful CPAs actively work and expand their referral network to secure a steady flow of new business opportunities. The main advantages of developing leads through referral sources are the following:

- The prospect is qualified *before* you devote resources to developing the relationship.
- The referral source has already presold you, your services, and firm.
- The prospect has a positive impression of you and the firm before you meet.
- The referral source will share background information on the prospect with you.
- The business development cycle is shorter.
- The cost of engaging the client is decreased.

---

[1] How Clients Buy: 2009 Benchmark Report on Professional Services Marketing and Selling from a Buyers Perspective *(Framingham, MA: Wellesley Hills Group, 2009) RainToday.com.*

[2] Bill Cates, Get More Referrals Now! *(New York, NY: McGraw-Hill, 2004).*

[3] Ibid.

Your attitude toward developing a strong referral network is important. Many accountants feel uncomfortable about asking for a referral. You may feel like you are imposing on a client relationship or you might be anxious about how the client will respond to your request for a referral. If you have done your job well and have exceeded your client's expectations, you have earned the right to ask. Furthermore, if you have taken the time to build a relationship based on trust, your clients will want to refer you to their business associates. It is the quality of the relationship that gives you the right to ask for a referral.

Demonstrate that you truly care about your client. Actively listen to their needs, pay attention to new legislation and industry trends that may affect their business and deliver on your promises. Provide solutions instead of an audit or tax return. This will enhance the lifetime value of the client relationship, as well as your ability to earn a referral. Look at a client's lifetime value in terms of the fees earned from the client, as well as the fees generated from referrals from that client.

It is also advisable to talk to your clients about what they expect from you. Summarize what they say and send them a recap of your discussion. Make it a point to ask clients about their expectations on an annual basis. As their needs change, so will their service requirements. You need to know what they want from you to be able to deliver.

In this chapter we will discuss the following topics:

- Developing a relationship based on trust
- Building a referral-based practice
- Identifying referral sources
- Strategies for developing strong referral source relationships
- Developing your perfect client profile
- The five-step referral script
- Resources for making qualified referrals
- Programs for meeting and developing referral sources
- Keeping in contact with referral sources
- Motivating firm members to develop referral relationships
- Tracking systems
- Social networking

Developing a Relationship Based on Trust

The foundation of all relationships is trust. Bringing a relationship to this level requires attention, meaningful dialogue, follow-through, and follow-up. To solidify the connection you make and increase the chances of gaining their acceptance, you need to focus on what is important and how you can help. If the person likes what they hear and know you are listening to their concerns, they will connect with what you are doing and saying and begin to trust you.

Once trust is established, it needs to be reinforced by what you do. It is essential that you deliver on the commitments that you make in a timely fashion. The absence of follow-through and follow-up will turn feelings of trust into insincerity.

Key Concept

The foundation of all relationships is trust. Bringing a relationship to this level requires attention, meaningful dialogue, follow-through, and follow-up.

Building a Referral-Based Practice

To build a referral-based practice, you must first decide that referrals are the best way to generate new business opportunities. Bill Cates identified five critical skills to building a referral-based business in his book:[4]

---

[4] *Ibid.*

Skill One: Adopt a Referral Mindset

When you have a referral mindset, referrals become a primary method for acquiring new clients and an integral part of your marketing plan. You will actively and strategically pursue referrals from clients and other business associates.

Skill Two: Enhance Your Referability

If you give consistent exceptional service, your clients will want to refer you to their associates. If you are not receiving referrals, you need to evaluate the level of service you provide, as well as the relationships that you have with your clients. Make it a point to work on enhancing these relationships.

Skill Three: Prospect For Referrals

Develop a client-centered approach to referral development. Focus on delivering so much value to your clients that they will want to bring that value to others. Doing so will help both you and your client feel comfortable with the referral process. It will also enhance the quality of the referral and increase the likelihood that your client will actively make the connection (an introduction via an e-mail, phone call, or meeting).

Skill Four: Network Strategically

Networking with the right people is important to building a strong base of referral sources. It is important to identify professionals that want to help and, more importantly, have the means to help. You need to educate potential referral sources on the value you can bring to a client relationship and what differentiates you from the competition. Define what type of client you are looking for so they clearly understand your target market.

You should have a mutually beneficial relationship with referral sources. Each person needs to help the other grow his or her business. Look for opportunities refer business back, whenever possible, or to introduce the referral source to a contact that they can benefit from meeting. If you cannot refer business to the referral source, look for other ways to help including: coauthoring an article, inviting them to sit on a panel of experts or speaking at a seminar.

Skill Five: Target Niche Markets

Develop a reputation for being an expert or the "go to" person in an industry or service area. Invest the time to become a "famous" person in that industry. Speak at seminars, write articles for trade publications and become a leader in an industry organization.

IDENTIFYING REFERRAL SOURCES

In most CPA firms, referrals from clients are the predominant source of new business. This is to be expected; your clients know you, the quality of your work ,and the value that you bring to the relationship. Your clients can be influenced and coached to refer effectively. If you target your most satisfied, connected, and influential clients and provide them with guidelines on the type of business opportunities you are looking for, they will refer you to good qualified prospects. The key is to clearly communicate your intentions so that you do not put your relationship at risk and they do not feel uncomfortable about referring you to their business associates and friends.

Referrals from centers of influence (COI) are generally the next most frequent source of new business. Seventy-five percent of the participants in the RainToday.com study[5] stated that they are very or somewhat likely to find a professional service provider from a referral from another provider. COIs are individuals who, because of their professional, business, or personal acumen; exercise influence over the decisions made by others. The following is a list of the most common categories of COIs:

- Lawyers
- Bankers
- Financial planners
- Insurance brokers/agents

---

[5] How Clients Buy 2009 Benchmark Report on Professional Services Marketing and Selling from a Buyers Perspective *(Framingham. MA: Wellesley Hills Group, 2009) RamToday.com.*

- Stockbrokers
- Trade and industry association executives
- Alumni/alumnae of the Firm
- Other Accountants

COIs can refer effectively and often. Your challenge is to enhance their image of you and your firm by consistently adding value to your relationship. Because you may not have the opportunity to refer enough business back to them, the value you bring to the relationship is important. You need to become a resource to COIs. For example, you may not have the opportunity to refer many cases to a divorce lawyer, but you can be there for them when they need answers to difficult tax questions or advice on the tax consequences of a particular situation. This will make the lawyer look good in front of their clients and associates, as well as enhance your relationship.

The niche and service specialties in your firm will determine your most productive COI. In addition to the ones listed previously, the following are examples of other referral sources:

Industry	COI
Construction	Surety bond agents
	Commercial real estate agents
	Institutional lenders
	Architects
	Engineers
Healthcare	Hospital administrators
	Insurance brokers/agents
	Medical billing professionals
Service	**COI**
Litigation Support	Litigation attorneys
	Judges
	Other accountants
International Tax	Tax attorneys
	Consulates/embassies
Feasibility Studies	Architects
	Developers

Inside referrers are individuals that you have a strong relationship with and you feel the most comfortable asking for a referral. You may or may not refer business to these individuals. Inside referrers are

- partners in your firm,
- other firm employees,
- vendors,
- board members,
- friends,
- relatives,
- neighbors.

These individuals are familiar with the benefit you provide and have contact with people that need your service. Educating them on the value-added services you provide, as well as establishing guidelines for referral development work well with inside referrals. You need to consistently remind this group of what you do and how you provide value.

Referral partners are individuals that refer to you often and effectively. They are a higher level COI because you agree to refer business to each other. You have an established relationship with these individuals and invest time in learning to refer business opportunities to each other. You also invest an equal amount of time working to refer one another. Referral partners give you the opportunity to define what type of prospect you are looking for and how to find them. Referral partnerships are a win-win situation for both parties.

⚷ Key Concept

In most CPA firms, referrals from clients are the predominant source of new business.

APPROACHES TO REFERRAL SOURCE DEVELOPMENT

An introduction or recommendation from a referral source can lead to a new engagement faster than any other marketing method. If done properly, the referral source will presell the prospect on the value of doing business with you.

Figure 24-1 is a list of the typical ways CPAs develop new business opportunities. In the middle of this list is the success line. This line separates the best methods to win opportunities from the least likely. Whenever possible, work above the success line because a higher percentage of qualified leads will come from opportunities derived from these activities. Multiple strategies should be implemented to keep your pipeline full of qualified leads.

The advantages of referrals coming from above the success line are

1. trust is built quickly.
2. the prospect is more likely to communicate their needs.
3. the prospect has a good impression of you before you even meet them.
4. it produces a client service orientation within your firm.
5. it takes 5–10 times less activity to win the engagement.

The disadvantages of referrals coming from the bottom of the list are

1. the prospect is skeptical about the true value you can bring to the engagement.
2. the likelihood of rejection is increased.
3. there is a high cost associated with securing new business.
4. it places more pressure on the development new business opportunities.
5. you will have to work much harder to develop new business.

FIGURE 24-1   TYPICAL WAYS CPAs DEVELOP BUSINESS OPPORTUNITIES

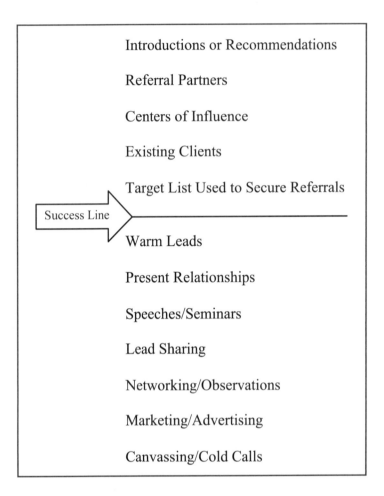

Strategies for Developing Strong Referral Source Relationships

The development of a strong referral relationship requires work and dedication. You should develop a strategy to move a relationship from the initial contact stage to the referral partner stage. You can do this by

- determining the wants and needs of the referrer.
- ascertaining if the referrer has the ability and interest in referring work.
- brainstorming to maximize the benefits to the referrer.
- determining specifically what you might want the referrer to do to find and introduce prospects to you.
- inspiring the referrer through referral success stories, client benefit stories, testimonials, vision or mission statements, and so on.
- developing a client profile.
- creating resources to help the referrer to easily and effectively identify referral candidates.
- targeting benefits to the referrer and prospects.
- preparing and making direct and specific requests to refer.
- scheduling meetings on a regular basis.
- developing an agenda for each meeting.
- following-up to move the referral process along.
- establishing goals and target dates.
- engaging in activities to build the relationship and develop a comfort level for referring business.
- presenting your referrer with a gift, doing them a favor, giving advice, helping them with a problem, or referring them new business.

- developing a relationship based on trust and value.
- becoming their friend.

> **♀ Key Concept**
>
> The development of a strong referral relationship requires work and dedication.

DEVELOPING YOUR PERFECT CLIENT PROFILE

You should be as specific as possible when you develop your Perfect Client Profile. Determine the revenue size, growth stage, number of employees, industry, niche, service needs, geographic market, and so on. Here are some examples:

> "I am interested in meeting the chief executive officer of a manufacturer of durable goods with sales revenues between $10M–$25M, especially if they have experienced a slow or declining growth rate. They could benefit from our profit enhancement services."

> "I am interested in meeting with the lead physician or practice manager of a four-to-eight doctor practice that has slow receivables because they are not managing their insurance claims well. This type of practice could benefit from our charge capture or account revenue management services."

> "I am looking to meet the chief financial officer of a construction company that is expanding into new markets and is having difficulty obtaining surety bonding. I can introduce them to surety agents that I have a strong relationship with and, if applicable, work with them to present their financials in a positive way."

Specific data to include in the client profile are the following:

- Annual sales revenue, number of employees, geographic area, industry, etc.
- Typical wants/needs of a prospect in a particular target market
- Services engaged by this type of company or individual
- Individuals using the service (that is, chief executive officer, chief financial officer, or audit committee chair)
- Decision maker at the company

Points that can be added to create urgency and need include the following:

- Mindset of the prospect
- Benefits they can realize by working with you
- Value you can bring to the relationship
- Short falls with the quality and service provided by their current account

THE FIVE-STEP REFERRAL SCRIPT

The following is a five-step referral script that has been proven to work with professionals who are marketing a high-value service with a long-term relationship.

1. *"I am expanding my practice and would welcome new clients. Would you feel comfortable introducing me to anyone of your caliber who might benefit from my services? I can assure you that I would do everything in my power to help them just as you hopefully feel I have served you."*

   This question will qualify the person for their willingness to refer work to you. It lets them know the direction you are going in and that you would like their assistance. By asking a qualifying closed-ended question that requires a "Yes" or "No" answer, you will know if the person is receptive and confident about referring you new business.

   If he or she is hesitant, you will need to spend more time qualifying the prospect and discussing the value you bring to each client relationship. At this time you might decide to develop a referral relationship with another person. This question will let you know exactly where you stand in the potential referrers eyes.

2. *"Since you would feel comfortable recommending me, let me give you a better description of my perfect client profile... Who do you know that might fit this profile?"*

   Question 2 identifies exactly what type of client you are looking for. Be as specific as possible. Discuss the value you can bring to this type of client. Use client success stories to make a point. By asking this question, you are asking the referrer to prequalify prospects for you based on their potential needs.

3. *"Tell me about the relationship you have with (prospect's name). On a scale of one-to- five, with five being that you value each other's opinion, where is your relationship at?"*

   With this question you are qualifying the referrer's relationship with the prospect. There must be a strong relationship (rated as a four or above) to proceed.

4. *"It sounds like you have a good relationship with (prospect's name). Would you take a few minutes to tell me more about it?"*

   Or

   "It sounds like it might not be an appropriate time for you to introduce me into your relation- ship with (prospect's name). Would that be a fair assessment?"

   Question 4 will give you the opportunity to learn more information about the prospect or make the decision not to move forward. If the referrer's relationship with the prospect is not as strong as you think it should be, it will produce a cold lead. This will require you to spend more time developing a relationship with the prospect. You goal is to obtain warm referrals or leads.

5. *"What would be the most appropriate way for you to introduce me to (prospect's name)?"*

   This question is critical. It will allow you to manage the process by suggesting a way for the referrer to introduce you. Your goal is to have the referrer engage in a conversation with the prospect about the value you can provide before the actual introduction and then be an active participant in the introduction. You will be more successful if the referrer participates in a lunch meeting, golf outing, or three-way conference call between you and the prospect. This way the refer- rer will be able to reinforce the reason why the introduction was made and act as your "sales force."

RESOURCES FOR MAKING QUALIFIED REFERRALS

Encouraging referral partners and clients to make referrals is only one step in the process. You must also ensure that your referral sources have the knowledge and materials needed to facilitate referrals. They need to know about your area of expertise, your firm, and the value you bring to each relationship. At a minimum, give your referral sources copies of your brochures, newsletters and other marketing collateral.

Whenever possible, educate your referral sources on your firm and services by hosting a seminar. Provide enough information for the referrer to intelligently discuss the value you can bring to the relationship. Make the information easy to understand and provide a "sell-sheet" or fact sheet. The sell-sheet should do the following:

- Briefly explain the service
- Describe what type of prospect you are looking for
- List benefits the prospect will realize
- Include high gain questions the referrer can use to qualify the prospect
- Identify competitive advantages

⚷ Key Concept

Ensure that your referral sources have the knowledge and materials needed to facilitate referrals.

Reward Referrers

Acknowledge all referrals received, even if they do not develop into a new business opportunity. Depending on the situation, call the referrer, write a thank you note or send a gift.

Establish a system to track referrals received, there value and outcome. Keep the referral source updated on your progress. Periodically review the referrals received with your source. Include the estimated fee and whether or not you won the engagement.

Reciprocate

Like you, most business people are looking for referrals to grow their business. Make sure that you reciprocate whenever possible. Track the referrals you give. Follow-up with the person you gave the referral to and determine the value and result. Include a discussion on the referrals you gave in your periodic reviews with your source.

Many CPAs believe that they are not in a position to offer as many referrals as they would like. That is why you should make the most of each opportunity. For example, if a client needs to finance the expansion of his facility, offer to help. Arrange an introduction to three different banks and accompany the client to the meetings. This will give you the opportunity to participate in the process, demonstrate your technical skills to the bankers and strengthen your relationship with your client.

PROGRAMS FOR MEETING AND DEVELOPING REFERRAL SOURCES

Now that you have learned the general principals of identifying and nurturing referral sources, here are some specific programs for developing a relationship with them.

Networking

Most CPAs devote time to networking at industry and trade associations, chambers of commerce, charitable organizations, and certified public accounting societies. Networking is the process of developing relationships before you need them so that you will be in the position to leverage that relationship when you have a need. One of the biggest shortcomings of networking is that most relationships stay on a superficial level. Conversations revolve around the weather, sports, news topics, and so on, without going down to the next level of detail. Even when the topic of business does come up, it is usually centered on one person telling another about his or her field without pursuing it in much more detail.

Another criticism of traditional networking is that most people who attend networking functions are there for one reason, to promote themselves and their business. They go into the function looking for "What's in it for me?" When involved in a conversation, they are listening to determine if the person is a prospect or if the person can help them. This focus results in individuals using the opportunity to sell themselves, instead of developing a relationship. Unless you spend time developing a relationship with the people you meet at a networking function, you will not have a high return on your investment.

> **♂ Key Concept**
>
> Networking is the process of developing relationships before you need them so that you will be in the position to leverage that relationship when you have a need.

NetWeaving

NetWeaving is a philosophy, as well as a set of learnable skills and strategies, developed by Bob Littell, a consultant from Atlanta, Georgia. It is a form of networking which focuses on helping others. Instead of looking for "What's in it for me?" the NetWeaver will approach the relationship with a different focus, "What's in it for them?" As result, stronger relationships are developed.

The essence of NetWeaving is helping others and in doing so, having the confidence to know that over time, you will also benefit. NetWeavers act without regard for what they will receive in return. A skilled NetWeaver is constantly on the lookout for ways to bring people together and to help people locate resources to meet their needs.

There are two key elements of NetWeaving. The first is learning to become a *strategic connector* of others—putting people together in win-win relationships—without gaining from the relationship.

The second element of NetWeaving is learning how to position yourself as a *strategic resource* for others. In other words, you become the "go to" person for getting something accomplished. Sometimes this means that you will be the resource provider. Other times it will mean that you will provide introductions from your *trusted resource network*—a broad group of experts in a variety of fields who have agreed to be a member of your network in exchange for you agreeing to be a part of theirs. The strength of the resources that you can provide your clients, associates, prospects, and friends are limited only by the strength of the people in your network.

Instead of spending time talking about them, the NetWeaver will ask high gain questions to discover information about another person, such as the following:

- How do you create revenue in your business?
- What does your best prospect look like?
- Tell me the story of how you landed your best client or customer?
- What are the strategic differentiators that make you unique?
- Who are the three or four people you would like to meet?

When communicating with other people, the NetWeaver is looking to determine:

1. Is there someone I know who would benefit from knowing or meeting this person?
2. Could this person provide information or resources to someone else I know?
3. Has this person impressed me so much that I need to get to know them better, and if they continue to impress me with their exceptional value, should I make them part of my trusted referral network?

Learning to listen for opportunities to help others can become the most valuable habit you will ever develop. In traditional networking you are looking for people to refer business to you. When you are in a NetWeaving frame of mind you are *talking* about referrals. It is not about getting someone to send you referrals, it's all about putting people together, and you are the referrer. There are four levels of giving referrals in NetWeaving. They are the following:

1. *Loaning your good name.* You simply give someone the name and contact information of someone else whom you believe that person would benefit from meeting. All you are doing is allowing the other person to use your good name as a means of entry. Everything else is left up to them.
2. *Loaning your good name plus a written introduction.* In addition to loaning your good name and reputation to one of the two people you are suggesting should meet, you also send an e-mail or a personal letter to the other person. Include an explanation of why you think the two would benefit from meeting, as well as a testimonial for the person you are referring with a biography or resume and information on his or her company.
3. *Loaning your good name, plus a written and telephone introduction.* In addition to the information in the level two referral, you follow-up with a personal telephone call to further validate the importance of the person's worth and the value of meeting the other person. You can also do this by means of a three-way phone introduction with both parties. The strength of the telephone call could eliminate the need for sending a note or e-mail.
4. *Hosting the introduction.* Even though the effectiveness and benefits derived from any of these levels of referral connections are good, they dwarf in comparison to hosting an introduction meeting. Hosting a meeting will give you the opportunity to provide an overview of why you feel the other two people would benefit from meeting each other. Hosting the meeting is the best form of giving a referral.

> ### 🔑 Key Concept
>
> NetWeaving is helping others and in doing so, having the confidence to know that over time, you will also benefit.

> ### 🔑 Key Concept
>
> Learning to listen for opportunities to help others can become the most valuable habit you will ever develop.

BUILDING A TRUSTED REFERRAL NETWORK

The individuals in your *trusted referral network* should be the "best of breed" in their service and industry. Since your reputation is on the line each time you give a referral, you need to make absolutely sure that the person you are referring will do an exceptional job. Third party testimonials about the quality of their work and recognition from acknowledged experts in their line of business are the best sources of this information.

People in your trusted referral network should

- demonstrate a high degree of integrity and sense of urgency.
- prove that they are competent at what they do.
- provide exceptional service that always exceeds your expectations.
- have a positive mental attitude.
- exhibit a need for accomplishment.
- develop a strong relationship and intangible bond with you.

In other words, you need to trust each individual in your network to consistently deliver high quality service.

When you are developing your trusted referral network you should search for the most qualified person in that area. Be very careful in your selection process if you really want your network to be powerful. If you put your network together properly, it will be a tremendous reflection on you.

Social Meetings

Meeting referral sources outside of the office is a good way to further develop your relationship. These meetings can take many forms, including the following:

- *Alumni/Alumnae functions.* Your alumni can be a good source for referrals. Host Alumni/Alumnae social events to keep in touch and invite them to attend continuing professional education programs. Keep them updated on what you are doing and new services. Introduce alumni to new team members. If the person has his or her own practice, develop a cross-referral relationship to generate new business opportunities for both firms. Make sure to add alumni to your mailing list for newsletters, firm announcements, and tax updates.
- *Breakfast, lunch, or dinner meetings.* Dining with a client or other referral source is the one of the most effective ways of solidifying your relationship and developing referrals. During meals, these referrals sources are relaxed and more likely to discuss their business and personal challenges. Frequently they will mention situations in which you can assist them or a business associate. Most likely they will ask about your firm, which will give you the opportunity to cross-sell services or ask for a referral.
- *Business-to-business mixers.* These meetings will give you, your partners, and other associates the opportunity to meet their counterparts at local law firms or banks. This type of event should be well organized to prove valuable. Prior to the meeting, an agenda should be established, allowing time for networking. The individuals in attendance should prepare a short introduction which would include information on their area of expertise, snapshot of a typical client, and a client success story. You might also consider a short presentation or seminar on a particular service as a subject for the meeting.

It is important to establish a follow-up action plan. You can assign people to each other prior to the event or request that the attendees choose someone afterwards. Follow-up can be in the form of a hand written note card; a social, networking, or educational outing; or simply adding the person to your mailing list. Without consistent follow-up, this method of referral development is low on the list of successful techniques.

- *Business referral clubs.* These organizations bring business people together for the explicit purpose of generating referrals from one another. Typically, there is only one member per industry or profession. Each member is required to give a certain number of referrals each month. A system is in place to track the number of referrals given by each member.
- *Civic, social, and trade associations.* Active participation in a few well chosen organizations can help you to generate referrals. Join organizations that attract members of your target market. Become actively involved by volunteering for committees which will give you visibility and the opportunity to meet people of influence in the organization.
- *Concerts, sports, theater, and other cultural or charitable events.* Special events will give you the chance to treat your referral sources. You can use this method to strengthen your existing relationship, thank them for a past referral, or as an opportunity to introduce you to their clients and associates. The perfect environment for this type of function is a luxury box at your local arena or VIP seating.
- *Golf outings.* If used correctly, golf outings are a powerful method of developing referral relationships. It is important to ensure that you are in the right foursome prior to the event. A good rule of thumb is to invite one referral source and someone that the referral source can benefit from meeting. You should ask the referral source to bring someone that you would like to meet. Avoid golfing with three other members of your firm.
- *Seminars.* Private seminars on a particular service that focus on the value you can provide are an effective way to generate new business opportunities. You can also host joint seminars with referral sources and invite each other's clients to attend. Another successful strategy is to invite your referral source to attend a seminar that you are giving with a guest. This can be a win-win situation for everyone. You have the opportunity to meet a prospect and showcase the firm, your referral source has the opportunity to spend quality time with the contact and the contact has the opportunity to learn new information.

KEEPING IN CONTACT WITH REFERRAL SOURCES

In addition to the techniques we have identified for developing and nurturing referral sources, it is important to establish a follow-up system. The following are ways to remind your clients and other referral sources of the value you provide:

- Send welcome letters to new clients.
- Thank clients in writing for the opportunity to serve them.
- Mail thank you letters to referral sources after every referral.
- Give a gift to those that have referred business to you throughout the year.
- Send a year-end thank you letter or card to clients and friends of the firm.
- Remember birthdays, anniversaries and other significant dates and facts.
- Present firm promotional items to clients and referral sources.
- Make a donation in the name of your clients or referral sources.
- Nominate clients or referral sources for an industry or service award.
- Publish general and niche specific newsletters.
- Periodically send a copy of the firm, service, or niche brochures.
- Send out mid-year and year-end tax planning letters or guides.
- Distribute articles and guides on relevant issues of interest.
- Buy a business book or complimentary subscription to an appropriate magazine for select clients or referral sources.

You should develop a "touch" plan to keep in contact with referral sources. Schedule at least four interactions (business or social, depending on the depth of your relationship) each year with key referral sources. Have breakfast, lunch, or dinner as frequently as possible. Because you need to touch some people more than others, schedule more interactions with members of your trusted referral network. These people are more likely to give you referrals than other sources. It is better to develop a close relationship with a small number of quality referral sources than to have casual contact with a large number.

> ### ⚷ Key Concept
>
> Develop a "touch" plan to keep in contact with referral services.

MOTIVATING FIRM MEMBERS TO DEVELOP REFERRAL RELATIONSHIPS

It has been suggested that most CPAs know what they should be doing to generate referrals, but they do not work at the process. This so-called marketing problem is really a management problem. The partner-in-charge of the firm or office must establish goals for each person based on their position at the firm. They must also provide employees with the training, tools and support to be successful.

There are lots of reasons why CPAs decide not to develop new business. Some of the most common excuses or obstacles are

- I do not have the time.
- It is not my responsibility.
- I do not think that I can be successful.
- I do not believe that selling is professional behavior for CPAs.
- I am not good at it.
- I became an accountant to provide technical services, not to sell those services.

Overcoming these objections can be a real challenge. The following are suggestions for encouraging employees to participate in new business and referral development:

1. Lead by example. If firm members see the partner(s) actively working on referral sources, they are more likely to view it as an appropriate activity.
2. Establish clear goals for each individual that are measurable and obtainable. Goals can be monetary or activity driven.
3. Provide training on relationship development, networking, and other marketing skills.
4. Establish a mentoring program and invite colleagues to meetings with your clients and referral sources.
5. Hire a marketing director or coordinator to develop personal marketing plans. Have that person meet with each individual on a quarterly basis to ensure that they are meeting the goals outlined in their Personal Marketing Plan. For more information, see chapter 5, "Developing a Personal Marketing Plan."
6. Give employees the tools that they need to market the firm. These include business cards for every employee, including the administrative team; "sell sheets" or service fact sheets; training for everyone on the firm's services; and expenses accounts, when applicable.
7. Reward and recognize people for their efforts. Offer a bonus program for new business, an incentive program for business development activities or a public recognition program. See chapter 33, "Effective Employee Incentive Programs: How to Bring Out the Best in Your Firm," for more information on incentive programs.

TRACKING SYSTEMS

As previously discussed, it is critical that you track the referrals in and out of your firm. Tracking systems are helpful for gauging activity levels and results. Whatever tracking system you use, make it simple to use and easy to maintain.

See appendix 24-1 for a sample *referral source data form*. This form can be used to record information on the individual including, his or her contact, personal info, relationship, company, and activity data.

Appendix 24-2 shows a sample *referral tracking form*. You can use this form to record data on referrals received and given, as well as detailed information on the referral, such as its estimated value, the results, and follow-up activities.

Client relationship management (CRM) systems, such as Seibel, Oracle, SalesLogix, Sage Accpac, Interaction, Microsoft Dynamics CRM, Salesforce, Netsuite, Sugar CRM, ACT, or Goldmine, can easily track new business, contact relationships and referrals. The forms in the appendixes can be used to collect data to input into a CRM system. The advantage of this type of computer program is that you can quickly determine who has a relationship with whom, as well as what was discussed with each contact and how the relationship is developing. You can also schedule meetings and reminders to follow-up with contacts. For more information on databases and CRM systems, see chapter 22, "Databases That Fuel Your Marketing Efforts."

Social Networking

There are many social networking sites that you can join to connect with people. The most popular for business purposes are LinkedIn and Facebook. Each allows you to post a personal profile and develop an online network. LinkedIn also allows users to post recommendations, which in essence is a referral testimony.

Twitter is another popular site to develop an online presence. You can post short messages, commonly referred to as "tweets," to people that are connected to you. Twitter gives you the opportunity to provide information of value to people in your online network quickly and efficiently.

Naymz is a reputation building network that allows up to 10 people to provide a reference for you. Based on your references and other factors, Naymz assigns a *RepScore* to your profile. Participating in Naymz is one way to establish your online creditability.

Even though social networking is becoming increasingly popular, people still buy from people they KNOW, LIKE, and TRUST. To make social networking work, you should

- target a specific audience—that is important to you and your firm.
- be a thought leader; provide valuable information of interest to your target audience.
- make quality connections—with people that are in the position to do business with you or refer business to you.
- encourage people to contact you—both on and offline.
- participate in online discussions; consider starting or participating in a blog.

For more information, see chapter 17, "Adding Social Media to Your Marketing Mix."

Conclusion

The ultimate key to the success of your referral source development program is adding value to the relationship. This value can come in many forms, such as giving qualified referrals or becoming a trusted resource. It is important that you follow-through and deliver what you promise, as well as follow-up and maintain frequent contact with each of your referral sources. In this chapter we have covered a wide variety of techniques you can implement to successfully develop new clients through referrals. It is important to remember that it is not the quantity of the referral sources or number of activities that you do, but the quality of those sources and activities. You will be more successful if you can develop a strong trusted referral network with a handful of people that provide exceptional service and are passionate about referring business to you, than a larger group with lower expectations.

Sources

The sections on NetWeaving, Building a Relationship Based on Trust and Building a Trusted Referral Network was summarized with the permission of Robert S. Littell author of *The Heart and Art of NetWeaving* (Atlanta, GA: NetWeaving International Press, 2003). Visit www.netweaving.com for more information.

Several of the concepts in this chapter were developed by Eric Taylor, author of *The Energy Passport and Your Best Year Ever – 12 Secrets & Strategies for Unlimited Success.* For more information about Eric Taylor and his programs visit www.MoveAhead1.com.

Some of the ideas presented in this chapter were originally written by Christian Frederiksen, CPA and Managing Partner of Frederiksen & Co., CPAs in Mill Valley, California for the first edition of this book.

Aubrey Wilson, *Practice Development for Professional Firms* (London: McGraw-Hill (UK), 1984).

SUGGESTIONS FOR FURTHER READING

Mike Schultz and John E. Doerr, *Professional Services Marketing*, (Hoboken, NJ: John Wiley & Sons, Inc.)

Jeffrey Gitomer, *Little Teal Book of Trust*, (Saddle River, NJ: Bard Press, 2008)

Jeffrey Gitomer, *Little Black Book of Connections*, (Austin, TX: Bard Press, 2006)

Keith Ferrazzi, *Never Eat Alone*, (New York, NY: Currency Doubleday, 20005)

Bill Cates, *Get More Referrals Now! The Four Cornerstones That Turn Business Relationships into Gold*, (New York, NY: McGraw-Hill, 2004)

Jeffrey Gitomer, *Little Red Book of Selling*, (Austin, TX: Bard Press, 2004)

Timothy L. Templeton, *The Referral of a Lifetime: The Networking System That Produces Results*, (San Francisco, CA: Berrett-Koehler Publishers, Inc., 2003)

Diane Darling, *The Networking Survival Guide*, (New York, NY: McGraw-Hill, 2003)

Robert S. Littell, *The Heart and Art of NetWeaving*, (Atlanta, GA: NetWeaving International Press, 2003)

Robert S. Littell and Donna Fisher, CSP, *Power NetWeaving: 10 Secrets to Successful Relationship Marketing*, (Cincinnati, OH: The National Underwriter Company, 2001)

Donna Fisher, *Professional Networking for Dummies*, (New York, NY: Wiley Publishing, 2001)

Bob Burg, *Endless Referrals: Network Your Everyday Contacts into Sales*, (New York, NY, McGraw-Hill, 1999)

Ford Harding, Rain Making, *The Professionals Guide to Attracting New Clients*, (Avon MA: Adams Media Corporation, 1994)

Aubrey Wilson, *Practice Development for Professional Firms* (London: McGraw-Hill (UK), 1984).

Dale Carnegie, *How to Win Friends & Influence People*, (New York, NY: Pocket Books, a division of Simon & Schuster, Inc., 1936)

ABOUT THE AUTHOR

Eileen Monesson, MBA, is a Principal with the Marketing Services Group at Cowan, Gunteski & Co., P.A. In this role she is responsible for strategic marketing planning, practice development, branding, and public relations. She holds a Master of Business Administration degree in Marketing and Computer Information Systems from the Lubin School of Business at Pace University and a Bachelor of Science degree in Marketing from Richard Stockton College of New Jersey. Ms. Monesson is an adjunct professor of graduate and undergraduate courses in public relations, managerial communications, and strategic management at Georgian Court University.

Appendix 24-1
Referral Source Data Form

Name _____

Title _____

Company _____

Address _____

Telephone _____ Fax _____

Mobile _____ Home Phone _____

Email _____

Personal Data (Birthday, Anniversary, Spouse, Children, Home Town, Secretary, Favorite Sport, Hobby, Drink, Other) _____

_____

Mailing List(s) _____

Principal Contact at the Firm _____

Other Contacts at the Firm _____

Relationships Outside of the Firm _____

Introduced By/At _____

Industry/Sales Revenue _____

Product/Service _____

Trusted Referral Network   Yes _____   No _____   Future Member _____

Activities

Date	Activity	Description	Follow-up/Comments

Activity Codes: A–Association Meeting, AC–Anniversary Card, B–Breakfast, BC–Birthday Card, BR–Brochure, C–Correspondence, D–Dinner, G–Gift, GO–Golf Outing, HC–Holiday Card, L–Lunch, OE–Other Entertainment, P–Promotional Item, M–Mailing, N–Nomination, S–Seminar, V–Visit

APPENDIX 24-2
REFERRAL TRACKING FORM

Team Member _____

Date _____

Please check one of the following:

Referral Received ☐   Referral Given ☐

To/From

Name _____

Company _____

Address _____

Phone _____

Fax _____

E-mail _____

Prospective Client _____

Company _____

Address _____

Telephone _____

Fax _____

E-Mail _____

Details

_____

_____

Estimated Value _____

Result _____

Send Thank You to _____

Type of Thank You

Card _____   Gift _____

Date Sent _____

Type of Gift _____

Follow-up _____

CHAPTER 25
Utilizing Seminars to Build Your Practice

Leisa Gill

Lattimore Black Morgan & Cain, PC

INTRODUCTION

Marketing, at its core, is about perception. Marketing is a process of creating *perceived value* in the eyes of your target audience. Marketing is also the process that drives lead generation for firms. In the context of providing professional services and, specifically, providing accounting, auditing, and tax services to businesses and individuals, your primary goal is to create, maintain, and increase the perceived value of your services in the eyes of your existing and prospective clients, potential referral sources, community and industry leaders, and even your competitors. This is true whether you are a local accounting firm marketing your services to small businesses, a regional or national accounting firm targeting middle-market and public companies, or a local solo practitioner who provides tax planning services to individuals.

Seminars, Webinars, and, more broadly, public speaking opportunities provide an ideal marketing vehicle for the accounting profession. For the purpose of this chapter, we are going to call these events. They present the opportunity to communicate useful information to clients and prospects while showcasing your skills and experience. Clients and prospects perceive this as "value" being delivered. Moreover, you or your firms association with events helps develop your reputation—how others perceive you—as an authority in your field. Participating in seminars, Webinars, and the like can be useful tools to emphasize your firm as a thought leader in a particular area. Your participation in these events helps create "brand" awareness, even if your brand is nothing more than your name and the "awareness" is the mere fact that individuals and businesses in your target market begin to associate you and your firm with your field of expertise. Whether you ultimately deliver real value to your existing clients and to the new clients that result from this process is a matter of your own professional practice. The primary goal of this chapter is marketing—developing perceived value in you, your firm, and the services you have to offer—through your development of and participation in events and public speaking opportunities.

By utilizing a speaking program in your firm you have the opportunity to build your practice and generate new business opportunities for your firm. One caveat, as with anything you do to generate awareness of your firm, services, and expertise, a thorough follow up program is critical to the success of any marketing vehicle or program. Through the development of this perceived value and, ultimately, your reputation and goodwill, business development opportunities will naturally follow.

This chapter focuses primarily on developing your own events and other speaking opportunities. There are a host of opportunities to participate with other organizations in their existing and planned events, conferences, trade shows, and similar forums, and of course you should be actively seeking out those opportunities for many of the same reasons described in this chapter. However, it is beyond the scope of this chapter to provide guidance on the benefits of your joining and participating in local chambers of commerce, trade and industry associations, and other similar organizations that also hold events. Rather, this chapter is targeted toward the individual CPA or accounting firm interested in creating their own event as a marketing vehicle specifically tailored to your target audience and specifically designed to meet your marketing objectives. When successfully organized, planned, developed, marketed, and executed, this type of seminar/event can be among the most cost effective marketing tools at your disposal.

This chapter will help you understand the entire process of seminar planning and the tasks and logistics involved. Whether you are planning a breakfast seminar in your office, a 60-minute Webinar, or a two-day conference at a destination resort, this will be a time intensive process that should not be taken lightly. The old saying of you get out of something what you put into it, definitely applies here. You will want to ensure a professional, problem-free event for both your speakers and your audience. A poorly planned and executed event will drain internal time and resources and can actually damage your goodwill and reputation. However, if you understand the scope of the project and plan, staff and outsource accordingly, and define a follow up process, you will reap the benefits of an incredibly enjoyable and effective marketing tool for you and your firm.

DEFINING OBJECTIVES

Marketing Objectives—What Are You Trying to Accomplish?

Planning, developing, and holding an event that is effective in meeting your marketing objectives requires significant planning and focus. Everything about your event from its topic and speaker to the venue and the ways your seminar is promoted and marketed, should be guided by the objectives you define at the beginning of the planning process.

Events are not an end in themselves—they are just a vehicle for achieving some predetermined marketing objectives. Some example are

- to communicate important new tax, accounting, or business information to your current clients in a timely and interesting manner;
- to showcase your services to a mixed audience of clients, prospects, and referral sources; and
- to increase your firm's visibility before a targeted industry group or profession.

Each of these objectives supports a second, more basic goal, which is to bring key clients, prospects and referral sources into closer contact with the firm. When a seminar's content and format are carefully planned, your partners and managers will have an opportunity to meet with these important people, and in so doing, strengthen existing relationships and create new ones.

Key Concept

Everything about your event from its topic and speaker to the venue and the ways your seminar is promoted and marketed, should be guided by the objectives you define at the beginning of the planning process.

Audience Objectives—Why Do They Want to Attend?

Once the marketing objectives of the seminar have been established, you must consider the information objectives for your seminar audience. What are the information needs of the people you are trying to target through your seminar? For instance, if you have determined in your marketing objectives that your goal is to draw senior executives representing a specific industry group or profession to your seminar, find out what these people are concerned about. One way to accomplish this is to telephone several key clients and interview them about their information needs. Other less direct approaches include speaking to industry experts or trade association leaders, or even sending out a survey with topic ideas for your target market to select and offer suggestions. The more you have your key audience involved in the building of the agenda, the more likely you are to have an event that is specifically focused on their needs, thus building a greater attendance.

Whatever the topic, the seminar must provide useful information that participants will perceive as valuable, and that is not readily available through other means. Whether you choose a new twist on a topic, focus on a particular sub-topic, or provide a unique event through the participation of particular industry or government experts, you should create an event that is distinguishable from other opportunities for your attendees. Often unique venues and networking opportunities provide the distinction necessary for a successful event.

Finally, even though one of your marketing objectives will undoubtedly be to showcase your firm's services and expertise, your topic must have legitimate educational value for the audience. Clients, prospects, and referral sources will not be impressed with an overt attempt to sell the firm's services. This is often where events fail. Step back from the process during the planning phase and assess how your event will be perceived by your potential audience. If you were in their shoes, would you consider this seminar as a mere sales pitch by the firm? Or would you view it as an opportunity to gain useful knowledge, obtain useful take-away materials, and take part in a beneficial networking event? Which would you rather attend?

> **? Key Concept**
>
> Clients, prospects, and referral sources will not be impressed with an overt attempt to sell the firm's services. This is often where events fail.

DETERMINING THE SEMINAR'S FORMAT

A wide variety of events exists and we will review the most useful ones here. The most important variables in deciding which format is best for your program are the targeted audience size, the length of the event, and the desired level of interaction between the speaker (or speakers) and the audience. As you review the following options, think back to your program's marketing objectives and audience objectives to determine which format would best accomplish your goals. Also consider the length of the program you are planning and the comfort of your attendees. Formats that might work for a one-hour breakfast seminar may be inappropriate for a full-day seminar with multiple speakers.

- *Lecture.* This is the traditional theater format most people are familiar with (the speaker is at the front of the room, usually on a platform, and the audience is seated in rows, facing the speaker). It is ideal when you plan to have a large audience and the subject matter is such that interaction between the presenter and the audience can be limited to a brief question and answer period at the end of the lecture.
- *Classroom.* The classroom format does not differ markedly from the lecture format, except there are narrow tables in front of each row of chairs so participants can comfortably follow handouts and take notes. This format is ideal when the subject matter is rather technical and it is expected that participants will want to take notes. This format should also be considered for any program that will last longer than approximately 90 minutes. In addition to providing a table for handouts and note taking, tables in today's classroom seminars are used to hold laptop computers, mobile devices, water pitchers, and refreshments. This set-up also makes it easier for attendees to step out of the seminar as needed without significant disruption. For seminars exceeding 90 minutes, your audience will be much more comfortable and attentive in this format.
- *Roundtable events.* The format of this type of event is suggested by the title; the audience and the speaker are seated around a large conference table. In this arrangement, the target audience is usually small—often no more than a dozen people. An ideal venue would be your firm's own conference room. This format should be utilized when you are trying to achieve a high level of interaction between the speaker and the audience. It is an excellent format, for example, when you want to hold a small seminar for executives from a particular industry or profession. Key clients and prospects who share a specific concern can hear from an expert and explore specific questions in depth. The speaker's formal remarks can be quite brief, and he or she can apply energy instead to answering questions and offering advice that has real meaning for those attending. On the other hand, this format can also be quite intimidating and create the impression of being "cornered" in a sales pitch in your offices. Potential attendees considering whether to attend will have a natural aversion to this format if they do not have a prior professional relationship with your partners.
- *Webinars.* This format is not geographically restricted and attendees need only log on or link into a Web site for the presentation. It can be as simple as a pre-recorded voice over PowerPoint or can be a live Webinar where you utilize a Web tool to take questions from your audience. Often this allows you to get information out quickly and cost effectively to varying sizes of audiences. Again, be sure you are providing a venue that fits your audience needs and composition. A Webinar may not be a solution for an older audience that might not be as technologically savvy.

Selecting Your Speakers

With your marketing objectives, audience interests, seminar topic, program length and format determined, you now must focus on selecting your speakers. Many professional service firms make the mistake at this early stage of deciding that they must limit their pool of potential speakers to their own firm. As discussed in this section, you should consider the length of your presentation, the type of information being presented, and the need to keep the interest of your audience and create an interesting and enjoyable experience.

Time Considerations

As a general rule, unless an individual presenter is very charismatic and engaging, he or she should not speak solo for more than 60 to 90 minutes, and preferably should be limited to 45 to 60 minutes. Audiences generally prefer variety to maintain their attention and interest. Consider whether a specific presentation or segment of your event could be presented by multiple speakers, or as a more casual conversation where multiple individuals have microphones and may interject whenever they prefer.

Use Your Best Speakers

While it is natural to think of asking one of your firm's more senior partners or managers to be a speaker or panelist at your seminar out of respect for their seniority or the size of their book of business, this is not always the best approach. Your most technically brilliant partner or your best rainmaker may not possess commensurate speaking ability, and could resort to using overly complex language (that is, accounting jargon) that is difficult for the audience to comprehend.

If you decide on an in-house speaker, be sure the chosen partner or manager will make an effective presentation. If his or her public speaking skills need improvement, arrange for the firm member to rehearse the presentation before a small audience. You might also consider asking a professional speaking coach to help with fine-tuning their presentation.

A key advantage in selecting an in-house speaker is that you will be working with a known quantity. Another benefit is that this partner or manager will be able to showcase your firm's expertise while on the podium. These are perfectly valid reasons for asking someone from inside the firm to make the presentation. If, however, you choose an in-house speaker just to save the price of an honorarium, remember that the firm must still absorb the cost of the presenter's preparation and presentation time.

Outside Speakers

Using an outside speaker has its own merits and disadvantages. An expert in a particular subject can give your seminar some added appeal. On the other hand, the speaker will represent his or her own organization. And, of course, you may have to pay an honorarium. By the way, don't confuse industry expertise and impressive credentials with the ability to inform and engage an audience. Ask to hear the candidate speak before committing (if you can't arrange to hear the speaker in person, try asking for an audio tape or video clip of one of his or her previous presentations).

Industry experts or high-profile executives who are also firm clients make up another possibility. By asking one of your own clients to be the guest speaker, you help strengthen the relationship that you already have with him or her, and you demonstrate to prospects in the audience that your relationships with clients are especially close. One disadvantage of this approach, of course, is that you could not ask a client to audition for you or to provide proof of his or her ability as a public speaker.

Moderated Panels—The Best of Both Worlds

You should also strongly consider the use of moderated panel discussions, which are usually very well received and generally obtain the highest ratings in post-seminar evaluations. A well planned panel composed of individuals from a variety of perspectives could be moderated by an individual in your firm, and could include an individual from your firm, one or more executives from your clients or other industry participants, noncompeting professionals such as lawyers or investment bankers, government officials and representatives, and academics. In this scenario, the moderator and panelists share proposed questions and topics that will be discussed prior to the seminar, so that panelists have a chance to consider their thoughts and responses on specific issues and topics. Similarly, if the subject matter is particularly complex, you minimize the chance of having an audience participant ask a question that a single speaker would be unable to answer.

The main thought to take away from this section and to remember when developing your own events is that you can meet your marketing objectives without limiting the seminar to speakers solely from your firm. The involvement of other professionals, business executives, and the like will lessen the likelihood that your seminar will be dismissed as a mere sales pitch for your firm, while still developing your reputation as an industry or topic expert. Moreover, you will build goodwill with the outside speakers and their firms, and will be perceived by your audience as a member—perhaps even a leader—of a broader network of complementary professional service providers and industry leaders.

> ### ⚑ Key Concept
>
> Consider the use of moderated panel discussions, which are usually very well received and generally obtain the highest ratings in post-seminar evaluations.

Venue Choices

The location chosen for your seminar is an important factor in an individual's decision to attend and is often overlooked. It is also potentially the largest source of expense and headache in your planning process. If you are planning a small seminar for clients and close contacts that will be held in your firm's conference room, then of course the complexity and risk will be reduced. On the other hand, entire books have been written for event planners on how to negotiate and mitigate risks when booking events at hotels and conference centers. The following subsections of this chapter will assist you in your process of determining the right venue for your seminar, and will provide some of the important factors to keep in mind when negotiating with off-site facilities.

Room Size

Audience size is, of course, one of the most important variables when it comes to choosing a seminar site. You want the room to be pleasingly full without overcrowding. An empty room will drain energy from the audience and make people think your seminar was not successful. An overcrowded room will simply be an irritant to everyone present.

Determining your actual audience size is easier said than done. If you have held multiple events in the past, then your prior attendance figures will be your best determinant of future attendance. There is no general rule on what response rate to expect from your invitations and the marketing of your event. As you consider facilities, you should keep in mind both minimum and maximum attendance figures for the event. The minimum figure would be the number of attendees below which you will choose to cancel or postpone the event. The maximum figure will be determined by the facility you choose. You should strive to ensure that your chosen facility has the ability to be flexible and accommodate your event within your determined range. It is easier to reduce the number of seats in a room than it is to squeeze an unanticipated 20 or 30 people into a room not meant for them. If, in the final analysis, you do find the room is going to be too large, it may be possible to utilize air walls, screens or potted palms to make the room seem smaller. This is an important item to review with hotel management when you are making your site inspections.

The largest risk in determining room size will arise if you are working in reverse—that is, you have a room in your firm or another company's offices that you want to use, and you are trying to determine the number of attendees that the room can hold. When making these estimations, you must consider the size of your staging area, and the format of your setup (lecture, classroom, etc.). There are online event planning resources that can help you in making these estimates.

If you determine to hold the event at a hotel or conference facility, they will have meeting planners who will be intimately familiar with their own facilities and the number of attendees that will work in any room for any given format. Indeed, if they are not able to immediately discuss this type of information with you, you should seek another facility or use extreme caution in proceeding. The process of holding an event at a hotel or other outside facility is complicated enough when everything works perfectly. Staff inexperience or lack of knowledge is an early warning sign of problems that are likely to come. A few words of caution—facilities can often put too many people in a room which can make for tight meeting space. Always fault on having more space than too little.

On-Site or Off-Site

Holding the seminar in your firm's offices, if appropriate for your program, can be beneficial because you have the chance to show off your people and your facilities. If your office has a board room or a lecture room that will seat the target audience comfortably, consider using it. If there is nothing suitable, perhaps another company has a room you could use. Banks and law firms are good candidates. As mentioned earlier in this chapter, however, step back and consider the event from the viewpoint of your target audience. If you would hesitate to attend because of any impression that you would be coming to a sales-pitch in another's company's offices, you should consider holding the event at an off-site facility.

If your event is being marketed to a large audience, or if you otherwise determine that holding the seminar on-site is not ideal, you should consider the range of off-site facilities that are available. These include not only hotels, conference centers, clubs, and convention centers, but also more unique venues such as museums, restaurants, and universities. Hotels, conference centers, and convention facilities book well in advance so you may need to contract with them for event facilities anywhere from two to six months in advance. Check your local calendar for other major conventions, sporting events, and the like, as these events may result not only in limited space availability but also increased room rental fees and food and beverage prices.

 Key Concept

> Holding the seminar in your firm's offices, if appropriate for your program, can be beneficial because you have the chance to show off your people and your facilities.

Negotiating Facility Costs

Negotiating with hotels, conference centers, and convention centers is an art form and covering all of the issues that must be addressed is beyond the scope of this chapter. Make an ally of the salesperson assigned to help you, and of course be sure and obtain bids from more than one facility. While there are many "industry standard" terms and conditions common to the event industry, competition usually rules the day and most items are, to some extent, negotiable. One of your first actions once you have contacted a potential facility should be to request a copy of their standard contract. There are a host of concepts and charges that are unique to this industry and that you should be familiar with. If the size of your event merits it, you may want to have an attorney assist in reviewing the contract.

- *Service charges, gratuity, and tax.* Most hotels and similar facilities add a service charge or gratuity to the price of each and every item for which you are charged. Sales tax is then added to the combined price after adding the service charge. This combination can easily add 25 percent to 35 percent to the otherwise expected price of everything you are purchasing from the hotel, whether it is the room rental fee or the price of a can of soda. Service charges normally run from 15 percent to 20 percent, and taxes are determined by your local taxing jurisdiction. Make sure you drill down on all pricing items and are clear about the total cost and exposure for each item or service you choose to purchase.

- *Cancellation policies.* The contract with your off-site facility will undoubtedly include a cancellation policy, usually a sliding scale depending on how close to the scheduled seminar date you cancel. While you do not want to enter into this process expecting to cancel a seminar, you may determine that it is necessary to do so. Be sure you understand and can accept the consequences at the outset.
- *Cutoff dates and attrition.* These concepts concern the estimated number of attendees and sleeping rooms included in your initial contract with the hotel or other facility, and changes in those numbers based on the actual number of people who register to attend your event. Before signing a contract with any facility, be sure you understand the consequences of increases or decreases in the number of attendees at your event, and make note of deadlines for notifying the facility of such changes. Failure to consider these constraints in your contract can result in substantial penalties and extra fees (to which service charges and gratuity will be added as well!).
- *Audio/visual fees.* This area is often overlooked as unimportant in the early stages of your planning process, but most professionals who are new to the event planning industry will be shocked (and perhaps outraged) at the terms, conditions, and prices involved at many hotels and conference centers. Your facility may have express restrictions on bringing in your own audio/visual equipment. On the other hand, they may charge you a fee to do so. Moreover, every individual piece of equipment will include a unit rental price and often a labor charge (again, which will be supplemented by service charges and taxes). You will likely find that the rental price for an LCD projector is around 50 percent of the price of a new projector! Rental fees for an extension cord may run $50 per day. The hotel may provide a podium free of charge, but they will then charge you $50–$200 for a microphone. Oh, and did you want that microphone connected to their house PA system, as opposed to your own speakers and amplifier? If so, add on another fee. Without being too tongue-in-cheek, the point here is that your audio-visual fees can run hundreds—and even thousands—of dollars, even for a simple half-day seminar. Compounding the problem is that many professionals gloss over these items in the initial contract, and do not appreciate everything that they need (and that will be separately priced) until the day before (or day of) the event. Carefully plan your audio-visual requirements for your event, and require the facility to provide an itemized price list for everything, including their prices and penalties for last-minute changes. Compare these prices to the prices provided by third-party audio-visual suppliers. And finally, negotiate!
- *Internet access.* If you plan on needing a connection to the Internet for any aspect of your seminar, be sure and discuss this thoroughly with the hotel or other facility. A welcome trend is that many hotels are installing wi-fi (wireless) Internet access throughout their facilities, often with access available to guests free-of-charge or for a nominal daily fee. However, these same hotels will charge you fees for this access ($350–$600).

EVENT PROMOTION

The methods you use to promote and market your event will depend on the target audience you wish to reach and your budget constraints. Among the various options you have to consider include

- word-of-mouth;
- invitations on firm letterhead;
- professionally printed invitations;
- brochures (PDF or printed);
- postcards;
- e-mail;
- advertisement (Web, print, etc.);
- media sponsorships/partnerships; and
- partner to client personal invitation/calls.

The best marketing method for your seminar will most likely be a combination of several marketing techniques. Perhaps the strongest promotion comes from partner or professional directly to the client or prospect. This direct, word-of-mouth promotion has the highest rate of return, yet it is commonly presumed that the "other guy" is promoting the event and that, since we share many of the same contacts, I do not need to do so. An easy way to encourage this type of promotion is to provide each professional in your firm with scripted communications that they can forward. This could be text promoting the event that can be dropped into a letter or e-mail.

Effective Marketing Pieces

Whether you choose to produce typeset invitations, professional 4-color glossy brochures, or an HTML e-mail advertisement, there are several concepts to keep in mind to help increase the effectiveness of your efforts.

1. Develop an invitation that is both informative and eye catching. Use language that appeals to the target audience. An invitation that is sent out on firm letterhead is fine, but one that is designed, typeset, and printed will make a better impression. While this may mean you have to spend more money, the extra cost will pay off in increased attendance and visibility for your firm.

2. The invitation should always specify how people can register. Provide a telephone number; a self-addressed, stamped registration card; a form coupled with an envelope; and a Web site and/or an e-mail address that can be used for registration. This will help improve your rate of response.

3. Whenever possible, ask partners to add a personal note, especially to new clients and important prospects.

4. Send out the announcements three to six weeks before the event (again, the amount of lead time needed depends on which region of the country you live in; allow more time in large metropolitan areas). If you are sending more than 500 direct mail pieces, consider using bulk mail and engaging a mail house to affix labels for you (if you choose this option, move your mailing deadline up, as bulk rate envelopes may be delivered a week to 10 days later than first class).

5. To increase the rate of response, send out reminder announcements one week before the event, and follow up with phone calls two to three days before the event. The reminders could be postcards (if within your budget) or e-mails. Phone calls from partners, managers, and staff will yield a higher response rate.

Utilize Online Event Planning Resources

In recent years, a wealth of online resources and solutions have been developed for the event planning industry. While you should always keep in mind your target audience and the impression made by your means of announcement, it may be the case that the most cost effective solution will be to utilize one of these online resources. As a bonus, many of these on-line companies also automate many of the registration and logistics tasks involved with event production, including tracking results and responses, notifying you of bad e-mail addresses, allowing on-line registration, and automating the distribution of reminders. A Web search for event or Webinar companies will undoubtedly yield a variety of choices to consider.

Your Target Mailing List

Your mailing list is extremely important, whether you are doing direct mail invitations or e-mail announcements. You do not want to wait until the mailing deadline arrives to find out whether or not you have a usable list of clients and prospects.

Many firms compile their client mailing list from billing addresses. The problem is that, while accurate, these records may only contain the name of the company and a mailing address—not the proper name of the CEO, the CFO, and the head of human resources.

If you plan to send invitations to prospects, where will you get your list? Again, a well-defined objective will help you determine who to target. With selection criteria in hand, you can consult mailing list brokers, local industry and professional associations, the chamber of commerce, and specialized yellow page directories. You should also scour the Internet for mailing list resources. When purchasing a direct mail or e-mail list, ask if there is a guarantee of the number of addresses that will be deliverable, and expect to pay more for a higher level of accuracy.

Special Considerations for E-Mail

If you have an e-mail address, you are probably quite familiar with spam—the term used to refer to unsolicited commercial e-mail. While there is a natural pejorative connotation associated with the use of unsolicited commercial e-mails, there is an important distinction between unscrupulous "spammers" who send out millions of e-mails per day and who strive to disguise and hide their identities, and the use of unsolicited e-mails in specific, targeted campaigns within the bounds of the law.

Most states also have regulations concerning the use of unsolicited e-mail and the Internet, and it is beyond the scope of this chapter to detail the varying regulations. Many people have very strong feelings about the use of unsolicited commercial e-mail, and this chapter is not taking a position on whether you should or should not use this means of promotion. However, this can be a very effective means of spreading information about your event if you do so in a constrained and deliberate manner. Of course, if there are any state or federal rules or regulations concerning unsolicited advertising by certified public accountants, you will of course be bound by those.

Publicity

Would your seminar topic or one or more of your speakers or panelists be of interest to the media? Send news releases to local dailies and business publications and invitations to select journalists. Of course, if you have promoted the seminar by offering clients exclusive information or advice, they may not be pleased to see the speaker's comments in the next day's business journal. Use discretion in inviting journalists, and always consider the information needs of your client first.

The cachet of exclusivity is also something to consider as you decide whether or not to publicize the seminar through newspaper ads or press releases. While this approach may yield a larger audience, you cannot be assured that those who are drawn to your program are ideal prospects for your firm. These kinds of considerations shouldn't prevent you, however, from taking photographs at the seminar, and then including a story in the next issue of your client newsletter.

SEMINAR LOGISTICS

Time of Day

When setting the date and time of the seminar, consider the needs of the audience. For example, if you are speaking to physicians, keep the presentation fairly short and hold the seminar on an evening. A financial planning seminar for working couples could be held at the end of the workday. By contrast, business owners and senior managers would probably prefer a breakfast or lunch meeting.

Length of the Program and Program Timetable

Again, the subject matter and information needs of your audience will be paramount considerations in determining the length of the program. You must also take into consideration how busy the target audience is and if they have pending deadlines that might prevent them from attending. For instance, no matter how critical the subject, an audience to be made up of private-practice physicians is not likely to sit still for a seminar that lasts more than two hours.

As you work to calculate the overall length of your program, consider the following elements:

- Registration and seating—allow up to 30 minutes for this phase of the seminar, especially if you are providing coffee and continental breakfast.

- The presentation—make sure your speakers and moderators understand how important it is for him or her to start and finish on time.
- Question and answer period—allow sufficient time for questions and answers following each particular speaker's or panel presentation.
- Reception—if appropriate, allow time for networking after the formal seminar presentations have concluded.

Seminar Materials and Take-Aways

You have successfully organized a seminar, and have a room full of individuals representing your target prospective client base and referral sources. You have their undivided attention for a few hours, and then they will leave, perhaps with a business card. If that description applies to your event, then you have missed one of the most significant opportunities available to you—the *take-away*.

The name is self-explanatory. Take-aways are the collateral and material that your attendees receive at the seminar. Normally, you will provide some form of handout for the seminar. At a minimum, you should provide copies of any PowerPoint slides with room for taking notes. However, where are these notes likely to end up at the end of the day? At best, if your attendee is an organized person, they may end up in a research file on the topic of your seminar. At worst, they'll either remain on the table at the conclusion of the seminar, or in the trash.

Depending upon your creativity and budget, there is a wide variety of effective ways to provide your attendees with a take-away will not end up out of sight and out of mind. And in case anyone may be thinking along another path at this point, no, we are not talking about mouse pads with your firm's name, baseball caps, seat cushions, or any of the other marketing junk that you often receive at conferences and trade shows. The idea is to provide a useful reference tool to your attendee that they will feel compelled to turn to in the future.

A seminar is first and foremost, in the eyes of your attendees, an educational event. Whether your seminar is one hour long or a full day or more, at a minimum you and your fellow professionals who are presenting the event should put together a package of material that provides a source of reference to which your attendees will turn in the days to come. Consider also who your target audience is, and what you would expect if you were in their shoes. An executive officer of a middle-market public company who is attending a seminar on forensic accounting and fraud detection will not be impressed by the same collateral that would work for an individual who attends a seminar on maximizing their personal income tax deductions.

In addition to preparing the actual material constituting the take-away—whether it be an outline, one or more papers or articles, or other reference materials—you should have the material professionally bound. There are a multitude of options, and a trip to your local print and copy shop is all that is required. Compare the impression made by a spiral bound set of material with a glossy cover, hard back, and table of contents, versus a set of materials copied in your office and stapled together.

With the need for many companies to be 'green,' there has been a definite rise in use of materials on CDs or on USB memory sticks. This is a very good idea as you can also load some of your firm's marketing materials on them as well. For a little more money you can have the CDs inserted into cases with a cover that is branded for your firm.

⚷ Key Concept

Providing seminar materials on CDs or on USB memory sticks allows you to "go green" with the added benefit of being able to load some of your firm's marketing materials on them as well.

Visual Aids

In prior years, books on this topic often discussed overhead transparencies, flip charts, and slide projectors. Today, there is essentially one standard for visual aids during seminar presentations—projected slides generated with Microsoft's PowerPoint software. Indeed, it is taken for granted that any seminar will include a PowerPoint presentation and that at a minimum the written handouts will include copies of the PowerPoint slides to be used during the presentation.

During the past decade, a wealth of research and scientific publications have explained that different people learn through different means. Some people learn best through aural means. Others are visual learners. Without delving to deeply into the science behind these results (which your author is quite unqualified to do), suffice it to say that, unless your seminar is a small, round-table event without a formal presentation, and except in the case of panel discussions, each of your speakers should prepare and use a PowerPoint presentation in conjunction with their speech.

Staffing for the Event

You will need staff to handle on-site registrations and check-in; assist your speakers; test your audio system, projector, and PowerPoint presentation equipment, and any other visual aid equipment; and to help seminar attendees find their seats. Designate one person as the troubleshooter whose sole responsibility will be doing what is necessary to assure the comfort of the audience. For example, if the air conditioning is set too low or too high, he or she should see it is adjusted. Proper lighting and sound should also be the troubleshooter's concern.

If your event is being held at a hotel or conference facility, you should meet one or more designated persons on the facility's staff who are responsible for promptly addressing your concerns. (Never hesitate to call for a second meeting just to provide confirmation on all the details.) At larger facilities, this may include specific individuals from the catering department and the audio-visual department, as well as a general facilities person. Make sure you know who to contact and how to contact them in the event of a problem.

Registration/Name Tags

Seminar attendees will expect name tags. Remember that this is also a networking event for them, and it is standard for all attendees, speakers, sponsors, and other participants to be provided pre-printed name tags. A supply of blank tags should be kept on-hand for walk-in registrations or to correct errors on the pre-printed tags, but other than those situations, attendees should not be expected to handwrite a name tag. Your local office supply store has name tag kits that can be fed through any ink jet or laser printer. There are also a number of on-line services that permit you to simply enter names or upload your registration list, and you will receive professionally printed name tags shipped to you within a matter of one or two days.

For added impact, add a ribbon on nametags that have a specific purpose, for example, speaker or sponsor.

Room Setup

If the seminar will be held on-site or in another facility without an on-site event planning department, then you may be responsible for setting up the room yourself. When setting up a room for a lecture-style presentation, consider the visibility of the speakers, and think about line of sight. If at all possible, arrange for a small dais to be placed at the front of the room, so every member of the audience can comfortably view the speakers and the presentation screen. Place chairs far enough apart to allow for the comfort of the audience.

If the seminar will be held in a classroom setup, you will arrange narrow tables in front of each row of chairs to allow participants to take notes. The ideal ratio of tables and chairs is two people for every 6 feet of table length. Many hotels try to place three people in this amount of space, but they can feel quite cramped, especially if the seminar lasts for more than two or three hours.

If you are holding your event at a hotel or conference center, they will have staff that is responsible for setting up and tearing down the room. You should clearly communicate your needs and expectations in advance of the event, and arrive 60 to 90 minutes prior to the time of arrival of the first guest (not the time of the first presentation) to ensure that the room is set up correctly.

Regardless of the site used, there should be a distinct check-in and walk-up registration area, usually one or more tables situated outside of the room in which the event will be held. These tables should look organized and not be in disarray—they are the first impression your attendees will have. Name tags and sign-in sheets should be organized and easily accessible, registration forms for walk-ins should be readily available, and the table should be consistently staffed. To continue to drive home your marketing message, you may choose to make available additional information on your firm, speakers, or sponsors at a table at the event.

Signage

If the event is to be held in a hotel, conference center, or other large facility where it is not self-evident how to find your event, make sure that there are signs in the lobby and other appropriate locations indicating the seminar's title, its sponsor, and the location. If the meeting rooms are difficult to find, directional signs allow for ease in finding, but also gives you more opportunity to share your firm name with traffic throughout the facility. The hotel should also be willing to place information about the seminar, including your firm's name, on the marquee.

Program Timetable

A minute-by-minute timetable is a virtual necessity if you want the seminar to go smoothly. When planning the timetable, allocate time to the following activities: equipment setup and testing (allow up to two hours before registration commences), registration and seating, the presentation, question and answer period, and reception. Make sure all key players, including the lecturers and program coordinators, have a personal copy of the agenda with assigned times. It is always a good idea to do a 'trial run' through the agenda and the speakers. Have a timekeeper at the event to help you stay on track. Attendees expect the event to end on time.

To Charge or Not to Charge

Whether or not your seminar should be free or should have a registration fee will depend on your budget and your marketing objectives. There are advantages and disadvantages to both situations.

As common sense would dictate, a free seminar will usually result in the largest attendance levels. If you have established specific maximum attendance levels and have made the event an invitation-only event, this may be easy to manage from both a budgetary and a marketing-effectiveness perspective. However, consider the impact on your budget if you have not set maximum attendance levels or monitored the number of registrations you have received, particularly for off-site events where you will be charged a per-head or consumption-based fee. As mentioned earlier, you may also be subject to penalty surcharges if your attendance levels are significantly above the numbers set forth in your contract.

A fee-based event, while usually resulting in lower overall attendance, often has the counterintuitive effect of *increasing* the number and quality of attendees who more closely fit your marketing objectives. It is a matter of the precept that nothing in life worth having is free. It is also a result of the fact that if your target audience needs the information you are offering, they will not think twice about paying for one or more of their representatives to attend. Many professionals will also attribute a higher value to an event, and will be less suspicious of a covert sales-pitch, when the event requires a fee.

Charging a fee will of course help your budget by allowing you to recover some or all of your expenses. Moreover, you will be able to enhance your invitations directed toward clients and identified prospects by offering them an opportunity to attend free-of-charge, compliments of your firm. Many clients believe that educational seminars are one of the benefits of being with your firm, so they may not attend your own firm's function if they are required to pay. This also provides your firm's partners and other professionals with a legitimate reason to call on clients, prospects, and other people in their business networks. By both inviting someone to attend and offering to "comp" their registration fee, you will have increased your goodwill with them even if they ultimately are unable or choose not to attend.

⚑ Key Concept

A fee-based event, while usually resulting in lower overall attendance, often has the counterintuitive effect of increasing the number and quality of attendees who more closely fit your marketing objectives.

WHAT ABOUT CO-SPONSORING?

In the age of joint ventures and strategic alliances, we cannot overlook the question of co-sponsoring events. As is always the case, there are several advantages, and disadvantages, to consider.

By co-sponsoring your seminar, you can save money, spread the risk, gain access to your co-sponsors' clients and marketing lists, and possibly build a close alliance between your firm and the other businesses sponsoring the event. You also reduce the risk that your seminar will be perceived solely as a sales-pitch by your firm. A potential disadvantage is a possible loss of control over the seminar's content and quality as you negotiate with the co-sponsors' management to develop a program that suits both of your respective clients' needs.

DEVELOP A BUDGET AND TIMETABLE

Your budget line items will of course depend on the kind of seminar you have planned, but the following checklist of possible cost items should be considered:

- Speaker fees and travel expenses
- Seminar room rental and equipment fees
- Refreshments (catering charges and equipment rental costs for tables and chairs)
- Mailing list charges
- Production and mailing of invitations and follow-up postcards (includes design fees, printing charges, postage and handling)
- Parking
- Name badges
- Handout materials, including folders and photocopy charges
- Planning time

The sample timetable in exhibit 25-1 is based on the assumption the seminar will be held at a hotel, 100 guests are expected, and the seminar will end with a reception. Remember, if your seminar will be held in a large metropolitan area, you may need to allow even longer lead times for some of these activities.

WHAT TO DO AFTER THE SEMINAR

The real marketing opportunity in seminars lies in what you do after the seminar is over.

Follow Up on Conversations with Attendees

If your partners and managers have been properly briefed, they will have spent their time at the seminar talking to clients, key prospects, and referral sources. After the seminar is over, they must follow up with each of these contacts. Requests for additional information or a meeting must be taken care of within a few days of the seminar. Even when no specific action is called for, partners and managers should call up their contacts and ask what they thought of the seminar. Did they find it useful? Would they like to attend other events in the future?

Follow Up on No-Shows

Those who were unable to attend should receive a brief letter (preferably personalized) expressing the firm's or partner's regret that they were unable to attend. A copy of the lecturer's handout materials should be included. Another tip: add all nonclient attendees to the firm's permanent mailing list, and flag them for pertinent mailings.

Evaluate the Seminar

It's not easy to measure the success of a seminar because many of the marketing outcomes are intangible. How do you quantify the goodwill generated among your clients? Can you measure the value of having established a mutual referral relationship with that hot new law firm in town? Difficult though it may be, evaluating the successes and disappointments of your seminar is well worth the effort. If nothing else, you will be able to refine your seminar

Exhibit 25-1
Sample Timetable for Organizing a Seminar

Days Before Event	Activity
60 – 90	Topic and speakers selected. Commence site inspections of hotels.
60 – 90	Select site. Contact hotel sales manager about requirements for food and beverages at reception.
45	Complete text for invitation/brochure.
35	Graphic design professional prepares invitation/brochure graphics.
30	Invitation/brochure to printer. Specify volume to be printed. Always ask for 10 percent above the number required for mailing list.
25	Mailing list is ready to use.
21	Mail invitations.
14	Contact hotel and discuss room arrangements, specifying equipment needs such as microphones, LCD projectors and screens, Internet access, room layout and podium.
10	Begin receiving RSVPs. If less than 1 percent of those invited have responded, mail out a follow-up postcard. Assemble take-away materials or have outside copy shop or printer prepare, as appropriate. Send news releases to local media if press is invited.
4	Individual speakers rehearse their presentations. Prepare name badges. Begin calling key clients and prospects who have not responded to the invitation.
3	Make reminder calls to individuals who have responded to tell you they will be attending. Contact media to determine which journalists will attend. Assemble press kits for them. Contact hotel and review all arrangements.
1-2	Assemble materials to take to hotel including take-aways, name badges, computer equipment, electronic copies of PowerPoints, and other supplies.
Day of Event	Arrive at the hotel at least 90 minutes before the beginning of the seminar. Inspect the rooms and make sure everything is in place. Ask about light switches, microphone volume controls, and a phone you can use to reach hotel management.

EXHIBIT 25-2
SEMINAR EVALUATION CHECKLIST

1. *Audience response*. What did seminar participants say about the program?

2. *The speaker*. How do we think the speaker did? Was he or she dynamic, informative, prepared? Did he or she handle audience questions well and stay around during the reception to answer additional queries?

3. *Location*. How was the facility? Was it comfortable? The right size? Did we get any complaints?

4. *Pacing*. Did we stick to the timetable we had planned? Did everything proceed smoothly?

5. *Refreshments*. How was the catering? What about cost versus value?

6. *Response rate*. What do we think of the turnout? Should we have done things differently to increase attendance?

7. *Marketing outcomes*. Did partners and managers make good use of the time available to them by meeting with clients, prospects, and referral sources? Were there any specific outcomes we should know about? What about media coverage—did we get any and was it positive?

8. *Budget*. Did we stay within our budget? If we did not, what was the cause of the overrun? What will we do differently next time?

♀ Key Concept

If your partners and managers have been properly briefed, they will have spent their time at the seminar talking to clients, key prospects, and referral sources. After the seminar is over, they must follow up with each of these contacts.

---

planning process and ensure that the next presentation is even better attended and more successful than this one was. Exhibit 25-2 contains a list of questions you might want to ask your partners and managers during the postmortem. Exhibit 25-3 is a sample participant evaluation form, which should be distributed and collected by the end of the seminar.

CONCLUSION

Using seminars or events to educate clients and prospects is always a worthwhile endeavor, and the information objectives of your event should be your first priority when planning an event. However, your desire to keep your clients educated, or to provide information to prospective clients and other professionals, is inherently driven by marketing desires—namely, your desire to maintain your existing client base and to develop new business. Great events are an excellent way to reach specific predetermined marketing objectives. To achieve both of these objectives takes good planning and hard work, but the results will be well worth the effort.

EXHIBIT 25-3
PARTICIPANT EVALUATION FORM

Dear Participant:

Thank you for attending this seminar. We hope you found the information useful and the format enjoyable. Won't you please take a few moments to answer the following questions? With your remarks and opinions, we can work to make each seminar an outstanding experience.

Thank you,
ABC Firm

Please rate this seminar on a scale of 1–5, with 5 being the highest rating, and 1 being the lowest.

	Excellent		Fair		Poor
Overall impression of the seminar	5	4	3	2	1
Seminar content	5	4	3	2	1
Speaker's skill as a presenter	5	4	3	2	1
Speaker's knowledge of the material	5	4	3	2	1
Your comfort at the facility	5	4	3	2	1
Quality of written materials	5	4	3	2	1

• What aspect of this seminar, or item(s) of information, did you find to be most useful? _____
_____

• Would you like to receive more information on this subject matter? Yes_____No_____

• What would you recommend we do differently at our next seminar? _____
_____
_____

• What subjects would you like us to address in future events?_____
_____

• Name (optional)_____

• Phone number (optional)_____

ABOUT THE AUTHOR

Leisa Gill is the Director of Marketing for Lattimore Black Morgan & Cain, PC, the largest regional CPA and professional services firm in Tennessee and was named the 2004 Marketer of the Year by CPA Marketing Report, a CCH Publication. In her role at LBMC she oversees all aspects of marketing for LBMC's eight additional affiliated companies. While her duties are mostly comprised of the day-to-day marketing strategies of the organization, she also helps coach and mentor professionals to understand the role of marketing in professional development. She has diverse experience in all areas of marketing. In addition, she has had significant experience in marketing campaign design and implementation. She is the past president for the national Association for Accounting Marketing (AAM) and is a frequent speaker for industry groups such as the AICPA, NorthStar Conferences, and AAM. In addition, her experience also includes working with a financial planning firm and a national publishing company of business newspapers.

APPENDIX 25-1
SEMINAR AND EVENT PLANNING WORKSHEET—CHECKLIST

The Seminar and Event Planning Worksheet provides a checklist of the details needed to plan an event.

Name of Event: _____

Type of Event:
- ____ Seminar
- ____ Tradeshow
- ____ Introductory Meeting
- ____ Lunch and Learn
- ____ Workshop
- ____ Networking Event
- ____ Other (explain below)

Time/Duration of Event: _____

Event Location:
- ____ *In-House*
  - ____ Classroom
  - ____ Conference Room
  - ____ Other (explain below):
- ____ *Off-Site*
  - ____ Hotel
  - ____ Banquet Hall
  - ____ Other (explain below):

Room Set Up Style:
- ____ Classroom (w/tables)
- ____ Roundtable
- ____ U-Shape
- ____ Auditorium (seats only)
- ____ Computer Lab
- ____ Other (explain below)

Database to be Used:
- ____ Firm Contact Mailing List (specify subset below (i.e., tax, healthcare, etc.)
- ____ Purchased Mail List
- ____ Other (explain below)

 # to be Invited: _____

Desired/Expected # of Attendees: _____

Materials Required:		Mail By:	Quantity:
	____ "Save the Date" Postcard	_____	_____
	____ Meeting Brochure/Registration Form	_____	_____
	____ Invitation Letter	_____	_____
	____ Registration Confirmation	__Mail __Fax __Phone __Email	_____
	____ Meeting Handouts	N/A	_____
	____ Marketing Brochures	N/A	_____
	____ Presentation (PowerPoint, etc.)	N/A	_____
	____ Attendance Sheet	N/A	_____
	____ Evaluation Sheet	N/A	_____
	____ Name Tags	N/A	_____
	____ Tent Cards	N/A	_____
	____ Signage	N/A	_____
	____ Follow Up/Thank You Letter	_____	_____
	____ Follow Up Information	_____	_____
	____ Other (explain below):	_____	_____

CPE
- ____ Forms for CPE
- ____ Once forms are complete, it will be added to Web site - check to confirm links

A/V Requirements:
- ____ Slide Projector
- ____ Screen
- ____ Microphone/Lavaliere
- ____ Internet Connection
- ____ Whiteboard/Blackboard
- ____ Overhead Projector
- ____ Flip Chart
- ____ Podium
- ____ VCR/Monitor
- ____ Other (explain below)

Food/Beverages:
- ____ Continental Breakfast
- ____ Lunch
- ____ Cocktail Hour/Hors d'oeuvres
- ____ Other (explain below)
- ____ Mid-morning refreshment break
- ____ Mid-afternoon refreshment break
- ____ Dinner
- ____ Wine Tasting

Meal Style:
- ____ Seated
- ____ Served in meeting room
- ____ Other (explain below)
- ____ Buffet
- ____ Served in separate location

Internal
- ____ Added to Web site - date:_____
- ____ Added to marketing calendar - date:_____

Press
- ____ Press release written - date:_____
- ____ Press release distributed - date:_____

Seminar and Event Planning Worksheet—Summary
The Seminar and Event Planning Worksheet provides an overview of the event while providing a high level explanation of the objectives, strategy, and follow up.

Name of Event:

Date of Event:

Event Objective:

Goals:

Target Audience [what industry, number expected]:

Who will attend from the firm:

Marketing Plan:

Challenges:

Follow up Plan:

Leads obtained:

CHAPTER 26
Building Opportunity Through Trade Shows

Colleen Rudio

Rudio Performance Management Group, LLC

INTRODUCTION

You've heard the statements, "Target Your Marketing, Create Niche Opportunities, Focus on Specialization." The challenge is determining how to accomplish this, identify what activities work best for your firm, and managing programs for efficiency and maximum effectiveness.

Today, many firms seek to create stronger connections with potential clients in a targeted industry or business sector. Among the myriad of marketing tactics available, one often embraced last is the trade show environment. Previously perceived as belonging to the world of retail marketing, trade show participation is one of the most cost-effective methods of direct industry contact supported by firms of all sizes. As we prepare to explore the various areas of trade show preparation, it is necessary to establish a brief foundation of how trade shows have evolved.

Historically, trade shows were a form of retailing primarily utilized by parties seeking direct access to specific industry based goods. In general, their purpose was to allow businesses of all kinds to come into direct contact with prospective consumers. As expected, "sales orders" obtained were the preliminary measurement factor. Creating a strong sales environment, staffing the booth with highly trained sales personnel, and approaching the show in a single-purpose manner often guaranteed success. Over the years, the intensity of customer relationship management broadened the trade show purpose and the overall approach in participating.

Today, trade shows are as varied as their sponsors. Whether sponsored by a local chamber of commerce, university, industry association or business development group, trade shows offer a multitude of opportunities for firms of all sizes. What are the benefits? Choose a trade show that successfully draws the audience you want and you will have the opportunity to target your marketing, create niche opportunities, and meet qualified prospects as you focus on specializing and branding your firm as a serious industry competitor.

In this chapter, we will explore the five primary areas of trade show participation; the plan, the team, the prospect, the show, and the outcome. Our goal is to provide a solid foundation allowing you to create and execute an effective trade show plan.

♀ Key Concept

> Choose a trade show that successfully draws the audience you want and you will have the opportunity to target your marketing, create niche opportunities, and meet qualified prospects.

SETTING GOALS FOR THE TRADE SHOW

As with any other marketing tactic, the first and most important step is to conduct a full analysis and establish goals. In other words, you need to define what you really want to accomplish at the show. A few possibilities are included in table 26-1.

Table 26-1   Sample Goals

Firm or Team Driven Goals	Product or Service Driven Goals	Industry or Client Driven Goals
• Expand the team's ability to speak in public	• Introduce new product or service offering	• Expand or reinforce existing relationships
• Expose new staff to establish or broaden industry focus	• Expand or promote utilization of product or service offering	• Secure future engagements, generate new leads
• Observe staff capabilities to develop relationships or implement skills training	• Increase fees within a specific product or service category	• Represent a solid commitment to specific industry group
• Broaden team's ability to network and secure new relationships	• Maximize utilization of resources or reallocate product or service expenses to trade show efforts	• Show appreciation to client or industry group through attendance, sponsorship, or special recognition
• Improve firm's visibility as a key industry provider	• Identify new product or service needs based upon trade show attendee surveys or interviews	• Obtain and retain "exclusive" industry representation
• Position firm as a key competitor within the target industry	• Test acceptance, fee structure, or introduction of new product or service	• Expand client view of firm as an educational or intellectual resource
• Recruit potential staff or interns	• Survey or obtain input regarding a product or service.	• Generate new or cultivate existing referral sources
• Introduce key, new, or specialized staff	• Gather leads for future product or service rollouts	• Conduct market research or a competitor analysis for future strategic planning

Whatever the goal, it is also important that you attempt to quantify it. For example, if your primary objective is to generate new leads, your objective statement might read like this: "Our goal is to generate new leads. We will have achieved this goal when we have collected the business cards of 50 A-level prospects, and have personally contacted each of those prospects within one week after the end of the trade show." Of course, this type of objective is much easier to quantify and measure than some of the others, like "Expand team's ability to speak in public." Nevertheless, the more precise you are in setting goals, the easier it will be to evaluate the results of your investment.

One word of caution, remain flexible when establishing goals relating to "sales" expectations. Trade shows are typically designed to facilitate exposure, especially when the product being marketed is something as abstract as professional services.

⚲ Key Concept

Remain flexible when establishing goals relating to "sales" expectations. Trade shows are designed to facilitate exposure, especially when the product being marketed is something as abstract as professional services.

DECIDING WHERE TO EXHIBIT AND CONDUCT AN ANALYSIS

Once you have decided what you want to accomplish by exhibiting, it is time to decide where to exhibit. Your best resource is your own firm's experts, industry specialists and marketing staff. If they are not aware of the target industry's key shows, substantial information is available at infoplease.com or other local, state or national association Web sites.

The next phase is to conduct a thorough analysis upon identification of your target shows. Some firms consider obtaining show literature or speaking to show organizers as sufficient review, others desire a full analysis. Although this is not an all-inclusive list, consider the following items as you determine if the tradeshow environment is right for you.

Show Organizer Analysis

- Determine the primary exhibit cost factors. Are they reasonable in comparison to like-kind shows? Are there fee packages that include conference registrations or other bundled benefits?
- How long have the current organizers been in business? Are they financially sound? Do they have a solid reputation in the trade show industry? Does the show have a long history—has it been around for years, or is this only its third or fourth season?
- Is there an exhibitor contract? What is the cancellation policy? How much is the deposit and does it secure requested space? Are spaces secured on a first come basis?
- Are there additional fees for technology, set-up, teardown, security, etc.? Are you required to use their designated vendors?
- What are the show organizers doing to promote the show? Are they writing up the show? What is the word on the street about the show? What do your clients in the target industry say about it?

Attendee Analysis

- Who are the past attendees? Has attendance grown or declined over the years? Are they the "primary" decision-makers?
- Do your clients or prospects attend the convention? Have you cross-sectioned your client list to determine attendee ratio?
- Are attendees encouraged to actively participate in the trade show? Have organizers changed their show format in the past two years?
- Are there additional opportunities to address attendees beyond the traditional "trade show" breaks? Are there frequent breaks? What is the distance between the exhibitor area and the educational area? Is there a clearly defined traffic flow? Are there show sponsored activities encouraging visitation to the exhibitor area?
- Are you provided a full attendee list? Is the list available prior to the trade show for preshow contact?

Exhibitor Analysis

- Who are the other exhibitors? If past exhibitors are not returning, do you have the ability to find out why?
- Do you have the ability to request or select booth placement?
- How many direct competitors attended in the past two years?
- How are other exhibitors communicating their messages? What was the audience response?
- Are there opportunities to provide give-a-ways? What are some common promotional items?

Product/Service Analysis

- What are the primary products or service you plan to promote? What is your presentation strategy? Are you planning a promotional "special"? If so, what are the terms, who is eligible, etc.? Can we provide any products or service specials profitably?

- Do you have specific material for selected products or services? How will you advertise? Are you conducting a full "visit our booth" campaign? Is this type of activity supported by organizers?
- What topics are being presented at the convention? Are there opportunities to present or host an educational session?
- Do you know what your competitor's lead products or services will be? Are you able to compete directly or do you need to adapt your approach?
- Are there specific products or services the industry is requesting? Is there an opportunity to interview past attendees to determine which products or services are most needed at this time?

Team Analysis

- Do you have adequate coverage for the show? Will your booth be represented by firm employees or is there an opportunity to partner with other industry vendors?
- What skills or characteristics are necessary to achieve your goals? Does your team have these skills or characteristics? Is there a need for specific training? Who can conduct the training? What are the cost factors?
- What are the primary and secondary goals for each team member?
- Is recruiting a goal? Who are your point people? Do you need to reserve a private room for interviews? Does the show organizers support or perhaps promote this factor?
- What is the schedule for team members? How many will you need to bring? What level of staff should be in attendance? What level of staff do other exhibitors bring?

There is one more prudent step you owe your firm before signing a contract for exhibit space. If time permits, walk the show yourself or obtain permission to walk another show in the same venue to determine how the organizers typically set-up the exhibit hall. This observation allows you to acquire important information you cannot glean from other methods of analysis. Now you are thoroughly prepared to begin establishing a budget and action plan.

DEVELOPING A BUDGET

All activities have resource limitations, whether identified limitations are the amount of people or the available funds, establishing a realistic budget is critical. The budget is a necessary foundation in determining whether your trade show participation will be viewed by others as a success. As a rule of thumb, it is common that your total out-of-pocket expense is five times the cost of booth rental expense.

To some, this number may seem excessive. Consider the following one-time or reoccurring expenses when preparing your budget. Keep in mind, the frequency and allocation of these expenses will vary depending on your firm, your trade show schedule, and your firm's desire to "capture" all related expenses to determine success.

- Trade show registration (reoccurring and should include set-up, technology, electrical, equipment rental, cleaning and freight handling fees. Note: In many cities, the wage rate for labor is usually set at union levels.)
- Conference registration (reoccurring per staff attending)
- Booth design and production (one-time if you own the booth, reoccurring if you rent the booth)
- Shipping (reoccurring)
- Promotional materials (one-time if you plan ahead and produce high quantity, reoccurring if you produce materials show by show)
- Specialty materials (reoccurring for customized show materials)
- Give-a-ways, prizes, or thank you gifts (reoccurring)
- Staff expense (reoccurring and should include time, travel, meals, lodging, entertainment, etc.)
- Advertising (reoccurring and should include design, agency fees, direct mail, trade publications, etc.)

Establishing and agreeing upon a budget is important. Keep in mind, your budget should incorporate some flexibility so you can respond or adapt to situations as they occur. The main purpose is to achieve your overall trade show goals. This might mean adaptations to your plan or budget. It is highly recommended to incorporate and gain understanding that a slight budget variation, typically 5–8 percent, may be necessary without additional approval.

ESTABLISHING A MANAGEABLE TIMELINE

Establishing a manageable timeline is important for several reasons. First, it allows for even distribution of tasks, which promotes the opportunity to engage all team members, thus creating stronger buy-in. Secondly, a timeline reduces the chance for error or rushed decision making at crucial moments. Following are examples of the types of tasks to be performed during a 12 month timeframe.

- *12 months before show date.* Attend the targeted show as an observer. This is a prime opportunity to walk the show floor, attend a few educational sessions, and meet the show organizers. Key points to observe include: show layout, level of booth interaction, type of booth attendees, session topics and quality of prospects. Prepare to follow-up with show organizers and request registration material.

- *10 months before show date.* Establish and obtain budget approval based upon observations, previous budget considerations, and desired outcomes. Booth design, ordering, and delivery can often take up to 6 months. Taking care of this important task early often allows for a higher level of creativity in the design stage and reduces unnecessary costs due to rush orders.

- *7–9 months before show date.* Typically, conference registration is announced within a 9 month period of the show date. Keep in mind, show placement is usually on a first-come basis, so register early. Once registration is secured, focus on activities that will engage show team. Conduct a strategic session to brainstorm how you will draw traffic to your booth, engage existing prospects or clients, maximize your time at the show or distribution of tasks.

- *6 months before show date.* Pre-show cultivation is an important task. It allows you to establish your firm in the eyes of show attendees. Mailing lists of clients and prospects can quickly be turned into pre-conference cultivation. A direct mail or e-mail program administered over several months will increase attendees' familiarity with your firm and traffic to your booth. Additional cultivation efforts include, offering to write an article in the association newsletter or industry publication, sending a series of e-mails that support your initiatives, seeking partnering opportunities with other vendors, and announcement of your participation at the tradeshow on your firm's Web site.

    Budget permitting, this is also the time to determine if you will purchase give-a-ways, gifts for key attendees, or special clothing for your team. Some exhibitors use such items to capture attention, while others give them out as a sort of keepsake after they have had the chance to talk seriously with the prospect. Consider using your firm logo, slogan, or booth theme and take advantage of all opportunities to unify your booth, your give-a-ways, and your team's appearance. This will further display your firm's professionalism and attention to the smallest of details.

- *3 months before show date.* Now is typically the time paperwork from the conference organizers starts to arrive. Submit orders early for labor, electricity, set-up/cleaning services, and so on. Most shows offer discounts when orders are placed early and unfortunately some elements are on a first come, first serve basis. Additionally, research opportunities to advertise in the trade show journal or industry publication. Focus the advertisement on visiting your booth, introducing your team or identifying a specific need. This is especially important if you have never exhibited at this show before.

- *2 months before show date.* As the show gets closer, the details seem endless. Following are some common details that should be addressed in the weeks prior to the show:

    — Based upon your team's schedule and coordination of logistics, meet with your staff and confirm who is going, how they will travel, and when they are expected to arrive. Ask show organizers about possible discounts offered to attendees on airfares and hotel rooms.

    — Schedule a preshow orientation and rehearsal for all booth staff. This session should be revisited just before the show opens to ensure that everyone delivers the same message and is working toward show objectives.

    — Confirm arrangements to ship your booth, if your firm owns one, or finalize rental agreements if you are renting.

    — Prepare a lead tracking form that your staff can use in the booth. The form should allow space for attaching the prospect's business card, an area to identify contact as high/med/low opportunity, and ample space to capture pertinent information. Consider including a short checklist of products/ services that should be incorporated into your follow up correspondence.

— Depending on the size of the show, you may want to arrange for someone to arrive at the show site one or two days early to supervise show labor, booth setup, or, if your booth has a technology element, placement and testing of equipment.

— Take time before the show begins to walk the floor. There are multiple benefits; it gives you the opportunity to introduce yourself and your firm to other vendors, identify potential business partners for future projects, familiarize yourself with your competitors approach, and gain better understanding of the number of sales messages attendees will receive. An often unspoken benefit, it gets the conference "walk around"out of the way and allows your team to refocus on your booth and your show objectives. Now it's time for the real fun to begin.

Working the Show

Professional, friendly, interactive, knowledgeable, proactive, concise, attentive, and interesting are just a few characteristics necessary to achieve success once the trade show begins. The question that plagues most trade show booth representatives is not, "Do I possess all or some of those characteristics?" It is, "How do I know what the attendees want to hear, want to know, or want to receive?"

Just as with any sales or prospecting interaction, the art of working a trade show booth can seem puzzling, especially to newcomers. Here are some tips on how to make your time and team more effective.

- *Establish and prepare your target list of prospects.* Before you attend the show, review the attendee list to decide what type of prospects you are seeking. Next, pre-select top prospects; research each using internet or pre-call preparation software such as First Research (www.firstresearch.com) or IBISWorld (www.ibisworld. com). Obtaining strong familiarity of attendees will assist to maximize your efforts, prepare you for a higher level conversation or narrow the focus to specific industry needs.

- *A well-organized, professional presence is important.* Most trade show organizers provide the standard eight foot table and two chairs per booth. Resist the urge to use them in the traditional manner. Stand at all times, take rest breaks outside the booth area if feasible, and actively welcome the attendees to your booth. Position your table along the side, allowing for more room and an easier flow of traffic. Most exhibitors make the mistake of "loading" the table with firm literature in large quantities. Leaving only a few copies of each piece of literature out on the table presents a more organized effort. Although these suggestions seem simplistic, they help promote a strong physical, professional presence that will ultimately set the tone for your conversations.

- *Make a good first impression.* Trade show industry surveys suggest that you have only seconds to capture the attention of attendees. Don't make the mistake of trying to give each person a complete list of the services your firm provides. Instead, devise a crisp one-sentence benefit statement that tells listeners "what's in it for them." This statement will provide the opportunity to focus on qualifying the attendees versus attempting to engage in extensive conversations. A good recommendation is to leave the technical details for a follow-up meeting or telephone call.

- *Questions lead to conversation.* To get a conversation started, ask an open-ended question. Never ask, "May I help you?" Most people are programmed to answer that question with a firm "no." Establish a bank of five to ten questions that can be asked to initiate conversation. Combine industry, firm, and general show questions that will help broaden your conversation and engage attendees. If your conversation is going to last longer than ten minutes, you should move to a more private area.

- *Develop an information tracking system.* Capturing critical information during a prospect conversation will determine the thoroughness of your follow-up. It is important to remember every person retains and recalls information differently. Visit with each representative from your trade show team to determine a tracking method that will work best for them. A common practice is to record prospect interests or concerns on the back of a business card. This method simplifies the tracking, is physically manageable, and provides an immediate information match for follow-up.

Properly working your booth is a critical factor in your overall success. In addition to the previous list of tips, here are some common errors that can occur and jeopardize your trade show success.

- Never assume your best prospects are the best dressed. Many important decision makers dress informally at trade shows to be inconspicuous or to relax while they are away from the office.

- Resist relaxing as the show progresses. Fatigue is typically the number one reason for this. Take regular breaks, maintain your energy level, and realize your prospects are watching.
- Use an appropriate tone of voice. Whether it's speaking too softly or trying to out-yell other attendees, trade show conversations are tricky. To maintain a professional tone, first pay attention to your prospect's tone and then adjust accordingly.
- Focus on positive show activities. As you may have already experienced, there are multiple opportunities to engage in show events or extra-curricular activities. When selecting what to participate in, remember to always maintain your professionalism, stay refreshed, and—once again—realize your prospects are watching.

Finally, when preparing your team for their booth experience, try to establish some basic ground rules and then allow each individual's personality to shine through. The success of the show depends primarily on your team and their interactions with attendees.

> ### Key Concept
>
> The success of the show depends primarily on your team and their interactions with attendees.

EVALUATING THE RESULTS

While capturing the costs of a trade show is a fairly simple task, it is not so easy to evaluate or clearly define its benefits. The challenge in evaluating a trade shows direct and indirect results is three-fold. First, it takes *time* to pursue all of the leads generated at the show, and some business may take a year or more to develop. Second, it is often difficult to assign an actual dollar *value* to such outcomes as increased visibility or new relationships. Third, firms often fail to *define* how they will evaluate short and long-term success factors.

You will be able to overcome these challenges by first establishing your evaluation factors. All involved partners should approve the components for evaluation. At anytime in the process, if situations occur that may positively or negatively impact the evaluation elements, they should be addressed immediately. Consider the following as a foundation in defining your evaluation process.

1. Define 3–5 primary and secondary goals for evaluation. Establish and obtain agreement on how evaluation will take place prior to the trade show.

2. Mirror your evaluation process with other trade show plan components. For example, evaluate financial results based upon budgeted items or evaluate contact results based upon verified attendee records.

3. Establish a method for involved firm members to report on any new client, or new business resulting from a trade show contact. Additionally, provide all involved firm members with a list of contacts, attendees, vendors to reduce contact origination issues.

4. Develop a tracking spreadsheet, or use your firm's contact management software, to track activity beyond the initial short term follow-up period.

5. Identify measurements for difficult factors such as visibility or name awareness. Utilize definable elements (such as, number of attendees at booth, frequency of name mentioned as sponsor, number of new relationships established) to communicate impact.

6. Incorporate overall evaluations to support trade show results where feasible.

7. Remain flexible in the evaluation process. It is often difficult to define or support why your team "feels" the trade show was a success or failure.

Although the process may seem lengthy, it is important to be sensitive to the need for review and authorization of all phases of the exhibit process. Based upon your firm's experience with trade show exhibiting, a multi-layer evaluation process may prove worthwhile.

BUILDING VALUE BEYOND THE TRADE SHOW

One common error that is certain to decrease your firm's return on investment is limiting your network development efforts to trade show attendees. The tendency to further limit your direct contact to only those positive interactions at the trade show will further threaten future trade show success. Upon completion of your initial trade show follow up plan, explore the various options that may exist to build on future trade show experiences. Each "key contributor" plays a significant and often over-looked role. Furthermore, they possess valuable trade show insight your firm can potentially utilize. The following list is not all-inclusive and you are highly encouraged to expand your targeted network based on the uniqueness of the trade show environment.

- *Association staff.* A true "key" to attendee information. This group is often a primary source in obtaining critical member cultivation characteristics. Establishing the relationship early in the planning process may afford you the opportunity to ask "what are the attendee's buying habits; are they the decision makers; how do the attendees prefer to be contacted; or what other trade shows are they likely to attend?" Building a relationship with association staff develops a direct line to the resource and information that may differentiate your firm.
- *Trade show coordinators.* Often the most "over-looked" group, trade show coordinators have a unique opportunity to observe and often independently discuss trade show successes and failures with attendees. Their ability to provide insight and value goes well beyond a single trade show. A quick follow-up call can provide additional information to further measure your trade show success. Questions such as "how did you feel the overall show went; what were some of the positive experiences or frustrations; are you aware of other shows with similar attendees, do you have plans for next year's event?" can further strengthen your final analysis.
- *Program/speaker coordinator.* Never taking a break from their responsibility, program coordinators are constantly on the look-out for the next hot-topic, qualified speaker, gifted presenter, or knowledgeable expert. Although engaging in conversation during the trade show may not be feasible, initiating contact as part of your follow-up plan often proves worthwhile. For example, sending a letter commenting on which programs you found most useful and offering a partner's expertise for next years trade show may open a door for a speaker position.
- *Other vendors.* Yes, they are targeting the same group of attendees, and some may perceive them as direct competitors. But, are they targeting them for the same reasons, and is there an opportunity to partner with them? We all know organizations attend trade shows for a multitude of reasons. This could be the opportunity to discuss why they are attending, who they are hoping to see, what they are offering, and if there is a natural connection between you and their organization. The benefit could be additional referral relationships, mutual client interaction, or direct sales opportunities.

Incorporating this level of follow-up broadens your ability to fully understand the trade show environment and how your firm can benefit. Applying an active and consistent approach to developing key relationships beyond trade show attendees will expand the bottom-line benefits to your firm.

CONCLUSION

As we have explored, exhibiting through trade shows is definitely not for everyone, or every firm. Although some partners may view it as the next step in being considered a progressive firm, there are obvious risks for consideration. Opportunities to explore trade show exhibiting exist at multiple levels. It is through careful research, planning, preparation, and follow-up that your firm will obtain the maximum benefit from each show you choose to invest in. The bottom line is you will only know the true value of exhibiting at a trade show after you have made the commitment.

ABOUT THE AUTHOR

Colleen Rudio is a results-oriented professional with over 20 years experience in professional service industries. Areas of expertise include strategic planning, project management, marketing and advertising, business development, and organizational development. Rudio developed the Montana Profit Enhancement Symposium, receiving national recognition for innovation in economic development for JCCS, P.C. She is a past board member for the Association for Accounting Marketing, served as marketing chair for CPAmerica International, and multiple Montana based organizations. She can be reached at colleen@rudiopmg.com or www.rudiopmg.com.

PART V:
The Handoff—Connecting the Dots between Marketing and Sales

CHAPTER 27
From Opportunity to New Client

Gale Crosley, CPA
Crosley+Company

INTRODUCTION[1]

Pursuing prospective opportunities will always be important to enable CPA firms to grow. In the new economy, this pursuit is more important than ever before.

This chapter discusses the process of pursuing opportunities in the most efficient and effective manner. Pursuing and landing more opportunities will enable a firm to increase revenues, gravitate up-market, expand technical and industry capabilities, provide opportunities to develop people with more complex and interesting work, and raise the visibility and stature of the firm.

QUALIFYING THE OPPORTUNITY

Before spending significant time pursuing an opportunity, it's important to assess whether it is really an opportunity—in other words, does it have sufficient business potential to be worth pursuing? If we look at the definition of an opportunity, we find that an unqualified opportunity (lead) is one where, based upon a conversation, we think the prospect might have a need for our services in the foreseeable future. A qualified opportunity (lead) is one where, based upon a conversation, the prospect has a need, and the prospect has potential—that is, the need is (1) painful enough to spend money to fix the problem, (2) the prospect has money available to fix the problem, and (3) someone has the authority to fix the problem.

In addition, the opportunity should fit a certain profile, fit within an acceptable level of risk, and appear to be able to pass the firm's client acceptance procedures. The profile should include positive responses to the following questions:

- Is this an industry where someone in the firm has expertise?
- Is this a service offering where someone in the firm has expertise?
- Is this an opportunity that we can handle geographically?

Qualifying the opportunity involves a call on the prospect (calls are usually in-person meetings, unless for some reason, such as geographic distance, this needs to be done by phone call), and discussing with the prospect the following five questions:

1. Why buy?

   In other words, why is the prospect considering buying or changing providers? This will give you clues about whether they are just superficially looking at alternatives to compare pricing with their current provider, or whether you have a serious chance of being considered.

2. Why now?

   You are trying to uncover something called an impending event, that is, a reason why they have to make the decision now, versus a year ago or a year from now. This will help you understand whether they are

---

[1] *This chapter is reproduced with permission from the AICPA's Management of an Accounting Practice Handbook, chapter 106, "Expanding Firm Capabilities."*

actually required to make a decision at this time before you expend significant effort, only to discover that they've delayed making a decision.

3. Why us?

Why is the prospect considering your firm? This line of questioning will reveal potential past relationships, current perceptions of your firm, and underlying agendas that can help you with strategy development. For example, it's relevant that a member of their board might have recommended that you be evaluated versus merely that they've heard about you in the business community.

4. Who else?

Who else is the prospect considering? This question is designed to reveal past and incumbent relationships. This is an important area of questioning because existing relationships represent one of the most challenging areas of competitive strategy in opportunity pursuit. The sooner you uncover and understand existing relationships with incumbents and other competitors, the better you can assess whether we have a real chance to win the opportunity, or whether you are probably not going to be a serious contender. This will help you decide whether to pursue the opportunity, and if so, how much resource you want to expend. If you find that there are existing, deep-rooted relationships, you may decide to opt out or conversely pursue with the objective of gaining experience and developing relationships, but not necessarily with the objective of winning an "unwinnable" opportunity.

Avoiding wasting resources on an unwinnable opportunity is so important that the questioning should not be cursory. It is recommended that you dig deep and ask the prospect several questions to uncover the nature of prior and existing relationships. This is where you can and should ask how much they are spending with their current provider. Even if they opt not to disclose the information, there is little to no downside to asking the question, and it's important to uncover as much information as possible to craft a pricing strategy.

5. Who cares?

This line of questioning is designed to reveal who will be involved in the decision making process. Some examples of specific questions are as follows:

- Who will be involved in the decision?
- What role will they play?
- Who might be affected by the decision?
- Will the board, the CEO, the CFO, or the controller be involved in the decision?

Again, it's important at this point to uncover all the potential players, so that your business development efforts are appropriately focused on the right parties. Spending time with the wrong players, who are not influential in the decision, is a waste of time and resources. Uncovering information about decision makers will enable you to craft a better pursuit strategy.

? Key Concept

Avoid wasting resources on an unwinnable opportunity by asking questions about prior and existing relationships.

Early on in an opportunity pursuit, asking lots of questions is acceptable. Because you aren't expected to know anything, this is your time to ask as many questions as you can without the risk of appearing uninformed or overly inquisitive because the prospect will expect you to ask many questions now. If you don't ask now, it's difficult once the pursuit has progressed further; it will look inappropriate and feel clumsy. So take this opportunity to gather as much detailed information as you can in these five areas. However, don't limit the discussion to these five questions. These questions will lead to others as you explore the information you need from the prospect.

It's recommended that you maintain an internal attitude of making sure you are convinced this is a real opportunity. Don't just hear what you want to hear, hoping that this is an opportunity when it really isn't. Ask the questions like a business person trying to determine if it's worth expending the firm's valuable resources to pursue the opportunity, not as a desperate professional who believes that any lead is a good lead! This attitude will insure that you look professional (not desperate), that you craft a better strategy (not one based upon what you wanted to hear), and that you deploy appropriate levels of firm resources (not just throw resources at the opportunity).

> **♀ Key Concept**
>
> Early on in an opportunity pursuit, asking lots of questions is acceptable. Because you aren't expected to know anything, this is your time to ask as many questions as you can without the risk of appearing uninformed or overly inquisitive because the prospect will expect you to ask many questions now.

> **♀ Key Concept**
>
> Ask questions like a business person trying to determine if it's worth expending the firm's valuable resources to pursue the opportunity, not as a desperate professional who believes that any lead is a good lead. This attitude will insure that you look professional (not desperate), that you craft a better strategy (not one based upon what you wanted to hear), and that you deploy appropriate levels of firm resources (not just throw resources at the opportunity).

LARGER OPPORTUNITIES

Larger opportunities are often more complex and, therefore, often require a team approach if the opportunity exhibits one or more of the following attributes:

- One or more competing accounting firms involved
- More than one prospect decision-maker
- Larger than your normal opportunity
- Longer to develop than your normal opportunity

Because each firm is different, we refrain from a specific fee size when defining "large" opportunities. The large opportunity should be worth your time to pursue, given the necessity to spend more time in pursuit of a more complex, multicompetitor scenario. To be worth your time, large or small, opportunities should always be qualified to avoid wasting resources.

STRATEGY DEVELOPMENT

Once you've determined that you have a qualified opportunity, as defined previously, you are ready to pursue the opportunity. If it is relatively small, you may be able to handle the opportunity yourself. However, larger, strategically significant, and more complex opportunities are best pursued with a team. The following information should be shared with pursuit team members. If you have gaps in your knowledge, you'll need to start the process of identifying those gaps and asking the prospect questions throughout the process to gather as much information as possible. Only then will you have the best strategy. The information to collect and share includes the following:

1. Area(s) of opportunity (services)

2. Decision making timeframe

3. Information collected in the qualification process

    a. Why buy?
    b. Why now?
    c. Why us?
    d. Who else?
    e. Who cares?

4. Decision making process

5. Knowledge of the prospect's business

6. Knowledge of interpersonal dynamics of prospect people involved in the opportunity

7. Other relevant information you've uncovered thus far

The decision-making timeframe is a crucial piece of information. Because you only have a given amount of time to build a relationship and exhibit technical expertise, it's important to know the timeframe. The more time you have, the better you can accomplish these objectives and increase your odds to win. If you have a short window and few existing relationships, it's more difficult to accomplish the objectives and secure the business. If you have a window that's very small (a few days or a couple weeks), test the timeframe with the prospect to see if you can secure more time to do the right job in "due diligence." If you can convince the prospect that you need more time to do the right job, generally, the odds to win go up in your favor. The only exception is where you are clearly the front runner, in which case trying to speed up the process and close the business is the best strategy. Remember, you get no "extra credit" points by being the first to get back with your proposal. Almost all selling activity occurs before the proposal is submitted, and you need to create as much time with the prospect as possible as you identify needs, links to solutions, persuasively communicate, and build a relationship.

Finally, if you are pursuing the opportunity as a team, the lead person should establish a protocol for ongoing communications (called strategic recalibration) with the other team members. This is composed of short conference calls with team members during the period of pursuit in order to keep the team activities on track. Strategic recalibrations are phone meetings typically lasting from 15–30 minutes (depending upon opportunity size). The objective is to review your current strategy and tactics and modify your approach. It is fairly typical to change course several times during a pursuit, especially with larger opportunities. As more information is revealed, you can highlight certain themes in your communications to the prospect and identify where you should spend your time cultivating relationships. For example, you'll often find out that the prospect's needs are different than you thought they were. Or you'll find out that certain decision-makers have more influence than others. As information is revealed, you will change course in your pursuit activities to better fit the situation and increase your odds to win.

⚷ Key Concept

The decision-making timeframe is a crucial piece of information. Because you only have a given amount of time to build a relationship and exhibit technical expertise, it's important to know the timeframe.

OPPORTUNITY PURSUIT

Once you've concluded that the opportunity is qualified and you've reviewed what you know (or shared, if you are working with a team), the following are the steps and best approaches with pursuit.

Stage I—Begin the Date

The primary objective of this stage is to establish the relationship. This is best done utilizing the following three principles:

1. *Properly penetrate the opportunity.* Determine who from the firm you should select to execute the first meetings, and who from the prospect company you are going to call on first. Your selected team member is not necessarily the best technical person. Depending upon with whom you're meeting, often the person who has the best odds of establishing a relationship and persuasively communicating is a better choice.

2. *Divide and conquer.* Initial meetings should occur one-on-one with the prospect, wherever possible. If not possible, then the second meeting should be one-on-one. Establishing a relationship is the primary goal of stage I, and relationships are built one-on-one and one-by-one. Subsequent calls throughout the opportunity process can include more than one person, especially to build technical credentials in multiple areas. But remember that prospects tend to reveal more information one-on-one and, as a result, you'll have an increased chance to develop a winning strategy, the more information you can uncover.

3. *Gather environmental information.* This is the process, over the first (several) call(s), of finding out key information about the prospect, the decision makers, and the decision making process. It is used to expand your knowledge of the prospect and enables you to put the opportunity in the right context of what else is going on in the business, the priority of this decision, who will influence the outcome, how severe your competition might be, and other crucial information. This can strengthen your pursuit strategy. The categories of information you should gather include the following:

   a. Business effect (of this decision)
   b. Decision makers
   c. Decision-making process
   d. Competitors
   e. Professional objectives
   f. Personal objectives

Your due diligence should uncover as much information in each of these categories as possible. Write your questions out before meeting with the prospect. Take good notes during the prospect interview(s), and use these notes to craft your proposal. Use the questions in multiple meetings if you have that opportunity. The nature of opportunity pursuit is to find out as much relevant contextual information as possible before the sell cycle ends. The more you discover, the better your strategy, and the higher your odds to win. The best rainmakers are very, very good at questioning techniques to uncover hidden information, as well as identifying and selling reasons to meet with the prospect more than once.

Stage II—Edge Out Other Suitors

The primary objective of this stage is to build the relationship. This is best done utilizing the following three principles:

1. *Create individual value propositions.* Identify the intersection of the prospect's professional and personal objectives and your offering(s) to design a compelling value proposition. Understand your competition's likely value proposition and strategically craft a value strategy which has the highest odds of winning. The better you understand the prospect's motivations, based upon personal and professional needs, the more you'll be able to link these to what your solution represents in the buyer's mind, and the better you'll be able to support a value-based (not price-based) proposed solution.

2. *Identify influence.* Determine who will be making the decision and their relative level of influence in the decision. Recalibrate your strategy and tactics based upon this information.

3. *Preview the proposal and pricing.* Work with the prospect by creating the draft proposal and sending it over for comment before finalizing. In this way, you'll make sure you've included all the prospect's issues and your point of view about them. In addition, discuss the probable pricing in a face-to-face meeting. Don't send pricing over in a document until you've discussed it first. If you send the draft over and haven't yet discussed pricing, note in the pricing section "To Be Discussed." You want the prospect to feel some ownership in the final proposal. In the pricing discussion, you want to discuss value, then reveal your proposed price, and observe his or her expression. This way, you'll be able to assess whether the prospect appreciates the value you are trying to build. You want to build as much value as possible and attempt to stay out of a pricing war.

Key Concept

The better you understand the prospect's motivations, based upon personal and professional needs, the more you'll be able to link these to what your solution represents in the buyer's mind, and the better you'll be able to support a value-based (not price-based) proposed solution.

Stage III—Propose a Marriage

The primary objective of this stage is to solidify the relationship. This is best done utilizing the following two principles:

1. *Identify exposure.* Assess who your finalist competitors are and recalibrate your strategy to position yourself against your competitors. If you know a competitor is going to use a particular strategy (such as, stressing strength in a particular area), you need to be able to position yourself as different, memorable, and a better fit. At this juncture, assess which prospect decision makers are your allies, neutral voters, or your detractors.

2. *Utilize allies.* Based upon your assessment of allies, neutral voters, or detractors, craft a strategy to neutralize your detractors and utilize your allies to influence neutral voters. Appeal to your ally to assist with persuading neutral voters to support your approach.

Collaborate to Close

The primary objective of this stage is to close the opportunity. This is best done utilizing the following two principles:

1. *Look for buying signs.* Questions about price and risk are usually signs that the prospect is ready to buy and that you are still in the running. The exception to this is when you weren't able to build value, and the prospect is just price shopping.

2. *Orchestrate your presentation.* Leave nothing to chance in the oral presentation. Rehearse all aspects before the final oral presentation.

Maintaining Contact

The time between the proposal submission and the decision is the most difficult. Before proposal submission, you have some control over the process. After proposal submission, the power shifts to the prospect's hands. Most CPAs are challenged with how to keep the lines of communication open with the prospect. But it is very important to figure out how to achieve this. One way is to set the stage with your ally before proposal submission by discussing how you recommend that you communicate with him or her once the proposal is submitted. The reason you want to keep the lines of communication open is that each decision maker usually has some objections about the proposal. You just might not know what they are. If you don't uncover and address them, you risk uncovering and addressing them in a group. This is much more difficult to do and has lower odds for success. Or you may never be able to uncover the objections. Business does not get closed until all objections are addressed.

When the prospect goes dark (won't return your messages), usually a few possible reasons include the following:

- The decision has been delayed
- Shifting priorities
- No need to make a decision immediately and, therefore, postponed indefinitely
- Requirements have changed
- Decision makers can't reach an agreement
- Politics are at play

> **Key Concept**
>
> The time between the proposal submission and the decision is the most difficult. Before proposal submission, you have some control over the process. After proposal submission, the power shifts to the prospect's hands.

TECHNIQUES FOR KEEPING THE RELATIONSHIP ALIVE

Before delivering the proposal, discuss the communications protocol after the proposal is delivered. For example, you may state that you'd like to call in a few days to get the buyers' reaction to the proposal, answer any further questions, and check in on where they are in the decision process. This gives you the ability to keep a dialogue going after proposal submission.

E-mails to decision makers are certainly acceptable after proposal delivery. You can ask how the decision process is going, when they'll be making a decision, and offer your availability to answer any questions they have. Delivering a proposal and disappearing can come across as not caring about the outcome. On the other hand, don't e-mail them daily! Asking the buyers about their decision timeframe will enable you to assess how often to check in with them.

Decision makers and other business people tend to favor either voicemail or e-mail. Unless you know the preference of the decision makers, leaving a voicemail and e-mail is perfectly acceptable. You can include verbiage in your voicemail such as, "I e-mailed you and thought I'd also leave a voice message." Or you could say, "As I mentioned in my e-mail..."

The important point is to use creativity and a sense of timing to keep the relationship alive and the lines of communications open. The decision makers are often considering many different factors in the decision process, and having the ability to clarify, restate, and persuade is a valuable skill in closing opportunities.

HANDLING OBJECTIONS

Objections by the prospect provide an opportunity to persuasively communicate. They represent questions or points of concern that, when successfully clarified, can strengthen the buyer's commitment to a solution.

Objections may be spoken or unspoken. Often prospects are hesitant to tell you things that might be perceived as negative. Therefore, it is essential to dig and identify all objections. The better you do this before proposal submission, the better off you are because, as previously mentioned, prospects often stop communicating once the proposal is submitted.

Objections occur in every opportunity cycle. They signal several of the following things:

- A question that needs clarification
- A comment, issue, or concern with your proposed approach
- Your services are still under consideration
- The prospect is moving closer to a decision
- An opportunity to hear feedback about you and your competitors
- An opportunity to differentiate your services

Objections are identified and flattened by returning to the questioning mode you used in stage I. Some suggested questions are as follows:

- Do you think our planned approach addresses your needs?
- What are your thoughts about our approach?
- Are the fees that we proposed within the range of your expectations?
- Are there any other issues that would prevent us from being seriously considered as your provider?

When you uncover an objection, consider doing the following:

1. *Restate the objection.* For example, "So, what I hear you saying is that you thought our fees would come in much lower than the other firms?"

2. *Acknowledge the prospects feelings.* For example, "I understand why you might perceive this." Then you could go further, stating, "This is a common misconception in today's unpredictable market."

3. *Ask open-ended questions.* For example, "We attempted to display our value in our proposal processes. Do you think we accomplished this?"

4. *Respond by describing feature/advantage/benefit.* For example, "You will find that the same focus and attention you experienced during the process is an example of the experience you will enjoy through our working relationship. We believe we can do this better than some of the larger firms and is the significant value of Jones & Jones, as a local firm."

5. *Test for reaction.* For example, "Does this make sense?"

The previous points are guidelines. Obviously, when handling objections you shouldn't sound stilted. And some are easier to handle than others. If you get stumped and can't think of a good answer, at least you know what the objections are, and you can work on them between your current meeting and the next one.

> **⚑ Key Concept**
>
> Objections by the prospect provide an opportunity to persuasively communicate. They represent questions or points of concern that, when successfully clarified, can strengthen the buyer's commitment to a solution.

NEXT STEPS

During the selling cycle, one of the most important things in pursuit is to identifying appropriate next steps. When you are meeting with a prospect, you should be attempting to identify logical next steps and persuading him or her to the advantage of executing the next step. What you accomplish during each step in the process is important to improving your chances of being awarded the business. If you do it right, your odds increase as you execute the steps. Stretching out or elongating the process lets you present your thought leadership in bite-size pieces. This permits the buyer to develop an appreciation for you and your offerings. Every time you're talking with a prospective client, focus on two things, both the objective of the meeting at hand and the appropriate next step. For example, you're meeting with a controller and a CFO. The CFO is much more ready to buy than the controller. Think for a second what the logical next step should be. It's not to return with a proposal, but rather to meet with each of them separately so you can uncover more clearly the needs of the controller and move him or her one step closer to commitment. Examples of other next steps are as follows:

- A return visit during which you present thoughtful responses to specific questions asked during the previous meeting.
- A meaningful e-mail in which you thank the buyer for his or her time and offer a suggestion for how to approach a particular challenge. In this case, you're not so much giving away the store as offering a hint of what you can bring to the table.
- A follow-up e-mail to which you attach additional information, such as an article you wrote, a description of a similar project, a testimonial, or a client reference, for example.
- A phone call in which you propose returning in order to discuss his or her needs further.
- A follow-up meeting with additional professionals to strengthen the relationship and continue to build credibility.

These and other next steps help the buyer get to know and trust you. But keep in mind that you may not know exactly which step is the right one until the current meeting unfolds.

THE PROPOSAL

The proposal represents a historical record of the findings from all of your meetings with the prospect, and the articulation of your strategic approach. It should not be used as a major selling tool, but rather as a support document which confirms the information you've already gathered from the prospect and reinforces the information the prospect already knows about you. Be careful not to use it to "sell" your services without first uncovering and then summarizing the prospect's needs, and articulating a value proposition based upon those needs. Many proposals incorrectly focus primarily on a firm's capabilities without first stating the prospect's objectives. This approach communicates to the prospect that his or her needs are not that important, and that you're putting your own agenda before his or hers. See exhibit 27-1, "Sample Proposal Overview (Executive Overview)," for an example.

For more information, see chapter 28, "Creating Proposals That Win."

MOST COMMON MISTAKES

Many mistakes can be made in opportunity pursuit. The following are the ones I've noticed the most in CPA firms:

- Not qualifying the prospect

    — Qualify early, often, and hard.

- The wrong person pursuing the opportunity

    — Many firms lead with the best technical person, rather than one who can best develop the opportunity.

- Group calls early in the cycle

    — Never builds a close enough relationship with the buyer.

- Complying with requests rather than digging for needs

    — Not understanding the true needs and the best value proposition results in the wrong strategy.

- Not setting up the right next step with a specific timeframe

    — Letting the prospect wander around without you and losing control and the ability to influence (as long as you're talking, you can influence).

- Not regrouping to continue to evolve the strategy

    — Failing to have the best strategic selling minds devoted to the best winning approach. Your strategy will stay static instead of dynamic as circumstances change.

- Not asking early and directly about competition

    — Not understanding who the competition is. They represent strategic options based upon why the buyer is including them (for example, different size firms, specialty firms like staffing companies or tax boutiques).
    — Not getting the prospect comfortable with talking to you about competition, which is key to later influencing the prospect.
    — Not putting yourself in an advisory capacity, which can be valuable in influencing the prospect.

- Not asking broad contextual questions which could reveal what will affect the buyer's decision
- Not confirming assumptions, such as

    — I thought he was the buyer.
    — I thought they were the competitor.
    — I thought that's what they wanted.

- Meeting only once or twice to find out all important information

    — You lose the ability to continue to influence the buyer.
    — The sales cycle is a process, not an event—and the process is to help shape, define, sort out, and influence the buyer's evolving understanding of the choices.
    — Decisions are always made in the context of other factors outside what's readily apparent.

- Not cultivating an advocate and "getting on the same side of the table" with him or her

    — Results in not having an ally to call in order to overcome objections after proposal submission.

FINAL WORDS ON BUILDING A RELATIONSHIP

When you are not in opportunity pursuit, but rather creating a long-term relationship with "suspects" or referral sources (those people who don't have immediate potential), you have all the time in the world. You might take them to dinner or sporting events and get to know them personally. When you are in the heat of opportunity development, building a relationship takes a different approach. This is not to say that you can't entertain when and if appropriate, but you usually have a very short sell cycle and have to get to know the prospect quickly. Relationship development, in this context, is much more about developing and displaying an understanding of their immediate needs, your proposed solution, and the value you represent. This should be front and center in your focus. Knowing them on a deep, personal level is secondary and, often, simply not possible. However, if you pursue the opportunity in a sophisticated manner using the previously mentioned principles, the prospect will assume that the professionalism you display in opportunity pursuit will translate into the professionalism they will experience if your firm is chosen to do the work. Many times, prospects cannot discern during a short sell cycle which CPA firm is the best alternative. They assume that all are qualified, or they wouldn't be talking to you. Therefore, the firm with the most experience doesn't necessarily win. If all firms have adequate experience to be considered, then the one which will most often emerge as the winner is the one who shows expertise in opportunity pursuit. Because there are almost always incumbent relationships that influence the buyer, it's important to quickly establish a relationship and show your expertise in opportunity pursuit in order to have a chance to level the playing field.

CONCLUSION

The following summarizes the key points in opportunity pursuit:

1. Before pursuing an opportunity, it must be qualified. In other words, is this really an opportunity? Remember, there are five questions:

   a. Why buy?
   b. Why now?
   c. Why us?
   d. Who else?
   e. Who cares?

2. Three stages exist in opportunity development. Stages I and II are to meet the prospect and develop needs (I — Establish the Relationship; II — Build the Relationship).

   Do not show up and talk about your firm (even if the prospect thinks this is what they want). This is true, whether it takes one call (meeting) or multiple calls to close the opportunity.

3. Do ask the prospect lots of questions at the beginning of the process (remember the five categories of questions mentioned earlier).

4. Try to elongate the process in order to build value and a relationship, except if you are winning, in which case, try to hurry up and close. Submit the proposal at the last possible moment.

5. Elongate by trying to figure out logical "next steps" in the sequence, rather than trying to accomplish everything in one call.

6. Remember to "divide and conquer." You want to get each decision-maker and recommender one-on-one.

When they "go dark" after you deliver the proposal, gently continue to nudge them by maintaining contact. Don't give up after a phone call or e-mail or two, or three.

ABOUT THE AUTHOR

Gale Crosley, CPA, is founder and principal of Crosley+Company and consults with CPA firms on revenue growth issues and opportunities. She graduated from the University of Akron, Ohio with a Bachelor of Science degree in Accounting, and is a CPA in Ohio and Georgia. Her background includes a unique mix of experience with two national CPA firms, and nearly 30 years in business development and senior management, including IBM and several small technology companies. She was formerly Executive Vice President of Business Development at a $250 million consulting firm, and was responsible for implementing revenue growth initiatives among 39 individual practices, 1,500 CPAs and consultants, a direct sales force and marketing department, and 100 rainmakers. Over her career, she has been responsible for developing high performance rainmaking organizations, bringing more than 30 offerings to market and closing dozens of multi-million-dollar opportunities. Her first book, *At the Crossroads*, chronicles the challenges and successes of a fictional CPA firm struggling with growth.

Exhibit 27-1
Sample Proposal Overview (Executive Overview)

> The following is an excerpt from an executive overview. This approach focuses on the prospect, displaying an interest and understanding of his or her needs, and addressing each need that you uncovered from meetings throughout the sell cycle. You'll be putting the prospect's needs first, before your own need to tell them about the greatness of your firm.

Mr. John Jones

Treasurer & CFO
Indiana Mutual Insurance Company
265 E. Water St.
Indianapolis, Indiana

Dear John:

Thank you for the opportunity to meet with you and your team. Over the last few weeks, we have attempted to identify financial related reporting and operational needs within your company, as well as to gain a real sense of the business objectives and goals for the organization. In this fashion, we believe we can better tie our recommendations and solutions for the audit and tax work into an understanding of the bigger picture. As a result, we believe that through the course of working with you, we can learn to understand your organization better—how decisions are made, what makes it tick, and the key drivers of your business. This will enable us to provide real value to your organization, especially in the audit and tax work. You will observe that we have focused upon your key issues to begin working with you to optimize your return on the investment made in your selection of a CPA firm.

Observations and Identified Needs

The needs that we found through our interviews were almost consistently voiced across the company. Although we found different priorities among different individuals, the discussion below summarizes what we have been able to learn within our brief acquaintance.

Our Recommendations

1. The need for an accounting firm with a level of understanding of the insurance industry and statutory and GAAP accounting procedures to perform audits of the company financial statements and the company benefit plans.

   Recommendation:

   We have selected a team of qualified individuals to work on this project who understand your industry. Partner-in-charge, Jeff Smith, has 22 years of public accounting experience as well as being the former CFO of a mutual insurance company. Paul Capers, senior-in-charge, was previously employed by KPMG and conducted audits of property and mutual insurance companies, including your company's financial audit and employee benefit plan audit.

2. Concerns that the fees are not commensurate with the level of service that the company is experiencing. We heard loud and clear that the company wants to be treated with outstanding service, rapid response, and respect for the dollar being spent with a CPA firm.

   Recommendation:

   Our fees for audit services and tax consultation will be clearly spelled out, both in discussions with you, as well as in our proposal. If questions arise that require additional work beyond the scope of the engagement, our policy is to first discuss the charges with you, and obtain approval at that time. Like you, we do not like hidden charges and are above board in everything we do.
   [Issue number three, etc.]

EXHIBIT 27-1
SAMPLE PROPOSAL OVERVIEW (EXECUTIVE OVERVIEW)
(CONTINUED)

Summary of Proposal Excerpt

The previous example is how all your proposals should start— either with an executive overview or a proposal summary. It should represent the culmination of all your discovery and due diligence during the process. The better you become at understanding the prospect's issues, the more you can include in the proposal. It can become a powerful document to enhance your selling efforts.

CHAPTER 28
Creating Proposals That Win

Dawn Wagenaar
Ingenuity Marketing Group, LLC

INTRODUCTION

Firms spend hundreds of hours writing and submitting proposals. Some are responses to requests for proposal (RFPs), some are ideas for services they are pitching, and some are "relationship proposals" when a client or potential client is considering a project and wants to see what they can offer.

Many, if not most, of the proposals we have seen are not compelling. Too many seem to speak in the language of, "we, we, we," instead of the "you" language that focuses on the potential client's challenges and needs. Prospects are concerned about two things: the work they want done and whether or not your firm is capable of doing it to their satisfaction. To create a winning proposal, you must do more than regurgitate your marketing brochure.

There are three parts to a proposal process: before, during and after. Miss one of these and your chances of landing the project or future opportunities will diminish.

By implementing the steps that take you through the proposal process in this chapter, you and your team will have a better understanding of who you are proposing to, what their true needs are, and how you can meet their needs, leaving no doubt in their minds that you are the right firm for the job.

The critical components of each phase are as follows:

Before

- Start with the end in mind
- Create a proposal process
- Assemble a proposal template
- Promote buy-in

During

- Alert and assemble the team that best fits the prospect
- Research thoroughly
- Develop a winning strategy
- Attend the prospect meeting
- Make the Go/No-Go decision
- Produce and deliver the proposal
- Prepare the oral presentation

After

- Send a thank you
- Stay in touch

BEFORE YOU BEGIN

Start With the End in Mind

To find out how your proposals stack up against the rest, collect copies of proposals and similar documents from other professional service firms and other industries. If you are a member of an association or have friends in the industry (at other firms), request copies so you can see how your firm compares against others. Review them and determine what could be changed within your proposal. Most CPAs have not seen what other firms and industries are doing; when they see concrete examples for improvement, they will be more likely to act.

Create a Proposal Process

Some of the criteria for a proposal process might include alerting marketing to develop a proposal within 48 hours of receiving an RFP. You could develop a proposal log that lists the prospect, project description, date logged, key team members and deadlines. Marketing could screen the prospect through acceptance criteria and also track wins and losses here. Responsibilities would be clearly defined. By developing this step-by-step process for each proposal, you won't be under the gun to "get something out." Here is an example of what that process might look like.

Proposal Log

Proposal Log:
Prospect:
Project Description:
Team Members Involved:
Date Received:
Date Due:
Follow up:
Won/lost: (if lost, schedule post mortem)
Reason for win/lose:

Proposal Process

Step 1:

A copy of or the original RFP gets sent to the marketing director immediately after receiving it to ensure a timely turnaround (if the original is sent, a copy will be made to highlight proposal requirements).

-OR-

After a prospective client meeting, if there is a need for a proposal, send marketing director any information gathered in the meeting in order to start the process.

Step 2:

Once the marketing director receives the initial information, they will contact the proposal requester for any additional information in order to fill out the RFP as completely as possible.

Step 3:

The marketing director will put together the proposal based on the proposal template or on the RFP (format should always be followed).

Step 4:

Partners or proposal requester will receive the first version of the proposal. They will review it and make any additions or changes. All changes will be made by the marketing director and reviewed with the proposal requester before sending out to the prospect.

Step 5:

Proposal requester will follow-up with the prospect according to timelines given in RFP.

Step 6:

Proposal requester will continue to follow-up until a decision is made and then pass along that decision to the team and the marketing director. If the proposal was not won, a post mortem phone call should be made either by the proposal requester or marketing director.

Assemble the Proposal Template

To ensure a consistent brand and message, it is best to develop some standard templates for hard copies and electronic versions for such things as firm history or the firm story, bios, case studies, table of contents, industry/niche introductions, appendixes and indexes to assist with quick assembly and a sharp, branded presentation.

Whether it is a hard copy or perhaps a PowerPoint presentation, add visual interest with graphs and tables. The human brain can process graphics five to seven times faster than text and responds to color and pictures. So, when the prospect is looking at (not reading) your proposal, the visual elements will pop out and set your firm apart. Many simple graphs can be created for a transition plan, an audit methodology timeline, project flows, work timeline, and a team chart—just to name a few.

You will also want to take great care in assembling your hard copy proposal by using a sturdy and professional cover and proper binding (no paperclips or staple in the corner). If you can, use the prospects logo on the cover—it is about them—while adding your own logo at the bottom.

Technology has also given you the chance to break out of the hard copy proposal standard and use things such as Webcasts, PowerPoint, social media or video casts to set yourself apart from the competition. Although, always be sure to follow the RFP guidelines first. If there is room for creativity, great, but don't blow your chance at getting the project because you didn't provide the information in the proper format.

If you don't have in-house writers, consider hiring a copywriter for a clear and dynamic message. And remember, professional does not mean boring. Almost all bios, for example, look exactly the same and do NOTHING to differentiate your firm or CPAs. Create bios that tell the prospect about your corporate culture and the personalities behind it.

Important Tip: If using the prospect's logo/brand, it is important to remember to ask permission to use it if you are including it on the proposal.

♀ Key Concept

Develop standard templates for hard copies and electronic versions of such things as firm history or the firm story, bios, case studies, table of contents, industry/niche introductions, appendixes and indexes to assist with quick assembly and a sharp, branded presentation.

Promote Buy-In

To promote buy-in of the improved (or even new) proposal process, select some go-getters to pilot it and then heavily promote their success in attracting new business. Eventually the change resisters will wonder what the go-getters are doing right.

DURING THE PROPOSAL

Alert the Team

Set a rule in the proposal process that an RFP or any type of proposal request cannot sit on a desk for more than 24 hours before alerting the marketing or proposal team. Your team in the proposal process should consist of the marketing director, partner/manager who brought in the proposal/RFP, other experts for a particular service offering, and an administrative person to assist in the proofing/formatting of the proposal. Make sure everyone brought in is aware of their role in getting the proposal ready for submission. A clearly defined proposal process (see earlier example) should keep everyone on task.

Bring every relevant team member in on proposal opportunities. If you are working to develop new business, marketing staff can do their jobs better when they understand the strategy. They can help the firm develop proposal language that is customized to that industry as well as create ways to differentiate your proposal from the rest.

The team should quickly weigh in on whether the project is worth going after or not. This might be based on industry expertise, return on investment, location or potential conflict of interest.

⚷ Key Concept

Set a rule in the proposal process that an RFP or any type of proposal request cannot sit on a desk for more than 24 hours before alerting the marketing or proposal team.

Research Thoroughly

There are many things you can find out about a potential client before the prospect meeting and before you spend time on a proposal. Go to the company's Web site, which usually presents the way they see themselves. You can find officers, boards, clients, services, the community they are in and what it is like, awards won, press they've gotten, and many other things. From this research ask yourself, what effect do they make in the marketplace?

Look for similarities between the prospect and your firm—similar memberships, charities, or missions—so you can form a kinship. Finally, meet with as many people in the company as you can, beyond the president to the controller and other key staff. Ask them what's important to them and their company. You will probably get all sorts of different answers on what's important but you will learn a lot and be able to customize the proposal to them much more than if you hadn't made the extra effort.

Develop a Winning Strategy

When you write a proposal document or prepare an oral presentation, brilliant prose and competitive pricing are certainly important. However, they will not be nearly as important as the ability to convey a keen understanding of the prospect's industry and particular problems and needs. The most important investment is in the following:

- Identifying the key decision maker(s)
- Discovering their needs/issues, both corporate and personal
- Determining how to provide solutions

Let's spend a little time on each of these key strategies:

Identify the Key Decision Maker(s)

In most small businesses, there will only be one or two key decision makers. In a larger company, the number of individuals involved in the decision-making process can be legions. While not all of them will have a vote, most will be in a position to influence the final outcome.

Regardless of the number of key players it is important to learn who will be involved in the proposal process and who will have the key decision maker's ear when the moment of truth arrives. These are the people you must meet to learn not only what the key decision makers want, but also what they expect from a new accounting firm. You must address all of these concerns in your proposal document and oral presentations.

The following is a list of possible decision makers and decision influencers. You might never encounter all of these individuals in any one proposal situation, but it is useful to think about this list when you are invited to propose.

- *Primary decision maker.* This is usually the CEO or CFO depending on the amount of power they actually have in the organization. The key is to find out who the decision maker is. He or she almost always has final say over the budget. Your best bet is to have a solid business relationship with this individual before entering into the bidding process. If this is not the case, find ways to establish rapport as soon as possible in the proposal process.

- *Influencer.* Typically, this is an old friend or longtime associate of the decision maker, someone he or she uses as a sounding board. In the case of a smaller business, this might be an outside attorney or a fellow Rotarian. If you can identify this individual, ensure that he or she knows your track record for serving similar businesses.
- *Advocate(s).* This individual has a strong personal motive for seeing that you succeed. Possibly an alumni of your firm, he or she speaks out on your behalf when the decision makers meet behind closed doors. Arm this person with all of the facts so he or she can make a convincing argument on your behalf. Keep him or her well informed throughout the proposal process. You may also ask for suggestions on how to approach the key decision maker(s).
- *Veto voter.* This can be anyone in the prospect's business who may have a personal reason for preferring another firm. He or she may influence key decision makers to put your proposal in the B pile. All you can do to counter this individual is to try to uncover his or her objections and address them.
- *Evaluator.* This is someone, usually in middle management, who has been asked to serve as a liaison with accounting firms. This individual may be asked to weigh proposals against some predetermined selection criteria and make recommendations. Work to gain this person's confidence in your credentials and working style. Find ways to encourage him or her to reveal the selection criteria being used before preparing the proposal.
- *Gatekeeper.* This is a high-powered secretary or administrative assistant who screens incoming calls and inquiries for the senior executive. Win this person's confidence and respect by treating him or her courteously and acknowledging the gatekeeper's importance.

Discovering the Prospect's Needs

Once the key decision makers and decision influencers have been identified, begin gathering as much information as possible about their accounting service needs. This needs analysis process precedes any attempt to prepare a proposal document or oral presentation. Here are the topics to address:

- Objective requirements for accounting services
- Short-and long-term goals for the business
- Concerns about problems in the business, such as poor performance in certain divisions or difficulty in controlling inventory
- Personal standards related to service excellence (see chapter 36, "Developing a Service Excellence Plan for Clients"), such as expecting to reach the engagement partner each time he or she calls (you can learn a lot by listening to how the prospect talks about his or her current accounting firm).

Almost all prospects, especially those being served by small to medium-sized firms, will be willing to meet you—at least once—to discuss their requirements. Make the most of these meetings. Develop interview questions that are open-ended, leading the interviewee to share as much as possible about the history of the company, the goals and frustrations of management, what they liked or disliked about their previous accountants, and so on. Remember, let them do most of the talking.

When you have gathered all of the necessary information, review the "12 Cs" listed subsequently and make sure you can answer each question with a "yes."

Key Concept

Once the key decision makers and decision influencers have been identified, begin gathering as much information as possible about their accounting service needs.

Selection Criteria: The 12 Cs

1. *Cost:* Do we know if our fee is in the acceptable range?

2. *Chemistry:* Do the key decision makers like and trust us?

3. *Comparable experience*: Is the prospect aware of our track record of serving clients with similar needs?

4. *Capabilities*: Do we have the staff and technology to serve this client effectively?

5. *Credentials*: What is our proof?

6. *Clear communication*: Have we established a pattern of effective communications?

7. *Client service commitment*: Have we shown that the prospect will be important to us? Also, are our references speaking well of us?

8. *Centralized control*: Can our service team members manage this work effectively?

9. *Competence:* Have we been able to prove we will do the right thing?

10. *Continuity*: Do we have a proven track record of low staff turnover?

11. *Creativity and initiative*: Can we show them we will always be looking for ways to help them reduce costs and increase profits?

12. *Contacts*: Do we know all the members of the prospect's decision-making group?

Never underestimate the importance of contacts. Contacts can make or break a proposal's success by providing information and supporting your firm as the preferred choice. It is therefore important that the proposal team identify their contacts within the prospective client's organization and decide how best to use them. The tactics of maintaining the managing contact should be integral to your proposal strategy.

Determining How to Provide Solutions

Now, you must explain how your firm's features translate into desired corporate and personal benefits, and then go on to prove you can deliver as promised.

A *feature* is the service or expertise the firm can provide (example: quarterly financial statements). A *benefit* is what the prospect gains as a result of receiving the service or expertise (example: the statements will be delivered within four weeks of the close of the quarter, enabling the client to satisfy lender requirements). To put it another way, features answer the question, "What?—What will the CPA firm provide?" and benefits answer the question, "What's in it for me or the company?"

Each time you describe a service, ask yourself: What will the decision maker *gain, save, do, or become* as a result of receiving this service?" For example, the decision maker might gain the ability to seek additional credit from a lender, or save 5 percent in overhead as the result of streamlined operations, or be free to focus on other concerns of the business such as overseas expansion. It is just as important to focus on the latter as it is to describe the former, so you should organize each selling point in this way:

- *Observation*. Make an observation or recommendation. Example: "You have expressed concern about the fact that changing auditors will add to the burdens of an already overworked staff."
- *Benefit*. Identify the benefits the client will receive by using your firm. Example: "We understand your concern, and can assure you that our team will minimize disruptions while supporting staff with workflow recommendations."
- *Feature*. Explain how your firm can solve the problem. Example: "We will provide a computerized questionnaire that can be filled out by your staff, at their convenience, before we arrive."
- *Proof*. Offer proof, using evidence, and whenever available, expert testimony. Example: "We employed this approach when we audited ABC, XYZ, and BBR, and they found it very effective. Bob Johnson, VP of finance at BBR, said our approach caused little disruption for his staff."

In short, a proposal document or oral presentation that starts off by detailing the prospect's goals and needs has a much higher chance of capturing attention and interest.

Attend the Prospect Meeting

If you want new business, meet the prospect. Submitting a solid proposal is great, but no piece of paper or presentation can start building the relationship or tell the prospect what you can do for them better that you can in a face-to-face meeting. One of the biggest benefits to the prospect meeting is determining whether or not you have a good rapport with the prospect and learning as much as you can about their needs and concerns. Here are several tips for preparing for the meeting.

- Review the previous research about the prospect.
- Listen, listen again, and listen some more.
- Go with the mindset that you want to learn everything about the prospect, including why they are looking for a new accountant.
- Make sure you know a lot about them before you say anything about yourself or your firm.
- People assume you have good credentials. They make a choice based on whether they like you and whether they think you will do a good job for them.
- Do not present your résumé. Focus on connecting with them by being intensely interested in their challenges and opportunities.
- When it is your turn to speak, talk about other clients you may have helped in similar situations. Offer free advice on the spot; it is the only way they will see you know what you are talking about.
- Tell them you are quite interested in working with them and ask when they would like to make a change. Get some specifics on their timeline.

When interviewing prospects, almost all of them will say that fee is an issue. This is only true if you haven't made them feel that they want you. By drilling down during your interview process—from the CEO to the controller to key project team members, you will begin to learn what they really want. It could really be continuity of personnel, more industry expertise or responsiveness.

 Key Concept

> When interviewing prospects, almost all of them will say that fee is an issue. This is only true if you haven't made them feel that they want you.

Make the Go/No-Go Decision

Each time a proposal opportunity arises, you should evaluate whether or not the prospect meets the firm's criteria for new clients after you've had the prospect meeting. Don't waste time preparing a proposal for someone that isn't a good fit for the firm. Before committing yourself to preparing a proposal, do the following:

> *Determine whether or not it is cost effective to submit a proposal.* In other words, what are your chances of winning the client? Will you be able to meet the prospect's service requirements, resolve his or her management issues, and compete on fees?

Exhibit 28-1, located at the end of the chapter, is a go/no-go worksheet that can help you decide whether or not it is cost effective to submit a proposal to the prospect at this time.

Remember, however, that even if the prospective client passes the go/no-go screening with flying colors, client assessment does not stop there. It continues through the proposal process, and in fact a major goal during the prospect meeting is to assess potential risk areas. Specific guidelines for client screening during site visits, staff interviews and the prospect meeting include the following:

- Determining the condition of the prospect's management, finances, and internal control
- Meeting the prospect's accounting and tax personnel to determine specific financial needs and the condition of accounting records
- Complaints about the current CPA

Produce and Deliver the Proposal

Although the proposal document is only one of several factors influencing the prospect's selection, it is highly important. This is the place where all of your research and planning come together and you tell the prospect you have heard their challenges and can provide solutions.

If the prospect was unclear about their direction or you feel a full proposal is overkill based on your meeting, submit a one page document. The document should (see Executive Summary following) outline what you see as their critical area of concern, how you can solve it for them, the benefit to them and what fee you will charge. This will often lead to more discussion and eventually a full proposal might be needed.

While a proposal document may not win the engagement for your firm, it can easily be the reason why you are eliminated from further consideration. Do everything required to ensure that your firm advances to the next round of evaluation (generally the oral presentation).

The purpose of the proposal document is to convey the following information:

- The CPA firm understands the prospect's business as well as its needs and expectations.
- The CPA firm meets all of the prospective client's selection criteria.
- The CPA firm differs—and is superior to—its competitors in ways that make it better qualified to meet the client's needs.
- The CPA is able to offer solutions.

The following four elements should be included in every proposal.

The Transmittal Letter

The transmittal letter can be an executive summary that highlights the key messages and selling points that are explored in much greater detail in the body of the proposal. Or it can be a brief introductory letter accompanied by a separate executive summary. Regardless of the form you choose, write this part of the proposal document last to ensure that it conveys the messages found elsewhere in the text. The transmittal letter should include the following elements:

- The CPA firm's appreciation for being considered
- A statement that conveys an understanding of why the prospect has requested a proposal
- A statement that conveys the firm's understanding of the engagement being discussed
- An affirmation concerning the CPA firm's genuine interest in working with the prospect

The transmittal letter is also the best place to ask for the business. Most accountants simply present their firm's credentials without conveying their eagerness to do the work, assuming the prospective client realized how interested they are. Never assume; if you don't ask for the work, the prospect may be forced to conclude some other firm is more interested.

The Executive Summary

Most of the time, the executive summary is the only section that is referred to and re-read. It should be prospect focused and address the prospect's needs and concerns. Explain how this engagement will benefit them and eliminate their pain. Avoid mentioning your company too much; prospects don't care that it's been around since the Roman Empire.

One of the biggest mistakes companies make in proposals is outlining generic capabilities rather than concrete solutions that reflect a true understanding of that client's business needs. It takes more time, but the executive summary is your primary opportunity to connect on a business and personal level with three or four relevant selling points.

The Body

This part of the proposal document goes to the heart of the matter, reviewing each of the prospect's requirements and building a convincing argument about why he or she should choose your CPA firm. If an RFP was submitted by the prospective client, the proposal team should follow it carefully, using its information requirements as an outline. If no RFP was provided, then the proposal team should organize its remarks so the issues of the greatest interest to the client appear first. As you prepare this section of the proposal document, remember to use the guidelines listed earlier concerning observation-benefit-feature-proof.

Appendixes

Use appendixes for the following:

- Descriptions of special services and fees for projects beyond the primary scope of the proposal
- Review of the firm, its history, resources, and methodologies
- A list of firm locations
- Service team biographies
- A list of representative clients, especially those in the prospect's industry
- References, article reprints, and relevant client testimonials

Remember that even this boilerplate material should be tailored to the unique needs of the prospect.

Leveraging References and Testimonials

Make sure references are current and in a similar industry. Prospects like to see clients that have used the same service. Testimonials and case studies are also a great way to talk about your company without speaking in the "we, we" language. Call references in advance of submitting the proposal so they can anticipate a call and engage with familiarity. Provide between four and six to ensure that the screening committee can reach at least a few of them quickly.

Before delivering your proposal, read the RFPs one more time. At least one of the screening committee members, if not more, is very attached to the RFP parameters. If they ask for 12 point Times New Roman, give it to them even if it does not fit your branding standards or format for proposals. Avoid proposals over 20 pages. Too long is just… too long. The ideal length is 10–14 pages.

You also want to follow the same sort of common sense rules when submitting electronically. Nobody wants to scroll through a 50 page PowerPoint presentation. Technology does give you the chance to differentiate yourself from the competition. If you are submitting your proposal online, send it with a video cast of the team members introducing themselves and start building rapport immediately.

Packaging of proposals, when done correctly, can definitely make an impression. A few examples include the following:

- For a travel agency or airline, put the proposal in a suitcase with destination stickers all over it.
- For a children's hospital, put it in a toy trunk with new toys.
- For a manufacturer, send the proposal in a toolbox.

The point is to use your creativity so that you spark their attention and set yourself apart from your competitors.

Deliver the proposal in person (if less than one hour away). Take a minute to ensure that it gets to the right person and express to that person your interest in the business. Call before you go to make sure it is a good time. Don't walk through the proposal (unless they have time and want to), simply hand it to the right person, thank them for the opportunity and tell them not to hesitate to call you if they have any questions. If you have to mail, never mail anything on Friday that you want to be noticed because Mondays are the largest mail days for businesses.

If you delivered it electronically, a phone call the next day to make sure they received it is always a good idea. You do not want your proposal to be sitting in some junk folder because a filter didn't let it get through their security wall. Regardless of the mode of delivery, it never hurts to follow up after a few days to see if they need any clarification on your recommendations. Even if you don't reach the person, it shows you are eager to earn their business.

ᵠ Key Concept

Your proposals should outline concrete solutions that reflect a true understanding of that client's business needs—even the boilerplate material should be tailored to the unique needs of the prospect.

ᵠ Key Concept

If you deliver a proposal electronically, a phone call the next day to make sure they received it is always a good idea.

Prepare the Oral Presentation

In oral presentations, impact and style are everything. We are not advocating form over substance, but you must accept the fact that the adage "the medium is the message" is highly relevant. After all, you are selling people, not a product that can be sampled or judged before it is purchased.

When making an oral presentation, assemble your team and develop a plan of action. At your first meeting, review the following questions, and take them into consideration as you prepare:

- Has anything changed since you delivered the proposal document?
- Are there any additional decision makers to be taken into account?
- How have the decision makers reacted to your proposal and those of your competitors?
- Which firm, if any, is in the lead?
- Are there any veto voters?

It is at this juncture that having an inside contact or advocate can be very helpful. Without one, you may have difficulty obtaining answers to some of the questions on this list.

To prepare your team, you will need to determine who will speak, what visuals you will need, and when you can get together to rehearse. Never send more people to the oral presentation than the number representing the prospect. The engagement partner should be in charge of the team. If the managing partner is present, he or she should defer to the engagement partner. The issues determine who speaks, not the relative seniority of team members.

PowerPoint, presentation boards, and handouts can greatly enhance your presentation. Use the highest standard in preparing them, but make sure they do not draw attention away from what your presenters are saying.

If you have team members who are uneasy about making an oral presentation, you should invest in one or more rehearsals. Choose an occasion when everyone can attend, and run through the presentation, trouble-shooting as you go. Ask someone in the firm to come in and hurl difficult questions at your team. Make everyone practice their responses until they are comfortable.

You may want to use a proposal coach—a person who can help team members develop polished presentation skills. Don't limit this person's role to helping with public speaking techniques. Find someone who can make a significant contribution to the proposal's content, strategy, and organization. If hiring is not in your budget, find someone inside the organization who can act as the proposal guru. This individual should have a record of success in making oral presentations.

While not everyone will have carefully reviewed your proposal, the presentation should not be a word-by-word recapitulation. If you have gotten this far, chances are good that management finds your capabilities acceptable. Now they will focus on whether or not you are best qualified to meet their needs.

Like any good business letter or report, an oral presentation has three parts:

- *Introduction.* Briefly review the challenges and solutions that you will discuss during the meeting, and then summarize what will happen immediately following the prospect's decision to retain your firm.
- *Body.* Focus on benefits, not features (services). Organize your presentation so the issues most important to the client are discussed first. This will help convince decision makers that you really do understand their needs.

  As in the written document, use the observation-benefit-feature-proof method, described earlier, to demonstrate your understanding of the prospect's business and industry. Explain how specific services will help achieve their goals. Finally, make it clear that you will do more than react; you will become an active member of the company's management team.
- *Closing.* Your team now has an opportunity to summarize key messages, review the differentiators that distinguish your firm from other firms, and ask for the work.

A question and answer period usually follows your prepared remarks and is the last opportunity you will have to overcome objections, whether expressed or implied, While your objective is to be hired, the decision makers are always looking for reasons to eliminate contenders. It is therefore important for you to confront objections in a highly competent manner and turn potentially damaging situations into new opportunities for demonstrating your strengths.

If decision makers want to interrupt your presentation and ask questions, encourage them. You will demonstrate your comfort with the process and with them.

Important Tip: Reading leadership bios to see what organizations or associations they belong to in their off hours can give you insight into their interests and affiliations. Also look at the firm profile or community page to see where they donate their time and money.

AFTER THE PROPOSAL

Send a Thank You

Regardless of how you believe you performed during the proposal, write a thank you note to the potential client, thanking them for their time. This will also enable one more contact for your firm to make a difference. Lobby for the job! Tell them how much you would enjoy working with them. Also, if you have not already, send a thank you note to the referral source.

Stay in Touch

Have the marketing staff call a project committee member regarding the winning or lost proposal to gain feedback for improving your next proposal. If you didn't get the project, plan a follow-up call about 15 months later. By that time, they might be ready for a change.

Consider the questions in exhibit 28-2, located at the end of the chapter, when debriefing a prospect or new client on your proposal process.

You can learn a lot from both a win and a loss. Don't let that feedback go to waste, share it with everyone who could benefit from hearing it and improve the process for next time. If you consistently hear you won the bid because you were technically stronger than the others, make sure that is a prominent piece of information in all future proposals. Remember, even if you don't agree with the reason they gave if you didn't win, perception is reality, and their perception is what matters.

⚷ Key Concept

You can learn a lot from both a win and a loss. Don't let that feedback go to waste, share it with everyone who could benefit from hearing it and improve the process for next time.

Celebrate

If you won the proposal, take time to celebrate your victory. It will boost firm morale for the next round of new business development.

CONCLUSION

Proposal writing is a bit of an art form; each one is individual, but the same essential elements have to come together to make it work. If you streamline your proposal process so you aren't recreating the wheel every time and go into each opportunity with the focus on the prospects' needs, not only will you be more efficient, but also more successful. Don't just send out proposals, send out winning proposals.

ABOUT THE AUTHOR

Dawn Wagenaar is principal of Ingenuity Marketing Group, and provides comprehensive marketing strategy for professional service firms across the country. She is the founder of several networking groups and a former chair of the Association for Accounting Marketing's annual conference. Contact her at Dawn@ingenuitymarketing.com, 651-690-3358 or visit www.ingenuitymarketing.com or www.marketingyourpeople.com to view additional articles.

EXHIBIT 28-1
THE GO/NO-GO DECISION

Company Name: _____

Work required: _____

Potential for additional work: _____

Year end:_____ Fees to be included in proposal? _____ Yes _____ No

Est. first year's fees: $_____ Est. discount expected (%): _____

Est. hrs to complete proposal: _____

Total est. cost to propose: $_____

Competition (other firms):

Their Strengths/Weaknesses	Our Response
_____	_____
_____	_____
_____	_____
_____	_____

Our major weakness: _____

Our major strength:_____

Probable key decision makers:_____

Our relationship with each of them: _____

Our Firms	Relationship
_____	_____
_____	_____
_____	_____

Arguments against proposing: _____

Do they meet our new-client acceptance criteria? _____Yes_____No

Why/Why Not? _____

Any special considerations: _____

_____

_____

Final decision: _____Propose _____ Decline to Propose

Recommended by: _____ Decision approved by: _____

EXHIBIT 28-2
POSTMORTEM QUESTIONS

Winning Proposal

1. What made you choose our firm over the others?

2. What were the most important criteria on which you based your decision?

3. Were our fees competitive?

4. How much of a role did our written proposal play in the selection process?

5. Was our written proposal similar in style and content to the other proposals you received?

6. What did the other firms do that you thought was good or helpful?

7. What did we do that you thought was good or helpful?

Lost Proposal

1. What was your overall and immediate impression of our firm's proposal? This would pertain to the appearance of the document, format and length.

2. As you reviewed the detail of our proposal, where did you perceive our strengths to be? Where did you perceive our weaknesses to be?

3. Where was your confidence level about our team's abilities to perform the services you requested? Why?

4. What made you choose the winning firm?

5. What were the most important criteria on which you based your decision?

6. What was the winning fee?

7. If possible, would you share with me who the winning firm was?

8. What should we do differently to improve our next proposal?

9. How much of a role did the written proposal play in the selection process?

10. What was the quality of our interaction with your management?

11. What did the other firms do that you thought was especially good or helpful?

CHAPTER 29
Win More New Business With Effective Sales Management

Rick Solomon, CPA
RanOne

INTRODUCTION

While many accounting firms invest considerable resources into their marketing efforts, they often overlook one critically important area, that is, sales management. Unfortunately, that oversight can significantly reduce their overall return on that marketing investment. Although most firms enjoy a reasonable degree of success in generating business opportunities, the conversion rate of those opportunities into new business is not nearly as high as it could be. The primary reason for this is that too little attention is being paid to developing selling skills and managing the sales process within the firm.

Properly managing the firm's sales efforts can have an enormous impact on a firm's growth and profitability. Managing the sales process means having an effective sales training program to provide the necessary skills, and then supporting the successful implementation of the selling process at the individual level. It also means integrating the firm's marketing activities with the selling process, and providing the necessary technology to measure and monitor ongoing results.

When a firm effectively manages its sales process, in addition to converting a higher percentage of opportunities into new business, it also serves to create many more additional opportunities that would otherwise go unnoticed. That's because increased attention to selling activities helps people more readily recognize opportunity when it presents itself. Best of all, a well-managed sales process results in a more profitable, thriving firm that is more rewarding to work for and more exciting to be a part of.

> **Key Concept**
>
> When a firm effectively manages its sales process, in addition to converting a higher percentage of opportunities into new business, it also serves to create many more additional opportunities that would otherwise go unnoticed.

IT STARTS WITH A TOP-DOWN COMMITMENT

Effectively managing the sales process in an accounting firm requires a solid commitment from firm leadership. Much like other more traditional processes such as preparing financial statements, tax returns, or conducting audits, the sales process needs to be thought through and properly managed to enjoy its maximum benefits and achieve its highest impact.

The importance that firm professionals place on engaging in sales activities, and ultimately the sales results they produce, will be directly related to the importance firm leadership places upon such activities. A carefully thought out and well managed sales process communicates to everyone that this is indeed a firm priority that everyone is expected to participate in. Clearly defined, reasonable expectations, along with the support and skills that increase chances for success, make it easier and more inviting for professionals to participate.

This chapter provides the guidelines and critical success factors that will make it easier to establish and manage an effective sales process. A well-functioning sales process will significantly increase the results of all your practice development efforts.

The topics we'll cover are as follows:

1. Challenges specific to accounting firms

2. The crucial difference between marketing and sales

3. Critical success factors for managing your firm's sales process
    a. Defining sales responsibilities
    b. Personal sales plans
    c. Sales training
    d. A uniform sales process
    e. Sales meetings
        i.   Accountability
        ii. Success transfer
        iii. Resolution of obstacles
    f. Sales leadership
    g. Sales tracking
    h. Motivating people

CHALLENGES SPECIFIC TO ACCOUNTING FIRMS

While generating new business is important to accounting firms, the truth is that most accounting firms are not sales oriented organizations. It's taken accountants many years to come to terms with the fact that selling is necessary to compete and grow in today's market. Despite that understanding, most accountants are not salespeople and for the most part, do not think or act like salespeople. While it is true that increasing numbers of firms are retaining sales professionals, and sales training is becoming more prevalent, most firms still do not consider themselves to be "sales organizations."

This explains why firm leadership is generally not well-equipped to develop and manage a sales process within the firm. If accountants are not salespeople, they are not likely to be good sales managers. Being an accountant and being a sales manager are two distinctly different roles, each requiring a different set of skills and experience. In a typical nonaccounting business, the selling process is led by professional sales managers with a top down sales process. Measuring systems are in place to monitor sales productivity. Salespeople readily accept these measurements as a primary means of determining their effectiveness.

It's quite different for accountants. All of our training and our primary responsibilities have nothing at all to do with sales. Accountants do not voluntarily become salespeople. Rather, they discover upon entering the profession, often to their dismay, that their professional development and success will ultimately depend upon their effectiveness in the sales area. This is scary news for most accountants. And, as accountants progress within the firm, there is an inherent resistance to being managed at all. Experienced professionals take great pride in independently managing their own set of clients, and have no desire to be told what to do.

To make matters worse, in a typical accounting firm, those who play a sales manager role are in reality accountants who often don't understand what sales management is about. So we end up with "sales managers" (accountants) managing "salespeople" (accountants) who are not proficient at selling and inherently do not want to sell. Is it any wonder that sales management in most accounting firms falls far short of its potential?

There Is a Solution

Where does this leave us? If our goal is to establish an effective sales management process, how do we proceed in light of these obstacles? Fortunately, there is a solution that can actually be quite effective, if properly implemented. The solution is based upon a new and different definition of "sales." Most accountants dislike selling because they define it as something that requires them to become someone or something they don't want to become. There's a belief that selling requires that we engage in "sales" behavior that does not feel professional or comfortable. Holding on to these beliefs, this old definition, is an unnecessary obstacle to success in selling. To achieve greater results, it is imperative to establish a different paradigm for what selling means in an accounting firm.

A new and more effective definition for selling is that it's simply about discovering the needs of a prospective client, and exploring solutions in a way that is mutual and respectful. When selling skills are more accurately defined as relationship building communication skills, resistance begins to melt away and professionals begin to see the development of the skills as an integral part of their professional growth. By letting go of "trying to sell something," and coming more from a place of service, as this definition implies, pressure is removed and results improve. When this new definition is embraced, exciting possibilities open up for both the professional and the firm.

The first step to making these changes is to recognize the importance of sales management, and to then begin developing and implementing an intelligent, effective sales management process in the firm.

Key Concept

> When selling skills are more accurately defined as relationship building communication skills, resistance begins to melt away and professionals begin to see the development of the skills as an integral part of their professional growth.

THE CRUCIAL DIFFERENCE BETWEEN MARKETING AND SALES

A discussion of the difference between marketing and sales is critical to understanding what the sales process in a firm must be designed to accomplish and how it needs to be managed. Here's a simple, practical definition of the difference between marketing and sales:

- Marketing includes those activities that a firm engages in, and the collateral material it creates, all for the purpose of generating opportunities for new business.
- Selling is the process we engage in to convert those opportunities into additional business.

Although they are often intertwined, essentially selling starts where marketing ends.

Understanding the difference between marketing and sales allows us to delineate between the two activities and to define our objectives and success criteria separately for each of these two areas. Marketing success is measured in terms of the number and quality of selling opportunities that have been created. Sales success is measured in terms of the number of qualified prospects who become clients, the number of new services purchased by existing clients, increases in billings, and increased market share.

For both marketing and sales activities to be successful, it is necessary to define a "qualified prospect." All too often firms will mistakenly accept just about any client who will have them. It is important for a firm to define its target clients and to create a profile of the ideal client. This definition would be used to determine whether or not the firm wants to pursue any particular opportunity. One of the many benefits of a well managed selling process is that it allows a firm a much higher degree of selectivity when it comes to acquiring clients.

The lack of understanding between marketing and selling, two distinct processes, explains why so little attention has been paid to sales management. A commonly held belief is that marketing, in and of itself, will create new clients. This is simply not true. In fact, this mistaken belief is a source of stress in many accounting firms. From the marketer's perspective, they have created an opportunity that is sometimes not converted into new business because of a lack of selling skills or proper follow-through on the part of the accountant. In other words, there is poor sales management. However, marketers may not always be forthcoming with these observations, because of their reluctance to insult a superior. From the accountant's perspective, the inability to convert an opportunity into a new client is generally attributed to a poorly qualified lead. While this might sometimes be the case, more often it is not.

By ensuring our professional team has the requisite selling skills, and helping them view selling much like any other process the firm engages in, considerable opportunity for improved results exists. In the final analysis, it is not the marketing effort that causes the client to hire the firm; it is the sales effort. It is the proper application of the selling process, from beginning to end, that most significantly affects the client's decision to engage or not. This is why sales management is so important. It's the final step in the process of client acquisition.

> **⚷ Key Concept**
>
> A well managed selling process allows a firm a much higher degree of selectivity when it comes to acquiring clients.

> **⚷ Key Concept**
>
> The proper application of the selling process, from beginning to end, is what most significantly affects the client's decision to engage or not.

CRITICAL SUCCESS FACTORS FOR MANAGING YOUR FIRM'S SALES PROCESS

Defining Sales Responsibilities

In many accounting firms, no mention of sales responsibilities exists until accountants reach a higher level position in the firm. This is unfortunate for a variety of reasons. It is not realistic to expect accountants to suddenly have any degree of competency or comfort with regard to selling skills, when up until this point they have strictly been focused on developing their technical skills.

The level of responsibility for participation in the sales process should vary depending upon the staff level. For new staff members, while it is not realistic to expect them to be engaged in direct sales activities, they should be developing core relationship building communication skills. Just as an entry level person's job description would include their expected technical professional responsibilities and development, that description should also include activities that will foster the development of relationship building communication skills.

The following is a list of sales related, communication oriented responsibilities that might be included in a professional's job description. The list begins with responsibilities for entry-level staff people, going all the way up to the partner level. By no means should this be considered an exhaustive list of responsibilities. Simply view it as a starting point, integrating your own ideas into it.

For an entry-level staff person, you might consider including the following:

- Work effectively as part of the client service team.
- Develop rapport with the firm's existing clients.
- Demonstrate an understanding of appropriate business etiquette, including proper forms of dress.
- Acquire basic competence in preparing business correspondence.
- Maintain contact with other professionals.

As professionals progress to higher staff levels, they should be expected to take on increased levels of responsibility for engaging in the sales process. In addition to the previously mentioned responsibilities, you might consider adding the following to their list:

- Identify additional service opportunities for existing clients.
- Communicate such opportunities to superiors.
- Attend professional and trade organization meetings to increase personal network of peer level business contacts.

At more senior staff levels, the list might also include things such as the following:

- Gain visibility among professional and trade organizations, or in some other way enlarge network of business contacts.
- Demonstrate ability to identify and discuss needed services to existing clients.
- Develop relationships with professional and other service providers of existing clients to expand potential business referral network.
- Participate in the development and implementation of a personal sales plan.

At the manager level, in addition to the previous list add the following:

- Assume responsibility for managing the client relationship and client satisfaction.
- Participate in the firm's marketing efforts including making presentations, writing articles, or in whichever activities they are most comfortable participating.
- Represent the firm in the community by holding high-level leadership positions in community based organizations.
- Begin identifying and converting sales opportunities for the firm by generating referrals from networks that have been established.

At senior manager and partner level, professionals should include the following:

- Establish specific goals to identify and acquire new business on their own and in conjunction with the marketing efforts of the firm.
- Be held accountable for fulfilling sales goals.

Personal Sales Plans

An integral part of the sales management process is to assist professional team members in setting sales goals that are consistent with each person's skills and level of selling responsibility. At the initial stages of development, it is more appropriate to set goals around time commitments and participation in sales-related activities, with little or no demand on results. As one progresses to higher levels in the firm, the focus should shift more to the results achieved from those activities, and less on the time spent doing them. Allow professional team members to allocate a specific amount of their time to engaging in such activities. This makes it easier for them to participate without concern about exceeding their time budget allocations. Time expectations should be clearly defined in each personal sales plan.

In establishing personal sales plans, take into account the capabilities and experience level of each person. Recognize that simple goals can be very challenging for many people because it requires them to go outside of their comfort zone. Goals should be established based upon mutual agreement and should help people stretch and grow. Overly aggressive goals can be counterproductive, as they tend to cause stress or fear. It is much more effective if sales goals are developed through a collaborative effort, as opposed to taking a directive approach. When the plan is completed, the professional should feel good about it. It should be a bit challenging and require some stretching, but still doable. It is incremental progress that we are looking for. The earlier in someone's career that we start this process, the better. As we'll describe later, these sales goals will serve as a basis for measuring and monitoring performance.

Once our professional team members have clearly identified expectations, we must provide the requisite training and support to increase their chances of success in fulfilling their responsibilities. It is not sufficient to give people responsibilities without the means to achieving them. Just as we don't expect our professional staff to develop technically without ongoing education, training, and supervision, it is unrealistic to expect the development of their relationship building communication skills without similar support. One of the most important components of providing such support is a good sales training program.

> **Key Concept**
>
> An integral part of the sales management process is to assist professional team members in setting sales goals that are consistent with each person's skills and level of selling responsibility.

Sales Training

One of the first and most important responsibilities in managing the firm's sales process is to provide appropriate, effective sales training at all levels in the firm. A common mistake made by firms is to not provide sales training as an integral part of a professional's training and development, and then suddenly expect them to successfully bring in new business. Not only is this unrealistic, but it sets people up for frustration and failure.

Of course, most accountants are not excited about the idea of sales training. As mentioned earlier, learning to sell is not something most accountants want to do. Rather than talking about "sales training," present the training as one designed to further develop relationship building communication skills. As professionals come to realize that this is an integral component of their professional growth, there begins to be considerably more acceptance.

A good sales training program will attempt to bring about changes in thinking, behavior, and communication habits that have been learned over a lifetime. To be effective, a sales training program should be implemented as an ongoing, incremental learning process, as opposed to some event based activity that takes place once in a while. It is critical that the sales philosophy and methodology of the sales training program be completely compatible with both the firm and individual professional values. If there is a disconnect from the process because it feels inconsistent with one's values, or if it causes a high degree of discomfort, intended results are less likely to be achieved. Chapter 31, "Sales Training: The Key to Better Service and Better Clients," goes into the subject in great depth, and should be carefully reviewed.

A Uniform Sales Process

A firm-wide sales training program can provide the foundation to establish a uniform sales process throughout the firm. With everyone using the same sales process, it's much easier for people to work together as teams. Let's say, for example, one part of the sales process is about discovering needs and another part is about presenting solutions. Two different teams might then be involved, each in one part of the process. When there is clarity as to how the pieces interrelate and where the firm is in the process with regard to any particular sales opportunity, collaboration is easier.

A uniform, firm-wide sales process also makes it easier for people to identify each component of the process, and to incrementally develop skills, while always being aware of how each piece fits into the big picture. As professionals increasingly understand and accept the selling process as something that feels consistent with their values and that is comfortable for them, its effectiveness is greatly enhanced.

Sales Meetings

Now that sales communication responsibilities have been identified for each level of staff, and appropriate training has been provided, we must focus on managing the sales process. Sales meetings are one of the most important ways to manage ongoing sales activities. Sales meetings should be segregated for each professional level in the firm to correspond with the degree of responsibility for that level. This also allows for a more manageable meeting size, allowing each person to participate. Ideally, the group size for a sales meeting would not exceed 15–20 people.

Regularly scheduled meetings, usually once a month, are adequate to support the process. Participants should be prepared at each meeting to discuss what sales activities they have engaged in and what results they experienced. The group facilitator should be a sales leader in the firm (see our discussion on "sales leader" later in this chapter).

Three key objectives exist that you want to accomplish at each sales meeting. They are

- accountability,
- success transfer, and
- resolution of obstacles.

Accountability

At each sales meeting, every professional should have an opportunity to commit to the group the specific sales activities they are planning to engage in before the next meeting. This would include such things as meetings or calls with clients, prospective clients, and referral sources. At subsequent sales meetings, each professional should report on the activities they engaged in, and the results they experienced.

Essentially, the results of sales activities fall into one of two categories. Either they experienced a success, or they ran into some obstacles, or possibly some combination of the two. Knowing they have to present to the group the results of their activities serves as a motivator to remain focused on meeting their commitments. Someone needs to be playing a "sales manager" role to hold people accountable for their commitments, and follow-up with those who do not attend the meeting.

Success Transfer

By sharing successes, everyone learns from the positive results of those who have successfully applied the process. It is often inspirational for professionals to know that their peers are achieving success with the process they might still be struggling with. When someone shares a success, they should be asked to explain specifically what they believe most contributed to that success. This sharing process is known as "success transfer," as everyone learns from the success of one person.

Sharing positive results and receiving acknowledgment in front of the group is rewarding in many ways. Hearing of the success of others sometimes serves to motivate people to have something positive to report at the next meeting.

Resolution of Obstacles

At the sales meeting, encourage professionals to talk about the obstacles they are experiencing in applying the sales process. By so doing, they quickly learn that facing obstacles is a natural, expected occurrence and is not a sign of failure, which most professionals fear.

When an obstacle is presented, input from the group should be solicited so that everyone's thinking is engaged in how they might address that obstacle. It is much more important for the group to be engaged in the process of resolving the issue than it is for the facilitator to give the "right" answer. Most importantly, the collective thinking process helps develop everyone's sales abilities.

Acknowledge each person who talks about their obstacles. Acknowledge them for applying the process and sharing the results, for being open to receive feedback, and for learning. This is a new process for everyone. We must do all we can to encourage people to share their issues and concerns. Reinforce and encourage this kind of behavior, as it is the formula for success.

Key Concept

Sales meetings are one of the most important ways to manage ongoing sales activities.

Sales Leadership

Another critical success factor to managing the selling process is to have one or more sales leaders who serve as a resource for anyone to talk about any selling situation. Whether it's pre-call planning, or post-call analysis, getting feedback and direction helps people learn to apply the selling process in action. The big question is "who should it be?"

While effective sales leadership plays such a critical role in improving sales results, it is often the area of greatest weakness in accounting firms. One reason for this is accounting firms are not sales organizations and generally do not employ professional sales managers; although, much to their credit, a growing number of accounting firms are addressing this weakness by hiring sales professionals. There is no doubt that these firms will quickly gain a competitive edge over nonsales oriented firms.

In a traditional organization, such as manufacturing or distribution, sales is a separate function with a complete hierarchy of sales leaders to whom full-time sales professionals report. The relationship between sales professional and sales manager is very direct, as are the sales professional's responsibilities.

Accounting firms are different. They are organized by service functions such as tax, accounting, auditing, and consulting. Professionals are reporting the results of their sales activities to higher-level accountants, not sales managers. As a result of these conditions, the most effective sales management structure for an accounting firm would be a sales management model in which selected, experienced professionals coach and develop the sales skills of the less experienced professionals in the firm.

Depending upon the size of the firm, it may designate one person as a sales leader, or have several sales leaders, one for each staff level. Another approach would be to have different sales leaders in each department. The primary responsibility of the sales leader is to be a resource and mentor to support everyone's selling efforts.

If your firm has a professional salesperson on staff, or a marketing director with sales experience, they might be an excellent candidate to serve in a sales leadership role. The ideal choice, whenever possible, would be to hire a professional manager, or a well-qualified salesperson in this position (see chapter 10, "A Buyer's Guide to Hiring a

Marketing Professional," and chapter 12, "The Case for Utilizing a Sales Professional."). The increased results they are likely to achieve should more than offset the additional cost of having them on board.

One of the essential requirements for the sales leader is that they must have a good track record with regard to their own selling activities. A successful salesperson does not necessarily make a good sales manager; even between those two rolls, you have different skill sets. If you are hiring someone from the outside, make sure their sales management experience is either in the accounting profession or some professional services capacity where relationship based selling is at the core of their experience.

A sales leader should have good coaching and mentoring capabilities. A good sales leader provides positive feedback and helps each person develop their own style and approach to sales. This sales leader should be the "go to" person for questions and issues that anyone is experiencing in applying the selling process.

Sales Tracking

Now that we have defined each person's sales responsibilities, provided sales training to help them develop the skills necessary to succeed, and are currently providing sales leadership and sales meetings to increase both support and accountability, we must have a system in place to measure and monitor sales results. As we have often heard, there is no management without measurement.

A well-designed sales tracking system can improve the effectiveness of the firm's selling efforts and can make the sales leaders' job much easier. Over the long run, a well-designed monitoring system can also provide useful information about how well the firm's various selling and marketing activities are working. The right monitoring system encourages people to think in terms of sales results, an important ingredient when trying to motivate people to become more creative in their selling efforts.

The type of software that would be used to track marketing and sales activities would be either *contact management software* (CMS) or *client relationship management* (CRM) software. There are a wide variety of solutions available to fit every budget and every level of need, from an individual to an enterprise-wide solution.

A growing number of firms are using Web-based SAAS applications, which are easily accessed remotely. By doing an Internet search on these names, as well as on "contact management software" or "client relationship management software," you can find a wealth of information on these and other solutions. Take the time to research each solution carefully and learn about its features. As with most technology solutions, there is a considerable investment of time, energy, and money in getting the software up and running. Make sure it's the right solution before you start.

For a sales tracking system to be effective, everyone involved must update the system on a daily basis with their sales activities. This is a necessary discipline in effectively managing the sales process. This is easier to accomplish when you use a Web-based application that can be remotely accessed. As an alternative, if your firm is new at this, and there's not too much sales activity, Excel can be used to collect and review information.

A good sales tracking system is a powerful tool to manage individual sales efforts while providing a firm-wide overview of sales activities and results. These systems make it easy to schedule follow-up activities; send marketing materials, articles, or letters to prospects; and much more. Sales tracking systems are a powerful, absolutely essential tool to managing the sales process. For more information, see chapter 34, "Marketing and Sales Metrics Matter: Measuring Results, Calculating Return on Investment."

Motivating People

Motivating accountants to engage in selling activities can be a challenge. In addition to the fact that accountants are not naturally motivated to engage in sales activities, selling can be challenging even for sales professionals. A negative, punitive approach to selling is generally ineffective, as it creates stress and may result in a very unpleasant working atmosphere. From a positive perspective, a significant motivator can be a well-crafted personal sales plan. Because the plan is collaboratively developed, it is likely that the professional will have a strong sense of commitment to achieving its objectives.

A good way to stimulate increased success in this area is to provide ongoing, positive reward and recognition for all sales activities in which people are engaged. Verbal recognition or other types of rewards for a job well done can work well. The power and impact of personal recognition is often overlooked.

Selling is a new and challenging area for most professionals. Positive acknowledgment means a great deal to those who receive it. Not to mention that it is an effective and very inexpensive way to reinforce and encourage positive performance. Building the self-esteem of your professional team is an important part of their individual growth and the firm's success.

There's also a more subtle impact that our approach to motivating professionals to engage in the selling process has on their actual performance. If we want people to sell from a place of service and integrity, we need to apply those same principles to engage them in the selling process. Not unexpectedly, some people will participate more than others in the client acquisition process. Let this be okay. We need people who are technicians to turn out the work, who do not necessarily have to become significant rainmakers. However, we must emphasize the development of relationship building communication skills for all professionals, whether or not they become actively involved in client acquisition.

Motivation will naturally occur as we continue to position the development of relationship building communication skills and engaging in sales activities as a natural part of professional development. It also helps for professionals to know that their success in developing the skills consistent with their personal sales plan will be a significant factor when it comes to promotion, and eventually membership in the firm.

At lower staff levels, while direct monetary rewards might play some role in the motivational process, it is generally not a significant one, and is not recommended. However, as professional growth and development becomes a more significant factor, and professionals advance and eventually become firm members, having some portion of their compensation directly related to their sales results can be an effective means of motivating growth in this area. It also sends the message that ultimately, producing sales results makes a difference in their success in the firm.

♟ Key Concept

Stimulate increased success by providing ongoing, positive reward and recognition for all sales activities in which people are engaged.

CONCLUSION

By implementing many of the previous suggestions, you should be able to substantially improve the sales results for your firm. Increased sales is not only about growing the practice and improving profitability, although, that by itself is great. It's also about shaping the firm exactly the way you want it to be. By creating a vibrant, highly profitable firm, you'll find it much easier to attract and retain top-quality talent because you have created a more exciting work environment, and can offer higher compensation because of your firm's increased profitability.

As you now realize, many things exist that need to be done to properly manage the sales process in your firm. Don't feel overwhelmed. Many of these items can, and should be implemented incrementally over time. Each step that you take will further improve the overall sales process and results.

As we expand our sales communication skills we not only grow as professionals, but we more competently serve our clients with an increased ability to discover and fulfill more of their needs.

Enjoy the process!

ABOUT THE AUTHOR

Rick Solomon has been on a mission for the past two decades: he's convinced that accountants are the key ingredient in helping businesses to succeed. He has taken this message, along with his innovative methods and programs, to thousands of professionals across the globe, helping them lead more lucrative and rewarding lives. Solomon is noted for bringing a dynamic and progressive approach to topics foremost in the minds of accounting and business advisory professionals, including firm development; marketing, selling and delivering services; and solving client problems in a way that leads to greater retention and profitability.

As a leading practice development consultant and CEO of RAN ONE Americas, Solomon works directly with accountants, advisors, industry experts and professionals. He received his bachelor's degree from the City

University of New York-Baruch College and began his CPA career at a New York City-based international accounting firm. He went on to build one of the fastest-growing CPA firms on Long Island. He has studied human behavior and motivation at the Sedona Institute in Arizona and has incorporated the knowledge of overcoming limiting beliefs and points of view as a unique ingredient in his training programs. Solomon has served on the faculty of the Esperti-Peterson Institute, a think-tank of the nation's leading estate planning attorneys. Solomon is the founder and lead facilitator of the exclusive Masters Program, a dedicated group of accountants experiencing quantum growth in their practices and their lives.

CHAPTER 30
Cross-Serving Clients: Integrating Sales and Service Delivery

Russ Molinar
Ernst & Young LLP

INTRODUCTION

Where is the best place to get revenue? The answer is fairly obvious—the best place to get revenue is from your existing clients. The old adages still ring true: "Your current client is your best client" and "It costs less to grow a current client than to find a new one."

The reasons for this is also fairly obvious. Existing clients

- know your firm's reputation and brand.
- currently pay fees to your firm for assurance, compliance or advisory services.
- enjoy one or more relationships within your firm.
- have some level of trust around the services and value that your firm can deliver.

This is different from a prospect or target—an individual or organization that typically has little to no knowledge, awareness, or degree of confidence or trust in your firm. If the best place to obtain revenue is from existing clients, why then do most accounting and professional service firms spend most of their marketing and business development efforts on prospects instead of clients? Why are they intent on focusing on attracting new clients rather than expanding their relationships with current clients?

There are three key elements to address in the ongoing discussion around cross-selling, or cross-serving, clients: (1) the concepts and considerations involved in cross-serving clients; (2) understanding and overcoming some of the internal barriers; and (3) how to effectively implement or enhance cross-serving efforts in your firm. We will address each of these in this chapter.

THE CONCEPTS INVOLVED IN CROSS-SERVING

In its simplest form, cross-serving can be defined as the process of identifying unmet client issues and needs and offering specific products, services, and solutions from your firm to fulfill their individual and organizational needs. It is the process of enhancing your relationships with clients by expanding the number of services provided to and fees received from your clients.

A number of key concepts, or constructs, exist in looking at the process of cross-serving clients. The most common ones are described in this section.

> **Key Concept**
>
> Cross-serving can be defined as the process of identifying unmet client issues and needs and offering specific products, services, and solutions from your firm to fulfill their individual and organizational needs.

Concept #1: Process Not Event

Perhaps the first concept is the notion that cross-serving is a process and not an event. Cross-serving does not merely happen on an annual basis, for example, at the audit planning event or during the presentation of the client's financial statements. It needs to be viewed as an ongoing process of taking the time to understand the client's organization—their objectives, strategies, initiatives and challenges—and to appreciate the needs and expectations of key executives, from both corporate and individual perspectives.

Concept #2: Problem-Solving Orientation

Another key concept in cross-serving is the inherent focus on understanding and recommending potential actions to address client issues and problems. Cross-serving begins with listening to clients to understand their overall goals, strategies, and key business initiatives. It involves a consultative selling approach—a problem-solution orientation—rather than a "menu-based" approach to outlining potential services your firm can provide to the client. Done correctly, cross-serving does not involve much "selling"; it simply involves helping your client address their problems through services and competencies that are already resident in your firm.

Concept #3: The Client Relationship Pyramid

What makes a "good" client? What should our client relationship objectives be from a firm perspective? Other than the obvious elements of a productive client relationship, such as paying on time and fair realization, one useful construct to consider is the three levels of the client relationship pyramid. The first level, or the base of the pyramid, involves securing the client or prospect's "mind share." The first step in the relationship process is to make the prospect aware of your firm's capabilities and services, have them consider you as a potential service provider. This "battle" for the client's mind is typically the responsibility of the marketing/communications function. Figure 30-1 illustrates the concept of the client relationship pyramid.

FIGURE 30-1 THE CLIENT RELATIONSHIP PYRAMID

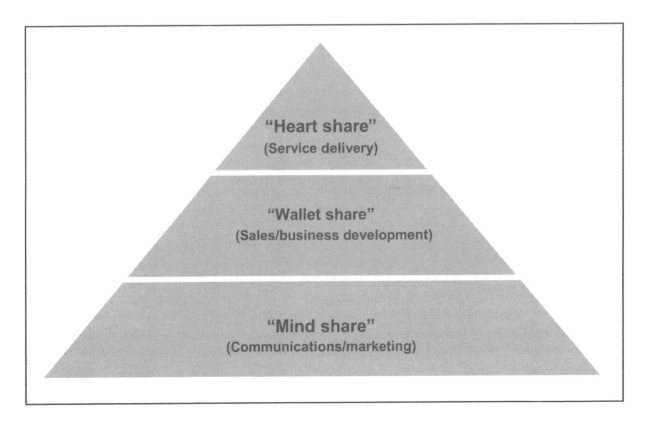

The second level of the pyramid involves the battle not for the mind, but for the client's wallet. Each client can essentially be viewed as a "market"—every client spends a certain amount of money on services from professional firms, including firms in accounting, consulting, human resources, information technology, law, and a host of others all across the alphabet. The question for your firm to consider is what percent of the client's wallet do you really own? What percent of the services that you could deliver do you actually provide to the client?

The third level, or pinnacle, of the pyramid involves the battle for the client's heart, or "heart share." After you own a piece of the client's mind and wallet, the next step is to develop and nurture client loyalty. Loyal clients look first to your firm to provide services, speak positively about your firm to others, and typically provide referrals of potential clients. Loyalty and "heart share" are driven by trust and the perceived value received from services delivered by your firm.

Reaching the top of the pyramid requires cross-serving. While some accountants may be concerned about the potential perception of selling services to audit and tax clients, the reality is actually much different. Some of the realities of cross-serving are listed below.

Reality #1: Clients Want Us to Bring Them Solutions

Most entrepreneurs and executives actively search for ways to improve their business. Many hire professional service firms at various times (or on an ongoing basis) to improve their operations, increase profitability, or to reduce risks. As a trusted advisor, clients expect their accounting firm to bring them potential services and solutions that can help drive improvements to their top line and their bottom line. They expect, however, potential solutions to their specific issues and problems, not just services that will grow our revenue base.

Reality #2: Clients Expect Us to Sell

Often the number one concern expressed by accountants around cross-serving is they don't want to be perceived as "selling" something to their clients. While there are independence issues to consider, the reality is that clients understand and appreciate the concept of selling. As successful entrepreneurs and executives, they sell every day and their organization's growth is dependent upon the effectiveness of their sales efforts.

Reality #3: Failure to Bring Ideas Is Actually a Client Disservice

If we fail to bring service opportunities to clients, not only are we suboptimizing our potential client relationship, but we are also not fully serving them as a trusted advisor. Using a retail example, let's say you go to the hardware store and buy a can of paint and a brush. At the checkout, the sales clerk asks you if you need a drop clop or paint thinner. Is that selling or a service to you as the customer? Reminding you of what you might need for your painting project is a service that might keep you from making an unwanted return trip to the hardware store later in the day.

So what is cross-serving? It is essentially the same as the more ubiquitous term of "cross-selling" but with two important differences: (1) serving implies the process is focused on client issues and needs, not what we have to sell; and (2) the notion implies an overall responsibility to bring ideas, insights, and service opportunities to help clients improve their business.

🔑 Key Concept

Cross-serving is different from cross-selling in two important ways: (1) serving implies the process is focused on client issues and needs, not what we have to sell; and (2) the notion implies an overall responsibility to bring ideas, insights, and service opportunities to help clients improve their business.

IDENTIFYING AND OVERCOMING INTERNAL BARRIERS

A number of potential internal barriers exist, both real and perceived, to effectively implement the concept of cross-serving clients in your firm. Some of the more common partner objections and challenges are outlined in this section.

Barrier #1: I Didn't Become an Accountant to Go into Sales

You've never heard this one before, right? When most accountants hear the word "sales," visions of used-car sales-men and alligator shoes are often the first images that pop into their heads. Accountants want to serve clients and don't want to feel pressured to sell services into their accounts.

This perceptual barrier is another reason to use the term "cross-serving" instead of "cross-selling" in your firm's efforts. The term will resonate more with your partners and practitioners. While most accountants do not believe (incorrectly) that "sales" is part of their job description, they all agree that client service is their number one priority.

While to some this may sound like "spinning" the issue, the way the concept is positioned is critical. Cross-serving will be received with interest and understanding, while cross-selling will likely be received with skepticism and doubt.

Barrier #2: Independence Considerations

Concerns about auditor independence are both perceived and real barriers to cross-serving initiatives. Remaining independent is imperative for an external auditor, and in cases for other types of advisors and consultants. Determining the types of engagements that can be provided to attest clients (and more importantly those that cannot be provided), along with the relative scope of nonattest work provided (for example, 1:1 ratio of attest to non-attest services) are important elements to address in any cross-serving initiative.

Enron and the Sarbanes-Oxley Act generated increased awareness around auditor independence, and publicly-traded organizations (as well as government and not-for-profit entities) often pay significant attention to nonattest services provided by the external auditor. Privately-held companies, however, often do not have the same level of independence concerns.

In addition, nonattest clients are outstanding targets for a cross-serving initiative. The real and perceived "independence threshold" is much higher for nonattest clients. And given that you already provide some type of advisory or consulting services to them, they are good candidates for expanding your service relationship.

Barrier #3: Lack of Leadership Reinforcement and Accountability

Another typical barrier to cross-serving initiatives is the lack of formal support from the partner group, including the firm's managing partner. In addition to providing executive sponsorship, it is also important to reinforce the importance of cross-serving clients. Sharing success stories is also a powerful way to reinforce the concept, including client examples and testimonials. Making sure that partners are measured and held accountable for cross-serving is also critical (see implementation section to follow).

Barrier #4: Marketing is Told to Stay Away from Clients

Many partners and accounting firms seemingly equate the marketing function with prospects. The perception is that marketing is what you "do" with prospects and that marketing and business development is not necessary for existing clients. Often, marketing is not encouraged to be involved with (and in cases even discouraged from involvement with) existing client initiatives.

Going back to the client relationship pyramid, the base is built on obtaining "mind share." And that typically is the responsibility of the marketing function. Cross-serving initiatives involve all levels of the pyramid—building mind share, wallet share, and finally heart share. In many accounting firms, however, there is no formal sales/business development function, or that responsibility is incorporated within the overall marketing function. So, why would this function be asked to ignore or stay away from client activities? The answer may be partly explained in the following paragraphs.

Barrier #5: Perception That "It's My Client"

Another barrier to cross-serving clients is the attitude of many partners that client relationships are owned by an individual partner and not the firm. Many partners subscribe to the belief that "it is my client but the firm's opinion." As a result, partners are very protective of their relationships and don't want other people "meddling" in their accounts.

Many partners are also troubled with insecure, and often irrational, fears. What if my client likes another one of my partners better than me? What if others find out that I don't have such strong relationships within my client as I claim to have? These issues often present significant challenges to cross-serving efforts.

Barrier #6: The Annuity Relationship Paradox

Another related perceptual barrier is the "annuity relationship" paradox. The thinking goes something like this: "I have had an ongoing compliance relationship with this client for many years, and I don't want to jeopardize it by bringing in someone else and having them not meet my client's expectations." This line of thinking may have worked better 10 or 20 years ago, when firms were not aggressively pursuing new clients and loyalty and relationships were perhaps a little more important than they are today.

In today's environment, the mindset of clients includes such typical questions as, "What have you done for me lately?" and "What value have you brought to my organization?" The only way to inoculate your clients from competitors is by diversifying the portfolio of services you bring to them—making your firm more indispensible.

IMPLEMENTING CROSS-SERVING IN YOUR FIRM

Implementing a formal cross-serving initiative in your firm is no simple task. It should not be taken lightly, and should not be delegated to only one function or person (for example, firm administrator, marketing director, junior partner). While there is no "secret recipe" for cooking up a cross-serving program, here are a few suggested action steps.

Step #1: Conduct a Current-State Assessment

The first step is a critical one, and one that is typically ignored or not even considered by many firms in implementing a cross-serving initiative. Put simply, you need to assess where your firm is currently with respect to your client relationships and define your overall service portfolio.

There are a number of key considerations and activities in this step, including the following:

- Do you have a defined list of services and engagement opportunities you can provide to clients? If not, you need to develop a comprehensive list and communicate it across your firm.
- Can you record and track those specific engagements separately in your time and billing system? For example, how do you record a specific engagement, such as an IT security assessment? Do you have a separate charge code or is it simply lumped under "other accounting services"?
- How many different types of services/engagements do you provide to your best clients? Two services? Five services? What is a reasonable indicator of effective "account penetration"?
- What percent of clients do you currently provide at least three types of services? (One way to look at this is across different business units within your firm. For example, a client may have four or five open engagements but if all of them are within the tax area, does that really constitute cross-serving?) How many clients are currently being served by three or more of your key business units or groups (for example, audit, tax, consulting, staffing, IT)?

Step #2: Establish a Steering Group

The overall initiative should be guided by a group of people from across your firm, and not simply driven by one individual. In looking at the overall composition of your steering group, here are a few considerations:

- *Senior partners.* Be sure to include a number of very senior partners who are well-respected in your firm. They will bring credibility to the effort, as well as ideas and insights from years of client service.
- *Cross-representation.* You should include people from several if not all of the key functional areas of your firm. Representatives from different groups will help drive adoption of your efforts.
- *Diversity.* A diverse group of people will also help drive implementation. Don't just load up on senior partners—for example, include aggressive junior partners or an "up-and-coming" senior or manager. You should also ensure you have appropriate gender and ethnic balance on your steering group.

- *Industry considerations.* If your firm specializes in more than one niche area, you may want to address this in the composition of your steering group. Cross-serving efforts could be somewhat different for government and not-for-profit entities compared to manufacturing and distribution companies.

Step #3: Define Scope and Establish Goals

The next step is to define the overall scope of your cross-serving initiative, including establishing specific and measurable goals. Your steering group should be involved in the process and consider topics such as the following:

- *Overall scope.* Will this initiative focus only on our largest accounts (for example, the top 20 percent of your client base)? Will we focus on expanding services only within our attest client base?
- *Program goals.* What are the goals and objectives for this effort? What are we trying to accomplish? What tangible and realistic goals (for example, to improve account penetration by XX percent in our priority accounts; deliver three or more types of services to at least 40 percent of our attest clients within the next 12 months) do we want to establish?
- *Individual/account goals.* How will we cascade the program goals down into smaller goals for individual practice units, key industries or accounts, and for individual partners as appropriate?
- *Accountability.* How will we make individual client service professionals (that is, coordinating partners and client relationship executives) accountable for achieving these goals?

Prior to deploying the initiative, it is important to establish firm, team, and individual goals around cross-serving. In looking at your existing audit clients, for example, let's say the nonaudit fees currently represent only 22 percent of the total fees, with core audit fees representing the remaining 78 percent. You could, for example, establish an overall firm goal of moving nonaudit fees from 22 percent to 30 percent of total fees. For some accounts and for some offices or industry sectors, however, that percentage may vary and be as high as 40 percent or 50 percent of total fees.

Step #4: Develop a Formal Cross-Serving Plan

A goal without a plan is only a wish. While establishing goals is important, it is equally critical for the steering group to invest time in developing specific strategies and tactics that will change and shape the behaviors that you want to reinforce in your cross-serving initiative. Some of the key considerations of the plan include the following:

- *Focus on change management.* Implementing an initiative like this is a change management effort. And change management efforts require a number of elements to be successful, ranging from active leadership support to ongoing reinforcement to build a cross-serving culture in your firm. Your steering group can help identify and monitor the key change management aspects.
- *Provide ammunition.* You simply can't tell your partners and staff to "go out and cross-serve." The firm, primarily through the support of the marketing or business development functions, needs to provide sales support materials to help enable issues-based client conversations. Typically this does not take the form of firm brochures or individual practice brochures, but tools and enablers to facilitate client conversations about their issues and ways in which your firm may be able to help. Customizable client meeting templates can help partners and teams guide conversations to uncover client issues and potential service opportunities.
- *Training and enablement.* Many of your partners may be uncomfortable in having consultative selling-type conversations with clients. If your firm has not conducted sales or service delivery training for your partners and staff, you may wish to consider this as part of your program. There are a number of relevant training and education programs, such as consultative selling skills, asking good questions, or small group facilitation skills. For more information about sales training, see 31, "Sales Training: The Key to Better Service and Better Clients."
- *Service education.* Another barrier to cross-serving efforts is the lack of knowledge (real or perceived) that partners and staff members have relative to the variety of service offerings available within the firm. Often, staff may be somewhat familiar with engagement opportunities such as cost segregation, but may not know the key questions to ask to uncover potential client opportunities.
- *Carrots and sticks.* People need motivation to do something outside of their normal activities, especially if it is outside of their comfort zone. Positive motivation (carrots) can take the form of public praise and

recognition, financial incentives, team or practice unit-based incentives, or other nonfinancial incentives. Accountability measures (sticks) can include specific goals or metrics (for example, account penetration indexes) for partners that should be factored into performance review discussions and compensation decisions. For more information about employees incentives, see chapter 33, "Effective Employee Incentive Programs: How to Bring Out the Best in Your Firm."

- *Targeting warm accounts.* An essential element to any change management effort is generating early successes. Working with the steering group, you may want to identify and prioritize existing clients that have an immediate need for consulting or advisory services. Potential client needs coupled with strong firm relationships may help you secure initial successes to help generate enthusiasm and support for the effort.

> **Key Concept**
>
> While establishing goals is important, it is equally critical for the steering group to invest time in developing specific strategies and tactics that will change and shape the behaviors that you want to reinforce in your cross-serving initiative.

Step #5: Roll It Out Across Your Firm

Another key step is to invest the appropriate time in formally launching the initiative across your firm. Developing goals and a plan are the forerunners to actually deploying the program across your various offices, practice units, and to various stakeholder groups (including practice support staff). A number of considerations may be relevant in implementing the initiative, including the following:

- What are the key messages you want to send that convey the importance of this initiative?
- How do you plan to communicate these messages to people in your firm (for example, e-mails, voice mail, face-to-face meetings, etc.)? (See chapter 32, "In-House Marketing Communications That Foster Success.")
- Who needs to communicate the key messages (for example, managing partner, practice unit leaders, geographic leaders) and how will they be reinforced on a periodic basis?
- What supporting training or information needs to be provided (for example, consultative selling skills, asking good questions) during the launch events or soon after?
- How will people be made accountable for program results (see the following)?

> **Key Concept**
>
> Developing goals and a plan are the forerunners to actually deploying the program across your various offices, practice units, and to various stakeholder groups (including practice support staff).

Step #6: Measure and Monitor Efforts

While establishing firm, team, and individual goals is important, measuring and monitoring progress towards those goals is equally critical. There are a number of considerations in measuring results, including the following:

- *Measure activities.* Tracking meeting activities is an important milestone on the way to revenue results. Meeting with clients on a regular basis is an essential ingredient to any cross-serving program, and is a good indicator of effort, progress, and relationship development—even if the results do not appear immediately.
- *Measure results.* Developing reporting systems—whether separate spreadsheet-based templates, or using existing billing and financial reporting systems—is needed to efficiently track progress and communicate results.
- *Recognize individuals/peer pressure.* Positively recognizing people who have been successful in cross-serving clients is a key enabler of change. Peer pressure—based on positive accolades, rather than negative shaming tactics—is a powerful motivator for people to act in professional services firms.

For more information on measuring results, see chapter 34, "Marketing and Sales Metrics Matter: Measuring Results, Calculating Return on Investment."

Step #7: Communicate Results and Share Success Stories

The final step in the process is to communicate the results of the initiative on a regular basis across the firm. It is also important to share success stories from two dimensions: (1) the internal perspective—how your firm's account team identified the opportunities and closed the engagements; and (2) the client's perspective—what the client's reaction was and how what you did for them helped them improve their overall business performance, reduce costs, or more effectively manage risks. Some of the considerations in this step include the following:

- *Ongoing reinforcement.* It is not enough to communicate results or examples once a year. Regular communications are needed to get the message through to time-challenged partners. In addition, consider varying the format of your communications—if e-mails and voicemails aren't working, consider hard copy materials, flash animations, or even record the information in an MP3 format for people to listen to the results on their desktop or iPod.
- *Credibility.* Sharing successes from well-respected partners can be extremely helpful. In addition, case studies or testimonials from either your largest and most respected clients, or in some cases your most difficult clients, can help to erase doubts about the program.

For more information about communicating results and sharing success stories, see chapter 32, "In-House Marketing Communications that Foster Success."

CONCLUSION

The best place to grow revenues is by concentrating on your existing client base. But client expansion, or cross-serving, does not happen automatically or through osmosis. It is an often neglected area of practice development for a number of reasons (both real and perceived), ranging from partners protecting their turf to concerns about auditor independence and the stigma of being viewed as trying to "sell" something to clients.

So what are the specific action steps in getting started? What are the key roles for partners and marketing professionals? Some of the key roles for developing and implementing a cross-serving initiative in your firm are briefly outlined here:

- *Executive sponsor.* The firm's managing partner needs to serve (vocally) as the lead sponsor for the initiative.
- *Champion.* Identify an effective rainmaker to serve as the champion, or spokesperson, for the effort.
- *Coach.* Identify someone to serve as a coaching resource to help partners prepare for and conduct effective client encounters. This could be the firm's business development director, marketing director, or one or more people from the steering group.
- *Program manager.* Assign someone to manage and monitor the effort. This could be the firm administrator, the marketing director, or a member of the steering group.

In summary, cross-serving needs to be viewed as an important strategic element of your firm's overall go-to-market strategy. As such, cross-serving warrants status as a formal initiative, or program, within your firm's strategic plan or overall marketing and business development efforts. If the best place to get revenue is from existing clients, then a formal, cross-serving program needs to be an integral part of your firm's go-to-market efforts.

ABOUT THE AUTHOR

Russ Molinar has been active in marketing, business development, and consulting for over 24 years, including the past 17 years with professional services firms. Currently, he is a Director in the Client Programs group within Ernst & Young's Global Markets organization. He has served in a variety of local, national and global roles for Ernst & Young for over 10 years. Previously, he served as the Director of Marketing & Practice Development for Plante & Moran, PLLC, one of the 12 largest accounting firms in the U.S. He also served as a consultant to professional service firms with PDI Global, Inc. and as the first Marketing Manager for Skoda, Minotti, Reeves & Co., a local accounting firm in Cleveland, Ohio. Russ has been active in the accounting marketing profession, including serving as past president of the Association for Accounting Marketing and being inducted into the Accounting Marketing Hall of Fame. Russ can be reached at 216.583.8816 or at russ.molinar@ey.com.

CHAPTER 31
Sales Training: The Key to Better Service and Better Clients

Rick Solomon, CPA
RAN ONE

INTRODUCTION

If you think sales training is just about learning to sell your firm's services, you're only half right. Developing your professional team's ability to bring in profitable new business, while critical to success and growth, represents only part of the story. A good sales training program provides essential *relationship building communication skills* that can have an enormous impact on the success of your firm. In fact, for many firms it turns out to be the missing link to achieving significant practice growth. In this chapter, we'll describe some of the benefits of a good sales training program, some hidden obstacles you need to be aware of, guidelines for choosing a sales training program, how to get the most from the program, pitfalls to avoid, and some thoughts on presenting the idea of sales training to your staff.

BENEFITS OF A GOOD SALES TRAINING PROGRAM

Grow or Re-Shape Your Firm

Bringing in profitable new business is always the primary reason for sales training. Whether your goal is to build a larger practice or to re-shape your existing practice, selling skills are equally important. Sales skills enhance your ability to bring in exactly the kind of clients you want. The more effectively we can acquire "choice" clients, the greater control we have in building our practice into what we truly want to be. It is unfortunate that many practitioners, lacking sales communication skills, end up with a practice that "happened to them," as opposed to building the practice they really want. It's never too late to change this. Having more choice in selecting new clients allows us to maximize our profits and increase the enjoyment of our practice. As a result, we get to spend more time engaged in work that is truly rewarding and doing so with people we enjoy working with.

> **Key Concept**
>
> Sales skills enhance your ability to bring in exactly the kind of clients you want.

Professional Team Development

Attracting and motivating key professional staff is critical to your firm's success and its future. Sales training provides a component to professional development that is all too often overlooked, and one that provides benefits well beyond what may be expected.

Reaching our full potential as professionals requires that we achieve mastery in two critical areas. The first is mastering our ability to deliver excellent technical services. Whether an auditor, tax advisor, or consultant, we must learn the relevant knowledge base and gain the experience that enables us to provide valuable, meaningful services to our clients.

The second area of mastery has to do with our relationship communication skills. These enhanced skills allow us to become better listeners, more effectively diagnose problems, see things from another person's point of view, more easily address concerns, build consensus, and so on. These new skills also provide an enhanced ability to communicate our value and our ideas, all of which are as critical to our success as our technical skills.

Not surprisingly, while most accountants are fairly strong when it comes to technical skills, they are often lacking in their relationship communication skills. Simply stated, no matter how good you are at what you do, if you are unable to communicate in a way that causes others to readily perceive your value and the results you are likely to achieve, you are not likely to be hired. Or, if hired, you are less likely to be paid for the full value that you bring. Increased success, at both the firm and individual level, is a natural by-product as professionals develop their relationship communication skills enabling them to establish productive relationships with clients, referral sources, and firm members.

Improve Client Relationships

Another added benefit to developing relationship communication skills is that client relations are likely to be considerably improved. This naturally occurs as professionals begin to ask more questions, engage in expanded conversations, and perhaps explore additional ways to help the client. Whether or not this results in an expanded engagement, clients are likely to appreciate the increased interest and focus on their business, improving their overall experience of your firm's value. This enhanced relationship makes the whole process of delegating work to your professional staff easier and more comfortable.

Improve Internal Communications and Relationships

Relationships within the firm can significantly improve as team members improve their basic communication skills. As people naturally begin to apply their new skills, they will be more open to listening, to understanding different points of view, will be more solution oriented, and so. In addition to establishing a more open, collaborative environment, there is an increased sense of relevance for professional team members. As a result, you've created a healthy, vibrant firm, all as a valuable by-product of a well-implemented sales training program.

Hidden Obstacles to Success

Before engaging in a sales training program, there are certain obstacles that must be recognized and addressed. Without doing so, we may be bound for failure before we start. The fundamental problem with sales training is that accountants do not view themselves as salespeople, and have no desire to become such. In fact, selling is often looked upon as being distasteful. Fortunately, there is a very different view of selling that is much more comfortable for accountants to accept. Before we discuss this different view, let's consider some hidden, commonly held beliefs about selling that are unnecessary obstacles, just so we can get them out of the way.

First is the belief that selling skills are something that one needs to be born with, as opposed to being learnable skills. That erroneous belief leads one to the conclusion that "I'm not a natural born salesperson, therefore I will never be good at selling." Such a conclusion only serves to inhibit the learning and development of selling skills. The truth is that selling skills can be learned by anyone who has the desire to do so. Once we find a process that we are comfortable with in a world that is aligned with our values, learning the process can be very enjoyable.

Another common obstacle is the belief that "to be successful in selling, one must engage in behavior that does not feel comfortable as a professional." To the extent we feel that selling means compromising our values and integrity as a professional, we won't do it. The idea of trying to control or manipulate another person for our own benefit has no appeal to most accountants. While we have all experienced various forms of this self-centered approach to selling, from a more enlightened perspective there is the possibility that selling can be done in a way that serves others, and is aligned with our core values and integrity as professionals.

Getting comfortable with the whole idea of selling is much easier once we let go of these two beliefs.

A DIFFERENT VIEW OF SELLING

Developing our sales communication skills can be exciting when we begin to see selling as a form of service from one human being to another. When, rather than trying to "close the sale," we recognize selling as a process of exploring needs and goals and engaging in a discussion of possible solutions, we are coming from a place of service. As we let go of attempting to close the sale, it allows an exploration of what is mutual. This results in a significant increase in comfort level for us and the client, and greater success in obtaining new engagements.

It is reassuring to know that what sells best is authenticity, people being real. Selling is not about being someone, or something, other than who you are. Nothing sells better than truth. As we let go of the idea that we are supposed to present a particular persona, or to create a certain image, or try to impress someone, we begin to relax more into being ourselves. As such, we are free to engage in relevant, productive dialogue with the client. With this approach, the client is more likely to have a higher perception of our value, and to be more inclined to work with us. Paradoxically, as we let go of wanting to sell anything, more people hire us because they perceive us as being more trustworthy.

 Key Concept

> It is reassuring to know that what sells best is authenticity, people being real.

Guidelines to Success

Here are some essential guidelines to follow, as well as pitfalls to avoid that will help insure you get the most from your sales training.

Sales training as an ongoing process. If you're looking for a "quick fix" sales training program that has lasting value, save your money. It doesn't exist. Sales training as an occasional event in a firm produces mediocre results, at best. To receive the many benefits a good sales training program offers, it is best to view sales training as an ongoing process. Sales communications skills are most effectively learned incrementally, over time. As team members have the opportunity to apply their new skills and get feedback, they eventually internalize their expanded skills and increased awareness.

To get the most value from a sales training program, make the commitment to provide ongoing support over an extended period of time. Minimally, a 12 month support period should be provided. Ideally, support for implementing selling skills should be ongoing. As with anything new, more support is needed initially, tapering off over time. Once a month sales meetings are the minimum level of support that should be considered on a long-term basis.

A good way to look at developing sales skills would be to compare it to learning to play a musical instrument or a sport. It starts with lessons from an experienced teacher, then practice, then feedback for correction and improvement, and then more practice. Anyone who wants to learn to play a musical instrument or a sport can do so. If you've ever learned to play an instrument or a sport, you know that eventually it becomes second nature. Your success in mastering these skills is directly related to your commitment to doing so.

Practical experience is part of the learning process. Silly as it may sound, we don't actually learn how to sell at a sales training seminar. Of course we can learn the steps in the process, such as how to conduct a meeting, present solutions, and address concerns, but we actually learn to sell by applying the process in real-life situations. This is why ongoing feedback and coaching support is critically important to help our team members to internalize and successfully apply selling skills on a continuing basis.

The process should be easy to personalize. No one selling style works for every person. Choose a sales training program that can easily be customized to fit different styles. Most people, and particularly accountants, are not likely to use a sales process or techniques that feel uncomfortable or unnatural to them. That's why sales training programs that teach you to see things from only one "right" perspective are often doomed to failure. Sales training programs are most effective when they provide the essential principles of each component of the process, explaining how it works and providing ideas on how to personalize the material. When accounting professionals feel comfortable with a process they can "own," they are much more likely to apply it and experience success.

Model behavior vs. delivering a commercial. The way you conduct a sales meeting and the behavior that you model often has more impact on the outcome of the meeting than what you actually say. That's pretty amazing when you think about it. Look for a sales training program that helps you model the relationship with the client in a way that allows them to experience, in the moment, the value that you bring. This is much more effective that trying to deliver a commercial about how wonderful your firm is, and all of its great capabilities. Effective relationship modeling creates a very different dynamic wherein the client is pursuing you, rather than you pursuing the client. In addition to being a much more effective approach to sales, it also is much easier for accountants since there's nothing they have to "sell."

Who in the firm should have sales training? Knowing that good sales training develops relationship building communication skills, it becomes clear that every person in the firm would benefit from developing these skills. However, it would not be appropriate for each person to go through the exact same sales training program. For those who are not, or will not be directly responsible for acquiring new business, their training should be focused around developing listening and questioning skills, communicating the firm's value in a way that is consistent with their position in the firm, and in general builds a positive client focused mentality.

A good sales training program can be modified to various staff levels and needs. It should inspire team members to create a compelling client experience, producing results that can be truly amazing. When everyone in the firm is aligned with serving clients and creating a positive experience of the firm, you have successfully created a "Sales Culture." In truth, a sales culture is not about selling things, but more accurately represents an atmosphere of "discovery" when it comes to client needs.

> ### ⚑ Key Concept
>
> To get the most value from a sales training program, make the commitment to provide ongoing support over an extended period of time.

> ### ⚑ Key Concept
>
> The way you conduct a sales meeting and the behavior that you model often has more impact on the outcome of the meeting than what you actually say.

DISCUSSING SALES TRAINING WITH TEAM MEMBERS

How you present the opportunity for sales training to staff has a significant impact on their degree of acceptance. If you tell staff that they must learn how to sell and that they are required to bring in business, you are likely to generate fear and resistance. There's no benefit to having people become overly concerned or fearful that they will suddenly have to bring in business, or engage in activities that are very uncomfortable to them. Being told that we must do something that we don't want to, something that we feel is inherently not part of our job, does not create a collaborative, productive atmosphere.

A much more effective approach is to let your staff know that you consider communication and relationship building skills to be an integral part of their professional development. As staff members learn to more effectively communicate their ideas, ask better questions, explore solutions, and so on, their selling skills are naturally developing.

Interestingly, the best sales results are achieved when we let go of the idea that we're trying to sell something, and simply look to serve others. As our professional team learns ways to more effectively explore the needs and concerns of clients and to discuss ways in which we might help them, they are becoming better at selling. When presented in this light, it makes it easier for professionals to embrace the learning of these new skills. Using this approach, increased sales become a by-product of this "How can I help you?" mentality.

> ### 🔑 Key Concept
>
> How you present the opportunity for sales training to staff has a significant impact on their degree of acceptance.

ESSENTIAL COMPONENTS OF A GREAT SALES TRAINING PROGRAM

There are a number of reputable sales training programs available to the accounting profession today. Following are some suggestions intended to guide you through the selection process for a sales training program. Among other things, it is important that you readily understand and feel comfortable with the overall selling process. If it's overly complicated, or doesn't feel logical, it's probably not a good choice.

Balance Between Structure and Flexibility

A good training program provides a step-by step selling process that is easy to understand and apply. While providing structure, the process must also allow for sufficient flexibility so it can be applied in a variety of situations, and by different people. Whether it's a meeting with an existing or prospective client, or a referral source, the process should readily adapt to the situation. It should also flow naturally and be an extension of how you might normally conduct yourself.

Building Relationships

The essence of an effective sales process for professionals must be rooted in building relationships. Look specifically at the relationship building components of the sales process to make sure that you understand and are comfortable with them. Beware of sales training programs that talk about the importance of building relationships, without giving you any specifics as to how. The best sales programs have relationship building components integrated into all the stages of the selling process. Following the process should be all that is necessary for building trust and establishing long-term relationships.

Discovering Needs

The most effective sales training programs are those that would have you begin the process by discovering the client's needs and wants before presenting your solutions. While we are often anxious to tell our story in an effort to convince clients of how much better we are than other firms, this is not an effective approach to selling. It is more important that we learn about the client, their needs and their goals, so we can later discuss our solutions in terms that are most relevant to them. If we want the client to experience that we can provide services that are relevant to their needs, we must first discover what those needs are.

> ### 🔑 Key Concept
>
> The most effective sales training programs are those that would have you begin the process by discovering the client's needs and wants before presenting your solutions.

Asking Questions

The questions you ask play a significant role in creating a high value perception and in causing the prospective client to experience the need for your services. A good sales training program, in addition to supplying some excellent questions, will provide an understanding of the structure and format of questions that can guide you in creating your own set of questions.

Asking good questions in the right way quickly brings the most relevant issues to the surface, motivating the client to action. The right questions also serve to positively position you in the prospect's mind, and can imply your capabilities without you having to say them. The proper use of questions significantly increases your chances for success in obtaining a value priced engagement.

Inquire in great detail about the types of questions and the guidance that is provided in helping your team members develop their own set of the effective questions.

Listening

Active, fully present listening is a critical success factor in conducting a sales meeting and in building long-term, trusting relationships. Be sure that your sales training program discusses the art of listening and provides practical tools and means by which you can effectively listen.

Unfortunately, listening is the easiest part of a sales program to skip over. That's because most of us naturally respond with thoughts such as, "I'm already a good listener. I understand the importance of listening. I don't need to be trained on how to listen." While all have the capacity to be excellent listeners, it is very seldom that we actually apply it. Make sure the sales training program that you select goes into some depth in this area. This will help everyone further develop their listening skills as they become more aware of the importance listening plays in selling process.

Exploring Solutions

There is an art to presenting solutions in a way that causes clients to recognize your ability to provide a solution, without actually solving any of their problems at that moment. Very often in an effort to impress a client, we will give away answers, or try to solve their problems on the spot. A good sales training program will provide a framework for you to explore possible solutions with a client in a way that convinces them that you know how to approach the situation, while also increasing their desire to work with you. The presentation of solutions should be a collaborative process, inviting client feedback to make sure you're on track.

When we start by discovering client needs and goals, we can more readily present our firm's capabilities and experience in terms relevant to the client. This can create substantial buy-in from the client. Be sure your sales training program integrates the "discovering needs" component into this "exploring solutions" component.

Addressing Concerns

When it comes to addressing client objections, accountants are generally not comfortable with a traditional sales training model that teaches us to "overcome" objections. There is a more natural approach to addressing client concerns that is much easier for accountants to apply.

Look for a sales training program that does not talk about overcoming objections, but rather provides collaborative ways to address them as a means of deepening the relationship and furthering the trust established with the client. By asking for an example of how a particular concern might be addressed, you can quickly observe the style of this aspect of the sales program.

Moving Forward

Accountants are not salespeople. That's why a selling process that requires us to "close the sale" is generally difficult to implement. This is the place where many sales programs provide slick techniques for closing that are uncomfortable for accountants to apply. Moving forward into a new relationship should be a natural outcome of the mutual exploration of how your services might benefit the client. If there is indeed mutuality, discussing engagement details and the nature of the relationship is simple and easy. Again, asking for an example of how the sale is closed will provide some idea of the approach used.

THREE SOURCES FOR SALES TRAINING

Sales training can be obtained from a number of sources. It is possible to have someone in your firm present the training, you can send people to an outside sales training, or you can hire an in-house sales trainer. In the following sections we discuss each of these options in some detail. Regardless of who provides the training, it is realistic to expect that each participant will invest somewhere between three and five training days per year in the initial year of training.

If you plan on using an outside resource for sales training, the best source for locating possible providers might be to talk to managing partners of other noncompeting firms. If you belong to an accounting association they might be able to make suggestions, as well as the managing partners of member firms.

In-house Resource

Using an in-house person can be a cost-effective approach to providing sales training. However, while there are many meaningful ways that successful rainmakers can contribute to the firm's sales training efforts, there can be some significant drawbacks to this approach. Being very successful at selling does not, in and of itself, make someone a good sales trainer. Training is a complex process, and a great deal has been written about how people learn, and accordingly, how they should be taught. If you decide to exercise this option, ask the designated trainer to participate in an instructor-training program. Many sales training organizations offer this kind of course.

One of the most common pitfalls to this solution is that team members will look at the rainmaker leading the group and think that they are supposed to be just like them, and do things the way they've done them. Also, rainmakers who are not experienced in providing sales training may be more focused on teaching their own particular style then they will be on helping each person discover their own style. All of this can create unnecessary obstacles.

There is an exception to this rule. If your firm has a capable presenter, access to a good sales training program with a facilitator's guide and participant handouts, this can then be a viable option. However, that same rainmaker could be well utilized in a sales training program presented by an outside trainer who would be willing to integrate the experience and perspective of that person into the training as a means of reinforcing some key principles.

Outside Sales Training Programs

Another option is to send team members to an outside sales training program. While there certainly are some good sales training programs available in this way, there are some drawbacks to this approach.

A basic problem with this option is that firms are often disappointed with the results of such training. The course participant returns to the firm enthusiastically utilizing skills learned, but since there is little or no encouragement and common understanding by others in the firm, the participant soon reverts to previous behavior. Another problem is that this is a piecemeal approach. Different people taking it at different times does not provide the same benefit to a firm as having people go through the same experience as a group.

There is also the issue of ongoing support and coaching. As stated previously, best results are achieved over time, with ongoing support. Pay close attention to the support being offered and plan on taking advantage of it. If the program does not offer ongoing support in an acceptable format, it might be better to choose a different program.

Hire a Sales Trainer for an In-house Program

Hiring a sales trainer to present the program in-house is often the most cost-effective way to provide sales training to the greatest number of people. One of the biggest advantages of hiring an outside sales trainer is that you will be working with a skilled professional who can help you determine the firm's specific training needs. From there, he or she can develop a customized training program.

With an in-house training program, there is the additional benefit of having everyone go through the same experience as a group. Because sales training programs often require communication among the participants, and everyone is going through the process together, these sessions also serve as an excellent team building experience. It's rewarding to see team members supporting one-another in the learning process.

If you decide to hire a sales trainer for an in-house program, you want to first determine how you will provide training to new team members as they come on board. It is important to make sure that everyone is trained in using the same selling process. This increases the effectiveness of the process and continues to develop a team approach to the client acquisition process. Ideally, additional training will be available on an individual basis either online, or in a public course.

Look closely at the ongoing support and coaching that is available. Again, the best results from any sales training program are achieved over time with ongoing support. Make sure it is readily available and easily integrates into everyone's schedule.

GUIDELINES FOR SELECTING THE RIGHT PROGRAM

Guidelines for selecting the right program are as follows:

- Make sure the sales training program you choose is aligned with the definition of selling that you are comfortable with. You can use the definition we provided as a basis for creating your own definition.
- Look for providers who have considerable experience in providing sales training, coaching, and ongoing support *within the accounting profession.*
    — Many well-known sales training providers will tell you that all sales principles are the same and would apply to any type of sale. While this is true to some degree, the simple reality is that accountants are not professional salespeople. We need an approach that is comfortable and is respectful of our values and integrity.
        o Many traditional sales training programs are not appropriate for accountants because they teach sales techniques and "tricks" that accountants not comfortable with, or perhaps an aggressive, tricky approach to closing the sale.
    — Established sales training organizations that have experience in the accounting profession understand these nuances and can make a tremendous difference in the level of acceptance of those accountants who are learning the system, and in their comfort in applying it.

- Look closely at the ongoing support and coaching that is provided by the sales training company. Beware of contracts that tie you to the provider for any length of time. A good sales support system should allow you to disengage if you feel you're not getting your money's worth.
- Talk to several other accounting firms that have been through their sales training program. Make sure at least one or two of those firms took the training program at least one or two years ago. Ask about the long term impact of the training program, how effective the support was, and the extent to which participants are utilizing the material on an ongoing basis.

BE CAREFUL ABOUT MODIFYING THE PROGRAM TOO MUCH

If you are using an in-house sales trainer, once you have selected a source for sales training, use caution if you are planning to modify their program to any significant degree. The program and support offered are likely to be based upon their experience of what produces the best results. If you believe in the sales training provider enough to hire them, trust their judgment when it comes to recommending the best program for your needs. Unless you have good reason change it, subscribe to the sales training program as it has been designed.

Many firms, in an effort to create their own version of sales training, inadvertently dilute the power of the program. If you feel it is necessary to make changes to the program, do so in collaboration with the sales training provider, and ask for their assurance that the effectiveness of the training has been maintained.

HOW CLIENTS MAKE BUYING DECISIONS

Understanding how people make buying decisions with regard to accounting services makes it easier to select the right sales training program. Fundamentally, the decision-making process is fairly simple. The decision to buy accounting services, or for that matter any service, has two significant components to it.

The first, often overlooked, component is emotional. Buying is essentially an emotional process. They buy "you" first, and then consider your services. If people don't like us, they're not likely to consider our services. Prospects always ask themselves, whether they realize it or not, "Is this someone I want to work with? Do they understand who I am and what I need? Do they care about me, or are they more self-focused?" One of the secrets to success in relationship based selling is that people do not buy our services because they understand what we do, but rather because they feel we understand them. Be sure your sales training program adequately addresses the relationship component in a way that is real, natural, and comfortable for accountants to engage in.

The second component to the buying decision is intellectual. Once the client is comfortable with you, they must be convinced that you have the technical ability, experience, and resources to provide services that will fulfill their needs. A good sales training program will show you how to present your solutions in a way that allows the prospect to experience your capabilities.

Key Concept

Understanding how people make buying decisions with regard to accounting services makes it easier to select the right sales training program.

Partner Endorsement

Participation in a sales training program will be greatly enhanced if everyone knows that it has the full support of all the partners. That's why it is very important to have partners present at the sales training. If your message is that sales training is important to the firm, you do not want to undermine that message by having partners who are not present. Of course, if it's impossible for a partner to be there, an explanation should be provided so that everyone knows they understand the importance of being there, but for a legitimate reason could not do so.

To take partner endorsement one important step further, partners should make it a point to take younger professionals out on sales calls. This is the best way for a partner to communicate the importance of developing sales skills. It's also a great relationship builder and mentoring process. There is a great deal younger professionals can learn from observing partners in action that can significantly enhance what they learned in the classroom.

Key Concept

Participation in a sales training program will be greatly enhanced if everyone knows that it has the full support of all the partners.

Costs and Return on Investment

When considering the cost of a sales training program, keep in mind that often the most significant portion of the cost is not in the training fees, but rather the combined hourly rates of all the participants. Also factor in the ongoing support costs for at least 12 months. It is not unreasonable to expect a first-year return on your investment in sales training of at least 100 percent of your total investment. That return would be measured in terms of additional annual billing generated as a direct result of the improved selling skills gained in the sales training program.

A word of caution. While minimizing expenses is always important, skimping when it comes to investing in a good sales training program may not be a good idea. If you think about it, one additional sale of moderate size can more than offset the incremental cost of a better program.

Conclusion

As you now know, there are many considerations to take into account when choosing a sales training program. You firm's investment in such a program is considerable, as is the time value and energy of everyone participating.

While the costs are not insignificant, the benefits can truly be enormous. Both at the firm level and at the individual level, sales training can have significant, far reaching effect that goes well beyond the added revenue and increased profitability of the firm.

It is extremely important that you take your time, and do the necessary research to select the right service provider. Once that decision has been made, take advantage of the full program and all its support, measure and monitor your results, make adjustments and improvements as you go along, and you will be virtually assured of a level of success that you have only imagined.

Good luck, and have fun in the process!

ABOUT THE AUTHOR

Rick Solomon has been on a mission for the past two decades: he's convinced that accountants are the key ingredient in helping businesses to succeed. He has taken this message, along with his innovative methods and programs, to thousands of professionals across the globe, helping them lead more lucrative and rewarding lives. Solomon is noted for bringing a dynamic and progressive approach to topics foremost in the minds of accounting and business advisory professionals, including firm development; marketing, selling and delivering services; and solving client problems in a way that leads to greater retention and profitability.

As a leading practice development consultant and CEO of RAN ONE Americas, Solomon works directly with accountants, advisors, industry experts and professionals. He received his bachelor's degree from the City University of New York-Baruch College and began his CPA career at a New York City-based international accounting firm. He went on to build one of the fastest-growing CPA firms on Long Island. He has studied human behavior and motivation at the Sedona Institute in Arizona and has incorporated the knowledge of overcoming limiting beliefs and points of view as a unique ingredient in his training programs. Solomon has served on the faculty of the Esperti-Peterson Institute, a think-tank of the nation's leading estate planning attorneys. Solomon is the founder and lead facilitator of the exclusive Masters Program, a dedicated group of accountants experiencing quantum growth in their practices and their lives.

PART VI:
Measuring Results, Communicating, and Rewarding Success

CHAPTER 32
In-House Marketing Communications That Foster Success

Jill R. Lock
Isdaner & Company, LLC

INTRODUCTION

Although we are more connected today with communication vehicles like PDAs, Twitter, and Facebook, it doesn't mean we are doing a good job of clearly communicating key messages essential to growing our practices. Just because we have more ways to connect, we often take for granted that our employees possess a clear picture of what's new in the organization, where our organization is heading, and what our employee's evolving role is in it. If we expect our employees to not only embrace marketing and business development, but to succeed at being our brand ambassadors, we must work proactively to provide them with clear and continuous communications reinforcing our marketing and sales initiatives.

In this chapter, we will provide you with a framework for building an effective internal marketing and sales communications function within your firm, including key components, ideas for implementing them, and the essential roles that firm and marketing leaders must play in bringing them to life.

> **🔑 Key Concept**
>
> Although we are more connected today with communication vehicles like PDAs, Twitter, and Facebook, it doesn't mean we are doing a good job of clearly communicating key messages essential to growing our practices.

WHY ARE IN-HOUSE MARKETING COMMUNICATIONS IMPORTANT?

Internal marketing communications, or, as it is often referred to in the accounting industry, *in-house or internal marketing,* is in its simplest form, the sharing of information inside the firm needed to educate, inspire, and engage your employees to market the firm to those outside the organization. Effective in-house marketing communications are more important than ever as firms strengthen their practice development efforts. In fact, strong internal marketing is essential to developing a marketing and sales culture within your firm, while building your brand outside the firm. A growing body of research amply demonstrates there is a link between internal marketing and profitability.

Internal marketing communications serve several key roles in helping your employees to grow your practice including the following:

- Providing employees with a clear vision for your firm's marketing and sales initiatives
- Strengthening employees' understanding of their role in marketing and sales within the firm
- Reinforcing your firm's value proposition and how to share it with others

- Understanding firm services, capabilities and expertise, and how to convey them to external targets
- Understanding the firm's brand and how to bring it to life inside and outside the firm
- Highlighting new external marketing initiatives and how to get more involved with them
- Celebrating new business wins and recognizing those responsible for the victories
- Offering tips, tools, and insights to win more new business
- Providing inspiration for employees to get more involved in business development efforts

> **♀ Key Concept**
>
> A growing body of research amply demonstrates there is a link between internal marketing and profitability.

INTERNAL MARKETING BEST PRACTICES

So what is needed for successful internal communications? *The Integrated Marketing Communications* department at Northwestern University conducted an Internal Marketing Best Practices study which identified six key characteristics that drive successful internal marketing programs. The six characteristics revealed in the study are as follows:

- *Senior management participation*
  Direct communication from c-suite executives and visible support from internal marketing leaders is necessary for effective internal marketing.

- *Integrated organizational structure*
  Most companies believe that it should encompass all communications with employees to maximize employee involvement and commitment.

- *Strategic marketing approach*
  When it comes to marketing internally, best-practices companies market to their internal constituents in a manner that parallels how it reaches out to acquire and retain customers.

- *Human resources partnership*
  For successful internal marketing, human resources staff must consistently seek to integrate innovative methodology to train, communicate, and foster feedback.

- *Focus on employee engagement*
  Employee engagement is a result of an efficient and collaborative work environment where employees feel involved and motivated.

- *Internal brand communication*
  All firms shared the basic principle that internal branding should inform and engage employees to consistently support brand initiatives.

These are important factors to consider as you look to strengthen your firm's internal communications. We will take a look at a number of these in the chapter.

COMMUNICATION MUST START AT THE TOP

For new initiatives like marketing and sales to be truly embraced throughout the organization, they must be endorsed by the firm's top leaders. Employees look to key leaders to gauge what is important and what is not top priority, as schedules are increasingly stretched to their limits.

The Role of Firm Leaders

Managing partners, niche partners, and executive committee members must find ways to incorporate key marketing messages into their regular routines. They must help facilitate the internal communications process with all levels of employees in all departments and support the role of the marketing professional. Whether at a new employee orientation, an annual firm day or a partner retreat, their support through positive remarks can give strength to marketing initiatives. Involvement of firm management in the internal marketing communications program will build excitement for the program and establish added credibility and value.

The Role of the Marketing Professional

For firms with marketing directors, the marketing professional is generally responsible for the overall internal marketing communications initiative. Success is achieved by positioning themselves as a leader through visibility, accessibility, and approachability. The spirit of marketing and the role each employee plays needs to be projected in a way that encourages participation. This requires communicating consistently, constantly, and with conviction. The marketing professional has to continually keep the employees informed about the industries and services offered by the firm. Employees need to understand not only what the firm's brand means but be comfortable in how to bring the brand to life through their actions. Marketing activities and accomplishments must be communicated to all employees on a regular basis. Consistent messages create expectations and add credibility to the process. Regular, ongoing communications demonstrate the priority and importance of the message, resulting in a strengthened marketing effort across the firm.

DUE DILIGENCE

It's important to have a clear understanding of the existing marketing and sales culture of the firm before developing an internal communications plan. For firms with marketing directors on board, conducting due diligence generally falls into their area of responsibility. If your firm does not have a marketing professional on board, you could consider asking a key rainmaker or a marketing committee to assume this task. You could also consider retaining an outside marketing consultant.

A wide assortment of employees should be surveyed to gain an understanding of the existing marketing and sales culture. Key industry leaders, partners, accountants on various professional levels, new hires, seasoned veterans and administrative staff should be included in the survey. The survey should include such information as strengths and weaknesses of the firm, reasons they selected to work at the firm, their view on marketing, motivating factors, and comfort level of various marketing activities. The results will allow you to develop the right plan that will fit nicely with the unique needs and personality of your firm.

INTERNAL COMMUNICATIONS PLAN

Just like an external marketing plan is essential to external marketing initiatives, an internal plan is the backbone of in-house marketing initiatives. As revealed by the *Internal Marketing Best Practices* study, best practices companies market to their internal constituents in a manner that parallels how they reach out to acquire and retain customers. This is an important consideration as your firm prepares its internal marketing plan.

Key components of the plan can include the following:

- Information vehicles
- Meetings and face-to-face connections
- Marketing tools
- Programs and training
- Measurement tools
- Resources
- Firm environment

Key Concept

Just like an external marketing plan is essential to external marketing initiatives, an internal plan is the backbone of in-house marketing initiatives.

Information Vehicles

One of the first steps in developing your communications plan is to select how you will get your messages out to employees. There are a number of vehicles for you to consider in the dissemination of information. It is important to select those that best suit your firm's culture. Employees need various vehicles for continual education about firm activities, services, and industries. The more of these vehicles used, and the greater the frequency of use, helps to build better informed staff. The firm's marketing director or communications director generally spearheads and implements these efforts. Consider these information vehicles:

- *Internal marketing & sales blogs.* A personal online sales/marketing journal that is frequently updated can enhance the firm communications. Employees can be updated about marketing events and activities with these blogs. Articles about marketing can be posted to the blog. The blog or Web log is a fast way to get articles and information up on the Web. Blogging may be done as often as desired—make sure it is relevant or it will lose its readership. Readers can leave comments so blogs provide an interactive format.
- *Marketing & sales sections on firm's portal or intranet.* A marketing and sales section can be added to the firm's portal or intranet. In this way, employees can read the latest marketing news and sales activities. The intranet can deliver news internally to the accounting firm and provide employees with an easily navigated window into the firm. Firm news can be communicated consistently and promptly to everyone at the same time with the intranet or Web portal.
- *Marketing updates.* Marketing updates can provide information about new clients obtained, clients and employees in the news, networking representation, new services offered, client success stories, employee promotions and nominations to boards, special programs, employees in the news, firm awards, etc. Marketing updates can serve to educate and motivate others to be involved in marketing activities. The key with these updates is to do them consistently and promptly. E-mail often works best as it can be delivered in a timely fashion. These can also be placed on the firm's portal or be left as voicemail messages.

    At Islander & Company, a recent marketing update communicated to staff at our firm was a success story about LinkedIn. One of our CPAs was contacted via LinkedIn in search of a job in the Philadelphia area. This CPA was relocating to the area and read our employee's information about the firm on LinkedIn.
- *Internal newsletters.* Depending upon the size of your firm and the locations of various offices of the firm, it may be beneficial to have an internal newsletter. It can be transmitted via the intranet, your internal marketing blog, or written and distributed. There are three different kinds of newsletters depending upon the purpose and audience you are reaching. These internal newsletters include the following:
    — The Professional Practice Newsletter. Generally produced monthly or quarterly and distributed to all partners, managers and accounting staff. Industry group leaders and service leaders may submit updates and plans of their groups to be included in this newsletter. New accounting software can also be highlighted as well as priority items of the various groups, or upcoming future services or events.
    — The Employee Newsletter. It is directed to all personnel and communicates information about new hires, progress, and direction of the firm.
    — The Partner/Manager Newsletter. It may include pertinent news articles, changes in the profession and issues facing the firm.

Meetings and Face-To-Face Connections

Meetings are crucial to internal communications. Face-to-face meetings have the highest impact because the message is animated in a variety of ways: facial expressions, tone of voice, and posture of speaker. However, meetings can be time consuming and it may be difficult to get all the staff together. When conducting meetings, they should be brief and relevant. Consider these in your internal marketing communications program:

- *Staff Meetings.* At staff meetings, it is important for firm leaders to offer inspirational marketing messages. Encourage employees to share their individual marketing efforts. The marketing professional can make brief presentations about a particular marketing aspect, service introduced, or client data. It is advantageous for the marketing professional to do this to increase their visibility while educating staff as to the role of the marketing professional in the firm. The marketing professional can bring employees into their presentations by remarking about a marketing success story by the employee and then the employee can be asked to elaborate on the story. The marketing professional should position her- or himself as a leader at these meetings and inspire others to discuss their marketing activities.

- *Marketing and pipeline meetings.* At marketing and pipeline meetings, members of the management team, niche leaders, and the marketing professional discuss opportunities for business and share the status of prospective business being pursued. Through this discussion, they develop strategies to obtain the prospect. Team members share what they know about the lead and their industry. They plan winning strategies with this information by working together using their expertise. This allows for opportunity management with a cohesive team approach. The marketing professional or managing partner may facilitate these regular meetings. Many firms hold them weekly.

- *Partner meetings.* Firm leaders should include marketing and business development updates at partner meetings. Marketing professionals should take an active role, positioning themselves as the marketing go-to resource. Topics could include new marketing initiatives, success stories, new business wins, and competitive intelligence, to name a few.

Marketing Tools

There is a variety of marketing tools that you can use to better help your employees understand your brand, and to use in marketing your services to those outside the firm. These marketing tools include the following:

- *Marketing plan.* The marketing plan identifies a firm's overall marketing and business development goals and objectives, and the strategies and actions it will use to work toward those goals. Regular updates that communicate how the firm is progressing toward the achievement of its goals will allow your employees to understand how far they have come in reaching targeted goals, and know what work is yet to be done. For maximum effectiveness, the plan should be updated annually. Well-integrated internal communications are the key to executing your marketing plans. For more information on developing a marketing plan, see chapter 4, "The Marketing Plan: An Audit-Based Approach."

- *Marketing tool box.* The tool box includes those communications materials used frequently by staff to promote the firm. Employees need to be educated about how to use each of these materials and when they are appropriate to use. They should also be informed when changes have been made.

  Internal communications materials include new account data sheets, proposal sheets, referral forms, and lost client data sheets. These forms/sheets help track new business, referral sources and lost clients. Information gained from these forms helps to measure past successes and determine sources of business. Premium gifts with the firm logo, brochure, fax sheet, firm fact sheet, biographies and business cards are all materials that are used externally and must all have a homogeneous appearance. Employees need to be educated about the availability of all the tools and the proper use of materials.

- *Marketing manual.* A useful reference tool is a detailed marketing manual. This manual can include sample client surveys, fact sheets, biographies, and a guide on how to network or present at trade shows, for example. It may also include tips on writing letters and preparing proposals, distributing premium items and cross-selling services. It's important to include copies of all client publications and promotional materials. Regular updates are encouraged, to help project a consistent image of the firm.

Programs and Training

Various types of programs and training can enhance your firm's internal communications. These can include the following:

- *Marketing orientation programs.* Each new employee should meet with the firm's marketing professional soon after he or she joins the firm. The marketing manual, which was discussed in the "Marketing Tools" section should be reviewed with the new employee. It is also advisable to inquire about the marketing background of the new employee as he or she may have utilized various skills in past positions that would be an asset to the firm.

At Isdaner & Company, we hold a marketing orientation session for new hires and interns. This session includes firm history, partners' biographies, services, high profile clients and a description of major marketing initiatives. As a result of this presentation, they have an increased understanding of the firm and will be able to better market the firm.

- *Marketing and sales skills development programs.* These programs facilitate the development of marketing and sales skills at various staff levels and in different departments across the firm. They create appropriate marketing and sales expectations for each employee and build core competencies needed to market and sell. Sessions can address various subjects from firm history and capabilities including services, industries, and size of clients served; how to network with referral sources; the basics of communications skills; how to project the best image when visiting with a prospect; and the basics of selling to cross-selling and advanced negotiations, to name a few. To be most effective, courses should build on each other. Shorter, more frequent sessions are more effective than longer less frequent sessions. These CPE courses also provide the opportunity to update your personnel on current marketing and sales initiatives in your firm. For more information on sales training, see chapter 31, "Sales Training: The Key to Better Service and Better Clients."

- *Industry Groups.* Employees need to know the expertise of the staff and the industries they serve. In this way, they can be fully aware of the range of expertise available at the firm and the proper referrals to be made. Constant and frequent communication needs to be made so all employees know the individuals within the industry groups and the type of clients served. Employees also need to know the background of the individuals in the groups. The more employees know, the better marketers they can be. This internal communications is essential.

At Isdaner & Company, we use "lunch and learn" sessions to highlight industries and invite client speakers to speak about their industry. So in addition to our employees talking about an industry and attending industry meetings, we invite clients in that industry to make a presentation. This has been well received by our employees and clients feel valued by being a featured speaker at this event.

- *Incentive Programs.* Incentive programs can help create a marketing culture within the firm. For the program to work, the concept must be embraced first by management. The program can help in enhancing client service, building new business and developing relationships, and assisting in recruiting efforts. The length of the program may vary according to the firm's objectives. For more on incentive programs, see chapter 33, "Effective Employee Incentive Programs: How to Bring Out the Best in Your Firm."

- *Value added client service programs.* It is always prudent to first serve your clients with excellent service before trying to obtain new clients. Existing clients are the best source for referrals, whether it is cross-selling new services to them or asking the clients to refer their friends to your firm. Value added client service programs help ensure that clients are receiving quality service from your staff and that the bond between the client and the firm is deepened. Such a program may include examples of superior service or introduce employees to client service standards. For more information on client service programs, see chapter 36, "Developing a Service Excellence Plan for Clients."

- *Team building programs.* Employees need to understand that the firm is a team and team players must work together toward a common goal. Team building is a process of enabling the team to achieve a common goal. By working together and using the strengths of individuals, the client bond becomes tighter and prospects and referral sources become aware of the full range of experts available. This increases the leads that the firm gets. Powerful and fun exercises may be used to communicate these concepts. Incentives should be established to facilitate these views. An outside facilitator or marketing professional can conduct these types of program. They can be an all day annual event in conjunction with shorter meetings throughout the year to insure the implementation of the team building concepts.

- *Employee recognition programs.* This type of program recognizes employee birthdays or special employee milestones or contributions. It can be as simple as an e-mail announcing birthdays of the month with a cake at a staff meeting to a more elaborate annual dinner/lunch program recognizing the milestones of various employees. At various anniversaries of employment, you may want to distribute special items with the firm logo or a gift certificate to the employee. The goal of the program is to show how the employee is appreciated and valued and an important addition to the team. This program can also aid in employee retention.

Measurement Tools

For employees to gauge how effective your marketing plans are, it's essential to report on your progress against the plan. There are a number of tools that you can use for tracking business and marketing initiatives including the following:

- *Data tracking.* Forms such as a New Account Data Sheet, Proposal Sheet, and Lost Client Form can be useful internally to track and measure the success of gaining clients in a particular industry group and understanding the reasons when the firm is not chosen for a proposal or a client is lost. Tracking data helps to measure the success of various marketing initiatives and also gives the firm a barometer of where it is has been and is headed. These forms should be updated to reflect any new services or industries. For more information, see chapter 34, "Marketing and Sales Metrics Matter, Measuring Results, Calculating Return on Investment."
- *Budget.* Before developing the budget, the firm must have goals and strategies to achieve those goals. A marketing plan will help in the development of the budget. Use the plan to estimate the cost of the activities outlined. If the firm is trying to establish itself in a new marketplace or service area, more money will need to be allocated to establish your market share objective. A marketing budget should be developed so each year, money can be specifically allocated to a particular marketing area and used as a measuring tool. Later, the budget will be evaluated to determine if the money was well spent. A budget should be developed annually. For more information on budgeting see chapter 8, "Budgeting Techniques for Today's CPA Firm."

> **Key Concept**
>
> For employees to gauge how effective your marketing plans are, it's essential to report on your progress against the plan.

Resources

There are a variety of resources that can be used to enhance internal communications including the following:

- *Employee surveys.* Various employee surveys can be developed depending upon the goals. If you want to initiate a marketing program or incentive plan, it may be helpful to survey the employees about their marketing strengths and weaknesses and key motivating factors. A participation activities survey to employees can identify areas of interest.
- *Research tools.* Before going on a prospect meeting, it is important to do as much research as possible to understand the prospect's industry and needs. Start first with searching the Web about the prospect. Also ask in-house if others know the prospect or people on the prospect's board or prospect's lawyer, banker, and so on. Various software programs are available to provide industry background and give benchmarking financial ratios. Many Web sites also feature information on nonprofits and public companies. Use all available tools to position your firm as a strong candidate for the prospect's business.
- *Marketing advisory groups.* Developing a marketing advisory group to include all levels of professionals in various service and industry groups can help in strengthening and transmitting the marketing message. This group can be a useful resource to the marketing professional for feedback on ideas and to influence the outcome of a program. The marketing professional should lead this group, develop the agenda items with group input and meet periodically.
- *Marketing idea fairs.* Because many great marketing ideas are initiated at the grassroots level, consider a marketing fair. The purpose of the fair is to recognize the creativity of your people. and allow all personnel to gain ideas that can be applied in everyday marketing. Categories of entries can include proposals, newsletters, advertising, press release programs, trade show activities, direct mail campaigns, referral programs, client service programs, and e-mail correspondence. A narrative should be submitted with each entry that includes all of the following category of the entry, description of the entry, target, costs, marketing objective, and marketing results. Share the results with our entire firm.
- *Communications audit.* This audit analyzes how communications are conducted by a department and office. Such an audit addresses method of transmission, timeliness of information and consistency of message.

Firm Environment

Your firm's office and its environment affect communication and send a strong message about who you are. Be aware of the image your environment is creating. The image should be consistent with your brand and how you want to be viewed.

- *Reception/conference rooms.* The reception area is the first area a visitor to your firm enters. The appearance of the area as well as how the visitor is greeted makes a lasting impression. The appearance of your reception area and the attention given to visitors has a great impact on the firm's image. Consider a streaming video with your firm's story on a flat screen monitor. Only carefully considered, current magazines and brochures should be displayed neatly on coffee tables. All visitors should be greeted in a friendly, pleasant manner. The receptionist is the Director of First Impressions as he or she is the first person the visitor sees as entering your firm. Make sure they take the role seriously and convey the appropriate image of the firm. The same care and attention should be given to your conference rooms. Make sure they speak volumes about your brand to visitors. Think about the furnishings and how they are maintained.
- *Other display areas.* Marketing materials can be displayed internally for the employees at a central meeting place such as the lunch room or employee lounge. It is helpful to display in the public employee area things such as news articles about employees and their family members and clients, inserts in newsletters, and breaking industry news. This display helps to keep everyone involved in the events of the firm and recognizes special achievements of employees and clients.

KEYS TO SUCCESS

Good internal communications are essential to your external marketing and business development efforts. Here are some keys to success to consider in your firm:

- Make internal marketing a top priority
- You can never over communicate—frequency is essential
- Start with a plan—one that parallels your external plan
- Establish an in-house marketing program before developing an external program
- Top leadership's ongoing involvement is essential
- Help employees understand their role in marketing the firm—start by helping them to understand how to bring the firm's brand to life
- Share consistent messages across the firm
- Consider a variety of communications vehicles—people process information in different ways
- Mix it up by adding new ways to communicate
- Make it fun

CONCLUSION

Each employee has a role in marketing and an impact on the way the firm is perceived to outsiders. This does not simply happen by chance. If we expect our employees to be the best marketing and brand ambassadors they can be, we must start inside the firm with a well-planned internal communications program. The goals of the in-house marketing communications program are to instill a consistent image of the firm by illustrating how each employee projects that image and to impart a sense of employee commitment to the firm by appreciating the contribution of each team member. When employees understand where the firm is heading, see the role they play in it, and receive recognition for their contributions, your firm will build a stronger marketing culture and ultimately achieve success through growth and profitability.

ABOUT THE AUTHOR

Jill Lock is the director of marketing at Isdaner & Company, LLC. In this position, she builds and facilitates internal and external marketing programs. Prior to joining the firm in 2003, Jill was the director of marketing at other regional accounting firms. She has more than 20 years of experience in the marketing of accounting firms. Jill has written numerous articles on business and communication topics for business and professional publications.

CHAPTER 33
Effective Employee Incentive Programs: How to Bring Out the Best in Your Firm

Lisa A. Rozycki
LR Marketing Group

INTRODUCTION

An *incentive program* is a planned activity designed to motivate people to achieve predetermined organizational objectives. In other words, it is a planned activity to encourage people to do what it is you want them to do.

In the accounting industry, many firms have the standard commission type structure paid to employees for bringing in new business and cross-selling services to existing clients.

Other incentive programs are activity based programs that are geared toward reaching firm goals—increasing business development activities, improving communication, and developing marketing cultures within firms, for example. Professionals are rewarded with money or merchandise for reaching a predetermined set of goals.

The benefits of developing an incentive program within an accounting firm can include

- increased sales,
- improved relationships,
- improved client service,
- enhanced client loyalty,
- amplified client retention,
- improved employee morale,
- strengthened employee loyalty and trust,
- improved communication between departments and service groups, and
- enhanced teamwork.

When developing an incentive program, several things should be considered including the structure of the program, the demographic makeup of the organization, what type of incentives would motivate employees to do what it is you want them to do, and the goals and objectives you want to achieve. This chapter will address each of these areas.

THE STRUCTURE OF AN INCENTIVE PROGRAM

There are generally three basic ways to structure an incentive program:

- *Open-ended.* This type of program allows anyone who reaches a specific goal to earn a reward. The standard structure for an open-ended program is to give each professional a specific goal, such as to conduct 10 business development activities a month. The open-ended approach generally gets better results since it gives you a better chance of motivating the majority of people in your firm who more than likely function at average, but not exceptional levels.

- *Closed-ended*. This type of program structure allows a predetermined number or a percentage of people to qualify for rewards. For example, in a closed-ended program, a firm might establish that only the top 10 participants would qualify for a reward or only the top 10 percent of achievers would qualify for a reward. Closed-ended programs are not as effective as open-ended programs because they tend to reward only the top performers who, more than likely, would have performed well in the program anyway.
- *Plateau*. This type of program offers rewards at different performance levels. For example, a staff accountant may have three different goal levels, appropriate for his or her staff level, to work towards in a program year. An example would be to use a point system whereby every time the staff accountant conducts a marketing activity he or she is awarded a set amount of points for that activity. That staff accountant works towards three incremental point goal levels that have been established for staff accountants as part of the guidelines of the program. Once he or she reaches a goal level, they are rewarded with an incentive award. The benefit of this type of program structure is that it motivates people to push themselves a little harder when they become close to achieving their next reward increment.

Understand the Lifestyles and Demographic Make-Up of Your Staff

Before developing an incentive program, it is important to understand your firm's culture so that you can tailor your program and the rewards accordingly. Conduct a survey to poll employees for their preferences. Find out what your employees value and what motivates them. Understanding the lifestyles and demographic make-up of your firm's professionals is key to the success of any incentive program. Each generation perceives the value of a gift or reward differently. Keep this in mind when selecting incentive pay, rewards, and how people are recognized for their achievements. The reward choices should provide enough options so that something is appealing to everyone. They should also be quick and easy to administer.

Cash Isn't Always King!

It may seem surprising to learn that cash isn't always the best incentive. People feel less comfortable talking about a cash award then a nice plaque or nonmonetary award such as a trip or a dinner at a fine restaurant. Noncash awards are more likely to be remembered. Many times, employees will spend cash awards on incidental items or to pay off household bills. If you asked them a year from receiving the monetary award what they spent it on, they probably wouldn't be able to recall. Employees also view monetary rewards as compensation and after a while feel that they are entitled to them regardless of the effort put forth.

Recognition Is an Important Component of Any Program

Recognition is defined by *Merriam-Webster* as "acknowledgement, special notice, or attention." It is an important component of an incentive program. When employees realize that their contributions are an important part of a firm's success, they are more likely to embrace the goals and objectives of the firm and its incentive program. Recognition can take many forms, from a managing partner announcing achievements at firm wide meetings to handing out personal notes of gratitude or certificates for reaching certain milestones. The value of recognition cannot be overstated. Recognition drives everything and can foster goodwill, recognize goal achievement, boost morale, reinforce positive behaviors, and promote teamwork among members of a firm. For more on effective ways to communicate employee recognition, see chapter 32, "In-House Marketing Communications That Foster Success."

⚷ Key Concept

When employees realize that their contributions are an important part of a firm's success, they are more likely to embrace the goals and objectives of the firm and its incentive program.

OBTAINING BUY-IN

When planning an incentive program, the first step is to obtain buy-in from the managing partner, other partners, and employees. Make sure all of the partners of the firm have been briefed on the concept and guidelines of the incentive program and have had the opportunity to provide input and approval.

Incentive programs are an important part of the psychological gratification of the professional and, therefore, need to be associated with the top management group. At the very least, include comments from your managing partner in promotional materials to participants.

FORM A TASKFORCE TO PLAN THE PROGRAM

When planning a program, form a taskforce of representatives from all levels of staff. Surprisingly, they will set tougher standards than a marketing director would. Yet, because they are members of the rank and file, staff usually respects their decisions. As the program progresses, your taskforce will be your internal sales team when pitching the program to staff.

You risk the exact opposite when the marketing director or executive committee creates the program. This is not to suggest that guidelines should not be tied to legitimate firm goals. As part of the task force, make sure you guide them and include this important consideration in your proposal to your management group.

The task force's job should be to work on the goals and objectives of the program, theme, promotional items, reward systems, and return on investment (ROI) measurements. Openly discuss everyone's concerns. Pay special attention to the obstacles that they see and their suggestions on what to do to overcome these obstacles. Vote on changes to the program and make sure the changes reflect the opinion of the majority of the taskforce members and not just a specific group, the managing partner, or marketing director.

Involve the taskforce in the program design, introduction, implementation, maintenance, and promotion of the program. They will take ownership and pride in the program if they have an active role in creating and promoting it. A successful incentive program requires teamwork—make your taskforce an integral part of your business development efforts.

DEVELOP A CLEAR SET OF GOALS & OBJECTIVES

The most highly motivated groups are those that have clearly defined goals. To motivate staff, set goals for every staff level that participates.

Design a program that reinforces the "real" goals of the firm. Many firms will talk about a specific goal but go on to design an incentive program predicated on something else. For example, a firm may kick off a contest by telling professionals that they want to build a stronger marketing culture and that the expectations are that they want people to become more involved in business development by trying marketing activities that they feel comfortable with. Then the incentive program is rolled out and the incentive measurement is on revenue generated for a certain time period. This usually happens because it is easier to evaluate revenue growth rather than an intangible like building a marketing culture. Don't take away from the future value of an incentive program in order to produce good, short-term results.

Goals should be realistic, achievable, and sincere. This is the key to building credibility for your program.

The incentive program objectives should contain four critical elements:

1. The desired activity or "what you want them to do"

2. The units of that activity that will be measured or "how they will do it"

3. The expected performance level or "goals for individuals or teams"

4. The time allotted to achieve the performance level or "how long they will have to work towards their goals"

Regardless of an employee's staff level, they should have an equal opportunity to achieve their goals. Don't use the same goal levels for staff accountants as you would managers, for example. Early on, a staff accountant is learning how to become a good business developer. The units of activity that would be measured for the staff accountant should be tied to the quality and quantity of his or her efforts as well as successes.

Designing an incentive program on the assumption that a staff accountant can successfully perform the same activity as a manager, will likely have a negative effect on their attitude toward business development later on in their career. He or she might not have the skill set to call on a prospect yet. Make sure that everyone has an equal opportunity to achieve.

Factors to Consider

Factors to consider include the following:

- *Cost vs. desired results.* Determine how much the firm is willing to spend to achieve the desired results. Management should view the incentive program as an investment in achieving the goals and objectives outlined, not an expense.
- *Timing.* Timing is critical to the success of your program. Kicking off a new program during tax season could be difficult.
- *Length.* The length of the program is important as well. A study for the Forum for People Performance Management and Measurement (Northwestern University) found that long-term programs outperform short-term programs. The study found that programs that ran for a year or more produced an average 44 percent performance increase, while programs running 6 months or less showed a 30 percent increase.
- *Individual or team effort.* Decide whether the participants will work in teams, as an individual or both. In a study done by the International Society of Performance Improvement entitled "Incentives, Motivation, and Workplace Performance," it was found that properly constructed incentive programs can improve performance by as much as 44 percent in teams and 25 percent in individuals. If you decide to run a team based program, make sure that each team includes participants from all staff levels, everyone feels they have an investment in attaining the team's goals, and each individual has a chance to be recognized for outstanding achievement.
- *Good appeal/perceived value.* Make sure the structure you choose appeals to a majority of your employees and everyone knows "what is in it for me."
- *Disqualification.* No one wants to disqualify a person from participating in an incentive program. It is advisable to have a review board to determine what is acceptable and what is not. By having a review board, you reduce favoritism and increase the fairness of the program.

Determine Your Budget

A successful program pays for itself. Determine your budget and the criteria to tie it back to your expected ROI. Budget for incentive costs, the number of participants, the promotional costs of educating and motivating employees, and the administrative costs of tracking performance and distributing rewards.

A rule of thumb: budget your costs based on a best-case scenario. In other words, what would you need to spend for every participant to reach his or her highest goal level? Your management group will not mind if you spend less than budgeted, but you will encounter problems if costs soar far beyond your budget, even if the program results far exceed expectations.

Write the Program Guidelines

Every incentive program has guidelines to provide a blueprint for exactly what you expect from the participants in the program. Your guidelines should specify precisely what is expected of people and cover every loophole you can think of, while remaining simple and easy to follow. Guidelines should specify the following:

- The timing and length of qualifying periods
- Who can qualify and at what level
- How people can meet their goals
- How they will be measured
- What will be awarded and when
- What is not included
- What actions will not be awarded
- What will cause disqualification

Be Flexible

Too often, contest rules and reward choices are too rigid. Because of the nature of the accounting business, review board personnel tend to want to view the guidelines in black and white. Flexibility is key to the success of any incentive program. For example, if the top reward is a cruise, but the winner gets seasick on boats, give them something of comparable value in place of the initial top prize. Likewise, trust people when they say they've accomplished a measurable activity. Constantly requiring them to provide proof that they attended an event or brought in a piece of business can be a real morale buster. Their actions may have been one of 10 that led to the piece of new business. If that is the case, split the reward with those that were involved or let the group decide how to divide it up. Treat people with respect and trust them until they give you a reason not to.

PROMOTE THE PROGRAM

There are a variety of ways to promote an incentive program to staff. Some examples include the following:

- *Teasers.* Teasers can be used at the beginning of an incentive program to peak the interest of participants. If the program has a theme, often times a promotional item or some type of communication piece related to the theme can be sent to participants or placed on their desks to peak interest in learning more about the program.
- *Kickoff.* The kickoff for a program is an important step. The goal should be to create excitement for the program and for everyone to understand the objectives clearly. It should be fun and exciting. Oftentimes, a theme-based program can provide for some creative ideas for a kickoff.
- *Guidelines booklet or information piece.* The guidelines of the program should be spelled out in an information booklet or as a section in a firm's intranet so that everyone has access to the program guidelines.
- *Standings mailer.* A standings mailer, especially if it is a team-based program, can be sent to an employee's residence. This often gets the family involved in cheering on the participant to achieve success within the program.
- *Newsletters.* Internal firm newsletters can be used to announce program guidelines and accomplishments of teams and members of the firm.
- *Meetings.* Firm-wide meetings, department meetings, or special celebrations can be used to provide recognition to participants for their achievements.
- *Final Mailer.* A final mailer can be used to thank participants for their efforts, announce firm wide and individual achievements, and to announce a new program, if appropriate.

EXTRA ELEMENTS TO BOOST PARTICIPATION

In order to maintain excitement for the incentive program throughout its life, other elements can boost participation. The following programs, for example:

- *Fast Start.* Extra measurement units can be awarded to participants for engaging in a certain activity at the start of a program. Some firms award them for a certain activity conducted during the kickoff event.
- *Sprint or Spurt.* Extra measurement units can be awarded to participants for engaging in a certain activity during a specific timeframe within the program. For example, extra measurement units can be awarded to an individual or team that submits so many client testimonials during a specific program week or month.
- *Fast Finish.* Bonus measurement units can be awarded at the end of a program year for participants who engage in a certain level of activity during the program year.
- *Service Bonus.* Extra measurement units can be awarded to participants for engaging in a certain activity that is related to a service group. For instance, participants can be awarded so many measurement units for handing in qualified leads for cost segregation study engagements during a specific timeframe.
- *Industry Bonus.* Extra measurement units can be awarded to participants for engaging in certain activities geared towards a specific industry niche during a specific timeframe.

Provide Training

Management at top-performing firms agree that training to equip employees at every level with the knowledge necessary to support their role in the organization's success is critical. Offer marketing training programs to arm your firm's professionals with the skills necessary to succeed. Include programs on your service offerings, industry expertise, and soft skills training on probing, listening, uncovering opportunities, providing excellent client service, living your firm's brand, networking, and building relationships, for example. According to the authors of *High Performance Sales Organizations,* these companies create a common language or brand in which all employees are trained so that they know their role in the organization's strategy. Activities are then developed to support their role in that strategy. For more information on sales training, see chapter 31, "Sales Training: The Key to Better Service and Better Clients."

Provide a Reporting System

Create a simple reporting system to capture results, such as a database, Excel spreadsheet, form, time entry code, etc. Make it simple. Everyone is very busy and most firms already have too many forms and reporting systems in place. Avoid using something so complex that is becomes an administrative nightmare for everyone involved, including you.

Have the review board evaluate the results on a timely basis. This will ensure that the program is fair.

Calculate Your Return on Investment

It is important to measure the ROI. If incentive programs are not carefully planned out and regularly evaluated, they tend to become viewed as an expense rather than an investment. At the end of a program, measure the tangible. Tangible measurements might include sales of new engagements, the increased number of new clients, new service sales, percentage of increase in market share, general profits, or client satisfaction ratings.

Measure the intangible. Look at how well your firm improves over time. Intangible measurements may include such things as better client service, client retention, client satisfaction ratings, employee satisfaction rates, computation of employees' action on the bottom line, training expenditures, turnover costs, improved morale, or decreased turnover. For more information on calculating ROI, see chapter 34, "Marketing and Sales Metrics Matter: Measuring Results, Calculating Return on Investment."

Evaluate the Results

The end of a program timeframe is only the beginning. A critical evaluation of the results can provide valuable information you can use for creating a more effective program in the future. Ask what concrete results were achieved. Was the budget justified given the ROI? Ask the people who participated in the program for suggestions for improvement. What is the qualitative data? Do you have new clients knocking at your door? Does your staff appear more marketing oriented and more effective at business development?

Conclusion

Incentive programs should be tailored to the unique needs of an organization. Goals and objectives should be established that are the "real" goals for the firm. Design activities and training geared towards reaching those goals. Communicate with your staff to find out what they value in order to plan for incentive pay, rewards and recognition. Is the value worth the extra "oomph" it will take to reach the set goals? Discover what your staff values and your firm will literally profit from it.

ABOUT THE AUTHOR

Lisa A. Rozycki is the founder and Principal of LR Marketing Group, a marketing consulting practice specializing in growing revenue of professional service firms through market analysis, planning and implementation, public relations, lead generation, and business development. Lisa has 28 years of marketing experience including 13 years in the public accounting industry. For more information on employee incentive programs, contact Lisa A. Rozycki at 610-582-0097 or lisa@lrmarketinggroup.com.

CHAPTER 34
Marketing and Sales Metrics Matter: Measuring Results, Calculating Return on Investment

Mitchell Reno
Rehmann

Tracy Crevar Warren
The Crevar Group LLC

INTRODUCTION

So your firm has developed a well thought-out marketing and sales plan, the team has embraced it, and implementation is underway. Nice going! But wait, there's another important thing you need to be doing to help ensure your firm's efforts are a success—that is, measuring your results. Unless you measure results, you can never truly gauge the success of your actions. And if you can't measure your results, you can never effectively manage your business development efforts, can you?

In this chapter, we will take a closer look at the importance of measuring your firm's marketing results, and explore some tools that you can use in calculating the return on your marketing investment.

THE AGE OF ACCOUNTABILITY

Over the past decade when it was not uncommon for firms to achieve double-digit growth on a regular basis, keeping tabs on their marketing results was just not a top priority for many firms. For years, the industry has grown comfortable with providing marketers a "pass" on demonstrating how their financial investments were providing positive outcomes to firms. As a result, many firms have become complacent in measuring lead generation and sales production, not to mention returns on marketing activities such as tradeshows and seminars.

In this new economy, however, internal accountability is more important than ever. Marketing is no exception. Partner groups from firms of all sizes now demand a better accounting of where investments are made and the impacts they have on their organizations' top and bottom lines. Marketing and practice growth professionals in accounting firms are challenged with the requirement of demonstrating the return on investment (ROI) for marketing, business development, and client retention programs.

A WIDER LENS

For firms to remain competitive, it's also critical to measure success of marketing investments in a much broader way today. Marketers and partners alike must focus on metrics that help them understand the return on investments at all phases of the business development pipeline. For example, we must examine ROI before leads are generated, during the pursuit process, and after new clients are acquired.

> **♀ Key Concept**
>
> Marketers and partners must focus on metrics that help them understand the return on investments at all phases of the business development pipeline.

WHY MEASURE?

"Without metrics to track performance, marketing and business plans are ineffective." according to Laura Patterson, author or *Metrics in Action: Creating a Performance-Driven Marketing Organization.* "Businesses need to know which success factors require measuring, and they must understand the differences between measurements (the raw outcomes of quantification), metrics (ideal standards for measurement), and benchmarks (the standards by which all others are measured)."[1]

We operate in an environment that thrives on measuring results. They enable us to assess progress against the achievement of goals. Just look at the way we manage our practices. We determine how well we are doing by measuring such areas as employee productivity, realization, and billings.

To get a clear picture about your marketing and business development efforts, you must apply the same types of measurements to your practice growth efforts. This sends a strong message to your employees that leadership is committed to sales and marketing. When they see the same metrics being applied to business development that is applied to practice management, they quickly realize that it is a priority just like billing and productivity.

GETTING STARTED

Patterson advises marketers to consider three metrics as a starting point for tracking performance. "Once companies are aware of their competitive position, their desired outcome, and what will take to achieve those outcomes, companies will be better able to identify the success factors, benchmarks, and appropriate metrics to meet their target."[1]

Let's take a closer look at steps your firm can take in adding better metrics as you are getting started.

Gain Agreement on What's Important to Track

Whatever the life cycle of the firm, partners and marketers must agree on what the firm's primary metrics for success should be. Too often, marketers make assumptions about what's most important to track for the short- and long-term. Marketing staffs must begin with the end in mind in all marketing endeavors. In most cases, this requires a strong marketing plan that identifies the key measures and metrics of success.

Here are some traditional favorites: client satisfaction, retention rates, sales, win rates, budget-to-actual spending, services provided per client, loss rate, brand awareness, referrals, leads, lead generation by source, proposals, and losses. Each year, marketers and partners should identify new or additional metrics that should become firm priorities. By doing so, the partnership will be provided all of the data required to make good practice growth decisions in coming years.

> **♀ Key Concept**
>
> Whatever the life cycle of the firm, partners and marketers must agree on what the firm's primary metrics for success should be.

Proper Alignment Is Critical

Practice growth and marketing professionals find the greatest degrees of success in developing strong metrics by first understanding what is most important to their firms. Too often, marketing professionals and partners are not

---

[1] *Laura Patterson, 'Classic Truths': If You Don't Measure, You Can't Manage: The Best Metrics for Managing Marketing Performance, (Marketing Profs LLC, October 23, 2007. The Marketing Profs "Classic Truths" article was first published on November 23, 2004), www.marketingprofs.com.*

aligned on what practice growth investments should accomplish. This stems from two common challenges: the role and job focus of the marketers and the state of the sales culture in an organization.

Marketers tend to have an ROI paradigm defined in most part by personal skill sets, interests, and capabilities. Partners, on the other hand, focus on metrics that relate to the firm's short-term priorities. Instead, both should be assessing the current marketing and sales culture of the organization to determine the metrics that are most appropriate.

> **Key Concept**
>
> Too often, marketing professionals and partners are not aligned on what practice growth investments should accomplish.

Follow the Money

Understand where you spend money and what the return on investment is for significant marketing expenditures your firm makes. Yes, that's easier said than done. Establish clear goals before the projects are underway. ROI is what partners and marketers should be talking about before an initiative is undertaken and at appropriate periods following execution of any strategic marketing expenditure. For example, make sure ROI is measured on direct mail and telesales efforts 3, 6, and 12 months after a program is concluded.

> **Key Concept**
>
> Understand where you spend money and what the return on investment is for significant marketing expenditures your firm makes.

One Size Doesn't Fit All

Firms of different sizes and life cycles also require different metrics of success. It's natural for smaller and 'younger' firms to focus on basic metrics instead of dedicating themselves to investing time and resources to capture complicated metrics. In general, the sophistication of the marketing department will also have an impact on the scope of detail of the marketing plans as well. As firms develop a greater level of complexity in their marketing plans, the scope of the metrics used should also grow in complexity.

Convert All Reports Into Numeric Outcomes

Marketers should make certain that there is as much focus on quantitative data as qualitative data in the reports shared with partners. The "numbers" are meaningful to everyone and are trusted more than generic rhetoric.

For example, 137 clients responded to the direct mail campaign to attend an open house, while 43 prospects and 67 referral sources attended the open house. In the first 6 months following the event, revenues were up 13 percent from client attendees against the same period during the prior year and referrals jump 52 percent from referral sources who attended the event. Six prospects who attended became clients with engagement contract values of $167,500 in first-year revenue.

Just Enough Is Just the Right Amount of Information to Provide

Service professionals are overwhelmed with information—the wrong information and oftentimes too much information. Thus, marketers must ensure that reports on practice growth and marketing metrics are concise and relevant to the leadership of firms. Marketing and business development reports should be customized to key audiences; such as, the board of directors, partners, service line/niche leaders, and firm-wide audiences. Marketers must determine what and how the people receiving reports want to receive appropriate updates. Leaders in firms should feel comfortable requesting marketing and business development updates on-demand, weekly, monthly, quarterly, and annually—as long as marketers have agreed upon the reporting approach.

LEVERAGE TECHNOLOGY TO CAPTURE METRICS

Marketing departments must integrate key metric capture within the natural workflow of the practice. From project management software to billing systems to common forms used by the firm, data must be captured when events occur and not after the fact.

Additionally, marketing staffs and partners are affected greatly by the technology that is available to capture metrics. From project management software to leveraging customer relationship management software, larger firms will generally have the ability to capture more complex metrics than smaller firms. Optimally, technology should be leveraged whenever possible to limit administrative resources and costs.

Samples of measures and metrics firms and their marketers should leverage include the following:

- *Completed marketing communications projects.* Marketers and partners alike should make certain that the basics are documented in a consistent and comprehensive manner. In most cases, that means simply capturing a review of the projects that marketing and practice growth departments are completing. Oftentimes, firms are unfamiliar with the scope of activities that marketing staffs involve themselves. A detailed report should be provided to the appropriate firm leaders periodically to outline the number and scope of completed work.

  Examples include the following: 1566 postcards on tax minimization to Boston market; FASB Interpretation No. 48 notification letters to 613 clients; and International Financial Reporting Standards media release to 53 media outlets with 6 stories printed.

- *Web and e-marketing statistics.* Clients, prospects, and referral sources now look to Web sites as a primary venue for collecting information on accounting firms. Each year, the sophistication of Web sites continues to evolve. Technology enhancements attract and keep visitors engaged in the sites. These technological improvements also affect a firm's ability to capture metrics on Web and e-marketing investments. Given the fact that Web sites are so important to our clients, prospects, and referral sources, it is critical to integrate Web and e-marketing tactics and strategies into all marketing strategies and campaigns.

  Examples include the following: counts of visitors to the site; repeat visitors to the site; penetration of each visit; average pages visited; length of site visits; data by page or section of the site; requested information from the site (such as white papers or other thought leadership data); blog and Twitter registrations; commerce data; survey responses and the data; path to access the site; and Google or search engine response data.

- *Public relations and thought leadership.* Brands are built off the reputations of talented and skillful leaders in professional service firms who provide thought leadership in their area of specialization or niche. However, measuring this area is often difficult or costly. See chapter 16, "Getting Your Name in Lights With Public Relations" for more information on Public Relations.

  Examples include the following: coverage data; column inches of coverage; number of people in audience at speaking events; comparative advertising value of media coverage; requests for additional information; and leads generated by media.

- *Brand awareness.* As a firm's leaders become better known, their personal brands begin to be reflected as the firm's brand. At a critical tipping point, larger professional service firms begin to focus on how to build the firm's brand through marketing communication and thought leadership initiatives. At this point in time, these firms begin to account for the brand's equity and value in the marketplace. For more information on branding see chapter 15, "Successfully Branding Your Firm."

  Examples include the following: aided and nonaided brand recognition research; brand equity valuations; and brand quality (qualitative impressions of the brand).

- *Referrals into and out of the firm.* Firms live and die by the maintenance of referral relationships with the legal and banking community. While firms like to believe these referral relationships are "owned" by the firm, these relationships are acquired, nurtured and harvested by key leaders in the organization. Measures and metrics of referrals into and out of the firm need to capture all of their efforts. To document referrals effectively, leaders must understand and hold themselves accountable to recording referrals in an agreed-upon system. Optimally, a contact relationship management (CRM) system can be leveraged to build a solid historical reference for the impact of these relationships. Reports should be provided to firm leaders on a monthly basis at a minimum to better determine how to nurture them effectively. For more information about referral relationships, see chapter 24, "Referral Source Development: The Most Powerful, but Under Utilized Business Development Tactic."

Examples include the following: referrals into the firm by organization and by individual; referrals out by office, service line and individual; referral conversion and close ratios; and referral balance between organizations.

- *Leads from all sources.* Of course, referrals from bankers, attorneys, clients, and friends of the firm are only one category of leads. Leads from all sources should be tracked for all new business opportunities. Optimally, firms should require that all client facing associates understand how and where to capture and track this information. From the front desk to partners interacting directly with prospects, associates need to be trained to ask prospects where they first learned about the firm or why they made contact with the firm. Firm marketing departments have historically focused on tracking leads generated from a variety of sources. In most organizations, lead generation is a core responsibility of the marketing department. Firms must make certain that leads are being tracked from all investments being made by the department. While this is not always easy to capture, it is critical to ensuring that future investments continue to be made in the right tactical areas.

  Examples include the following: leads by source (phone, direct mail, seminars, banker referral, social media campaign); lead close ratios; lead volume; time to convert to sale by lead source; subscribers to newsletters; and requests for additional information.

- *Budget-to-actual spending.* Marketers should always 'follow the money' and understand how spending compares to actual investments budgeted. It is critical to be able to provide explanations of variances in either direction (of being over or under any line item). CPAs are comfortable and confident in talking about budgets. Marketers need to match this level of enthusiasm for numbers and spend more time monitoring budgets and preparing documentation to analyze spending patterns and trends. The ability to demonstrate how and why investments have been made are powerful to maintaining the firm's ongoing support to invest in practice growth. For more information on budgeting, see chapter 8, "Budgeting Techniques for Today's CPA Firm."

  Examples include the following: budget to actual by dollars and percent variance to budget by line item are the most common budget tracking and reporting approaches.

- *Sales pipeline and proposals.* Firms are comfortable responding to requests to prepare proposals and to present them to demonstrate their technical superiority as compared to competitors. However, too often, firms only look at the win or loss rate on proposals. Most fail to analyze how their pursuit teams are performing in this stage of the sales process. Some firms have begun to invest in surveys of won and lost opportunities to better understand how to compete more effectively in the proposal process. These research efforts can be powerful in helping to identify how to improve proposals and presentations to increase win rates. Ultimately, firms need to measure all stages of the sales process to manage an effective pipeline process in the organization. Just as a tax or audit has a method to follow for successful execution, the sales pipeline is a documentation source for monitoring and executing a successful sales process. For more information on proposals, see chapter 28, "Creating Proposals That Win."

  Examples include the following: volume and value of opportunities at all stages of the sales process; volume of proposals; dollar value of proposals; average proposal values by service line, niche, sales team or service team/individual; value and percentage of open or pending proposals; proposal win and loss ratio; and surveys that report on how successful the firm is in presenting data in the proposal.

- *Win and loss data.* It seems obvious that wins and losses need to be tracked. Often, a firm will leverage the time and billing system to track sales growth of existing clients as well as new clients in the system. However, marketing and sales teams need to ensure that CRM systems are also capturing data from the entire sales process. Sales results are critical to individuals, service lines, niche groups and offices or profit centers. Firms should develop systems that allow them to capture and synthesize this data through the use of business intelligence software and CRM tools. As important as tracking the win is, it is similarly important to track losses of both clients and new prospects. Firms must collect data to understand why they win and lose business. These metrics can help shape practice growth and pursuit strategies as well as the future investments related to them.

  Examples include the following: win and loss volume; win and loss rate; percentage of sales goals to budget; billing increases to prior year; sales by individual, service line, campaign, niche or profit center; and sales cycle time from lead identification to close.

- *Share of client.* As firms continue to diversify their practices, offering a variety of consulting and financial services, measuring the organization's ability to capture more "share of wallet" is critical. Most firms want to sell more to existing clients in a dual effort to drive additional revenue and make it more difficult for the client to end the relationship with the firm. As firms sell more services to a client, it becomes easier to retain the client if an unplanned or unexpected event challenges the vendor-client relationship. For more information, see chapter 30, "Cross-Serving Clients: Integrating Sales and Service Delivery."

Examples include the following: services delivered per client; rate of additional sales; revenue retention statistics; annual revenue growth by client; and profitability by client and service line.

- *Client satisfaction.* Clients who are totally satisfied are more likely to be loyal to the firm, purchase more services and refer business. Thus, the most powerful metric for firms to measure on an ongoing basis is client satisfaction. A variety of methods can be used to monitor satisfaction from individual interviews to formal survey systems. For more information about tools to measure client satisfaction, see chapter 35, "Gaining Client Feedback to Strengthen Your Practice."

Examples include the following: overall satisfaction; satisfaction with partner, team and firm; satisfaction in areas of responsiveness, quality of deliverable, proactive effort, communication and fees; likelihood to retain; and likelihood to refer.

> ### 🔑 Key Concept
>
> Marketing departments must integrate key metric capture within the natural workflow of the practice.

Add New Metrics Over Time

Each year, marketers and partners should identify new or additional metrics that should become firm priorities. Use your updated marketing plans to help you identify new metrics. By doing so, the partnership will be provided all of the data required to make good practice growth investments in coming years.

Communicate Results

Now that you have gathered these results, it's important to communicate them to your employees on a regular basis. It helps professionals to understand how the firm is progressing in achieving its growth goals. Use a variety of communications to share the results. For example, share the results in meetings such as pipeline meetings, niche meetings, or management meetings, and add them to your internal marketing e-newsletters and internal blogs. For more information about internal communications, see chapter 32, "In-House Marketing Communications That Foster Success."

> ### 🔑 Key Concept
>
> Each year, marketers and partners should identify new or additional metrics that should become firm priorities.

Conclusion

If you expect marketing and business development to become a part of your firm's landscape, you must measure it just like other key indicators such as billing and productivity. These measurements allow you to gauge the effectiveness of your marketing and sales programs. Over time as these results can provide valuable information about which marketing programs are most effective and which ones need some reshaping in the future.

ABOUT THE AUTHOR

Mitchell Reno is a principal at Rehmann, a Midwest-based CPA, consulting and financial advisory firm. He was the Association for Accounting Marketing's 2006 Accounting Marketer of the Year and his firm has been recognized with more than a dozen national awards for accounting marketing excellence. Mitch has presented nationally on a variety of marketing topics. You can contact Mitch at mitch.reno@rehmann.com.

See "About the Editor" for more information on **Tracy Crevar Warren**.

PART VII:

Delivering and Measuring Client Service

CHAPTER 35
Gaining Client Feedback to Strengthen Your Practice

Linda Slothower
Contryman Associates, P.C.

Julie S. Tucek
Legacy Professionals, LLP

INTRODUCTION

How do you know when a client is unhappy with you or your firm? Unless you ask for feedback from your clients, you may never know. Many clients will simply find another provider and you may never learn the real reason they left. Most importantly you will never have an opportunity to correct the problem for other clients who may be experiencing a similar problem.

Fortunately, in addition to identifying problem areas for your firm, client satisfaction research may also help you learn your areas of strength and why your clients recognize them as valuable. Client satisfaction research, in the form of surveys, focus groups, and one-on-one interviews, can help you discover the thoughts, attitudes, and perceptions of your clients. Results can even be incorporated into performance evaluations, proposals and other marketing materials, or used to identify cross-selling opportunities.

When administered properly, the results may be used to set marketing and client service goals for the firm, as well as to establish valid benchmarks against which future performance can be measured. Client satisfaction research can also help firms identify new service opportunities and highlight superior firm qualities and attributes. From there, you will be able to develop marketing and communications programs that tell the story of your firm's strengths in ways your clients will find to be believable and that will build the perception of value for the services you provide.

In this chapter you will learn about the benefits of client satisfaction programs, different types of programs, some advantages and disadvantages of each type of program, and you will also see samples from CPA firms around the country who have successfully implemented client satisfaction programs.

GETTING STARTED

Before You Begin, Commit to Acting on Survey Results

The most prevalent reason people give for not responding to a survey is that they believe nothing will change, no matter how they respond on the survey. So, it is most important to be prepared to act on the responses received even when the information does not agree with your perceptions. Survey results can be extremely powerful, sometimes devastatingly so. In fact, it is important that partners understand they might not always like the responses generated by the survey but they must be prepared, nevertheless, to act on those responses.

A failure to follow through with assurances that client comments and suggestions will be acted on could have a more negative effect on the firm's image than never asking for input in the first place. In many cases, acknowledging the fact there are problems and making a public commitment toward resolving them will be well-received.

To overcome this, include in your plan a system for communicating. After responses are received, address how you plan to correct the problems and how you will handle suggestions and complaints. If surveys are submitted anonymously, consider using client newsletters, Web sites, and other mass communication vehicles to tell clients how you plan to move forward. For surveys that are signed, or are conducted face-to-face, communicate with respondents directly and personally. By doing this, client satisfaction research can be a powerful tool in enhancing your relationship with your clients.

> **♀ Key Concept**
>
> It is most important to be prepared to act on the survey responses received even when the information does not agree with your perceptions.

Develop Research Goals and Objectives

To realize all of the benefits of client satisfaction surveys, begin by developing goals and objectives for the research project. Possible goals may include the following:

- To obtain a better understanding of our clients' expectations of our firm, our people, products, and services.
- To determine our clients' level of satisfaction with our firm, our people, products, and services.
- To learn about our clients' perceptions of quality in the services they have utilized.
- To acquire information that can be used in shaping new products and services.
- To foster goodwill among our clients toward our firm by demonstrating our interest in their opinions about the quality of service we deliver.
- To learn about our client's willingness to provide potential new client referrals.

Broadcast Goals and Intentions—Both Internally and Externally

Once established, the firm's survey goals and objectives should be disseminated throughout the firm. This is particularly important when you plan to use the results in partner or staff performance reviews.

Clients and other groups with a stake in the survey and its results should also be notified. This is particularly true in the case of those who might later be asked to participate in the survey. An effective letter or client newsletter article can help stimulate interest in the process and help you achieve a higher rate of response. Exhibit 35-1 shows a sample letter that can be sent in advance of the actual survey.

Primary Types of Research

There are two broad types of client satisfaction research methods, those involving direct contact and those implemented through indirect means. In-person (direct contact) research includes advisory boards, other focus groups and one-on-one interviews. Indirect includes printed and mailed surveys or comment cards and electronic surveys that are distributed via e-mail or posted on a firm's Web site.

Although there are elements common to all of these research methods, there are certain advantages and limitations inherent in each type. A comparison of these "pros" and "cons" can be found in exhibit 35-2. For our purposes in this chapter, we will refer to all methods of client satisfaction research collectively as "surveys."

Exhibit 35-1
Sample Letter Sent Prior to Sending a Written Survey

[Date]

[Name]
[Address]

Dear [First name]:

During [months], we will be conducting a client satisfaction survey and asking our clients to share their views with us. We are writing to inform you that you will be asked to participate, and to express our hopes you will agree to do so.

The purpose of the survey is to obtain your opinions regarding the quality of service you have been receiving from [firm name], and to learn how well we are meeting your expectations. The survey will only require a few minutes to complete, but will provide us with valuable information needed to ensure that the services we provide you and other clients are of the highest quality.

Once the results of the survey have been tabulated and analyzed, we will prepare a detailed plan of action to address and improve any problem areas that have been identified, and to develop new service areas that are needed by our clients.

(Optional) In order to ensure respondent confidentiality, we have retained an outside firm to receive and compile the survey's results. Consequently, the self-addressed, stamped envelope that will accompany our written survey will be addressed to [name of firm].

We want to thank you in advance for your time and participation. You are a valuable client and we appreciate your help and your advice.

Sincerely,

[Partner in Charge]

Exhibit 35-2
Comparison of Benefits of Client Research Tools

	Pros	Cons
Mailed Surveys	• Gather information from a statistically large number of respondents • Available for response at any time • Can be anonymous so respondents may be more open with their responses	• Relatively expensive to design, administer, and tabulate • Limited number of open-ended questions • No opportunity to ask for clarification or read nonverbal cues • Proliferation of written surveys may make people less apt to respond • Most influential clients may not take time to respond • Perception that response may not change a perceived problem • No personal contact • May be submitted anonymously so you have no way to follow up on individual concerns or requests
Online and E-mail Surveys	• Gather information from a statistically large number of respondents • Least expensive to distribute • Can be anonymous so respondents may be more open with their responses • Available at any time for responses • Very low cost investment • Can personalize via e-mail to each respondent • Can follow up immediately • Tabulation of results is immediate because of the tools available	• No opportunity to ask for clarification or read nonverbal cues • Limited number of open-ended questions • Proliferation of online surveys may make people less apt to respond • Most influential clients may not take time to respond • Perception that response may not change a perceived problem • No personal contact • May be submitted anonymously so you have no way to follow up on individual concerns or requests

EXHIBIT 35-2
COMPARISON OF BENEFITS OF CLIENT RESEARCH TOOLS *(CONTINUED)*

	Pros	Cons
Focus Groups	• Learn responses of selected/best clients, referral sources • Able to probe for more information and read non-verbal cues • Most influential clients may be more apt to participate because of personal contact and feeling of honor • If positioned correctly and handled well, can lead to improved relationship with client • Provides opportunity to follow up with individuals who have expressed specific concerns	• Statistically smaller group so answers may not be representative of all clients • One or two members may sway perceptions of others, positively or negatively • Specific time frame—participants cannot answer questions at any convenient time; they must attend at the set time • Provides little anonymity
One-on-one Interviews	• Learn responses of selected/best clients, referral sources • Able to probe for more information and read non-verbal cues • No other participants to influence responses • Most influential clients may be more apt to participate because of personal contact and feeling of honor • If positioned correctly and handled well, can lead to improved relationship with client • If handled correctly, could uncover additional services the client needs from your firm • Provides opportunity to follow up with individuals who have expressed specific concerns	• Statistically smaller group so answers may not be representative of all clients • Specific time frame—participants meets with you at set time (could be seen as positive or negative) • Time consuming to set meetings with many clients • Provides no anonymity

DESIGNING SURVEY AND INTERVIEW QUESTIONS

Determining which topics and issues to cover in a survey is a lot like going to an all-you-can-eat buffet. A little of absolutely everything is nice but if you really indulge yourself, you won't have a clear memory of anything you ate.

To get started, you may want to gather a team to develop the survey. Include a cross-section of people from your firm in this process including your managing partner.

The first step for the team is brainstorming. Have your work group write down topics and issues related to the goals of your firm. Then prioritize the list. Try to limit yourself to no more than a dozen key issues. Listed below are some sample items to consider.

- Overall quality of service
- Promptness in delivering the service
- Accessibility and responsiveness of partners and staff
- A demonstrated interest in the client's business, and in solving the client's problems
- Industry expertise
- Value of services
- Effective communications about any delays
- Aggressive attitude in providing recommendations and finding solutions to problems
- Competence and friendliness of all relevant firm personnel
- Suggestions for improving service
- Referrals
- Firm image
- Awareness of other firms' services
- General remarks

Design questions so they are clear and unbiased. Questions for interviews and focus groups should be open-ended to enhance dialogue. A sample survey with cover letter is presented in appendix 35-1.

If no one in your firm has experience in writing surveys and managing the data collection and reporting process, you may want to consider the services of a consultant with proven expertise in the field to help you develop your survey questions or to manage the entire survey process.

DECIDING WHO TO SURVEY

Who should be surveyed? Much will depend on your research objectives. A general opinion survey could be distributed to a majority of the firm's clients, whereas service- or industry-specific research could be directed just to those meeting specific criteria. This can include industry or profession, fee range, service utilization, partner responsibility, or "A" client versus "B" client list.

While surveying all clients would give you the most accurate picture, this is not always a realistic option because of the cost involved. A random sampling of 25 percent to 50 percent of the client group should allow for a statistically accurate sample. Just like an audit, you must balance the investment with the desire to obtain technically reliable actionable data.

ESTABLISHING A BUDGET

Client satisfaction research can be costly. While the method you choose will affect your budget, consider these costs associated with this type of project:

1. Planning meetings to determine the topics/issues to be addressed and which clients will be surveyed.

2. Professional time to write the survey instrument and interview/focus group questions.

3. Data processing time to design a database for tabulating responses.

4. Tabulation of responses, data entry, and processing.

5. Preparation and presentation of a written report.

6. Time to write and postage to send thank you notes, if participants are identified.

7. Use of outside consultant to conduct survey, if needed.

8. Costs associated with survey tools like Zoomerang or Survey Monkey. Note: if using such tools, many of these listed costs, such as tabulation, data entry, and reporting, are not a factor because of the sophistication of the online tools.

Additionally, for mailed surveys you will have the expense of printing charges to produce the survey and cover letter along with outgoing and incoming envelopes and postage. E-mailed surveys will require that you collect or update the e-mail addresses of all clients involved and then set up an e-mail "group" for distributing the survey along with any reminders or follow up communication. Depending on the sophistication of your firm's database, much of this legwork may already be done.

One way to learn whether written survey questions will work is to test them in advance with a very small group of clients. While this process will add more time to the research process, the effort will certainly be worthwhile. It is only after you have reviewed the sample responses and attempted to tabulate them that you will learn whether or not your clients understood your questions. You could avoid the frustration of mailing out 500 surveys and tabulating the results, only to discover that 90 percent of the respondents misinterpreted some of your most important questions.

For focus groups or one-on-one interviews, you will incur costs for printing and mailing letters to invite participation. The partner or firm contact must also take time to call or make a personal visit to the key clients invited. Compensation or gifts for interview or focus group participants could add to your budget as well as rental of a site for meetings, audio or video equipment for recording sessions, and catering of meals and refreshments for focus groups.

WRITTEN SURVEYS

Because written surveys enable you to gather information from a large number of respondents, they may offer the highest degree of statistically reliable data. Surveys can be completed at any convenient time within the survey period. And the survey instrument can be designed to provide anonymity so that respondents may answer more candidly.

While offering some advantages, there are challenges to surveying clients, especially for traditional mailed or electronic surveys. At one time a firm that surveyed clients was unique. Today, with improved data management capabilities, many organizations including CPA firms routinely distribute surveys to their clients. Mailed surveys can be relatively expensive to design, administer, and most notably, to tabulate. Many firms elect to keep the number of open-ended questions to a minimum, which can limit responses. Additionally, because you have no direct communication built in, you will be unable to ask for clarification on an issue or read nonverbal cues with any written survey.

Another very real problem with written surveys is that the people who have and take the time to reply may not be your best clients—the clients whose opinions you would value most. Would you expect the CEO or CFO of a large corporation to fill out a survey and return it to you?

An alternative to mailing surveys is to e-mail surveys to clients or to post the survey on your firm's Web site. Online surveys can provide your clients a forum for voicing their opinions at any time providing an opportunity for ongoing feedback. Of course you will have to establish a system for ongoing collection and response, and revise your reporting methods. You will also have to publicize the availability of the online survey and frequently encourage clients to complete the survey. You may wish to offer clients the option of replying to your survey in the format of their choice, online, by e-mail, or by U.S. mail when you send them a printed survey.

Some firms send the survey to clients upon completion of the engagement, so the process is ongoing. This allows for one-on-one follow up once they respond. But, more importantly, it allows the client to give immediate feedback when the impression is still fresh.

With new tools such as Survey Monkey and Zoomerang, the online survey program has gotten a lot easier to manage. Feedback is immediate and with the increased use of e-mail, your response time can also be immediate. The costs associated with such tools are minimal compared to the cost of the hard-copy survey. Many firms are using a combination of e-mail and mailed methods to allow the client to respond in his or her preferred format. Even if you collect written surveys, they can quickly be entered into the online survey such that the results are integrated and again, nearly immediate. Both Survey Monkey and Zoomerang have a powerful tabulation program built into the survey program, allowing you to forward results to others and slice and dice the results in many different ways. This is a big change from the old days of surveying clients.

EXHIBIT 35-3
SAMPLE RESEARCH TIMETABLE: WRITTEN SURVEYS

Week	Activity
1	Establish survey goals, parameters, and budget.
2 – 3	Develop rough draft of the survey instrument. Determine participants and target sample size. Obtain partner review. Pretest the survey. Compose cover letter.
3	Begin developing mailing list/database of clients to be surveyed. Prepare mailing: Handle printing of survey, postcard, etc. Order self-addressed or business reply envelopes.
5 – 6	Produce individualized cover letters. Have them signed, and complete the mailing.
7 – 10	Gather surveys; compile and tabulate data. Send reminder postcards or e-mails to those who have not completed the survey. Send thank you letters or thank clients via firm newsletter.
11 – 13	Prepare a report of survey findings.
13	Present the research findings and facilitate a partner action planning workshop.
14	Determine action steps to be taken to improve client satisfaction.
15	Present research findings and action steps to all employees.

The sample research timetable in exhibit 35-3 will help guide you when you begin the written survey process.

How long should the written or e-mail survey be? If your survey is longer than two pages, you can expect the rate of response to drop off sharply. It is best to make your questions very concise to keep the overall length of the survey to an absolute minimum.

 Key Concept

Because written surveys enable you to gather information from a large number of respondents, they may offer the highest degree of statistically reliable data.

Improving Response Rate

Response rates will vary. Consider the following recommendations to improve your rate of return for a written survey:

- When mailing the survey, include a *personalized* cover letter from the client's partner or principal contact, along with a postage paid return envelope. This letter should have an original signature if at all possible. Digital signatures don't carry the same clout as personal ones.
- Thank clients for their business in the letter.
- Always use first class mail.
- Indicate a return date in the letter and on the survey.
- Mail reminder postcards or e-mails approximately seven days following the survey distribution. See exhibit 35-4 for example.
- Include an assurance of confidentiality, that as an accounting firm, you will not share a client's responses or personal information with any person or organization outside your firm.
- Send thank you letters immediately. If the survey is anonymous, publish an article in a client newsletter or on your website soon after the completion of the survey process. See exhibit 35-5 for a sample article. (This last suggestion won't increase your response rate this time around, but may help when you repeat the survey.)

EXHIBIT 35-4
SAMPLE REMINDER COMMUNICATION

**HAVE YOU COMPLETED [NAME OF FIRM]'S
CLIENT SATISFACTION SURVEY?**

Recently, you received a client satisfaction survey from our firm. Your comments are important to us, as they will help us to determine how we can improve our services to you.

If you haven't already done so, please take a few minutes to complete the questionnaire and return it to us [or the outside firm address]. If you need another copy, call us and we will mail or e-mail another one to you or [if applicable] it is also available online at [firm's Web site].

Thank you for your time and input!

EXHIBIT 35-5
SAMPLE NEWSLETTER ARTICLE

THANK YOU CLIENTS!

Over the last couple of months, many clients were called upon to give us their input on the level of satisfaction with our services and to offer us their advice on improving the products and services offered by [name of firm].

Because of your insight, we have made many changes and improvements throughout the firm. Some of hese include

> [List two to four changes or improvements being made that were most requested and/or will affect the most clients.]

We are so pleased to report that [give example of positive statistics uncovered in the survey. Example: 98 percent of our clients who responded said they feel satisfied or very satisfied with the value of service we provide to them.]

Again, thank you for your input. If you have additional comments or recommendations on the quality of service or the services offered by [name of firm], please feel free to call me personally at [telephone number].

[Signature and name of partner-in-charge or managing partner]

Ideas to increase response rates for an online survey:

- Double check electronic survey links to ensure they work
- Personalize the e-mail
- Thank the client for their business in the e-mail
- Indicate a deadline in the e-mail
- Send thank you e-mails as soon as the client responds
- Comment on the client's feedback in the response

Anonymity?

There are advantages and disadvantages to an anonymous survey. One advantage is that respondents *might* offer a more honest and open assessment of the firm's performance. A key disadvantage is that respondents who have a specific complaint might feel frustrated because they will not be assured of having their concern addressed. The biggest advantage to not making the survey anonymous is that you can respond immediately to the client if you know who he or she is. Some firms choose to allow respondents the option of identifying themselves if they want to be contacted about a particular issue.

Electronic surveys can be designed so respondents can remain anonymous, or have the option to reveal their identity.

If you want to allow respondents to remain anonymous in written surveys, but wish to track responses by some other criteria, for instance by partner or manager, you can use a different color paper for the surveys sent to each manager's clients or use another more sophisticated tracking system such as numbering. This allows the respondent to remain anonymous while allowing you to track responses for an individual's clients or for a particular type of client vs. another type.

Focus Groups

A formal focus group study is an ideal method for gathering qualitative information from a relatively small group of individuals—usually 8–12. This approach offers 2 significant advantages. First, it allows the facilitator to be face-to-face with the respondents. The facilitator can therefore probe for more detail on specific issues and make note of relevant nonverbal cues. Obviously, these benefits cannot be realized in a written survey.

Like interviews, a clear disadvantage of the focus group approach is that the sample size is relatively small. It is not always safe to assume the opinions gathered from the focus group represent the views of the entire client base. You might consider using a focus group or interviews in conjunction with written surveys. For example, by meeting with a focus group first, you can develop an agenda of areas of concern that can be explored more fully in a written survey. Or, conduct the written survey first, and then use focus groups or one-on-one interviews to get more detailed information about issues identified through the written survey.

Focus Group Selection

How are participants selected and how do you get them to participate? As with other client satisfaction research methods, much will depend on your research objective. If your goal is to determine overall client satisfaction, then it is best to include a good cross-section of your client base. If, on the other hand, you want to learn more about perceptions of a particular practice group, say the audit practice, you might instead select the firm's top audit clients in terms of billings.

You might want to develop an advisory board—a focus group that consists of some of your best clients and referral sources. Members of this group are selected because their opinions are most highly regarded. As an ongoing focus group, the same people may meet periodically or some members may change, but the group would always consist of some of your most influential and valuable clients and referral sources—people whose success in running their own businesses you admire. The term *advisory board* has a connotation of higher level input and clients may feel honored to be invited to join.

The firm's partners can help identify which of their clients may be interested in participating in an advisory board, other focus groups, or in one-on-one interviews. They can also identify which would be most candid and forthright, without monopolizing the conversation in a focus group session. Though an initial letter of invitation may be used (see exhibit 35-6 for a sample letter) partners should always initiate contact with, and then act as liaison to the clients who are involved in the focus group process.

Often focus group and interview participants are compensated for their time, though a small, thoughtful gift may be a sufficient reward. The amount of compensation or value of gift may be limited by rules set by the Board of Public Accountancy in some states.

Focus Group Facilitation

Who should facilitate your focus group? Focus groups are only as good as their facilitators. Marketing directors with experience working with focus groups may be able to facilitate your research. However, a trained outside facilitator with no vested interest in the outcome of the study may be a better choice. These outside facilitators are less likely to inject a bias into the final report. A good facilitator will also assure that everyone in the room has equal time to offer opinions, and can move the group promptly from one topic to the next, so that all pertinent issues are covered in the time allowed.

Avoid using a partner or manager in the firm as a facilitator, unless he or she comes from another office and has had little or no prior contact with the focus group participants. Respondents will be far more likely to air their grievances if they feel their remarks are not directed to someone in the room with them at the time.

EXHIBIT 35-6
SAMPLE INVITATION TO JOIN FOCUS GROUP

[Date]

[Name]

[Address]

Dear [First name]:

We want to ask for your input and advice. We value your business experience and respect the day-to-day problems you face. By inviting you to share your experience with us, we hope to learn ways that we can serve you even better in the future.

[First name], I'm writing to invite you to join in a focus group [or advisory board] for our firm, which will help us identify the things that are important to you. It means we'll be able to find out what you really need and value from your accounting firm.

This focus group will offer you a chance to tell us what we have to do to become a better firm for you and our other clients. You'll have an opportunity to give us the feedback we need to continue to provide you the service you want and deserve.

We've invited only a small, select group of clients. I'll be giving you a call in a few days to find out if you are willing and available to participate. We can discuss the details and talk about any questions you may have at that time.

We have asked [Name of facilitator and his/her position or description of his/her expertise] to run the meeting for us. As the facilitator(s), he/she/they will ensure that the meeting is impartial and objective and will collect all your feedback, good and bad.

The date we are planning to host the focus group is [date] from [times]. Please take a look to see if this date works for you.

I look forward to talking with you soon and to hearing your feedback and advice.

All the best,

[Client/Referral Source Contact in Firm]

Interviews may be conducted by a marketing director, by a well-informed consultant, or by a partner or manager who, again, has had little previous contact with the client to be interviewed. A recently retired, well-respected partner may also be an option.

☘ Key Concept

Focus groups are only as good as their facilitators.

Conducting a Focus Group

It is recommended that focus group sessions and interviews be conducted off-site. There are several advantages to this approach. First, the discussion will be held on neutral territory, thus enabling participants to be more objective, and at the same time more forthcoming in expressing their opinions. Second, interruptions and distractions can be minimized.

Ideally, focus group discussions should not last more than 90 minutes, with 2 hours as a maximum. After about 90 minutes the chances for participant burnout increase exponentially and their responses may become increasingly negative. Regardless of the length of the session, always provide beverages and snacks.

Summarizing the Focus Group Responses

In a focus group situation, it is far more difficult to ensure the participants' anonymity. Because the survey population is so small, a shrewd reader may be able to link specific remarks to their source. However, the focus group facilitator can be asked to compile a report without attributing remarks to any particular individual. And, as with written surveys, you should follow through with whatever procedure you told the focus group participants you would employ. Again, always follow up with a thank you letter that expresses your appreciation for the participant's involvement, and promises to report findings as soon as they have been tabulated and analyzed.

Focus group questions are similar to those used in one-on-one interviews, a sample of which can be found in appendix 35-2.

Recording the respondents' remarks is a critical component in the success of the process. Facilitators must be able to focus all of their energies on doing just that—facilitating and probing for more details when circumstances warrant it. If they must instead concentrate on taking notes, they will not be able to do a good job of obtaining important information for you.

To successfully accomplish this, some firms elect to use an electronic recording device. When you record focus group sessions, always offer to "go off the record" and turn off the recording device if someone wants to make a comment for which anonymity is imperative. An alternative would be for the facilitator to be teamed with an additional person who would serve as a note-taker and additional observer. This may be a good system whether or not you record the session.

ONE-ON-ONE SURVEYS

One-on-one interviews are the most personal type of surveys. Unlike the focus group setting, the individual will not be influenced by the comments shared by other participants. Interviews are limited by the number of people that you can realistically meet with in person. Phone interviews can increase the number of clients you reach but diminish some of the main advantages of face-to-face meetings.

Selection of Participants and Interviewer

Client selection for one-on-one surveys is similar to selecting focus group participants. There are many options for who will interview the selected clients.

To ensure that your client will be forthcoming about positive as well as the negative aspects of their experience with your firm, it is best for the client's service provider not be the interviewer. Options might be a partner who doesn't work with the client or a marketing professional from your firm, who is also without a significant relationship with the client. Some firms team up the managing partner and the marketing director for this process. Another consideration is a recently retired professional in your firm. An outside consultant may be an option for these interviews, but it may be difficult to give them enough background on your firm to be as effective as an insider from your firm.

The traits that make a good one-on-one interviewer would, of course, be someone who is a good listener. A good interviewer would also be someone who knows enough about your firm to answer questions but with the good judgment not to be defensive or to argue with the client. The best person to lead these interviews will be able to effectively communicate how much your firm values the client's opinions. The clients who are chosen should be made to feel very special to have such attention paid to him or her.

INTERPRETING SURVEY RESULTS

Data from focus groups will be compiled by the focus group leader (and the note-taker, if applicable) or the interviewer for one-on-one surveys to get an accurate recap of what was learned. For written surveys, an administrative assistant may be utilized for tabulating results. For online surveys, the tabulation is no longer an "extra." It is included in the program.

The results will be reflected in a report written to summarize findings soon after the survey is completed so that no details are forgotten. To get an objective summary, you may want to consider using a relative "outsider"—either an outside consultant or someone in your firm who has little or no direct client contact, no hidden agenda nor incentive to misrepresent the findings.

The report should include the following:

- A review of the survey process: the motive for the study, who was involved in developing the topics/issues covered, how the survey group was selected, the percentage of those surveyed who responded (written surveys), and any common characteristics of the survey pool
- A summary of findings
- The raw data, in table form
- Specific remarks written to open-ended questions (written surveys) or a summary of remarks made in focus groups or one-on-one interviews
- Cross-tabulations—tabulating for specific service groups, partners, shareholders, or managers, etc.
- List of participants unless the survey was completely anonymously
- Report on the follow up and next steps

Post-Analysis Activities

As suggested earlier, the way in which a firm publicizes and acts on the findings of its client satisfaction research is as important as conducting the survey.

One urgent aspect to acting on survey results is when a problem was brought up or a specific request was made by a survey respondent. Those issues must be addressed as soon as possible. As was mentioned earlier in this chapter, you must be ready and willing to act on any issues identified in the survey. Almost immediately after the survey has been tabulated, firm management should report the survey's most significant findings to all personnel. While it is important to highlight some of the best news the survey has disclosed, it is also vital to be candid about any negative comments or criticism expressed by respondents. A significant exception would be any criticism directed at an individual. This kind of comment should be addressed in private. Survey results can be released in a report, or better yet, presented at a staff meeting, enabling staff members to ask questions and discuss the implications in general terms.

The firm's partners and managers (or an executive group) should meet to review the survey results in greater depth. At this meeting the group should reach consensus about how they will capitalize on the areas of strength and how they will work to resolve areas of weakness. As was the case in the first round of evaluating the survey results, the group's decisions should be broadcast to firm members as soon as possible.

Once concrete action steps have been agreed upon, it is time to communicate with your clients, or at least with those individuals who participated in the study. Here candor is vital, even if it can sometimes be disagreeable. There is no harm in pointing out how well your firm did in the survey, but it is also important to own up to areas of weakness and then to outline the steps that will be taken to improve them.

Specifically, each client who participated should be thanked and, if at all possible, contacted by the partner on the account. If you surveyed most or all of your clients, the best way to communicate with them in a more general way would be through a letter, or through an article in the firm's client newsletter or on your Web site. If, on the other hand, you utilized focus groups or one-on-one interviews, and targeted a specific area of concern, it may be better to communicate directly, usually in a face-to-face meeting with each of the clients involved.

Key Concept

> Almost immediately after the survey has been tabulated, firm management should report the survey's most significant findings to all personnel. While it is important to highlight some of the best news the survey has disclosed, it is also vital to be candid about any negative comments or criticism expressed by respondents.

Conclusion

There are several items you may want to keep in mind to ensure the success of your research process. Obtain the full commitment of your firm's management team before embarking on this process. The hours and dollars committed can be significant, and everyone involved should have a full understanding of the process and the importance of it.

Always thank clients for participating, and find a way to report the results of the study to them as quickly as possible. Make sure you inform them of any action steps you will be taking as a result of the survey process. If you promise confidentiality to participants, enforce your promise rigorously.

Finally, remember that the research processes described are only as good as what your firm does with the findings.

ABOUT THE AUTHORS

Hired as the firm's first marketing professional, **Linda Slothower** has been Marketing Director for Contryman Associates, P.C. for 11 years. The firm has conducted surveys, one-on-one client interviews, and has found the greatest value in advisory boards, which they have conducted at each of their five main offices across Nebraska for the past 7 years. Linda is a graduate of the University of Nebraska—Kearney. In addition to her marketing duties, she has developed a Web-based accounting career planning process, the Professional Excellence Path, which was released in 2009.

Julie Tucek is the Marketing Director at Legacy Professionals, LLP, a Chicago-based niche CPA firm with 19 partners, 140 professionals, and offices in Munster, IN and Minneapolis, MN. Julie has been with the firm for 12 years. She currently serves as President of the Board of Directors of the Association for Accounting Marketing. Tucek has been named by *Accounting Today* as one of the 100 Most Influential People in the accounting industry. She is also active as a member and on committees at the Union League Club of Chicago and Association Forum of Chicagoland. Prior to joining Legacy, Julie was the Marketing Director at a regional CPA firm in Virginia. Julie is a graduate of Saint Mary's College in South Bend, Indiana.

APPENDIX 35-1 SAMPLE WRITTEN SURVEY AND COVER LETTER

[Date]

[Client Name]

[Company]

[Address]

Dear [name]:

[Firm name] is committed to providing high quality service to our clients. To help us achieve and sustain that goal, we would like to know your views regarding the level and quality of our service.

Please take a few minutes to complete the enclosed client satisfaction survey and let us know how we're doing. Your honest answers will help us identify our strengths as well as those areas that need improvement. Please return your completed survey by [date] in the enclosed self-addressed (stamped) envelope. [or: We have contracted with an independent firm to assist us in this effort, therefore, please return your responses in the enclosed envelope addressed to (name of firm).] [If applicable: You may also complete this survey online at (Web address).]

Thank you in advance for taking time to complete this questionnaire. The satisfaction of our clients is very important to us and we value your opinion.

Sincerely,

[Partner Name]

[Firm Name]

Enclosures

Sample Client Satisfaction Survey

Please answer the following questions to the best of your ability, using the following key:

VS – Very Satisfied
S – Satisfied
SS – Slightly Satisfied
SD – Slightly Dissatisfied
D – Dissatisfied
VD – Very Dissatisfied

How satisfied are you with the firm in the following areas? (Please circle one number for each answer.)

	VS	S	SS	SD	D	VD
Overall quality of service	5	4	3	2	1	0
Responsiveness to your needs	5	4	3	2	1	0

continued

Appendix 35-1 Sample Written Survey and Cover Letter
(continued)

	VS	S	SS	SD	D	VD
Timeliness of work and service	5	4	3	2	1	0
Communicating with you regarding any delays in the work or service	5	4	3	2	1	0
Keeping you informed on new tax legislation, business topics, etc.	5	4	3	2	1	0
Providing recommendations and solutions to your business problems	5	4	3	2	1	0
Understanding of your business	5	4	3	2	1	0
Knowledge of your industry	5	4	3	2	1	0
Competence of firm personnel	5	4	3	2	1	0
Professionalism of firm personnel	5	4	3	2	1	0
Firm personnel making you aware of other areas in which the firm can assist you	5	4	3	2	1	0
Firm personnel are accessible when needed	5	4	3	2	1	0

(optional)

Do you read the firm newsletter?	Yes _____ No_____					
If yes, how satisfied are you with our Firm communications?	5	4	3	2	1	0

What do you like best about working with our firm? _____

What do you like least about working with our firm? _____

Have we ever asked you to recommend us?   Yes _____ No_____

APPENDIX 35-1 SAMPLE WRITTEN SURVEY AND COVER LETTER (CONTINUED)

Would you give us referrals if asked?   Yes _____ No_____

If no, why wouldn't you recommend our firm to others?

_____

_____

_____

_____

Please check the services we currently provide to you:

_____Auditing

_____Tax planning and/or preparation

_____Management advisory services

_____Accounting services or small business services

_____Computer consulting

_____Other _____

_____

_____

Please indicate your annual professional accounting fees:

_____ Less than $500

_____ $501 – $1,000

_____ $1,001 – $2,500

_____ $2,500 – $5,000

_____ Over $5,000

Is there anything else you think the firm should know about how we can improve our service to you?

_____

_____

_____

Please return by [date]

THANK YOU FOR SHARING YOUR THOUGHTS!

APPENDIX 35-2 SAMPLE FOCUS GROUP/INTERVIEW QUESTIONS

Client Profile (complete this information prior to the meeting/interview)

Services provided: _____

Firm client since: _____ Partner-in-charge: _____

Staff member(s) involved: _____

Has there been staff turnover for this client? _____

Payment record (30, 60, 90, 120 days): _____

Other comments: _____

_____

1. What do you expect from your accounting firm?

2. What's the most important factor to you in choosing an accounting firm?

3. Compared to other accounting firms you have dealt with, how satisfied are you with the quality of work and services provided by [firm name]?

4. Why did you choose [firm name], and why do you remain a client?

5. What could [firm name] do to become your ideal accounting firm?

6. What would have to happen for you to break your ties with our firm?

7. Now, more specifically, please offer your recommendations on how [firm name] can improve in the following areas:

   a. Timeliness of service

   b. Responsiveness to your needs, questions, calls

   c. Advice that will help you better run your business

   d. Understanding of your business and industry

   e. Communication regarding project status, opportunities, delays, etc.

   f. Clear explanation of fees

8. What do you expect from our firm personnel who work with you?

9. Is there anyone in particular who has provided exceptional service to you or your company?

10. Please give us your recommendations on how [firm name]'s people could be of better service to you.

11. Have you ever recommended [firm name] to anyone?

12. If you referred business to this firm, what have those clients reported back to you about the firm?

13. If no, would you be comfortable recommending [firm name], should the opportunity arise?

14. Are you aware that [firm name] offers a wide variety of services such as: [list with description/explanation of benefits of each service]

15. Do you have any other recommendations or suggestions for [firm name]?

16. (Optional) How do you feel about the focus group/advisory board process?

CHAPTER 36
Developing a Service Excellence Plan for Clients

Susan Wylie Lanfray
ERE LLP

HOW IMPORTANT IS SERVICE?

What do our clients expect of us, in a society where fast food restaurants make sure you "have it your way"; theme parks recruit and train employees to ensure a consistent experience for visitors; and high-end retailers use sophisticated customer relationship systems to earn lifetime customers? What do our clients value in their relationships with us?

Numerous surveys across the country tell us that CPA firm clients don't just expect their accountants to be technically competent—they are looking for value in two ways: through the quality of the professional service and the quality of service delivery.

Several years ago, the West Coast accounting firm Moss Adams asked their clients the following questions: "If you consider that your accounting firm provides you value in two ways, professional value through its professional services, and client-service value, how do you rate their relative importance?" and "If the total value is a pie, how big a piece of the pie is client service?" Their research showed that the client service slice of the pie was considered by clients to be 50 percent to 75 percent of the total value of their relationship. Since then, they have continued informally to ask this question of their clients with the same results. Clearly, service performance makes a difference to clients.

If you accept the premise that people expect professional competence from their service providers, are accustomed to service excellence in their other buying experiences, and place as much or greater value on your service delivery as on the service itself, then client service is strategically critical to your firm's long-term success.

Excellence in client service will give your firm a competitive advantage when it is integrated into your strategic plan and built into your communications and engagements with every client and potential client.

A strategic view of client service is focused both externally and internally with the following:

1. A clear and well-communicated vision of the aspects of service that clients value

2. A process for integrating client service into client engagements and the business development process

3. A training approach that integrates service training with professional skills training

Although an integrated approach applies to both individual and business clients, this chapter will focus on business clients. We will discuss steps for defining client service excellence within your firm and introduce a model framework for the plan based on six dimensions of client service. We will offer practical tips for integrating the client service dimensions into client engagements, business development, and staff training, and provide additional tools to help you embed client service excellence into your firm's culture.

⚲ Key Concept

CPA firm clients don't just expect their accountants to be technically competent—they are looking for value in two ways: through the quality of the professional service and the quality of service delivery.

> ⚷ **Key Concept**
>
> Excellence in client service will give your firm a competitive advantage when it is integrated into your strategic plan and built into your communications and engagements with every client and potential client.

Getting Started

The first step is to develop a shared vision of what client service excellence means for your firm and those you serve. Conducting surveys, interviews, and focus groups will provide you with insight into the aspects of client service that clients (existing, prospective, and former); partners; and staff members value the most. Collecting this data is important to your plan's success for two reasons: (1) without research, assumptions about what clients value is likely to be off the mark, and (2) this must be a *shared* vision; the participation of partners and staff will help them to understand the strategic value of a client service plan, and support its implementation.

The external survey is not intended to measure client satisfaction. Its purpose is to benchmark the firm's present service level and learn what would be necessary to bring that service to a higher level of value. Questions in the client interviews and survey are focused on finding out what your firm is doing well, what can be done better, and what frustrations the client may have felt in dealing with the firm. Face-to-face interviews and focus groups are most effective, because they allow interaction with clients and can result in more in-depth, qualitative information. Written (or electronic) surveys provide benchmark data against which future surveys can be compared. In either case, participants should represent a sampling of key clients, at-risk clients, and former clients across all practice/service areas and including businesses of varying sizes.

Internal surveys are best done in focus groups. ERE, LLP created a "Blueprint for Client Service Excellence" through a series of focus group sessions in which every member of the firm participated. Each session began with a discussion of their personal expectations as consumers and how they felt when they experienced excellent and poor service. The focus group participants then drew parallels to the firm's client relationships and what the clients experience in their interactions with the firm. Each group established baseline service guidelines and identified what it would take to go beyond baseline expectations and achieve service excellence.

Points to cover in internal focus groups or surveys with professional and administrative staff include asking them to rank the current level of service and list in order of priority what they believe clients expect from the firm. It also would include follow-up questions such as "What do you think we could or should do to have clients give us a '10' in service value? What is hindering us from doing that?"

Your goal in the entire interview/survey process is to identify the "moments of truth" in your business processes and relationships—those moments when clients see your professional service and client service combine to provide them with a unique value that sets you apart.

The Dimensions of Client Service

You will use what you learned from the surveys and interviews to define the service aspects or dimensions that form the framework for your firm's client service plan. Think of the dimensions as the service "tools" your firm can apply to every client relationship. Everyone in your firm can use these tools in his or her role with clients.

Each firm will have differences in the selection and expression of the dimensions that reflect its shared vision of client service excellence. Below are six that were described by Steve Greenberg in "The Marketing Advantage II: New Ideas on Getting and Keeping Clients":[1]

1. We understand your business and industry and demonstrate our knowledge in the services we provide to you.

2. We consistently anticipate your needs by making suggestions and offering services of value to you.

3. We foster open and active communication between our firms that contributes to the value of our services.

---

[1] *Steve Greenberg, The Marketing Advantage II: New Ideas on Getting and Keeping Clients (New York, NY: American Institute of Certified Public Accountants, Inc., 1998).*

4. We are visibly committed to your success by our attitude, performance, and services.

5. If a problem arises in our services, you can be confident that it will be addressed and remedied.

6. We will not surprise you.

These are not in any order of priority; all of the dimensions are important. Each service dimension is a unique tool that your staff must understand and know how to apply in client settings. The following sections provide descriptions of the six dimensions of client services with examples of their applications in client service situations.

Industry Knowledge and Understanding of Client's Business

Niches are built on this strategy, and there are a number of vendors with Web-based tools that make it possible to enhance your industry-specific accounting or consulting knowledge with industry research and analysis. But the application of this dimension means going beyond that to exceed clients' expectations. The truth is that in many industries, having a niche is no longer a competitive advantage because of the growing number of competing service providers marketing within the same niches.

Creating distinction means going further than industry knowledge and developing a unique understanding of your client's situation within the industry niche. This means first understanding the client as an individual, not as a member of a group or niche. According to David Maister, consultant and co-author of *The Trusted Advisor*,[2] you should be listening to your client with one question in mind: "What makes this person different from any other client I've served?" Our natural tendency, he says, is to hear only what is said that matches something we recognize and have worked with before, so that we can use the familiar words, approaches and tools we are experienced with. The purpose of listening is to build the trust that is essential to your success as an advisor. Only then does the process begin in which the advisor helps the client to identify and clarify the ideas, issues and problems unique to his or her situation, and then build a picture of how the end result might look.

Your conversations with the client should enable you to answer the following:

- Do I have a clear understanding of the client's strategic goals and plans?
- Have I listened carefully for what's different in this situation?
- Do I know what options the client has considered and how he or she feels about them?
- Have we explored the risks and uncertainties before we agreed on a solution?
- Does everyone on the engagement team share a common understanding of the client's plans, so that our professional services can be shaped with the client's goals in mind?

Even within the framework of compliance work, you can make a difference. As part of your pre-engagement planning, armed with knowledge of the client's strategic goals, ask the client's management team to participate in a planning session that focuses on shaping the compliance work to contribute to their company's goals. For instance, an agreed-upon additional analysis of their revenues in line with strategic goals would be more easily accomplished in the course of the audit than as a separate consulting project. Your efforts, just in asking, will not go unnoticed by the client, even if you cannot identify special steps to take.

> **? Key Concept**
>
> Creating distinction means going further than industry knowledge and developing a unique understanding of your client's situation within the industry niche.

Recommendations of Value

This dimension of client service is well understood in our profession. It flows from your understanding of clients' businesses and goals. This dimension also clearly links to your professional service value, the other piece of the pie,

---

[2] *David Maister, Charles H. Green, Robert M. Galford,* The Trusted Advisor *(New York: Touchstone, 2000).*

when you deliver focused professional services that contribute to clients' success. One client described the essence of this dimension as "When we have a trusting relationship, I expect you to make recommendations to me. I don't consider that selling. It's your responsibility to me as long as your recommendations have value. I don't ever want to have to say to you at a later date, 'Why didn't you tell me that?'"

One way to regularly integrate this into a client relationship is to schedule two or three meetings a year with the client for the sole purpose of having the client review their business plans with you. Keep the meeting to 90 minutes and focus on the agenda. Your role is to listen and achieve a full understanding of the client's views. In certain industries, it is a given that you should be attending, if not presenting at, the client's board meeting when the results of the annual audit are discussed.

A good management letter with even two or three solid suggestions or observations gives you an opportunity to continue the conversation with the client. You or your staff will involve the client in drafting the letter so it is complete and accurately addresses the issues, and you will meet face-to-face for a discussion rather than mailing the letter.

Open Communication

We all know that communication is at the heart of our client relationships, yet we often fail to create overt, proactive plans tailored to each client's situation. When clients don't get what they want, it is because their desires have not been communicated or understood clearly and solutions were not built around those desires. Two of the most common reasons clients complain are because you or the client did not take time to confirm expectations or the client perceives you as indifferent.

Do you ask your clients about communication preferences? Does everyone serving the client understand the client's requirements? Do you make special arrangements for contact during certain times with the client? For example, do you offer the client's accounting staff the opportunity to call their contacts at your firm any time they have a question? To be able to call without the concern of incurring fees unless agreed upon? How often do you stop by your client's office, or call on the telephone, just to ask how things are going? You will be surprised at what you can learn from these kinds of contacts and you should do everything possible to encourage them.

Communication is a two-way street: your clients must feel assured that they can reach key engagement partners and staff when needed. How hard do you make it for your clients to contact you? Can you be reached by phone after hours? Do you return calls and e-mails the same day you receive them? Do your clients know whom to call when you are not available?

Lastly, has your marketing staff tailored your firm mailings so that clients receive only what is relevant, delivered in the media (mail, e-mail, Web-based) and frequency each client prefers? Customer relationship management (CRM) and database software allow you to customize your communications and gives everyone in the firm access to that information.

> **♀ Key Concept**
>
> When clients don't get what they want, it is because their desires have not been communicated or understood clearly and solutions were not built around those desires.

Commitment to Clients' Success

This is the most intangible dimension of client service, but it may be the most powerful in the long run. We define it for our staff as the client's belief that they are more successful as a result of their relationship with us than they would be with any other firm. When we've asked clients to help us understand this dimension, they say things such as the following: "You are always there when we need you." "Whenever we have a problem, even if it's outside your services, you ask, 'How can we help?'" "It feels like your service was designed specifically with us in mind."

Do you help clients make new connections that help their business? Do you show the clients you are thinking about them after the engagement? Do you make recommendations that reduce your fees? These are all examples of the kind of commitment that clients value.

Problem Resolution

Think of service failures as unmet client expectations. Even though you do not want this situation in the first place, it is a valuable chance to show the client that you stand behind your performance. Some research shows that a business' ability to properly recover from a service failure can actually create added loyalty in the client's mind. Service failures can be unpleasant, but they are also a golden opportunity to show the client that you are accountable.

People always remember when you recover by going beyond their expectations to fix or correct the situation. Have a methodology in place for handling service failures such as this five-step approach: (1) Recognize it, (2) Admit and own it, (3) Apologize, (4) Fix it in a way that exceeds expectations, and (5) Work out a way to avoid it happening again.

You should plan to review your service performance once a year and in person with your clients. For example, the engagement manager can give clients a sheet of paper entitled, "How can we make your life easier?" Clients are asked to write down everything they observed during an audit that the firm could do differently to make their lives easier. At the end of the job, there will be items that you could—and will—change on the next engagement. Keep in mind that this dimension of client service is also about little improvements that the client nevertheless sees as attention to their needs.

> **Key Concept**
>
> Think of service failures as unmet client expectations.

No Surprises

Clients expect us to keep them totally informed of the progress on their engagement and the status of fees. They expect us to have an "early warning" system that alerts us adequately so that we can avoid surprising them. Clients hold you accountable when they say, "You should have known." What systems do you have in place to avoid surprises? Does everyone serving the client know the due dates and act as an early warning monitor? Do you ever surprise clients with fees?

One way to add significance to this dimension of client service is to make a direct guarantee to the clients that you will not surprise them with fees; if they are surprised, they do not have to pay the fee. That puts the burden on you to make sure, before you start the work, that clients have a clear understanding of the fee or how the fee will be determined.

Integrating the Dimensions of Service Into Client Engagements

Now that you know the six tools you have to work with, how can you use them in practical ways that clients will value? I recommend service value planning, an integrated approach to client service that involves creating and implementing a firm-wide process for applying the service tools in each client engagement. It is during this step that you translate the theory of client service into tangible benefits to each client. An effective service value plan is made up of the following three elements:

1. Team planning

2. Client feedback and acceptance

3. Service value plan

Team Planning

The foundation of a service value plan starts with a meeting of the engagement team to evaluate the client's current situation, discuss lessons learned from the past, and anticipate changes that will influence the service situation. Use the six dimensions of client service described in the preceding section as a checklist to raise questions around each dimension. Use this meeting to develop a common understanding of the client's situation and preliminary ideas for client service continuity and improvement.

Table 36-1 serves as an example of the kinds of questions about each dimension that the team should be asking itself in order to search for improvement opportunities.

Table 36-1 Client Service Dimensions— Example Questions to Consider

Service Dimensions	Questions to Consider
Understanding clients' business and industry	• What are the client's strategic plans? • Who else at the client's business do we need to talk to so we understand more? • What has changed in the company, industry or marketplace that may affect the client's plans? • What research can we do to help us? • Does everyone on the team know what he or she needs to do?
Anticipating needs and making recommendations	• What recommendations did we make last year? • What is the status of those recommendations? • What will we focus on this year? • What are the client's priorities? • What will the needs be two to three years from now? How can we set the stage for those? • Who else should we talk to?
Open and active communications	• What communications problems did we experience? • Do we need new communications links with client contacts? • How often are we in contact outside the engagement? • What other methods of communications can we employ? • Are there people outside the company with whom we need to build communications lines? • Does the client have the right access to people in our firm?
Visible commitment to client's success	• Did we have an opportunity to demonstrate commitment last year? • What extra efforts can we make this year? • Is there a bold step we should consider? • Are there any "red flags" in the client's operations that will require extra attention on our part?

Table 36-1 Client Service Dimensions—
Example Questions to Consider (continued)

Service Dimensions	Questions to Consider
Prompt problem resolution	• What service failures (no matter how small) did we experience last year? How were they resolved? • What are our concerns about this year? • Has anything changed for the client or for us that alerts us to potential service failures? • What were the results of the client service interview? • Do we understand the concerns (if any) of other people we work or interact with at the client?
No surprises	• Did any surprises occur last year? • Where are we at risk of surprising the client? • Does the engagement letter clearly describe agreed upon services, fees, deadlines (if any) and payment terms?

Client Feedback

With the preliminary opportunities identified from the team meeting, meet with the client to obtain their views on your service performance, and share your views from the team planning. Again, you can use the six dimensions of client service as an agenda to interview the client about their views. You can start by saying, "We know that service is an important part of our relationship. I want to ask you about six aspects of our performance last year so we can continue to find ways to improve our performance. By the end of our meeting, I want us to have a shared view of the service improvement opportunities that exist and joint plans for realizing them. Nothing is too small or too large to discuss."

Don't let fear inhibit you from having this kind of conversation with your clients. I have had people explain their reluctance to do this because it might actually raise doubts in the client's mind, as if asking the client about service performance might elicit a recounting of too many problems. Nevertheless, *if you are truly going to make client service part of your competitive advantage, then you have to be able to have a talk about it with your clients, period.*

Now that you have your preliminary views and the client's views, you can create the service value plan. This is a single-page document that describes the three to five priority steps you plan to take to increase your service value. Exhibit 36-1, "Sample Service Value Plan," is an example. Note that the items indicate the dimension of service affected.

Once the plan is complete, your service team members need to be briefed on their role in delivering the plan, and the client needs to be briefed on your promises. Yes, this approach has its risks, namely that you will not deliver on your promises. I believe that the failure to make such promises in the first place is a greater risk.

This written service value plan is a concrete promise to the client that you will follow through with these steps and you expect to be evaluated at the end of the engagement. You have elevated service performance to an integral part of your total relationship with the client.

Exhibit 36-1 Sample Service Value Plan

> **Service Value Plan**
>
> XYZ Accounting Firm
>
> To be more valuable to this client, the XYZ Accounting Firm will take the following steps in the coming year:
>
> 1. *Communications:* All new engagement team members will be introduced to their contacts and tour the client's facility 30 days prior to the audit. The partner will schedule this.
>
> 2. *Suggestions of value:* Our partner-in-charge and the client's controller will meet to find ways to reduce the client's need to prepare special work papers for the audit. We will find more ways to use the client's existing information system. This will be completed 30 days prior to the audit.
>
> 3. *No surprises:* Each week during the audit, the partner will brief the client on our progress and budget compliance.
>
> 4. *Commitment to client's success:* In May, we will provide a two-hour briefing to the stockholders and key management on the topic of retirement planning.

Business Development and the Dimensions of Service

The dimensions of service excellence play an integral part in business development and the proposal process. Having an established client service plan is the key to consistently delivering on stated and implied promises made during the "courtship" phase of your relationship.

There is no better beginning than to be helpful right from the start, to show an interest in learning about the prospective client's situation and goals, to communicate clearly and to follow up promptly. In your firm, do the professionals engaged in the selling process prepare questions and research information that will initiate a meaningful discussion? Do your written proposals directly discuss the information you learned during the sales call and link it back to your firm's capabilities?

How are you demonstrating your firm's service difference? By actually showing the value your firm provides (rather than simply talking about it), the prospective client is previewing the level of service he or she can expect to receive as a client of your firm.

> **🔑 Key Concept**
>
> Having an established client service plan is the key to consistently delivering on stated and implied promises made during the "courtship" phase of your relationship.

Training for Integrated Service

The kind of service delivery that clients describe as "noticeably superior" doesn't just happen. It is the result of a systematic process that includes training. Just as you develop the professional capabilities of your staff, you have to develop their service capabilities.

Formal training focused on service should be integrated into your firm-wide continuing professional education (CPE) and delivered at the appropriate time in your staff's development. In addition, staff should accompany partners to client assessment meetings as often as possible, since there is no better training than actually observing the process.

Table 36-2 illustrates an approach that uses service training as a curriculum.

TABLE 36-2 SERVICE TRAINING CURRICULUM

Topic	Training Objective	Position
Overview of client service	• What clients expect • Your roles during your career • The firm's policies and practices • The firm's client service standards	Professional and administrative staff
Fundamentals of client contact	• Handling yourself in the client's facilities • Problem resolution • Effective communication skills	Staff Seniors Administrative staff with client contact
Business development	• Consultative selling skills • Client needs assessment	Managers Partners
Conducting a client interview	• Listening skills • Understanding clients' expectations • Facilitating an interview	Seniors Supervisors
Managing a service team	• How to organize for service delivery • Defining your team's responsibilities • Evaluating your team's performance • Creating a service value plan	Supervisors Managers
Coaching service performance	• Individual coaching skills • Training skills	Managers Partners

If service is truly half your value to clients, it seems reasonable to invest time in service training, especially when you consider the time we already invest in professional CPE. Four to eight hours each year is recommended at every professional level, and at least four hours for administrative staff with client contact. In addition to the training's actual value to your staff, you are also sending a clear message that service performance counts. For more information on training, see chapter 31, "Sales Training: The Key to Better Service and Better Clients."

CONCLUSION

To embed client service excellence into your firm's culture, you will be touching almost everything you do and how you do it. You may also want to take the final step (if necessary) and change your evaluation and compensation process in order to support it. When you determine partner distributions at the end of the year, does the partner who brings in a new client receive greater recognition than the partner who brings in twice as much additional work from an existing client whose loyalty has been built through consistently excellent client service? We learned that selling more to existing clients in the normal course of great client service should be recognized in tangible rewards for the real value it delivers to our firm.

One would like to think that clients look for professional competence. In many cases, however, it is *how* clients are treated that determines the success of the relationship. With client service comprising at least half of our total value, this area is too important to leave to chance. You simply cannot assume that the people in your firm will take it upon themselves to deliver a high level of service to clients. Instead, you must formalize your client service program by defining it.

ABOUT THE AUTHOR

An industry veteran, **Susan Wylie Lanfray** knows how to get things done. As director of marketing at ERE, she has hands-on experience with every aspect of professional services marketing including: creating and executing brand strategy, integrated marketing campaigns, practice growth plans, niche-building programs, public relations and community outreach programs, client service and loyalty programs, a company-wide CRM system, and pipeline and business development reporting systems, as well as working one-on-one with partners on personal business development plans. After beginning her career in business-to-consumer advertising, she spent ten years as marketing director at one of the top 20 U.S. accounting firms before joining ERE in 2000 as their first marketing director. Susan is an active member of CPAmerica and currently vice-chair of the Marketing Executive Committee. A long-time member of the Association for Accounting Marketing (AAM), she served a three-year term on AAM's national board of directors, and is a co-chair of its New York Metro Chapter, which she helped to create in 1995.

CHAPTER 37
Letting Go: Evaluating and Firing Clients

Mark Koziel, CPA
AICPA

INTRODUCTION[1]

An evaluation of your client list is a healthy process for firms of all sizes. As firms change structure, size and expertise, evaluating the client list becomes a necessary annual exercise to implement firm strategy and vision. Some clients can't keep up with the price increases that come with firm growth and, inevitably, a firm will outgrow some of its clients. Or, a firm may choose to keep these clients and avoid the price increases and lose profitability. In either instance, firms need a formal policy for reviewing the client list annually and taking appropriate action.

Firms that sacrifice profitability to keep clients will eventually need to add staff to grow the firm but may be unable to offer market salaries to qualified candidates. The solution may not lie in hiring more staff, but rather in reducing the client load or redistributing the amount of time spent on each client's work.

While visiting a variety of firms across the country, I have observed a direct link between staffing issues, salary issues, and client evaluation. As a former recruiter, I understand the difficulties smaller firms encounter in competing with larger firms in terms of salary. The demand for the existing talent pool continues to outpace supply. This leaves firms in the difficult position of needing to fire clients that do not fit the firm's direction.

> **Key Concept**
>
> Firms that sacrifice profitability to keep clients will eventually need to add staff to grow the firm but may be unable to offer market salaries to qualified candidates.

RANKING YOUR CLIENTS

Each firm must know and understand its clients to determine if they are worth keeping and if the firm is charging the market rate for its work. The AICPA Private Companies Practice Section (PCPS) offers a standard Excel template, available to section members and reprinted in this text as appendix 37-1, that is easily adaptable for evaluating a client based on pricing, timing, stress, risk level, and overall satisfaction. Clients are ranked A, B, C, and D. An A is the most valuable client, and a D is the least valuable. Ideally, a firm does not want D clients and the C clients are borderline—not necessarily worth letting go. Once the Cs and Ds are addressed, the firm can focus on converting the B clients into As. Practitioners should spend the most quality time on the A clients, providing all the work they possibly can for them.

The template includes six key areas for rating each client:

- *Job risk/complexity.* This rates client risk and the potential liability a client brings to the firm. Whether it is an audit client in a high-risk industry, management attitude or lack of controls, or a tax client that constantly pushes the limit on deductions and income reporting, some clients pose a higher risk to the firm than others.
    Rating Scale: 5 = No Risk; 4 = Below-Average Risk; 3 = Average Risk; 2 = Above-Average Risk; 1 = High Risk.

---

[1] *This chapter is reprinted with permission from the January 2008 issue of the Journal of Accountancy.*

433

- *Job recovery/profitability.* Each firm must decide what recovery percentage is acceptable. Many firms determine profitability based on hours billed and amount of effort put into a job. The PCPS has a recommended recovery percentage in the scoring system. Firms that look at client profitability based on other key performance indicators (KPIs) can change the criteria to reflect their own KPIs.

  Rating Scale: 5 = 100% or more; 4 = 90%–99%; 3 = 80%–89%; 2 = 75%–79%; 1 = 74% or less.

- *Referral source/client tie-in.* This factor is important to the firm's overall profitability. Clients can be a firm's best referral source, and this source should be used. Some jobs, such as those in the not-for-profit sector, are the results of relationships with other clients. It is important to quantify the referred client in the client evaluation process. A client that has been referred by an A client can still be a D client. If a referred client is a D, the firm should keep the referring client in the loop as to why your firm is unable to serve the D client. Very likely, the A client will understand because it is a business as well.

  Rating Scale: 5 = Excellent referrer/tied to an A client; 4 = Occasional referrer/tied to another client; 3 = Possible referrer if asked; 2 = Tied to another client; 1 = No referral/no tie.

- *Additional potential services.* This criterion is highly valuable and potentially profitable. The potential to provide additional services for a client could improve that client's current rank if it is below an A.

  Rating Scale: 5 = Could be doing more; 4 = Some additional opportunities; 3 = Full now, but future potential; 2 = Reached full potential; 1 = Does not value what we do now.

- *Timeliness of Payment.* This factor is highly quantifiable and like job recovery, there are no exceptions to the ranking.

  Rating Scale: 5 = 30 days or less; 4 = 31–60 days; 3 = 61–90 days; 2 = 90–120 days; 1 = more than 120 days.

- *Client satisfaction.* This does not refer to the client's satisfaction, but rather the firm's. How much satisfaction and enjoyment is there in working with the client? It is important to know how client management and client teams treat your employees.

  Rating Scale: 5 = Great to work with and our team enjoys them; 4 = Good environment; 3 = OK job that we get through; 2 = Can be stressful at times; 1 = Client does not respect us and treats our people poorly.

The template provides an automatic calculation based on the overall score to determine if the client ranks as an A, B, C, or D. Three of the six criteria are based on statistical evidence; one can be considered engagement objective; and two can be considered subjective. This puts some science in the process since four of the six criteria can be more difficult to argue, but can still make the process negotiable within the firm.

Parting Ways

Dealing with the D clients can be extremely difficult and emotional, especially for multi-partner firms where partner compensation is often tied to the wrong performance measures. Ultimately, the goal is to reduce the number of D-rated clients to improve the profitability of the practice and allow firms to spend more time with their A clients. August Aquila, author of chapter 4, "The Marketing Plan: An Audit-Based Approach," and co-author of *Compensation as a Strategic Asset: The New Paradigm*, notes that "many firm partner compensation agreements call for compensation based on partner revenue contribution to the firm, and not to the profitability the partner generates for the firm. You will never get a partner to give up a D client if it is going to hit him or her in the pocket."

If this is the case in your firm, consider revising the partner compensation to add performance measures beyond revenue contribution (see exhibit 37-1, "Compensation Criteria").

ᚦ Key Concept

The goal is to reduce the number of D-rated clients to improve the profitability of the practice and allow you to spend more time with your A clients.

Exhibit 37-1 Compensation Criteria

Resist opposition to letting go of clients by encouraging other compensation measures in a firm. As part of an overall compensation survey, August Aquila and Coral Rice, authors of *Compensation as a Strategic Asset: The New Paradigm,* asked practitioners to consider the following 16 criteria for compensation. While the list is not exhaustive, it does provide the breadth of criteria that firms can consider beyond revenue.

- Book of businesses
- Client or book gross profitability
- Community involvement
- Cross-selling
- Fees collected
- Firm management responsibilities
- Industry experience/expertise
- Managed charge hours
- Mentoring and training employees
- New business development (origination)
- Ownership percentage
- Professional involvement
- Realization
- Seniority
- Technical expertise
- Utilization

Two factors that typically make a D client not worth saving involve job risk and client satisfaction. If the client has high risk or treats the firm or its staff, or both, poorly, the firm is better off without the client. For these D clients, the determination is that, no matter what, they have to go. Keep in mind that some D clients are willing to work with the firm to improve the relationship. These clients are worth upgrading to C's. The AICPA *Management of an Accounting Practice (MAP) Handbook* contains sample client termination letters. Once the D clients are gone, the firm can focus on moving the C clients up to Bs and the B clients up to As.

The "D" Client Meeting

For D clients that require a face-to-face meeting, the team member in charge of the engagement relationship should set up the discussion. He or she should be prepared for two possible outcomes: first, the client will agree and your firm should help the client find another CPA firm to work with; or, second, the client will ask what it will take to continue the business relationship. The team member must have the new terms ready, including new price, payment, and workload. This gives your firm the ability to control the situation and to price the engagement accordingly. The firm should require a double-digit price increase if this situation occurs. I know of some firms that ask for a 20 percent to 30 percent price increase from their D clients and get it.

If payment terms are an issue, the firm should require the client to become up to date with any outstanding payments due, ask for a deposit on any future work, and establish a monthly payment schedule for the client, explaining that the monthly payment schedule will help the client's cash flow and budget.

If client satisfaction is low, firm management should discuss this issue with its team members before the client meeting and then establish new expectations with the client. These expectations may include when the work will be ready, what the expected condition of the work will be, and how the client will treat the team. The conversation with the client will likely be similar to the examples provided in the sample client termination letter in exhibit 37-2. As difficult as the conversation may be, it is necessary to help your practice grow. Follow up with a letter to the client confirming your discussion and detailing your termination action, and send it via a delivery method that will provide you with documentation that the client received the letter on a specific date.

Exhibit 37-2
Sample Client Termination Letter

Reprinted with permission from chapter 204, "Client Engagements," of the Management of an Accounting Practice Handbook. © 2010 AICPA.

Date

Ms. Helen Green, CEO
Company Name
Street Address
City, State, and Zip Code

Dear Ms. Green:

We have enjoyed working with you on your tax and accounting matters over the past years. As our firm has grown and developed, we have the need to consider how we can best serve our clients. To continue to strive to give outstanding professional service, we have reluctantly come to the conclusion that we can no longer serve some of our clients. Therefore, regrettably, we need to ask that you engage another accounting firm to provide your personal and business tax and accounting services for the year ended December 31, 20XX.

We will be glad to assist your new CPA with any matters with which they may have questions. In that event, please drop us a note authorizing us to release information to your new CPA.

We thank you for your patronage and wish you every success in your business.

 Sincerely,

John Smith, CPA

SMITH, JONES & DOE

Improving the Rankings

Once a firm commits to streamlining its client list, the focus can shift to improving the rankings of the remaining clients as described here.

- *Job risk/complexity.* Some clients who make "the cut" may still have high job risk or high job complexity. If job complexity is based on a difficult industry, your firm should consider partnering with another firm that has expertise in that industry. Conducting an additional partner review for an extra level of comfort on the risk and providing additional training to team members on the complex areas of the engagement may solve this issue.

- *Job recovery/profitability.* Consider the current responsibility flow of the engagement and begin the process of pushing work down. Assigning a rising manager as lead on the engagement to reduce partner involvement at higher rates will increase profitability. The firm should review engagement parameters, meet with team members to educate them on services included or not included in the current arrangement, and follow up with the client to reinforce the engagement parameters and alert them to areas that are no longer included and need to be priced separately. Team members must be knowledgeable of pricing techniques to improve client profitability and have the ability to price additional services outside the scope of the current engagement. Refer to the "Additional Potential Services" section to increase the number of services priced more profitably than the current engagement.

- *Referral source/client tie-in.* Firm management must use all clients that scored a three in this category as the top source of potential referrals and conduct a team meeting to discuss ideas on asking for referrals. If your firm provides a written client satisfaction survey, add a line to ask for a referral. The firm managers should meet regularly with the client to discuss business and to ask, in person, for a referral. Develop a referral reward system to encourage referrals (the reward should be nonmonetary and low cost, but memorable). For more information on referrals, see chapter 24, "Referral Source Development: The Most Powerful, but Underutilized Business Development Tactic."

- *Additional potential services.* The firm should hold a planning meeting with every client that scored a four or higher in this area to discuss the client's business. Your firm may be missing many opportunities with that client simply because the client didn't know you could help in a specific area. Don't be afraid to ask, even if you don't provide all services. Firms that have set up a referral service with other providers for services they do not offer will ensure that their clients call them first for any business service. This way the firm can pick and choose the business services they would like to provide to their clients. For more information, see chapter 30, "Cross-Serving Clients: Integrating Sales and Service Delivery."

- *Timeliness of payment.* The firm should request a deposit from slower-paying clients and offer a monthly payment option to assist with cash flow and budgeting. Consider accepting credit card payments (combined with the monthly payment option, you can negotiate an "until further notice" acceptance, which also helps with client retention).

- *Client satisfaction.* The firm should conduct a meeting with team members to discuss all clients that scored a three or less in this area and meet with the client to report the issues addressed by the team members. You must put together a joint plan to improve the relationship.

Clients should be evaluated annually. Once the current client list is evaluated, the firm can establish parameters for accepting new engagements. This process allows the firm to set the bar higher and improve its profitability, team member compensation, and general satisfaction in the work performed.

Key Concept

Once a firm commits to streamlining its client list, the focus can shift to improving the rankings of the remaining clients.

ABOUT THE AUTHOR

Mark Koziel is Director of Specialized Communities and PCPS/Firm Practice Management at the AICPA. He oversees the development, ongoing improvement, and delivery of services to members in PCPS/Firm Practice Management and the Financial Planning, Technology, and Forensic & Valuation Services interest areas, including the PFS, CITP, ABV and CFF credentials. He frequently speaks on CPA issues around the country.

Prior to joining the AICPA, Mark Koziel served three years as Director of Media Planning for a political consulting firm after finishing his 12 year public accounting career in a variety of accounting, auditing, and consulting roles at a large local accounting firm in Buffalo, NY.

Mark was an active member of the Buffalo Chapter of the New York State Society of CPAs. Mark was one of the founding members of the Young CPAs committee and served as Chair for two years before being appointed to the Buffalo Chapter Board and serving as President for the 2003–2004 Fiscal Year, one of the youngest Presidents in the history of the Buffalo Chapter.

Mark was named one to the Top 100 Most Influential People in Accounting by Accounting Today in 2008 and 2009.

Mark earned a BS in Accounting from Canisius College.

APPENDIX 37-1 CLIENT EVALUATION TEMPLATE

This template was originally published through the AICPA Private Companies Practice Section's Firm Practice Center and is reprinted here with permission.

The client evaluation has been designed to provide guidance in ranking your clients based on set criteria. It is critically important that you answer honestly for each client and criteria. A client's value is determined far beyond just recovery and timeliness of payment and this worksheet will help you determine the best and the worst of clients within the firm. Its been said the clients that contribute 20% of our profits, tend to consume 80% of our time. This exercise will help you re-focus and quantify the better clients of the firm, set the base for the clients we should focus more of our attention to, and show us clients that have the potential of moving up the scale.

Once the ranking process is complete, the next step is to look at the "D" clients and discuss how you will let them go, so you have more time and energy to do more work for your "A" clients and work to increase your "B" and "C" clients up the ranking.

Instructions:

1. List all clients of the firm. You can provide a list for each partner if you prefer, but it will be important to have all clients in one master list when done, so comparisons can be made.

2. If you need more rows than provided, insert the required number of additional rows in between rows that have already been formatted, then copy and paste the formulas from both columns H and I into the new rows. Column H automatically calculates the average score. Column I automatically calculates the A, B, C or D ranking based on the results of Column H.

3. Sort the list, first by column I, then by column H, then by column A. This will give you the list by rank.

4. Determine the plan to fire the D clients that we need to purge from the firm. Then determine a game plan for providing more services to the A clients, then B, then C.

5. Repeat this exercise on an annual basis.

Definitions:

Job Risk/Complexity—an audit client in a high risk industry, management attitude or lack of controls, or a tax client that constantly pushes the limit on deductions and income reporting, we know there are some clients that pose a higher risk to the firm than others.

Job Recovery/Profitability—This criteria seems to be the key focus for many firms and can be self explanatory. The difference lies in what recovery percentage is acceptable for each firm. PCPS has a recommended recovery percentage in the scoring system. For firms who look at individual client profitability based on other key performance indicators(KPI) outside of hours and effort can change the criteria to reflect their individual KPIs.

Referral Source/Client Tie In—This criteria becomes important to the overall profitability to the firm. Clients can be our best referral source and we should take advantage of that. Some jobs such as in the Not-For-Profit sector are clients due to a relationship with another client. It's important to quantify that in the process. Just because we do work for a client that may have been referred by an "A" client doesn't mean they are safe from being let go. If a client comes in as a "D", you need to first have the difficult conversation with the "A" client and tell them why you can't service the "D" client anymore, before telling the "D" client you can no longer do the work. Chances are, your "A" client will understand, since they are after all, business people.

Appendix 37-1 Client Evaluation Template (CONTINUED)

Additional Potential Services—This criteria can be highly valuable and profitable. In addition to ranking the current status, this will also be the base of where to begin the improvement process after you free up capacity. While some may say this is subjective, if there is more than one owner or manager in this process, there can be more opportunity for open discussion.

Timeliness of Payment—This is fairly self explanatory and very quantifiable. Like Job Recovery, there are no exceptions to the ranking.

Client Satisfaction—This isn't how satisfied the client is with us. This criteria deals with our satisfaction and enjoyment in working with the client. More importantly, do your team members derive enjoyment and satisfaction from the work. In addition to overall work enjoyment, it is also important to poll team members to see how client management and client teams treat our people.

continued

APPENDIX 37-1 CLIENT EVALUATION TEMPLATE (CONTINUED)

Client Evaluation

Client Name	Job Risk/ Complexity	Job Recovery/ Profitability	Referral Source/ Client Tie in	Additional Potential Services	Timeliness of Payment	Client Satisfaction	Score	Rank
	5 = No Risk	5 = 100% or more	5 = Excellent referrer/Tied to an "A" Client	5 = Could be doing a lot more	5 = 30 days or less	5 = Great to work with and our team enjoys them	A Client = 25-30	
	4 = Below Average risk	4 = 90-99%	4 = Occasional referrer/Tied to another client	4 = A few additional opportunities	4 = 31-60 days	4 = Good environment	B Client = 20-25	
	3 = Average Risk	3 = 80-90%	3 = Possible referrer, if asked	3 = Full now but future potential	3 = 61-90 days	3 = OK job, we get through it	C Client = 15-20	
	2 = Above Average Risk	2 = 75-80%	2 = Tied to another client	2 = Reached full potential	2 = 90-120 days	2 = Can be stressful at times	D Client = 14 or less	
	1 = High Risk	1 = 75% or less	1 = No referral/No tie	1 = doesn't value what we do now	1 = over 120 days	1 = Client hates us and treats our people poorly		